Brazilian Agricultural Development, 1890–1950

Earl Richard Downes

Brazilian Agricultural Development, 1890–1950

Educators, Capitalists, and Cold Warriors

palgrave
macmillan

Earl Richard Downes
Georgetown, Texas, USA

ISBN 978-3-031-76991-7 ISBN 978-3-031-76992-4 (eBook)
https://doi.org/10.1007/978-3-031-76992-4

This Palgrave Macmillan imprint is published by the registered company Springer Nature Switzerland AG
The registered company address is: Gewerbestrasse 11, 6330 Cham, Switzerland

Preface

My experience as an American Filed Service exchange student in Quito, Ecuador, left me with a myriad of questions about the role of the United States in Latin America. Four decades of experience allowed me to gain a broader perspective. I became particularly intrigued with assessing with the economic import of the United States on the region in general and, in particular, upon Brazil which I had visited early in my professional career. What were the main parameters of the relationship? How did the United States affect the economic growth of Brazil?

Time would prove that addressing these issues would not come easily, but the opportunity to study Brazil later in life allowed me to explore my questions on a broader scale. Scrutiny of a period of expanding contacts between the United States and Brazil soon revealed strong interaction through trade, investment, education, technical information, and political designs—vital pieces of the U.S.-Brazil economic relationship, with important social ramifications. As my study progressed, the obvious prominence of rural components drove the focus of my research from anterooms of diplomats and ledgers of accountants into the nooks and crannies of the nation's vast countryside. The principal object of my furious scribbling and photocopying soon became agriculture—the growing, harvesting, and processing of foodstuffs or fiber. Aside from the ever-present academic deadline, the critical role of agriculture in Latin America's economies imparted an urgency to my combing of the already crumpling record.

When I retired from classroom responsibilities, the focus of my research expanded beyond Brazil's First Republic (1890–1930) to the more recent experience. I seized upon the luxury of time to explore robust archival collections and repositories of digital and printed data. It is soon evident that there is no study on the broad history of interaction between the United States and Brazil related to agriculture, nor is there a general history of Brazilian agriculture itself. I then expanded the scope of my study to explore how agriculture fared from the earliest days of Brazil's republic until the end of its unfortunate experiment with military government. To explain the linkages between Brazil and the United States in establishing the new reality of Brazilian agriculture, I found it necessary to provide a broader account of Brazil's agricultural development.

I have sought to portray perspectives on multiple issues. How did innovations generated through U.S. contacts alter pre-existing economic and social arrangements expressed in the national institutional structure, if at all? How did new agricultural technology alter the nation's economic and social development? Who promoted the adoption of new technology? What were the motives of Brazilian politicians and agriculturalist as they considered alternatives for the nation's agriculture? Equally, what were the motives of U.S. agriculturalists and policymakers as they reviewed the state of Brazil's agriculture? Finally, who benefited from innovations introduced into the agricultural sector and what were the unintended consequences, if any?

This study will not answer all these questions or those that confronted me long ago during my adventures on the streets of Quito. I am hopeful, though, that it will provide insight into the role of the United States in the economies of Latin America, and especially Brazil. Perhaps I have shed some light on answers to relevant questions. If so, I will have completed my quest.

Georgetown, Texas
October 2023

Earl Richard Downes

Acknowledgments

I am deeply obligated to many dedicated scholars, archivists, and librarians who have supported my research. I am particularly indebted to my dissertation advisor, Richard Graham, who decades after orienting my original work continued to be supportive of approaches and material. He and Thomas F. McGann inspired me both with their own works on similar topics and their personal advice and direction. I am deeply indebted to multiple U.S. and Brazilian scholars who oriented my original research in the 1980s for my dissertation on U.S.-Brazil relations during Brazil's Old Republic (1890–1930). These include Walt W. Rostow, Jose Honório Rodrigues, Ana Celia Castro, Eulalia Maria Lehmeyer Lobo, Stanley R. Hilton, and John W. F. Dulles.

I am especially grateful to Benjamin Harris Hunnicutt Jr., Wilbur K. Hunnicutt, and George Hunnicutt for sharing memories of their father and his accomplishments. I have fond memories of my meeting with Joaquina de Assis Brasil, who discussed her father's ideas about modernizing Brazil's agriculture. Sylvio do Amaral "Bi" Moreira of Belo Horizonte shared valuable material on the history of the Escola Agricola de Lavras. Eduardo King Carr, a descendant of nineteenth-century U.S. immigrants and former dean of the Lavras school, generously shared his perspectives on the roles of Americans in Brazil.

I have benefited from the assistance of multiple individuals. Inez Schuh, widow of G. Edward Schuh, graciously answered my queries about her late husband's role as an inspired promoter of Brazilian agricultural education. Professor Terry Roe, Director of the University of Minnesota's Center for International Food and Agricultural Policy, provided valuable insights on agricultural development. Professor Claiton Marcio da Silva of the Universidade Federal da Fronteira Sul in Chapecó, Santa Catarina, Brazil, provided valuable suggestions about documentation of Nelson Rockefeller's activities at the Rockefeller Archive Center.

Equally worthy of my gratitude are the staffs of libraries and archives in Brazil and the United States especially the staff of the Nettie Lee Benson collection of the University of Texas for access to its world premiere collection of materials on Latin America. I also thank the Universidade Estadual de Campinas, for online access to works of its graduating students and technicians of the digital archive of the Brazil's National Library for access to over 11 million pages of Brazilian newspapers and magazines, as well as to technicians of the Hathi Digital Trust.

I especially thank my dear wife Natividad and our children for their unfailing good humor, understanding, and cooperation throughout this extended venture. As is standard for historians of Brazil, I have confronted spellings later abandoned in orthographical reforms. I have retained the original spelling in all citations and formal titles to facilitate access to sources, but used the modern spelling of all other words, including designations of geographical regions. All translations are mine unless otherwise noted. Of course, I remain solely responsible for interpretations and any errors contained therein.

Contents

1 **Introduction** 1

2 **The Brazilian Agricultural Reform Movement** 11
The Promoters of Agricultural Reform 14
Political Action to Reform Agriculture 21
The Re-institution of the Ministry of Agriculture 24

3 **Agricultural Diversification and U.S. Ties: The Technicians** 29
The Origins of U.S. Ties 29

4 **The Range Cattle Industry** 43

5 **The Great War and Increased Production, 1914–1919** 51
The Wartime Stimuli 52
The Federal Government Raises Support Levels 62
Acquiring Technology and Raw Materials 64
The Social Impacts of Increasing Production 67

6 **The U.S. Role in Promoting Increased Production** 81
Cotton 81
Cattle and Beef 103

7 **The Strengthening of U.S. Ties to Brazil's Agricultural Education** 115

8 Epitácio Pessoa, Cotton and Beef, 1919–1922 137
Brazil at War's End 137
The Regional Priorities of President Epitácio Pessoa 140
Aiding the Northeast Through Anti-Drought Measures 144
Improving Cattle and Beef Processing 156

9 The Center-South Adapts to New Conditions, 1922–1930 169
Restoring Support Level for Coffee 169
Cotton: The Advantages of the Center-South 173
The Center-South and the Cattle and Meat Packing Sectors 182

10 Education, Extension Services, and Mechanization, 1922–1930 191
Rolfs' Extension Services 191
Benjamin Hunnicutt: Extension Services and Mechanization 196
Brazil and Mechanized Agriculture in the 1920s 202

11 Elite Factionalism and the First Republic's Downfall, 1922–1930 211
Withdrawing Support for Anti-Drought Works in the Northeast 212
Further Challenges to the Cotton of the Northeast 216
Compensating Factors 222
The Cattle Sector in Rio Grande do Sul 231
Political Implications of Regional Inequalities 234

12 Vargas: Institutional Restructuring, 1930–1937 245
Combating the Commodities Crises 247
Sustaining Political Support from the Cattle Sector 258
Restructuring Agricultural Research and Education 260
Conclusion 268

13 Vargas: The Cotton Alternative and the United States, 1930–1937 271
William Clayton and Brazilian Cotton 275
The Implications of the Cotton Boom 281

14 The *Estado Novo*, Agriculture and the United States, 1937–1942 285
The Estado Novo and Agriculture 286
Expanding Federal Support for Agriculture 293
Changes in the International Environment and Agriculture (1937–1939) 298
Agriculture's Role in Rise of a De Facto Alliance (1939–1940) 305

15 Wartime Agricultural Cooperation, 1942–1945 319
The Joint Food Commission 320
Implementation of the Agreement 326
Gaining Support for U.S. Agricultural Practices 338
The Demise of the Commission 342
Brazilian Agriculture at War's End 344
Conclusion 346

16 Industrialization and the Agricultural Revolution, 1945–1950 349
Agriculture and the New Reality 350
Rockefeller Renews His Engagement 359
Rockefeller's Programs for Brazilian Agriculture 360

17 The New Model: Capital and Technical Assistance 369
Conclusion 379

Bibliography 381

Abbreviations Used in the Text

ABCAR	Associação Brasileira de Crédito e Assistência Rural
ACAR	Associação de Crédito e Assistência Rural
AEP	Arquivo Epitácio Pessoa, Instituto Histórico e Geográfico Brasileiro, Rio de Janeiro
AHI	Arquivo Histórico de Itamaratí (Foreign Ministry), Rio de Janeiro
AISL	Arquivo Ildefonso Simões Lopes, Centro de Pesquisa e Documentação de História Contemporânea do Brasil (CPDOC), Fundação Getúlio Vargas, Rio de Janeiro
ANP	Arquivo Nilo Peçanha, Museu da República, Rio de Janeiro
APMG	Arquivo Público do Estado de Minas Gerais, Belo Horizonte, Minas Gerais
ARGS	Arquivo do Estado do Rio Grande do Sul, Porto Alegre, Rio Grande do Sul
ARS	Arquivo Raul Soares, Centro de Pesquisa e Documentação de História Contemporânea do Brasil (CPDOC), Fundação Getúlio Vargas, Rio de Janeiro
BPAU	Bulletin of the Pan American Union
BP-SUA	John Casper Branner papers, Stanford University Archives, Palo Alto, California
BRUA	Brown University Opening the Archives: Documenting U.S.-Brazil
CDdG	Coleção Domício da Gama, Instituto Histórico e Geográfico Brasileiro, Rio de Janeiro
CPDOC	O Centro de Pesquisa e Documentação de História Contemporânea do Brasil, Fundação Getúlio Vargas, Rio de Janeiro

CPN	Comitê de Produção Nacional
CSHS	Colorado State Historical Society, Denver, Colorado
EBW	Embaixada Brasileira, Washington
EGA	Ernesto Geisel Archive, Centro de Pesquisa e Documentação de História Contemporânea do Brasil (CPDOC), Fundação Getúlio Vargas, Rio de Janeiro, Brazil
Encl.	Enclosure
FAS	U.S. Foreign Agricultural Service
FRUS	Foreign Relations of the United States
GVA	Getúlio Vargas Archive, Centro de Pesquisa e Documentação de História Contemporânea do Brasil (CPDOC), Fundação Getúlio Vargas, Rio de Janeiro, Brazil
GPO	United States Government Printing Office
HMRC	Houston Metropolitan Research Center
Impr. Nac.	Imprensa Nacional
L	Lata [box]
M	Maço [book]
MAG	Ministerio de Agricultura., Industria e Comercio
N	Number
ONI	U.S. Navy Office of Naval Intelligence
PHRA	Peter Henry Rolfs Archive, University of Florida Libraries, Gainesville, Florida
RAC	Rockefeller Archive Center, Sleepy Hollow, New York
RC de "JC"	Retrospecto Comercial do Jornal do Comercio
RJ	Rio de Janeiro (city)
RG	Record Group
SNA	Sociedade Nacional de Agricultura
SNI	Serviço Nacional de Informações
SP	São Paulo (city)
SRB	Sociedade Rural Brasileira
SWC	Southwest Collection, Texas Tech University, Lubbock, Texas
USACG	U.S. Consul General, Rio de Janeiro
USC	United States Consul
USDA	United States Department of Agriculture
USDA	United States Department of State
USE	United States Embassy
USNA	United States National Archives, Washington, D.C.
USBFDC	United States Bureau of Foreign and Domestic Commerce
WSHA	Wyoming State Historical Archives, Cheyenne, Wyoming

List of Figures

Fig. 2.1 Indexed production and unit value, Brazilian coffee exports, 1890–1914 (*Source* Calculated from Fundação Instituto Brasileiro de Geografia e Estatística, *Séries estatísticas retrospectivas* Vol. 3 (Rio de Janeiro: IBGE, 1987), p. 312) 12

Fig. 2.2 Revenue from Sugar Exports, 1890–1913 (foreign currency) (*Source* Calculated from Fundação Instituto Brasileiro de Geografia e Estatística, *Séries estatísticas retrospectivas* Vol. 3 (Rio de Janeiro: IBGE, 1987), p. 307) 14

Fig. 2.3. Revenue from Rubber Exports, 1890–1914 (foreign currency) (*Source* Calculated from Fundação Instituto Brasileiro de Geografia e Estatística, *Séries estatísticas retrospectivas* Vol. 3 (Rio de Janeiro: IBGE, 1987), p. 309) 14

Fig. 3.1 Indexed production cotton and other crops, São Paulo, 1894–1911 (*Source* Calculated from "The economic situation of São Paulo," *Brazilian American*, 4, No. 95 (Aug. 20, 1921), 23. See also Wilson Cano, *Raizes da concentração industrial em São Paulo*, p. 63) 41

Fig. 5.1 Indexed unit values and value trends of Beans and Corn, 1912–1917 (*Source* Calculated from Haddad, "Growth of the Brazilian Real Output," p. 44) 55

Fig. 5.2 Indexed production and unit values of Brazilian Raw Cotton, 1912–1917 (*Source* Calculated from Haddad, "Growth of the Brazilian Real Output," p. 49) 55

Fig. 5.3 Indexed Unit Values and Value Coffee and Rubber, 1910–1916 (*Source* Calculated from Haddad, "Growth of the Brazilian Real Output," p. 56 56
Fig. 5.4 Value of select Brazil Food Exports, 1915–1917 (US Dollars) (*Source* Calculated from *Wileman's Brazilian Review* and *Commercio Exterior do Brasil* by Arthur H. Redfield in *Brazil: A Study of Economic Conditions since 1913*, pp. 22, 24, 61) 78
Fig. 6.1 Brazilian apparent domestic consumption and indexed s prices of raw cotton, 1913–1916 (metric tons). Apparent domestic consumption is production, plus imports, minus exports (*Sources* Imports and Exports from Brazil, Directoria Geral de Estatística, *Resumo de várias estatísticas,* pp. 48, 56. Production and prices estimated by Haddad, "Growth of Brazilian Real Output," pp. 56–57) 83
Fig. 6.2 Cotton production of Northeast versus São Paulo, 1911–1918. Data from Brazil, Serviço de Algodão, Ministerio de Agricultura, Industria e Commercio, reported in USDA, *Foreign Crops*, Vol. 10, No. 25 (June 22, 1925), pp. 745–746 86
Fig. 8.1 Brazilian Cotton: Total exports and unit values, 1918–1922 (*Source* Calculated from Instituto Brasileiro de Geografia e Estatística, Repertório Estatístico do Brasil, Quadros retrospectivas No. 1 [Rio de Janeiro: Serviço Gráfico do Instituto Brasileiro de Geografia e Estatística, 1941], p. 87) 156
Fig. 8.2 Brazilian exports of and unit value of chilled and frozen beef, 1919–1922 (*Source* Brazil, Ministerio da Fazenda, Directoria de Estatística Commercial, *Commercio Exterior do Brasil, Janeiro a Dezembro 1919, 1920, 1921, 1922, 1923* [Rio de Janeiro: Estatística Commercial, 1924], pp. 110–111) 164
Fig. 9.1 Brazilian coffee production and prices, 1922–1930 (*Source* Calculated from Instituto Brasileiro de Geografia e Estatística, Repertório Estatístico do Brasil, Quadros retrospectivas No. 1 [Rio de Janeiro: Serviço Gráfico do Instituto Brasileiro de Geografia e Estatística, 1941], p. 85) 171
Fig. 9.2 Destinations of Brazilian cotton production, 1920–1926 (*Source* USC-São Paulo to SS, Dec. 26, 1928, RG 166, Box 57, USNA) 178

Fig. 9.3 São Paulo cotton production, 1919–1930 (*Source* Rui Henrique Pereira Lima de Albuquerque, *Capital comercial, indústria têxtil e produção agricola: as relações de produção na cotonicultura paulista, 1920–1950* [São Paulo: HUCITEC; Brasilia: Conselho Nacional de Desenvolvimento Científico e Tecnológico, 1983], p. 116) 179
Fig. 9.4 Quantity and value of animals slaughtered in São Paulo Packing Houses, 1922–1930 (*Source* São Paulo [state] Boletim da Directoria de Industria e Commercio, cited in USC-São Paulo to SS, July 14, 1931, Box 65 RG 166, USNA) 186
Fig. 9.5 São Paulo Packing House Production of Frozen versus Fresh Beef, 1928–1930 (*Source* São Paulo [state] Boletim da Directoria de Industria e Commercio, cited in USC-São Paulo to SS, July 14, 1931, Box 65 RG 166, USNA) 187
Fig. 9.6 Volume and price per ton of Brazilian Frozen Beef Exports, 1922–1930 (*Source* Brazil, Ministerio da Fazenda, Directoria de Estatística Commercial, *Commercio Exteriordo Brasil,* [Rio de Janeiro: Directoria de Estatística Commercial, 1931]) 188
Fig. 9.7 Destination of exports of chilled and frozen beef from São Paulo Packing Houses, 1929 (*Source* São Paulo [state] Boletim da Directoria de Industria e Commercio, cited in USC-São Paulo to SS, July 14, 1931, Box 65 RG 166, USNA) 188
Fig. 11.1 Exports and average price per ton of cotton exported from Brazil, 1922–1930 (*Source* Brazil, Ministerio de Fazenda, *Relatório 1925*, p. 9. *Source* Brazil, Ministerio da Fazenda, Directoria de Estatística Commercial, *Commercio Exterior do Brasil* (Rio de Janeiro: Directoria de Estatística Commercial, 1931)) 222
Fig. 11.2 Cotton production in three leading Northwestern Producing States, 1922–23 to 1929–30 (*Source* Rui Henrique Pereira Lima de Albuquerque, *Capital comercial, indústria têxtil e produção agricola: as relações de produção na cotonicultura paulista, 1920–1950* (São Paulo: HUCITEC; Brasilia: Conselho Nacional de Desenvolvimento Científico e Tecnológico, 1983), p. 116) 225

Fig. 11.3 Domestic and foreign cotton exports from Pernambuco, Ceará, and Rio Grande do Norte 1923 to 1929 (*Sources* Recife data from Directoria Geral de Estatística quoted in *A Provincia* [Recife], Jan. 16, 1930, p. 3. Data on Rio Grande do Norte from state presidential messages complied by Itamara de Souza, *A República Velha no Rio Grande do Norte 1889–1930* (Natal, RGN: Editora da UFRN, 2008), p. 80. Ceará data from *Annuarios Estatísticos do Ceará* quoted in Memoria do Ceará, *Ceará—A Crise Permanente do Modelo Exportador 1850–1930* (Fortaleza, CE: Instituto da Memória do Povo Cearense, 1989), pp. 206–207. (No data are available for Pernambuco for 1923 and 1924.)) 226
Fig. 11.4 Value per ton Frozen Beef and Charque, Rio Grande do Sul, 1922–1930 (Source: Rio Grande do Sul, Departamento Estadual de Estatística, *Anuario Estatístico do Rio Grande do Sul 1938/39; 1941* (Porto Alegre: DEE, 1939/1940; 1942) cited in Sigfried Emanuel Heiser, *As Relações de Comércio do Rio Grande do Sul – Do Século XIX a 1930* (Porto Alegre: Secretaria de Coordinação e Planejamento, 2004), pp. 109, 122) 231
Fig. 11.5 Production of Frozen Beef versus Charque, Rio Grande do Sul, 1922–1930 (Source: Rio Grande do Sul, Departamento Estadual de Estatística, *Anuario Estatístico do Rio Grande do Sul 1938/39; 1941* (Porto Alegre: DEE, 1939/1940; 1942) cited in Sigfried Emanuel Heiser, *As Relações de Comércio do Rio Grande do Sul – Do Século XIX a 1930* (Porto Alegre: Secretaria de Coordinação e Planejamento, 2004), pp. 109, 122) 232
Fig. 12.1 Indexed prices for coffee, sugar, and cocoa, 1928–1939 (*Sources* Coffee and Cocoa prices from Instituto Brasileiro de Geografia e Estatística, Reportório Estatístico do Brasil, Quadros Respectivos, No. 1 (Separata do Anuário Estatístico do Brasil, Ano V, 1939/40 (Rio de Janeiro: Serviço Gráfico do Instituto Brasiliero de Geografia e Estatística, 1941), p. 23. Sugar prices from Brazil. Instituto do Açúcar e do Álcool, *Anuário Açucareiro 1939* (Rio de Janeiro, Brasil Açucareiro, n.d.), p. 95) 248
Fig. 12.2 Allocations of central government expenditures for sugar cane cooperation fields, c. 1933–1939 (*Source Anuário Açucareiro 1939*, p. 57) 251

Fig. 12.3	Brazilian coffee production and export, 1931–1945 (*Source* Charles C. Mueller, *Das Oligarquias Agrárias ao Predomínio Urbano-Industrial: Um estudo do Processo da Formação de Políticas Agrícolas no Brasil* (Rio de Janeiro: IPEA/IPES, 1983), pp. 225, 227)	256
Fig. 12.4	Total Area Planted in Coffee (millions of hectares) 1931–1945 (*Source* Brazil Instituto Brasileiro de Geografia e Estatística. *Estatísticas Históricas Do Brasil, Séries Econômicas, Demográficas e Sociais de 1550 a 1985* (Rio de Janeiro: IBGE, 1987), p. 291)	257
Fig. 12.5	Federal versus States' Allocations on Superior Education, Scientific Institutes and Experimentation in Agriculture, 1935 (*Source* Brazil. Ministério da Agricultura, *Relatório 1934–1935*, p. 169)	268
Fig. 13.1	Ratio of cotton to coffee prices and cotton acreage in São Paulo state, 1924–1937 (*Source* Compiled from reports of the São Paulo Merchandise Exchange and the Ministry of Agriculture. Cited in Percy K. Norris, *Cotton Production in Southern Brazil.* U.S. Department of Agriculture Office of Foreign Agricultural Relations (Washington DC, Sept 1939), p. 16)	274
Fig. 13.2	Cotton production in São Paulo versus Northeastern States, 1924–1925 to 1936–1937 (*Source* Percy K. Norris, *Cotton Production in Southern Brazil.* U.S. Department of Agriculture Office of Foreign Agricultural Relations (Washington DC, Sept. 1939), p. 7)	280
Fig. 13.3	Price per pound for U.S. and Brazilian Cotton, Liverpool, 1926–1927 to 1935–1936 (*Source* U.S. Department of Agriculture. *Agriculture Statistics 1937* (Washington, DC: GPO, 1937), p. 100)	283
Fig. 14.1	Wheat Production in Santa Catarina, Rio Grande do Sul and Brazil Overall, 1939–1943 (metric tons) (*Source* Brazil. Instituto Brasileiro de Geografia e Estatística. *Anuário Estatístico do Brasil Ano VI—1941–1945* (Rio de Janeiro: Instituto Brasileiro de Geografia e Estatística, 1946), p. 96)	296
Fig. 15.1	Indexed prices for key food goods in Brazil's 22 capital cities (1941–1945) (*Source* Calculated from Instituto Brasileiro de Geografia e Estatística. Conselho Nacional de Estatística. *Anuário Estatístico do Brasil Ano VII 1946* (Rio de Janeiro: Serviço Gráfico do IBGE, 1947), pp. 357–60)	324

Fig. 15.2 Destination by region of subsidies distributed by the Brazilian-American Food Production Commission, 1944 (Source: TS, "Ministerio da Agricultura, Trabalhos em Execução nos Estados e Respectivas Dotações Orçamentarias," Getúlio Vargas Archive, Centro de Pesquisa e Documentação de História Contemporânea do Brasil (CPDOC), Fundação Getúlio Vargas, GV MinA,44.06.00) 336
Fig. 15.3 Indexed change in production major crops, average production 1940–1944 versus 1935–1939 (*Source Brazil*: Agricultural Production and Trade Statistics (Washington, DC: USDA, 1951), p. 7) 346
Fig. 16.1 Indexed average price increases for various crops, 1946–1950 (1945 = 1.00) (*Source* Calculated from Fundação IBGE, Estatísticas históricas do Brasil: séries econômicas, demográficas e sociais de 1550 a 1988 2nd ed. Rev. of Vol. 3 de Séries Estatísticas Retrospectivas (Rio de Janeiro: IBGE, 1990), pp. 322–24, 326, 327, 329, 330, 332, 335) 351
Fig. 17.1 Average increases in production for various crops, 1945–49 versus 1940–44 (Average production 1940–44 = 1.00) (*Source* Calculated from Tables 6, in Dwight R. Bishop, *Brazil: Agricultural Production and Trade Statistics* (Washington, DC: U.S. Dept. of Agriculture, Office of Foreign Agricultural Relations, 1951), p. 6) 375
Fig. 17.2 Average increases in area cultivated for specific crops, 1945–49 Compared to average 1940–44 plantings (1940–44 average—1.00) (*Source* Calculated from Table 4, in Dwight R. Bishop, *Brazil: Agricultural Production and Trade Statistics* (Washington, DC: U.S. Dept. of Agriculture, Office of Foreign Agricultural Relations, 1951), p. 4) 376
Fig. 17.3 Average increases in production versus average increases in cultivated area for specific crops, 1945–49 (1940–44 averages compared to 1945–49 averages) (*Source* Calculated from Tables 4 and 6, in Dwight R. Bishop, *Brazil: Agricultural Production and Trade Statistics* (Washington, DC: U.S. Dept. of Agriculture, Office of Foreign Agricultural Relations, 1951), pp. 4, 6) 377

List of Tables

Table 5.1	Agricultural material distributed by the National Production Committee, 1918–1919	65
Table 5.2	Material purchased by the Carlos Moreira Mission to the United States April 1918	67
Table 5.3	Seeds distributed by the National Production Committee, 1918–1919	68
Table 11.1	Highways and Carriage Roads constructed by the Inspectoria Federal de Obras Contra as Seccas, 1919–1925	224

CHAPTER 1

Introduction

An analysis of the historic transformation of Brazil's agriculture offers insight for planners, investors, producers, and consumers alike. Understanding how Brazil shifted its focus from prioritizing a few export crops to sustaining a diversified range of products can suggest ways to overcome the daunting challenges facing global agriculture in the twenty-first century. And, given the historically close ties between the United States and Brazil related to agriculture, a review of the evolution of that relationship can suggest how international ties may influence the agricultural destiny of today's developing nations.

Historians have heretofore addressed segments of the relationship without delving deeply into the agricultural aspect, except for occasional treatment of issues arising from the coffee trade and through narrowly focused dissertations.[1] Agriculture appears as a complement to studies

[1] Joseph Robert West offers a lengthy account of entrepreneurial and scientific ventures by foreigners in Brazil during the nineteenth century in "The foreigner in Brazilian technology, 1808–1900" [microform] 1949. Other works analyze the activities of North American businesses and tycoons, including Elizabeth Anne Cobb's, *The rich neighbor policy: Rockefeller and Kaiser in Brazil* (New Haven: Yale University Press, n.d.); Lincoln Gordon and Engelbert L. Grommers, *United States Manufacturing Investment in Brazil: The Impact of Brazilian Government policies, 1946–1960* (Boston: Graduate School of Business Administration, Harvard University, 1962); Mauricio Font. *Coffee, Contention, and Change in the Making of Modern Brazil* (Cambridge, B. Blackwell, 1990); Greg Grandin, *Fordlandia: The Rise and Fall of Henry Ford's Forgotten Jungle*

E. R. Downes, *Brazilian Agricultural Development, 1890–1950*,
https://doi.org/10.1007/978-3-031-76992-4_1

that compare Brazilian and U.S. national identities, inspired by the 1954 classic of Clodomiro Vianna Moog, *Bandeirantes e pioneiros: Paralelo entre duas culturas* (Rio de Janeiro: Editora Globo, 1954). Multiple dissertations and monographs on aspects of Brazil's agricultural history have been completed at Brazilian, U.S., and other universities. Unfortunately, this body of literature fails to treat the broad history of interaction between the United States and Brazil related to agriculture.

Historians have likewise failed to provide a comprehensive treatment on the role of agriculture in Brazil's development. Historians of Brazil's economy have long focused on the structural deficiencies of export agriculture and the inequities of a commodities export system as explanations of Brazil's relative lack of material progress. One persistent theme of this historiography has endowed various crops as constituting the defining factor for major periods, or "cycles," of Brazilian history, drawing from Portuguese historian João Lúcio de Azevedo's 1928 work, *Épocas de Portugal Econômico* (1928). In 1938, statesman and educator Alfonso Arinos de Mello Franco presented a series of lectures to Uruguayan audiences in which he declared that "in chronological order from the sixteenth to the twentieth century, we can divide the history of the Brazilian economy into cycles: (1) the cycle of Brazil wood; (2) the sugar cycle; (3) the gold cycle and (4) the coffee cycle. These were the main products, the successive sovereigns of our economy."[2] Pioneer economic historian Roberto Simonsen, writing in 1937, also embraced the commodity cycles in defining Brazil's economic history. For Simonsen, the focus on primary products meant that Brazil's economy at the end of the colonial period was characterized by goods in "an elementary stage of elaboration, to which there have not been integrated economic factors of high importance."[3]

The "cyclical boom and bust" concept became an accepted element of Brazilian economic historiography. In 1977, the third edition of Pontifical Catholic University professor Mirecea Buescu's *Evolução Ecônomico do Brasil* focused on the notion of a "cycle" as characterized by the

City (Metropolitan Books, 2009); and Susan McDonald, "'Development' as an Issue in Brazil-United States Relations, 1946–1954" (Diss.: Florida State University, 1986).

[2] Afonos Arinos de Melo Franco, *Sintese da história econômica do Brasil* (Salvador, Bahia: Aguiar & Souza, 1958), p. 24.

[3] Roberto Simonsen, *História Econômica do Brasil 1500/1820* (São Paulo: Companhia Editora Nacional, 1957), p. 390.

supremacy of a certain export that "creates a dependency of the entire economy in relation to this product."[4] A comprehensive view of Brazil's economic history, published in 2001 by a prominent Brazilian diplomat and historian, adopted similar terms to explain Brazil's economic history. Paulo Roberto de Almeida cites "the cyclical fluctuations of commodities primaries export-basically coffee, sugar, and cotton, complemented by tobacco, and cacao and erva-mate, besides rubber during one period," as determining "not only the pace of development in Brazil, but also the integration of each of the productive zones with other regions of the country and their relative degree of external economic integration, that is, of the opening to flows of foreign goods and services."[5]

Complementing the emphasis on the cyclical nature of the production of mainly agricultural commodities is a view that the structural weaknesses of the system of their production have not only defined Brazil's history but have left Brazil tied to a colonial past of inequities, at both national and international levels. Leading this field of interpretation is Caio Prado Junior, whose 1942 *Formação do Brasil Contemporâneo-Colônia* characterized Brazil's colonial history as a system designed to exploit Brazilian resources to "satisfy the international trade of some tropic good and precious metals on a grand commercial scale."[6] For Caio Prado, elements of Brazil's agricultural economy—the large estate, monoculture, and slavery—were the pillars of a single socio-economic system. This system persisted beyond the colonial era with arrival of the Empire, as "Brazil continued to be a producer of primary products for the foreign markets, as it always had been; it would not overcome this fundamentally colonial status."[7] He blamed export agriculture for the maintenance of a Brazil's traditional socio-economic structure. Caio Prado's views on Brazil's economic history gained him a permanent status

[4] Mircea Buescu, *Evolução Econômico do Brasil* 3rd ed. (Rio de Janeiro: APEC 1977), p. 24.

[5] Paulo Roberto de Almeida, *Formação da diplomacia econômica no Brasil: as relações econômicas internacionais no Império*. (São Paulo: Editora SENAC [Brasilia]: Fundação Alexandre de Gusmão, c2001), p. 73.

[6] Caio Prado Junior, *Formação do Brasil Contemporâneo colônia* 1st ed. 1942. 14th edition (São Paulo: Editora Brasiliense, 1976), p. 359.

[7] Caio Prado Junior, "A Guide for the Historiography of the Second Empire," in E. Bradford Burns, ed., *Perspectives on Brazilian History* (New York: Columbia Univ. Press, 1967), p. 95.

in Brazilian historiography, considered a "vigorous and constant reference in our economic historiography."[8]

The structural weaknesses of Brazilian agriculture also figured prominently in the writing of Celso Furtado, who in 1949 joined the economic team of Raul Prebisch at the Economic Commission for Latin America (ECLA). Furtado embraced the structuralist theory that asymmetric relations in the global capitalist system generated an underdeveloped periphery where equitable economic growth could be generated only by giving priority to domestic market development. His *Formação Econômica do Brasil* (1953) argued that dependence upon foreign customers created slave-based societies and economies such as Brazil's. To overcome the consequent lack of low-priced food for domestic needs, it was necessary to create a comprehensive agrarian reform.[9] The focus on the central role of structural deficiencies in Brazil's economic past has been sustained by prominent scholars, both Brazilian and foreign. Fernando Novais's 1986 work, *Portugal e Brasil na Crise do Antigo Sistema Colonial,* embraced the notion of a colonial economy designed to meet the metropole's needs, especially the accumulation of capital.[10] Former President Fernando Henrique Cardoso's work, *Dependency and Development in Latin America*, co-authored by Enzo Faletto and released in its latest version in 1997, retained the focus on the unequal relation between the center and periphery in the world economy. Meanwhile, non-Brazilian historians of Brazil's economy have also embraced cyclical and structuralist approaches.

[8] Tamás Szmrecsányi, "Retomando A Questão Do Início Da Historiografia Econômica No Brasil," *Anais do V Congresso Brasileiro de História Econômica e 6ª Conferência Internacional de História de Empresas,* Sept. 2003, p. 9. See also Renato Moscateli, "Um Redescobrimento Historiográfico Do Brasil," *Revista de História Regional,* Vol. 5, No. 1 (Summer 2000), 187–201 and Leandro Braga de Andrade,"A Historiografia sobre o debate acerca da economia colonial brasileira," Universidade Federal De Ouro Preto Instituto De Ciências Humanas E Sociais, II Encontro Memorial, Nov. 2009, http://www.ichs.ufop.br/memorial/trab/h10_5.pdf; Nícia Villela Luz, "A história econômica do Brasil no Período de 1830 a 1930: Abordagens e problemas: Um ensaio bibliográfico," in Carlos Manuel Pelaez and Mircea Buescu, *A Moderna História Econômica.* (Rio de Janeiro: APEC, 1976) p. 204.

[9] See Yedda Linhares, pp. 42–43; Geisa Maria Rocha, "Celso Furtado and the Resumption of Construction in Brazil: Structuralism as an Alternative to Neoliberalism," *Latin American Perspectives*, Vol. 34, No. 5, (Sep. 2007), 132–34.

[10] Leandro Braga de Andrade, "A Historiografia," p. 4.

This study adopts a different approach. It draws from the tenets of institutionalism, especially New Institutional Economics. This framework arose during the 1980s and 1990s to analyze why some nations' agricultural sectors developed more quickly than others. Such a paradigm presents essential elements of the development paradigm of agricultural development.[11] It recognizes that fomenting technological change in agriculture is a complex process that requires a suitable institutional base for commencement and sustainment. It recognizes that efforts to transform agriculture require institutional and political support, as well as organized long-term research to develop solutions appropriate for the climatic, social, and ecological setting. Social and economic factors are also critical, as is the level of education, which, according to a pioneer of agricultural technology transfer, "influences the supply of cognitive skills available to understand the new technology."[12] The failure of U.S. agricultural missionaries to instill systemic change in China's nineteenth-century agriculture is instructive. They strove for decades to alter traditional farming methods without realizing that technical knowledge alone was insufficient. Without "changes in the wider policy, society, and economy," including a supportive infrastructure, their suggested technical improvements failed to have an impact outside the laboratory and the experimental field.[13]

The New Institutional Economics allows for consideration of the wider context of institutions that reflect the economic, social, and political reality of the developing nation. As pointed out by a recent

[11] Christopher B. Barrett, "The Economics of Agricultural Development: An Overview," in Christopher B. Barrett, ed., *Agricultural Development: Critical Concepts in Development* Studies (London: Routledge, 2011), p. 36.

[12] See G. Philip Robertson, Vivien G. Allen, George Boody, Emery R. Boose, Nancy G. Creamer, Laurie E. Drinkwater, James R. Gosz, Lori Lynch, John L. Havlin, Louise E. Jackson, Steward T. A. Pickett, Louis Pitelka, Alan Randall, A. Scott Reed, Timothy R. Seastedt, Robert B. Waide, and Diana H. Wall, "Long-term Agricultural Research: A Research, Education, and Extension Imperative," *BioScience*, Vol. 58, No. 7 (July/ August 2008), 640–45; G. Edward Schuh, "Methods Used in Transferring Technology from the Laboratory to the Producer: Economic Considerations," in *Proceedings of the International Symposium on Biotic Stress of Barley in Arid and Semi-Arid Environments*, The Department of Plant Pathology, Montana State University, and The International Center for Agricultural Research in Dry Areas. Aleppo, Syria, July 30 -August 2, 1990, pp. 9–10.

[13] Randall E. Stross, *The Stubborn Earth: American Agriculturalists on Chinese Soil, 1898–1937* (Berkeley: University of California Press, c1986), p. 216.

study of the role of institutions in agricultural development, "the institutional structure of the agricultural sector is a complex socio-economic system containing economic, organizational, legal, moral and ethical elements."[14] With respect to agribusiness, the New Institutional Economics encourages consideration of "the role of institutions and coordination mechanisms other than prices...." It urges exploration of "the institutional frame that affect the mechanisms of governance" of agribusiness systems, incorporating "legal analysis, business management and economics and its application to agriculture."[15] Institutions of relevance to agricultural development include those that define relations between land and labor, credit and interlinked transactions, marketing and insurance, as well as "cooperatives, technology and the state."[16] Applying perspectives generated by New Institutional Economics can suggest existence of institutions that stimulated or restrained Brazil's agricultural development, thereby illuminating the primary catalysts of the process.

Employing New Institutional Economics also requires a judgment about the nature of the Brazilian state, a subject imbued with competing epistemological orientations. My review of the course of agricultural development during the period of this study suggests that distinct types of corporatism provided the framework for relations between capital, labor, and the state. Even though the concept of corporatism has undergone various mutations since it's returned to the analytical scene in the 1970s, interaction related to Brazil's agriculture in general reflected control by the state through various interest groups or organizations.[17] Howard Wiarda has argued that Brazilian corporativism, marked by representation

[14] Petro Putsenteilo, Yuriy Klapkiv, Vitalii Karpenko and Irina Gvozdecka, "The role of institutions in the development of agriculture," *Bulgarian Journal of Agricultural Science,* Vol. 26, No. 1 (2020), 23.

[15] Decio Zylbersztajn, "Agribusiness Systems Analysis: Origin, Evolution and Research Perspectives," *Revista de Administração,* Vol. 52 (2017), 115–16.

[16] Pranab Bardham, ed., *The Economic Theory of Agrarian Institutions* (New York: Oxford University Press, 1989).

[17] There are multiple interpretations of the nature of the Brazilian state since the end of the monarchy. For a review, see Bolivar Lamounier, "Brasil. La formación de un pensamiento político autoritario en la Primera República: una interpretación," Vol. 16, No. 62 (July–Sep. 1976), 253–79. On corporatism, see Cláudia M. R. Viscardi, "Corporativismo e Neocorporativismo," *Estudos Históricos,* Vol. 31, No. 64 (May–Aug. 2018), 243–256 and Bruno P.W. Reis, "Corporativismo, Pluralismo e Conflito Distributivo no Brasil," *Dados,* Vol. 38, No. 3 (1995), 417–57.

of various "functionally determined units... and directed by the state," is a legacy of the "Iberic-Latin tradition."[18] It is a "format of intermediation" whereby "groups or functional categories" exercise a "monopoly of representation [and] directed fundamentally at the bureaucracy of the state."[19] In his pioneering 1974 essay, Phillipe C. Schmitter offered two varieties of corporatism based on the degrees of state control. Societal corporatism is found "imbedded in political systems with relatively autonomous, multilayered political units" and "open, competitive political systems." State corporatism practices "central bureaucratic power" where elections are "nonexistent or plebiscitary; party systems are monopolized by a weak single party; executive authorities are ideologically exclusive and more narrowly recruited."[20]

The corporatist model best explains the relations between Brazil's agriculture and the state during the period of this study. The First Republic manifested societal corporatism. Subsequent governments through to the collapse of the military-led government practiced state corporatism in varying intensities. The experience is consistent with the relationship between corporatism and agricultural development as pointed out by Spanish agronomist and sociologist Eduardo Moyano Estrada. Based on his study of the evolution of Spanish agriculture, Moyano concluded that corporatism is the response of the agrarian sector to its loss of hegemony to industrialism in modern societies. Moyano judged the "corporatization of the agrarian sector" as the "tendency of the articulation of diverse interests through large organizations." This, he argued, was "an observable fact in developed agriculture."[21] In a discussion of the role of corporatist model in Brazilian agriculture, Antonio Cesar Ortega points out that corporatism "modifies the system of agrarian interest representation to

[18] Howard J. Wiarda, "Corporatism and Development in the Iberic-Latin World: Persistent Strains and New Variations," in Fredrick B. Pike and Thomas Stritch, *eds., The New Corporatism: Social-Political Structures in the Iberian World* (Norte Dame, IN: Univ. of Notre Dame Press, 1974), pp. 10, 12.

[19] Eli Diniz and Renato R. Boschi, "O Corporativismo na Construção do Espaço Público," in Renato R. Boschi, *Corporativismo e Desigualdade: A Construção do Espaço Público no Brasil* (Rio de Janeiro: Rio Fundo Editora, 1991), p. 13.

[20] Philippe C. Schmitter, "Still a Century of Corporatism?" *The Review of Politics*, Vol. 36, No. 1 (Jan. 1974), 104–105.

[21] Eduardo Moyano Estrada, *Corporatismo y Agricultura: Associaciones Profesionales y Articulación de Intereses en la Agricultura Española* (N.P.; Instituto de Estudios Agrarios, Pesqueros, y Alimentarios, 1984), p. 103.

make it compatible with the economic transformations that have vertically integrated agriculture and industry."[22]

Considering Brazil's agricultural development within such a framework benefits from the explosion of research on Brazil's agricultural history underway since the early 1980s. As summarized by Yedda Linhares, previous accounts of Brazil's agricultural history were "relatively small and reduced to a few titles, covering the whole complex or some product, a certain technique, manpower and other topics. Everything is incomplete, sometimes nothing but suggestions, and [there are] basically ignored issues such as the case of land, waiting for research." She decried as "incredible" that so little scholarship embraced Brazil's agricultural history, especially since "almost until yesterday," agriculture had served as Brazil's base.[23]

Despite the volume of new research on Brazil's agricultural history, to date there is no general history of Brazil's agriculture that would update Luis Amarals's 1958 two-volume study, *História geral da agricultura brasileira, no tríplice aspecto político-social-econômico*. However, subsequent analyses by scholars and official Brazilian and multinational organizations have provided much needed additional context. Bahian Tamás Szmrecsányi attempted to rectify that situation with his 1990 pamphlet-sized summary, *Pequena Historia da Agricultura Brasileira*, while observing that "the economic history of agriculture in Brasil continues to be, in many aspects, a virgin area for rigorous research and in-depth studies."[24] Additional insights have been provided by multiple studies of Brazilian agriculture published by EMBRAPA and independent scholars. The recent study on Brazilian agriculture by Herbert S. Klein

[22] Antonio Cesar Ortega, "Corporatism and New Forms for Representing Agricultural Interests: Theoretical Approach," *Revista de Economia e Sociologia Rural*, Vol. 36, No. 4 (Oct. Dec. 1998), 156.

[23] Maria Yedda de Linhares, *História da agricultura brasileira: combates e controvérsias* (São Paulo: Brasiliense, 1981), p. 8. An exception is Alice Canabrava's *O Algodão em São Paulo, 1861–1875* (São Paulo: T.A Queiroz Editor, 1984), praised by Tamás Szmrecsányi as being "strictly academic and professional," in "Retomando A Questão Do Início Da Historiografia Econômica," p. 15. Yedda de Linhares added her own contributions by addressing the issue of land tenure in Brazil's agrarian history, authoring with Francisco Carlos Teixeira da Silva, *Terra Prometida: Uma História da Questão Agraria no Brasil*. (Rio de Janeiro: Campus, 1999).

[24] Tamás Szmrecsányi, *Pequena História da Agricultura Brasileira* (São Paulo: Contexto, 1990), p. 9.

and Francisco Vida Luna, *Feeding the World: Brazil's Transformation into a Modern Agricultural Economy* (New York: Cambridge University Press, 2019), presents an impressive compilation of data and perspectives on the more recent course of the sector. However, the work provides few details on how exogenous factors, especially those of U.S. origin, may have contributed to the transformation of commercial agriculture. In the opinion of one reviewer, the work avoids "important political aspects of agricultural 'modernization,' and the social and environmental costs involved."[25] In another reviewer's opinion, the work "is not a social or political history" and fails to explain "why certain changes happened—and in particular, who was responsible for them."[26] These perspectives and theoretical guidelines offer an enticing framework for presenting a balanced view of the rich history of interaction between Brazilians and Americans related to Brazil's agriculture.

[25] Chris N. Lesser, "Review of Feeding the world: Brazil's Transformation into a Modern Agricultural Economy," *Environmental Politics*, Vol. 30, No. 3 (2021), 483.

[26] Eve E. Buckley, "Review of Feeding the World: Brazil's Transformation into a Modern Agricultural Economy," *The American Historical Review*, Vol. 125, No. 4 (Oct. 2020), 1478–79.

CHAPTER 2

The Brazilian Agricultural Reform Movement

During the forty years of Brazil's First Republic (1890–1930), Brazilian agriculture responded to pressures from the global marketplace and domestic reformers to make modest adjustments to its structural reality. The accepted truth that Brazil was an "essentially agricultural" nation dictated the First Republic's agrarian elites' response to major problems undermining their major cash crops—coffee and sugar. By the turn of the century, both were suffering severe crises. Coffee cultivation suffered from the twin scourges of declining productivity in some zones and excessive worldwide production. Virtually at the same time, sugar growers found it increasingly difficult to compete in the U.S. market with sugar from Puerto Rico, Cuba, and the Philippines. The rubber boom in Pará and Amazonas for a time compensated for declining export revenues, but the cyclical nature of rubber prices and then their complete collapse after 1910 only intensified the economic dilemma facing the regional elites charged with maintaining national as well as regional prosperity.

Early in the First Republic coffee began its fall from the privileged position it had enjoyed since the mid-nineteenth century. Massive new investment in the bean had quadrupled the number of coffee trees in production in Western São Paulo between 1886 and 1900.[1] Overall

[1] Thomas H. Holloway, *The Brazilian Coffee Valorization of 1906: Regional Politics and Economic Dependence* (Madison, WI.: The State Historical Society of Wisconsin, 1975), p. 27.

E. R. Downes, *Brazilian Agricultural Development, 1890–1950*,
https://doi.org/10.1007/978-3-031-76992-4_2

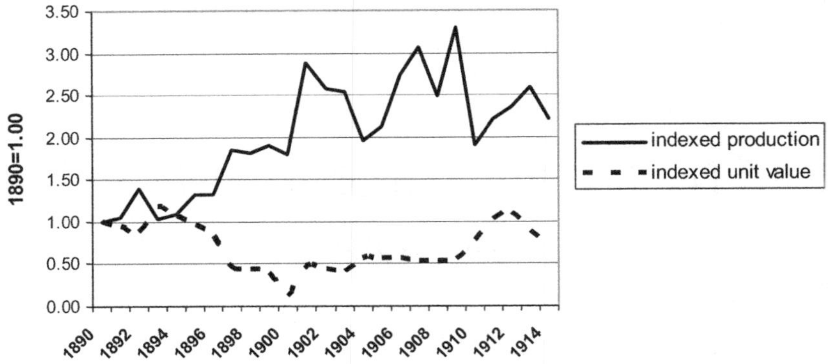

Fig. 2.1 Indexed production and unit value, Brazilian coffee exports, 1890–1914 (*Source* Calculated from Fundação Instituto Brasileiro de Geografia e Estatística, *Séries estatísticas retrospectivas* Vol. 3 (Rio de Janeiro: IBGE, 1987), p. 312)

production exploded from 10 million sacks in 1896 to over 23 million sacks by 1907, creating an "avalanche of coffee rolling through the markets, crushing everything, in an unparalleled devastation."[2] Coffee prices in milreis crested in 1894 and then began a gradual fall that became a headlong plunge by 1897, entering 20 years of general depression. By 1897, the price of coffee in New York dropped to half its 1890 price.[3] Action the Brazilian government took in 1898 to shore up the *milreis*, in response to foreign pressures, created further problems for coffee producers. The combination of a harder currency and lower prices caught planters in a "double squeeze," dramatically lowering their revenue in local currency. Figure 2.1 depicts the increase in output and dramatic fall in prices, measured in pounds sterling, between 1890 and 1914.

Regions tied to sugar cultivation faced an equally bitter future. Sugar had provided more than 25% of Brazil's export revenue during the early nineteenth century, but the Brazilian product found by the 1890s that it

[2] Augusto Ramos, *O café no Brasil e no estrangeiro* (Rio de Janeiro: Santa Helena, 1923), p. 527.

[3] V.D. Wickizer, *The World Coffee Economy with Special Reference to Control Schemes* (Stanford, CA.: Food Research Institute, Stanford Univ., 1943), p. 139; Affonso de E. Taunay, *Pequena história do café no Brasil* (Rio de Janeiro: Departamento Nacional de Café, 1945), p. 549.

could not compete with lower cost producers in Cuba and the Philippines. Sugar prices and exports dropped decidedly, and after 1900 Brazilian sugar producers were forced to depend upon the internal market. Sugar's decline spread economic malaise in Pernambuco, Alagoas, and Sergipe, as well as the Campos region of Rio de Janeiro state.[4]

The rubber boom of the 1890s presented an even less durable source of national revenue. The dependence of the rubber production upon wild trees sprinkled throughout the Amazon valley reduced benefits to other regions of the nation, except for the ability to charge federal import taxes on goods purchases through rubber exports. The cyclical nature of rubber prices, and finally their complete collapse after 1912, smothered any hope that rubber could provide Brazil with long-term benefits (Fig. 2.2).[5]

The uncertain futures of coffee, rubber, and sugar forced elites of those regions most affected to search for alternatives. Simultaneously, increases in urban population stimulated the notion that agriculture for domestic use could become profitable. The result was an alliance of elites from regions capable of producing foodstuffs for the domestic market with those in depressed regions seeking alternative economic activities. Their solution proved entirely consistent with long expressed but little practiced Brazilian thinking: diversify production from the soil. Their actions and the economic reality of the times created a broad-based movement for agricultural reform with monumental domestic and international implications. Aside from gradually gaining acceptance for the idea that Brazil could be something other than the "República do café," this movement eventually played an influential role in shifting Brazil away from its traditional European reference point. Diversifying production from Brazil's soil meant increasingly closer economic ties with the world's greatest agricultural nation of the time: the United States (Fig. 2.3).

[4] Carone, *A República Velha*, I, p. 52; Robert M. Levine, *Pernambuco in the Brazilian Federation: 1889–1937* (Stanford, CA.: Stanford Univ. Press, 1978), pp. 21–31; José C. Gnaccarini, "A economia do açucar: Processo de trabalho e processo de acumulação," in Boris Fausto, ed., *O Brasil Republicano, I: Estrutura de poder e economia (1889–1930)* (São Paulo, DIFEL, 1975), pp. 311–9; Peter L. Eisenberg, *The Sugar Industry in Pernambuco: Modernization without Change, 1840–1910* (Berkeley, CA.: Univ. of California Press, 1975).

[5] Barbara Weinstein, *The Amazon Rubber Boom 1850–1920* (Stanford, CA.: Stanford Univ. Press, 1983), pp. 112, 140–5.

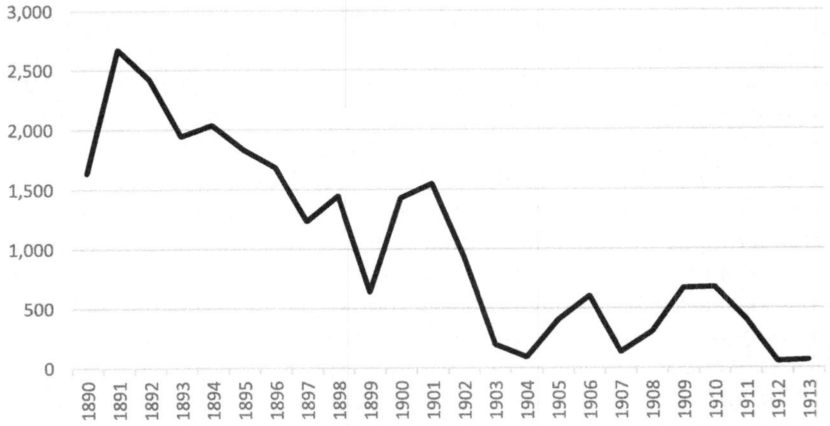

Fig. 2.2 Revenue from Sugar Exports, 1890–1913 (foreign currency) (*Source* Calculated from Fundação Instituto Brasileiro de Geografia e Estatística, *Séries estatísticas retrospectivas* Vol. 3 (Rio de Janeiro: IBGE, 1987), p. 307)

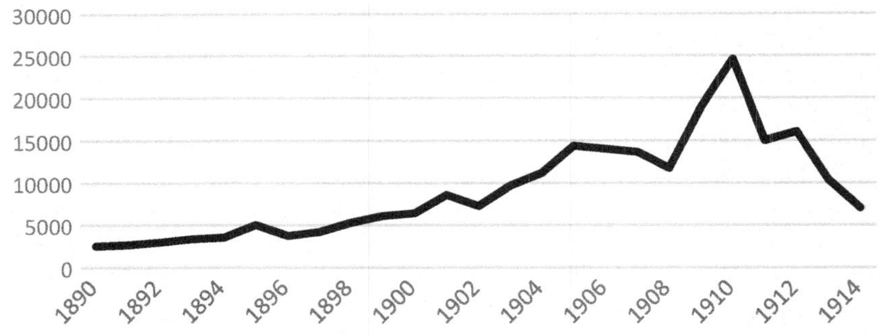

Fig. 2.3. Revenue from Rubber Exports, 1890–1914 (foreign currency) (*Source* Calculated from Fundação Instituto Brasileiro de Geografia e Estatística, *Séries estatísticas retrospectivas* Vol. 3 (Rio de Janeiro: IBGE, 1987), p. 309)

The Promoters of Agricultural Reform

Three distinct types of individuals transformed the diversification movement from vague notions to concerted action. One was the technically minded resident of the declining coffee areas who presented empirical evidence in favor of diversification, or "polyculture." These reformers worked from both within the state government apparatus and without, but had received a technical or scientific education, rather than the law degree customarily a necessity for success. A second major proponent of diversification was the professional politician seeking to enhance the prosperity of his regional power base. These occupied both federal and state posts and attempted to establish tariff mechanisms and federal support to offset the costs involved in diversification. A final group interested in diversification were elite members of areas dependent upon coffee seeking a hedge against further disturbances in the coffee market.

Engineer Américo Werneck (1855–1927), a concerned property owner in southern Minas Gerais, became the state's agricultural secretary in 1898. He had raised the unpleasant issue of the overproduction of coffee in 1892, pointing out "our error … in thinking that this land can live only from the cultivation of coffee." Coffee's profits, in his opinion, left the country too rapidly, through an "exaggerated importation" that upset all financial calculations.[6]

Similar in training and motivation was Luis Pereira Barreto, a medical doctor who became a vocal champion of the new empiricism for Brazilian agriculture. He preached and practiced the new sermon of a diversified agriculture and became an ardent apostle of polyculture. Like most Brazilians of the time, Pereira Barreto credited agriculture with a central importance in the nation's life, once writing that "Everything we are, everything we possess, we owe to agriculture." Agriculture provided "all the riches and elegancies of modern life." Unfortunately for man, the "breast of soil does not become fertile" unless man first conquered the brute force of nature, Science, however, applied by man through his intelligence, would make the "physical agents … our holy allies in the struggle to make the land bear fruit."[7] For, in the last analysis, it was not the land "which produces but, instead, the head of man."[8]

[6] Fabio Francisco de Almeida Castilho, "Américo Werneck: O Haussman de Águas Verturosas," *Annais do XXVI Simposio Nacional de História (ANPUH)* (July 2011), p. 2; Americo Werneck, *O Brasil, seu presente e seu futuro* (Petropolis: "Gazeta de Petropolis," 1892), p. 60.

[7] Quoted in Luis Amaral, *História geral da agricultura brasileira no triplice aspecto político-social-ecónomico* (São Paulo: Editora Nacional, 1939), I, 425.

[8] Roque Spencer Maciel Barros, *A evolução do pensamento de Pereira Barreto* (São Paulo: Grijalbo, 1967), p. 191. For Pereira Barreto's advocacy of wine production, see Graciela de Souza Oliver, "Debate cientificos e a produção de vinho paulista, 1890–1930," *Revista Brasileira de História*, Vol. 27, No. 54 (Dec. 2007).

The fruit that Pereira Barreto envisioned would be something other than coffee. And he began to prescribe a variety of medicines for Brazil's agricultural illnesses but focused on "polyculture." In over 100 articles in the *Provincia de São Paulo* and *Estado de São Paulo* newspapers, he argued that coffee should be replaced by other crops and industries, such as wheat, alfalfa, and "dozens of products which, if we overcame ignorance and complacency, we could export." Further, only exploitation of multiple crops could attract the immigrants and capital needed to broaden Brazil's economic perspectives. He cited the lack of technical and scientific agricultural education as a serious drawback to change in Brazilian agriculture. Only radical educational reform would deliver Brazil from the "kingdom of the law school graduates" and reorient education to studying natural laws. Brazil remained tied to a colonial economy despite its fertile soil and agreeable climate because "religious intoxification" had smothered scientific instruction. Fervently anti-Jesuit, Pereira Barreto urged a national technical and scientific education based on the U.S. example. "North America is showing us the road to follow," he wrote in 1901. In his view, the U.S. educational system had brought that country "prosperity, knowledge and power."[9]

A second major advocate of diversification was professional politicians seeking to enhance the prosperity of their regional power bases. These occupied both federal and state posts and championed tariffs and federal support to offset the costs inherent in diversification. Foremost was Joaquim Francisco de Assis Brasil, a prominent Rio Grande do Sul rancher and politician generally remembered more for his political activity

[9] Barros, *A evolução do pensamento*, pp. 189–90, 210–1, n. 34, 213; Mario Roberto Ferraro, Teresa Cristina Magro, and Demostenes Ferreira da Silva Filho, "A Gênise da Modernização da Agricultura em São Paulo," *Revista Ciência Agrícola* (Belém), No. 47 (Jan-Jun 2007); Amilson Barbosa Henriquez, "Um 'Orgão dos Agricultores Brasileiros': Algumas propostas da Moderna Agricultura na *Revista Agrícola* paulista (1895–1907," *Revista Crítica Histórica*, Vol. 2, No. 4 (Dec. 2011).

than his agrarian activism.[10] On his first foray into public life as a delegate to the provincial legislature in 1886, he spoke in favor of aiding the state's cattle sector—"our principal wealth, our principal source of income." Other industries may arise, he admitted, but "cattle raising will never disappear in our Province." In his opinion, this created an obligation upon the provincial legislature to improve the cattle industry. Fulfilling this goal was difficult, though, since provincial assemblies in the centralized Empire held little true power or authority. Change required a new arrangement, not among the legislators or party leaders, but in the nation's institutions.[11]

Assis Brasil soon gained the stature needed to advance his campaign for rural reform. As a loyal and active Republican and effective orator, he soon rose to national prominence. He established the first modern Brazilian agricultural interest group, the Sociedade Brasileira para a Animação da Agricultura (Brazilian Society for the Encouragement of Agriculture), in Paris, out of his concern for the precariousness of Brazil's coffee-based economy. In the society's inaugural session, he called attention to the "danger, each time greater, recognized by eminent Brazilians, of [having] only one support, of not [being able] to count on anything but coffee." Relying solely upon coffee overlooked the "eventuality of a great reduction in price or the impossibility of export because of an international or civil war."[12]

The Society became a European outpost of Brazilian agricultural improvement and the first manifestation of corporatist activism in Brazilian agriculture. It purchased agricultural equipment, publications, breeding animals, and seeds for shipment to its members in Brazil and

[10] The study of Assis Brasil's political philosophy gained momentum with the return of democratic government in post-1985 Brazil. See Paulo Brossard, ed., *Idéias políticas de Assis Brasil* (Brasilia: Senado Federal; Rio de Janeiro: Fundação Casa de Rui Barbosa, MinC, 1989) and *J.F. de Assis Brasil*, 2nd ed., (Porto Alegre: Est Edições, 2004); Carlos Reverbel, *Assis Brasil*, 2nd ed. (Porto Alegre: IEL, 1996); José Antônio Giuisti Tavares, *Representação Política e Governo: J.F. de Assis Brasil Dialogando com os Posteros* (Canoas: Universidade Luterana do Brasil, 2005); Joseph L. Love, *Rio Grande do Sul and Brazilian Regionalism, 1882*–1930 (Stanford, CA: Stanford Univ. Press, 1971), p. 225. Assis Brasil's diplomatic service is recounted in Joaquim Francisco de Assis Brasil, *Assis Brasil um diplomata da República* (Rio de Janeiro: CHDD/FUNAG, 2006).

[11] Quoted in Fortunato Pimentel, *Joaquim Francisco de Assis Brasil: Emérito Agricultor* (Porto Alegre: Santa Teresinha Ltda., 1950), pp. 101–2.

[12] Assis Brasil, *Cultura dos campos*, p. xiii.

sought political patronage. By 1910, it boasted 428 members and, in that year alone, forwarded to Brazil 243 breeding animals of various species. Its membership represented the unity of purpose of agricultural, commercial, and governmental agencies. Individuals and groups later prominent in the agricultural reform movement lent support: Paulistas Carlos J. Botelho and Augusto Ramos, U.S. missionary Benjamin Hunnicutt, and agricultural associations in São Paulo, Rio de Janeiro, and Santa Catarina. Various state governments and the federal government, along with newspapers *O Estado de São Paulo* and *A Noite* [Rio de Janeiro], contributed funds.[13]

Assis Brasil continued his campaign to advance Brazilian agriculture from his diplomatic post in Lisbon, where he published, in 1897, what became the Bible of progressive Brazilian agriculture: *Cultura dos campos*, a primer on soil weather, plants, fertilizers, drainage, irrigation, wheat, rye, barley, oats, rice, and alfalfa.[14] Assis Brasil hoped his book would lead to increased production and greater government support for agriculture, especially better agricultural education and greater farm mechanization. The book endorsed the increased use of modern farm implements, especially on large farms to replace individual laborers using hoes. Cultivators,

[13] Pimentel, *Assis Brasil*, pp. 4, 5. For an example of the society's search for patronage, see its letter to Nilo Peçanha, Jan. 30, 1904, L-270, ANP, seeking Peçanha's "valuable support." The distance of the Sociedade Brasileira para a Animação da Agricultura from Brazil lessened its influence in domestic politics, however, provoking Edgard Carone to dismiss the society as "aristocratic and rare" in A *República Velha, I: Instituições e classes sociaes (1889–1930),* p. 161. For a list of the society's contributors, see MS, "Sociedade Brasileira para a Animação da Agricultura: Histórico da Sociedade," pp. 1–26, SNA. The Society's actions reflected the continuing importance of European ties to Brazilian agriculture before World War I, even as linkages to U.S. educational institutions were increasing, as noted in Chapter 2. Some Brazilians seeking agronomist degrees traveled to French or Swiss schools. For example, A. Gomes Carmo went to France to conquer a "heavy" agricultural engineering degree, returning to Brazil in 1893 to become a prominent publisher of agriculturally oriented material. See A. Gomes Carmo, *Considerações historicas sobre a agricultura Brasileira* (Rio de Janeiro: Serviço de Publicidade Agrícola, Ministerio da Agricultura, 1939), p. 89. Likewise, earlier in the century the president of an ephemeral agricultural club in the Paraíba Valley region of Rio de Janeiro state praised French and British agricultural practices but made no mention of U.S. methods. See Laura J. Pang, "The State and Agricultural Clubs of Imperial Brazil, 1860–1889," (Diss. Vanderbilt 1981), p. 69. Information about agricultural conditions in other countries reached Brazilvia Paris, such as an article on U.S.wheat cultivation published in Brazilafter appearing in *Monde Moderne* of Paris. "A cultura de trigo nos E.U.," *A Lavoura*, Vol. 2 (1899), 216–7.

[14] Assis Brasil, *Cultura dos campos*, p. ix.

plows, and weeders improved farm efficiency by doing "more and better work." Especially effective were implements made by the large U.S. manufacturing companies, such as Deere and Company of Moline, Illinois, available at a "relatively insignificant" price.[15] Meanwhile, *Cultura dos campos* reached a large audience, with over 37,000 copies sold.[16]

Another regional politician promoting diversification of agriculture was Rio de Janeiro state's Nilo Peçanha. Peçanha was aware of the problems of a tottering sugar economy because of his upbringing in Campos and education in Pernambuco. He became even more concerned about dependence upon traditional crops when he became governor of Rio de Janeiro state in 1903. The sugar industry in Peçanha's home region of Campos was suffering from inferior quality and low productivity. Receipts from coffee taxes had fallen to half their 1898 level, as coffee prices and the extent of cultivation itself had receded. Peçanha chose to remedy the situation by promoting agricultural diversification within the state, an option reflecting his conviction that agriculture constituted the prime source of national wealth. For Peçanha, the very term "production" implied goods brought forth from the soil. Rather than promoting industrialism, Peçanha was committed to reviving the agricultural sector from its comatose state.[17] As he explained to the Rio de Janeiro state legislature, "the first duty of the State, before caring for the cities, is to care for the field, promoting means of developing them, educating their populations, opening roads ... defending production and increasing the public wealth."[18] He sought diversification through subsidies, technical assistance, and even protection of the state's domestic market through taxes on the agricultural products of other states.

The third group interested in diversification consisted of elite members of areas dependent upon coffee seeking a hedge against the increasingly obvious dangers of reliance on coffee. These were mainly *paulistas*, or residents of São Paulo state, attempting to use the state's resources to support research on alternatives to coffee in the heartland of Brazilian

[15] Assis Brasil, *Cultura dos campos,* pp. xv, 234–5.

[16] Pimentel, *Assis Brasil,* p. 4.

[17] Ana Maria dos Santos, "Agricultural Reform and the Idea of 'Decadence' in the State of Rio de Janeiro, 1870–1910," (Diss. Univ. of Texas at Austin, 1984), p. 219.

[18] "A política da terra," *Boletim da Sociedade de Agricultura de Pernambuco*, Vol. 10 (1916), 330. See also Robert Edward Russell, "Nilo Peçanha and Fluminense Politics, 1889–1917" (Diss.: The Univ. of New Mexico, 1974), pp. 98–99.

coffee production. They were responding to tremors of the coffee market that began to send aftershocks into the heartland of the Brazilian coffee production since 1898. At a meeting of *paulista* planters in Campinas on March 25, 1899, Duarte Rodriguez urged caution. "The nation and principally coffee cultivation," he noted, "is passing through the sharpest of crises," provoking "uneasiness in the *paulista* society and the Brazilian Society in general." In search of a solution, "some individuals have mounted an attractive horse called polyculture" and, although they "know not to what species he belongs, they proclaim that thereupon lies salvation."[19]

The tenuous nature of its coffee-based economy prompted São Paulo's state government to take the first tentative steps toward diversification. In 1897, it reorganized the agronomic station at Campinas, founded ten years earlier, and charged it with stimulating crops other than coffee. By 1904, its director Gustavo D'Utra was strongly advocating "the need to cultivate, alongside coffee, another vegetable that would increase the resources" for the state's "already notable progress and development." That "vegetable" was cotton.[20]

Extensive reform of the state's agricultural support system soon followed, spearheaded by a prominent member of the *paulista* elite, Carlos J. Botelho. As the state's secretary of agriculture from 1904 to 1908, he began to reorient *paulista* agriculture toward "intensive cultivation and polyculture as remedies for the economic crisis stemming from the extensive monoculture of coffee."[21] During his lifetime, he received the distinction, shared by Assis Brasil and Nilo Peçanha, as being one of the "leading figures" of the "regenerative movement" of Brazilian agriculture.[22]

[19] "O Congresso de Lavradores Paulistas," *A Lavoura*, Vol. 1 (1899), 13–14.

[20] Gustavo D'Utra, *Cultura do algodoeiro* (São Paulo: Redacção da Revista Agrícola, 1904), p. 2.

[21] Quoted in Carlos Borges Schmidt and José Reis, *Rasgando horizontes: A secretaria de agricultura no seu cinquentenário* (São Paulo: Directoria de Publicidade Agrícola, 1942), p. 312.

[22] "Mais uma etapa," *Brasil Agrícola*, Vol. 4 (1919), 3.

Political Action to Reform Agriculture

Transforming agricultural diversity from an idea to a reality, though, required political pressure exerted through vocal and strong representatives of agricultural interests. With the downfall of the monarchy, the Ministry of Agriculture had been abolished as the new republic's leaders turned their eyes, if only momentarily, toward industrialization. Despite the lack of national direction, local agricultural interests began organizing "comícios agrícolas" or agricultural assemblies that sponsored expositions of farm products. While agricultural societies organized during the Empire remained in existence in Bahia, Pernambuco, and Rio de Janeiro states, local and regional agricultural interests suffered from lack of representation at the national level.

In 1897, a coalition of regional elites seeking to increase federal support of agriculture in general and alleviate the effects of lower coffee and sugar prices formed the first truly national Brazilian agricultural lobby, the Sociedade Nacional de Agricultura (SNA) [the National Agricultural Society]. In May 1896, with coffee prices plummeting, 47 individuals met in Rio de Janeiro to establish a "common center" to serve "as a point of support for all and any effort of agrarian improvement in our country."[23] When formally organized the following January, the SNA described itself as "an association of farmers [*lavradores*] and friends of farming" promoting:

1. agricultural unions, rural credit banks, and cooperatives;
2. demonstration fields, practical agricultural schools, veterinary posts, rural industries, and other agricultural institutions;
3. the perfection of rural labors through the practice of agronomy.

The Society planned to fulfill these goals through public conferences, publications in the daily press, agricultural congresses and expositions, and distribution of plants and seeds. Not the least of its objectives was "representation to the public powers and to the farmers, calling for the means necessary for national agricultural progress."[24]

[23] Poliano, *A Sociedade Nacional de Agricultura*, p. 26.

[24] *A Lavoura*, Vol. 9 (1905), 118–9. As France's minister of agriculture, member of parliament and prime minister, Meline promoted agricultural protectionism in reaction to the low prices of the 1889–1892 depression. His major accomplishment was an 1892 tariff

The formation of the SNA—the second manifestation of the private corporatist state in Brazilian agriculture—institutionalized the agricultural reform movement through a coalition of regional elites dedicated to increasing federal support of agriculture in general and alleviating the effects of the coffee and sugar crises. The SNA's early proposals suggest that the lobbying group represented producers of foodstuffs as well as the traditionally strong coffee and sugar sectors. In short, the SNA sought to create a federal infrastructure that would support regional agricultural economic development.

The SNA moved quickly to generate public support and political pressure on behalf of agricultural interests. In its first year, it sponsored dozens of public conferences on agricultural matters and founded a magazine (*A Lavoura*), supported initially by member contributions and later by government subsidies.[25] New agricultural societies sprang up in Bahia, Pernambuco, Ceará, Paraná, and Rio de Janeiro states. The SNA's first major step toward influencing policy occurred through sponsoring of the Primeiro Congresso Nacional de Agricultura (first national agricultural congress) in 1901.[26] The most significant accomplishment of the congress was promotion of the right of agricultural interests to organize and receive preferential treatment from the state.[27] They would then benefit from the right to buy and sell goods, and therefore bypass intermediaries and their often steep commissions. As juridical entities, the unions remained exempt from any onus, presumably in the form of taxes. The Syndicato Central de Agricultores (the Central Union of Farmers), based in Rio de Janeiro and strongly associated with the SNA, saved members between five and 40% of the cost of imported and national supplies.[28]

that protected food products but yielded to pressures from manufacturers by allowing free entry of industrial raw materials. See Michael Tracy, *Agriculture in Western Europe* (New York: Praeger, 1964), pp. 68–75.

[25] Ignacio Tosta, *Organização agronômca. Parecer da Comissão de Finanças sobre o orçamento do Ministerio da Industria, Viação e Obras Públicas para o exercício de 1906* (Rio de Janeiro: Cia. Litho-Typographia, 1905), p. 46.

[26] SNA, *Annaes do Congresso Nacional de Agricultura*, I, 2, 11, 21, 225–6.

[27] *A Lavoura*, 9 (1905, 149; See decree 979 of Jan. 6, 1903, published *in Boletim da Sociedade de Agricultura de Paraná,* Vol. 1, No. 5 (1918), 145–50.

[28] *A Lavoura*, Vol. 14 (1910), 412.

Meanwhile, the SNA began to display its growing political influence. In 1903, the Ministry of Industry authorized the SNA to act as its agent to import seeds and purebred animals, supported by a 100 *contos de reis* subsidy. In 1904, the Câmara de Deputados approved an SNA proposal to grant unions postage-free mailing of seeds and correspondence and an exemption from import taxes, transforming the SNA into a major source of supplies. By 1908, it had distributed over a million fruit trees, over 77 tons of seeds for forage plants, and tons of seeds for cotton, rice, beans, corn, wheat, and potatoes.[29]

The SNA's example stimulated the founding of similar state-level agricultural societies that pressured for concessions and subsidies from state governments. Buoyed by legal recognition and tangible economic benefits, agricultural societies spread to all states and pressured for concessions and subsidies from state governments. The Alagoas agricultural society, founded in May 1902, immediately petitioned the state congress to reduce export taxes and lower freight rates on the state railroad and the national shipping agency, Lloyd Brasileiro. Farmers in Minas Gerais established the Sociedade Mineira de Agricultura in 1909, later to obtain important state subsidies. Meanwhile, the national organization continued to grow. By 1911, the SNA had enrolled over 4,000 members.[30]

The power of these interest groups and the difficulties of importing large quantities of foodstuffs in a falling coffee market stirred support for protective tariffs for agricultural products. The treatment of rice exemplifies the experience of other crops stimulated by agricultural protectionism. Rice was a traditional but not dominant part of the Brazilian diet, outpaced by manioc-derived staples in the North and corn in the South. Colonial accounts mentioned consumption of rice, and by mid-nineteenth century Brazil exported rice from Maranhão, Pará, Bahia, Rio de Janeiro, and São Paulo. The spread of coffee soon pushed rice aside, though, and in São Paulo by 1870 coffee had taken over land previously used for rice. With the rise of the coffee economy and population increases, Brazil had begun to import rice by the final decades of the nineteenth century.

[29] Poliano, *A Sociedade Nacional de Agricultura*, pp. 42, 44, 51.

[30] *A Lavoura*, Vol. 13 (1909), 113.

An 1896 doubling of the tariff on rice had little effect on imports,[31] but subsequent tariff increases, pushed by agricultural interests, finally sufficed to guarantee protection and stimulate widespread rice cultivation. An amendment to the 1903 tariff law introduced by the deputy from Maranhão, the traditional stronghold of Brazilian rice production, raised tariffs by fifty percent. A 1905 law boosted tariff rates by another 33% and added a fifty-percent surcharge to be paid in gold. Tariffs now equaled half the wholesale cost of rice, and rice imports dropped from over 100,000 kilos in 1902 to less than 7,000 kilos in 1908. While not momentous in per capita terms, the protection spawned a domestic rice sector that would grow significantly throughout the First Republic.[32]

The Re-institution of the Ministry of Agriculture

The political power of regional elites concerned with Brazil's agricultural destiny showed itself in the re-institution of the Ministry of Agriculture. Reviving the Agriculture Ministry had been a recommendation of the 1901 national agricultural congress, using concepts transmitted from Washington by Assis Brasil. Early in 1901 Assis Brasil had forwarded a report to the Foreign Ministry outlining activities of the U.S. Department of Agriculture. The editor of the *Jornal dos Agricultores* obtained a copy of his report and urged participants in the agricultural congress to advance the idea of a Ministry of Agriculture. Cristiano Cruz, a federal deputy, agronomist and advocate for the sugar cane industry, from Maranhão, failed to gain sufficient support for a bill to that effect in 1902. In 1904, deputy Joaquim Ignacio Tosta forwarded the proposal to the SNA for comment. It recommended at least a separate agricultural department within the existing Ministerio de Industria, Viação e Obras Públicas.[33] Cristiano Cruz's original proposal gained presidential support in 1905

[31] Paul I. Mandall, *The Rise of the Modern Brazilian Rice Industry* (Stanford, CA.: Food Research Institute, 1971), pp. 166–7; "A lavoura Paulista de cereaes," *Revista de Commercio e Industria*, Vol. 3 (1917), 59.

[32] Mandall, *The Rise of the Modern Brazilian Rice Industry*, pp. 167–8. Law 1,452 of Dec. 30, 1905, established a 50% tariff to be paid in gold for food crops and some industrial products. See Wilson Cano, *Raizes da concentração industrial em São Paulo* (Rio de Janeiro: DIFEL, 1977), p. 61. n. 67.

[33] See "Dados sobre o desaparecimento e a ressureição do Ministerio da Agricultural (1892–1906–1909)," in AISL, 06.12.29. SNA's failure to support an independent agriculture ministry may be understood in the challenge that such a ministry would have

when President Rodrigues Alves, attuned to the crisis in his own state of São Paulo, advocated re-establishment of the agency. While admitting that "the agricultural societies in this city and others are lending very good services and awakening private initiative," the complex needs and problems of agriculture, especially the need for populating our territory," make it necessary, he said, to create a Ministry of Agriculture.[34] The following year Congress authorized creation of a secretary of state for agriculture, industry, and commerce. When agricultural reformer Nilo Peçanha became president in 1909, he ordered creation of a full-fledged Ministry of Agriculture.

The objectives of the re-established ministry complemented trends already established by boosters of agriculture. The first head of the ministry called for "new products and new markets," supported by "colonization … that fixes the colonist to the soil" and attention to "polyculture" and "pastoral" industries.[35] New laws authorized separate directorates within the ministry to enhance federal government support for diversified agricultural products. Within one year of the ministry's founding, laws created separate offices for agricultural inspection, consultation, weather services, and the distribution of plants and seeds and a special directorate to assist the cattle industry.[36]

Federal subsidies, vocational training, and field instruction directed toward supporting diversified agriculture soon became realities. Soon after assuming office Agriculture Minister Adolpho Miranda witnessed President Peçanha sign decrees that authorized a 200 *conto de reis* subsidy to stimulate export of Brazilian fruit. They also authorized workshops for agricultural apprentices and assistance for ranchers interested in importing purebred animals. Perennial concerns about agricultural schooling generated the first congress of agricultural education on São Paulo during May

represented to SNA's growing power and influence, as funds allocated to the SNA through subsidies would probably have been channeled through the agricultural ministry instead.

[34] Quoted in *A Lavoura*, Vol. 9 (1905), 2.

[35] "Dr. Rodolpho Miranda," *A Lavoura*, Vol. 13 (1909), 427.

[36] Celso Peçanha, *Nilo Peçanha e a Revolução Brasileira* (Rio de Janeiro: Editora Civilização Brasileira 1969), p. 71; Brazil, Serviço de Informação Agrícola," *1° centenario do Ministerio da Agricultura, 1860–1960* (Rio de Janeiro: Ministerio de Agricultura, 1960), p. 65.

25–30 under chairmanship of Assis Brasil.[37] By 1912, agricultural apprentice schools were operating in Barbacena, Minas Gerais; Setubal, Alagoas; Iguarape-Assue and Guimaraes, Maranhão; and Tubarão, Santa Catarina. A contemporary observer reported that the schools were "greatly developed," giving "very satisfactory results," with numerous applicants for admission. The ministry also set up experimental stations for improving wheat and sugar cane cultivation and initiated instruction for farmers in several states in the East and South. To remedy the lack of trained agronomists, the federal government decreed creation of the Escola Superior de Agricultura e Medicina Veterinaria in the city of Rio de Janeiro.[38]

Indicative of the broad scope of the ministry's program—and its lack of information on Brazil's agriculture—was its survey of the agricultural resources of *municipios* on a state-by-state basis. The objective of the surveys was to develop "a register or inventory of everything that could interest our farmers and ... facilitated the proper disposition of labor and capital, [whether] foreign or national." Surveys catalogued local agricultural conditions, listing crops, costs of land and labor, size and economic activities of towns, weather, and often the most prominent farmers with the *municipio.* Surveys proceeded slowly but provided a wealth of agricultural information. The survey for the state of Goiás took over two years to complete, from June 19, 1910, to November 2, 1912, but presented detailed information on the agricultural conditions of 43 *municipios.*[39]

[37] "1° Congresso de Ensino Agrícola em São Paulo," *A Evolução Agrícola*, Vol. 2, No. 24 (1911), 21–26.

[38] "Dr. Rodolpho Miranda," *A Lavoura*, Vol. 13 (1909), 427–8. and "'A acção do Ministerio de Agricultura no desenvolvimento econômico do pais,' Conferencia do Dr. João Maria de Lacerda, São Joao d'El Rey, Dec. 15, 1912,"*Boletím* [MAG], (1913), 151; See also Brazil, Ministerio da Industria, Viação e Obras Públicas, Relatório 1909, Vol. I (Rio de Janeiro: Imprensa Nacional, 1909), 36–40; Brazil, Ministerio de Agricultura, Industria e Commercio, *Relatório 1911*, Vol. I (Rio de Janeiro: Oficina da Directoria Geral de Estatística, 1911), pp. 43–44; Marco Arlindo Amorim Melo Nery, "Da Escola a Aragem da Terra: A Gênese do Ensino Agrícola Primário Federal no Brasil (1910–1934)," V Congresso Brasileiro de História da Educação (2008), www.sbhe.org; Graciela de Souza Oliver and Silvia Fernanda de Mendonça Figueiroa, "Características da institucionalização das ciências agrícolas no Brasil," *Revista da SBHC*, Vol. 4, No. 2 (July-Dec. 2006).

[39] Brazil, Serviço de Inspecção e Defesa Agrícola, *Questionarios sobre as condições da agricultura dos municipios do Estado de Goyaz* (Rio de Janeiro: Serviço da Estatistica, 1913), p. iii.

The Brazil being surveyed differed in important ways from the Brazil that had witnessed the end of the Empire. The traditional lure of the land as the source of all wealth combined with the hardships of the coffee, sugar, and rubber sectors to release the nation from its fixation with those traditional crops. Outspoken idealists and pragmatic reformers traced a new route to prosperity through fields bowing with cereals and pastures replete with bellowing animals. Special interest groups functioned as members of a privately directed corporatist lobby to pressure national and state politicians for favors that would subsidize the diversification movement and make new crops truly profitable. Guiding the government's response to the call for diversification of Brazilian agriculture were technically oriented reformers who proclaimed the potency of technology and science. Bureaucrats and reformers alike looked to the latest "processes which modern science adapted and demonstrates"—in the 1912 words of Minister of Agriculture Toledo—to "resolve all problems."[40] This search for the latest in technical information about the exploitation of the nation's soil would turn Brazilian eyes toward the United States.

[40] Brazil, MAG, *Introducção ao Relatório da Ministerio da Agricultura, Industria e Commercio para … 1912,* (Rio de Janeiro: 1912), p. ix.

CHAPTER 3

Agricultural Diversification and U.S. Ties: The Technicians

The Brazilian goal of wringing new wealth from the land led to the employment of U.S. technicians to aid a diversified agriculture. The faith in U.S. technical expertise adopted by Brazilian students in U.S. universities and already expressed by Assis Brasil, Pereira Barreto, and others embodied a general notion that Brazil could benefit by adapting the ways of U.S. agriculture. In an evolutionary process, those regional elites most interested in reform began to invite U.S. agronomists and geologists to Brazil to participate in or even lead the diversification movement. U.S. emissaries of private capital soon joined in an uncoordinated but thorough "invasion" of the Brazilian countryside, welcomed and even encouraged by technically trained Brazilian bureaucrats who admired U.S. ways.

The Origins of U.S. Ties

Brazilian decisions to seek technical education in the United States during the last two decades of the Empire expanded contacts with U.S. natural scientists. U.S. universities offering a technical education, especially Cornell University in Ithaca, New York, became an alternative to the traditional law school or European university for sons of elite families. The success of U.S. geologists who participated in multiple explorations into the Brazilian hinterland in the 1860s and 1870s led to their incorporation into scientific institutions where they gained status as reliable

E. R. Downes, *Brazilian Agricultural Development, 1890–1950*,
https://doi.org/10.1007/978-3-031-76992-4_3

analysts of Brazil's natural assets. Two who had accompanied Cornell professor Charles Frederick Hartt as students during expeditions in the 1870s became especially active in strengthening U.S. ties during the First Republic.

Orville Derby served as the geologist for the province and state of São Paulo from 1886 to 1905. In 1907, the ministry named him as head of the newly created federal Geological and Mineralogical Service of Brazil (Serviço Geológico e Mineralógico do Brasil), charged with studying the nation's mineral resources and gathering information for public works and communications projects. Derby remained in close contact with another former student of Hartt: John Casper Branner. Branner had traveled extensively in Brazil in the 1870s and 1880s and retained his interest in Brazil as a professor at Stanford University. He participated in extensive excursions there in 1899, 1907, and 1911. Based upon experiences in Brazil, Branner authored a geology textbook "expressly prepared for the use of Brazilian students" that recognized Orville Derby, "to whom the country and the geological world owed so much."[1] The *Jornal do Commercio* described the book as marking "a revolution in our method of teaching this science."[2] Branner also became an important advocate of teaching Portuguese in the United States and authored a Portuguese grammar text.[3]

Branner's close contact with Derby soon produced a long stream of Stanford graduates to occupy key positions in Brazilian government service.[4] First of several hired through the Branner-Derby connection was Horace F. Williams, employed by Derby in 1892 as a geologist and topographer. He collaborated with Derby on a topographical survey of the state

[1] John C. Branner, *Geologia elementar preparada com referência especial aos estudantes brasileiros* (Rio de Janeiro: Laemmert, 1906), pp. 5–6. Branner also owed a great deal to Derby. As Branner's agent, Derbytranslated a portion of Branner's textbook and wrestled with the publisher's financial troubles. See Derbyto Branner, Feb. 12, 1902, July 6, 1903, Box 31, Folder 139, Branner papers, Stanford University Archives (hereinafter referred to as BP-SUA.).

[2] Quoted in "Some Brazilian Americans," *Brazilian-American*, July 4, 1922 (special edition), 27.

[3] *Brazilian-American*, Vol. 5, No. 129 (1922), p. 11.

[4] Branner took great interest in his students' careers. He sought practical experience for them while they studied and tracked their careers after graduation, often recommending students to specific employers. See Frank Robert Jackle, "John Casper Branner and Brazil" (Diss. Stanford Univ. 1967), p. 84.

of São Paulo and, when Derby became director of the federal geological service in 1907, Williams became his assistant.[5]

Derby soon employed more Americans to assist in a major government undertaking: attenuating the impact of droughts that regularly punished the Northeastern states of Piauí, Ceará, Rio Grande do Norte, Paraíba, Pernambuco, and Sergipe, as well as parts of Bahia. As early as 1710 droughts scorched the area, returning in 1792, 1825, 1845, 1877–79, 1898, and 1900. The Northeast's dissatisfaction with relief measures attempted during the Empire gave the Republic's politicians important political leverage. In 1906, they succeeded in having the federal government establish the Superintendencia dos Estudos e Obras contra as Seccas (Superintendency of Studies and Works Against the Droughts), renamed in 1909 the Inspetoria de Obras contra as Seccas (Inspectory of Works against the Droughts) within the Ministerio de Industria, Viação e Obras Públicas.[6]

The basic assumption of the anti-drought campaign was that hydrographic measures could overcome nature's refusal to provide a constant water supply. Minister Miguel Calmon reasoned that the first steps in the campaign were "a new map of the states in question" and a "geological reconnaissance to have a better knowledge of the supply of water and the problem of irrigation."[7] In doing so, he was perhaps influenced by the

[5] Derbywrote to Branner that he was "exceedingly obliged to you for sending us so good a man [Williams.]" Derby to Branner, Aug. 24, 1892, Box 23, Folder 89, BP-SUA.; See also "List of American subjects in employ of the Brazilian Government," enclosure to U.S. Embassy, Rio de Janeiro (hereinafter cited as USE-RJ) to the Secretary of State (hereinafter referred to as SS), p. 1, Oct. 1, 1912, RG 59, 810.01/5, USNA (hereinafter cited as USNA.).

[6] For effects of the 1877–79 drought, see Roger L. Cuniff, "The Great Drought: Northeast Brazil, 1877–1880," (Diss. Univ. of Texas at Austin, 1970), p. 284. See also Joaquim Alves, *Historia das Secas (Séculos XVII a XIX* (N.P.: Edições do "Instituto do Ceará," 1953), p. 241; Anthony L. Hall, *Drought and Irrigation in Northeast Brazil* (Cambridge, Eng.: Cambridge Univ. Press, 1978), pp. 5–6; Albert O. Hirschman, *Journeys Toward Progress: Studies of Economic Policy-Making in Latin America* (New York: Norton, 1973), pp. 22–26; Nicolas Gabriel Arons, *Waiting for Rain: the politics and poetry of drought in northeast Brazil* (Tucson: Univ. of Arizona Press, 2004), pp. 28–38.

[7] Brazil, Inspectoria de Obras contra as Seccas, *Geografia, geologia, supprimento d'agua, transportes e açudagem nos estados orientaes do norte do Brasil: Ceará, Rio Grande do Norte, Parahyba*, by Roderic Crandall, 2nd. ed. (1923: rpt: N.P.: Departamento Nacional de Obras contra as Seccas, 1977), p. xi. Irrigation in fact benefited mainly large landowners and smallholders with property nearby. Most of the low-income agricultural population received few benefits, except from wages from employment on the projects themselves.

opinions of Oswaldo Benner Weber, director of the weather observation station in Quixeramobim, Ceará, from 1896 to 1905. Weber reasoned that the region's problems stemmed not from a lack of rain, but from a poor distribution of existing rainfall. Weber felt strongly that "rational agriculture" employing the "North American system of dry-farming" could transform Ceará into a great productive state that would "never again suffer the effects of a drought."[8]

Minister Calmon then began the search for a "professional, specialist in the matter" to apply dry farming in the arid areas.[9] Calmon asked Derby to obtain "an agricultural sharp to look over the *secca* region with reference to dry farming methods."[10] He also invited Derby to use his geological service to conduct a comprehensive survey of the Northeast. Derby then arranged for the survey with the head of the drought service, geologist Miguel Arrojado Lisboa, a graduate of the Escola de Minas of Ouro Preto, and an acquaintance of Derby for years. In 1901, Derby called Arrojado Lisboa "a very good friend" and "a very good fellow indeed, one of the best that has come out of the Escola de Minas."[11] The two kept in touch through the years, and when Derby became head of the geological service, he arranged for an appointment for Arrojado Lisboa. When the government formed the Inspectoria de Obras contra as Seccas in 1909, Arrojado Lisboa became its head. Derby's geological service—a unit of the Ministry of Agriculture—was to carry out the

See Hall, *Drought and Irrigation*, pp. 5–6 and Eve Elizabeth Buckley, "Drought in the sertão as a natural or social phenomenon: establishing the Inspetoria de Obras Contra as Secas, 1909–1923," *Boletim do Museu Paraense Emilio Goeldi Ciencias Humanas*, Vol. 5, N. 2 (May-Aug. 2010).

[8] Brazil, Inspectoria de Obras contra as Seccas, *Geografia, geologia, supprimento d'agua*, pp. 49, 51 On Weber, see Carlos H. Oberacker, *A contribuição teuta a formação da nação brasileira* (N.P.: Presença, 1985), p. 315.

[9] Miguel Calmon, "Introducção ao Relatório do Ministerio de Indústrias, Viação e Obras Públicas … 1917," in Miguel Calmon du Pin e Almeida, *Idéias econômicas de Miguel Calmon*, introduction by Francisco de Assis Barbosa. (Brasilia: Senado Federal, 1980), p. 276.

[10] Derby to Branner, Mar. 27, 1907, Box 38, Folder 172, BP-SUA.

[11] Derbyto Branner, Aug. 31, 1901, Box 31, Folder 139, BP-SUA.

survey under his immediate supervision using funds allocated to Arrojado Lisboa's Inspectoria de Obras contra as Seccas.[12]

At this point American technicians became integral to the anti-drought program. Geologist Roderic Crandall joined Derby and Williams after visiting Brazil in 1907 as an unpaid assistant to Branner, at the time surveying an interior region of Bahia. Crandall had studied under Branner and received his M.A. at Stanford in 1906.[13] Crandall surveyed portions of Bahia, Sergipe, and Alagoas in 1907, reporting his findings to both Branner and Derby. While his focus was on geologic features, he peppered his accounts with details of the harsh conditions imposed by the drought and offered suggestions about the water supply that Derby "had put into Portuguese for Calmon who took a fancy to it."[14] He collaborated with Horace Williams in 1910 in composing a map of Ceará and published an exposé of the Northeast's geological and economic conditions, *Geografia, geologia, supprimento d'agua, transportes e açudagem nos estados orientaes do norte do Brasil: Ceará, Rio Grande do Norte, Parahyba*, with 34 specific recommendations to mollify consequences of future droughts.[15]

The Dry Farming Technician. Calmon's search for a dry farming expert added another dimension to U.S. participation in the anti-drought campaign and epitomized Brazilian faith in U.S. technicians. Dry farming techniques had become widespread in the late nineteenth century in the United States west of the 98th meridian from Texas to Montana. Dry farmers compensated for low rainfall by planting only a portion of

[12] Derby to Branner, Feb. 21, 1907, Mar. 27, 1907, Box 38, Folder 172, Branner papers, SUA; Brazil, Inspectoria de Obras contra as Seccas, *Geografia, geologia, supprimento d'agua*, p. xi.

[13] Jackle, "John Casper Branner," p. 109, n. 1.

[14] Roderic Crandall, Ltr. to John Caspter Branner, Sept. 8, 1908, in "Notes of Roderic Crandall on the Geology of Bahia, Sergipe, and Alagoas, Pernambuco and Ceará, 1907," p. 60, BP-SUA.

[15] Brazil, Inspectoria de Obras contra as Seccas, *Supprimento d'agua no Nordeste do Brasil por Geraldo A. Waring* Publication no. 23 (Rio de Janeiro: Inspectoria de Obras Contra as Seccas, 1912), pp. 3–4. U.S. technicians offered technical recommendations but felt compelled to record other dimensions of the drought problem. Geologist Crandall explained that "a great part of the causes of the existing unfavorable conditions are sociological and... represent obstacles as difficult to overcome as those of a technical nature," Brazil, Inspectoria de Obras contra as Seccas, *Geografia, geologia, supprimento d'agua*, p. 47.

their land and using fallowing and drought-resistant varieties of seeds.[16] During the early years of the twentieth century dry farming congresses provided the forum for an exchange of information among interested parties, including the Brazilian government. Lourenço Baeta Neves of Minas Gerais represented Brazil at the second Dry Farming Congress held in Cheyenne, Wyoming, in February 1909, where he explained that "the Brazilian government wishes to try the dry farming process" that "results so well in your country, when properly applied."[17] Baeta Neves became an active proponent of dry farming. Members of the congress elected him to a post for the next meeting, and, when he returned to Brazil, he convinced at least one state agricultural society to endorse dry farming as a solution to Brazil's agricultural problems.[18]

In 1911, the Brazilian government hired dry farming expert Vernon T. Cooke based upon a recommendation of Derby. Englishman Cooke had migrated to the United States in 1880 and, after some time in Oregon, gained recognition in Wyoming as an expert in dry farming. The Cheyenne Board of Trade engaged Cooke in 1906 after he successfully demonstrated the potential of dry farming by raising respectable crops of wheat and barley. When Wyoming named him state director of dry farming in 1907, he began to travel throughout the state explaining techniques of plowing, sowing, and harrowing essential to successful dry farming. Testimonials included in reports published by Cooke provided evidence of his success.[19]

Cooke accepted the Ministry of Agriculture's invitation to direct Brazilian attempts at dry farming in September 1911. The offer came with

[16] Gilbert C. Fite and Jim E. Reese, *An Economic History of the United States*, 3rd. ed. (Boston: Houghton Mifflin, 1973), pp. 421–2. On dry farming, see Mary W. W. Hargreaves, "The Dry Farming Movement in Retrospect," *Agricultural History*, Vol. 51 (1977), 149–72.

[17] *CheyenneDaily Leader*, Feb. 24, 1909, p. 5, col. 3.

[18] "Sexto Congresso Internacional de lavoura secca," *A Lavoura*, Vol. 15 (1911), 116–7; "Lavoura secca," *A Lavoura*, Vol. 15 (1911), 302–3.

[19] *Jornal do Commercio*, Nov. 24, 1915, enclosure to USE-RJ to SS, Nov. 30, 1915, RG 59, 332.113/95, USNA. For Cooke's background, see MS, "U.S. Bureau of the Census, Thirteenth Census of the United States: 1910–Population, Laramie, Wyoming," Sheet in WHSA, and V. T. Cooke, "What is Dry Farming?" *Wyoming Industrial Journal*, June 1910, 6; *The Wyoming Tribune*, Jan. 30, 1907, p. 7, col. 3; "Dry Farming in Wyoming," *The Cheyenne Daily Leader*, Feb. 25, 1909, p. 8, cols. 1-4. Carl V. Halberg, "Dry Farming in Wyoming," www.wyohistory.org.

the handsome salary of $1,000 per month (as much as Cooke had earned in his entire year with the Cheyenne Board of Trade) for the first three months, free transportation for himself and his family to Brazil, and use of a farm for experiments.[20] Upon Cooke's arrival in Brazil, the Ministry of Agriculture dispatched him to Pernambuco, Rio Grande do Norte, and Ceará where, he reported, it was possible to conduct dry farming "with absolutely certain results."[21] By October 1912, Cooke had installed a demonstration field in Garanhuns, Pernambuco, to grow "all types of fruits and vegetables, besides other plants found in the arid and semi-arid zones of the United States." While most seeds and other equipment needed could be found within Brazil, Cooke requested barbed wire and seeds from the United States.[22]

Cooke apparently enjoyed some success, though at one point he offended the sensibilities of the SNA. Members of the SNA were unimpressed with Cooke after he postponed demonstration of his techniques and left Rio for the Northeast without explanation. When he returned and finally conducted a demonstration, members found it "deficient and lacking interest," especially given Cooke's promise to demonstrate elaborate procedures of "soil hydrodynamics and hydrotactics." Cooke's performance led some SNA members to question his competence and the government's judgment in entrusting him with "the solution of such an important problem."[23] Cooke, however, enjoyed the support of the agriculture minister and efforts at dry farming expanded. In August 1912, his contract was renewed for another year, and the following year Minister of Agriculture Pedro de Toledo publicly praised his work. Toledo appointed Cooke and Brazilian Eduardo Braga as Brazil's representatives to the 1913 International Dry Farming Congress in Oklahoma City.[24] Other U.S. dry farming consultants followed Cooke's example and opened dry

[20] MRE to EBW, Sept. 21, 1911, M-235, 4, 2, AHI.

[21] Brazil, MAG, *Introducção ao Relatório do Ministerio da Agricultura, Industria e Commercio .... 1912*, p. xxvii.

[22] Brazil, MAG, *Relatório do Ministerio da Agricultura, Industria e Commercio ... 1913* (hereinafter cited as Relatório) (Rio de Janeiro: Impr. Nac., 1913), I, 43.

[23] "Acta da 439ª Sessão da Directoria da Sociedade Nacional da Agricultura," *A Lavoura*, Vol. 18 (1914), 63–64.

[24] Pedro de Toledo, "A situação Agrícola industrial do Brasil," *A Evolução Agrícola*, Vol. 5, No. 54 (1913), 18–19.

farming demonstration fields in Pernambuco and Macahyba, Rio Grande do Norte.[25]

The Cotton Technicians. Other U.S. agronomists soon assumed leadership of public and private initiatives to increase production of crops other than coffee and sugar. In the Northeast, the federal government complemented its anti-drought efforts by intensifying support for improving the nation's Brazilian cotton crop. In the early years of the twentieth century, increased foreign demand and the rise of a protective tariff for raw cotton stimulated a renewed Brazilian interest in the crop. Annual cotton exports increased 34% between 1900 and 1909 compared with the average for the previous ten years. Cotton reappeared in western Minas Gerais and enjoyed renewed popularity in the Northeast, as the value of exports from Pernambuco doubled between 1902 and 1906. Even the tiny Sergipe shipped an average of over 15,000 bales outside its borders annually between 1910 and 1914.[26]

With the rebirth of the Ministerio da Agricultura, the federal government took a more active interest in cotton production, especially in the Northeast, home of the long-fibred Mocó strain. Agriculture Minister Toledo sent prominent Northeasterner José de Sa Pereira to Egypt to find out why Egyptian cotton rated higher prices than Brazilian cotton. He returned to blame lack of proper seed preparation in Brazil, cultivation by persons ignorant of agricultural principles, and improper processing as causes of the lower prices for Brazilian cotton. To "inoculate" cotton cultivation with "new blood, new life" required courageous government action, including sending a professional to study cotton cultivation in the United States, Mexico, and Jamaica, participating in international cotton groups and exhibitions, allowing tax-exempt import of seeds, and promoting better processing plants.[27]

[25] Memorandum, "Citizens of the United States in employ of Other American Governments," Mar. 28, 1913, RG 59, 810.01/, USNA.

[26] Stein, *Brazilian Cotton Manufacture*, pp. 46, 198; Daniel de Carvalho, "O Algodão em Minas," *in Annaes da primeira conferência,* I, 100; Apolônio Peres, "O Algodão e sua indústria em Pernambuco," in *Annaes da primeira conferência*, II, 381; Manoel de Carvalho Nobre, "O Algodão em Sergipe," in *Annaes da primeira conferência,* I, 441.

[27] José de Sa Pereira, "O Algodão no Egypto," Brazil, MAG, *Relatório*, *1911*, II, 103, 105.

The federal government then made a strong commitment to improving Northeastern cotton. In 1912, Congress authorized creation of an experimental station for the intensive cultivation of cotton in Maranhão, near the São Luiz to Caxias Railroad. By 1913, the government identified a 200-hectare site for the station near the municipio of Coroatá, Maranhão, once a "great center of cotton production." Although long in decline, the area in 1913 still stood as an important cotton producer.[28]

The Brazilian government then contracted U.S. agronomist Edward C. Green, who had over a decade of experience in teaching about agriculture and developing new crops, to serve as chief of the station's vegetable biology section. A native of Detroit, Green graduated from Michigan Agricultural College in 1897 and lectured on "practical entomology" at the University of Illinois. He taught agriculture and directed an agricultural experimental farm at Texas A&M from 1903 to 1907, leaving to take charge of a USDA "Pomological Garden" at Brownsville, Texas. In his positions, Green experimented with a variety of crops and published pamphlets highlighting his findings, including an "Horticultural Survey of Gulf Coast" (1907), "The Possibilities of Citrus Culture in Texas" (1911), and reports on onions, strawberries, tomatoes, and the use of fertilizers. In 1911, he accepted a position with the Bureau of Plant Industries of the USDA.[29]

Green arrived in Rio de Janeiro on May 25, 1913, and began a laborious study of Brazilian cotton. He spent a month and a half visiting various textile mills in Rio de Janeiro, and then traveled north, pausing at cotton establishments in a variety of states. Green found it much easier to point out the deficiencies of Brazilian cotton than to bring about immediate changes in cultivation practices. Green's own deliberate pace in arriving at the experimental farm effectively prevented him from establishing new directions during his one-year contract, since preparation on the current year's crop was already underway. As a result, Green found it

[28] Ltr. m., Article 72 of Law 2,544, Jan. 4, 1912. See Brazil, MAG, *Introducção ao Relatório, 1912*, lxxv; Brazil, MAG, *Relatório, 1913*, I, 24.

[29] *Longhorn* [Texas A&M University], 1903. 25-26; *The Eagle* [Texas A&M University], Mar. 1903; Apr. 11, 1907; University of Illinois, *The Semi-centennial Alumni Record of the University of Illinois.* (University of Illinois -Urbana-Champaign campus), n.d.), p. 801.

difficult to accurately compute the actual costs involved in raising cotton according to modern methods, one of his primary tasks.[30]

Green encountered other problems but remained optimistic about the potential for Northeastern cotton. He became frustrated with the idiosyncrasies of the Brazilian bureaucracy and claimed to have supported the initial plantings at Coroatá out of his own pocket, since government funds became available only a month or two after optimum planting time. He also complained that low salaries and overdue payments for government employees forced many to seek work elsewhere, crippling the experimental station's efforts. Bureaucracies remained indifferent despite "the best agricultural possibilities of the world." Green's work lay incomplete when his contract expired in June 1914, but he continued experiments with the crop on a five-hectare plot he acquired on his own. These experiments included use of cotton seed from the United States.[31]

Green managed to conduct enough experiments to convince him that Brazilian cotton's various ailments were completely curable, especially with better and more carefully selected varieties of seed. He frequently blamed the "degenerate type of cotton planted" for making a good harvest impossible and argued that careful seed selection over a variety of years might produce a "fine, prolific cotton." He reasoned that with "improved care and selection," the best native Paraíba cotton might even surpass the finest Egyptian variety.[32]

Thomas R. Day was a 1902 graduate of Texas A & M University who traveled to Rio de Janeiro in 1914 under contract with the Leopoldina Railway Company. The Leopoldina was originally a Brazilian firm but had fallen into hands of British creditors in 1897 after failing to pay off seven million pounds worth of bonds marketed in London. The railway expanded during the early years of the new century to become the country's most extensive privately-owned railroad.[33] Its lines reached out from the vicinity of Rio de Janeiro into that state's agricultural regions and then into southern Minas Gerais. The crisis of coffee naturally affected

[30] Achilles Lisboa, "Do Algodão," *Boletím* [MAG], Vol. 4, No. 2 (1915), 35–36; Brazil, MAG, *Relatório, 1914*, I, 199.

[31] Edward C. Green, "Meios de desenvolver a cultura algodoeira no Brasil," in *Annaes da primeira conferência*, I, 300-1.

[32] Achilles Lisboa, "Do Algodão," pp. 51–52.

[33] Richard Graham, *Britain and the Onset of Modernization in Brazil, 1850–1914* (Cambridge, Eng.: Cambridge Univ. Press, 1968), pp. 56–57.

the line's revenues, and in 1911 its Brazilian director João Teixeira Soares reported that "the region served by the company's lines was that which suffered most with the excessive fall in the prices of coffee and sugar."[34] The company felt compelled to seek "diminished dependence upon one crop–namely coffee" as a source of revenue for the company's lines.[35]

Director Teixeira Soares viewed possible remedies for the Leopoldina's troubles through the eyes of a *fazendeiro* with a technical background. He was an engineer who had designed the railroad climb from the port of Paranaguá to the city of Curitiba in Santa Catarina. Around the turn of the century, he had acquired farms in Paraná and Santa Catarina and invested much in making them profitable through "scientific methods."[36] The solution for the railroad's economic challenges in Teixeira Soares's view lay in stimulating new crops in the region, but unfortunately the government had failed to set up demonstration fields and "the farmers do not have the necessary instruction to introduce improvements in their cultivations."[37]

His campaign to improve the Leopoldina's revenue by diversifying and improving agriculture in the region it served turned him toward the experience of the United States, and he hired agronomist Day. Day was a Texan who liked to quote Texas governor O. M. Robert's statement that "civilization begins and ends with the plow."[38] Day had a varied past, having worked as a teacher in east Texas, then as a farmer in the northern Texas community of Dalhart, followed by a stint in real estate in El Paso, but he never lost his interest in agriculture. When he became chief of the Industrial Department of the Leopoldina, he set up an experimental station at the Bemfica farm in Macuco, Rio de Janeiro. By late 1914, he was offering the region's *fazendeiros* seeds of the principal forage

[34] The Leopoldina Railway Company Limited, *Relatório da Directoria relativo ao anno de 1911. ...* (Rio de Janeiro: Jornal do Commerico, n.d.), p. 11.

[35] "Leopoldina Railway Company (Limited)," *The Times*, May 20, 1911, p. 24, col. 6.

[36] For his background see Charles A. Gauld, *The Last Titan: Percival Farquhar, American Entrepreneur in Latin America* (Stanford, Ca.: Stanford Univ. Institute of Hispanic-American and Luso-Brazilian Studies, 1964), pp. 164, 184; C. Arruda Betrao, "Uma fazenda modelar," *Brasil Agrícola*, Vol. 3 (1919), 3.

[37] Leopoldina Railway, *Relatório* 1911, p. 10.

[38] T. R. Day, *Manual de algodão: meio século de experiencia em Texas e no Brasil*, 3rd. ed. (N.P.: n.p., 1926), p. 149. Roberts governed Texasfrom 1878 to 1883. For Day's background, see *Bulletin of the Agricultural and Mechanical College of Texas*, Vol. 1 July 1913, p. 203; June 1915, Third series, No. 6, 239.

plants, including spineless cactus, alfalfa, Texas peanut, cowpeas, corn, and sorghum.[39]

Agronomist Day became another advocate for closer economic ties between Brazil and the United States based upon agriculture. During a trip to Texas after several years in Brazil, Day pointed out that Brazil had a "marvelous future," not only because it could produce cotton, but especially since it was "almost unbelievably rich in minerals, including diamonds, gold and silver, to say nothing of natural gas and petroleum." Brazil also held "wonderful" forests, with "multiplied millions of virgin pine and the most valuable hard woods in the world ... awaiting the time when American timber becomes exhausted." To exploit Brazil's natural potential, U.S. machinery of every type—gins, presses, plows, harrows, planters, among others—was being introduced throughout the country. All this meant that "with each succeeding year, the demand for American-made goods of all kinds becomes greater." All the "Latin countries to the south," including Brazil, were "very soon to be out best customers," he explained.[40]

U.S. technicians engaged in the campaign against the droughts provided technical assistance critical to a Brazilian-led diversification movement within the nation's agriculture that was beginning to show results. By the middle of the second decade of the twentieth century, the Brazilian countryside was beginning to exhibit the fruits of new agricultural priorities. The falling price of coffee triggered action by interest groups, outspoken advocates of change, government, foreign and domestic capitalists, and others who saw potential wealth in producing crops other than the traditional coffee and sugar.

Contemporary statistical data and statements provide evidence of the success of the diversification efforts. Production figures for the state of São Paulo show how the "crisis caused by over-production" of coffee slowed coffee plantings and "permitted the restoration of polyculture."[41] (See Fig. 3.1.) Recent changes in the Brazilian countryside were so profound that Miguel Calmon, speaking as vice president of the SNA before the second national agricultural congress in 1912, characterized them as

[39] T.R. Day, *Plantas forrageiras* (N.P.: Repartição Industrial de Leopoldina Railway, 1915), pp. 62–63.

[40] Interview in *The Houston Chronicle*, Nov. 29, 1924.

[41] "The economic situation of São Paulo," *Brazilian-American*, Vol. 4, No. 95 (Aug. 20, 1921), 23.

the "revolution which has happened in the nation's agriculture."[42] He glowed with figures that indicated the nation had within a decade gone from a large-scale importer of corn to nearly meeting its own needs for the grain. Others saw new rays of optimism for Brazil. Minister of Agriculture Toledo reasoned that Brazilian farmers had been chastened by the "periodic crises that have afflicted" traditional crops and begun to "cast hopeful glances at the attempts of polyculture."[43]

Agricultural diversity, in the 1912 hyperbole of Rio Grande do Sul President Borges de Medeiros, had "presented itself in all exuberance, offering the observer an enticing aspect of variety, in a great number of species."[44] Brazil even began to export small quantities of corn, rice, and beans, mainly to neighboring Uruguay.[45]

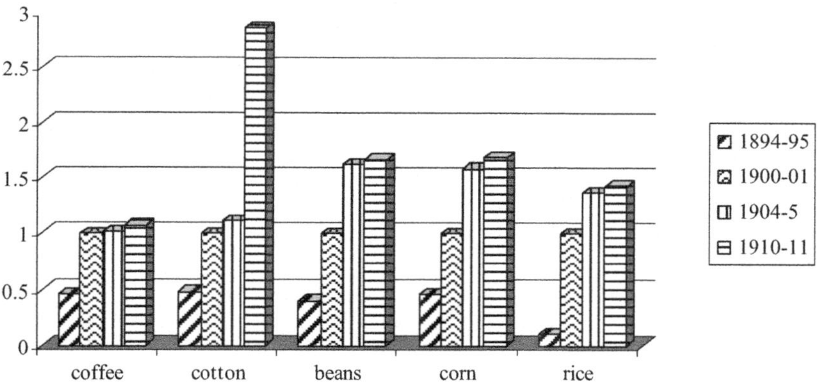

Fig. 3.1 Indexed production cotton and other crops, São Paulo, 1894–1911 (*Source* Calculated from "The economic situation of São Paulo," *Brazilian American*, 4, No. 95 (Aug. 20, 1921), 23. See also Wilson Cano, *Raizes da concentração industrial em São Paulo*, p. 63)

42 Miguel Calmon, *Ideas econômicas*, p. 339.

43 Brazil, MAG, *Introducção ao Relatório, 1912*, p. 50.

44 Rio Grande do Sul, *Mensagem*, 1912, p. 50.

45 Brazil, Directoria de Estatística Commercial, *Commercio Exterior do Brasil: Exportação, Importação, 1913–1918* (Rio de Janeiro: Estatística Commercial, 1919), Vol. I, pp. 546, 570, 600.

The technicians' presence in early twentieth-century Brazil also presaged a higher level of economic contacts between the United States and Brazil. Brazil's search for individuals prepared in soil sciences and the latest in soil technology shifted its attention away from its traditional fascination with Europe and toward the world's most productive agricultural nation. Responding to Brazilian initiative and changing conditions, by 1914 U.S. geologists, topographers, and civil engineers were scouring the gritting backlands of the Northeast for ways to improve rural life. Others sought to improve cotton cultivation or diversify crops in the area served by the nation's largest private railroad. While a fading U.S. agricultural frontier released individuals eager to mold Brazil according to the dominant perception of its economic destiny, conditions within Brazil imbued those tied to diversified agriculture with optimism based upon their own accomplishments and upon those of the model they admired, the United States. The European crises of 1913 and 1914 and the consequent reduction of Brazilian exports to that region would only temporarily dampen Brazilian spirits. Soon the war encouraged still closer ties with the United States and heightened Brazilian expectations that diversified agriculture could indeed fulfill the dreams of its advocates and their commercial allies.

CHAPTER 4

The Range Cattle Industry

Private U.S. capital also envisioned the profitability of applying U.S. agricultural techniques to opportunities implied by a reawakened Brazil. It responded to contemporary versions of an established theme: that Brazil was a natural utopia awaiting the products and capital of industrial North America. In 1901, Marie Robinson Wright's *The New Brazil* boasted that Brazil "promises to be an important factor in the political and commercial development of the western continent." It was a place of "inexhaustible" resources, containing "vast stores hidden in the mines or growing out of the fertile soil" of "priceless value." Wright called for "the application of commercial talent and much capital," to provide "substantial pro fit" to the investor and to improve "the world at large from the stimulated growth and activity of trade."[1] Theodore Roosevelt later summarized the popular notion about Brazil: "the United States can help Brazil, both with her capital and manufactures, and, in return, we need from Brazil many of her raw products."[2]

The availability of large tracts of Brazilian land made Brazil an attractive destination for an assortment of entrepreneurs and capitalists. Tracts of

[1] Marie Robinson Wright, *The New Brazil: Its Resources and Attractions, Historical, Descriptive and Industrial* (Philadephia: George Barnie & Son, 1901), p. 13.

[2] Quoted in José Custodio Alves de Lima, *Aproximação racional entre o Brasil e os Estados Unidos da America* (São Paulo: n.p., 1918), p. 9.

E. R. Downes, *Brazilian Agricultural Development, 1890–1950*,
https://doi.org/10.1007/978-3-031-76992-4_4

land in the United States suitable for homesteading or for grazing range cattle had begun to disappear by the turn of the century. The Homestead Act of 1862 had provided hundreds of thousands of settlers with arable, productive land, but by the turn of the century many homesteaders found only less productive, arid land available. A major study of federal land policy pointed out that by 1912 "the remaining public land was of such a nature that a settler under homestead conditions was not ordinarily able to make a living during the five years required in residence."[3]

Congress modified the homestead laws to adapt to new conditions, but the image of the extensive and almost mystically fertile land of Brazil provided a sharp contrast not lost to many businessmen. U.S.-based colonization companies hoped that the image of bountiful Brazilian land would inspire prospective migrants to invest in the immense tracts of land under their control. One company attempted to lure settlers to over one million acres of land it claimed to own on the Jauaperi River one hundred miles upstream from Manaus. Despite the continual heat and drenching humidity of the areas, the Brazilian Products Company of New York promised settlers that the "air was temperate and balmy, not sultry and oppressive," and that the soil there was of "almost unparalleled fertility," not like the "comparatively exhausted soils" of the eastern United States. An investment would guarantee a house and ten acres of land and, even more importantly, the chance to benefit from the company's exploitation of the myriad varieties of hard and soft wood, wild fibers, nuts, and "free fodder" for raising cattle.[4]

[3] Benjamin H. Hibbard, *A History of Public LandPolicies* (New York: Peter M Smith, 1939), p. 395. See also Paul W. Gates, "Homesteading the High Plains," *Agricultural History,* Vol. 51 (1977), 109–33.

[4] Brazilian Products Company, *South America*(N.P.: Brazilian Products Co., ca. 1915), pp. 3, 7. Even if they adapted to the oppressively hot and humid climate, prospective settlers would probably have had to wrestle their lands from the Indigenous residents in the area who, in the late nineteenth century, were reportedly "intractable" and suspect in the disappearance of a missionary attempting to convert them. See De Santa-Anna Nery, *The Land of the Amazons*, George Humphrey, trans. (New York: E.P. Dutton, 1901), p. 43. The Brazilian Products Company never had a chance to exploit the concession. By 1916 the resident of Amazonas state, an original partner in the enterprise, had decided to allow a "political adherent" to assume control of the property. This provoked a salvo of acrid letters from the company's lawyer to the State Department, unsuccessfully demanding that "you order a U.S.gunboat to the Jauapery Riverat once." Stephen M. Hoye to SS, Apr. 6, 1916, NA 332.115B73; Apr. 25, 1916, NA 332.115B73/20; June 20, 1916, NA 332.115B73/6, RG 59, USNA.

The vast expanses of Brazilian land also held promise for the range cattle industry. In the late nineteenth century, the pressure upon U.S. public land mounted, adding to the woes of a range cattle industry beset by overproduction and low prices. The experience of British cattle companies is illustrative. From 1893 forward, the disappearance of cheap public lands that were the foundation of their profits forced several companies established in the 1880s to liquidate. By 1920, only one, the Matador Cattle Company, remained.[5] Meanwhile, Brazil's empty hinterland and its government's new willingness to assist the cattle sector seemed to offer a uniquely profitable alternative, especially to the ubiquitous U.S. entrepreneur, Percival Farquhar. Although generally remembered more for creating a financial house of cards based upon Brazilian railroad expansion, Farquhar played a significant role in introducing U.S. methods into the Brazilian cattle industry. His vehicle was the Brazil Land, Cattle and Packing Company, one of the multitude of companies Farquhar established within his financial labyrinth.

This company's appearance in Brazil represented the power of European capital and the relevance of the U.S. agricultural experience within the Brazilian environment. Its capital originated in France and Belgium, as the company was an outgrowth of the Brazil Railway Company.[6] But the experience and techniques the company employed in Brazil derived from the United States. British capital had long been employed in the U.S. cattle industry, and the decision to organize the Brazil Land, Cattle and Packing Company was in essence an extension of the British investor's experience in the United States.[7]

The company's hiring of Murdo MacKenzie as its manager in Brazil embodied the company's plans to build from its North American experience to obtain success in Brazil. MacKenzie was a Scotsman who, after brief ventures as a law student and banker, had managed a half-million-acre estate in Scotland. In 1885, he accepted a position as assistant manager of the Scottish-owned Prairie Cattle Company headquartered in Trinidad, Colorado. In 1891, he assumed management of the Matador

[5] Richard Graham, "The Investment Boom in British-Texas Cattle Companies, 1880–1885," *The Business History Review*, Vol. 34 (1960), 424, 443–5.

[6] Robert T. Swaine, *The Cravath Firm and its Predecessors 1819–[1948]*, (New York: N.P., 1946–1948) Vol. II, p. 154; "As industrias animaes no Brasil," *Revista de Commercio e Industria*, Vol. 5 (1919), 6.

[7] For a view of the British experience see Graham, "The Investment Boom."

Ranch, which at that time controlled over 5 million acres in Texas and nearby states. MacKenzie became a naturalized U.S. citizen during his years on the Matador while managing multiple aspects of the ranch's business, ranging from protecting cattle from tick infestation to negotiating sales with Armour and Swift packing houses in Chicago and Ft. Worth. He also found time to represent the cattle sector's broader interests as head of the Texas and Southwestern Cattle Raisers Association from 1901 to 1903.[8]

The astute Farquhar recognized that MacKenzie's experience in the United States would make him an important asset for the new company. Farquhar met MacKenzie in Denver in 1911 where he explained to him, as MacKenzie later told an interviewer, that the company had been organized to take advantage of cheap Brazilian land with abundant grass land and plentiful rain. Improving the immense Brazilian herd by infusing new stock would furnish the missing ingredient needed to make Brazilian beef competitive and allow it to satisfy the world's growing demand for beef. MacKenzie at first refused a "fabulous offer," but the 61-year-old rancher eventually signed a five-year contract. The silver-tongued Farquhar convinced him with discussion of the company's $25 million credit and promises of sweeping authority in organizing the company, purchasing of land and cattle, planting pastures, and erecting a packing house near São Paulo.[9]

Once committed to the enterprise, MacKenzie lost no time in putting together a Brazilian cattle empire based upon his U.S. experience. In late 1911, he sent his son and three trusted associates to Brazil to locate suitable lands for the enterprise. Among their purchases were large parcels of land in Mato Grosso, where in 1911 and 1912 the company paid cash for over 500,000 hectares of land purchased from 17 different families. Together with purchases in Paraná and Minas Gerais, total land under the company's control soon surpassed four million hectares.[10] The company proved no less ambitious in its purchase and importation of cattle. MacKenzie, who in March 1912 had reached São Paulo, reported

[8] Mary Whatley Clarke, "Murdo MacKenzie Makes Cattle History in Western World," *The Cattleman*, Vol. 38, No. 1 (1951), 80–81.

[9] C.L. Douglas, "Cattle Kings of Texas," *The Cattleman*, Vol. 23, No. 7 (1927), 16.

[10] T.G. Crittenden, "Statement regarding the 'Taquarussu' Fazenda," Aug. 9, 1920, in "Presidência da República, 'Ministerio da Viação e Outros,'" N-44, AEP; Douglas, "Cattle Kings," 16.

eleven months later that "we have now on our books 80,000 head of cattle... purchased, received and branded in less than six months."[11] By April 1913, MacKenzie could hardly contain his optimism. He wrote to a friend that recent purchases had pushed the total cattle under the company's control to 230,000 head and that "by the time we are through... we shall have about double this number." The cattle were "very much superior" to those he had found in southern Texas, prompting MacKenzie to judge that crossing domestic cattle with imported Shorthorn or Hereford "can show splendid results."[12] True to Farquhar's design, MacKenzie began to import purebred stock from Texas and Iowa. By mid-1912, over 900 had arrived through the port of Paranagua, where MacKenzie personally supervised off-loading. From the port, the cattle traveled in express trains directly to the company land in Santa Ana da Parahyba.[13]

MacKenzie even received the endorsement of former President Theodore Roosevelt, who visited his "old friend" at Morungava, Paraná, shortly after his quixotic search for Brazil's "River of Doubt." To Roosevelt, MacKenzie's operation proved remarkably "typical of all that was best in the old time 'far West,' in the days when I knew it as cattle country." Roosevelt reported that "half the employees were men from Western ranches, from Montana, Colorado, Texas or elsewhere" and that their company was "carefully breeding upward, following precisely the same course which in Texas... has effected a complete substitution of graded beef and dairy cattle for the old longhorns."[14]

In the company's drive to improve the quality of the Brazilian herd, it probably benefited from special credits integrated into the new Ministry of Agriculture's budget. Forward-leaning ranchers of the Minas Triangle were already seeking to improve the quality of their herds, importing Zebu cattle from India as an alternative to the long-established Caracu breed. A 1911 federal law authorized a subsidy ranging from $1,700 to $60,000 for companies establishing model breeding farms. The law also provided free transportation to Brazil for cattle intended for use in

[11] Murdo MacKenzie to John McBain, Feb. 14, 1913, p. 2, MCCP, CSHC.

[12] Murdo MacKenzie to R. C. Anderson, Apr. 7, 1913, p. 3, MCCP, SWC.

[13] Roy Nash, *The Conquest of Brazil* (1926; rpt. New York: Biblo and Tannen, 1968), pp. 269–70; *A Lavoura*, Vol. 16 (1912), 157.

[14] Theodore Roosevelt, *A Book-Lover's Holiday in the Open: Ranch Life and the Hunting Trail*, Vol. 4 of *The Works of Theodore Roosevelt*, ed. Herman Hagedorn (New York: Charles Scribner's Sons, 1924), pp. 84–85.

reproduction. Proof of the government's interest in the matter was the payment to the state of Minas of 331:600$ in 1914 for transportation of imported cattle to the state. The federal government also established veterinary posts in cattle raising areas and in 1913 decreed a subsidy of 500$ for each rancher with more than 200 head of cattle who constructed a cattle dip.[15]

MacKenzie's actions, along with those of Cooke, Green, Hunnicutt, Day, and others, had diverse impacts on Brazil and its ties with the United States. In a broad sense, their presence may have weakened the arguments of Brazilian industrialists and nationalists who urged caution or disapproved of closer economic ties with the United States. Brazil's Ambassador in Washington, Domicio da Gama privately expressed wariness of U.S. economic power. Da Gama was "one of the most intimate friends" of the baron of Rio Branco, the foreign minister many believe favored strong U.S.-Brazilian relations.[16] Despite da Gama's ties with the Baron of Rio Branco, soon after reporting to Washington, he wrote President Hermes that the United States "judges itself different and superior to" the other American Republics. "Manifestations of friendship," he cautioned, "soon turn out to be a calculation of interests." So great was U.S. economic power, and so important was the U.S. position as a purchaser of Brazilian coffee, that Brazil stood in danger of becoming "a simple economic province of the United States."[17] Philosopher Alberto Torres also disapproved of strong economic ties with the United States. Torres acknowledged that "political and economic interests can justify more intimate or more frequent trade, with any country." However, "control over [a nation's] seas and economic life, adsorption of its banking systems and commercial, industrial, and transport industries" reflected "North American hegemony" that "could not be accepted by any other Republic of this part of the globe." For Brazil, he wrote, "the

[15] See Joana Medrado, "Do Pastoreio a Pecuária: A invenção da modernização rural nos sertões do Brasil Central" (Diss: Univ. Federal Fluminense, 2013); *RC do "JC,"* 1914, pp. 183, 448, 48. The 1911 federal law was specifically designed to inject foreign capital into the industry, since it specified payment in either dollars or pounds.

[16] Helio Lobo, *Brasilianos & Yankees* (Rio de Janeiro: Pimenta de Mello, 1926), p. 167; E. Bradford Burns, *The Unwritten Alliance: Rio-Branco and Brazilian-American Relations* (New York: Columbia Univ. Press, 1966).

[17] Domício da Gama to Marechal Hermes, Dec. 29, 1911, P-5, L-648, CDdG.

United States could be neither partner nor model."[18] Other nationalists refused to apply the "essentially agricultural" theorem to Brazil's future and argued against the export of raw materials, especially iron ore.[19]

But their actions also probably reinforced the thinking of Brazilians who espoused a faith in free trade and respect for the rapid growth of the northern nation. These believed that a strong U.S. presence would bring benefits through exploitation of Brazil's natural resources. Even Eduardo Prado, author of a book criticizing the notion that the United States had anything in common with Brazil, admired U.S. economic potential. In his *A ilusão americana* [The American Illusion], he chided the United States for failing to contribute its capital and labor to Brazilian development. The United States was "the richest soil in the world inhabited by the most energetic race of the human species," but "we should ask," he said, "what help have they been for the development of the national prosperity of Brazil?"[20] An anonymous bureaucrat in the newly formed Ministry of Agriculture expressed similar thoughts in 1913. Brazil needed an "intertwining of commercial relationships with the United States" to guarantee a flow of capital to exploit "the variety of industries that are appropriate for us," he wrote.[21]

A third segment of informed Brazilians interpreted increased U.S. technical support for Brazilian agriculture as merely part of a broader and beneficial adaptation of the U.S. economic model. This viewpoint found highly vocal support from a Brazilian civil engineer who had graduated from the University of Syracuse (New York), José Custodio Alves de Lima. Alves de Lima actively sought to increase economic ties between the two countries as an employee of the national shipping line, Lloyd Brasileiro, and then as a Brazilian consular official. Overlooking broad differences in class structure and enormous difficulties of transportation, Alves de Lima felt that Brazil should exploit the U.S. market and follow the example of the U.S. economic experience. Alves de Lima wrote from New York in 1910 that "Americans are a people who do not haggle over

[18] Quoted in A. Saboia Lima, *Alberto Torres e a sua obra* (Rio de Janeiro: Labor, 1918), p. 63.

[19] William S. Callaghan, "Obstacles to Industrialization: The Iron and Steel Industry in Brazil during the Old Republic," (Diss. Univ. of Texas at Austin 1981), pp. 180–1.

[20] Eduardo Prado, *A ilusão americana*, 3rd. ed. (São Paulo: Typographia Salesiana, 1902), pp. 258, 254.

[21] Brazil, MAG, *Relatório, 1913*, I, cxii.

the price of an object" and who were "a very rich people who soon will know not what to do with their private and public fortune." He urged Brazil to develop and export oranges to the United States where the consumer would not hesitate "to pay even double the intrinsic value of the article."[22] Moreover, the United States offered its example as a "new and virile nation," a model that Brazil should follow for "our material and intellectual formation."[23]

[22] José Custodio Alves de Lima to Nilo Peçanha, Jan. 13, 1910, L-11, P-1, N-21, ANP.

[23] José Custodio Alves de Lima, *Cartas americanas* (Rio de Janeiro: Impr. Nac., 1914), p. 7. See Alves de Lima to Peçanha, Nov. 25, 1918, L-23, P-2, N-76, ANP, recommending the Foundation Company of New York. See also Alves de Lima, *Aproximação racional entre o Brazil e os Estados Unidos da America* (São Paulo: n.p., 1918). Alves de Lima also lobbied intensely to stimulate U.S.investment in the exploitation of Brazilian rubber in the 1920s. See Barry F. Machado, "Farquhar and Ford in Brazil: Studies in Business Expansion and Foreign Policy," (Diss. Northwestern Univ. 1975), pp. 237–8.

CHAPTER 5

The Great War and Increased Production, 1914–1919

The death and devastation rocking the European countryside during World War I momentarily broadened and strengthened Brazil's agriculture reform movement. While remaining a rescue mission for besieged rural elites, agricultural diversification became a national crusade for a truly wealthy Brazil. Prominent Brazilians convinced elite associates that conditions in Europe meant Brazil would be "swimming in gold" if only the state assisted production from its mines and fields.[1] The prospect of commercial gain from Brazil's rural products gave new momentum

[1] Congresso Nacional, *Questões econômico-financeiros: Trabalhos do Deputado Paulista Dr. Cincinato Braga* (São Paulo: Duprat & Co., 1915), pp. 35, 55. Analyses of the war's impact on Brazil's economy focus almost exclusively on whether the diversification and expansion of Brazilian industrial activity during the war establish the supposed benefits of externally driven "shocks" to the Brazilian economy. See Wilson Suzigan, *Industria Brasileira: Origem e Desenvolvimento* (São Paulo: Editora Brasiliense, 1986), pp. 23–29; Nicia Vilela Luz, *A luta pela industrialização do Brasil* (São Paulo: Editora Alfa Omega, 1975), pp. 152–153; Francisco M.P. Teixeira, *História econômica e administrativa do Brasil* (São Paulo: Ática, 1989), pp. 132–133; Flavio Rabelo Versiani and Maria Tereza R.O. Versiani, "A industrialização brasileira antes de 1930: uma contribuição," in *Formação Econômica do Brasil*, eds. Flavio Versiani and José Roberto Mendonça de Barros (São Paulo: Saraiva, 1977), pp. 121–142; and Warren Dean, *Industrialization of São Paulo, 1880–1945* (Austin: Univ. of Texas Press, 1969), pp. 83–104. The impression that the war created a financial crisis stems from a focus on sharply reduced federal revenues, based upon import taxes, without an analysis of state revenues, based largely upon export taxes. At least two postwar analysts argued that the Brazilian states benefited from the war. See Ramalho Ortigão, "Situação econômica-financeira do Brasil,"

E. R. Downes, *Brazilian Agricultural Development, 1890–1950*,
https://doi.org/10.1007/978-3-031-76992-4_5

to the diversification movement. Agricultural societies, commercial associations, and political leaders used the state's resources to lower costs through subsidies and adoption of better techniques and raw materials. As the Federation of Commercial Associations of Brazil pointed out, the "great crisis" was "before anything else an economic crisis" and "its solution, therefore, resides in the expansion of agricultural endeavors."[2] Such conviction—coupled with higher demand in the form of higher prices—paved the way for a massive increase in agricultural activity by 1917. Bolstering alternatives to coffee, sugar, and rubber seemed to offer a bright future for the "essentially agricultural" nation.

The Wartime Stimuli

Stoking the firebox of this new Brazilian locomotive was increased domestic and international demand for many Brazilian raw materials and foodstuffs. The interruption of international trade raised prices for previously unglamorous products added momentum to the agricultural diversification movement and pushed the slumping coffee and rubber sectors further to the sidelines. In a complex process, agricultural societies, commercial associations, and political leaders used state and federal resources to boost agricultural production through grants and subsidies. These were designed to raise foreign exchange and increase revenues for the First Republic's semi-autonomous states, but the South and South-Central regions benefited more than the Northeast. The process created a new prominence U.S. technical information, equipment, technology, and, in some cases, markets. While prewar initiatives established bases for a more diversified agriculture and a stronger U.S. position within the Brazilian economy, wartime conditions consolidated both tendencies and gave them seemingly permanent natures.

Revista de Commercio Industria, Vol. 7 (1921) 215–22; Affonso Costa, "Os estados e a crisis," *Boletím* [MAG], Vol. 10, No. 2 (1921), 83–86. For a balanced discussion of the Brazilian government's wartime fiscal policy, see Winston Fritsch, "Brazil and the Great War," (Diss. Pontifica Universidade Católica de Rio de Janeiro, 1984). For a broad view of Brazil's actions during the war, see Francisco Luiz Teixeira Vinhosa, O *Brasil e a Primeira Guerra Mundial (A diplomacia brasileira e as grandes potências)* (Rio de Janeiro: Instituto Histórico e Geográfico Brasileira, 1990).

[2] "A situação econômica e financeira," *O Progresso*, Vol. 3, No. 23 (1915), 8.

The European war pushed domestic Brazilian commodity prices higher in response to two factors: higher world market prices and new internal demand created by reduced imports. Worldwide prices for raw materials and foodstuffs had been rising since 1896 because of an imbalance between world population growth and global production of foodstuffs and raw materials. The disruption of international trade and European agricultural production during the war intensified this imbalance and pushed prices even higher. The war withdrew much of Europe's cropland and pasture from production and created a manpower shortage that crippled the continent's agricultural supplies. European countries sought to import necessities they formerly produced, stimulating agricultural expansion in various nations, including the United States, Canada, and Brazil.[3]

Since Brazil participated in the world market for raw materials and foodstuffs as both seller and buyer, prices for Brazilian goods rose accordingly. Prices for industrial raw materials and foodstuffs for domestic consumption also rose, though, because of the need to produce substitutes for goods imported prior to the war. Potato imports shrank from nearly 30,000 tons in 1913 to 8,000 tons in 1915, and then to a mere 4,000 tons in 1916. Imports of wheat and wheat flour fell by over 100,000 tons between 1913 and 1915. The real price of rice jumped 138% over its 1914 value in just a year. Real corn prices increased by 28% between 1914 and 1916. Real bean prices rose 33% between 1912 and 1916. (See Fig. 5.1.) Production of cotton textiles rose during the war precisely when importing raw cotton became problematical. Real prices for raw cotton increased by 79% between 1914 and 1916. (See Fig. 5.2.) Meanwhile, prospects for coffee revenues continued dim. After a brief recovery from 1910 to 1912, coffee prices returned to their lackluster performance of earlier years in 1915.[4] Rubber increased slightly in price from 1914 forward, but never reached its previous price level. (See Fig. 5.3). President Wenceslau Braz Pereira Gomes, the nation's political

[3] Walt W. Rostow, *The World Economy: History and Prospect* (Austin: Univ. of Texas Press, 1978), pp. 162, 202, especially 195; 299–304.

[4] For pessimism on coffee's future, see João Nacio da Costa Prazers to Raul Soares, Aug. 29, 1914, 1914–08-28, ARS; "A situação do café," Annex 1 to Associação Commercial de Santos to MRE, June 28, 1915, M-313, 1, 29, AHI, and Brazilian Consul, New York, to Nilo Peçanha, May 11, 1916, L-45, P-1, N-46, ANP; MS, Nilo Peçanha, "A Presidente," n.d., L-45, P-1, N-50, ANP.

leader for most of the war, and his Minister of Agriculture João Pandia Calógeras, typified the federal government's view of the situation. Like most First Republic presidents, Braz had progressed from a predominantly rural background through the labyrinth of *coronelismo* politics to national prominence. The bulk of his experience and political power base lay in southern Minas Gerais, an area highly susceptible to changes in coffee prices.[5] Braz felt strongly that Brazil needed to exploit "other sources of gold," such as cotton, cattle raising, textile fibers, tobacco, and cacao to which "we have attached little attention." While iron and steel industries remained long-term goals, Braz was convinced that increasing agricultural production would compensate for falling coffee and rubber returns much more quickly.[6]

Minister Calógeras, a geologist graduated from the Ouro Preto school of mines and former federal deputy from Minas Gerais, promised federal support for diversified production shortly after the war's outbreak. As a federal deputy, he had disagreed with supporting traditional products by attacking a plan to "valorize" rubber. As Minister of Agriculture, he pledged to support exporting peanuts, leather, wood, cotton, tobacco, cacao, sugar, and rubber. In 1915, he estimated that Brazil could triple its annual harvests and bring nationwide prosperity by "direct cooperation of the government," since "farmers by themselves will never have the means to put into practice" modern farming techniques.[7] Energizing his ministry to aid diversified production, Calógeras ordered printing of a large poster for display on every farmer's wall in 1916. The "Guia do Agricultor no Brasil" listed simple instructions for 25 crops, including distance between rows, number of seeds per hectare, planting seasons, and many other details, especially the probable profit of each crop. The

[5] John D. Wirth, *Minas Gerais in the Brazilian Federation, 1889–1937* (Stanford, CA.: Stanford Univ. Press, 1977), p. 92.

[6] Biblioteca da Câmara do Commercio Internacional do Brasil, *O problema econômico e financeiro do Brazil: (Impresões de uma palestra com o Sr. Dr. Wenceslau Braz)* (Rio de Janeiro: Edifício da Bolsa, 1915), pp. 3–4. See also Darcy Bessone de Oliveira Andrade, *Wenceslau: Um pescador na presidência* (N.P.: Sociedade de Estudos Históricos Dom Pedro II, 1968), pp. 165–6.

[7] Bibliotecas da Câmara do Commercio Internacional do Brasil, *O problema econômico do Brasil* (Rio de Janeiro: "Jornal do Commercio," 1914), p. 12; Brazil, MAG, *Relatório, 1915*, Vol. I, xvii-xviii. On Calógeras, see Percy A. Martin, trans., ed., *A History of Brazil*, by João Candia Calógeras (Chapel Hill, NC: Univ. of North Carolina, Press, 1939), pp. x-xii.

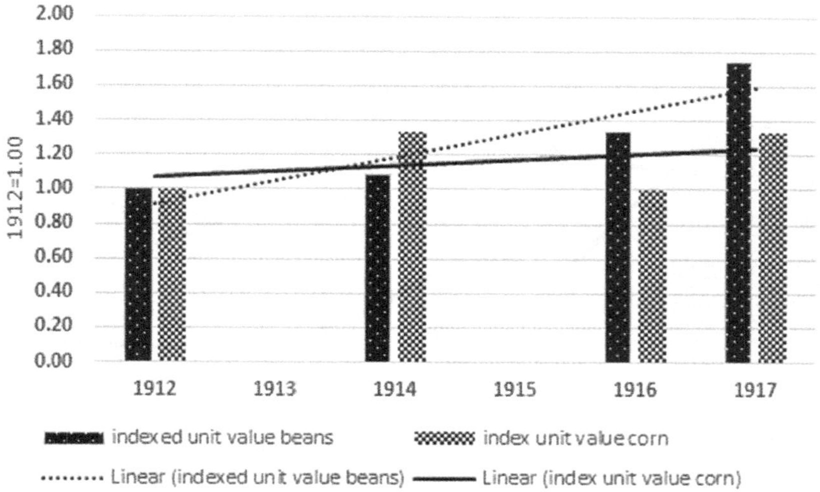

Fig. 5.1 Indexed unit values and value trends of Beans and Corn, 1912–1917 (*Source* Calculated from Haddad, "Growth of the Brazilian Real Output," p. 44)

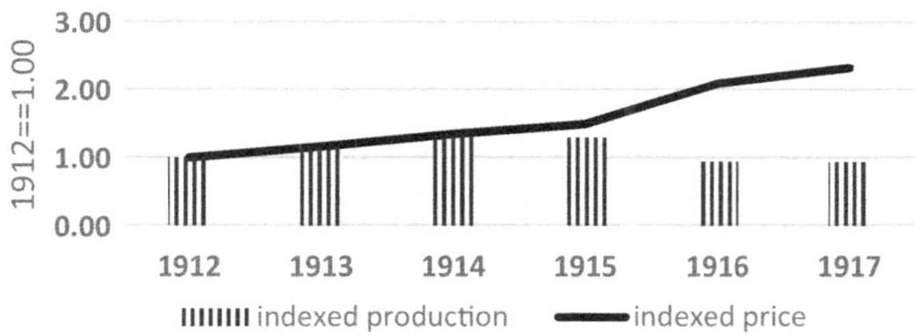

Fig. 5.2 Indexed production and unit values of Brazilian Raw Cotton, 1912–1917 (*Source* Calculated from Haddad, "Growth of the Brazilian Real Output," p. 49)

federal ministry also supplied modern implements, loaning over 2,000 plows and cultivators to farmers in 1915.[8]

More effective in the push for increased production, given the power of states in the decentralized First Republic, were state political leaders

[8] "Guia do Agricultor no Brasil," 17.00.00/1, AISL.

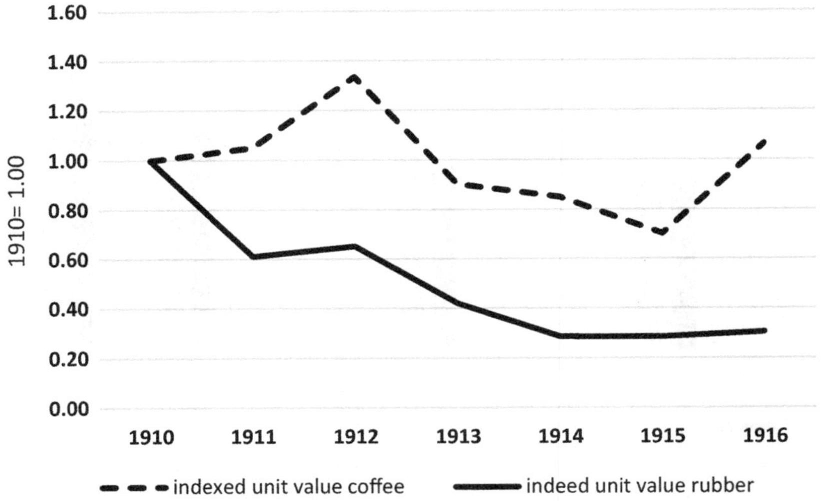

Fig. 5.3 Indexed Unit Values and Value Coffee and Rubber, 1910–1916 (*Source* Calculated from Haddad, "Growth of the Brazilian Real Output," p. 56

concerned about filling the state coffers. Beyond benefits for its rural elites, the states saw the heightened demand for Brazil's natural products as creating literally golden opportunity to increase revenues by stepping up production of raw materials and foodstuffs. Their price increases made sales outside of these states economically feasible, important because taxes on goods shipped beyond state borders figured prominently in the states' revenue. São Paulo obtained important revenues from export taxes, mainly on coffee, and Minas Gerais counted on export taxes for about half its revenues during most of the First Republic.[9] The same was true in Ceará, where the government was reportedly "anxious to increase the cotton production" for export.[10] Paraná earned important sums from

[9] Joseph L. Love, *São Pauloin the Brazilian Federation, 1889–1937* (Stanford, CA.: Stanford Univ. Press, 1980), p. 244.

[10] Arno S. Pearse, *Cotton in North Brazil, being the Report of the Journey through the States of Ceará, Maranhão, and Para* (Manchester: Taylor Garnett Evans & Co., n.d.), p. 29.

export taxes on agricultural and extractive products, especially from erva-mate.[11] Nationwide, export taxes provided almost half of the states' total revenues between 1914 and 1916.[12]

Raising state government incentives to expand production of cotton, cattle, cereals, and minerals held the prospect of creating multiple increases in export taxes charged on such products. By 1915, the combined effects of higher demand and potential benefits for producers and state coffers moved the states into action. São Paulo state established prizes in December 1915 for colonists who would produce the best and largest crops of cereals for the next three years. In return for planting at least five hectares in cereals and one and one-half hectares in potatoes, the state offered agricultural implements and partial dispensation from payments for their land.[13] A circular distributed throughout the state soon thereafter urged planting of cereals and other food crops, as well as raising cattle and hogs and developing dairy products. The acting state secretary of agriculture prodded mayors and heads of local agricultural committees to encourage "the emergence, alongside the great cultivations of coffee, of plantings of cereal and other food products" for both export and internal markets.[14]

Paraná's state government provided farmers with seeds for wheat, rye, corn, rice, cotton, and agricultural implements at no charge or at cost. One contemporary observer praised the state president's efforts to "strive boldly" to develop "multiple sources of richness that, in the near future,

[11] *Mensagem*... [Paraná], Feb. 1, 1917," quoted in *Brasil Industrial*, Vol. 2, No. 4 (1917), 10.

[12] Brazil, MAG, *Relatório, 1922*, p. 169. The states' dependence upon export taxes generated considerable controversy. One federal official interested in promoting orange cultivation urged support for fruit growing since export taxes on fruit could represent "many dozens of contos de reis" for the producing states' treasuries. See Affonso Costa, "Exportação de Frutas," *Boletím* [MAG], Vol. 5, No. 3, (1916), 80. Others opposed the taxes because they led to endless feuding between the states and higher prices for Brazilian products in international markets. Américo Werneck, in 1917 engaged as an adviser to Nilo Peçanha, termed them the "great disorganizer of the economy and finances of the Republic." See Werneck to Peçanha, June 22, 1917, L-45, P-2, N-22, ANP. José Custodio Lima, consular inspector for Brazil in North America, denounced export taxes as "asphyxiating barriers" contributing to the "crises of our principal products," in *Revista de Industria e Commercio*, Vol. 1, No. 8 (1915), 192.

[13] São Paulo [State], *Boletím de Agricultura*, Vol. 17, No. 6, (1916), 409, 411.

[14] "Circular do Dr. Secretário da Agricultura," *A Evolução Agrícola*, Vol. 7, Nos. 78–79, (1916), 20–21.

will constitute the greatness of our land."[15] The Minas Gerais government also subsidized a wide variety of agricultural activities. On the eve of the war, it purchased and distributed 1,500 copies of *ABC do Agricultor*, a primer on agricultural methods.[16] The state secretariat of agriculture became a "center of information about natural riches" and supported experimental farms for cotton, fruits, and tobacco.[17] As in Paraná, the Minas government imported seeds and implements and sold them at cost. The official state newspaper dedicated a special issue to improving cultivation of various crops in November 1915 and made copies available to farmers in other states.[18] Extensive credits began to provide the infrastructure for a revived cattle industry. The state appropriated large sums to import breeding cattle, grow quality pastures, award prizes at cattle fairs, erect tick baths, and operate veterinary posts to provide ranchers with free vaccine for their animals.[19]

In Rio de Janeiro, Nilo Peçanha, returning in early 1915 to another two-year stint as state president, advanced his long-standing goal of diversifying the state's agriculture. In 1915, his state authorized a 100 *conto de reis* subsidy for planting new crops and extending existing crops, including wheat, corn, rice, manioc, cotton, fruits, English potato, cacao, and textile fibers. Agronomist Day complemented Rio de Janeiro state's actions along the Leopoldina's routes. With his experimental farm firmly established, Day began excursions to introduce new crops to the area's farmers. On one such foray on July 14, 1915, he addressed over 2,000 farmers. Through an interpreter, Day informed them of successful plantings of cowpea, Sudan grass, peanuts, English potato, several types of cotton and melons, as well as his efforts to improve local beef and

[15] Raul Gomes and L. Rocha Junior, *O milho no Paraná* (Curitiba: Papelaria Globo, 1918), p. 4.

[16] Minas Gerais, Secretaria de Agricultura, "Fazendas modelo, campos de demonstração... 1913–1916," p. 41, S.A. 163, APMG.

[17] Minas Gerais, Secretaria de Agricultura, *A agro-pecuaria mineira: sua história, sua evolução* (N.P.: Secretaria de Estado de Agricultura de Minas Gerais, 1979), p. 33.

[18] Minas Gerais, Secretaria de Agricultura, "Rascunhos de oficios,"N-190, Mar. 10, 1916, S.A. 125, APMG.

[19] Minas Gerais, Secretaria de Agricultura, A agro-pecuaria mineira: sua história, sua evolução (N.P.: Secretaria de Estado da Agricultura de Minas Gerais, 1979), p. 33. Minas Gerais, Secretaria de Agricultura, "Rascunhos de ofícios," N-190," Mar. 10, 1916, S.A. 125, APMG. Minas Gerais, Secretaria de Agricultura, "Livro de créditos," S.A. 166, APMG.

swine by importing purebreds. Day's efforts proved successful. Shortly thereafter a visitor reported that "the encouragement of agriculture" had helped convert the Leopoldina to profitability. Brazilian farmers along the railroad's routes were soon imitating the demonstration farm's methods with satisfactory results.[20]

Amazonas state had special reasons to promote agriculture as it confronted dwindled rubber income and scarce shipping. The region could no longer afford the luxury of imported food nor expect to sustain itself through income from rubber. An August 1915 state law placed a three to six percent export tax on rubber "to foment agriculture... that inexhaustible fountain of public wealth." The state set aside funds for 3,000 copies of *ABC do agricultor*, one hundred subscriptions to the practical agricultural magazine *Chácaras e Quintais*, published in São Paulo, and for buying agricultural machines, fertilizers, and insecticides in the United States. Such measures reduced production costs and provided further incentives for landowners to increase production of non-coffee crops.[21]

Brazil's wartime agricultural diversification program shifted gears and changed drivers in 1917 as Brazil moved toward belligerency. Federal and state government officials quickly recognized the opportunity created by Brazil's June 1, 1917, decision to abandon neutrality and side with the United States. In June, Agriculture Minister José Bezerra informed farmers that "the worldwide shortage of foodstuffs of prime necessity" assured "highly remunerative prices" for those who would "intensify our agricultural production, principally of those articles that constitute the base of the public's food supply." Shortly thereafter, Bahia's state agricultural bulletin reminded farmers that it was "very convenient... to plant abundantly, as much as for internal consumption as for export, diverse cereals, especially corn, beans and rice." Such plantings would meet "the European demand, [which] in this moment is enormous" while providing

[20] RC do "JC," 1915, p. 189; Thomas R. Day, "Relatório sobre os trabalhos da repartição industrial no segundo trimestre de 1915," L-40, P-2, N-38, ANP; Lillian Elliott [Joyce], *Brazil, Today and Tomorrow* (New York: MacMillan, 1917), p. 147.

[21] "Food for Brazil," NYT, Aug. 20, 1914, p. 12, col 4; Amazonas, *Mensagem, 1916*, pp. 177, 114.

ample opportunity "to earn money" because "the high prices will remain for a long time."[22]

The SNA pressured the federal government to assume a new leading role through a series of conferences driven by their corporate members. Through its lobbying, producers and merchants obtained official sponsorship for making Brazil the "granary of the Allies" and increasing output of meat and cotton.[23] Its vice president, Miguel Calmon de Pin e Almeida, who in previous years as minister of industry, transportation, and public works had hired Derby and other U.S. technicians to raise Brazilian output, became a strident advocate of increasing cereals' production by adopting U.S. techniques. In late June, he termed the "intensification of our production of cereals" of equal importance with "our military organization." To increase production, Calmon announced that the SNA would promote U.S. techniques of cereals' production, where "great quantities of seeds were distributed." He also cited the need to adopt the U.S. method of transporting cereals in bulk, thereby cutting processing costs.[24]

Calmon's activism stood to benefit regions represented by the SNA's membership, especially the Northeast and the South. Miguel Calmon's power base lay in Bahia, where agricultural diversification had removed sugar from its dominant economic and political position. (The 1920 census would show that only 6% of Bahia's farms raised sugar cane, while nearly 14% raised rice, 46% grew beans, and 49% produced corn.) Santa Catarina, home of a subsequent SNA president, Lauro Muller, also stood to receive substantial benefits from federal sponsorship of increased cereal production.[25]

Under Calmon's leadership, the SNA began a concerted push for more government subsidies. As with cotton production the previous

[22] *O Milho*, Vol. 1, No. 9 (1917), 2; "Aviso útil," *Boletím da Agricultura, Commercio e Industria* [Bahia], Vol. 1, No. 1 (1917), 37.

[23] Quoted in "Informações diversas," *Boletím da Agricultura, Commercio Industria* [Bahia], Vol. 1, Nos. 6–7 (1917), 75.

[24] *Diário de Minas*, June 30, 1917, p. 1, cols. 5–6.

[25] Brazil, Directoria Geral de Estatística, *Resumo de várias estadísticas ecônomo-financeiras* (Rio de Janeiro: Typographia de Estatística, 1924), pp. 20–24. On Calmon's power base, see Eul-Soo Pang, *Bahia in the First Brazilian Republic: Coronelismo and Oligarchies, 1889–1934,* (Gainesville: University Presses of Florida, 1979), pp. 151–2. Muller probably played a less prominent role in the production drive because of his dismissal from the foreign ministry less than two months earlier.

year, the SNA organized a conference to pressure the federal government to increase its collaboration based upon goals suggested by the SNA. The SNA proposed holding the Primeira Conferencia Nacional de Cereaes (First National Cereals Conference) in conjunction with the Terceira Exposição Nacional de Milho (Third National Corn Exposition), set for Curitiba, Paraná, in August 1917. The SNA hoped the conference would "bring solutions to the present needs of cereals' cultivation" by discussing ways to intensify the production of foodstuffs, improved processing methods, including support for foodstuffs' production from federal, state, and municipio governments, and how to organize county or regional expositions and stimulate organizations similar to the already established corn clubs.[26]

At the conference, Vieira Souto specified what government support was needed for agriculture's expansion. He proclaimed that the war "had created the propitious moment for the rural prosperity of Brazil." After alluding to the military mobilization of Europe, Vieira Souto urged Brazilians to "mobilize our economic resources" to take advantage of the "current situation [which is] exceptionally advantageous for the production of foodstuffs," and prepare for a postwar "commercial campaign of those raw materials" used by civilian industry. He urged the federal government to undertake multiple tasks: supply selected seeds, equipment, fungicides, and printed instruction on how to plant, fertilize, harvest, and process each crop. "Thus," Vieira Souto summarized, "the federal government... will give uniformity to the expansionist mechanism." State and local governments, meanwhile, would direct the campaign within each region, distributing information and material received from the federal government, adding "whatever they can furnish, with costs borne by the state treasuries." Concerning labor, this situation created a demand that all potential workers, "whether men or women, young children or youths, even the elderly," sacrifice rest and leisure to dedicate themselves to increasing production.[27]

The conferees emerged from days of deliberations with blueprints for an agricultural mobilization of Brazil, based upon a new national-level organization to funnel assistance from all government levels to the

[26] L. Marques Poliano, *A Sociedade Nacional de Agricultura: Resumo histórico* (Rio de Janeiro: Sociedade Nacional de Agricultura), p. 56.

[27] "Conferência Nacional de Cereaes," *Brasil Agrícola*, Vol. 2 (1917), 239–41.

producer. A "competent central nucleus" at the federal level was to forward seeds, equipment, fungicides, and propaganda material to similar state and municipal organizations. Inherent in this arrangement was the call for the government to bear much of the costs. The federal government was to furnish seeds free of charge to small farmers (working four or five hectares or less) and at cost to large farms. Federal, state, and local governments were to pay for transport of seeds from ports or collection points in the states.[28]

To complement these arrangements, the SNA called for more instruction in agriculture. Not only were the fundamentals of agriculture to be emphasized throughout the education system, but also each *municipio* was to employ an instructor to work with local producers. The federal government and the states were also to mobilize their inspectors and instructors, even by contracting agronomy students yet to graduate from agricultural schools. The conference also called for a drastic increase in credit for small and intermediate farmers, for expositions and the institution of agricultural clubs promoting new products. The SNA declared itself ready to offer "a patriotic service" by supporting each of these initiatives.[29]

The Federal Government Raises Support Levels

The federal government reacted quickly and positively to the conclusions of the cereals conference and pressures of the times. On August 16, President Braz issued a decree authorizing the executive to "aid and develop national production."[30] The decree gave the executive broad authority to use the "most convenient means," whether they be guarantees, fiscal measures, or contracts to increase national agricultural production.[31] The federal government soon took stronger action to transform the cereals conference's recommendations into reality. On October 29, 1917, President Braz told Brazilians that the three-day-old state of war between Brazil and Germany required them to "intensify as much as possible the

[28] "Primeira Conferência Nacional de Cereaes," *RC do "JC,"* 1917, 199.

[29] "Primeira Conferência Nacional de Cereaes," *RC do "JC,"* 1917, pp. 199–200.

[30] Decree 3316, see Max Fleuiss, *História administrativa do Brasil*, 2nd. ed. (São Paulo: Melhoramentos de São Paulo, 1922), p. 739.

[31] TS, José de Araújo Góes, "Memorial," n.d., 12.00.00, AISL.

production of the fields." Such an effort was necessary, he warned, not only to prevent the hunger "knocking at Europe's door" from affecting Brazil as well, but also to make Brazil the "granary of the Allies."[32]

Braz then implemented one recommendation of the cereals conference and instituted the Comité de Producção Nacional (CPN) (National Production Committee) to spearhead the expansion of agricultural production. The CPN represented an alliance of agricultural and commercial interests acting under government sponsorship. Members included representatives of the SNA, the commercial associations of Rio de Janeiro and Santos, the Centro Industrial of Rio de Janeiro, and the Liga do Commercio of Rio de Janeiro. The Ministry of Agriculture retained control of the committee chair. Vieira Souto became "executive delegate" of the committee.[33]

The CPN soon endorsed specific measures to facilitate production and export. In November, it approved government storage of cereals at port facilities "at minimum rates." It also approved guarantees of minimum prices for agricultural products to be offered by the states with approval by the federal government. It endorsed the recommendations of the cereals conference and, in its meeting on November 22, authorized the government to import machines, implements, and tools used in farming and ranching for provisioning at cost to private parties. The CPN also exempted barbed wire and other fence materials from import duties and learned of President Braz's approval of "minimum, fixed, and uniform" freight rates on railroads and shipping lines "independent of the distance" from growing areas to port of export.[34] The committee also extended its reach through "Executive Delegates" in each state. The agriculture ministry invited each state president to name a state coordinator of CPN activities. Each state was to report needs of each *municipio*, transmit requests for loans of agricultural implements, and oversee the supplying of seeds and insecticides at the local level.[35]

[32] Quoted in "Informações diversas," *Boletím da Agricultura, Commercio e Industria* [Bahia], Vol. 1, Nos. 6–7 (1917), 75.

[33] "O Comité da Producção Nacional: As medidas aconselhadas," *A Lavoura*, Vol. 21 (1917), 430.

[34] "O Comité da Producção Nacional: As medidas aconselhadas," *A Lavoura*, Vol. 21 (1917), 433.

[35] Dias Martins, untitled document stamped "Escriptorio do Delegado Executivo: da Producção Nacional," n.d., pp. 3–6, 09.07.00, AISL.

The state delegates also became agents of implementing one of the CPN's major activities: distribution of propaganda urging increased production through voluntary means. As the cereals conference had recommended, the federal government through the CPN assumed a significant role in alerting farmers to the opportunities opening to them. On December 12, 1917, it ordered 20,000 posters for display in federal, state, and municipal officers, town halls, schools, railroad stations, movie houses, and post offices. The five-color poster displayed a patriotic appeal to make the land yield more fruit.

The CPN generated exhortations and information to accelerate the production drive. Its slogans transformed envelopes, packages, and boxes into subtle reminders of patriotic duty and potential profits. Those adopted included: "Help our allies and ourselves, raising the national production of cereals and [other] foodstuffs," and "The soil is the fatherland; cultivate it and make it become rich and powerful."[36] Its booklets provided practical instructions. Paulo Vieira Souto authored *Amendoim* (the Peanut), *A cultura de arroz* (Growing Rice), and *A cultura de guando* (Growing Pidgeon Peas). Benjamin H. Hunnicutt also collaborated with *Instrucções para a cultura de milho* (Instructions for the Cultivation of Corn), *A criação do porco no Brasil* (Raising Pork in Brazil), and *Algodão e o algodoeiro* (Cotton and the Cotton Plant).[37] The committee also distributed substantial amounts of implements, seeds, and insecticides. (See Table 5.1).

Acquiring Technology and Raw Materials

Other elements of increased production that the Brazilians sought from the United States were the technology and raw materials of production: thousands of tons of seeds, insecticides, and agricultural implements. By 1915, the United States supplied 90% of Brazil's imported plows and 76% (by value) of all imported agricultural equipment. A U.S. commercial agent traveling in Brazil in 1916 noted that "the great bulk of the implement business in Brazil has gone to American manufacturers." U.S. agricultural implements were more prominent than European in a

[36] "Propaganda Agrícola," *Boletím de Agricultura* [São Paulo], Vol. 19 (1918), 682–3.

[37] Dias Martins, untitled document stamped "Escriptorio do Delegado Executivo: da Producção Nacional," n.d., pp. 13–14, 09.07.00, AISL.

Table 5.1 Agricultural material distributed by the National Production Committee, 1918–1919

Item	*Make*	*Amount*
Tractors	Big Pull	7
Tin Plate (for canning)		10,014 sheets
Cultivators	Planet Jr	60
Plows	Faquhar, Clipper	994
Corn thrashers	Sterling, R. H., Gem	86
Iron posts		2,604
Barbed wire	Strong	776 roles
Root breakers		303
Cotton seeders		2
Seeders	Planet Jr., Banners	59
Sulfur		75,452 kilos
Copper sulfate		5,267 kilos
Cupric Arsenic		6,881 kilos
Syringes		389
Axes	Collins	961

Source "Material agrário despachado pela Superintendência para diversos portos do território nacional," Apr. 3, 1920, 06.12.29, AISL

1916 article advising farmers on choosing a plow. The "Pluto" plow of B. F. Avery and Sons, Louisville, Kentucky, and plows by the Oliver and Deere companies met requirements of simplicity, low cost, and maneuverability.[38]

Under such conditions, the limited imports of U.S. agricultural implements became a priority concern of the Braz government and the CPN. To remedy the situation, the Minister of Agriculture charged special agent Carlos Moreira with the mission of making substantial purchases of material to support the expansion effort. Moreira visited implement factories during his February to July 1918 trip to the United States and obtained over 1,000 tons of seeds, thousands of simple and complex agricultural instruments, and important amounts of purebred animals and insecticides. (See Table 5.2). Moreira's success in purchasing an important quantity of

[38] USBFDC, *The Market for Agricultural Implements in Brazil* (Washington: GPO, 1917), pp. 53, 59; Arthur Torres Filho, "A escolha de um arado," *Brasil Agrícola*, Vol. 1 (1916), 305–7; 371–3.

raw materials despite restrictions on U.S. exports attests to U.S. willingness to make concessions favoring stronger postwar economic ties. The federal government's funding of over 90% of the \$464,000 cost of the purchases highlights its dominant role in this process.[39]

This material bolstered the CPN's support of higher production to respond to higher foreign demand and compensate for imports interrupted by the war. In addition to distributing over 200,000 publications and 44,000 posters and illustrations, the CPN dispatched almost 2,000 tons of seeds of cereals and industrial crops and significant quantities of agricultural implements, barbed wire, and insecticides. (See Table 4.2).[40]

Moreira's initial request for authorization to purchase some of the material desired by the Brazilian government conflicted sharply with export controls imposed by the War Trade Board and the Food Administration to guarantee U.S. domestic food supplies and prevent surreptitious trading with enemy firms. Moreira appealed to the Ministry of Agriculture and soon obtained permission for his purchases through the intercession of Ambassador and hints of even closer ties with the United States. Morgan quickly notified the State Department of Brazil's plans to "stimulate local production" while confidentially noting that "the Brazilian delegation will place some thirty Brazilians in agricultural schools in the United States if Dr. Moreira's mission is successful." The State Department's Foreign Trade Adviser then obtained authorization for exporting rye, barley, and oat seeds as well as "the special approval of Dr. Hoover and Dr. Taylor" of the U.S. Food Administration to export 500 tons of wheat seed and 200 swine (Table 5.3).[41]

[39] Three states placed orders through Moreira: Minas Gerais (\$34,755), São Paulo (\$2,420), and Rio Grande do Sul (\$80). Brazil, Ministerio da Agricultura, Industria e Commercio, *Serviços Prestados pela Delegação Executiva da Producção Nacional (Rio de Janeiro:* Papelaria Mendes, 1918), pp. 45–46.

[40] Delegado Executivo da Producção to Ministro da Agricultura, Aug. 11, 1919, 09.00.00 I8, AISL.

[41] "Missão Carlos Moreira," p. 251; USE-RJ to SS, Apr. 5, 1918, RG 59, 632.119/440, USNA; W. K. May [War Trade Board], to Julius G. Lay [DS], Apr. 9, 1918, RG 59, 632.119/1389, USNA; SS to USE-RJ, Apr. 22, 1918, RG 59, 632.119/440.

Table 5.2 Material purchased by the Carlos Moreira Mission to the United States April 1918

Item	*Type or manufacturer*	*Amount*
Animals		
Cattle	Guernsey and Jersey	40
Swine	Duroc	226
Seeds		450 tons
Spring Wheat		50 tons
Common barley		5.5 tons
Malt barley		5.5 tons
Chevalier barley		30 tons
While barley		50 tons
Red rust-proof oats		50 tons
Forage and food vegetables		11 tons
Implements		
Tractors	Big Pull	10
Cultivator	S.L. Allen, Farquhar	1,794
Plows	S.L. Allen, Farquhar, Perlin and Orandoff	3,295
Sowing machines	S.L. Allen	4,200
Weeders	S.L. Allen	209
Root cutters	Faquhar, Da Root	35
Corn thrashers	Faquhar, Da Toot	310
Cotton sowing machines	Not listed	20
Metallic syringes	Not listed	1,000
Axes	Collins Co	1,000
Sickles	" "	10,000
Root breakers	" "	4,000
Pickaxes	" "	2,000
Spades	" "	1,500
Forks	American Fork and Hoe	2,000
Pitchforks	" " "	1,000
Insecticides		
Cupric Arsenic		1 ton
Sulfur		2.25 tons
Copper sulfate		6 tons

Source "Missão Carlos Moreira aos Estados Unidos," Brazil, MAG, *Relatório, 1918*, pp. 251–5

The Social Impacts of Increasing Production

By war's end, it was clear that higher prices also had important social costs. The urban poor suffered from food shortages. The state offered former slaves and the unemployed residence in "agricultural colonies"

Table 5.3 Seeds distributed by the National Production Committee, 1918–1919

Crop	*Amount (kilos)*
Wheat	1,516,216
Barley	74,948
Rye	73,454
Bean	54,033
Corn	29,085
Rice	11,102
Cotton	38,085
Potatoes	38,904

Source "Executivo da Producção Nacional," *Brasil Industrial*, 3, No. 25 (1919), p. 69

where they would support higher production. Juvenile penile institutions focusing on agriculture enrolled youthful offenders who endured an austere lifestyle while serving as low-cost labor for the state and large landowners. Meanwhile, the benefits of higher prices for Brazil's commodities accrued primarily to producers and state treasuries.

Labor. Setting up a committee with contacts at the state level, formulating propaganda statements, and distributing seeds and equipment did not suffice to increase production. The need for increased labor, with reduced immigration caused by the wartime situation, called for increased utilization of available national laborers. These included the unemployed, victims of drought, and even minors.

Before the war the federal government had made serious efforts to increase the labor supply from both internal and external sources. Falling immigration since 1897 and the opportunities available to immigrants to acquire property for themselves had created concern among owners of large properties about the availability of rural labor. Immigration had slowed drastically since 1897, when over 146,000 immigrants arrived in Brazil. Between 1898 and 1906 an average of fewer than 60,000 immigrants per year entered Brazil. Immigrants also began to work their own land; by 1905 immigrants owned 14% of all rural properties in São Paulo. One São Paulo official spoke for plantation agriculture when he pointed out that immigration had originally increased the rural labor supply, but by then [1917] had led only to increases in small property owners. He reasoned that the problem became one of "knowing how agriculture, without abundant immigration, can receive the laborers it needs."[42]

The federal government stimulated more immigration with some success, at least until war's outbreak. In 1907, it established the Serviço de Povoamento do Solo Nacional (the Service for Populating the National Soil), and immigration rose through 1913. The war raised an immense barrier for potential immigrants. Immigration during the war years plummeted to less than one-fourth that of the five years before the war. While 679,968 immigrants reached Brazilian shores between 1910 and 1914, only 155,800 foreigners migrated to Brazil from 1915 through 1920. Such figures, as an anonymous Ministry of Agriculture official reasoned in 1921, showed the "enormous decline of laborers we suffered exactly in the moment of the country's great economic effort."[43]

The growing conviction that immigration would not increase rural Brazil's labor supply led to formation of the Serviço de Protecção aos Indios e Localização de Trablahadores Nacionaes (Service for Indian Protection and Placement of National Workers) in 1910. This service sought to tie poor Brazilian *mestiços* and former slaves to the land by offering them vacant lands (*terras devolutas*) in return for activity on the land. Each worker was to receive transportation for himself, family and baggage to the center, as well as tools, plants, and seeds, and three months of assistance for maintaining the family along with a year's free medical attention. The settler was to plant and harvest crops on between 25 and 50 hectares of land that he eventually would be able to purchase. Descendants of former slaves would in theory benefit from the program, according to one official of the placement service. Against the "picture of misery" that was slavery, the Serviço de Localização de Trabalhadores Nacionaes would relocate the "descendants of the martyrs of slavery"

42 Immigration statistics from *Revista de Imigração e Colonização*, Vol. 1, (1940), 228. Thomas H. Holloway, *Immigrants on the Land: Coffee and Society in São Paulo, 1886–1934* (Chapel Hill, N.C.: Univ. of North Carolina Press, 1980), pp. 146–9; São Paulo [State], Departamento Estadual do Trabalho, *Localização dos trabalhadores nacionaes* (São Paulo: Typographia Brasil, 1917), p. 6.

43 Brazil, MAG, *Relatório*, 1921, p. xi. On the establishment of the Serviço de Povoamento, see Maria Tereza Shorer Petrone, "Imigração," in Boris Fausto, ed., *História geral da civilização brasileira*, Tome I, Vol. II (Rio de Janeiro: DIFEL, 1978), 99.

in a work of "atonement and fraternity" and incorporate them into the "economic expansion of the time."[44]

The calamities of nature added to the supply of national laborers available to expand production. The searing 1915 drought not only devastated the Northeast's cotton production, but it forced many impoverished farmers to migrate to new lands with federal government's assistance. In the latter half of 1915, 4,461 individuals received federal assistance in migrating from the Northeast through Rio de Janeiro to work on private farms or government colonies.[45]

The war's first year also witnessed additional efforts to create farmworkers from urban sources. As the director of the Serviço Nacional de Povoamento commented in 1915, the "lack of work in the industrial centers, cities and public works" justified returning the unemployed to farming "where they would be converted to efficient factors of national prosperity."[46] Over 60,000 workers from Rio de Janeiro and state capitals returned to the countryside under federal sponsorship between 1915 and 1920.[47]

To supplement the supply of laborers generated by agricultural colonies, the federal government instituted youth training farms under the *patronato agricola* program. In doing so, it adopted a program beneficial to state-supported agricultural activity in Minas Gerais, where the Instituto João Pinheiro for youths ten to eighteen had been functioning at the state model farm at Gamelleira, near Belo Horizonte, since 1909. The institute's stated purpose was to "take control of the minor in danger

[44] Decree 8,072, June 20, 1910, *Leis do Brasil*, 1910, I, 949; David H. Stauffer, "The Origin and Establishment of Brazil's Indian Service, 1889–1910," (Diss. Univ. of Texas at Austin, 1955), pp. 287–8. The role of the Indigenous people in increasing agricultural labor is less clear. Unlike the national workers, the Indigenous people received all material from the government free of charge and therefore were less likely to work outside their properties. The same bureaucracy directed both the Indigenous person and the national workers' programs through 1931, however. See Stauffer, "The Origin and Establishment," p. 287.

[45] Brazil, MAG, *Relatório, 1915*, I, 63.

[46] Dulphe Pinheiro Machado [Serviço de Povoamento], to MRE, Sept. 25, 1915, M-292, 4, 5, AHI. It is unclear how the unemployed reached the countryside, but reference to their "parasitic" lifestyle, in the same letter cited here, might indicate that some were in petty criminals given a choice of farm work or jail.

[47] Brazil, Serviço de Povoamento, *Extrahido do Relatório do Ministro da Agricultura de* 1921 (Rio de Janeiro: Vilas Boas, 1922), p. XXX.

of perversion, or already corrupted and, after an education period, return to society a man healthy in body and soul." The *patronato* concentrated on agricultural instruction because of "the highly educative worth of farm work" and its favorable effects upon "the physical and moral development of the student."[48]

Despite such lofty statements, the schools functioned as a combination reform school and agricultural training center. Internees provided low-cost labor for the state's agricultural farm and, on occasion, for influential farmers in the immediate region.[49] Agricultural labor occupied much of the internees' time, as noted by a visitor to the institute a year after its founding. In fields that had been "dry and barren, one can see the beginnings of a rice field that the children have watered with love and dedication, making it grow green and beautiful," he reported. The minors received a salary for their work, although its major portions supported the institution itself. Internees kept a mere five percent of their salary while the institute deposited twenty percent in a savings account in their names for use upon release. The institute received the remaining three-fourths of the internee's salary, with portion dedicated to a reserve for founding of similar institutions.[50]

In early 1918 the federal government adopted the *patronato agricola* as a nationwide institution. A February 28, 1918, decree noted the need to "impel the movement of the country's economic transformation" and "the duty of the government to increase the rural population and form the true Brazilian farmer." As in Minas, the decree cloaked its provisions in noble social terms, reminding the nation of the need for a "work of social and economic foresight by employing in the formation of the rural community... minors abandoned or without means of support."[51] Specific

[48] "Ensino Agrícola," *Boletim* [MAG], Vol. 18, 2, No. 1 (1929), 93. On patronatos and the formation of workers in Minas Gerais during this period, see Miguel Gonzalez Arroyo, "The Making of the Worker: Education in Minas Gerais (1888–1920)," (Diss. Stanford Univ. 1982), 21-A. The first U.S. juvenile farm opened in 1826 outside Boston. Late nineteenth-century reformers instituted several types of rural juvenile reformatories in upstate New York. See Jack Holl, *Juvenile Reform in the Progressive Era: William R. George and the Junior Republic Movement* (Ithaca, N.Y.: Cornell Univ. Press, 1971), pp. 246, 225, 231.

[49] Minas Gerais, *A assistência a infância desvalida em Minas Gerais* (Belo Horizonte: Imprensa Oficial do Estado de Minas, 1930), pp. 46–47.

[50] Minas Gerais, *A assistência a infância*, p. 7.

[51] Decree 12,893, quoted in Brazil, MAG, *Relatório, 1918*, pp. 144–5.

instructions issued a month later allowed youths between ten and eighteen years to be interned "for the least amount of time possible."[52] Once in the *patronato*, youths were to be taught to read and write and the rudiments of history, but the bulk of the three years of instruction was to encompass agricultural topics. These included growing cereals, use of implements, seeds and fertilizers, the feeding and care of farm animals, and other practical knowledge useful to farm operation. In case of misconduct, students were not to be punished corporally, but merely isolated, fined, or forced to do extensive manual labor.[53]

The population of the *patronatos* grew rapidly. By the end of 1918, more than 1,100 internees lived in ten *patronatos*, located mainly in Rio de Janeiro and Minas Gerais, but also with one each in Santa Catarina and Rio Grande do Sul. In at least one case, the *patronato* worked closely with a local political boss who was also a large landowner. The "Delphim Moreira" *patronato* came into existence in July 1918 on the property of "Colonel" Jeronymo Guedes Fernandes in Sylvestre Ferraz, Minas Gerais. Eighty internees at the *patronato* helped care for and harvest 32,000 trees of oranges and other fruits on the property.[54]

Urban Unrest. While generating momentum for the agricultural diversification, the increased export of beef from *frigoríficos* in Rio de Janeiro and São Paulo, along with exports of beans and the reduced imports of wheat, soon imposed a social cost upon the Brazilian urban population. Prices for agricultural products at the farm level had risen by an estimated 28% between 1914 and 1916 and commodity speculation and hoarding probably lessened the supply and raised prices still further. A subsequent report estimated that total pork and beef supplied to São Paulo butchers by two meat-packing plants, the Barreto and Continental products operations, declined in 1917 in comparison with the previous year—beef by seven percent and pork by about 13%. Fresh meat delivered to Rio de Janeiro dropped 15% from 1916 to 1917 and continued to fall through 1919. As the U.S. naval attaché explained in mid-1917, "the war has produced in this country a great increase in the cost of everything, but especially foodstuffs. The laboring class, already poorly paid, are unable to

52 "Instrucções orgânicas dos Patronatos. ...," Brazil, MAG, *Relatório, 1918*, p. 146.

53 "Instrucções orgânicas dos Patronatos. ...," Brazil, MAG, *Relatório, 1918*, p. 146.

54 "Patronatos Agrícolas," Brazil, MAG, *Relatório, 1920*, p. 90; Octavio Gomes de Moraes Vasconcelos, "Notas," *Boletím* [MAG], Vol. 14 (1925), 325–6.

live on their old pay, due to these increases, and this has produced great unrest."[55]

The drive to increase production in the textile sector added further tension, and in June and July 1917 strikes began to occur among workers in major São Paulo textile mills encouraged by anarchists and a São Paulo newspaper, *A Gazeta*, that blamed "trusts organized to export food" for the high cost of living.[56] As many as 100,000 persons may have participated in strikes and violent confrontations in late June and mid-July, including an attack upon the police station to free striking workers. The U.S. naval attaché reported that the outbreak of strikes "was a very serious affair and culminated in riots in which machine guns were used, and with deadly effect."[57] So bloody were confrontations that "about two hundred soldiers and police were killed" and although the number killed off the "rioting populace... was never given out, it must have been upwards of thousand," he reported. The police picked up several hundred strikers and arranged for deportation of several foreigners labeled as agitators.[58] From São Paulo, strikes spread to Rio de Janeiro, Porto Alegre, and Bahia, while other cities remained "in the throes of labor disturbances" as "discontent is quite general over the entire country."[59] The number of strikes decreased toward the end of the year, but the government remained concerned.

In addition to repressive measures, the government began to intervene heavily in the food supply to stifle further urban unrest. In May 1918, the federal government restricted slaughtering to only those cows over ten years old, provoking a loud protest from ranchers. The following month the government modified the decree, prohibiting slaughter of those heifers under eight years old. This action was necessary, in the

[55] Leite Linhares, *História política do abastecimento*, p. 42; TS, Franklin Almeida, "Relatórios do Dr. Franklin de Almeida relativos. ...," Annexo N 12.00.00 II 18, AISL; "Abastecimento de carnes," *Boletím* [MAG], Vol. 10, No. 1 (1921), p. 85; U.S. Naval Attaché to ONI, "General Internal Conditions," Aug. 8, 1917, ONI files, WA-7, Brazil.

[56] Cristina Roquette Lopreato, *O espírito da revolta: a greve geral anarquista de 1917* (São Paulo: Annablume, 2000), pp. 46–77.

[57] U.S. Naval Attaché, "General Internal Conditions," p. 2.

[58] See Leite Linhares, *História política de abastecimento*, pp. 40–41; Warren Dean, *Industrialization of São Paulo*, 1880–1945 (Austin: Univ. of Texas Press, 1969), pp. 165–6; Boris Fausto, *Trabalho urbano e conflito social (1890–1920)* (São Paulo: DIFEL, 1976), pp. 157–8, 192–6.

[59] U.S.Naval Attaché, "General Conditions," p. 2.

opinion of the Minister of Agriculture, to "save the animal stock" and to prevent having to pay "exorbitant prices for this article of prime necessity."[60] In June 1918, the federal government took an additional measure to relieve pressure on food prices. On June 12, the president decreed creation of the Commissariado de Alimentação Pública [Public Food Commissioner's Office]. President Braz cited the need to prevent a rise in the "high cost of living already felt in some populous centers of the country" while still maintaining a high amount of varied exports.[61] He charged the office with weekly monitoring of food stocks and food prices and granted it power to buy or requisition food when the public good so dictated. Braz placed former Senator Leopoldo Bulhões at the head of the commission.

The Food Commissioner ran into a steady headwind of opposition from groups with conflicting interests. Sugar growers were particularly combative since the commission restricted sugar exports, and retailers charged prices higher than those allowed by the semi-monthly price guidelines published by the commission. The office did requisition beef from the Brazilian Meat Company [Frigorífico Anglo] plant at Mendes, Rio de Janeiro, and performed enough of a function to justify its continuation beyond the armistice. The food commission overall seems to have had limited success, though, as strikes broke out in Rio de Janeiro and Niteroi in August 1918 and wholesale food prices continued to climb. Strong police action and negotiations with those labor leaders not deported soon quelled further massive outbreaks of unrest. Despite the food commission's actions, worker discontent continued after the war, but none of the strikes had the furor of the 1917 confrontations.[62]

The strikes emphasized the inequities inherent in the program of increasing rural production to meet foreign demand. Urban workers found the cost of living increasing more rapidly than wages and suffered substantial deprivations because they could not pay the higher prices set by increased foreign demand. Furthermore, their urban living conditions

[60] "Pecuária," *RC do"JC,"* 1918, p. 316; *Revista de Commercio e Industria*, Vol. 4 (1918), 217.

[61] "A criação do Commissariado da Alimentação Pública," *RC do "JC,"* 1918, p. 269.

[62] Franklin de Almeida, "Abastecimento de Carnes," *Boletím* [MAG], Vol. 9, No. 1 (1921), 83–92; Leite Linhares, *História política do abastecimento*, pp. 43–54; John W. F. Dulles, *Anarchists and Communists in Brazil, 1900–1935* (Austin: Univ. of Texas Press, 1973), pp. 43–87.

prevented supplementing cash wages with crops grown on subsistence plots. Rural labor also received few, if any, benefits from the national production program. Despite the push to increase agricultural production, rural wages fell, probably because of declines in coffee production. The institution of *patronatos* and agricultural centers may have provided youths with certain skills and workers with plots of land, but conditions were onerous and far more benefits accrued to the state and powerful landowners than to the individuals. Rural workers may have used subsistence plots and land between coffee rows to supply food and raise cash crops for sale, but deficient credit and marketing mechanisms prevented significant earnings.[63]

The Beneficiaries. Landowners, ranchers, merchants, and capitalists received substantial benefits from the production program. With government subsidizing costs of seeds, transportation, equipment, and occasionally labor, landowners could plant extensively and reap the profits of higher prices. Given economies of scale, those with the larger land areas probably received higher benefits than owners of lesser properties. Ranchers selling to packing houses, especially those in Rio Grande do Sul and the Minas "triangle" near São Paulo, also benefited from higher meat prices, given the lack of monopsonist conditions in each area. Capitalists, both foreign and domestic, who invested in the meatpacking industry undoubtedly obtained strong profits from the wartime conditions. Moreover, the prominence of foreign capital in the sector assured proportionately high profits for foreign capitalists. The prominence of merchants in the movement to increase production testified to the benefits inherent in the marketing process.

Years of diversifying production and closer economic ties with the United States had been profitable for some Brazilians. Brazil's August 4, 1914, decree that "the exportation of war material from Brazilian ports to any of those powers at war, is strictly forbidden" had nevertheless allowed trade in coffee, foodstuffs, and other raw materials with

[63] The cost of food in Rio de Janeiro increased by over 50% between 1912 and 1917. See Leite Linhares, *História política do abastecimento*, p. 87. Haddad estimates that coffee production fell by 7% between 1914 and 1915, rose slightly in 1916, and then fell 12% below its 1914 level in 1917. See Haddad, "Growth of Brazilian Output," p. 65. Between 1914 and 1917 rural wages fell by about 10% compared with those of 1913. See Fernando Bastos de Avila, *Economic Impacts of Immigration: The Brazilian Immigration Problem* (The Hague: Martinus Nijhoff, 1954), p. 89.

neutral and belligerent alike.[64] Between 1914 and 1916, Brazil accumulated considerable trade surpluses, as imports diminished and new exports brought a shower of revenue upon Brazilian producers and upon states charging export taxes. Trade surpluses for 1915 reached nearly $110 million and remained at $71 million for 1916 and $74 million for 1917. Although coffee still accounted for a high percentage of exports, exports of foodstuffs also had generated significant revenues. For example, Brazil exported 34,000 tons of beans to France in 1916, and overall been exports for that year stood at nearly 45,000 tons, with a value of $3.4 million, 138 times the value of bean exports in 1915.[65] Fig 5.4 depicts the value of selected non-coffee food exports for 1914 to 1917 (1917 is included because exports depended upon planting done in 1916).

States with diversified agricultural bases became suddenly prosperous. While São Paulo state continued to suffer budget deficits, Rio de Janeiro state achieved a "remarkable recovery from the adverse financial conditions" of the immediate prewar period. The president of Rio Grande do Sul remarked in 1916 that the "economic situation of the state is sufficiently pleasing," citing a 12% rise in exports accompanied by a 16% drop in imports. The state's largest bank, the Banco da Provincia, as well as the Banco Pelotense and the Banco do Commercio, all issued the maximum twelve percent dividends to stockholders in 1915. Overall, the states enjoyed export taxes for 1915 and 1916 that averaged 28% higher than the 1914 total.[66] Pelotense and the Banco do Commercio both issued the maximum twelve percent dividends to stockholders in 1915. Overall, the states enjoyed export taxes for 1915 and 1916 that averaged 28% higher than the 1914 total.[67]

Rural municipios in Southern and South-central Brazil floated on a rising tide of prosperity buoyed by higher demand for rural products. The Rio Grande do Sul *municipio* of São Francisco Paula da Cima da

[64] Decree 11,037, Aug. 4, 1914, attached to USE-RJ to SS, Aug. 11, 1914, RG 59, 762.72 1N39/77, USNA.

[65] Trade figures compiled from consular reports by Arthur H. Redfield in USBFDC, *Economic Studies Countries during the War: Brazil: Study of Economic Conditions since 1913* (Washington: GPO, 1920), pp. 22, 69.

[66] Love, *São Paulo in the Brazilian Federation*, pp. 302–3; *The Financial Times*, Mar. 1,1916; Rio Grande do Sul, *Mensagem, 1916*, pp. 24–25, Brazil, MAG, *Relatório 1923*.

[67] Love, *São Paulo in the Brazilian Federation*, pp. 302–3; *The Financial Times*, Mar. 1,1916; Rio Grande do Sul, *Mensagem, 1916*, pp. 24–25, Brazil, MAG, *Relatório 1923*.

Serra, in a region producing cattle and pine products, reported strong surpluses in its 1915 and 1916 accounts despite increased spending and no increases in tax rates. Prices for land suitable for cultivation or feeding cattle in Minas Gerais's *zona da matta* rose considerably. The "agricultural and pastoral prosperity" of the area also "elevated county incomes and increased comfort on the [region's] farms."[68] In western Minas, the government of Uberaba ordered paving of the town's main streets, and vehicles were so numerous that "only counting automobiles there are more than a hundred."[69] Increased income from "wartime prices reached by various commodities of national production, such as cotton, sugar, cereals, beef and leather" caused a "strong increase in the hundred."[70] As an early 1917 editorial noted, the war shook off agriculture's "secular apathy" and placed it "in a situation of being able to develop itself" with only indirect government subsidies.[71]

Prosperity eluded only the traditionally impoverished Northeast. Although higher sugar prices provided relief for Pernambuco, the Northeast's hopes that cotton would create new levels of wealth foundered on the realities of geography, climate, and market. Despite insect plagues, scorching drought, and a primitive transportation network, the Northeast insisted that somehow its arid land, too, could become a fountain of wealth. The value of other states' exports increased markedly between 1913 and 1917, while exports from Rio Grande do Norte, Paraíba, Alagoas, and Espirito Santo fell. Even states that gained from the wartime conditions could not match the spectacular increases registered by Southern and South-Central states, whose exports swelled by as much as 400% in value between 1913 and 1917. Residents of Picos, Piauí, summed up the Northeast's plight in a March 1915 telegram to the

[68] Vicente Blancato, *As forças econômicas do estado do Rio Grande do Sul 1° centenário da independência do Brasil, 1822–1922* (Porto Alegre: Livraria do Globo, 1922), 267;"Preço das terras de cultura," *Boletím* [MAG], Vol. 12, No. 3 (1923), 130.

[69] *Jornal do Commercio* [São Paulo], May 11, 1917, 4,cols 1–2.

[70] *Jornal do Commercio* [São Paulo], May 11, 1917, 4,cols 1–2.

[71] Central Industrial do Brasil, *Relatório diretoria paraense apresentado a assembléia geral ordinária do anno de 1922* (Rio de Janeiro: Jornal do Commercio, 1928), 197; Associação Commercial de Rio de Janeiro, *Momento econômico-financeiro. (Representação das clases productores)* (Rio de Janeiro: Typografia do "Jornal do Commercio," 1917), p. 7; "Ensino Agrícola," *Industria e Commercio*, Vol. 1, No. 10 (1917), 16.

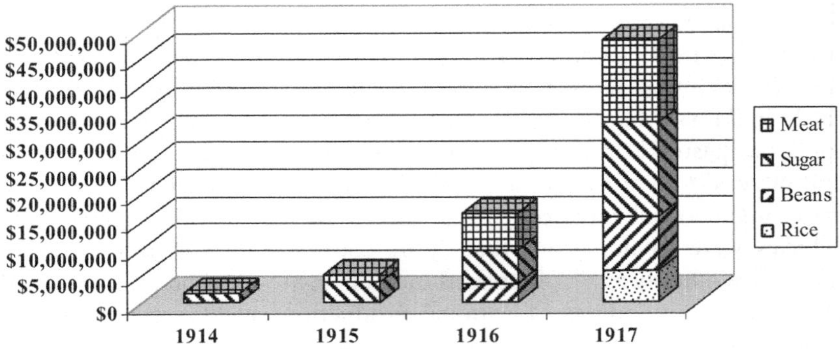

Fig. 5.4 Value of select Brazil Food Exports, 1915–1917 (US Dollars) (*Source* Calculated from *Wileman's Brazilian Review* and *Commercio Exterior do Brasil* by Arthur H. Redfield in *Brazil: A Study of Economic Conditions since 1913*, pp. 22, 24, 61)

Ministry of Transportation pleading for government assistance to overcome the "scourge" of a "poor zone entirely without resources, [where people were] dying of hunger, emigrating without a sure destiny, [and where even] the cattle [were] condemned to disappear [by] lack of pasture, water, everything."[72]

Higher prices for previously unattractive commodities intensified prewar initiatives of the federal government to support diversified agriculture. Higher state revenues from increased commodity production reinforced the traditional belief that wealth stemmed primarily from natural resources. It also raised the stature of advocates of "polyculture" arguing for decades that diversification of Brazil's agriculture rested upon sound economic rationale. Institution of a special federal government committee to encourage production through subsidies constituted another example of the First Republic's experience of societal corporatism. The First Republic's federal government assumed an activist role in response to a coalition of regional interests, a striking elevation of central government intervention in agriculture compared with practices of the

[72] Affonso Costa, "Os estados e a crise," *Boletím* [MAG], Vol. 10, No. 2, (1921), 85; Telegram to "Ministerio de Viação, Rio," from Picos, Piauhí, Mar. 10, 1915, in Inspectoria de Obras Contra as Seccas, Ministerio de Viação, Maço 296, Brazilian National Archive.

Empire. When economic and political conditions returned to normalcy in the early 1920s, elevated expectations of the benefits from diversified agriculture persisted. Unfortunately, these would conflict with the regionalism guiding the First Republic's political decisions, setting the stage for considerable maneuver and tension.

CHAPTER 6

The U.S. Role in Promoting Increased Production

Increasing and diversifying Brazil's agricultural production required intense interaction between elites promoting state and regional interests exercised through a newly activist federal government and special-focus interest groups. Institutional revitalization facilitated increased production of a variety of raw materials, including beans, rice, pork, cacao, lumber, tobacco, wheat, and others. Illustrative of the mechanics of the diversification movement are the campaigns to stir production of three specific commodities—cotton, corn, cattle, and beef. The national experience regarding these products between 1914 and 1919 portrays the complexity of that interaction as well as the increasing dependence on U.S. ties to make diversification a reality.[1]

Cotton

The drive to increase the size and quality of Brazil's cotton crop intensified with the onset of war, mirroring the approach taken during the U.S. Civil War. President Braz considered cotton cultivation one of the

[1] The United Statescontinued to be Brazil's best market for coffee. However, coffee offered a discouraging prospect during this period in contrast with other raw materials and foodstuffs. Coffee's share of the total U.S.-Brazil trade fell from 54% in 1913 to 41% in 1917. See USBFDC, *Foreign Commerce and Navigation of the United States1918* (Washington: GPO, 1919), pp. xii, 74.

E. R. Downes, *Brazilian Agricultural Development, 1890–1950*, https://doi.org/10.1007/978-3-031-76992-4_6

great unfulfilled opportunities of Brazilian agriculture. Before the war, he noted that "the improvement of the cotton industry and its exploitation on a large scale would bring us incalculable advantages, since one is dealing with a raw material with an ever-increasing consumption." Braz felt that increases in demand in England and the United States meant that "cotton cultivation should, therefore, merit the zealous attention of public officials."[2]

With the war, the textile industry responded to opportunities to exporting finished cloth to new markets and easy financing with increased production and a consequent upswing in the demand for raw material. One observer reported that textile mills were so active in 1915 that "the national supply of cotton is not sufficient for their needs," causing a significant price rise.[3] Textile exports increased to areas cut off from European sources of supply, such as Argentina and South Africa. Domestic demand also rose as traditional imports became unavailable. When a Brazilian utility company was unable to import insulating cords, the America Fabril company began producing a plaited yarn that met the company's needs. Cotton prices reacted predictably, prompting the Centro Industrial do Brasil, representing mainly textile producers, to protest the "unreasonable rise" in price. Abuses were also predictable. While "prolonged droughts" received primary blame for a decreased supply, rumors circulated in Rio de Janeiro that a "local trust" had formed "with the object of keeping up these prices as much as possible and of 'cornering' the supply."[4]

The new demand prompted unprecedented federal intervention in cotton production. As one federal official surmised, "it is cotton, gentlemen, which starting now can begin to raise us from ruin." The federal government established the Serviço do Algodão (cotton service) on February 15, 1915, and shortly thereafter contracted U.S. cotton expert Edward C. Green, originally hired in 1913 as a technical expert at the Coroatá, Ceará experimental farm, as its director with a $400

[2] Quoted in Miguel Calmon du Pin e Almeida, *Idéias econômicas de Miguel Calmon*, intro. Francisco de Assis Barbosa (Brasilia: Senado Federal, 1980), pp. 425–6.

[3] Elliott, *BrazilToday and Tomorrow*, p. 265; Stein, *Brazilian Cotton Manufacture*, pp. 106–7.

[4] Warren Dean, *Industrialization of São Paulo, 1880–1945* (Austin: Univ. of Texas Press, 1969), p. 96; Arno S. Pearce, *Brazilian Cotton* (Manchester, Eng.: International Federation of Master Cotton Spinners and Manufacturers, 1923), p. 29; *RC do "JC,"* 1915, p. 273; USACG to SS, Nov. 20, 1915, RG 166, Box 56, USNA.

per month salary. As Minister of Agriculture Calógeras explained, four centuries of experience had demonstration that "Brazil is predestined to be one of the world's greatest cotton producers." The cotton service would convert this capacity to reality by assisting in the cultivation, processing, and sale of the product. Instead of relying upon official experimental stations and demonstration fields, the service would "follow the North American example" and collaborate predominantly with private producers. Calógeras accepted Green's judgment that Brazil could standardize its production "within a very few years and at very little expense."[5] Green told the U.S. Consul General in Rio de Janeiro that "great portions of Northern Brazil contain vast areas that furnish ideal conditions, both of climate and soil, for cotton growing (Fig. 6.1)."[6]

Green drew upon his U.S. ties to support his campaign to improve the quality of cotton seeds for Brazilian farmers. Green observed that during the U.S. Civil War, cotton seeds imported from the United States had yielded better crops than domestically available seeds. The "degenerate"

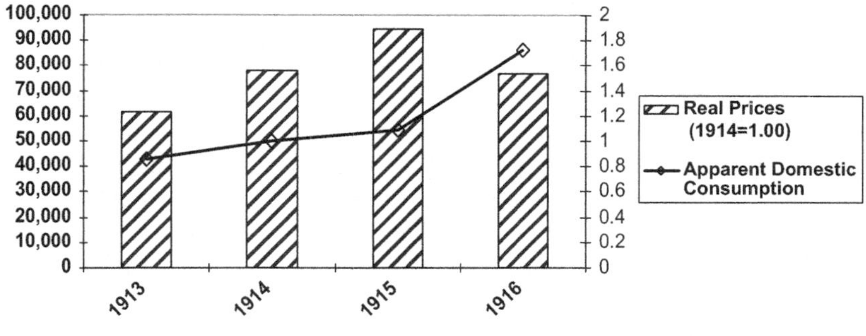

Fig. 6.1 Brazilian apparent domestic consumption and indexed s prices of raw cotton, 1913–1916 (metric tons). Apparent domestic consumption is production, plus imports, minus exports (*Sources* Imports and Exports from Brazil, Directoria Geral de Estatística, *Resumo de várias estatísticas,* pp. 48, 56. Production and prices estimated by Haddad, "Growth of Brazilian Real Output," pp. 56–57)

[5] Achilles Lisboa, "Do Algodão," p. 37; USACG to SS, May 17, 1915, RG 59 832.61331/3, USNA; Green, "Meios de desenvolver," in *Annaes da primeira conferência*, II, 315–7, 309.

[6] U.S. Consul- Rio de Janeiro, "The Cotton Situation in Brazil," Apr. 1, 1915, in "Foreign Agricultural Economics," RG 166.2, Box 56, p. 2.

nature of available seeds obstructed the cotton service's plan to increase cotton. Improved seeds alone, in Green's opinion, could double the productivity of Brazilian cotton plantings.[7] To resolve the seed problem, Green traveled to the United States on behalf of the Brazilian government to acquire large amounts of cotton seeds. He also sought implements and insecticides essential for large-scale cotton production. In early September 1915, he obtained assistance of the USDA's plant industry service and visited cotton seed farms in Virginia and South Carolina.

Green encountered considerable resistance to selling cotton seed for export. During a chance encounter in Washington, the governor of a cotton-producing state expressed surprise that the United States would export cotton seed to a potential competing producer. Through his responses Green showed his acceptance of U.S. industry's vision of the role of the United States in the hemisphere. Green told the governor that, with a developed cotton culture, Brazilian farmers would purchase more U.S.-made farm equipment. The "liberal policy of practical cooperation" would convince Brazilian farmers of the benefits of close U.S.-Brazilian commercial contacts.[8] Thus, Green reasoned, "the agricultural prosperity of Brazil is the commercial prosperity of the United States."[9] A South Carolina seed grower refused to sell Green any seeds at all until Green arranged for USDA to encourage the sale. Not all potential suppliers of seed balked. The W.A. Myatt Company of Raleigh, North Carolina, offered to furnish Green "improved early maturing varieties of Upland cotton."[10] Green eventually purchased seven and a half tons of Upland "Columbia" seeds from the Pedigreed Seed Company of Hartsville, South Carolina, a company formed in 1914 by David R. Coker to grow superior Upland cotton. After fulfilling additional instructions to buy seeds for corn and forage grass, Green returned to Brazil in early January 1916.

The cotton service's demise shortly after Green's return represented the government's frustration with poor results of its efforts in the Northeast. Despite the federal government's actions and subsidies offered by the governments of Ceará and Bahia, Northeast cotton production

[7] Green, "Meios de desenvolver," II, 315–17, 309.

[8] Edward C. Green, "Relatório ...," *Boletím* [MAG], Vol. 5, Nos. 1–2 (1916), 7–16; Brazil, MAG, *Relatório, 1915*, I, 23–24.

[9] Green, "Relatório," 10.

[10] W.A. Myatt Jr. and Co. to EBW, Sept. 1, 1915, M-234, 2, 4, AHI.

languished, and national production for the 1914 to 1917 period failed to equal the 1913 output.[11] The failure stemmed from a variety of factors. The return of the horrific drought to the Northeast in 1915 drove laborers and small producers from cotton lands. Of the 800,000 in the state of Ceará who made their living from agriculture, the drought affected over 400,000.[12] Cotton production suffered from the flight of small landholders, the mainstay of the Northeast's cotton crop. The rigors of drought and various insect plagues ruined "extensive cotton fields on the shores and backlands of Rio Grande do Norte" in 1915.[13] Even production of the region's perennial cotton decreased during the drought. Beset by unfavorable conditions, cotton production fell significantly and exports from the Northeastern states fell drastically during 1915.[14]

Insects devastated cotton crops even after the drought subsided. Most harmful the Pink Boll Worm caterpillar (*Gelechia Gossypiella*), with a voracious appetite for cotton bolls. First notice of the pest came in late 1915, when Ceará native Ildefonso Albano collaborated with Edward Green and Brazilian entomologist Carlos Moreira of the Museu Nacional to identify the insect. Controversy arose over its origin, and an anonymous article hinted that Green himself may have been responsible for its arrival in Brazil. Whatever its origin, the caterpillar further decimated the Northeast's cotton crop.[15]

[11] Ceará offered a substantial bonus for large producers and Bahia authorized cotton producers free use of up to 50 hectares of state land. See Ceará, *Mensagem, 1917*, p. 33; Bahia, Secretaria da Agricultura, Industria, Commercio, Viação e Obras Públicas, *Boletím da Agricultura, Commercio e Indústrias*, Vol. 1, No. 1 (1917), 52–53; Figures from the Serviço do Algodão published in *A Lavoura*, Vol. 28 (1924), 426.

[12] "As seccas do Nordeste e a agricultura," *Brasil Agrícola*, Vol. 2 (1917), 365–6.

[13] Stein, *Brazilian Cotton Manufacture*, p. 47; Eloy de Souza, "A irrigação na economia geral do Nordeste," in *Annaes da primeira conferência*, II, 112.

[14] Juvenal Lamartine, "O Algodão no Rio Grande do Norte," in *Annaes da primeira conferência*, II, 233; William W. Coelho de Souza, "O Algodão no Maranhão," in *Annaes da primeira conferência*, II, 107; Ildefonso Albano, "A cultura algodoeira no Ceará," in *Annaes da primeira conferência*, II, 183.

[15] Ildefonso Albano, "A nova praga do algodoeiro," in *Annaes da primeira conferência*, II, 361–4; "Devemos importar sementes do estrangeiro?" *Brasil Agrícola*, (1916), 347; Manoel de Carvalho Nobre, "Algodão em Sergipe," in *Annaes da primeira conferência*, II, 437.

A final factor debilitating the Northeast's cotton production was the inadequacy of the region's transportation system. Its railroad system reached only a portion of the cotton-producing region. Roads were little more than primitive paths hacked through the underbrush. As a federal deputy from Rio Grande do Norte explained, in his state "the lands most appropriate for cotton cultivation and that produce the best fiber are those in the interior, where the rails of the railroad have yet to arrive."[16] Transportation in the Northeast, in the opinion of U.S. geologist Roderic Crandall, remained identical with that of Egypt 2,000 years earlier and consisted mainly of donkeys. In Minas Gerais, a farmer with enough resources to plant cotton refused to do so because his land lay twenty kilometers from the nearest rail station. High transportation costs consumed potential profit, leading him to ask, "How can we [then] earn money by planting cotton? (Fig. 6.2)."[17]

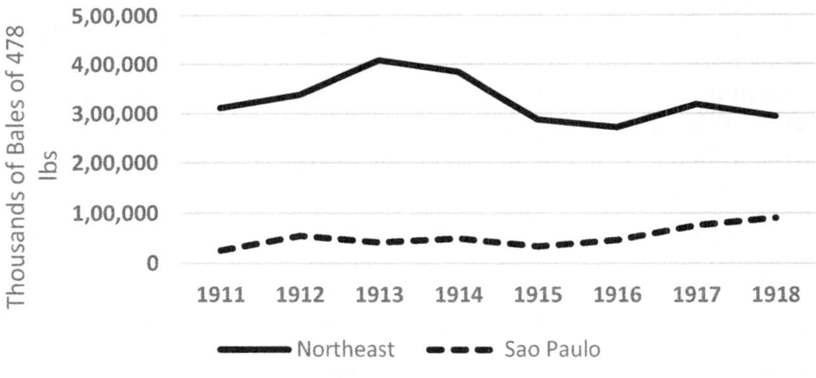

Fig. 6.2 Cotton production of Northeast versus São Paulo, 1911–1918. Data from Brazil, Serviço de Algodão, Ministerio de Agricultura, Industria e Commercio, reported in USDA, *Foreign Crops*, Vol. 10, No. 25 (June 22, 1925), pp. 745–746

16 "Recursos económicos do Estado do Rio Grande do Norte," *Boletím* [MAG], Vol. 17, 1, No. 6 (1928), 745.

17 Brazil, Inspectoria de Obras Contra as Seccas, *Geografia, geologia, supprimento d'agua.... 1923*: rpt. N.P.: Departamento Nacional de Obras contra as Seccas, 1977), p. 53; Álvaro da Silveira, "A producção das boas sementes de Algodão em Minas," *Brasil Agrícola*, Vol. 2 (1917), 58.

Problems caused by drought, pests, and the lack of transportation begged solution. Commercial associations and agricultural groups under the SNA's leadership organized the wide-ranging Primeiro Congresso Nacional de Algodão (first national cotton conference), in the first two weeks of June 1916 in Rio de Janeiro. Its purpose was to propose "methods of a practical range and immediate utility to increase cotton production amongst us." The cotton conference symbolized both the disorganization of Brazil's cotton-growing efforts and the intensity of aspirations of those seeking to make Brazil a first-rate cotton producer. After a solemn opening by President Braz and his cabinet in the Biblioteca Nacional on June 1, the conference addressed all aspects of Brazilian cotton growing, from planting, to transportation, to marketing, through deliberations of twelve committees. Committee membership represented leading lights of progressive Brazilian agriculture, including Epitácio Pessoa, Ildefonso Simões Lopes, Gustavo D'Utra, Carlos Botelho, Augusto Ramos as well as U.S. agronomists Green and Hunnicutt.[18]

Northeastern cotton interests used the conference to lobby for more government assistance. Trajano Saboia Viriato de Medeiros, a Ceará native, argued for increased federal support for cotton production. As an elite member from a depressed region, Viriato de Medeiros typified those who advocated reform of the First Republic's agriculture. Grandson of a *coronel* of the Empire, nephew of a senator, and son of a municipal judge, Viriato de Medeiros graduated from Rio de Janeiro's Escola Polytechnica in 1886 and worked for various Brazilian railroads at Engenho de Dentro outside Rio de Janeiro. He diversified his interests by planting cotton in Altino, Pernambuco, in 1915. He enjoyed favor in government circles. By early 1916 his company—Companhia Industrial de Algodão e Oleos—acquired a government contract to install cotton balers and cotton seed oil presses in the North.[19]

Trajano de Medeiros was keenly interested in improving processing of cotton and extracting maximum benefits from the crop. Speaking

[18] *Annaes da primeira conferência*, I, 14; "Commissões especiaes da conferência algodoeira," in *Annaes da primeira conferência,* I, 47–48.

[19] For Medeiros's background, see USE-RJ to SS, Nov. 7, 1917, pp. 2–3, RG 59, 632.119/83, USNA; and Guilherme Studart, *Diccionario Bio-Bibliographico Cearense* (Forteleza, Ceará: Assis Bezerra, 1915), I, 157–9. For Medeiros's contract, see MAG to MRE, Apr. 26, 1916, M-292, 4, 6, AHI.

to delegates at the Cotton Conference, he singled out opportunities for improvements within each segment of the cotton industry. In the ginning process, the long-staple cotton of the North suffered because gins used there were designed for short-staple cotton. The lack of hydraulic baling machines and the different capacities of those few machines available complicated transportation and marketing. Processing cotton seed was especially deficient. Most seeds remained far from marketing centers because of lack of transportation and only a few plants were equipped to take complete advantage of the seed. Most seed oil factories discarded the remainder of the seed after extracting the oil, ignoring the chance to form cakes for cattle fodder from the residue. In the manufacture of cotton seed oil, "there is everything left to do," he reported. He recommended federal action to improve seed qualities, transportation, availability of credit and subsidies to stimulate increased cotton production.[20]

The conference's recommendations reaffirmed their members' faith in the ability of Brazil to produce cotton in both the Northeast and the South on a large scale, and they solicited favorable government treatment toward that end. Lower taxes and freight rates, increased government assistance, establishment of cotton exchanges, and provision of credit on more liberal terms were the most salient. Of importance to U.S.-Brazilian commercial relations, the conference endorsed the results that the Upland Big Boll variety had achieved in the Southern Brazil. It also recommended purchase of simple and inexpensive plows, cultivators, and sowers made by the Allen Manufacturing Company of Philadelphia.[21]

Soon after close of the conference, the federal government granted important new subsidies for cotton production. President Braz ordered creation of agencies of the Banco do Brasil in Sergipe and Maranhão to extend credit to producers and installation of powerful cotton presses in Northern ports to facilitate transporting cotton on the national shipping line, Lloyd Brasileiro. At the end of 1916, Congress authorized creation of standard official cotton types and subsidies for installation of cotton processing mills and presses at railroad stations and other points the states deemed appropriate. It also required the federal government to aid small farmers by arranging their acquisition of gins and hand cotton oil presses.

[20] Trajano S. V. de Medeiros, "O Algodão—sua indústria, e commercio no Brasil - situação atual e medidas para melhorarl-a," in *Annaes da primeira conferência*, I, 5–62, 585–8.

[21] "Conclusões aprovadas," in *Annaes da primeira conferência*, I, 106–7.

The Ministry of Agriculture also moved to instruct workers in eradicating the Pink Boll Worm.[22]

As Brazil moved toward planting its third wartime cotton crop in early 1917, the links between improving the crop and ties with the United State became stronger. In the Northeast, not only did existing ginning practices depend upon American-made gins but improving the product by better ginning meant purchase of another U.S.-made gin, the McCarthy Roller Gin, designed especially for long-staple cotton. Brazilians decided in 1916 to purchase U.S. equipment to increase the number of cotton balers and seed presses in the Northeast. Portentous of later developments, many Northeastern Brazilians interested in the proliferation of cotton saw the automobile as the most practical solution to cotton's transportation problem.[23]

A major factor in cementing ties with the United States based upon cotton was the focus on making cotton cultivation profitable in the São Paulo region, a process already underway by 1917. São Paulo enjoyed obvious advantages over the Northeast: the lack of periodic droughts, lesser insect infestation, and an extensive transportation network already in place. As in the 1860s, São Paulo farmers also found cotton to be a profitable complement to coffee, often planting it between rows of coffee trees. More importantly, cotton proved less labor-intensive than maturing coffee trees that required "manuring .... very expensive work." As a result, many owners of decaying São Paulo coffee plantations converted their lands entirely to cotton, since their soil was still "good enough to produce a fair cotton crop" while requiring less labor than coffee.[24]

[22] "O Algodão," *Brasil Agrícola*, Vol. 1 (1916), 556; "Conferência algodoeira," *Boletím Agrícola* [Pernambuco], Vol. 10 (1916), 307; "Algodão," *RC do "JC,"* 1916, p. 244. As in most case for government mandates, there are no accounts that measure the actual results from these provisions.

[23] For visions of the automobile in cotton's future in Brazil, see an interview with Domingo de Sampaio Ferraz, *Imprensa* [Natal, Rio Grande do Norte], n.d., quoted in RC do "JC," 1917, p. 273; Trajano de Medeiros, "O Algodão," in *Annaes da primeira conferência*, I, 575, 586; José Eurico Martins, "O Algodão no nordeste," in *Annaes da primeira conferência*, II, 153; Diogenes Caldas, "O Algodão no estado da Parahyba," in *Annaes da primeira conferência*, II, 295.

[24] Arno S. Pearse, *Cotton in North Brazil, Being the Report of the Journey through the States of Ceará, Maranhao and Para* .... (Manchester, Eng.: Taylor Garnett Evans & Co., n.d.), p. 113.

The São Paulo state government had taken steps to improve the outlook for "white gold" earlier in the century. Agronomists at the Instituto Agronômico of Campinas began to shift their attention to a non-native type of cotton as experiments with long-fibred cotton proved that plant's inability to adapt to São Paulo's climate. Experimenters focused on the short-stapled Upland variety, which existed in over 650 species and made up the heart of the U.S. cotton crop. The Campinas station began testing varieties of Upland from 1910 forward, producing up to 2.7 kilos per hectare from Upland by 1912. Agronomist and director of the Piraçicaba Agricultural School Emilio Castello studied cotton in the United States for six months in 1911 and returned with a variety of seeds for experimentation.[25]

The São Paulo government also created incentives to revive cotton production. Through a 1911 decree creating cooperative fields to promote cotton cultivation, the state furnished everything necessary (except land) to grow cotton, including a pair of mules, a plow, and selected seeds. In return, the farmer agreed to cultivate cotton for three years and furnish the state with the seeds harvested, while selling the cotton on his own terms. Wary of adapting native cotton to the region, the state imported Upland Big Boll seeds from the United States. By 1914 twenty tons of seeds from these cooperative fields and twelve tons of seeds imported from the United States sustained expanded production under state sponsorship. The state installed ten demonstration fields, insisting upon the exclusive use of the Big Boll type of Upland cotton.[26]

By 1916 experiments with a wide variety of cotton types in southern Brazil established that the U.S.-centered Upland cotton was the most adaptable to the region. Agronomist Day now began to promote the growing of cotton along the Leopoldina Railway Lines. He reported that local farmers were interested in planting cotton and by 1915 had obtained the "first cotton from American seeds … which we believe will

[25] Gustavo A.P. D'Ultra, "Condições da cultura do algodoeiro no estado de São Paulo, e seu futuro," in *Annaes da primeira conferência,* I, 129; J. Arthaud Berthet, "Culturas experimentaes do algodoeiro feitas no Instituto Agronômico de Campinas, estado de São Paulo," in *Annaes da primeira conferência*, I, 146; *PAU*, Vol. 34 (1912), 110.

[26] Paulo de Moraes Barros, "O problema do Algodão," *Revista da SRB,* Vol. 4 (1924), 117; Brazil, Serviço do Algodão, *Possibilidades da cultura algodoeira no Brasil por William W. Coelho de Souza* (Rio de Janeiro: Imprensa Nacional, 1922), p. 24; RC do "JC," 1914, p. 183; "Relatório do Inspector J. R. Zamith," *Boletím de Agricultura* [São Paulo], 16 (1915), 55–56.

satisfy the highest expectations."[27] His plantings proved successful. The following year he sold 665 kilos of cotton seed to the Minas Gerais government. Day even bred his own brand of cotton, a variety of Upland Big Boll that compatriot Green termed "Day's Pedigreed." Day claimed this variety was "the most resistant, productive and adaptable" to conditions of southern Brazil. He concluded that the "southern region of Brazil is not appropriate to the development of the Seridó or Mocó cotton" prevalent in the Northeast."[28] In 1916, the Minas government contracted U.S. agronomist John W. Haddon of Newton, Mississippi, to teach cotton cultivation and establish cotton demonstration fields statewide.[29]

Experiments in São Paulo yielded similar conclusions. Specimens of Upland cultivated at the Campinas agronomic station in 1915 and 1916 yielded over four times those of long-staple cottons similar to those traditionally grown in the Northeast. The former director of the Campinas station concluded in 1916 that "the best varieties for the climate of São Paulo, are, without a doubt, those of the [Upland] Big Boll" because of its "relatively large, robust and strong plants" and production of "large capsules" of cotton.[30] The state distributed over 23,000 kilos of Upland Big Boll seeds in 1916 and only 750 kilos of other varieties. As Agronomist Coelho de Souza later explained, São Paulo would "never be able to cultivate the long staple species ... native to the hot backland of the Northeast." In São Paulo, he noted, "it will be possible only to plant the American species."[31]

[27] Thomas R. Day to Director Gerente, Leopoldina Railway, July 2, 1915, L-21, P-1, N-2, ANP.

[28] Minas Gerais, Secretaria de Agricultura, "Fazendas modelo," S.A. 163, p. 109, MGPA; Thomas R. Day, *Manual de Algodão: Meio século de experiencia em Texas e no Brasil*, 3rd ed. (N.P.: n.p., 1926), p. 24.

[29] Minas Gerais, *Mensagem, 1917*, pp. 62–63. The state of Minas Gerais contracted Haddon on May 27, 1916, to teach cotton cultivation and establish demonstration plots. See Minas Gerais, *Mensagem, 1917*, p. 63. Haddon remained an employee of the state until 1922, when he returned to Mississippi to "interest American investors in the opportunities for the cultivation of cotton and sugar cane in Minas Gerais." See *Brazilian-American*, Vol. 5, No. 118 (Jan. 22, 1922), p. 17.

[30] J. Arthaud Berthet, "Culturas experimentaes," in *Annaes da primeira conferência*, I, 147; Gustavo A.P. D'Utra, "Condições da cultura," in *Annaes da primeira conferência*, I, 129.

[31] "Sementes distribuídos em 1916," *Boletím de Agricultura* [São Paulo], Vol. 18 (1917), 686; Brazil, Serviço do Algodão, *Possibilidades da cultura algodoeira*, p. 24.

The cotton sector strove to advance its position under the new conditions created by the transfusion of new raw material, equipment, and expertise. As noted in Chapter 4, before Brazil entered into the war, state political leaders had become increasingly sensitive to the opportunities presented by cotton. While vacationing in his native Minas Gerais, federal deputy (and future national president) Artur Bernardes had recognized the opportunity the war would present for cotton. From Viçosa Bernardes asked the Minas secretary of agriculture Raul Soares to secure "a good quantity of cotton seeds" to distribute to farmers around Viçosa. Bernardes informed his close friend and political confidant of the "great number of requests" from farmers in the region that had "exported cotton to the United States during the war of secession."[32]

Farmers were reacting to cotton's respectable price rise, aided by higher levels of assistance from the federal government stemming since the June 1916 cotton conference. By 1917, real cotton prices were edging toward more than twice their 1914 level, causing renewed faith in cotton in both the North and South. Paraiba's state senator Epitácio Pessoa credited the high cotton prices for a rise in the state's income in early 1917. Camillo de Holanda established Paraíba's own cotton service in October 1917, and the higher price prompted renewed cultivation even in Pará, where official estimates later pegged the 1917 production at 82 tons–the first respectable crop in nearly 20 years. Likewise, São Paulo state's 1917 production rose 38% above the 1916 crop.[33]

Cotton's higher prices represented the pull of three factors: the continuing problems caused by drought and pest in the Northeast, the boom in the internal textile industry brought about by high tariffs and the war, and the increased demand for raw cotton in foreign markets. Cloth production rose another 73 million meters in 1917, and demand from foreign

[32] Arthur Bernardes to Raul Soares, Apr. 6, 1917, 1917.06.04, ARS. Soares had been a friend of Bernardes since school days and was to be an important political supporter. See Bruno de Almeida Magalhaes, *Arthur Bernardes, Estadista da República* (Rio de Janeiro: José Olympio Editora, 1973), pp. 33–37.

[33] Haddad, "Growth of the Brazilian Real Product," pp. 56–57; Epitácio Pessoa to Camillo de Holanda, Apr. 1917, P-12, N-63, AEP; João Mauricio de Medieros, "O Serviço de Defesa de Algodão. .... " *Annaes da Conferência Internacional algodoeira,* I, 397; Brazil, Serviço de Inspeçcão e Fomento Agrícola, *Relatório 1925* (Rio de Janeiro: Papelaria Americana, 1927), p. 60; Octavio Pupo Nogueira, "A indústria algodoeira em São Paulo," *Annaes da Conferência Algodoeira Internacional* (N.P.: n.p., ca. 1922), II, 337.

customers—especially Great Britain—also drove cotton production.[34] Great Britain's thirst for cotton proved nearly insatiable, stimulating new planting and efforts to improve processing of the Brazilian product. Shortages of U.S. cotton in Britain caused by the ravages of submarine warfare and higher priorities for military cargo threatened to produce a "chaotic scramble for the limited supplies" of short-staple cotton available. The British government formed the Cotton Control Board on June 28, 1917, to parcel out supplies by limiting production to no more than 70% of a firm's capacity. In early 1918 this figure shrank even more, as plants using U.S.-grown cotton were restricted to operating at only 50% capacity.[35]

Brazilian suppliers soon attempted to fill part of this void. Individual states sought to seize the opportunity to accelerate cotton development—especially of the short-staple U.S.—grown variety preferred by British customers. In 1917 Brazil exported 6,000 tons of cotton, with 87% of that going to England, and in February 1918 the Brazilian Consul General in Liverpool urged a greater Brazilian effort. In his view, conditions of the British market should translate into increased cotton production in the Brazilian Northeast, "predestined by nature to be one of the great depositories of the product."[36] In August 1917, U.S. agronomist Haddon recommended that the Sociedade Mineira de Agricultura obtain quality seeds, foster publication of practical guides to cotton cultivation, and encourage use of agricultural implements. In Haddon's opinion, Minas Gerais could produce an annual cotton crop worth over US$60 million, double the value of the state's coffee exports. Shortly thereafter the state government purchased 20 tons of short-staple "Upland Big Boll" cotton seeds from a São Paulo firm. That same year

[34] StanleyJ. Stein, *The Brazilian Cotton Manufacture: Textile Enterprisein an Underdeveloped Area, 1850–1950* (Cambridge: Harvard Univ. Press, 1957), pp. 107–9, 194–7.

[35] Hubert D. Henderson, *The Cotton Control Board* (Oxford: Clarendon Press, 1922), pp. 1–2, 23.

[36] "Exportação do Algodão," *RC do "JC,"* 1917, p. 262; Oscar Correia, "O problema de Algodão na Inglaterra," *Boletim* [MAG], Vol. 7, No. 2 (1918), 43. This represented about 8% of the 1917 crop. See Haddad, "Growth of Brazilian Real Output," p. 56.

cotton farmers in Paraíba doubled the area under cultivation in cotton in anticipation of a high return.[37]

The federal government also increased its support for cultivating and processing domestic cotton. To combat the continuing problems with the quality of cotton processed, the CPN recommended on November 29, 1917, that the federal government assist the states in establishing processing mills through long-term, low-interest financing. Shortly thereafter, the federal government issued a decree to implement the CPN's advice, making ample reference to the U. S. example and granting privileged positions to specific enterprises. President Braz noted the recommendations of the CPN as he reminded Brazilians that the value of Texas' cotton production alone surpassed that of all Brazilian agricultural goods, including coffee. Furthermore, the Northeast's population was equivalent to that of Texas and its area capable of growing cotton even larger, and with proper incentives the region could double the value of its exports, in his opinion. To do this, however, required creation of experimental stations and processing mills with presses in the producing states. Such measures, along with a careful selection of seeds, would yield valuable revenue and allow domestically grown cotton by-products, such as cottonseed oil, to substitute for more expensive imported commodities.[38]

The decree granted Brazilian engineer Trajano Saboia Viriato de Medeiros, already a recipient of important concessions, a concession for installing cotton processing and pressing mills in Pernambuco, Paraíba, Rio Grande do Norte and Ceará. Trajano de Medeiros was to install three mills in Pernambuco: two in the interior alongside existing rail lines, and a third in Recife. Mills in the other states were to be situated along major rail lines or, in the case of Rio Grande do Norte, river routes. The decree required each mill to process 180 tons of raw cotton and produce 120 tons of cotton seed monthly, the latter to be transformed into cooking oil and seed cakes for cattle fodder. For each mill in the interior, the

[37] TS, Parahyba do Norte, "Relatório … Diogenese Caldas," p. 18, 20.03.0.2, AISL; "Sessão de 22 de Agosto," *Boletím Mensal da Sociedade Mineira de Agricultura,* Vol. 1, No. 7 (1917), 149–53; See entry for Sept. 24, 1917, p. 68, Minas Gerais, Secretaria de Agricultura, "Fazendas modelos, campos de demonstração … 1913–1916," S.A. 163, APMG.

[38] Decree 12,981, Apr. 24, 1918. See Brazil, Serviço do Algodão, *Actos relativos ao Serviço do Algodão* (Rio de Janeiro: Impr. Nac., 1925), pp. 12–18.

concessionaire was to maintain an experimental farm to teach cotton cultivation to local farmers and furnish them proper seeds. The concessionaire received considerable assistance in return for meeting such requirements. The federal government pledged 75% financing at six percent interest payable in ten years. The Ministry of Agriculture was to pay all duties on imported equipment. Such provisions were to lapse if the equipment were not installed and functioning within eighteen months of the decree.[39]

Other initiatives to stimulate cotton production sprang up in both the public and private sectors. The federal government's Serviço de Agricultura Prática distributed over 18 tons of seeds in 1917 and made plans to provide 200 tons—enough to plant 6,600 hectares—for the 1918 crop. In May 1918 the chief of the CPN personally sent 400 kilos of cotton seed to the president of the Paraná agricultural society. The seeds were a hybrid of Pernambucan and "Big Boll" varieties and were to suffice for planting 100 hectares in cotton. Shortly thereafter, a private corporation dedicated to planting cotton formed in Curitiba. The Sociedade Anônima Paraná Agricola subscribed 70:000$ from "men of responsibility" in Curitiba in its first meeting on August 19, 1918. The firm noted that cotton was becoming the "true substitute of coffee" and acquired enough seeds from São Paulo to forecast a 1919 harvest of 300,000 kilos of unginned cotton.[40]

Corn. The interlacing of U.S. technical experience and Brazilian economic interests also occurred in production of foodstuffs, especially corn. As noted, the price of corn rose substantially between 1914 and 1916, reflecting the need to substitute for declining imports of wheat. Wheat had been grown in quantities in southern Brazil since colonial times, but climactic conditions and limited transportation prevented its widespread cultivation at an economical cost, forcing Brazil to import massive amounts of the cereal, principally from the United States and Argentina. The wartime shortage of shipping reduced this trade. By 1915

[39] Decree 12,981, Apr. 24, 1918. See Brazil, Serviço do Algodão, *Actos relativos ao Serviço do Algodão* (Rio de Janeiro: Impr. Nac., 1925), pp. 12–18.

[40] "Distribuição de sementes e mudas," *RC do "JC,"* 1917, p. 201; *Boletím da Sociedade de Agricultura do Paraná*, Vol. 1, No. 5 (1918), 136; "O algodão no Paraná," *Boletím da Sociedade de Agricultura do Paraná*, Vol. 2, No. 3 (1919), 383–4.

wheat and wheat flour imports had fallen by 100,000 tons.[41] A second major incentive for increasing corn production was the prospect of export, a notion that became a reality by 1916. Producing more corn would also provide cheaper fodder for the nation's cattle and aid efforts to export beef. A national campaign to increase corn production began in late 1914, and at its heart were U.S. methods, equipment, and the U.S. missionary directing an agricultural school in Minas Gerais.

Corn, or maize, had long served as a staple of the Brazilian diet and an important animal fodder. For many segments of Brazil's population, corn furnished necessities of life. Immigrant workers on coffee plantations planted much corn on their own between rows of coffee bushes. Such corn provided an important staple of the Italian immigrants' diet and provided for chickens and pigs kept by the settler.[42] Corn was also important to sharecropping. Farmers using land on the Jaguara farm near Morro Velho, Minas Gerais paid their rent in corn, a "common practice throughout the country."[43] A 1905 census of Sao Paulo state's agriculture counted over 37,000 farmers in the state who planted corn. Only 21,000 planted coffee. Corn farmers produced over 800 million liters of the crop. Prewar population growth and protective tariff measures stimulated a rise on corn production. Subsequent estimates suggest Brazil's population grew by nearly eight million, or nearly fifty percent, between 1898 and 1913, from 16.7 to 25.8 million.[44] Rapid population growth required equal strides in the supply of food and forage crops, including corn. As with rice, the 1905 tariff adjustment spurred improvements and increases in Brazilian corn production.

Brazilian agronomists sought to improve corn even before the war. One of the first to experiment with corn on a scientific basis was Gustavo

[41] Brazil, Directoria Geral de Estatística, *Resumo de várias estatísticas*, pp. 54–55; Caio Prado, Junior, *The Colonial Background of Modern Brazil*, trans. Suzette Macedo (Berkeley: Univ. of California Press, 1971), p. 193.

[42] Thomas H. Hollaway, *Immigrants on the Land: Coffee and Society in São Paulo, 1886–1934* (Chapel Hill, NC: Univ. of North Carolina Press, 1980), p. 89. Benjamin Hunnicutt estimated that humans consumed only 40% of Brazil's corn crop, while the remainder was used as animal food. See Benjamin H. Hunnicutt, *O milho: Sua cultura e aproveitamento,* 2nd Ed. (Lavras, MG: Imprensa Gammon, 1933), pp. 233–4.

[43] G. Chalmers to C.F. Kup, Aug. 27, 1914, in SJdRMCA.

[44] Francisco Vidal Luna, Herbert S. Klein, and William R. Summerhill, "A Agricultura Paulista em 1905," *Estudos Econômicos, São Paulo,* Vol. 44, No. 1, (Jan. - Mar. 2014), p. 156; Brazil, Directoria Geral de Estatística, *Resumo de várias estatísticas*, pp. 54–55.

D'Utra, at the Campinas agronomic station. In 1900 D'Utra received seeds of several varieties of corn growth in the United States from Orville Derby.[45] There is no record of the results of D'Utra's work, but, in the southern Brazil, Assis Brasil soon advanced the quality of Brazilian corn through his own research. Shortly after returning from Washington, Assis Brasil set about improving native corn, which he called *milho crioulo*. He described it as an accidental hybrid between hard corn of the yellow or red variety, grown in the Rio de la Plata region, and corn native to Rio Grande do Sul known as *catetão*. Assis Brasil's goal was to make the corn more nourishing as cattle fodder, and in 1915 he pronounced successful development of a slightly heavier and yellower breed of corn. The corn received his name: *milho Assis Brasil*, adding to his credibility as a spokesman for the cattle sector and diversified agriculture.[46]

While experimenters searched for a better Brazilian corn, production began to respond to growing demand. São Paulo's corn production nearly doubled from 5.6 million bags in 1901 to 10.9 million bags harvested in 1915. The opening of rich new farmland in Paraná at the turn of the century pushed corn production upward. The *municipio* of São Pedro de Mallet, Paraná, produced over 17 million liters (586,000 bushels) only five years after its formal establishment as a *municipio*. Other recently formed *municipios* in the state also reported large expanses of land dedicated to corn production.[47]

Despite this trend, Brazil still suffered from a deficit of corn supplies and, between 1910 and 1912, imported an average of over 4,000 metric

[45] Derbyhad ordered the seeds from a New York vendor for the geological service's botanical garden, where "a good number of native fruits, medicinal, timber, forage and ornamental plants" were cultivated. See Derby to Branner, Mar. 2, 1900, Box 29, Folder 89, BP-SUA.

[46] "Cultura do milho," *A Lavoura*, Vol. 4 (1900), 269–83; J.F. Assis Brasil, "Memorandum sobre o Milho A.B.," in Pimentel, *Joaquim Francisco de Assis Brasil*, pp. 59–61. Assis Brasil probably did most of his work on his palatial estate at Pedras Altas, Rio Grande do Sul, that he acquired in May 1904. See "O solar de Pedras Altas," in Pimentel, *Assis Brasil*, pp. 53–56. For Assis Brasil's reputation as an expert on corn, see a speech by the Brazilian commercial attaché in the United States printed in *Revista de Commercio e Industria*, Vol. 7 (1921), 29.

[47] "The Economic Situation of São Paulo," *Brazilian-American*, No. 95 (Aug. 20, 1921), 23; "Situação econômica dos municipios do Estado," *Boletím da Sociedade de Agricultura de Paraná*, Vol. 1 (1918), 101.

tons of corn, mostly from Argentina.[48] Among those impressed by Brazil's inability to meet its need for corn was the young director of the Lavras Agricultural School, Benjamin H. Hunnicutt. When Hunnicutt arrived in Rio de Janeiro in 1907, he was surprised to see an Argentine ship busily unloading corn and vowed to contribute to increasing Brazil's corn production.[49] Hunnicutt returned to the United States in 1912 and collected pictures of local corn expositions and attended the National Corn Exposition in Columbia, South Carolina. Returning to Brazil, he offered observations about corn exhibits and corn cultivation in a letter to the editor of a popular agricultural magazine, *Chácaras e Quintais*.[50]

Editor Amadeu A. Barbiellini, who would become a dedicated advocate of more and better corn production, responded enthusiastically and proposed that Hunnicutt produce a similar corn exposition in Brazil. Within a few days, Hunnicutt forwarded to Barbiellini a suggestion that the exhibit take place with cooperation of the São Paulo government or the Paulista agricultural society. He also thought that major implement houses of São Paulo would donate prizes and suggested forming corn clubs (*clubes de milho*), instrumental in promoting corn cultivation among U.S. teenagers. He also enclosed his first article on improving corn production. It advocated improved instruction through corn clubs, expositions, and magazine and newspaper articles. He also urged adoption of mechanization, fertilization, crop rotation, improved seed selection, improved breeds of corn, and better handling and transportation.[51]

Hunnicutt's ideas quickly gained endorsement of the Brazilian government and plans for the exhibit advanced rapidly. Agriculture Minister Calógeras applauded Hunnicutt's ideas, assuring "his collaboration" toward obtaining "immediate results" in the quantitative and qualitative improvement of the nation's corn crop.[52] In July 1915, the Primeira Exposição Nacional de Milho (first national corn exposition) opened at the Paulista agricultural society, with Hunnicutt as its director. The

48 "Iª Exposição Nacional de Milho," *Chácaras e Quintais*, Vol. 10 (1914), 325.

49 Personal interview with Benjamin H. Hunnicutt, Jr., Aug. 13, 1982.

50 Hunnicutt, *O milho*, 2nd ed., p. 155.

51 J.F. Velho Sobrinho, *Diccionario Bio-Bibliographico Brasileiro* (Rio de Janeiro: Irmãos Pongetti, 1937), II, 72; "Iª Exposição de Milho no Brasil," *Chácaras e Quintais*, Vol. 10 (1910), 324.

52 Calogeras to Hunnicutt, n.d., *RC do "JC,"* 1914, p. 184.

exposition marked the first step toward increased national attention and government support for the "commoner cereal." At the exposition, Hunnicutt advanced his idea of forming a national corn club to intensify corn production nationwide and show the advantages of mechanical cultivation. *Chácaras* editor Barbiellini agreed to promote the association and invited Assis Brasil to become the club's first national honorary president, with Hunnicutt to serve as the club's presiding officer.[53]

Club chapters could be established wherever ten or more members expressed an interest. Corn club strength and the prestige of corn as a crop gained considerably through the second national corn exposition, held in Belo Horizonte July 19 through 21, 1916. Hunnicutt served as the technical director of the show, where prominent farmers and politicians buzzed over row after row of corn ears carefully aligned on tables at the public archive. State President Delfim Moreira opened the display along with Hunnicutt, Raul Soares, the state secretary of agriculture, Fidelis Reis of the Minas agricultural society, Eduardo Cotrim, a spokesman for the cattle sector, Ildefonso Simões Lopes and Hannibal Porto, both from the SNA, Hegreville Hintz, later director of Paraná's Club de Milho, as well as numerous other farmers and bureaucrats. In the inaugural address, Secretary Soares challenged all raising corn to accept "the necessity of adapting and assimilating the modern agricultural processes which account for the prosperity of so many enlightened countries." Corn was important, he proclaimed, because it supported beef, bacon, and lard production and provided food for the "less fortunate" masses of the populace. Modern production techniques and improved transportation would transform Brazil into an exporter of corn, following U.S. and Argentine examples. Soares praised the corn exhibit's contribution to the "golden vision of our patriotism," where we can see the "Brazil of tomorrow" arise "great, opulent and happy, from the intelligent and dignifying treatment of the earth."[54]

Hunnicutt used the exposition to promote ideas and equipment popular in the United States. He urged government support for the corn clubs, a necessity since farmers were awakening from their "secular

[53] "Club Nacional de Milho," *Chácaras e Quintais*, Vol. 13 (1916), 165–7. *O Milho*, Vol. 1 (1917), 6.

[54] TS, Raul Soares, "A segunda exposição nacional de milho," [speech], 14/17.00.00.00/3, pp. 1, 3, ARS.

sleep" and looking toward the government to support modern agricultural instruction. The prizes he arranged for the best ears constituted a veritable catalog of popular U.S. farm implements: "Planter Junior" cultivators, made by the S. L. Allen & Co. of Philadelphia, Avery plows of B. F. Avery Co., Louisville, Kentucky, Wiard plows from Batavia, New York, plows from the Oliver Chilled Plow Works, South Bend, Indiana, and cultivators from the Deere Company of Moline, Illinois. The Leopoldina Railroad also awarded prizes for the best products in areas it served.[55]

Hunnicutt's campaign to promote corn cultivation had a strong impact in Paraná. Raul Gomes's book *O milho no Paraná*, published in Curitiba in 1918 drew heavily from Hunnicutt's *O Livro de Milho*. Hunnicutt's national corn club concept received important support from the Paraná government. Already by 1916, the state government passed a law offering subsidies of from 30 to 100 *milreis* for three farmers in each *municipio* who cultivated corn according to instructions of the national corn club.[56] An acquaintance of Hunnicutt became engaged in promoting organization of corn growers. Hegreville Hintz, who had graduated from Piraçicaba during Clinton Smith's tenure, returned from the 1916 corn show to promote corn club chapters in Paraná. The club founded a monthly publication, *O Milho,* published in Portuguese, German, and Polish, with the first edition appearing in October. By December 1916, enthusiasts had founded eleven regional and one local corn club with 1,160 members. Club members wrote to Hunnicutt for advice, read his answers at club meetings, and ordered his book on how to grow corn.[57]

Farmers in other areas expressed an interest in the corn club idea and increased corn production. Pernambuco's *Boletím Agricola* reproduced Hunnicutt's article from *Chácaras e Quintais* and reminded readers that the "rich cereal [was] one of the principal factors of U.S. prosperity," with an annual production valued higher than Brazil's total annual exports. Barbiellini reported interest in corn clubs spreading to Recife, Rio Grande do Sul, Goiás, and Bahia. Even President Braz became interested in the corn clubs' activities. The idea proved so popular that in Manaus a Club da Seringueira, or Wild Rubber Club, formed to promote cultivation of

55 "Exposição Nacional de Milho," *A Lavoura*, Vol. 20 (1916), 110.

56 # Law 1,636 of Apr. 5, 1916. See Paraná, Secretaria de Fazenda, Agricultura e Obras Públicas, *Relatório do Exercicio 1915–1916* (Curitiba: 1917), p. 113.

57 *O Milho*, Vol. 1, No. 1 (1916), 21; Vol. 1, No. 3 (1916), 15; Vol. 1, No. 2 (1916), 17.

wild rubber. By early 1917 Hunnicutt reported to the SNA that the national corn club had 1,500 members in Paraná and 2,000 members nationwide.[58]

A total of 257 prizes went out to owners of winning entries at the third exposition in Curitiba in August 1917. At the fourth exposition, held in Rio de Janeiro between 10 and 15 August 1918, Minister of Agriculture Pereira Lima predicted that Brazil could "increase on an incalculable scale the planting of this rich cereal, transforming it into energy for the worker, provident wealth for the granaries, into beef, bacon, and pork." Hunnicutt, president and organizer of the exposition, also called attention to the benefits of corn production while his wife demonstrated various dishes prepared from the cereal. A member of the Club Nacional de Milho who had represented Bahia at the national exhibits went on to organize an exposition of corn in Bahia in December 1919.[59]

Increased demand for corn and efforts of Hunnicutt and others to promote corn production yielded dramatic increases in output, even by the 1917 harvest. Available statistics on corn production between 1914 and 1917 tend to confirm the early impact of the war which, in Barbiellini's opinion, "valorized even more [previously] undervalued corn."[60] A study of the 1917 corn harvest concluded that "it would be advantageous from the economic point of view, to develop ... the internal and external" possibilities of corn, "one of Brazil's most extensive crops."[61] The study estimated that the nation's corn harvest had risen 20% between the 1914 and 1917. Because of corn's already widespread cultivation, this increase represented a gain of nearly one million metric tons. Based upon an average of productivity of between ten and fifteen quintais per hectare, such an increase would have required planting of between 67 and 100 thousand new hectares of corn. Total shipments of corn arriving at Rio de Janeiro's Centro Commercial do Cereaes rose sharply by 1917. From

[58] "O Milho," *Boletím Agrícola* [Pernambuco], Vol. 10, No. 2 (1916), 89; *Chácaras e Quintais*, Vol. 13 (1916), 412–3; Amazonas, *Mensagem, 1916*, p. 118; *Jornal do Commercio*, Feb. 28, 1917 [p.m. edition], p. 3, col. 3.

[59] ; "Quarta Exposição Nacional de Milho," *Brasil Agrícola*, Vol. 3 (1919), 226; "Primeira Exposição de Milho na Bahia," *Brasil Agrícola*, Vol. 5 (1920), 15–18.

[60] "Iª Exposição Nacional de Milho," *Chácaras e Quintais*, Vol. 10 (1914), 324.

[61] Brazil, Directoria Geral de Estatística, *Estimativa da producção do milho no Brasil (Safra de 1916–17)* (Rio de Janeiro: Typographia da Estatística, 1918), p. 28.

an average of 47 million kilos of corn arriving between 1907 and 1910, corn shipments reached 51 million in 1915 and 55 million in 1917.[62]

State statistics also indicate an upshot in corn cultivation. Corn production in Rio Grande do Sul state increased over 75,000 tons between 1915 and 1917. In São Paulo state, corn production increased by 1.2 million sacks, or 11% between 1915 and 1917. Paulista farmers were cultivating corn "on a large scale, employing machines identical to those used in the United States." Higher corn prices prompted a 1916 São Paulo planting "much greater than those of the previous two years." Even Hunnicutt's agricultural school participated. From the 1916 harvest Hunnicutt sold 5,000 liters of selected seed corn at 250 reis per liter and "could have sold twice as much." In early 1917 he wrote: "This year I calculated that we will have 10,000 liters and I proposed that we ask double the price."[63]

Increased corn production created the prospect of export by mid-1916. The Foreign Office informed the Brazilian Ambassador in Washington that Brazil would soon have a "great harvest of corn [and rice] which we need to export."[64] For the first time in recent history, Brazil began exporting corn, shipping almost five thousand tons to Britain in 1916, with another 150,000 sacks going to waste because of the lack of ocean going vessels.[65] With the massive increase of the harvest of 1917, not only did exports increase, but the price of the grain dropped by over 10% between 1914 and 1917.[66]

Hunnicutt's efforts to promote corn production transformed him into an important landmark on the landscape of Brazilian agriculture. Publisher Barbiellini termed him the "right man in the right place."

[62] "Iª Exposição Nacional de Milho," *Chácaras e Quintais*, Vol. 10 (1914), 324; Haddad, "Growth of Brazilian Real Output," p. 51; Brazil, Directoria Geral de Estatística, *Resumo de várias estatísticas*, p. 30. The estimate is probably high because much corn was traditionally planted among rows of other crops. Figures for deliveries calculated from Centro Commercial de Cereaes, *Relatório, 1910* (Rio de Janeiro: Imprensa Nacional, 1911), annexes 2, 4, 5 and 6; Relatório, 1916–1917, annexes 3, 4, 7, 15, and 18.

[63] Hunnicutt to East Brazil Mission, Feb. 9, 1917, in "Minutes, Directorate," GIA.

[64] MRE to EBM, June 6, 1916, M-235, 4, 3, AHI.

[65] Bazil, Directoria de Estatística Commercial, *Commercio Exterior do Brasil: Exportação, importação, 1913–1918* (Rio de Janeiro: Estatística Commerical, 1919), I, 600; "Producção e exportação de milho," *Boletím* [MAG], Vol. 14, 1, No. 2 (1925), 294; "A lavoura paulista de cereaes," *Revista de Commercio e Industria*, Vol. 3 (1917), 58.

[66] Haddad, "Growth of Brazilian Real Output," pp. 56–57.

Observers at the Second National Corn Exposition termed him "indefatigable," and the SNA made him an honorary member a few years later. A former student of Hunnicutt's who became a pioneer in Brazilian agriculture summarized the meaning of Hunnicutt's promotion of corn. José Garibaldi Dantas noted that, while Hunnicutt had not introduced corn to Brazil, "he was the one who dignified its cultivation." Furthermore, he "gave a new economic aspect" to the crop, teaching the country "its food value" and thus increasing demand for corn. Hunnicutt's work with corn alone, in Dantas's opinion, sufficed to raise Hunnicutt to a position of national esteem.[67]

Cattle and Beef

Increased corn production supported another Brazilian foodstuff sector stimulated by wartime conditions: the raising of cattle. Rising beef prices and the increased U.S. import of beef had turned eyes of potential beef producers toward Brazilian cattle on the eve of the war. The chief of the USDA's Bureau of Animal Husbandry explained in 1913 that "the domestic supply of meat in the United States" had shown "an alarming decrease," causing the United States to "look to the foreign field for relief." The Secretary of Agriculture ordered a survey of South American livestock and meat industries to see if its beef could safely be imported into the United States. While the report rated Argentine beef more favorably, the U.S. Consul in Rio de Janeiro countered shortly thereafter that Brazil could still compete in the international market because of cheaper lands.[68]

New market conditions and the abundant stock of cattle encouraged a review within Brazil of the potential for exporting beef. During the colonial era raising cattle to satisfy demands of the internal market had been a principle economic activity. Herds thrived in the Northeast until devastated by a late eighteenth-century drought. Although Minas Gerais had substantial herds, Rio Grande do Sul became the chief supplier of the

[67] "Iª Exposição Nacional de Milho," *Chácaras e Quintais*, Vol. 10 (1914), 324; *Acrópole* [Lavras, M.G.], Sept. 23, 1979, p. 1, col. 1.

[68] A.D. Melvin, "The South American Meat Industry," in *Yearbook of the USDA 1913* (Washington: GPO, 1914), p. 347; *RC do JC*'," 1914, p. 182. The United States imported over $253 million in meat products from foreign packing houses in 1912, 1913, and 1914. See *Yearbook of the USDA 1914* (Washington, GPO, 1915), p. 652.

beef needs of the Northeast because of its ample pasture and numbers of cattle. Production of dried beef, or charque (jerky), became an economic mainstay of Rio Grande do Sul, and remained so throughout the nineteenth century. The dawn of the Republic brought a depression in the charque industry, as the abolition of slavery disrupted a secure market. Higher taxes and competition from higher-quality Uruguayan beef also created serious challenges. Early in the twentieth century, ranchers in Rio Grande do Sul organized and considered financing a *frigorífico*, or chilled packing plant, to export to the world market. At their disposition was the largest portion of the over 24 million cattle in Brazil: a herd of over 6.6 million animals, including, as noted in Chapter 3, improved breeds recently developed by the Brazil Land, Cattle, and Packing Company.[69]

Despite the plentiful stock of cattle in Rio Grande do Sul, foreign and domestic entrepreneurs found more favorable conditions in São Paulo state. Large stocks of cattle were accessible; there were an estimated 6.3 million head of cattle in nearby Minas Gerais and another 1.8 million in São Paulo itself. The growing population of the city of São Paulo offered a ready domestic market, and the state's rail and port facilities guaranteed access to export markets. Such opportunity was not lost on paulista Antônio da Silva Prado, who opened the first modern meat packing plant in Brazil. Prado, from one of São Paulo's leading coffee planting families, had been Minister of Agriculture in the 1880s, mayor of São Paulo from 1899 to 1910, served as president of the Paulista railroad, which he promoted, and initiated glass, leather, and bottle factories. In 1910, he formed a partnership with immigrant entrepreneur Alexandre Silciliano and built the Companhia Frigorífico e Pastoril de Barretos, which opened at the terminus of the Paulista railroad in 1913. In the plant's first year, it processed over 25,000 cattle for the São Paulo metropolitan region.[70] Foreign capital soon built the second modern packing plant in Brazil, also in São Paulo. The Sulzburger Company of Chicago invested

[69] Caio Prado, *The Colonial Background*, pp. 213–4; Sandra Jahaty Pesavento, *República Velha Gaúcha: Charquiadas, frigoríficos, criadores* (Porto Alegre: Movimento, 1980), pp. 29–78, 94. On links between slavery and the charque industry, see Fernando Henrique Cardoso, *Capitalismo e escravidão no Brasil meridional* (São Paulo: DIFEL, 1962).

[70] For estimates of cattle, see Pesavento, *A República Velha Gaúcha*, p. 94. Dean, *Industrialization of São Paulo*, p. 45; Annex N to TS,"Relatório do Dr. Franklin de Almeida relativo as abesticimento de carnes, 1920," 12.00.00 I 18, AISl; Elliott, *Brazil Today and Tomorrow*, p. 140; Darrel E. Levi, "The Prados of São Paulo: An Elite Brazilian Family in a Changing Society, 1840–1930," (Diss. Yale 1974), p. 268.

$240,000 in a joint venture in 1912 with Farquhar's Brazil Land, Cattle, and Packing Company. The company, known as Continental Products, in 1913 began constructing a packing plant in Osasco, near São Paulo, capable of processing from 800 to 1,000 steers and 1,000 hogs daily.[71]

Conditions in the world market soon stimulated further expansion of *frigorífico* capacity. Soon after the war began the French initiated imports of large amounts of frozen beef to feed mobilized armies and prevent complete decimation of its livestock. An analyst with the USDA predicted that the war would push meat prices higher. "Meat in America will be a rarity before the war ends," the official warned.[72] In late 1914 an emissary of Continental Products visited the Osasco plant site and reported that "this is the most opportune time to make money on the Continental on account of war conditions" since the company "could secure large contracts from the French government."[73] The company's future was so tied to the war that "Sulzberger had to get out" and the company "had to get rid of any [German employees] in Brazil" so that Western nations would consider buying Continental's products, according to a knowledgeable observer.[74]

Brazilian firms soon entered the international market. In November 1914, a Brazilian company notified the British consulate in Rio de Janeiro

[71] "The Cattle and Meat Industry of Southern Brazil," *Bulletin of the Pan American Union,* Vol. 41 (July-Dec. 1915), 504; "Cattle Raising in Brazil," *The Times*, July 29, 1914, p. 19, col. 6. The Brazil Land, Cattle and Packing Company held 77 and ½% of the stock in Continental Products. Journals of W. Cameron Forbes, Series II, I, 101, Manuscript Division, Library of Congress. Despite the companies' interlocking nature, there were clashes of interest, especially after interests represented by Farquhar went into receivership in November 1914. Although the Cattle Company sold cattle to Continental Products, the Sulzberger interests complained that MacKenzie asked too high a price. See "Meeting with Forbes ... June 20, 1915," in U.S.Congress, House of Representatives, *Report of the Federal Trade Commission on the Meat Packing Industry. Part II. Evidence of Combination Among Packers*. House Doc. 1297. 65th Cong., 2nd Sess. (Washington: GPO, 1918), pp. 223–4.

[72] Michel Auge-Laribe and Pierre Pinot, *Agriculture and Food Supply in France during the War* (New Haven: Yale Univ. Press, 1927), pp. 73–75; *New York Times*, Dec. 19, 1914, p. 1, col. 2; "Meeting Held in H Office ... Nov. 17, 1914," in U.S. Congress, House of Representatives, *Report of the Federal Trade Commission*, pp. 229–30; Forbes Journals, Series II, I, 102, Manuscript Division, Library of Congress.

[73] "Meeting Held at H Office ... Nov. 17, 1914″ in U.S. Congress, House of Representatives, *Report of the Federal Trade Commission*, pp. 229–30.

[74] Journals of W. Cameron Forbes, Series II, I, 102, Manuscript Division, Library of Congress.

that it was prepared to ship 1,000 tons of beef monthly to Britain. The following month the first export of chilled beef from Brazil–1,415 kilos—left Santos for Europe.[75] Another Brazilian *frigorifico*, the Caçapava (São Paulo) packing house sensed the opening of new markets. In December, it asked the Ministry of Agriculture to obtain the weekly prices in foreign markets of frozen beef, corned beef in cans and barrels, salted meats, bacon, salami, hams, and sausages through Brazilian consulates in the United States, England, France, Germany, Italy, Portugal, Argentina, and Uruguay. The firm sought prices of other material as well, hoping to market "every class of articles of Brazilian make which our industries can export."[76]

The first full year of warfare witnessed continued efforts to make Brazilian beef more competitive in Europe. A prominent politician in Rio Grande do Sul noted that improvements in the stock would be "a benefit compensating any sacrifice" and was "a condition required by the cold packing industry."[77] The Brazil Land, Cattle, and Packing Company continued its program of improving the Brazilian herds. The company introduced a variety of agricultural implements, including tractors and 26-inch disk plows, to improve fodder for its immense herds in Mato Grosso. It used its extensive lands in Mato Grosso, Paraná, and Minas Gerais as open ranges where imported Herefords cross-bred with the local Caracu cattle. The "improved" stock then undertook a trek reminiscent of early cattle days in the United States, a 60- to 90-day journey to the Paraná or Paranapanema rivers. The cattle then retreated to pasture for three to six months to recover lost weight. In early 1915, Murdo MacKenzie drove 1,000 head of cattle to the railhead at Barretos, where he sold them to the Continental Products. A Cattle Company representative reported that between 28,000 and 35,000 cattle were available that year.[78]

The new *frigorificos* exploited both foreign and domestic markets successfully. So profitable were the cattle and meat-packing fields that the two Farquhar-related enterprises survived the collapse of the Farquhar

[75] "Brazilian Beef for Britain," *The Times*, Nov. 6, 1914, p. 3, col. 4.

[76] Caçapava Packing House to MAG, Dec. 1914, M-292, 4, 5, AHI.

[77] Rio Grande do Sul, *Mensagem, 1915*, pp. 28–29.

[78] *RC do "JC,"* 1915, p. 190; Roy Nash, *The Conquest of Brazil* (1926; rpt: New York: Biblo and Tannen, 1968), p. 262; "Meeting with Forbes ... June 20, 1915," in U.S. Congress, House of Representatives, *Report of the Federal Trade Commission*, pp. 223–4; MacKenzie to R.C. Sanderson, Apr. 1, 1915, MCCP, SWC.

Empire in November 1914. Continental Products and the Brazil Land, Cattle, and Packing companies continued to operate in receivership. Continental Products opened its first plant in Osasco in May 1915 and the following month exported 22 tons of frozen beef to the William Archer and Company of Smithfield, London. The beef arrived in good condition, prompting new orders for 300, 500, and 1,000 tons.[79] Such exports formed the bulk of Continental's business in 1915, but the internal market also proved profitable. Continental slaughtered nearly 23,000 cattle for export while sacrificing an additional 15,000 cattle for the São Paulo market. Prado's Barretos plant also served both markets, as meat from over 25,000 cattle processed at the plant fed the São Paulo market, while slightly under 15,000 head of cattle were processed for export.[80]

The high demand for beef products also created a related enterprise exploited by foreign and domestic businesses alike: cattle fattening. Ownership of land near a railhead was the main prerequisite for entering this lucrative enterprise. Once cattle were ready for slaughter, they traveled via rail to canning plants or *frigorificos*. A foreign businessman explained privately that "the fattening business as carried out in this country is very remunerative, giving 30% or more clear profit." Risks were considerable, though, since "a reliable person with vaqueiro has to be sent into the wild country with sufficient money to buy up 2,000 to 3,000 head of cattle."[81] But extensive land was available, a condition obvious to a man of ambition in Minas Gerais. In October 1915, an individual sought state approval for purchasing (at a reduced rate) several leagues of public lands "to turn them fertile by immediate exploitation." He also endorsed the state's efforts to obtain "immediate benefits" and "quick profits" by improving the existing cattle breed.[82]

State and federal government subsidies continued to support modernizing the cattle industry by reducing costs for importing breeding cattle and plant machinery. Minas Gerais continued state subsidies for the cattle industry and provided another one hundred *contos de reis* to subsidize importing purebreds in 1916. The federal government committed to subsidizing cattle imports in a May 1915 law. Soon thereafter, congress

[79] "Industria das carnes frigorificadas. ...," *Annaes da SRB*, 1 (1920), 190.

[80] Brazil, MAG, *Relatório, 1915*, pp. 40–41.

[81] G. Chalmers to C.f. Kup, Aug. 27, 1914, p. 6, SJdRMCA.

[82] Manuel Bernardes to Raul Soares, Oct 1, 1915, 1915.10.10, ARS.

decided to assist the cold storage and meat export trade by approving duty-free import of material for modern packing plants and slaughterhouses. Subsidies for transporting cattle allowed movement of 1,400 cattle at government expense on the government-owned Central do Brasil railroad in both 1914 and 1915. Minas exempted existing and future small meat canning plants from export taxes for up to two years. São Paulo and Rio Grande do Sul offered similar incentives to the meat-packing industry.[83]

Higher prices and government subsidies increased production of canned and chilled meat during the first years of the war. One observer reported doubling of the number of canning factories and the production of canned meat from 1914 to 1916. Exports of canned meat increased by more than 100 tons during the same period.[84] Even fresh meat supplied to Rio de Janeiro increased by 4,000 tons between 1914 and 1916, when it reached 53,268 metric tons.[85] Exports of frozen meat also rose dramatically. From the little more than one ton exported in late 1914, total frozen beef exports reached over 33,000 tons in 1916, including over 2,000 tons to the United States. Processing cattle by-products also increased. In the first eleven months of 1916 Brazilian tanneries produced 10,000 tons more leather than during all of 1914. Cattle killed under federal supervision increased fourfold—up to 176,000 animals—from 1915 to 1916.[86]

The demands of potential foreign customers also began to shape relations between the Brazilian government and the meat packing industry,

[83] Minas Gerais, *Mensagem, 1915*, p. 119; Minas Gerais, Secretaria de Agricultura, "Livros de créditos relativos a despesas com gado, postos zootécnicos e auxílio a indústria pastoril, 1916–1925," S.A. 166, APMG; *The Times*, Aug. 31, 1915, p. 13, col 4; Law 11,579 of May 12, 1915, see Max Fleiuss, *História Administrativa do Brasil*, 2nd ed. (São Paulo: Melhoramentos de São Paulo, 1922), p. 705; Brazil, Estrada de Ferro Central do Brasil, *Relatório, 1915*, p. 143; Law 664, Sept. 15, 1915, *Colecção das Leis e Decretos do Estado de Minas Gerais 1915* (Belo Horizonte: Imprensa Oficial de Minas, 1915), p. 47; Love, *São Paulo*, p. 258.

[84] Henry R. Armory [Special Agent for the War Trade Board], reported these data, but failed to indicate his sources. USE-RJ to SS, June 27, 1918, RG 59, 632.119/834, USNA.

[85] "Abastecimento de carnes," *Boletím* [MAG], Vol. 10, No. 1 (1921), 85.

[86] "Commerico de carnes," Boletím [MAG], Vol. 8, No. 3 (1919), 118, USBFDC, *Brazil: A Study of Economic Conditions Since 1913,* p. 35; Brasil Directoria Geral de Estatística Commercial, *Commercio Exterior do Brasil,1913–1918*, I, 488–9; *Brazilian-American*, Vol. 4, No. 82 (1921), 13.

as exports of many packing plants sensitized them to demands of foreign markets. The USDA's announcement that all beef imported into the United States after January 1, 1915, would have to pass inspection caused concern at the Continental Products plant at Osasco. In late 1914 company representative, C. W. Patton and a U.S. Embassy official met with Agriculture Minister Calógeras, who promised funding for federal meat inspectors, a function previously managed by *municipios*. A federal decree in early 1915 provided for ten animal inspectorships throughout the nation, satisfying the USDA's requirements at least temporarily.[87]

Brazilians abroad also sought to attract foreign capital to the meat packing and cattle sectors. The Brazilian Consul General in New York told delegates to a Washington conference in December 1915 that he favored injection of foreign capital into cattle raising. Opportunities for foreign capital in Brazil no longer were concentrated in transportation and mining ventures, but instead were appearing in "the utilization of her very rich soil" by transforming Brazil into "the greatest producer of beef." Among the "great teachings of the current great European conflagration," he surmised, was that meat for human consumption was "ever more scarce [and] increasing progressively in price." Brazil's "almost immeasurable fields with excellent and abounding pastures, good water" and much "free land" contrasted sharply with opportunities for cattle development in Argentina and the United States. Consul Pinheiro promised to cooperate with the USDA in providing details to any interested party on how to invest in Brazil.[88]

New foreign investors responded to wartime conditions assuming, mistakenly, that demand would remain vigorous even after the war. The first was a British company financed by the Vestey brothers, who later invested heavily in exporting Argentine beef. In September 1916, "Frigorifico Anglo" purchased the buildings and grounds of the former

[87] USE-RJ to SS, Nov. 23, 1914, RG 59, 611.005/40–32, USNA; USE-RJ to MRE, Nov. 23, 1914, M-280, 2, 14, AHI; Calógeras to Sub-secretario de Estado, MRE, Nov. 28, 1914, M-292, 4, 5, AHI; Laws 11,460, 11,462, Jan. 27, 1915, see encl. 1, "Diseases of Cattle. ..." to USE-RJ to SS, Sept. 20, 1915, RG 59, 611.005/117,USNA.

[88] H.C. de Martins Pinheiro, "Investments of Capital in Brazil," in Glenn L. Swiggett, ed., *Transportation, Commerce, Finance and Taxation, Section IX of Proceedings of the Second Pan American Scientific Congress* (Washington: GPO, 1917), pp. 625–7. See similar statements by Brazilian businessman Manuel de Barros Moreira in *The Quarterly*, Vol. 1 (1917), 6. For his background, see "Prominent in Pan American Affairs," *BPAU*, Vol. 38 (Jan.-June 1914), 693.

Brahma brewery in Mendes, Rio de Janeiro state. Soon thereafter, agents for "one of the largest Chicago packing plants" visited Brazil and reportedly made a large purchase of cattle grazing land and began planning for a modern packing plant. The first decisive move by U.S. investors took place a few months later. The Armour Company's recently formed subsidy, Companhia Armour do Brasil, purchased a beef jerky plant in Livramento, a town near Rio Grande do Sul's border with Uruguay.[89]

The Armour decision reflected optimism generated by a U.S. government-sponsored visit to Brazil. Armour was connected to the American International Corporation (AIC) whose officers had toured Brazil in 1916 as part of the "Return Visit Committee" set up by the Pan-American Financial Conference of May 1915. J. O. Armour, heir to the company founded by his father, also served as an AIC director and probably gained first-hand knowledge of Brazil's potential from the AIC's vice president, Richard P. Strong, and from Thomas W. Streeter, vice president of the AIC's Latin American Corporation. Both had visited Brazil in 1916. Under the AIC's auspices, the Armour and Sulzberger companies announced plans to invest in the meatpacking in South America. Armour decided to open a plant in São Paulo at a reported cost of US$10 million, capable of slaughtering 1,200 cattle and 3,000 hogs per day. The plant would consist of 25 buildings with nearly 25,000 square feet housing a canning plant, ice factory, sausage factory, oil, fertilizer, and box factories—all served by two rail lines.[90]

The federal government also continued its support of the cattle and beef sectors after Brazil's June 1917 decision to end neutrality. The political power of the cattle sector guaranteed that the federal government would continue to support the cattle industry as it had in the initial stages of the war. In 1917 the Ministry of Agriculture passed out free of charge over a million doses of vaccine to prevent various cattle diseases. Laws passed later in the year granted free use of public lands in Rio Grande

[89] "Sociedade Anônima Frigorifico Anglo," *Annaes da SRB*, 9 (1929), 712. Peter H. Smith, *Politics of Beef in Argentina: Patterns of Conflict and Change* (New York: Columbia Univ. Press, 1969), p. 113; "Cattle Boom in Brazil," *Washington Post*, Nov. 19, 1916; Pesavento, *Republica Velha Gaúcha*, p. 131.

[90] USE-RJ to SS, Sept. 12, 1916, RG 59, 832.51/129, USNA; Harper Leach and John C. Carroll, *Armour and His Times* (New York: D. Appleton-Century Co., 1938), pp. 349–55; *NYT*, Apr. 13, 1917, p. 17, col 2; May 25, 1917, p. 16, col 2; "A 10-million dollar faith in Brazil," *Brazilian-American*, Vol. 4, No. 82 (May 21, 1921), 6; "Frigorífico Armour de S. Paulo," *Annaes da SRB*, 1 (1920).

do Sul for cattle fattening to rancher groups or packing companies. The CPN recommended that the government subsidize installation of live cattle markets in the principal cattle states.[91] As publicist Paulo Barreto explained, with the war Brazil discovered that "in Mato Grosso alone there are more cattle than in all of Argentina." According to cattle advocate Eduardo Cotrim, Brazil was using its "immense natural pastures" and "considerable herds" not only to "minimize the sufferings of the populations of the Allied nations," but also to "capture a decisive factor of wealth" of great benefit to Brazil's economy.[92]

The packing industry added significant new capacity—foreign and domestically owned—following Brazil's decision to break its neutral stance. In late May 1917 the Chicago meat-packing firm of Armour and Company, already owners of a plant in Rio Grande do Sul, decided to build a *frigorífico* in Brazil and began purchasing lands in São Paulo state. In August, the Companhia Frigorífica de Santos received authorization for a packing plant using 1,000 *contos* as capital. Only in that same month did the Frigorífico Anglo formally establish itself in Brazil, even though in the previous year it had purchased facilities outside of Rio de Janeiro. In March 1918 Wilson and Company invested in a packing plant in Rio Grande do Sul.[93]

The influx of new capital after mid-1917 gave the meat-packing industry new structure and intensity, although it would be several years before the Armour plant began operation. In addition to plants near metropolitan regions, the industry began to locate near the immense herds of Rio Grande do Sul. There, Armour, Swift, and then Wilson and

[91] "Pecuária," *RC do "JC,"* 1918, p. 313; "O Comité da producção nacional: As medadas aconselhadas," *A Lavoura*, Vol. 21 (1917), 435.

[92] João do Rio, *Adiante!* p. 77; "Pecuária," *RC do "JC,"* 1918, p. 315. Cotrim, a staunch supporter of the cattle sector, had much in common with other advocates of reform of Brazilian agriculture. A native of Rio de Janeiro state, Cotrim graduated from the Escola Polytechnica as a civil engineer. He became the "chefe politico" of an area traditionally dependent upon coffee (Resende, Rio de Janeiro state) and vice president of the SNA. See "Dr. Eduardo Cotrim," *Brazil Agrícola*, Vol. 4 (1919), 44–45; Eduardo Augusto Torres Cotrim, *Industria pecuária: Conferências do Dr. Eduardo Cotrim* (Rio de Janeiro: Impr. Nac., 1911).

[93] *Brazilian-American*, Vol. 3, No. 62 (Jan. 1, 1921), 29; "Junta Commercial," *Revista de Commercio e Industria*, Vol. 3 (1917), 292; "Sociedade Anonyma Frigorifico Anglo," *Revista da SRB*, Vol. 9 (1929), 712; Brazil, Ministério do Trabalho, Industria e Commercio, *Sociedades mercantis autorizadas a funcionar no Brasil (1808–1946)* (Rio de Janeiro: Departamento Nacional de Indústria e Commercio, 1947), p. 54.

Company began to transform beef jerky plants into modern canning and chilling factories. By 1918 nearly 40% of all cattle slaughter in Brazilian packing plants took place in Rio Grande do Sul, versus 36% in São Paulo. The new capacity also reflected the increased role of foreign capital in the meat-packing sector. Whereas in 1915 and 1916, more cattle were slaughtered in the Brazilian-owned plant at Barretos than at the foreign-owned Continental plant, by 1918 the reverse was true. Foreign-owned firms controlled 83% of cattle slaughtered in the packing plants that year.[94]

The increased investment stepped up the pace of cattle killed for export and domestic consumption, and the packing plants enjoyed boom years in 1917 and 1918. The Anglo-Brazilian Meat Company, a British-based firm that began Brazilian operations in 1915, sacrificed over 130,000 cattle in 1917, while Continental Products prepared over 100,000 cattle for market. Nationwide, total cattle sacrificed in packing plants in 1917 rose from 380,792 in 1917 to over 434,000 in 1918, a 14% increase. Exports of chilled beef also rose dramatically—to over 66,000 tons in 1917 (double the 1916 total) and remained high in 1918, with over 60,000 tons shipped abroad. Exports of canned beef likewise rose from 6,000 tons in 1917 to over 17,000 tons in 1918. Despite high exports, the internal market remained the primary market, purchasing 57% of the 1917 production.[95] *Frigoríficos* in Rio de Janeiro and São Paulo continued as the major source of chilled beef exports, while plants in Rio Grande do Sul concentrated on canned beef. Only in 1919 did Rio

[94] Calculated from "Commercio de carnes," *Boletím* [MAG], Vol. 3 (1919), 117. For figures on the 1913–1916 slaughter, see TS, "Relatórios do Dr. Franklin de Almeida relativos ao abastecimento de carnes, 1920," Annexo N, 12.00.00 II 18, AISL.

[95] *Brazilian-American*, Vol. 4, No. 82 (May 24, 1921), 13; "Os frigoríficos brasileiros," *Revista de Commercio e Industria*, Vol. 5 (1919), 215; "Commercio de carnes," *Boletím* [MAG], Vol. 8, No. 3 (1919), 117–8; Brazil, Directoria Geral de Estatística, *Resumo de várias estatísticas*, p. 48; Maria Yedda Leite Linhares, *História política do abastecimento: uma problemática em questão (1530–1918)* (Brasilia: BINAGRI: 1979), p. 209. As with most on Brazilian agricultural production, sources differ on exact totals. The first three sources listed above agree on general trends, however, with differences only on the kill attributed to each plant. The Brazilian participation in the world market was marginal in comparison with U.S. and Argentine exports. The United States exported over 204,000 tons of beef in 1917 and over 398,000 tons of beef in 1918. Argentinaexported 450,000 tons of beef in 1917 and nearly 800,000 tons of beef in 1918. See USDA, *Yearbook of the USDA 1921* (Washington: GPO, 1922), p. 683; Peter H. Smith, *Politics and Beef in Argentina: Patterns of Conflict and Change* (New York: Columbia Univ. Press, 1969), p. 69.

Grande do Sul begin exporting chilled beef, and then providing only about 14% of the total chilled beef exported.[96]

The European war integrated U.S. technicians, equipment, and capital into Brazil's agriculture. U.S. agronomists, technicians, and educators became critical to developing Brazil's cotton and corn cultivation. Imports of U.S. cattle, meat-packing machinery, and capital facilitated access of Brazilian beef to world markets. U.S. and other foreign investors preferred São Paulo, without neglecting the extensive herds in Rio Grande do Sul. While much product met domestic needs, export markets grew faster and offered the alluring prospect of continued profit. The process reinforced the notion that technical information and expertise from the United States could benefit Brazil's agriculture. When Brazil sought to capitalize on wartime market conditions following war's end, U.S. ties related to increasing agricultural production would remain important.

[96] "Carne congelada," *RC do "JC," 1918*, p. 311; Sandra Jahaty Pesavento, *República Velha Gaúcha: Charquiadores, criadores, frigoríficos* (Porto Alegre, RGS: Movimento, 1980), p. 147. Jerky remained the mainstay of the Rio Grande do Sul beef industry. In 1918, more than one half million cattle were slaughtered in the state's beef jerky plants. See Pesavento, *República Velha*, p. 145; "Commercio de Carnes," *Boletím* [MAG], Vol. 8 (1919), 117.

CHAPTER 7

The Strengthening of U.S. Ties to Brazil's Agricultural Education

Better cotton seed selection and adapting agriculture to drought conditions would aid the Northeast and improved cattle breeding and processing benefited the Center-South, but nationwide gains in agricultural production using modern techniques remained crippled by a lack of trained agronomists. The reforms destined to improve agricultural education instituted with the resurrection of the Ministry of Agriculture in 1910 bore little fruit. The Ministry served mainly as an intermediary, pledging to donate land and buildings to support state and local government as well as private initiatives. The federal Escola Superior de Agricultura e Medicina Veterinaria opened in 1910 but closed in 1915, and a 1921 federal government report lamented that "few states have worried themselves with the maintenance of agricultural education."[1] Eleven of the 16 agricultural engineering courses established during the first 15 years of the First Republic were not functioning by 1915. Though Brazilians considered their land an "essentially agricultural" nation, working too close to the soil remained reminiscent of slavery. One estimate placed the number of graduates of the "liberal professions," including lawyers, doctors, and engineers at 15,000 annually in the immediate pre-World War I era. Meanwhile, the nation

[1] Brazil, Directoria Geral de Estatística, *Relatório* .... (Rio de Janeiro: Typographia da Estatística, 1921), p. 336.

E. R. Downes, *Brazilian Agricultural Development, 1890–1950*,
https://doi.org/10.1007/978-3-031-76992-4_7

produced only about 300 agronomists a year.[2] One agronomist who graduated in 1917 explained that many farmers "did not believe very much in agronomic sciences" while non-agronomists with political sponsorship often garnered public positions in agricultural service.[3] A foreign observer noted in 1921 that many young men obtained government agricultural positions "through influential political persons" even though they were "entirely unfit to undertake agricultural work."[4]

Reform of agricultural education using the example of the United States had been another of the recommendations of the 1901 national agricultural congress. The congress lamented deterioration of the Instituto Imperial Bahiano de Agricultura, created in 1859, where funding shortages prevented teaching of modern agricultural methods. The congress reasoned that since Brazil had attempted to imitate U.S. political institutions, it should also look toward the U.S. experience in agricultural education. The participants gave special attention to the "State agricultural fund of the "Moril bill" of 1862 and subsequent appropriations in 1890 that had created 43 agricultural schools. "Brazilian farmers," the recommendation added, "hope that the political powers of their country will not refuse them that which only the Indians of North America have yet to receive," the opportunity for an adequate agricultural education.[5]

Reforms at the Piraçicaba Agricultural School. Brazilian superior-level agricultural education then underwent gradual reform that oriented it toward the U.S. example, and agricultural schools in São Paulo and Minas Gerais especially drew heavily from contracts with U.S. agronomists. The state of São Paulo's Piraçicaba agricultural school originated in 1892 with a grant of land from fazendeiro Luiz Vicente de

[2] Rodrigo Sarruge Molina, "Primeiras Escolas Agrícolas no Brazil: Limites e Falências (1877 A 1936)," *Revista HISTEDBR On-line*, Campinas No. 46 (June 2012), pp. 319–20; Luis Amaral, *História geral da agricultura brasileira no tríplice aspecto político-social-economico* (São Paulo: Editora Nacional, 1939), I, 415; Brazil, Directoria Geral de Estatística, *Relatório* .... (Rio de Janeiro: Typographia da Estatística, 1921), pp. 336–37.

[3] Interview, José Figueiras Sobrinho, *Campus* [Escola Superior de Agricultura de Lavras], Sept. 11, 1977, p. 2.

[4] Arno S. Pearse, *Cotton in North Brazil, Being the Report of the Journey through the States of Ceará, Maranhao and Pará*.. (Manchester, Eng.: Taylor Garnett, n.d.), p. 80.

[5] Sociedade Nacional de Agricultura, *Annaes do Congresso Nacional de Agricultura.... 1901* (Rio de Janeiro: Impr. Nac., 1907), I, 29, 216; "Escola Superior de Agricultura e Medicina Veterinaria," *A Lavoura*, Vol. 17 (1913), 227.

Sousa Queiroz, grandson of the largest landowner in the province of São Paulo. Souza Queiroz had studied in France and Switzerland for 16 years, returning to Brazil in 1873 to assume control of his family's textile business and agricultural properties. Convinced of the need to modernize Brazil's agriculture, he sought state assistance after unsuccessfully attempted to found a practical agricultural school on his own in 1891–92. Limited financial support from the state government hindered its growth over the following decade, despite valiant efforts of contracted Belgium agronomist Leon Alphonse Morimont to design and implement a practical agricultural school based on a European model adapted to Brazilian needs. The state-operated school began to function in 1901, focused on a combination of theoretical teachings and practical work carried out on a model farm and experimental fields. Its small student body initially fell under the tutelage of Brazilian professors, but when Carlos Botelho became state secretary of agriculture in 1904, he instituted reforms that included contracting foreign instructors. Botelho, whose son was studying at Cornell, strongly admired the United States and was convinced that the United States offered the "highest percentage of educational elements for the Brazilian model of agricultural education."[6]

These reforms initially produced a hybrid model combining instruction in practical matters by U.S. instructors with European instructors focusing on theoretical subjects, but soon the U.S. model became firming implanted on the school's program. U.S. agronomist Eugene Davenport had participated in Luiz de Queiroz's unsuccessful effort to establish an agricultural school in 1891–92. Though Davenport returned to his homeland, the first professor of agriculture at the state school, Luciano de Almeida, named in 1902, received his education in the United States. But the foremost conduit of U.S. practices was Clayton Dewitt Smith, contracted in 1908 to direct the school by Botelho himself. Smith left an enduring imprint by instilling an emphasis on practical instruction during his four and a half years as the school's director.

[6] Mario de Sampaio Ferraz, *Piracicaba e sua Escola Agrícola* (Brussels: Verteneuil & L. Desmet, 1911), pp. 55–59; A. de Padua Dias, "O ensino Agrícola I no estado de São Paulo," *Boletim* [MAG], Vol. 14, 2, No. 1 (1925), 52–53; Marly Therezinha Germano Perecin, *Os Passos do Saber: A Escola Agrícola Prática Luiz de Queiro, O Esforço para Implantar o Ensino Técnico de Segundo Grau na Agricultura, 1891–1911* (São Paulo: Editora da Univ. de São Paulo, 2004), pp. 181–301, 307, 333–367.

Smith had studied agriculture with the first group of Brazilian students to study at Cornell, graduating in 1873. He went on to teach at Purdue and then directed agricultural experimental stations in Arkansas, Minnesota, and Michigan. On behalf of São Paulo, Carlos Botelho offered him a tidy $8,000 per year to serve in Brazil. During Smith's tenure, the school created chairs of rural economy and rural engineering, the latter dedicated to rural construction, draining, and road building. Smith termed his vision for the school's program as the "Gentlemen's Farmer's Project" and dedicated himself to guiding the rigorous preparation of agronomists while teaching political economy, where he stressed the "relationship of agriculture with commerce and industries in general and [with] political institutions."[7] Two individuals later prominent in Brazilian agriculture received their training during Smith's term at the school. Both originated in regions undergoing crises; both would become leaders in the diversification movement. William Coelho de Souza, from Maranhão, later prominent in the development of Brazilian cotton, graduated in 1909. The following year Artur Torres Filho, from Campos, Rio de Janeiro state, a pioneer in the Ministry of Agriculture, received his agronomist degree.[8]

When Smith returned to the United States at the end of 1912, many U.S. practices remained stamped on the school. U.S. influence at the school continued when Emilio Castello, who had traveled and studied extensively in the United States, became director following Smith's departure. Several years after Smith's departure graduating seniors solemnly planted a tree in honor of their class "in imitation of what is done in the academies of agriculture in the United States," a practice instituted by Smith.[9] Piraçicaba students demonstrated their abilities with farm implements to participants in a 1917 road-building conference in Campinas. A 1920 summary of the school's curriculum noted that the students

[7] Quote from R. Fernandes Silva, "Escola Agrícola 'Luiz de Queiroz,'" *A Evolução Agrícola*, Vol. 1, No. 9 (1910), 18. See also Love, *São Paulo,* pp. 79–80; Ferraz, *Piracicaba,* p. 71; Padua Dias, "O ensino," p. 53; Escola Superior de Agricultura "Luiz de Queiroz," *ESALQ* Vol. 75, pp. 121–2, 143. Carlos Botelho asked his son, a student at Cornell, to have his instructors recommend a candidate to direct Piraçicaba and one recommended Smith, then teaching at Michigan College. See Antonio Carlos Botelho to Joaquim Nabuco, Jan. 3, 1908, and C. D. Smith to Joaquim Nabuco, Mar. 27, 1908, both in Joaquim Nabuco Papers, AHI.

[8] "Os amigos de Brasil Agrícola," *Brasil Agrícola*, Vol. 2 (1917), 34.

[9] "Ensino Agrícola," *Brasil Agrícola*, Vol. 1 (1916), 377.

received 206 hours of practical work to accompany 96 hours of theoretical study, as "constant practical exercises" accompanied all instruction.[10]

The Institution of the Lavras Agricultural School. U.S. agronomists also proved prominent in the orientation of agricultural education in Minas Gerais during the same period. A young U.S. agronomist established a small privately-run agricultural school in the outskirts of the rural town of Lavras, in the gently rolling hills of the state's western region. The school originated from activities of Presbyterian missionaries who ministered to U.S. citizens who migrated to Brazil following the Civil War. While rejecting the consequences of the war, many American families who settled on land in Santa Barbara, São Paulo province, retained their cultural and religious heritage. In 1869 the U.S. Presbyterian Church (Southern) sent missionaries to Campinas to attend to the spiritual needs of the American immigrants and to convert as many Brazilians as possible. Crucial to their conversion efforts was a school, founded in 1870, to "reach many, men and children, who belong to the laboring classes." Apparently, the laboring classes had little time or no incentive to attend school, as shortly thereafter this mission turned its attention to the upper strata of Brazilian society and in 1872 broke ground for a "Colegio Internacional."[11]

The school functioned in Campinas for twenty years until yellow fever in the region prompted a search for a healthier climate. This carried its rectors to Lavras, Minas Gerais, where the Instituto Evangélico established two schools, the Gynasio de Lavras and the Colegio Carlota Kemper.[12] The Instituto initially had no facilities to teach agricultural education, but its rector Samuel R. Gammon nourished "the desire to provide those graduates destined to agricultural life" a course that would "prepare them to take advantage of the natural riches of the land."[13]

[10] Mario de Sampaio Ferraz, *Piracicaba e sua Escola Agrícola*, 2nd. ed. (São Paulo: Tipographia Brazil de Rothschild, 1916), p. 87; F.T. de Souza Reis, *O ensino na Escola Agrícola "Luiz de Queiroz" de Piracicaba* (São Paulo: Sociedade Editora Olegario Ribeiro, 1920), pp. 49, 144; *Jornal do Commercio* [São Paulo], June 1, 1917, p. 4, col. 3.

[11] Robert L. McIntire, *Portrait of Half a Century: Fifty Years of Presbyterianism in Brazil(1859–1910)* (Cuernavaca, Mex.: CIDOC, 1969), pp, 14–15, 21–22.

[12] *O Agricultor*, Vol. 1, No. 1 (1922), 34.

[13] Gammon Institute [Lavras, Minas Gerais], *O Instituto Gammon, no pasado e no presente* (Lavras, M.G.: Imprensa Gammon, 1950), p. 13. Gammon himself was from rural stock in the United States. The Gammon family was living in rural Retreat, Wythe County, Virginia, when "Sam" sold off his expected inheritance in the family properties,

Gammon, who originated from rural stock himself and kept a small garden to meet the school's needs, hoped to improve the conditions of agricultural production and rural life in general. He was impressed with the abilities of one of his helpers, a black named Zacharias Silva. Brooding over the future of Zacharias, Gammon discounted the value of "ancient languages" and considered teaching him to farm more intelligently. His contacts with *fazendeiros* in the region also probably convinced him that agricultural education would attract more students, offset costs, and support his missionary goals. He benefited from the collaboration of a Lavras *coronel* and city councilman, José Custodio da Veiga, a convert to Protestantism. As he later explained, founding the agricultural school and the adjacent farm "would do much toward solving our problem of self-help and of placing within reach a large number of boys and girls the benefits of the school."[14] In the opinion of local political leaders, instituting an agricultural school would not only overcome help the community overcome illiteracy, it would also provide a greater supply of trained agriculturalists.[15]

In 1907 Gammon arranged for a professional agronomist to augment the teaching staff and direct the curriculum toward agricultural education. Benjamin H. Hunnicutt (1886–1962) labored intensely for the next 45 years to improve and diversify Brazilian agriculture. Hunnicutt originated from a Southern family deeply committed to agriculture whose patriarch, Dr. James Benjamin Hunnicutt, had been undersecretary of agriculture for Georgia, professor of agriculture at the University of Georgia, and owner and editor of the *Southern Cultivator*. The senior Hunnicutt instilled in his son a "love of the affairs of agriculture" that carried him from his birthplace in Turim, Georgia, to Mississippi State College, where he graduated with an agronomist degree in 1905. After

including several farms, to establish the institute in Lavras. Samuel R. Gammon to author, July 1, 1983.

[14] Gammon to Hunnicutt, Nov. 20, 1924, in GIA; Benjamin H. Hunnicutt and William Watkins Reid, *The Story of Agricultural Missions* (New York: Missionary Education Movement of the United States and Canada, 1931), p. 149; Michelle Pereira da Silva Rossi, "'Dedicado Á Gloria de Deus e ao Progresso Humano': A Gênese Protestante da Universidade Federal de Lavras—UFLA (Lavras, 1892–1938)," (Diss: Univ. Federal de Uberlândia, 2010), p. 53.

[15] Silva Rossi, "'Dedicado Á Gloria de Deus," pp. 58–59.

graduation, Hunnicutt farmed family properties in the Atlanta suburbs, marketing his produce in Atlanta.[16]

Hunnicutt soon discarded business opportunities for a more venturesome calling as an agricultural missionary, becoming one of a small cell of U.S. agronomists who became "agricultural crusaders to serve among the needy peoples of the world."[17] Hunnicutt's original destination had been India, but a disease outbreak there and Gammon's call for an agronomist in Brazil changed his plans. Originally a Methodist, Hunnicutt changed his religious affiliation to Presbyterian to be compatible with the sponsor of his work in Brazil. He arrived in Rio de Janeiro on December 21, 1907, and soon joined Gammon in organizing an agricultural school on land adjacent to the Instituto Evangélico with Zacharias Silva as one of the first students. The school soon received a boost from the state and federal subsidies. In response to a proposal from the Board of Curators, Minas Gerais agreed in February 1910 to support ten youths at the school with a subsidy of 500 *milreis* each per school year. The federal government also began subsidizing the school that year with a five *conto de reis* grant. The school was sufficiently organized by November 1910 to prompt the Board of Curators to charge Hunnicutt with obtaining state authorization to confer the title of Agrônomo on its graduates.[18]

As the 23-year-old dean of a nascent agricultural school, Hunnicutt began his extensive career as a fervent apostle of diversified Brazilian agriculture. He drew from his previous experience and apparently boundless energy to promote new agricultural techniques in the classroom and beyond. He saw each of his students as "centers of activity and leadership" on behalf of Brazilian agriculture, cherishing their successes and suffering through their failures.[19] He required all his students—including

[16] Benjamin H. Hunnicutt, *O milho: sua cultura e aproveitamento*, 2nd. ed. (Lavras, M. G.: Imprensa Gammon, 1933), p. vii; Ronald Hilton, ed., *Who's Who in Latin America* 3rd. ed., *Part VI, Brazil* (Stanford, CA.: Stanford Univ. Press, 1948), p. 114. Benjamin H. Hunnicutt, "Duas decadas do desenvolvimento Agrícola do Brasil," *O Agricultor*, Vol. 4, No. 1 (1927), p. 9.

[17] Some hundred agronomist-missionaries eventually formed the International Association of Agricultural Missions. See Hunnicutt and Reid, *The Story of Agricultural Missions*, pp. 16, 158–74.

[18] Benjamin H. Hunnicutt, Jr. to author, June 8, 1983. TS, "Report of the Lavras Agricultural College for the Year 1924," p. 4, in GIA.

[19] Hunnicutt and Reid, *The Story of Agricultural Missions*, p. 151; Hunnicutt, "Duas decadas," 22.

Zacharias Silva—to do practical work on the school's farm and assist with experiments seeking to adapt new crops to the Brazilian soil. He squeezed financial support for the school and for his long-range goals from Brazilian government bodies through unceasing correspondence and meetings with local, state, and federal officials. His stamina often carried him into the early hours of the morning, setting out his visions of the future of Brazilian agriculture through correspondence and publications.[20] Hunnicutt's actions during the next 20 years at the Lavras School reflected a mix of intense spiritual commitment and devotion to improving the human condition through modernizing agriculture. He credited "Divine Providence" with taking him to Brazil but devoted his attention to improving human life through "better transportation facilities, better and more numerous rural schools, country hospitals and state health services for rural districts, [and] better agricultural credit."[21]

Student life at the Lavras school represented a mixture of serious scholarship and moral restraint. One Sunday evening in June 1911, five students left the school grounds without permission to attend a theater presentation. Three of the five were "repeat offenders" and were suspended from the school for the rest of the year, while the others received two week's suspensions.[22] Despite such challenges, enough students became committed to the school's programs to allow the development of a four-year program with Hunnicutt as its principal professor. The earliest fruits of his efforts came in 1914 with graduation of the school's first agronomists. As with other initiatives to reform Brazil's agricultural education in which North Americans figured prominently, the Lavras school adopted a North American emphasis on a combination of science, land, and agriculture, along with at least one hour daily of practical work on modern cultivating techniques.[23]

Hunnicutt also became a prominent advocate for diversifying Brazilian agriculture through increased ties with the United States. Like many of his Brazilian contemporaries, Hunnicutt considered Brazil "an essentially agricultural country," since "for some time to come, a large share of Brazil's wealth will come from the soil in the form of agricultural

[20] Personal interview with Benjamin H. Hunnicutt, Jr., Aug. 12, 1982.

[21] Hunnicutt, "Duas decadas," 9; Hunnicutt and Reid, *Agricultural Missions*, p. 148.

[22] Minutes, June 12, 1911, in MS, "Minutes of the Mesa de Curadores," GIA.

[23] Silva Rossi, "'Dedicado Á Gloria de Deus," pp. 72–74, 83.

products."[24] While Brazil someday would industrialize, in the meantime it needed to export primary products to maintain a favorable balance of trade, especially since Brazil was "a new country that needs great capital for rapid and sure development." U.S. agricultural equipment could make that production more efficient, as could the knowledge of U.S. agricultural techniques, in Hunnicutt's opinion.[25]

Sponsoring Brazilian Students at U.S. Universities during Wartime. Even as Hunnicutt's venture in Minas Gerais was gaining stature, the Brazilian federal government opted to turn to U.S. universities to meet the shortage of agronomists experienced during the wartime production boom. The federal government also recognized the need for more trained agronomists to direct the expansion movement. Given positive experience with U.S. university-level education related to agriculture since the late nineteenth century, and the inaccessibility of institutions in war-torn Europe, this meant turning to the United States. The United States became a source of more agricultural technicians, but also of agricultural education that met the Brazilians' needs. Prior to the war, Brazilian agricultural students continued to frequent European schools, but some had turned their attention to the United States. Jorge Tibiriça, a prominent paulista coffee planter and politician, had graduated from a German school, but in 1906 sent his son to study agronomy at Cornell. Three Piraçicaba graduates who had studied in Belgium, France, and Italy in 1913 noted their need to go beyond theoretical studies and become involved in practical work, recommending that they be allowed to travel to the United States following their European study.[26]

With the war's outbreak, government sponsorship of agricultural studies in the United States expanded. Amazonas authorized state support for one year's study in the United States for the top two state residents graduating from São Paulo's Piraçicaba school.[27] Several Brazilian

[24] Benjamin H. Hunnicutt, *Brazil Looks Forward* (Rio de Janeiro: Instituto Brasileiro de Geografia e Estatistica, 1945), p. 51.

[25] Benjamin H. Hunnicutt, "Os aspectos internacionaes da agricultura," *Revista da SRB*, Vol. 5 (1924), 179.

[26] "Um novo engenheiro Agrícola," *A Lavoura*, Vol. 10 (1906), 569; Federico Shumacher, "Relatório sobre os estudos feitos pelos estudantes agrônomos do Estado," *Boletím de Agricultura* [São Paulo], Vol. 15 (1914), 82.

[27] "Prêmios de viagem aos agrônomos," *Brasil Agrícola*, Vol. 1 (1916), 346–7.

agronomists traveled to the United States for training and technical information under government sponsorship. Former São Paulo secretary of agriculture Paulo de Moraes Barros traveled to the United States in late 1916 to "visit colleges and institutions of agricultural instruction" and see cattle farms raising the Devon breed. That same year a 1915 graduate of Hunnicutt's Lavras school, Valbert de Lima Pereira, visited U.S. government agricultural activities and veterinary posts, and agronomist Sebastião Mossoroense da Gloria obtained government support to continue studies in the United States.[28]

By early 1918, the demands for production increases led to a large-scale federally funded scholarship program. The federal government chose a trusted bureaucrat to recommend guidelines for a large-scale program. Carlos Moreira was a distinguished government entomologist who had worked closely with U.S. technicians. Moreira had entered the Museu Nacional in 1888 at age 19. He soon authored a series of publications on entomology, rising to direct the museum and then the Instituto Biológico de Defesa Agricola (Biological Institute for Agricultural Protection). He served as secretary to a U.S.-Brazil commission studying Brazil's coal needs known as the White Commission and translated the commission's massive report. On January 18, 1918, the federal government sent him to the United States to perform various missions associated with the economic expansion, but especially to "choose the best agricultural schools" for an extensive scholarship program.[29]

Commitment to conducting such a program in the United States stemmed from a variety of sources. The program was an extension of prewar federal government sponsorship of a small number of scholarships for agronomists training abroad. The decision also reflected the difficulties of study in Europe during the war and President Braz's open admiration for the U.S. educational system. Like Luiz Pereira Barreto, Braz linked the material progress of the United States with the practical nature of

[28] BEW to Third Assistant SS, July 8, 1916, RG 59, 033.3211/72, USNA; SS to USC-Para, May 12, 1916, RG 59, 033.3211/711, USNA; SNA to President Wenceslau Braz, Oct. 23, 1916, published in *A Lavoura*, Vol. 25 (1921), p. 107.

[29] Paulo de Miranda Ribeiro, "Professor Carlos Moreira," Museu Nacional, Rio de Janeiro, *Publicações Avulsas*, No. 3. (Rio de Janeiro: Impr. Nac., 1947), pp. 3–4; "Missão Carlos Moreira aos Estados Unidos," Brazil, MAG, *Relatório, 1918*, p. 248. Moreira was a devoted and tireless civil servant. In January 1933 he requested retirement, noting that in 44 years of service he had taken only one month of vacation, in November 1894. Carlos Moreira to Ministro da Agricultura, Jan. 16, 1933, 07.00.000 II 9, AISL.

U.S. education. While interim president of Minas Gerais in 1909, Braz remarked that "those who study the organization of instruction in North America will understand that there lies one of the most perfect bases of the astonishing progress of that country." Braz admired most what he perceived as a sense of action inculcated by "learning by action [which is]... the substance of the American methods: the laboratory, the shop and the fields constitute the base of instruction." Braz felt that Europeans "confess openly the failure of their educational institutions," recognizing that they lacked the "necessary practical mold." As a presidential candidate in 1913, he reaffirmed his faith in the North American example, especially concerning the country's agricultural needs.[30]

Moreira undoubtedly had Braz's support when he departed to examine U.S. schools in early 1918. Moreira visited six schools recommended by the USDA: the universities of Illinois, California, Oregon and Pennsylvania, Cornell and the Texas Agricultural School (Texas A&M). He judged two especially useful for Brazil's purposes: the University of Illinois, because of Eugene Davenport's previous experience in São Paulo, and the Texas school since "the nature of the crops under experimentation and study there most resemble ours."[31] Moreira also calculated the cost per student under a plan of study in U.S. schools. Within months after his return, the first contingent of Brazilian agricultural students departed for the United States to study the latest agricultural technologies—from soil preparation to product marketing. The Ministry of Agriculture's budget for 1918 included funding for up to 50 students annually.[32]

The students quickly became channels for transmitting the latest agricultural techniques practiced in the United States. A Brazilian student at the University of Illinois sent back suggestions for experiments on soils; another offered practical advice on growing rice using irrigation. A son of

[30] Darcy Bessone de Oliveira Andrade, *Wenceslau: Um pescador na presidência* (N.P.: Sociedade de Estudos Históricos Pedro II, 1968), pp. 109, 110, 165; see also an interview in the Apr. 16, 1914 edition of the *Jornal do Commercio*. On prewar programs, see Gammon Institute, Minutes of Board of Directors, Nov. 21, 1910, "Livro Primeiro," GIA; Brazil, MAG, *Escola de Agrícola annexo ao Posto Zootechnico Federal de "Pinheiro"* (São Paulo: Vanordem, 1912), p. 11.

[31] "Missão Carlos Moreira," p. 261.

[32] One-third were to study "mechanical or electrical arts," while the remainder were to study agriculture or veterinary sciences. See "Ensino téchnico," *RC do "JC" de 1917*, p. 203.

a Rio Grande do Sul cattle rancher supplemented studies at the University of Illinois with 15,000 miles of travel within the United States. Upon advice of Assis Brasil, he focused on constructing silos for storing cattle fodder. Another member of the same family purchased pigs and Hereford cattle from a Kentucky firm for shipment to several ranchers in the Rio Grande do Sul. Several visited meatpacking plants in St. Louis and Chicago. Although plant owners usually "kept their secrets carefully," they allowed the Brazilians to tour the plants through intercession of the chief of the Bureau of Animal Husbandry of the USDA. Practical instructions on processing fruit crops came from Brazilian students at Berkeley and Gainesville.[33]

The students also transmitted admiration for organizational and technical aspects of U.S. agriculture. Landulpho Alves de Almeida reported to Minister of Agriculture Simões Lopes that the United States was "rich and powerful," with agriculture an important factor "of the wealth and prosperity" of "this great country." He wrote in glowing terms of the state governments' extension programs, of youth clubs associated with agriculture, and of federal and state subsidies for road construction. Brazil's government, in Alves de Almeida's opinion, "has only to gain [by] sending youths graduated from our establishment of professional instruction to study the conditions of American agriculture."[34]

Other Brazilian scholarship students expressed admiration for agricultural mechanization. Djalma Hess observed the production and use of farm instruments with great interest. After extensive visits to factories producing agricultural machinery, he traveled to an Aurora, Illinois, farm and observed uses of agricultural machinery for three months. He concluded that agricultural machinery permitted a considerable decrease in labor needs, important for countries "vast and rich [but] with a less

[33] *Boletím* [MAG], Vol. 9, No. 2 (1920), 70–82; Mario Magalhaes, "O arroz, cultura pelos processos de irrigação," *Brasil Agrícola*, Vol. 5 (1920), 105–12; Guilherme Echnenique Filho, "Como se construiu um dos primeiros silos no Rio Grande do Sul," *Criador Paulista*, Vol. 17, No. 3 (1923), 41; Guilherme Echnenque Filho to Idefonso Simões Lopes, June 11, 1920, 14.12.15, AISL; "Brazilian Students in America," *Brazilian American*, Vol. 2, No. 41 (1920), 41; Octavio Gomes de Moraes Vasconcelos, "Fructos Semitropicaes," *Boletím* [MAG], Vol. 9, No. 3 (1920), 77–98; Felisberto Camargo, "A manga, o abacaxi, e o abacate," *Boletím* [MAG], Vol. 9, No. 3 (1920), 21–26.

[34] Landulpho Alves de Almeida to Ildefonso Simões Lopes, July 25, 1917, pp. 4, 12–19, 14.12.15, AISL. Alves de Almeida apparently received sponsorship prior to the large-scale program, as well as via the February 1918 decree.

dense population, those like our Brazil." Hess later became a strident advocate for mechanizing cotton cultivation. Octavio Peres wrote from Athens, Georgia, that Brazil should import more U.S. tractors, "the only way to give our agriculture the machines that it needs so much."[35]

The wartime expansion of agricultural output also required the immediate presence of technicians. Again, the Brazilian government turned to the United States and hired several technicians to direct the cultivation of promising crops. In early 1917 the government contracted specialists in pear, peach, apple, and tobacco production, and an entomologist and a phitopathologist from the United States.[36] Adding to the impact of U.S. agronomists counseling or directing private and public efforts to increase cotton, meat, and corn production, these advisers extended U.S. agricultural practices across the broad front of the Brazilian agricultural effort.

Founding a State Institution of Higher Agricultural Education in Minas Gerais. The third channel for adoption of U.S. practices in agricultural education occurred following Brazil's wartime experiment with diversified agriculture. Minas Gerais state President Artur Bernardes had long criticized Brazil's agricultural practices and advocated innovative approaches in agriculture during an extended political career. As a federal deputy in 1907, he had proclaimed that Brazil's agriculture was so "anchored to the routine that we cannot compete with other nations." While those "were aware of the employment of all the agricultural machines and all the new processes of agriculture," Brazilians still cultivated the earth "with a rude and primitive force" that was unproductive while exhausting workers. Once elected president of Minas in 1918, he called for "ambulatory practical instruction" undertaken by "professors of unequivocal aptitude." While he thought those hired could be "from here or foreign lands," he stressed admiration for U.S. agricultural education, noting that the U.S. system "has perfected agronomy and

[35] Djalma Eloy Hess, "Ensilagem," *Boletím* [MAG], Vol. 11, No. 2, (1922), 75, 81; *Jornal do Commercio* [Recife], p. 3, col. 6; Octavio Peres, "Algumas notas sobre o tractor nos Estados Unidos," *Brasil Agrícola*, Vol. 4 (1919), p. 228. The students also became vehicles for increased personal and economic ties between the two nations, especially by their substantial support for the Brazilian Student Association, reminiscent of the student organization founded at Cornell in the 1870s. Organized in June 1913 by Brazilians studying in Ithaca, Troy, Syracuse, and Schenectady, New York, the students' association boasted over a hundred members and published its own magazine, *O Estudante Brasileiro*.

[36] "Fructos Brasileiras, ou exóticas," *Brasil Agrícola*, Vol. 2 (1917), 43.

agricultural production [there] has grown astonishingly."[37] He reiterated support for adopting new techniques: machinery, soil science, the careful use of fertilizers, and seed selection as well as agricultural instruction "given by teachers going from farm to farm" once installed as president of the state.[38]

As state president, Bernardes became personally involved in creating a higher level of agricultural education for his state. In early June 1920 Bernardes asked for assistance from close friend Raul Soares, formerly the Minas state Secretary of Agriculture, then serving as the Pessoa administration's Minister of the Navy. Soares made known Bernardes's plan to hire "a professional of recognized competence to organize and direct" the establishment of the eventually school. The individual was to "select the site of the college, oversee its development and become director and be aided by a corps of American instructors." Minas offered a monthly salary of $1,000 as well as moving expenses for whomever accepted the position. To meet the state's need for numerous skilled agronomists, Bernardes envisioned a well-staffed and equipped institution with 300 to 500 students, far beyond the trickle of agronomists provided by Hunnicutt's Lavras school, the less than two dozen graduated annually from the Luiz de Queiroz school at Piraçicaba, or a similar number returning from the federally funded scholarship program.[39]

U.S. Ambassador Morgan and State Department officials urged fulfillment of the request. Ambassador Morgan remarked that it was "an unusual opportunity ... for making known our agricultural methods in Brazil" and urged that "a specialist be selected and [placed] in the field at the earliest possible moment." Undersecretary of State Norman H. Davis stressed the importance of naming a U.S. agronomist for the post in forwarding the request to the Secretary of Agriculture. However, filling the position faced difficulties. The chief of the USDA's Experimental

[37] *Brasil Industrial*, Vol. 2, No. 15 (Jan 1918), p. 12.

[38] Artur Bernardes, *Ideias políticas de Artur Bernardes*. Intro. Norma de Góes Monteiro (Brasília: Senado Federal; Rio de Janeiro: Fundação Casa de Rui Barbosa, 1984), p. 82; *Jornal do Commercio*, Oct. 19, 1921, translated and reported in USE-RJ to SS, Nov., 1, 1921, 832.00/220, RG 59 USNA.

[39] For total graduates of all programs, see Guy Decapville, "O Ensino Superior Agrícola no Brasil," *Revista Brasileira de Estudos Pedagógicos*, Vol. 72, No. 172 (Sept. Dec. 1991), p. 232; Raul Soares to Azevedo Marques [Minister of Foreign Affairs], July 9, 1920, E20-07–09, ARS; USE-RJ to SS, June 9, 1920, RG 59, 832.4237/3, USNA.

Stations Bureau undertook the task reluctantly, arguing that qualified candidates for such a position "were receiving even larger salaries in this country." At least one prominent agricultural educator turned down the position. Eugene Davenport, Dean of the Illinois College of Agriculture who had advised São Paulo on its agricultural education three decades earlier, responded that it was "impossible" to undertake the mission. Several months later, Florida citriculturist Peter H. Rolfs accepted the position. Rolfs was "just of type of man for the position," in the opinion of the USDA's Allen. In Allen's view, Rolfs had the "vision and judgment ... faith and courage coupled with patience and perseverance" needed for the venture.[40]

The fifty-five-year-old dean of the Florida Agricultural College of the University of Florida had compiled a distinguished career mingling technical work in botany with teaching botany and horticulture. Rolfs graduated from the Iowa State College with a Master of Science degree in 1891 and taught at Florida and Clemson agricultural colleges and experimental stations. He served as the plant pathologist in charge of the USDA's tropical laboratory in Miami between 1901 and 1906, and in 1906 became director of the Florida Agricultural Experimental Station. In 1913 he became also the director of agricultural extension for the University and two years later he was named dean of the Florida Agricultural College. He held all three positions simultaneously until departing for Brazil in 1921. Rolfs had authored multiple books and pamphlets on horticulture and citriculture, including a 255-page book on *Vegetable Growing in the South for Northern Markets*, (1895), a 309-page work *Subtropical Vegetable Gardening* (1916), and pamphlets on growing mangoes, pineapples, citrus, Rhodes grass, and corn, among other crops. Four plant species, varieties of oak, milk weed, and fungi, as well as a whitefly native to Florida, bore Rolfs' name.[41]

[40] Memorandum, Division of Latin American Affairs, USDS, June 10, 1920, N832.4237/10, RG 59, USNA; Eugene Davenport to Norman H. Davis [Undersecretary of State], Aug. 20, 1920, 832.4237/8, RG 59, USNA; E. W. Allen to P.H. Rolfs, Nov. 24, 1920, Albert A. Murphree Papers, University of Florida Archives, Gainesville, Florida.

[41] TS, "Peter Henry Rolfs, Biographical Sketch," Box 3, PHRA. Rolfs was the second son of a Danish immigrant who had settled in Iowa. The family was apparently oriented toward agriculture, as a junior brother George taught horticulture in his later years at the Oklahoma Agricultural College at Stillwater. P. H. Rolfs to George Rolfs, Apr. 26, 1932, Box 2, PHRA.

If Rolfs' qualifications were obvious, his motives in accepting the position remain obscure. Undertaking a long-term project far from familiar grounds at a senior age effectively ended Rolfs' career in the United States. The challenge of founding an agricultural school in a nation reputedly on the verge of greatness may have attracted him. "We are pioneers in this type of education … and pioneers make a lasting impression," he later told one of his periodic assemblies of students and faculty, alluding to Lindberg, Hoover, Rockefeller, and even Clinton D. Smith, the agricultural educator prominent in the development of São Paulo's Piraçicaba school. He was engaged in "Herculean work" and "proud to have a part in the war against ignorance."[42]

Rolfs shared the views of Hunnicutt, Green, and Day that Brazil stood to benefit from the products of U.S. industrialism while Brazil concentrated upon improving the production of raw materials. Interviewed after several years in Brazil, Rolfs noted that "this is the moment for the United States to establish the most intimate economic relations with the countries of South America, principally with Brazil, whose resources in raw materials are most abundant." This was necessary because the United States "has gone from the status of a raw material exporting country to an exporter of manufactured products" and the Latin American markets "where the competition with the British and French is already great," demanded U.S. attention. He never considered Brazil able to challenge the U.S. economic position. The United States, he reasoned, had "nothing to fear from Europe or any other country" because of the high productivity of U.S. agriculture. He informed his students that one day's labor on a U.S. farm yielded from three to five times as much crop output as a day's labor on European farms.[43]

Rolfs and his family left for Brazil in January 1921 and arrived in Rio de Janeiro a week before carnival. Accompanying Rolfs were wife Effie and daughter Clarissa, a 1920 graduate of Florida State College for Women. Clarissa left her job as a high school teacher of home economics because, as she later wrote, "I couldn't let my folks come so far without me." She aided her father as a typist, librarian, and then translator, although she continually chafed against what she considered unjust treatment for

[42] MS, "Student assemblies 1927–28," July 19, 1928; Mar. 7, 1928, Box 1, PHRA.

[43] "O Brasil visto por um estrangeiro ilustre," *Gazeta de Notícias*, Mar. 8, 1925; MS, "Student assemblies 1927–28," Mar. 27, 1928, Box 1, PHRA.

women in Brazil.[44] After touring Rio de Janeiro, they transferred to Belo Horizonte where Rolfs began to fulfill his contract.

Rolfs' first task was to select a site for the college. Preliminary studies had narrowed possible sites to four *municipios*, all within the populous Zona da Matta region of southeastern Minas Gerais. Rolfs examined nine locations in Ubá, Tio Branco, Ponta Nova, and Viçosa, and selected one near Viçosa. Soil characteristics, availability of water, and proximity to rail lines and urban areas figured prominently in his calculations. Another factor may have been that Viçosa was Artur Bernardes's hometown, although Rolfs insisted that "Dr. Bernardes twice warned me that I should not allow the fact that he was born in Viçosa to prejudice me in this matter." Rolfs reported privately while "other localities are more advantageous from an agricultural standpoint," their temperatures were "oppressively warm." Viçosa's climate and temperature were more favorable—"very similar to that encountered at Miami, Florida."[45]

Rolfs quickly developed personal contacts with Brazilian public officials and U.S. agronomists. Soon after arriving in Brazil, Rolfs visited the Escola Superior de Agricultura e Medicina Veterinaria in Niteroi, the Luiz de Queiroz school at Piracicaba, and the Lavras agricultural school, taking copious notes on their facilities and programs. He worked closely with João Carlos Bello Lisboa, the Brazilian engineer appointed in December 1922 to oversee the school's construction. Bello Lisboa, who later would become the school's first Brazilian director, translated Rolfs' early speeches and writings into Portuguese. The two worked well together, as Rolfs publicly praised "his friend" before the SNA as "The Right Man in the Right Place."[46] Within months of his arrival, at a demonstration of the "Fordson" tractor at Gameleira, Rolfs met John Haddon, employed by the Minas government since 1916. Rolfs also

[44] Clarissa Rolfs to "Katherine," June 20, 1921, Box 4, PHRA. For her view on the low status of women in Brazil, see also her letter to Dr. Jose Monteiro Ribeiro Junqueira, July 14, 1931, Box 4, PHRA.

[45] TS, "Speech to Sociedade Nacional de Agricultura, Dec. 15, 1923," Box 7, PHRA; P. H. Rolfs to Dr. Leon Dominion, Bureau of Latin American Affairs, USDS, Jan. 7, 1924, 832.4237/17, RG 59, USNA.

[46] Minas Gerais, Universidade Rural do Estado de Minas Gerais, *Escola Superior de Agricultura: Origem, desenvolvimento, actualidade* (Viçosa, M.G.: Universidade Rural do Estado de Minas Gerais, ca. 1968), p. 9; "Ensino Agrícola," *A Lavoura*, Vol. 27 (1923), 819–20.

visited the Ministry of Agriculture in Rio de Janeiro, where on one occasion he was escorted by Moacyr de Souza, who had studied for two years at Cornell. Rolfs also conversed frequently with Bernardes to ascertain the desires of Minas Gerais and make the agricultural school compatible with the state's educational system.[47]

Rolfs and his family moved to Viçosa in early 1923 to supervise the school's development, but progress was slow. Shortages of construction material caused by preparation for the Centennial Exposition in Rio de Janeiro slowed work. By December 1923, the main building was under construction and six of the twenty buildings were completed. More than a dozen agricultural experiments had been conducted, including some with Wheatland oats. The school staff, and presumably Rolfs himself, were holding weekly demonstrations for local farmers on the benefits of mechanized cultivation.[48]

Rolfs gradually established a program that stressed the practical over the theoretical and incorporated both Brazilian and foreign perspectives. His brief experience in Brazil had convinced him that "to try and transplant an agricultural school from the United States to Minas Gerais without modifications would have had without a doubt disastrous consequences." Rolfs' program reflected Bernardes's original concern for the school, echoed by his successor as state president Raul Soares, to "acquire and disseminate useful agricultural knowledge." Instead of immersing students in a study of science per se, Rolfs advocated teaching those scientific truths "directly related to the production of better harvests and better animals." It was "of little or no importance," explained Rolfs, "for an agricultural student to know if a whale is a mammal or not." But knowing the characteristics of the pink boll worm cotton pest or being able to recognize a particular sugar cane pest was of great importance. Only through teaching applied science could the school fulfill its true purpose: "to prepare men especially to direct the services on a farm and to direct rural industries."[49]

The plan of instruction reflected that philosophy. Twelve areas of instruction evolved: veterinary medicine, animal husbandry, agronomy,

[47] MS, "Trips 1921," Box 4, PHRA.

[48] Ensino Agrícola," *A Lavoura*, Vol. 27 (1923), 822. P. H. Rolfs to Dr. Leon Dominion, Bureau of Latin American Affairs, USDS, Jan. 7, 1924, 832.4237/17,USNA.

[49] "Ensino Agrícola," *A Lavoura*, Vol. 27 (1923), 820–3.

horticulture, plant and insect pests, soils, agricultural mechanics, chemistry, silviculture, Portuguese, Brazilian history, and mathematics. Three hundred to 500 students entered the four-year program at age sixteen or above. The books that Rolfs and his staff selected reflected a mix of Brazilian and foreign thinking. Works on technical subjects included Rudolpho von Ihering's *A fauna brasileira*, and *Atlas de fauna,* Benjamin Hunnicutt's *O porco*, *O milho,* and *O suino*, but also J. Simões Lopes's *Cultura de arroz*. Brazilian scholars figured more prominently in historical and literary texts, including José Francisco de Rocha Pomba's *Historia do Brasil* and the *Historia da literatura brasileira* by Sylvia Romero.[50]

If the school's curriculum represented a blend of foreign and Brazilian teachings, personally Rolfs found much that conflicted with his values. Rolfs cautiously denounced the agrarian elite for their lack of social conscience and inattention to the needs of rural Brazil. As director of the school, Rolfs sought to impart moral values. Rolfs felt that "morality, honesty, sincerity and simplicity" were "qualities of the highest order and should have preference over any other in a teaching establishment." This was required because, he said, "an educated thief is much more menacing to society than an ignorant one." He stressed such concerns to his students during one of the school's periodic assemblies. After carefully praising the current state and national hierarchy, Rolfs blasted the "old order" for leaving "the vast majority of the citizens illiterate [and] ... over half of the rural people without shoes." The old order was crumbling, though, and the Viçosa school could "make men and citizens worthy of the great state of Minas." In a later address he emphasized the school's duty to "make citizen workers of the great state of Minas." Rolfs attempted to show the way by arranging evening literacy classes for the school's manual laborers.[51]

Rolfs blamed Brazil's economic woes partially on the lack of morally strong agriculturalists. He decried Brazil's position as a sugar producer, surpassed by "the little island of Cuba, less than one-fourth the size of Minas, [which] exports more sugar than all of Brazil." Likewise, the Malay states' production of "80% of the world's rubber supply" shamed Brazil, less than fifty years earlier the world's greatest rubber

[50] MS, "Minutes, meetings, 1927–1928," July 30, 1927, Box 1, PHRA.

[51] "Ensino Agrícola," *A Lavoura,* Vol. 27 (1923), 820; MS, "Address to students," Aug. 1, 1927; MS, "Student assembly," Sept. 15, 1928, both in Box 1, PHRA.

producer. This "deplorable condition" existed because Brazil had "sucked the life-blood out of the greatest of all industries–agriculture." Brazilians produced "marvelous architecture" and "medical men ... sought by the highest courts of the world," but not one "agriculturalist of international renown."[52]

While these words may have sought to inspire impressionable students, Rolfs offered a similarly negative view of Brazil's rural environment in private. In a confidential report sent in 1930 to the state secretary of agriculture, Rolfs offered a stinging denunciation of rural illiteracy and government neglect of rural needs. "The greatest waste that occurs today is the waste of human life and effort," he wrote. The "foundation" for such waste lay "in the illiteracy of the masses," caused by a "government which inhibits education among the common people." The deep historical roots of the problem demanded strong corrective action, in Rolfs' opinion. The "unenviable situation" stemmed from a "highly centralized government which fell under its own weight in 1889." The "individual was nothing," and "absolute subservience was the means of self-preservation." He urged compassion for laborers, foremen, and many in higher positions since all have "never been taught efficiency or cooperation ... always waiting for someone higher up to tell them how, when and what to do."[53]

Rolfs busied himself during the school's construction with constant inspection visits, but he also took personal interest in Brazil's citrus cultivation. He judged that Brazil had an opportunity to "transform oranges into gold" by capturing the May through September market for oranges in the United States when native oranges were unavailable. He collaborated with Felisberto Camargo, who had studied citrus culture for two years at Gainesville as part of President Braz's scholarship program and who saw the opportunity to export Brazilian fruit, heretofore sold only locally and to Argentina and Uruguay. While in Florida, Camargo had supplemented his studies with practical experience, spending two-and-a-half months in 1920 at a modern processing plant operated by the Winter Haven Citrus Grove Association. When he returned to Brazil, he directed construction of Brazil's first orange packing house at São Gonçalo, near

[52] MS, "Address to students," Aug. 1, 1927, Box 1, PHRA.

[53] TS, P. H. Rolfs, "Report to Secretary of Agriculture, Lands, Colonization and Public Works of the State of Minas Gerais," pp. 1, 7–8, May 1930, Box 2, PHRA.

Rio de Janeiro. The plant was "constructed primarily with the view of exporting oranges to the United States."[54] Rolfs worked with Camargo to test the feasibility of his export plan. He went with Camargo to São Gonçalo where the pair selected 200 crates packed with 37,344 oranges for shipment to the United States in December 1922. When this shipment arrived in good condition, Camargo arranged for shipment of 200 more crates to Montevideo. Camargo was convinced that transforming "our routine and barbarous methods of cultivating and packing" would lead to the conquering of "new and more lucrative" markets.[55]

Rolfs became more involved in the Brazilian effort to develop citrus culture on his first return visit to the United States. From December 1924 to March 1925, Rolfs renewed old acquaintances in Gainesville, Ames, and Washington, and emphasized Brazil's economic potential. In speeches to alumni and university clubs, Rolfs downplayed the importance of recent political disruption. Brazil will still be the "greatest economic power of the world," he told the Lions Club of Ames. He returned to Brazil with citrus shoots for the Viçosa school. These included 65 shoots of Florida oranges, along with grapefruits, tangelo, kumquat, tangerine, avocados, apple, pear, prunes—a total of shoots from 865 plants. Rolfs probably used those slips and others from Brazilian trees to furnish interested parties with large numbers of citrus shoots.[56]

By August 1926, Rolfs fulfilled the main purpose of his contract, the founding of the agricultural college. After five years of construction and preparations, classes began with 25 students. On August 26 the Brazilian and U.S. flags unfurled over a sprinkling of the nation's and the state's highest authorities. President Bernardes used the occasion to list the changes required of Brazil's agriculture. Brazil must "lower the costs of

[54] TS, P. H. Rolfs, "Report to U.S. Horticultural Board," n.d., Box 1, PHRA; "Exportação de laranjas para Nova York," *Boletím* [MAG], Vol. 13, No. 2 (1924), 75-78; Camargo would later cooperate extensively with U.S. business and scientific ventures in Brazil, including the Fordlandia project and the Tropical Plant Research Foundation. See "Felisberto Camargo," *Grande Encyclopedia Delta*, 1970, IV, 1223; W. A. Horton, "A riqueza florestal do Brasil," *Boletím* [MAG], Vol. 17, 2, No. 6 (1928), 962.

[55] "Exportação de laranjas para Nova York," *Boletím* [MAG], Vol. 13, No. 2 (1924), 76, 78, 82.

[56] TS, P. H. Rolfs, "Primeiro Relatório do Director da Escola Superior de Agricultura e Veterinaria de Minas Gerais," 1925, Box 2, PHRA; A. Magarinos Torres, "O estado sanitario das plantas procedentes dos Estados Unidos. ...," *Boletím* [MAG], Vol. 14, No. 6 (1925), 701–7.

agricultural and diary production by the general use of machinery, by the knowledge of soils suitable for each culture, by the careful use of fertilizer, by the selection of seeds, by a more perfect packaging of products, by the improvement of cattle and their proper treatment and by a more profitable use of industries derived from cattle raising." Such actions would fulfill his economic vision: Brazil, before anything else, "has to be a great agricultural country."[57]

These three pillars of Brazil's agricultural education were thus firmly established along the North American model. Over the next several decades, their graduates would prove critical to improving the productivity and production levels of Brazil's agriculture within a capital-intensive framework.

[57] Universidade Rural de Minas Gerais, *Escola Superior de Agricultura*, pp. 9–11; *Jornal do Commercio*, Aug. 29, 1926. Bernardes's exact words were: "Aperfeiçoando-se os métodos da cultura, o Brasil, antes de tudo, tem de ser um gran país Agrícola."

CHAPTER 8

Epitácio Pessoa, Cotton and Beef, 1919–1922

Politicians and bureaucrats in the immediate postwar abandoned the nationwide orientation of the diversification movement to appeal to narrow regional interests. Like many Brazilian producers, merchants, politicians, and foreign investors, political elites in the Northeast and South assumed that Europe's devastated conditions would sustain elevated prices for favored commodities. Their efforts to support continued profitability of two products that had received new attention during the war—cotton and beef—were to founder despite ample government support. Elites in the Northeast and South would prove unable to counter falling cotton and beef prices, a weakened national currency and renewed interest in coffee. The regionalist approach to Brazil's agriculture returned with all its excesses, exposing a grave weakness that gradually undermined the existence of the First Republic.

Brazil at War's End

Brazil at the end of World War I stood at the summit of an economic roller coaster. "The war created many economic advantages for Brazil," as a Brazilian government publication intended for potential U.S. investors proclaimed in 1918. It proudly related that "the demand on the part of the belligerents for our foodstuffs and raw material stimulated agricultural

E. R. Downes, *Brazilian Agricultural Development, 1890–1950*,
https://doi.org/10.1007/978-3-031-76992-4_8

and industrial production to an output far in excess of our past records."[1] Individual states continued to enjoy strong increases in economic activity in the immediate postwar period, buoyed by sustainment of wartime production and prices for products that had created a flood of new revenue. Compared with 1914, state export tax receipts combined stood 44% higher in 1919. By that year, total state tax receipts rose to 166% of their 1914 level. Rio Grande do Sul's total exports had increased to 136% of the 1917 total. Overall state receipts doubled between 1917 and 1921. In 1920 Minas Gerais President Artur Bernardes proclaimed advances in economic growth stemming from increased production in agriculture and cattle raising, "the inexhaustible sources of its [the state's] wealth." Bernardes saw agriculture as being particularly healthy, each year "increasing the area under cultivation, improving existing crops, and attempting the planting of new varieties." Rio de Janeiro reported that "the financial situation is absolutely satisfactory," with a 64% revenue surplus for 1919. The president of tiny Sergipe proclaimed that "It is not exaggerated to say that Sergipe is passing through a phase of frank prosperity." Cotton-producing Paraíba was also enjoying a strong surplus at war's end, based upon "the exploitation of its natural sources of wealth."In early 1920, the president of Santa Catarina boasted that revenues had increased by as much as 29% every year between 1914 and 1919. He called the increase in revenues "truly impressive," the product of the "excellence of our economic conditions."[2]

Concern soon began to arise, however, that higher prices might not survive in the postwar era. A 1916 editorial in Porto Alegre's *O Progresso* had asked if "the end of the war will bring a decline in the orders for refrigerated beef?"[3] The author responded that the contrary would be true, because of the "entry of the Central European countries into the

[1] Brazil, Ministry of Agriculture, Industry and Commerce, *What Brazil Buys and Sells* (Rio de Janeiro: Imprensa Nacional, 1918), p. III.

[2] Brazil, MAG, *Relatório, 1922*, p. 169; Rio Grande do Sul, *Mensagem, 1917*, p. 97, *Mensagem 1920*, p. 74; "Rio Grande do Sul: A obra do Dr. Borges de Madeiros," *Industria e Commercio*, Vol. 7, No. 70 (1922), 60; "O estado de Minas Gerais: A mensagem presidencial," *Brasil Industrial*, Vol. 4, No. 30 (1920), 60; "As finanças do estado de Rio," *Brasil Industrial,* Vol. 4, No. 32 (1920), 49; "O estado de Sergipe. …," *Brasil Industrial*, Vol. 3, No. 29 (1919), 99; "A ótima situação financeira e econômica do Estado de Paraíba," *Commercio e Indúustria*, Vol. 3, No. 30 (1918), 27; "Estado de Santa Catharina," *A Lavoura*, Vol. 24, No. 8 (August 1920), 347.

[3] "O mercado mundial de carne," *O Progresso*, Vol. 4, No. 35 (1916), 2.

sales market" with the end of the war. The magazine retained a favorable outlook at war's end. "The lack of products of prime necessity is immense in all of Europe," it reasoned. Brazil had increased its agricultural production, "selling it for prices never before reached," and its "inexhaustible natural resources can and should place it at the height it deserves and that peace predestines." The observation, the journal remarked, was not "optimism on our part," but rather a "cold and positive fact."[4] A member of the Sociedade Nacional de Geografia argued that "fruit culture, fishery, the extractive industries, steel, mining, and all those admirable resources... demand our activity, our energies, with the same vital tension of the *bandeirantes.*" In the Amazon region, higher wood prices created the impression that the "fever of reconstruction" in Europe would create an "exceptional moment" for exporting high-quality lumber. Even vegetable oils, in one view, would be in high demand. As coal remained expensive and "mineral oils" used more often as a fuel, "all oil-bearing seeds will find an increasingly easier placement in worldwide markets, at highly compensative prices." Planting castor oil seeds, therefore, "is a sure way of earning money."[5]

Those who contributed to the wartime effort felt strongly that Brazil could reap substantial profits through the export of primary products following the war. Luis R. Vieira Souto, head of the Comité de Producção Nacional, admitted in 1919 that "without a doubt there must be a decline in the prices of some goods that lately reached fantastic prices." However, he pointed out, "this decline will never again make them fall as low as...the pre-war level." Most of all, Europe would be involved in a "long and difficult transition," marked by the "scantiest production of foodstuffs and raw materials." Until normal production resumed, Brazil and other American nations could reap the benefits "of the large field of possibilities opening before us in Europe" if only Brazil would exploit "with tenacity the productive power of the Brazilian soil." Such "almost

4 "Perspectiva animadora," *O Progresso*, Vol. 8, No. 65 (1919), 51.

5 Antônio de Almeida, "As possibilidades econômicas do Brasil depois da guerra," *Brasil Industrial*, 2, No. 23 (1918), 45; Luciano Pereira, *Coisas brazileiras* (Rio de Janeiro: Albuquerque & Neves, 1920), p. 26; "O commercio de mamona," *Revista de Commercio e Industria*, Vol. 3 (1917), 413. The bandeirantes were adventurous Brazilians who scoured the Brazilian interior from the sixteenth century in search of riches and fame. For a discussion of their supposed similarity to U.S. frontiersmen, see Clodomiro Vianna Moog, *Bandeirantes e pioneiros: Paralelo entre duas culturas* (Rio de Janeiro: Editora Globo, 1954).

indefinite" productive power and Europe's inability to meet its needs meant increasing prosperity for Brazil. "Let us develop, therefore," Vieira Souto suggested to state production commissioners, "the cultivations of those goods which we know will be exportable and let us also intensify the raising of cattle."[6] Increasing production of beef, pork, wood, oil-bearing fruits, and cotton would prolong the wartime prosperity Brazil had enjoyed.

The Regional Priorities of President Epitácio Pessoa

The nation's first postwar president shared the optimism about Brazil's place in the postwar world. Epitácio Pessoa was a native of cotton-producing Paraíba and head of a clan-like political machine that struggled to control state politics. His clan solidified that control while he served as a federal senator between 1912 and 1918, reminding the nation, in a banquet speech in October 1917, that the problems of the North-east and the periodic havocs of the droughts had been ignored. He lamented misapplication of funds allocated to combat the droughts' effects, complaining that they had been "spent in the defense of the less vital interests of other territorial places."[7] While heading Brazil's delegation to the Versailles peace conference, Pessoa was elected to the national presidency, left vacant by the January 1919 death of president-elect Rodriguez Alves and the illness of Vice President Delfim Moreira. In his new office, Pessoa was prepared to extend patronage politics to the national level by trumpeting the economic gospel of the time. He judged "development of the resources of the land" as "the most important factor in the prosperity of any nation." He forecast that maintaining efforts for foodstuffs and raw materials after the war's end would require a special effort to defend and develop Brazil's products.[8]

[6] "A producção mundial e a situação dos mercados," *Revista de Commercio e Industria*, Vol. 5 (1919), 327–8.

[7] See Linda Lewin, *Politics and Parentela in Paraiba: a Case Study of Family-based Oligarchy in Brazil*(Princeton, NJ: Princeton Univ. Press, 2014), pp. 308–348. Francisco G. de Queiroz, *Epitácio Pessoa* (Manaus: Governo de Estado de Amazonas, 1965), pp. 36–37.

[8] Quoted in *O Paiz*, May 7, 1919, translated encl. to USE-RJ to SS, May 10, 1919, 033.3211/16, RG 59, USNA.

Pessoa visualized Brazil's agricultural future through a Northeasterner's eyes. He soon evidenced his interest in promoting both cotton and his native Northeast through intense support to both. He pledged to do "everything he could to make cotton one of her [Brazil's] large export products." Like Assis Brasil and Nilo Peçanha, Pessoa desired to enhance the economic power and prestige of his region. He decided to use the presidency to improve transportation and port facilities, but especially for Northeasterner Pessoa, Brazil needed to strive for the "extinction of the droughts."[9]

Pessoa first had to confront the realities of a bureaucracy ill-equipped to provide substantive aid to agriculture. The challenges confronting the 10-year-old institution were numerous, detailed in a forty-page confidential memorandum prepared for president-elect Rodrigues Alves in September 1918 by João Pandiá Calógeras. Calógeras was a trusted civil servant who had served as Minister of Agriculture in 1914 and 1915 and Minister of the Treasury from 1915 through 1917. He became Pessoa's Minister of War, affording him the opportunity to comment on advice he had prepared for Pessoa's predecessor. The ministry could be best understood, wrote Calógeras, by recognizing that sections incorporated into the ministry in 1909 from other ministries were well-staffed by functionaries accustomed to performing their tasks. On the other hand, officers charged with new tasks undertaken by the ministry—and those most related to agricultural development—were suffering from a "low level of professional competence." Several new directories had often become "shoals for the shipwrecked of every profession" whose credentials were marked by an "admirable indifference to technical knowledge."[10]

Calógeras detailed pervasive deficiencies. One section that should have been staffed by technical experts had become the site of "confusion, waste, and pretentious unproductiveness," while "bureaucracy and inefficiency" reigned within the Information Service, reduced merely to providing handouts and "insufficient clarifications."Lack of coordination

[9] A postcard available in Rio de Janeiro in early 1919 depicted Pessoa in a stately gaze against the backdrop of a blossoming cotton plant. Attached to USE-RJ to SS, May 10, 1919, 033.3211/16, RG 59, USNA; Arno S. Pearse, *Brazilian Cotton* (Manchester, Eng.: International Federation of Master Cotton Spinners and Manufacturers' Associations, 1923), p. 9; Pessoa, *Pela Verdade!,* p. 50.

[10] João Pandiá Calogeras, *Problemas de administração: Relatório confidencial apresentado em 1918 ao conselheiro Rodrigues Alves sobre a situação orçamentaria e administrativa do Brasil* (São Paulo: Companhia editora nacional, 1938), pp. 173, 185.

among the various experimental stations was especially troubling. "In the current situation," he remarked, "by abuse, each director of a zootechnical [animal husbandry] post or a model farm acts by himself, without connection to efforts of those in similar establishments creating ties, only, by a decision of the Minister." Calógeras also criticized the lack of scientific support for agriculture. He recommended multiple remedies, concluding that it was "little wonder" that public opinion and informed observers held that the ministry was "so downcast and so discredited."[11]

The Pessoa administration addressed the need for more trained agronomists by continuing to rely upon foreign training. Before war's end, Pessoa's future Minister of War Calógeras had observed that "we will only have real and useful agronomic instruction [by] contracting professionals from foreign lands, preferably those from the United States." However, he noted, it was a work to be accomplished "after the war."[12] The short-term solution was continuation of the foreign scholarship program initiated during the war. Agriculture Minister Ildefonso Simões Lopes justified support for the program as the "most rapid and economic of processes to construct the body of professionals" needed for the country's agricultural needs. He vowed to sustain support for students already dispatched to France and the United States. Students were to be embarked upon two years of study, receiving an allowance of 100 dollars a month.[13]

In the United States, Brazilian agricultural and veterinary students sponsored by the federal government soon joined a vibrant organization of Brazilian students who provided mutual support through local "colonies," conferences, and correspondence. The "Brazilian Students Association," founded during the war, boasted its own publication (*O Estudante Brasileiro*), a national slate of officers, and an annual national congress. It advocated teaching Portuguese in the United States and

[11] Pandiá Calogeras, *Problemas de administração*, pp. 193, 198, 207–8, 215.

[12] João Pandiá Calógeras, *Problemas de administração: Relatório confidencial apresentado em 1918 ao conselheiro Rodrigues Alves sobre a situação orçamentaria e administrativa do Brasil* (São Paulo: Companhia editora nacional, 1938), p. 204.

[13] Brazil, MAG, *Relatório 1920*, pp. XL-XLII; Perhaps he was reacting to the origins of those 26 then studying in the United States under the program and selected by the administration of Wencelau Braz of Minas Gerais. Most originated from São Paulo, Minas Gerais, and Rio de Janeiro states. Only five were from Northeastern states and three from Rio Grande do Sul. See "Brazilian Students Arrive in New York," *The South American* (December 1918), p. 13.

used its magazine to share personal news, perspectives on national and international events, and observations on agricultural and engineering topics in 1,000 copies per edition. News from colonies in the June 1920 edition feature snippets from Ann Arbor (Michigan), Urbana (Illinois), Baton Rouge (Louisiana), Ada (Ohio), Madison (Wisconsin), Gainesville (Florida), Ithaca (New York), Berkeley (California), and College Station (Texas). A June 1921 edition listed 34 agronomists or veterinary students among nearly 300 members present in the United States, of whom five were female. Gainesville-based student José Cavalcanti Hardmann, who authored an essay on plant mutations, would help found a sugar cane mill in Pernambuco in 1928. Agronomist student Octavio Gonçalves Peres, from Pernambuco, studying in Columbia, South Carolina, would later become director of *Bahia Rural* magazine and a prominent advocate of change in Brazil's rural sector. In his 1920 essay, he stated that "I foresee the day when we can make scientific investigations on our own soil, a day that will mark a new era for Brazilian Agriculture."[14]

Scholarship students swelled the association's membership, occupied important posts in the organization, spoke before civic groups about Brazil with a collection of slides maintained by the association, wrote letters to prominent U.S. newspapers, and organized conferences about Brazil on a variety of campus. Personal ties forged through U.S. agronomists in Brazil increased through the study program: José Garibaldi Dantas lived in the home of Benjamin Hunnicutt's uncle during his study in Athens.[15] The program continued on the eve of the assumption of office of the Bernardes government. The Pessoa administration

[14] Member rosters are in *O Estudante Brasileiro*, Vol. 1, No. 6 (Apr. 1920), 65–68; Vol. 1, No. 7 (June 1921), 18–21; José Hardman Cavalcanti, "Importancia da Selecção dos Escudos na Propagação Artificial das Plantas," *O Estudante Brasileiro*, Vol. 1, No. 8 (Nov. 1922), 23–24; "Usina Central Olho D'Água—Pernambuco," www.onordeste.com; Octavio Gonçalves Peres, "O Estudo de Terrenos nos E. Unidos," *O Estudante Brasileiro*, Vol. 1, No. 6 (Apr. 1920), 65–68; *Diário Carioca* (Nov. 26, 1933), p. 10.

[15] Cristovam B. Dantas (Lavras 1919) served as "Eastern Vice President" in 1922–23. José Hardman Cavalcanti (Piraçicaba 1921) presided over the "Committee of Information and Refutations" the following year. See *O Estudante Brasileiro*, Vol. 1, No. 7 (1921), 1; No. 8, (1922), 1; "Colônia Brasileira de Athens, Ga.," *O Estudante Brasileiro*, Vol. 1, No. 7 (1921), 31–32; Personal interview with Benjamin H. Hunnicutt, Jr., Aug. 14, 1982; "Uma associação de estudantes brasileiros nos Estados Unidos," *Brazilian American*, Vol. 3, No. 56 (1920), 27–29.

dispatched 52 students to Europe and 29 to the United States in a decree published with only nine days remaining in government.[16]

Aiding the Northeast Through Anti-Drought Measures

Pessoa's most ambitious program sought to leverage his new political power to implement a wide-scale program to combat effects of the droughts—a program that borrowed heavily from U.S. experience, one Pessoa admired. Pessoa had developed a favorable disposition toward the United States as a beneficiary of U.S. efforts to secure a position of prestige for Brazil at the Versailles conference, where he had been the chief Brazilian delegate, and its successful lobbying for the Brazilian positions at meetings of the U.S., British, French, and Italian representatives, known as the "Council of Four." At a Versailles dinner, U.S. President Woodrow Wilson proclaimed that he was "gratified tonight to think of the hours I have had the pleasure of spending with Mr. Pessoa." Pessoa's U.S. visit enroute to Brazil allowed for increased Brazilian-U.S. economic and financial ties. In a lunch with the "South American Group" of U.S. bankers, he expressed hopes "to have a better understanding of American financial methods with a view to having in the future closer financial relations with the United States." Such ties would supplant the prominence of British bankers, Brazil's prewar financial agents. Indicative of U.S. businesses' interest in Brazil was the flood of invitations to Pessoa received at the State Department. General Electric, Goodyear, and Goodrich vied with the chambers of commerce of major U.S. cities and even the Mid-day Luncheon Club of Springfield, Illinois, to host Pessoa. Pessoa journeyed to Washington instead, to be feted at a banquet at the Pan-American Union and a dinner cruise attended by 175 "Brazilian and U.S. officials" aboard the presidential yacht. Pessoa left for Brazil, according to a State Department official, "impressed by the United States and its power and energy."[17]

Pessoa's U.S. visit was at least partially motivated by a desire to gather information on U.S. irrigation and cotton-growing techniques. As a U.S.

[16] Brazil, MAG, *Relatório 1923*, pp. 537–8, 541–2.

[17] SS to USE-RJ, July 18, 1919, 711.32/23a, RG 59, USNA; File 033.3211/101–86, 1919, RG 59, USNA; *The South American*, Vol. VII, No. 7 (June 1919), 16; Vol. VII, No. 9 (July 1919), 7–8; SS to USE-RJ, July 18, 1919, 711.32/23, RG 59, USNA.

official at Versailles reported, "Pessoa wants to leave for Rio as soon as possible but desires very much to see the cotton industry and dry farming and irrigation development." In addition to proclaiming Brazil's wishes to "develop more and more the relations of every kind, which bind her [Brazil] to the United States," Pessoa sought information on cotton cultivation, requesting copies of U.S. "laws, regulations, plans and monographs relative to irrigation and cotton" during his brief stay.[18]

Shortly after returning to Rio de Janeiro to assume the presidency—after first stopping in his native Paraíba—Pessoa ordered extensive studies in the drought region and reaffirmed the federal commitment to alleviating the impact of the droughts. Recalling the examples of Texas and other regions, Pessoa called for "permanent irrigation" of up to a million hectares to allow the Northeastern farmer to plant multiple crops. The plan drew extensively from recommendations created by technicians hired by the Inspectoria Federal de Obras Contra as Seccas (IFOCS) following its creation in 1909. These had impressed Senator Eloy de Souza of Rio Grande do Norte. Souza had experienced the devastation caused by the droughts in his native state and traveled to Egypt in 1910 to study cotton cultivation. He drew from works of Roderic Crandall, a U.S. engineer contracted by IFOCS to recommend remedies for the drought-based on the region's geology. In 1911, Souza drafted legislation for an extensive anti-drought program for the Northeast using, as he explained, the structure of the U.S. Bureau of Reclamation. The proposal he presented to the Câmara dos Deputados on August 30, 1911, entitled "Um problema nacional–projeto de justificação," called for large-scale irrigation to facilitate cultivation of rice, sugarcane, tobacco, and forage grasses, but especially cotton. The proposal lay dormant for eight years, but in 1919 it became the basis for Pessoa's action plan to combat the effects of the droughts.[19]

[18] USE-Paris to SS, May 19, 1919, 033.3211/101, RG 59, USNA; *NYT*, June 22, 1919, p. 9, col. 1; EBW to SS, June 20, 1919, 033.3211/139, RG 59, USNA.

[19] Vingt-un Rosado, "Roderic Crandall: Um Mossoroense da California," Acervo Virtual Oswaldo Lamartine de Faria, www.colecaomossoroense.org.br; Eloy de Souza, "A irrigação na economia geral do Nordeste," SNA, *Annaes da Primeira Conferencia Algodoeira*, Vol. II (São Paulo: Secção de Obras doi "Estado de São Paulo," n.d.), pp. 130–140; Maria Conceição Maciel Filgueira, "Eloy De Souza: uma interpretação sobre o Nordeste e os dilemas das secas" (Natal, RG: EDUFRN, 2011), p. 23. Souza requested works of the U.S. Bureau of Reclamation through the Brazilian Embassy in

Pessoa proposed that Congress authorize loans, dedicate two percent of the nation's budget and that states contribute from two to five percent of their budgets to fund the massive irrigation project. When Congress approved the proposal on December 25, 1919, the way stood open for yet more contacts between the United States and Brazil based upon Brazil's natural resources.[20]

Pessoa enjoyed the assistance of an accomplished rice farmer from Rio Grande do Sul, Ildefonso Simões Lopes. Like many proponents of more vigorous federal support for diversified agriculture who had pushed for reform a decade earlier, Simões Lopes was a regional politician from an area with little relation to coffee. Son of a prominent rancher and owner of a charque factory and trained as a civil engineer at Rio de Janeiro's Escola Politécnica, he had directed the waterworks in his native municipio of Pelotas, served in the state legislature, and become a major rice farmer using modern techniques. He was active on the committee dealing with agriculture as a federal deputy between 1913 and 1919, joining the SNA. Like Pessoa, Lopes embraced the logic of raising Brazil's production for export, affirming in his first report as Minister that the "expansion of our foreign markets" should be "at this time, the object of greatest concern."[21]

Simões Lopes recognized the magnitude of the challenges facing his ministry. In reporting on the proposed budget for the agriculture ministry as a federal deputy, he had identified the lack of an "articulated and powerful organization" and the insufficient number of trained personnel. Since rich farmers educated their sons in the "liberal professions," and there were insufficient positions for "poor agronomists," he queried: "where will we obtain, therefore, the necessary personnel?" As minister, he lamented that the ministry's professional staff included only 79 agronomists and 30 veterinarians, less than 10% of total employees.[22]

Washington, including C.J. Blanchard's publication on reclamation and irrigation, "The Spirit of the West." BEW to SS, June 26, 1916, Maço 234, 2, 6, #6354, AHI.

20 "Obras contra as seccas," *RC do JC,"* 1919, pp. 97–99; USC-Pernambuco to SS, Aug. 20, 1921, p. 2, 832.61/6, RG 59, USNA.

21 Ricardo Vieira Lima and Luciana Quillett Heymann, *Da monocultura a o agribusiness: a história da Sociedade Nacional de Agricultura (SNA)* (Brasilia: Embrapa Informação Tecnológica, 2005), p. 135. Brazil, MAG, *Relatório,* 1920, p. LXIII.

22 Brazil, MAG, *Relatório* 1919, pp. XVII, XVII.

Many of the ministry's programs under Simões Lopes' direction stood to aid the nation's South or Northeast. The ministry remodeled seed farms in Paraíba—the president's native state—and the southern state of Santa Catarina. Improvements in sugar cane cultivation that would benefit the Northeast as well as support for cultivation of wheat in southern states gained special attention. Support for improving cattle would aid the Center-South, home to the largest herds. Most prominent, though, were efforts to promote cultivation of Northeastern cotton. In March 1920, President Pessoa ordered re-institution of the Serviço do Algodão, extinct since 1916, placing its headquarters in his native Paraíba. He named Northeasterner (and 1909 Piraçicaba graduate) William Wilson Coelho de Souza as director and arranged congressional authorization for new experimental stations and demonstration fields. These included two fields in Rio Grande do Norte and experimental stations in Paraíba, Piauhí, Pará, and Maranhão. He ordered reconstruction of flood-damaged experimental stations at Coroatá, Maranhão, where Edward Green had experimented in 1913 and 1914.[23]

Another crucial element of the pro-Northeastern policy was Pessoa's drive to provide water for cotton and other crops in the Northeast, a program that soon assumed enormous proportions. By 1922 the federal government had constructed more than a thousand kilometers of roads, nearly 200 reservoirs, 126 wells, and 163 kilometers of railroad. Improvements in port works at Forteleza, Natal, and Paraíba were also an important part of the project. Irrigation projects "studied or in construction" in 1922 included works to irrigate 750,000 hectares in Rio Grande do Norte, Ceará, and Paraíba through dozens of major and minor dams. Such projects would prove especially beneficial for cotton. Improved

[23] William Wilson Coelho de Souza, "Intensificação da cultura do Algodão: Serviço Federal do Algodão," *Annaes da Conferência Internacional Algodoeira*, I, 469–76. While placement of the Cotton Service in Paraíba was justified in terms of ensuring technical assistance to planters, communications with Rio de Janeiro and especially disbursement of federal government credits, supplies, and equipment provided difficult. See Superintendente, Serviço do Algodão, to Ministro da Agricultura, Indústria e Commercio, July 19, 1921, 20.03.10 5, AISL.

infrastructure and the ability to plant food crops on the same land during the off-season would increase the region's prosperity, it was hoped[24]."[25]

Pessoa's support of increased cotton cultivation in the Northeast responded to both domestic and international demand. As noted earlier, Brazil's textile industry had expanded explosively in the early twentieth century, doubling the number of cotton mills and spindles between 1905 and 1921 and consuming over 90% of the nation's production of cotton between 1915 and 1919.[26] Especially supportive of Pessoa's interest in developing cotton in the Northeast was British interest in more Brazilian cotton. Britain had purchased 78% of Brazil's 623,900 bales of cotton exported since 1909. In the postwar, it once again saw Brazilian cotton as a welcomed alternative to imports from its traditional supplier—the United States. In early February 1920, adjustments in exchange rates forced the price of U.S. cotton upward for British buyers. Forecasts predicted a more than fifty percent cut in British purchases of U.S. cotton, important given the nearly 1.5 million bales of U.S. cotton purchased during the last five months of 1919. At the same time, the spread of the voracious boll weevil in cotton lands in the U.S. South further threatened the supply of U.S. cotton for British buyers. During the war years, the weevil had destroyed up to 14% of the U.S. cotton crop. By 1920 it consumed an estimated 20% of the crop.[27]

[24] Arno S. Pearse, *Cotton in North Brazil, Being the Report of the Journey through the States of Ceará, Maranhão and Pará, Together with a Synopsis of the Whole of Brazil's Cotton Potentialities*, pref. Miguel Calmon (Manchester, Eng.: Taylor Garnett Evans & Co., n.d.), pp. 58–62; Trajano S. V. de Medeiros, "O valor econômico dos trabalhos de açudagem e irrigação do nordeste," *Annaes da Conferencia Internacional*, II, 352–3.

[25] USC-Pernambuco to SS, Apr. 25, 1923, p. 21, 832.6113/4, RG 59, USNA; "A Sociedade Nacional de Agricultura e o Beneficiamento do Algodão," *Brasil Agrícola*, Vol 6, No. 2 (Aug. 1921), p. 59.

[26] StanleyJ. Stein, *The Brazilian Cotton Manufacture: Textile Enterprise in an Underdeveloped Area, 1850–1950* (Cambridge, MA: Harvard Univ. Press, 1957), p. 101; Export taxes cited in "The Brazilian Cotton Industry," USDA, *Foreign Crops and Markets*, Vol. 10, No. 25 (June 22, 1925), 761; Centro Industrial de Brasil, *A Industria Brasileira de Tecidos: Conferencia realizada em 12 de Junho por Dr. J. Costa Pinto...* (Rio de Janeiro: Typografia do Jornal do Commercio, 1916), p. 48.

[27] Export figures compiled from *Commercio Exterior do Brasil* cited in "The Brazilian Cotton Industry," USDA, *Foreign Crops and Markets*, Vol. 10, No. 25 (June 22, 1925), 762. The boll weevil proved its power in the United States from 1920 to 1923 when it forced substitution of other crops for cotton and massive migration of Southerners who had depended upon cotton for subsistence. See USDA, *Yearbook 1922* (Washington:

Britain then began searching for new sources of cotton, and Brazil appeared to be a willing and capable supplier. Brazil produced not only short-staple cotton but also long-stapled cotton suitable for the "ever-increasing fine spinning sections of the Lancashire mills." Industrialist Roberto Simonsen outlined Brazil's capabilities at the September 4, 1919, meeting of the International Cotton Committee (ICC) in Paris and invited the ICC to send a study mission to Brazil. The ICC accepted the invitation at its November 1920 meeting, clearing the way for a survey of Brazil's cotton potential.[28] Cotton service director William Wilson Coelho de Souza reinforced British fears about U.S. cotton in a booklet featuring Brazil's potential he prepared for the visitors, noting that the boll weevil "is spreading every day moreover the North American territory threatening to completely destroy the plantations," leading to the "completely hopeless outlook of cotton production in North America." Meanwhile, Brazil stood ready to offer the industrial world "with every safety a plentiful production of cotton…."[29]

The expedition of Arno S. Pearse of the International Federation of Master Cotton Spinners Associations further encouraged Brazilian cotton producers to supply the British market. Pearse arrived in Brazil in March 1921 and received assurances of support from President Pessoa and Minister Simões Lopes. During his six-month stay, Pearce visited over 1,000 cotton fields during a 7,500-mile journey by rail, auto, riverboat, and horseback through the hinterlands of São Paulo, Minas Gerais, Bahia, Alagoas, Sergipe, Pernambuco, and Piauí. He returned in late 1922 to complete his mission, traveling nearly 6,000 miles through Maranhão, Ceará, Pará, as well as other Northeastern states visited earlier, once again as a guest of the Brazilian government.[30] Pearse had support of interpreter and Brazilian cotton expert Oscar K. Piquet, a representative of

GPO, 1923), p. 714; John D. Helms, "'Just Looking for a Home: The Cotton Boll Weevil and the South" (Diss. FloridaStateUniv. 1977); *NYT*, Feb. 5, 1920, p. 3; Feb. 10, 1920, p. 23.

28 Pearse, *Cotton in North Brazil*, p. 54; *NYT*, Nov. 11, 1920, p. 23, col. 2; Arno S. Pearse, *Brazilian Cotton*, pp. 9, 210–211; "O Algodão Brasileiro," *Revista de Commercio e Industria*, Vol. 6 (1920), 572.

29 Brazil. MAG, *Possibilities of the Cotton Culture in Brazil by William Wilson Coelho de Souza* (Rio de Janeiro: Papelaria Brazil Quitanda, 1920), p. 8.

30 Pearse, *Brazilian Cotton*, p. 9; *Cotton in North Brazil*, p. 11. Decree 15,959, Feb. 10, 1923, authorized 50:000$ to fund the mission. See Brazil, MAG, *Relatório, 1923*, p. 432.

the Centro Industrial de Brasil, who had traveled to the United States in 1916 to acquire presses for processing cottonseed oil. In the opinion of one U.S. diplomat, Piquet had "long experience in the cotton districts of the United States."[31]

Throughout these odysseys, Pearse proclaimed his faith in Brazil's natural resources and especially in its ability to produce cotton. Brazil, in his view, was "a country which will be self-supporting in a very short time, and her natural resources have destined her to become the most powerful nation in the whole of South America." He told the SNA after his first mission that "the conditions of climate and soil... in Brazil are probably more favorable to cotton cultivation than in any other part of the world." He termed Brazil's outlook especially promising since the United States "has evidently come to the extreme limit of its capability."[32]

Pearse's recommendations reached a wide audience. The report from his first trip was published in 4,000 Portuguese and Italian copies, of which all but 50 had been purchased by late 1922. During his second trip, the indefatigable Pearse encouraged even the legendary Padre Cicero—faith healer and political leader—to improve his cotton production. The pair met for five hours at Joazeiro, Ceará, accompanied by 500 of the mystical priest's followers. Pearse found Cicero "extremely intelligent," perhaps because "he soon realized the advantages resulting from the growing of just one variety of cotton" instead of the "mixture generally adhered to in Ceará."[33]

Ironically, implementing Pearse's recommendations to stimulate production to suit the British market rested on greater technical collaboration with the United States. Modern U.S. equipment was already proving important in improving processing of the Brazilian crop. Gins from the Continental Gin Company of Birmingham, Alabama, were prominent in Trajano de Medeiros's plants. That firm's oilseed plant

[31] Ltr, MAG to MRE, Apr. 26, 1916, Maço 292, 4, 6, AHÍ; TS, "Study of Cotton Culture in Brazil," Mar. 31, 1921, USDA, FAS, "Narrative Reports (1904–1939)," Box 56, USNA.

[32] Pearse, *Cotton in North Brazil*, p. 21; "A cultura de Algodão em São Paulo," *Annaes da SRB*, Vol. 1 (1921), 804–5; Pearse, *Brazilian Cotton*, pp. 212, 222.

[33] José Maria Fernandes, "Classificação do Algodão e formação dos typos commerciaes da fibra," *Annaes da Conferência Internacional*, II, 87; Pearse, *Cotton in North Brazil*, pp. 53-54. The Italian edition was probably designed for immigrants considering planting cotton as a cash crop Whether those who purchased the book were predominantly laborers or smallholders is unclear.

at Pirapora, Minas Gerais, produced fodder for goats and cattle using machines made by the V. Anderson Company of Cleveland. Other modern ginning factories at Limoeira and Rio Branco, Pernambuco, used gins made by the Munger Hull Company of Dallas. All the ginneries Pearse visited in Quixadá, Ceará, used "American Eagle" gins.[34] The 1920 census recorded the presence of 570 Eagle or Continental gins in use for cotton processing.[35]

Pessoa's plans to improve the Northeast's fate through an immense irrigation project increased direct U.S. involvement in enhancing cotton production. Along with two British firms, U.S. companies garnered an important part of the contracts to implement the irrigation project. In August 1921, the Dwight P. Robinson Company of New York City received a contract to build five large dams in Ceará and Paraíba states that would require one million cubic feet of concrete. The company started work in mid-1921 and by the end of 1922 had employed a monthly average of over 7,000 people and imported over two million dollars in material. The largest dam, Poço de Paus, 64 meters high and 610 meters in length, was to irrigate 22,000 hectares. There the company built a village for 10,000 persons and positioned three air compressors, 24 Ingersoll-Rand jackhammers, and even four Baldwin locomotives. The largest dam in terms of area to be irrigated was the Orós dam on the Jaguaribe River, designed to water 60,000 hectares.[36]

U.S. technology and experience also permeated the efforts of a Brazilian firm organized to take advantage of favorable conditions and the availability of government support. The Sociedade Algodoeira do

[34] Pearse, *Cotton in North Brazil*, pp. 32, 42; Pearse, *Brazilian Cotton*, 98, 129–30.

[35] Brazil, MAG, Diretora Geral de Estatística, *Recenseamento do Brazil Realizado em 1 de Setembro de 1920. Vol. III. Agricultura. Instrumentos e machinas agrarias dos estabelecimentos ruraes. Beneficiamento da producção* (Rio de Janeiro: Typ. da Estatística, 1927), p. XXVII.

[36] *NYT,* Aug. 18, 1921, p. 23, col. 2; Pearse, *Cotton in North Brazil*, p. 50, table facing p. 62; Untitled notebook, n.d., Book 61, "Obras do Nordeste - Seccas," pp. 8–10, AEP. Another aspect of U.S.involvement in the project may have occurred in the financial realm. Ernst Hambloch, in his *His Majesty the President: A Study of Constitutional Brazil* (London: Metheun, 1935), p. 149, argues that much of the $50 million loan contracted by the Brazilian government in 1921 with Dillon, Read & Company of New Yorkwas destined to finance the irrigation project. Contemporary press accounts, however, stated that the loan was to support electrification of the Central do Brasil railroad. See *NYT,* June 9, 1921, p. 21; Aug. 30, 1921, p. 23.

Nordeste Brasileiro (SANBRA) drew heavily from the U.S. experience with cotton. The firm was organized with a 1:000$ initial investment from Pinto Alves & Companhia, an established Pernambuco export house. The company acquired rights to an earlier concession to establish cotton mills in four *municipios* in Pernambuco and Paraíba states. The federal government extended funding to complete its mills through a credit of 500:000$ payable with six percent interest in ten years. As with earlier concessions to Trajanos de Medeiros, SANBRA had to commit itself to intensified cotton production. Each mill was to process between 5.2 and 10 tons of cotton daily and 120 tons of cottonseed oil monthly in adjacent plants. The company was also to maintain an experimental farm of at least 200 hectares at each mill to produce cotton seeds for distribution to local farmers through the Serviço Federal do Algodão.[37]

The technical director of the firm outlined plans to incorporate U.S. concepts and equipment into its operations. Not only would "cotton clubs" be formed "in the model of the American corn clubs," but also the company was installing advanced processing machinery made in the United States by the McCarthy Company. Access to new cotton lands would result from extensive use of Ford vehicles on roads built by two Caterpillar tractors. Completed installations later boasted systems purchased from Continental Gin and Munger companies. SANBRA also soon employed one of the first participants in the federal scholarship program to study cotton in the United States. Octavio Peres had studied cotton at Georgia State College of Agriculture from late 1918 until June of 1919 when he traveled to Texas A & M to study the cotton industry and agricultural education. He became the first professional agronomist to direct one of SANBRA's seed farms.[38]

Another prominent example of the engagement of U.S. technical experience to increase supplies of Northeastern cotton for the British market

[37] See advertisement, Pearse, *Cotton in North Brazil*, p. xvii; José F. Brandão Cavalcanti, "Em prol do Algodão," *A Lavoura*, Vol. 24 (1920), 267–70; See Decree 14,330, Aug. 26, 1920, in Brazil, Serviço Federal do Algodão, *Actos relativos ao Serviço do Algodão* (Rio de Janeiro: Impr. Nac., 1925), pp. 19–21. See entry for Green in *The Semi-centenniel Alumni Record of the University of Illinois* (Chicago, IL: R.R. Donnelly & Sons, c1919), p. 880.

[38] José F. Brandão Cavalcanti, "Em prol do Algodão," 270; Octavio Goncalves Peres, "Relatório," *Boletím* [MAG], Vol. 9, No. 1 (1920), 39–52; "Serviço do Algodão," *Boletím* [MAG], Vol. 15, 1, No. 3 (1925), 321.

was the case of Edward C. Green. Green had acquired extensive experience with long-staple cotton native to the Brazilian Northeast. He had remained in Natal, Rio Grande do Norte, farming and selling cotton as a private individual. Through Green's contacts, Fernando Pedroza, a former employee of the Ministry of Agriculture in Rio Grande do Norte, partnered with U.S. entrepreneur Clarence B. Wharton and formed Wharton, Pedroza e Companhia in 1918. Green and Pedroza were both engaged in attempting to improve a local variety of cotton at experimental farm when Green introduced Pedroza to Wharton. The company they founded became engaged in classifying local cottons and traveling throughout the state, where friends of Pedroza brokered cotton on a commission basis and financed small producers. His mission was to increase the quantity and quality of the Northeastern cotton crop by propagandizing among growers and promoting modern processing techniques. Evidence of its faith in U.S. cotton expertise (but not in Green himself) was the company's calling upon another U.S. cotton expert to verify Green's experiments before making a large investment into increased cotton production.[39]

Federal government support for cotton in the Northeast also provided opportunities for U.S. manufacturers of cotton processing equipment, duly informed by reports from U.S. diplomats fully engaged in promoting sales of U.S. equipment and agricultural supplies. The U.S. Consul in Pernambuco advised the State Department of appropriations in the federal budget for 1921 for "the establishment of cotton gins and cotton presses at the principal railroad stations which ship cotton or at suitable interior points." The Consul noted that U.S. manufacturers of "cotton ginning, cotton pressing, and cottonseed oil machinery would do well to correspond directly with the private companies concerned." Identities and addresses were provided.[40]

The twin foreign pillars of Brazilian cotton expansion became even more evident at the Conferencia Internacional Algodoeira (International Cotton Conference) held in Rio de Janeiro from 15 to 20 October

[39] http://historiarn.blogspot.com/2012/05/fernando-gomes-pedroza-E-industria.html; "A SNA e o beneficiamento do Algodão," *Brasil Agrícola*, Vol. 6 (1921), 59; USC-Pernambuco to SS, Oct. 19, 1922, 832.6132/9, RG 59, USNA.

[40] TS, USC-Pernambuco, "Opportunities for the Sale of Cotton Machinery in Northeastern Brazil," Jan. 24, 1921, in RG 166.2, "FAS—Narrative Reports," Box 54, USNA.

1922, under sponsorship of the Ministry of Agriculture. U.S. delegates to the conference represented sources of technical information and capital; British delegates represented potential consumers. The British delegation, meanwhile, included representatives from the English Federation of Master Cotton Spinners Association, the Oldham Cotton Spinners Association, the Textile Institute of Manchester, and several private firms located in Manchester and Liverpool.[41]

The British delegates stressed their faith in Brazil's potential as a cotton producer. Oxford University professor John A. Todd warned that continuing worldwide demand and decreases in the U.S. crop created a "vital need for an increase in production." Other possible producers—Egypt, British India, Russia, and China—remained unable to meet Europe's demand. Brazil, he concluded, "is the country that offers the best possibilities for an immediate increase in production." Similarly, the vice president of the English Federation of Master Cotton Spinners Associations asserted that the United States, supplier of 60% of Britain's cotton, would soon consume its entire production. In the meantime, countries interested in cotton production should consider "creating an organization dedicated to this necessity." British Ambassador to Brazil Sir John Tilley likewise termed the "development of cotton cultivation in Brazil preeminently important" and pledged his country's assistance.[42]

Information from the United States sustained the conference's technical discussions. Cotton magnate Trajano de Medeiros presented a lengthy exposition on cotton classification that was mostly a translation of recent USDA bulletin. Brazilian agronomists just returned from study in the United States further elaborated techniques of cotton classification, citing experiments in North Carolina, Georgia, Louisiana, and Arkansas. U.S. delegate Youngblood expressed interest in "being able to contribute to the adoption of scientific methods used in the United States," later noting that "fifteen Brazilian boys" were studying at his Texas school.[43]

[41] USE-RJ to MRE, Oct. 3, 1922, M-280, 3, 2, AHI; Henry C. Wallace, Secretary of Agriculture, to SS, Aug. 15, 1922, 561.32/C1/7, RG 59, USNA; "Representantes junto a Conferencia Internacional Algodoeira," *Annaes da Conferencia Internacional*, I, 33.

[42] John A. Todd, "Abastecimento de Algodão," *Annaes da Conferência Internacional*, I, 186–7, 193; J. M. Thomas, "A cultura do Algodão nas colonias Britannicas," *Annaes da Conferência Internacional*, I, 234; "Sessão Inaugural," *Annaes da Conferencia Internacional*, I, 68.

[43] Trajano S. V. de Medeiros, "Classificação de formação do typos comerciase do Algodão no Brasil," *Annaes da Conferencia Internacional*, I, 115–42; José Maria

Fulfilling the Pessoa government's goals for improving production of Northeastern cotton proved elusive. The decline in the value of Brazilian currency from 1920 forward and consequent decline in the unit value of exports, including cotton, forced drastic reductions in the federal budget and the budget of the Ministry of Agriculture, leaving the cotton service with inadequate funds to implement its plans. Director William Wilson Coelho de Souza delineated the challenges he faced as head of the cotton service in a presentation to the 1922 cotton conference. After dutifully praising the Pessoa administration, he lamented that the total funds available to him for improvements in cotton in all 12 states assisted by the federal service amounted to less than French government spending to support cotton cultivation in a single African colony. He detailed challenges confronting restoration of the Coroatá experimental station, neglected since its creation in 1912. A flood in 1919 had destroyed what neglect had already damaged. He explained that rehabilitating a single experimental farm required construction of a telegraph line and road to access the farm as well as fencing to prevent drought-famished cattle from devouring the plants. It was also necessary to eradicate previous plantings of cotton to establish consistent grading and plant other crops as part of a crop rotation scheme. "Everything had to be done," he reported.[44]

The vagaries of weather and pestilence continued to create wide variations in the productivity of cotton lands in the Northeastern states. Production in Pará and Pernambuco decreased between 1919 and 1922 remained about the same in Alagoas, Sergipe, and Bahia, but increased in Maranhão, Piauhí, Ceará, Rio Grande do Norte, and Paraíba. Depressed prices for the commodity tarnished Pessoa's dream of a Northeast made prosperous by export of "white gold." Though the nation's cotton exports increased through 1922, the average value per ton, measured in pounds sterling, fell by over 30% (Fig. 8.1).[45]

Fernandes, "Classificação do Algodão e formação dos typos commerciaes da fibra," *Annaes da Conferencia Internacional*, II, 87–112; Heitor Airlie Tavares, "Pequenas sugestões ao aperfeiçoamento do Algodão no Brasil," *Annaes da Conferencia Internacional*, II, 7–39; "Sessão Inaugural," *Annaes da Conferencia Internacional*, I, 76; *Brazilian Business* [American Chamber of Commerce for Brazil, Rio de Janeiro], Vol. 2, No. 11 (1922), 9.

44 William Wilson Coelho de Souza, "Intensificação da Cultura do Algodão Serviço Federal do Algodão," in *Annaes da Conferência Internacional*, II, pp. 469–477.

45 Brazil, Ministerio de Fazenda, *Relatório... 1925*, p. 9. Cotton production figures cited in U.S. Department of Agriculture, *Foreign Crops and Markets*, Vol. 10, No. 25, (June 22, 1925), 746.

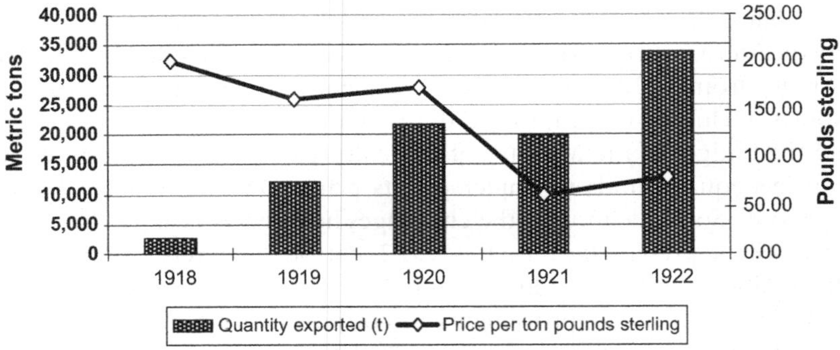

Fig. 8.1 Brazilian Cotton: Total exports and unit values, 1918–1922 (*Source* Calculated from Instituto Brasileiro de Geografia e Estatística, Repertório Estatístico do Brasil, Quadros retrospectivas No. 1 [Rio de Janeiro: Serviço Gráfico do Instituto Brasileiro de Geografia e Estatística, 1941], p. 87)

More problematical for the fate of cotton in the Northeast were disputes that arose between Pessoa and other regional elite members regarding selection of his successor, a perennial Achilles heel of the First Republic. The dispute centered on whether Pessoa would endorse Artur Bernardes, the president of Minas Gerais. Bernardes had won the March 1922 national presidential election with support of politicians from his native state and São Paulo but faced continued opposition from supporters of losing candidate Nilo Peçanha. In a meeting at the Catete palace on May 1, 1922, Pessoa refused to endorse Bernardes and left for Europe immediately after turning over the presidency to Bernardes on November 15. The stage was set for an abrupt reversal of the federal government's approach to cotton cultivation.

Improving Cattle and Beef Processing

Equally daunting were challenges faced by Pessoa and other advocates of sustaining the market positions that Brazilian beef had attained during wartime. Even so, his Minister of Agriculture remained optimistic about sustaining global market participation for Brazil's meatpacking industry. Ildefonso Simões Lopes supported initiatives to benefit the cattle industry, especially in his native South. Shortly after assuming his ministerial position, proposed improvements of Brazil's cattle through importation of breeds adaptable to Brazil's various regions. He ordered publication of an extensive report of U.S. practices in the cattle industry by scholarship student Landulpho Alves de Almeida, who had traveled Forth Worth, Texas, and Chicago, Illinois, to observe cattle auctions and expositions. Alves de Almeida urged that supporting the traditional charque industry was unwise: "Instead of providing assistance to the creation of charque processing plants, a primitive process for the conservation of beef for export, we should work in the sense of giving advantages to the industrial firms that establish *frigorificos* in the diverse breeding zones of the country." He believed that "our herd could support a greater export than what we have done," and higher levels of export would increase prices enough to fund new investment. This iterative process to improve the herd through the importation of breeding cattle and careful cross-breeding, along with better pasture grasses, would allow for year-by-year gains for Brazil's cattle industry.[46]

Foreign investors who had entered the cattle sector during the war expressed similar sentiments. Writing in 1920, Frank B. Carter of Armour do Brasil argued that Brazil's numerous local cattle breeds "have shown themselves to be ideal animals upon which to start constructing breeding and the development of improved frigorífico cattle." Brazil's abundant land meant that "the number of cattle now found can be doubled several times" since the climate was "ideal for cattle raising." Imported pure-breds had "adapted themselves to the Brazilian climate amazingly well and produced splendid results," he reasoned. Beyond land and climate, adequate fodder was available from "more than twenty varieties of corn" that was "of the highest quality." Further, "native labor" was "interested in cattle and eager to learn improved methods of management." Since livestock production was "a crop which returns a cash income every year without fail," Carter was convinced that "stock raising is sure to become the leading industry in this great country."[47]

Leopoldo Plaut, Carter's counterpart in the Continental Products company, was equally positive about prospects for Brazil's beef industry.

[46] Brazil. Ministerio da Agricultura, Industria e Commercio. Serviço de Informações. *Relatório apresentado pelo Agronomo Landulpho Alves de Almeida ao Diretor Geral de Agricultura como Profissional Envidado pelo Ministerio de Agricultura aos Estados Unidos de America do Norte*....(Rio de Janeiro: Typografia Vilas-Boas & C., 1920), pp. 55, 82,83.

[47] Frank B. Carter, "The Passing of the Longhorn," *Yearbook of the American Chamber of Commerce for Brazil, 1920* (Rio de Janeiro: n.p., 1920), pp. 117–22.

He described cattle-raising conditions in Brazil as "ideal," with "virgin land to be bought at reasonable prices," and forecast that Brazil would soon offer serious competition for the Argentine beef industry.[48] SNA member Hannibal Porto judged the meat-packing industry integral to "this burst of prosperity and solid wealth" and therefore "worthy of all support from public powers and the frank admiration of the nation." An official of the Ministry of Agriculture boasted that the "pastoral industry" was "developing each day more, [and is] not far from the period in which it will be, perhaps, the most opulent basis for the country's wealth and prosperity."[49]

The interest of U.S. investors and the prosperous outlook for the sector opened the door for at least one case of abuse—the "Pan American Cattle Exchange Company." The company had organized in late 1919 through "Barão B. de Beszedits" in collaboration with the U.S. Consul in São Paulo, Charles L. Hoover. In September 1919 de Beszedits obtained a letter of introduction from Hoover describing him as "one of the most successful stockholders in this region." With Hoover's endorsement, de Beszedits attended the International Livestock Exposition in Chicago in November 1919 and convinced the USDA to purchase cattle and hogs for shipment to Brazil. By late 1920, the company had received 44 purebred animals and housed them temporarily at a federal veterinary post at Moóca, São Paulo. In addition to de Beszedits, the company listed among its officers several leading U.S. cattle and pork breeders, former USDA officials and assorted U.S. bankers and businessmen. To devote more attention to the venture, Consul Hoover resigned his post in April 1920.[50]

Hoover's cooperation lent legitimacy to the enterprise, if only temporarily. In early January Hoover asked the Department of State to instruct Ambassador Morgan to certify to the Brazilian Ministry of Agriculture "the names and numbers of shares of the first four shareholders of the Company as shown on the attached certification." Even though the Department dutifully sent the telegram to Morgan, such

[48] "Acta da 57ª Reunião. ...," *Annaes da SRB*, Vol. 1 (1920), 326–7.

[49] Hannibal Porto, "A influência dos frigoríficos no futuro de S. Paulo," *Annaes da SRB*, Vol. 1 (1920), 125 "A criação do gado no Brasil," *Revista de Commercio e Industria*, Vol. 5 (191), 176.

[50] Memorandum, Office of Solicitor, USDS, Nov. 16, 1921, 123H76/124, RG 59, USNA; "Importação de reproductores," *Annaes da SRB*, Vol. 1 (1920), 359–62.

maneuvers failed to shield the company from attacks stemming from its exaggerated promises of marketing all U.S. merchandise in Brazil, falsely claiming ownership of extensive lands, and privately implying possession of a concession to import U.S. goods duty-free. The São Paulo police surmised in December 1920 that the company was presenting false statements in its prospectus. The State Department's trade advisor soon thereafter judged the whole operation a fraudulent "wild-cat promotion scheme." Simultaneously, a Brazilian businessman with a personal interest in the matter began to raise the specter of scandal through denunciations in Rio de Janeiro newspapers. By April, Hoover himself became disenchanted, informing the State Department that "they had concealed things from me" and "were in the hole about $40,000." Hoover judged the venture "a complete failure and [that] the money invested will be a complete lost [sic]."[51]

By the end of the war, genuinely financed foreign firms dominated the *frigorífico* business, although preparation of meat for local markets, especially in small towns and rural regions, remained largely in the hands of Brazilian firms. So prominent were foreign firms in the *frigorifico* business that one of the Brazilian students sent to the United States to study agriculture reported that "constantly we see the most important national industries fall into the hands of foreigners." The meat-packing industry, he reported, had been "entirely turned over to foreign capital and professionals, creating a brutal and crushing competition for the two or three national [i.e., Brazilian-owned] meat-packing plants."[52]

Foreign companies advanced their interests by supporting creation of a corporatist lobby to defend the meat-packing industry. Packers and exporters formed the Sociedade Rural Brasileira (SRB), or Brazilian rural society, in early 1919. The SRB modeled itself after the Argentine rural society in terms of goals, but many of its founding members represented foreign cattle and meat-packing firms. At the organization's leadership stood Eduardo da Fonseca Cotching, a Brazilian who admired the Argentine rural society. He chaired a May 20, 1919, organizational meeting in São Paulo. Members tasked with devising statutes of the society included A. S. Midlam, director of Armour do Brasil, Leopoldo

[51] C. L. Hoover to SS, Jan. 17, 1921, 832.5034/9, RG 59, USNA; SS to USE-RJ, Jan. 17, 1921, 832.5034/9, RG 59, USNA; W. E. Embry to USBFDC, Jan. 17, 1921, 832.5034/10a, RG 59, USNA; Memorandum, Office of Solicitor, USDS, Nov. 16, 1921.

[52] Guillerme Echnique Filho, "Relatório," *Boletím* [MAG], Vol. 8, No. 3 (1919), 60.

Plaut, director of the Continental Products Company, H. O. Bernsau, director of Armour do Brasil's "Anastacio" farm, along with representatives from Leon Israel & Company, an import–export firm. Eleven days later the group approved a charter with Fonseca Cotching's as president, Armour representative Midlam as first secretary, and Continental Products representative Plaut as director of the society's library.[53]

The SRB's statues pledged the society to secure state and federal subsidies for breeders and importers of purebred European cattle—Shorthorn, Hereford, Devon, among others. The society especially hoped to obtain an improved transportation network, removing the "principal impediment" to cattle and meat-packing industries. Tax exemptions and preferences for its members on imports, exports, immunizations of animals, and on "any other business concerning cattle-raising" were high priority goals.[54] The society founded its own magazine and soon sought the ears of influential politicians, thus giving the dominant foreign interests in the meat-packing industry a legitimate channel into the Brazilian political process.

There was little any interest group could do, though, to overcome endemic difficulties within the cattle sector itself. Despite the exuberance of the early postwar period, problems soon began to appear. Exports of frozen beef continued strong through 1920, averaging over 57,000 kilos each year from 1918 through 1920. Problems then began with a

[53] Other members of the committee on statutes were Julio de Mesquita Filho, son of the editor of *O Estado de São Paulo* newspaper, and Dr. Carlos A. Monteiro de Barros, a prominent fazendeiro associated with the export sector. Sociedade Rural Brasileira, *Estatutos 1930* (São Paulo: Irmãos Ferraz, 1930), pp. 6–7, 15; Autómovel Club de S. Paulo, *Annuário 1921* (N.P.: N. p., n.d.), p. 49. Various historians have argued that the SRB viewed the support of coffee as its priority activity. For Flavio M. Heinz, the SRB "prioritized as an activity the defense of coffee growers of São Paulo and neighboring states." Flavio M. Heitz, ed., *Por outro História das Elites* (Rio de Janeiro: Editora FGV, 2006), p. 127, n. 8. Drawing upon the archive of the *O Estado de São Paulo*, Joseph Love credits coffee planter interests with the most strength in the SRB, Joseph L. Love, *São Pauloin the Brazilian Federation, 1889–1937* (Stanford: Stanford Univ. Press, 1971), p. 225, n. 40. Its initial actions show that the SRB intended to support primarily the cattle sector. Only when coffee proved more profitable as the 1920s progressed did the SRB become more of an advocate of planters' interests. Ranchers played a more prominent role in the founding of Argentina's rural society than they did in the SRB. See Peter H. Smith, *Politics of Beef in Argentina: Patterns of Conflict and Change* (New York: Columbia Univ. Press, 1969), pp. 33, 47–51.

[54] "Industria das carnes frigorificadas. ...," *Annaes da SRB*, Vol. 1 (1920), 191; *Annaes da SRB*, Vol. 1 (1920), 381.

cattle plague that tainted the reputation of Brazilian beef abroad. Overflowing stocks of canned and frozen beef in European warehouses cut demand even further. The initial sign of problems emerged as Brazilian beef began to lose its competitive position in foreign markets. In 1920 the Brazilian commercial attaché in Italy warned that Brazilian exporters must "confront the struggle with the substitute" and pay special attention to a "good presentation of the article and an absolute guarantee of its quality." The following year, the government acknowledged problems in placing Brazilian beef in foreign markets, admitting that its inferior quality, along with excessive state export taxes, placed Brazilian beef in a difficult position. Without improvements, the Brazilian product would be "expelled by less expensive and better merchandise," the article warned.[55]

Problems soon accumulated. In early 1921 a cattle plague began to claim cattle in regions producing for the packing plants. The first instances of the disease appeared among cattle delivered for sacrifice to the Continental Products plant in Osasco. Some "fatal cases" were registered there, as cattle arrive in an advanced stage of the disease, "some of them even without teeth."[56] The number of infected cattle was substantial, requiring a Ministry of Agriculture team of 15 veterinarians, 40 functionaries, and 138 workers to disinfect pastures and bury dead animals. The sickness killed 600 cattle in Cotia, near São Paulo. In another, 72 cattle were sacrificed. As news of the infestation spread, so did repercussions. In April, Argentina and Uruguay banned import of meat originating in São Paulo, as did Santa Catarina and Rio Grande do Sul. European buyers quickly did the same, as Italian authorities refused to allow discharge of frozen beef from a steamer in Genoa in early May. Despite Brazilian insistence

[55] Brazil, Ministerio da Agricultura, Industria e Commercio, Directoria do Serviço de Inspecção e Fomento Agrícola, *Aspectos da Economia Rural Brasileira* (Rio de Janeiro: Oficinas Graphicas Vilas Boas, 1922), p. 17; *Revista de Commercio e Industria*, Vol. 6 (1920), 199; "Abastecimento de carnes," *Boletim* [MAG], Vol. 10, 1 (1921), 86.

[56] Guy A. Roberts, "A peste bovina em S. Paulo," *Annaes da SRB*, Vol. 1 (1921), 531; Roberts, educated at Kansas City Veterinary College, Cornell and Pennsylvania universities, responded to the state of São Paulo's request to hire a U.S. veterinarian. At the time of the investigation, he was employed by the Veterinary Institute of São Paulo. He later went to Lavras to teach veterinary medicine. See EBW to MRE, Dec. 10, 1918, M-235, 3, 7, AHI; *O Agricultor*, Vol. 2, No. 9 (1923), 9.

that the beef originated from cattle killed before outbreak of the disease, the Italians steadfastly refused to accept the shipment.[57]

Further weakening the demand for Brazilian beef was the overstocked condition of the European market. By 1921 European cold storage houses "were full of frozen meats of all kinds" while local cattle production was recovering and beginning to provide fresh beef. Large stocks of canned beef also encouraged the Europeans to reduce purchases of foreign beef, including that from Brazil. To make matters worse for Brazilian beef exporters, in 1921 French authorities downgraded Brazilian beef to "third category," comparable with beef from South Africa, and an inspector with the Dutch government rendered a highly negative report on its quality, further discouraging prospects of exporting to Europe.[58]

By mid-June 1921, the crisis could not be ignored. Armour closed its ten-million-dollar plant in July 1921 only six months after its opening. As the plant's manager explained, its principal purpose had been to prepare beef for export to Europe but with high European stocks and recovering herds, the daily kill at the plant dropped to 50 to 60 cattle per day, forcing its closure. Continental Products also shut down operations, prompting the San Paulo Railway to cut its office staff by 25%. These moves left the city of São Paulo "glutted with British and American unemployed." Although the cattle disease was reportedly under control by August, conditions for the cattle market throughout the interior of the country remained "very precarious." Some 50,000 cattle awaited buyers in Campo Verde, Mato Grosso, just one market town, and the SRB began to talk of setting up a fund for supporting cattle prices similar to that for coffee.[59]

Predictably, prices for Brazilian beef plunged. By 1922 prices for Brazilian beef had dropped so low in France, England, and Germany that production for those markets was uneconomical. Italy resumed imports

[57] Alpheu Grage to Ildefonso Simões Lopes, Apr. 1921, 12.00.00 III 25, AISL. In the *Murillo* case, the U.S. Embassy in Rio de Janeiroattempted to intercede for Swift, Armour and Wilson—to no avail. See USE-RJ to USE-Rome, May 13, 1921, and USE-RJ to MRE, May 31, 1921, both in M-280, 3, 2, AHI.

[58] Brazil, MAG, *Relatório, 1921,* p. lvii; Isalto Costa, *As nossas exportações: um inquérito na Europa* (São Paulo: "O Estado de São Paulo," 1922), pp. 34–36.

[59] "O frigorífico Armour," *Annaes da SRB*, Vol. 1 (1921), 108; Roy Nash, *The Conquest of Brazil* (New York: Biblo and Tannen, 1968), pp. 267–8; *Brazilian-American*, 4 No. 49 (1921), 15; "As condições do commercio do gado," *Annaes da SRB*, Vol. 1 (1921), 1089.

in early 1922, but purchases were decreasing even there. Prices on the Brazilian domestic market also dropped dramatically, from 900 to 950 reis per kilo on the São Paulo market during the war to 650 reis per kilo by March 1922. As the agriculture ministry explained the following year, the cattle industry found itself "in the arms... of a double crisis in 1921 and 1922 of [low] prices and the prohibition of entry of our animal products in the principal foreign countries."[60] By 1922, the crisis forced the sector to depend primarily upon the internal market.

The cattle sector and its supporters responded by intensifying efforts to improve the herd, but differences arose as to which breeds would create the best results. The manager of the Brazilian Meat Company blamed the lack of demand on the low quality of Brazilian beef, complicated by high state taxes. In November 1921 Armour reported to the SRB that the company had purchased five mixed-breed Devon cattle with an average weight of 496 kilos and yielding over 61% meat. The beef was to be sent directly to the London market "so that that great cattle market can once and for all be convinced that Brazilian beef should not be judged inferior or rejected." In Armour's opinion, such an example showed conclusively the desirability of "improving our cattle [by] breeding with purebred bulls such as Hereford, Devon and Shorthorn." The president of the SRB encouraged continued import of purebred cattle as a cure for the crisis (Fig. 8.2).

Paulo de Moraes Barros judged that "Brazil has a lesson to learn from the failure of the packing plants and refusal of the world to buy Zebu beef." Brazil needed to "substitute foreign blooded stock" to build its cattle industry "up on a big scale... within twenty years." In Minas Gerais, U.S. missionary and educator Hunnicutt supported those who favored importing purebreds. According to a visiting USDA commission, Hunnicutt and his assistant were "perhaps doing more than anyone else to spread the gospel of pure-bred livestock in Brazil." Meanwhile, improving the herd through selective breeding of the native Caracú breed became an alternative for other Paulista ranchers who enjoyed the support of the state secretary of agriculture in their efforts.[61]

[60] Hughes, "Brazilian Meat Industry," *Bulletin of the American Chamber of Commerce, S. Paulo*, Vol. 3, No. 3 (1922), 2; Brazil, MAG, *Relatório, 1923*, p. xiv.

[61] F. B. Carter to SRB, n.d., in "Carnes Brasileiras," *Annaes da SRB*, 1 (1921), 1087; TS, "Live Stock Production near Lavras, Brazil," [August 1920], RG 166, Box 64, USNA;

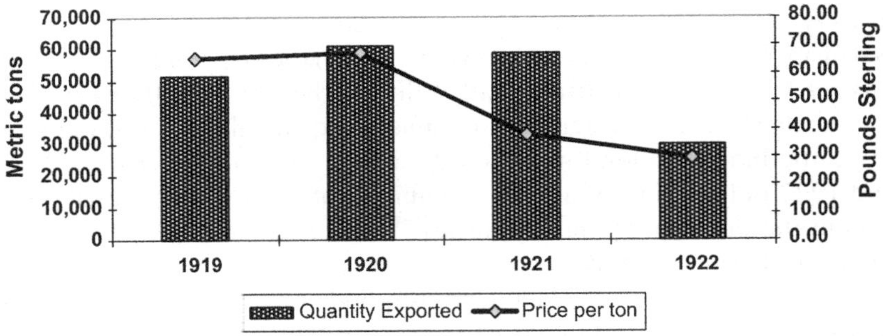

Fig. 8.2 Brazilian exports of and unit value of chilled and frozen beef, 1919–1922 (*Source* Brazil, Ministerio da Fazenda, Directoria de Estatística Commercial, *Commercio Exterior do Brasil, Janeiro a Dezembro 1919, 1920, 1921, 1922, 1923* [Rio de Janeiro: Estatística Commercial, 1924], pp. 110–111)

Proponents of improving the Brazilian herd by importing Zebu cattle offered an alternative. Led by stock raisers within the Minas triangle, an arrow-shaped outcropping of rich grasslands of Minas Gerais situated between the states of São Paulo and Goiás, Brazilian ranchers imported 5,500 Zebu cattle directly from India between 1904 and 1921. They initially faced resistance to inclusion of Zebu cattle at stock shows, but Zebu gained acceptance based on the claim that the animals adapted more easily to Brazil's climate. The agriculture ministry's September 1922 cattle exposition in Rio de Janeiro featured "noble" breeds from Holland, Switzerland, France, Argentina, and the United States, as well as purebreds raised in Rio Grande do Sul, São Paulo, Rio de Janeiro, and Minas Gerais, but a Zebu raised by a Paulista stockman won the prize as the show's best animal.[62]

A prominent cattleman with experience in the United States became conciliator between competing factions advocating improvements in the Brazilian herd. In the opinion of Fernand Ruffier, the best short-term solution lay in setting aside discussions on cattle genetics and focusing on feeding and processing of cattle already available for market, including

Joana Medrado, "Do Pastoreio à Pecuária: A invenção da modernização rural nos sertões do Brasil Central" (Diss.: Universidade Federal Fluminense, 2013), p. 11.

62 Medrado, "Do Pastoreio à Pecuária," pp. 88–158; Brazil, MAG, *Relatório,* 1922, p. 88.

those crossed with Zebu cattle. Between 1902 and 1906, Ruffier had worked on the "Far West" cattle ranch of Abel Borden of Pierce, Texas, a prominent Zebu cattle advocate. During the war, Ruffier became a featured speaker at cattle expositions and conferences on ways to improve the Brazilian herd. He followed progress of the U.S. cattle industry through contacts with the U.S. Consul in São Paulo, requesting folders "referring to several breeds of stock raised in U.S. (Guernsey cattle, Shropshire sheep, etc.)."[63]

In August 1922 Ruffier reported to the SNA on results of a five-month mission to study the U.S. cattle industry, undertaken at request of the Minister of Agriculture. Ruffier's travels to Colorado and Texas and consultations with his former employer in Pierce and other packing houses in Texas and Brazil confirmed his opinion that Zebu cattle was an effective remedy for the maladies of Brazilian beef. He reported that the directors of the Amour and Swift plants in Brazil were convinced that "during a long period of time" the central Brazil region "would not be able to create worthwhile cattle without the utilization of the exceptional qualities of Zebu cattle." He ridiculed efforts to transplant Herefords to Mato Grosso. The white-faced cattle so often sought refuge from summer heat in lakes that neighboring ranchers asked if they represented a "new amphibious breed."[64]

Particularly hard hit in the crisis was the beef industry of Rio Grande do Sul, where production of chilled and frozen beef was almost entirely exported to foreign markets. Like the Northeast, the cattle-dependent South suffered from erratic prices for its principal commodity. While advantages of São Paulo allowed it to side-step the effects of falling cattle prices, Rio Grande do Sul fell headlong into an economic abyss. The drop in demand and falling prices created a crisis atmosphere among cattle raisers. Although exports continued strong through 1921, in 1922 the state's *frigorífico* production dropped to one-tenth of the 1921 figure, from 32.5 tons to a mere 2.9 tons. The cataclysmic collapse in demand left ranchers with pastures full of cattle, provoking one rancher in the Rio

[63] Ltr., Fernand Ruffier to USC-São Paulo, May 11, 1919, Consular Reports, São Paulo, Vol. 84, RG 84, USNA.

[64] Medrado, "Do Pastoreio à Pecuária," p. 158: "Industrial Pastoril," *A Lavoura*, Vol. 26, Nos. 9–11 (Sept.-Oct.-Nov. 1922), 237–41; Fernand Ruffier, "Cattle Raising in Brazil," *The Field Illustrated*, (July 1922), p. 444.

Grande do Sul *município* of Uruguaiana to seek the Minister of Agriculture's aid to institute "urgent measures to save us from the painful and critical current situation." The "great decline in the price of cattle" had provoked a crisis "endured by the pastoral class." Faced with "ludicrous prices" offered by packing plants, ranchers were forced to sell once again to jerky plants even though their product suffered from strong Argentine and Uruguayan competition in the internal market.[65]

Gaúcho ranchers caught in the crisis formed an interest group in late 1921 to pressure state and federal politicians. The Federação das Associações Rurais do Rio Grande do Sul (Federation of Rural Associations of Rio Grande do Sul) began to seek relief, as did one of its member organizations, the Federação Rural. It complained to the national congress that the southern states stood on the brink of "complete ruin" because of conditions in the cattle market. It sought a protective tariff to discourage import of cattle products as well as granting the beef jerky industry the same privileges enjoyed by *frigoríficos*. They especially clamored for establishment of a bank, the Banco de Crédito Rural Hypothecario, to expand credit for the pastoral sector.[66]

Politicians from Rio Grande do Sul carried the petition to the congress with little result. Joaquim Osorio, former president of the Sociedade Agricola de Pelotas and now a federal deputy, complained that, although Rio Grande do Sul had acquired control over the railroad and port facilities vital to the cattle industry, lack of an adequate banking system prevented "defense" of the sector. High interest rates and the lack of long-term credit stifled sector's growth. "With a banking apparatus that permits the defense and growth of the cattle-raising industry," he argued, the State could guarantee the "economic expansion of Brazil."[67] The erratic prices and generally much lower exports of frozen beef from Rio Grande do Sul forced a renewed reliance on sales to jerky plants.

The efforts of Northeasterner Pessoa and his Ministry of Agriculture, led by progressive Gaúcho farmer Ildefonso Simões Lopes, to fortify

65 D. M. Reit to Ildefonso Simões Lopes, Feb. 23, 1922, 12.00.00 AISL; Rio Grande do Sul state figures cited in USC-PA to SS, May 8, 1929, Box 64, RG 166, USNA.

66 Sandra Jahaty Pesavento, *República Velha Gaúcha: Charquiadas, frigoríficos, criadores* (Porto Alegre: Movimento, 1980), pp. 211–5; Federação Rural do Rio Grande do Sul to Congresso Nacional, Mar. 14, 1922, 12.00.00, AISL.

67 Brazil, Câmara de Deputados, *Annais, 1922* (Rio de Janeiro: Impr. Nac., 1923), IV, 105.

Brazilian cotton and beef in world markets faltered on conditions they could little control. The establishment by foreign investors in the beef and cattle sector of a corporate identity to lobby for their interests—the Sociedade Rural Brasileira (SRB)—had little impact. The difficulties of transforming the practices of Northeastern cotton cultivators and overcoming problems of Brazilian beef during a three-year mandate were overwhelming. Attempts by the federal government to improve the quality and volume of a wide variety of commodities, including foodstuffs, corn, tobacco, silk, honey, and, explained here in detail, cotton and beef, involved continued contacts with U.S. sources of raw materials, technical information, capital, and management in the hopes of gaining high revenues from foreign markets. Meanwhile, the wartime alliance of elites from regions capable of producing foodstuffs for the domestic market with those in depressed regions seeking alternative economic activities was fracturing along regional lines.

CHAPTER 9

The Center-South Adapts to New Conditions, 1922–1930

Efforts of political elites from the Northeast and South to stimulate products relevant to their regions between 1919 and 1922 ignored the political realities of the First Republic. With their departure from political power, between 1922 and 1930, the Minas Gerais-São Paulo *café com leite* (coffee with milk) political alliance redefined the nation's priorities. Mineiran Artur Bernardes, National President from 1922 to 1926, oriented Brazil's economic policy toward supporters in the Center-South, especially coffee growers. Paulista Washington Luiz Pereira de Souza ratified and solidified a coffee-centric orientation during his presidency from 1926 to 1930 while promoting the state's cotton production. The process consolidated the Center-South's position as the hub of innovation for agriculture while the Northeast and extreme South remained challenged by nature and custom. The successful adaption of innovative technologies, through strong foreign—and especially U.S.—ties, became central to improvements in São Paulo's cotton cultivation and the cattle and beef sectors throughout the Center-South region.

Restoring Support Level for Coffee

The revival of coffee prices in the 1920s and support from politicians from Minas Gerais and São Paulo had conflicting impacts on diversification efforts in the Center-South. Coffee prices had begun to recover in the

E. R. Downes, *Brazilian Agricultural Development, 1890–1950*,
https://doi.org/10.1007/978-3-031-76992-4_9

final days of the war when a severe frost in 1918 reduced the supply. The resumption of international trade increased demand, and then a briefly successful valorization scheme prevented excess supply from swamping the market. Coffee prices doubled between 1918 and 1919, and by 1920 the coffee stock was exhausted. The forecast of an overflow crop in 1920–21 forced prices down momentarily and brought about renewed valorization efforts with support of President Pessoa, anxious to retain São Paulo's backing for his drought-relief program. Consequently, Pessoa painted the issue as having "national" instead of merely state importance.[1]

During the Bernardes administration, the valorization plan served up important short-term benefits. Real coffee prices continued their upward climb and by 1926 stood at nearly double their 1914 level (see Fig. 9.1). Total foreign exchange earnings from coffee exports increased by more than fifty percent for the entire 1921–1930 decade, compared with the previous decade, far outpacing the fifteen percent increase in the volume of exports. Federal monetary policies multiplied the impact of higher coffee prices, increasing revenues from coffee and other goods even further. Liberal growth of the money supply and devaluation of the *milreis* from 1920 through 1925 increased local currency revenues from coffee exports. In local currency, the price of coffee rose by 700% between 1917 and 1924.[2]

The 1926 inauguration of São Paulo's Washington Luiz Pereira de Souza, in accordance with the accepted practice of rotating the national presidency between Minas Gerais and São Paulo, heralded the return of political support for coffee cultivation. Washington Luiz had served as President of São Paulo state between 1922 and 1926, when the state assumed the primary role in defense of coffee prices from the federal

[1] Joseph L. Love, *São Paulo in the Brazilian Federation, 1889–1945* (Stanford, CA.: Stanford Univ. Press, 1971), p. 47; Affonso de E. Taunay, *Pequena história do café no Brasil (1727–1927)* (Rio de Janeiro: Departamento Nacional de café, 1945), pp. 531–2, 549; Annibal Villanova Villela and Wilson Suzigan, *Government Policy and Economic Growth of Brazil, 1889–1945* (Rio de Janeiro: IPEA/IPES, 1977), p. 119; Epitácio Pessoa, *Pela Verdade!* (Rio de Janeiro: Livraria Francisco Alves, 1925), p. 181.

[2] Thomas H. Holloway, *Immigrants on the Land: Coffee and Society in São Paulo, 1886-1934* (Chapel Hill: Univ. of North Carolina Press, 1980), pp. 177, 181; *Brazilian Economic Studies*, 121; Taunay, *Pequena história do café*, p. 549. For effects of a devalued milreis on the coffee sector, see Joseph L. Love, *Rio Grandedo Sul and Brazilian Regionalism, 1882-1930* (Stanford: Stanford Univ. Press, 1971), p. 113.

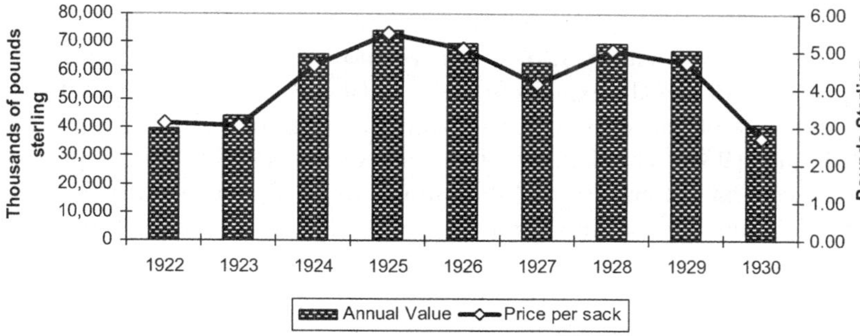

Fig. 9.1 Brazilian coffee production and prices, 1922–1930 (*Source* Calculated from Instituto Brasileiro de Geografia e Estatística, Repertório Estatístico do Brasil, Quadros retrospectivas No. 1 [Rio de Janeiro: Serviço Gráfico do Instituto Brasileiro de Geografia e Estatística, 1941], p. 85)

government through creation of the Instituto Paulista da Defesa Permanente do Café in 1924. The Institute—renamed the Instituto de Café do Estado de São Paulo in 1926—prevented price oscillation by regulating and financing storage and sale of coffee exported through the port of Santos. Coffee profits and new planting soared, creating a productive capacity by 1930 that stood 50% above that of 1918. The resulting boom benefited planters, exporters, and the coffers of the state of São Paulo alike, as coffee export taxes often provided over 50% of the state's income. São Paulo's state revenues measured in 1912 *contos de reis* more than doubled between 1920 and 1927. During the 1920s, São Paulo garnered 36.1% of income obtained by all Brazilian state governments. As Joseph Love emphasizes, "São Paulo's revenues were huge even by Brazilian standards."[3] Minas Gerais, which produced 20% of the nation's coffee crop, and Rio de Janeiro state, producing eight percent of the crop's output, also benefited from higher coffee prices and export taxes levied at ports in each state.[4]

[3] Wilson Cano, "Da Decada de 1920 à de 1930: Transição Rumo à Crise e a Industrialização no Brasil," *Revista EconomiA*, Brasilia, DF, Vol. 13, No. 3b (Sept.-Dec. 2012), 902; Holloway, *Immigrants*, pp. 46–47; Love, *São Paulo*, pp. 246, 265, 302. São Paulostill had to pay out significant sums on foreign loans, adding to an overall deficit in the state's accounts. See Love, *São Paulo*, pp. 304–5.

[4] For a detailed discussion of the coffee support schemes, see Winston Fritsch, *External Constraints on Economic Policy in Brazil, 1889–1930* (Pittsburgh, PA: Univ. of Pittsburgh

Coffee also regained its prominence in Brazil's foreign trade. Once again coffee dominated Brazil's exports, moving from only 37 and 31%, respectively, of Brazil's exports in 1917 and 1918, to account for between 60 and 76% of the value of the nation's exports in every year between 1921 and 1930. The United States remained Brazil's most important customer, and coffee resumed its importance in Brazilian exports to the United States, accounting for up to 87% of U.S. imports of Brazilian products.[5]

Coffee's profitability had both negative and positive effects on agricultural diversification within the Center-South. Brazil imported more foodstuffs each year from 1925 to 1927 than it had in 1913, including from 10 to 95 thousand tons of cereals other than wheat. While land devoted to coffee production nearly doubled between 1926 and 1928, land planted for corn production fell steadily after 1925, as did corn production itself. The growing of rice, another crop that saw its price slide, failed to keep pace with population growth. Even Hunnicutt, long an advocate of cultivating foodstuffs, offered advice on growing coffee, in his words, "a lucrative crop."[6] On the positive side, higher coffee prices provided funds for an aggressive state effort to improve local cultivation of cotton. The general prosperity and robust infrastructure of the Center-South region encouraged investors to foster improvements in the cattle and beef sector. Absent a national plan for agricultural development, regional politicians facilitated the improvement of products relevant to their political bases.

Press, 1988), pp. 53–169; Almir Pita Freitas Filho, "A política de defesa permanente do café na década de 1920 e o Instituto do Fomento e Economia Agrícola do Estado de Rio de Janeiro: notas para uma história institucional," *Anais do XXVI Simpósio Nacional de História-ANPUH*, São Paulo (July 2011).

[5] USBFDC, *Commerce Yearbook 1924* (Washington: GPO, 1925), p. 522; 1926, II, 84; 1930, II, 78. Taunay, *Pequena história do café*, p. 549.

[6] "A producção Agrícola no Brasil," *Boletím* [MAG], Vol. 18, No. 1 (1929), 65–68; USBFDC, *Commerce Yearbook 1930* (Washington: GPO, 1930), Vol. II, 73; "Cultura de arroz no Brasil," *Boletím* [MAG], Vol. 17, No. 2 (1928), 739–86; Benjamin H. Hunnicutt, "A defesa do cafe," *O Agricultor*, Vol. 5, No. 3 (1926), 7.

Cotton: The Advantages of the Center-South

Coffee's prosperity had some positive effects on São Paulo's agricultural development. The state's favorable economic conditions allowed for expanded state support for developing a variety of non-coffee crops. In 1925, the state created a service dedicated to researching disease-resistant sugar cane varieties and supporting the state's sugar industry. The Serviço de Defesa da Canna de Assucar was endowed in 1928 with a 50-hectare experimental station at Piraçicaba. Between 1927 and 1929, the sugar service distributed nearly 500 tons of cane shoots.[7] In 1927, the state expanded the functions of the Instituto Agronômico to include furnishing seeds and saplings to the state's farmers, studies on animal fodder, and conducting research with a variety of crops at experimental sub-stations throughout the state.[8] It also began supporting citriculture by founding the Serviço de Citricultura within the Instituto Agronômico. Among crops that benefited from the state's more robust institutional support for agriculture was cotton. São Paulo's cotton so benefited from scientific experimentation and significant foreign investment that it became to be considered as a viable alternative to the state's long-held focus on coffee.

Cotton had long been planted in São Paulo, and wartime conditions had provoked its appearance among the endless files of coffee plants, even more so after a 1918 freeze destroyed thousands of coffee trees. Tenants in established areas of the state and those purchasing land in the Northwestern zones of the state planted cotton among beans and corn as a cash crop. On the immense coffee plantation of Carlos Schmidt, one of the "kings of coffee," cotton planting was so advanced that agronomist Day estimated that some 4,000 arrobas would be harvested in 1919.[9]

Postwar São Paulo's raw cotton production continually surpassed earlier levels and occasionally even challenged production levels of the Northeast. The state's 1919 cotton crop was the largest in recent

[7] São Paulo[state], Departamento de Fomento da Produção Vegetal, *Exposição do Cincoentenario da Immigração de São Paulo: estatística e publicações* (São Paulo: Secretaria da Agricultura, Industria e Commercio do Estado de São Paulo, 1935), pp. 1–4; São Paulo [state*], Mensagem 1930*, p. 40.

[8] Carlos Borges Schmidt and Jose Reis, *Rasgasando Horizontes: a Secretaria da Agricultura de S. Paulo no seu Cinquentenário* (São Paulo: N.P., 1942), pp. 38–72.

[9] Arno S. Pearse, *Brazilian Cotton* (Manchester, Eng.: International Federation of Master Cotton Spinners and Manufacturers' Association, 1923), pp. 84–88; "A cultura do algodoeiro em São Paulo," *Brasil Agrícola*, Vol. 3 (1919), 58.

history—three times the 1918 harvest and 31% of national production. Nationwide, later estimates indicated that cotton production increased by 23% between 1916 and 1918. The 1919 crop registered a booming 37% rise over the 1916 figure.[10] While the Northeast still produced 67% of the crop, no single state matched São Paulo's output that year. In 1922 Ceará and Paraíba grew more cotton than São Paulo, but São Paulo regained its position as the top producing state in 1923.[11]

The crop's success stimulated new plantings and visions of cotton-based prosperity. The U.S. Consul in São Paulo reported in 1923 that many small farmers "are not only starting cotton plantations in addition to the cultivation of other crops," but even "devoting their entire attention to cotton." Even "many owners of extensive tracts of land," noted the consul, "are starting cotton growing on a large scale."[12] São Paulo's cotton-producing capabilities evoked high praise from the ubiquitous Arno S. Pearse during his tour of Brazil. Speaking at São Paulo's Cinema Central on May 17, 1921, he praised the productivity of São Paulo cotton—higher than that of India, Egypt, or the United States. He stressed that "fertile lands, a climate with regular seasons, rainfall, excellent railways [and] well-equipped seaports" were allowing São Paulo to produce cotton "without fearing any competitor." In his opinion, only greater state support for education and experimentation in cotton, as well as increased private or public interest in seed farms and demonstration fields, were necessary for São Paulo to fulfill its potential. Pearse urged greater government support for education and experimentation in

[10] "A prensagem do Algodão para exportação," *O Progresso*, Vol. 7, No. 67 (1919), 61; Pupo Nogueira, "A indústria algodoeira em São Paulo," *Annaes da Conferência Algodoeira Internacional* (N.P.: n.p., ca. 1922), Vol. II, 337; Brazil, Serviço do Algodão, *Possibilidades da cultura algodoeira no Brasil por William W. Coelho de Souza* (Rio de Janeiro: Impr. Nac., 1922), p. 20; Figures from the Serviço do Algodão quoted in *A Lavoura*, Vol. 28 (1924), 426.

[11] Brazil, Directoria Geral de Estatística, Synopse da Agricultura, Vol. 7 of *Recenseamento do Brasil... 1920* (Rio de Janeiro: Typographia da Estatística, 1922), pp. 82–83; *A Lavoura*, Vol. 28 (1924), 511; "Cotton producing in Brazil," *Monthly Bulletin of the British Chamber of Commerce*, Vol. 7 (1925), 459; See state production statistics cited in USC-SP to SS, Dec. 28, 1928, and USE-RJ to SS, Mar. 26, 1930, both in Box 57, RG 166, USNA.

[12] USC-SP to SS, Sept. 15, 1923, Box 57, RG 166, USNA.

cotton, as well as increased private or public interest in seed farms and demonstration fields.[13]

The prosperity of São Paulo funded continued research to do just that—based, as in the past, on U.S. technical information and equipment to meet the demand from European and internal markets for short-staple cotton. Shortly after the 1922 cotton conference, São Paulo State President Washington Luiz authorized the Instituto Agronômico at Campinas to devote more attention to all aspects of cotton production in the state, including seed production and distribution, soil treatment and crop protection. Former federal cotton service chief Coelho de Souza, who had left the cotton service in February 1923, became director of the state's newly created cotton section in December 1923 and promptly set about to increase seed production. His assistant, Raimundo Cruz Martins, had studied cotton in various parts of Mississippi and returned in late 1923 with sufficient seeds to begin breeding experiments. Using techniques acquired in the United States, Cruz Martins supervised crossing of a variety of U.S.-grown cottons in the 1924 and 1925 harvests. His experiments led to the successful adaptation of two Texas Upland cotton types to the São Paulo environment.[14]

The federal government also invested in cotton research using São Paulo as a base. It authorized an "experimental station" for cotton (and jute) in January 1923, commencing a search for the best variety for soil to be found in São Paulo and elsewhere. The Piraçicaba station had been planting cotton in a haphazard manner earlier but began an experimental plan in 1923 based upon those conducted at U.S. cotton stations. Scholarship student and 1919 Lavras graduate Cristovam Dantas returned from the United States with 18 varieties of cotton seeds to obtain a more resistant but abundant and uniform strain. Two years of experiments following "the system adopted by the 'Central Station' of Texas" on 60

[13] "A cultura de Algodão em São Paulo," *Annaes da SRB*, Vol. 1 (1921), 803–5.

[14] *Boletím Algodoeiro*, Vol. 1, No. 4 (1923), 23; Raimundo Firmino Cruz Martins, "'Breeding' de algodão," *Boletím* [MAG], Vol. 13, No. 6 (1924), 37–57; "Acção dos serviços oficiaes em prol do algodão nestes últimos tempos," *Revista da SRB*, Vol. 10 (1930); Benjamin H. Hunnicutt, *Brazil: World Frontier* (New York: D. Van Nostrand, 1949), p. 121; "Homenageando os pioneiros da cultura e commercio do algodão," *Correio Paulista*, Apr. 28, 1935, p. 4.

alqueires of land yielded seven types—"all noble varieties cultivated in North America"—successfully adapted to São Paulo's environment.[15]

The increasing concentration of Brazil's textile industry in São Paulo also provided strong incentives for further development of the state's cotton. Following the war, São Paulo state became the center of Brazil's textile industry. Whereas in prewar Brazil São Paulo had consumed less cotton than Northeastern states, in the three years after the war São Paulo's mills used from five to ten times the cotton consumed by Northeastern mills. Between 1905 and 1920, the number of plants in São Paulo increased by three-fold and the total number of spindles by a factor of five.[16]

The appeal of São Paulo's Upland cotton in foreign markets encouraged the state and possible producers. The German delegate to the 1922 cotton conference emphasized his nation's interest in São Paulo cotton. "Germany has," he remarked, "the greatest interest in the development of cotton cultivation in Brazil, but especially in the intensification of cotton production in the state of São Paulo." São Paulo's medium and short-staple cotton resembled "almost completely" the U.S. cotton purchased by Germany, and the German delegate urged the Brazilian government to devote "energetic initiative" to developing cotton, a crop with "the most brilliant perspectives for the future."[17]

British investors agreed that cotton's future could be found in the South. The Brazil Plantations Syndicate Ltd. decided to invest in cotton production in southern São Paulo and northern Paraná in mid-1924. Backers based their decision upon precise information on Brazilian cotton, as Lord Lovat, a leading figure of the 1924 British financial mission, was one of the Syndicate's directors. Other helpful information came from Edward C. Green, praised by Syndicate officials for placing "his knowledge of Brazil... at our disposal in all our negotiations." Dr. Emilio Castello, former head of the Piraçicaba school and who had spent six

[15] Arno S. Pearse found some 40 hectares of different species under cultivation there in 1921. Pearse, *Brazilian Cotton*, p. 83; "O trabalho experimental na Estação Experimental de Piraçicaba," *Boletím* [MAG], Vol. 14, No. 6 (1925), 728; Octavio Domingues, "Estação Experimental de Piraçicaba," *Revista da SRB*, Vol. 6 (1925), 259–61; Vol. 6 (1926), 142; USC-SP to SS, May 4, 1925, RG 166, Box 57, USNA.

[16] Figures cited by USC-SP to SS, Nov. 24, 1922, 832.61321, RG 59, USNA.

[17] Oscar G. Mors, "O interesse da indústria....," *Annaes da Conferência Internacional*, II, 323.

months studying cotton in the United States, became one of the syndicate's "managers."[18] Support came from the federal government through a decree (16,396 of February 27, 1924) authorizing loans, freight reductions, and tax exemptions to companies that would raise and process cotton. Companies receiving such favors were obligated to plant at least 1,000 hectares of cotton annually and maintain machinery that small cotton farmers could use to process their crops. The U.S. Consul in Rio de Janeiro linked the decree to British investors and Arno S. Pearse, since "it is generally understood that his purpose in coming to this country was to organize a company to engage in large scale production and ginning of cotton."[19]

Demands from foreign customers for heightened cotton production conflicted with growing domestic demand. The British Chamber of Commerce expressed its concern in 1924: "The consumption of Brazilian cotton in national mills in greatly increasing year by year, a factor which has considerably restrained export." Between 1920 and 1927, and despite a crisis within the textile industry caused by a rise in British cloth imports, domestic industry consumed an average of over 77% of the nation's cotton production, including over 89% of the crop in 1926[20] (see Fig. 9.2).

Merchants, a pioneering agronomist, and the state bureaucracy sought to strengthen São Paulo's cotton during the final four years of the First Republic despite shifting market conditions. Cotton prices in 1926 remained in a downward spiral that had begun in 1924, dropping from a high of 26$000 per arroba (15 kilos) of unginned cotton in 1924 to 8$000 in 1926 for the same amount.[21] The lower prices reflected a crisis in the textile industry caused by the restrictive monetary policy of the Washington Luiz government and the flood of cheap textile imports from British mills. Higher coffee prices also may have encouraged some planters

[18] *Bulletin of the Pan American Union,* No. 34, (Jan.-June 1912), 110; *Wileman's Brazilian Review*, May 21, 1924; "Brazilian Plantation Syndicate," *The Times*, Oct. 20, 1925, p. 21, col. 4.

[19] U.S. Consul-Rio de Janeiro to SS, Mar. 12, 1924, RG 166, Box45, USNA.

[20] British Chamber of Commerce Brazil, *Monthly Bulletin*, Vol. 6, No. 63 (June 1924), 60.

[21] Prices quoted from the Centro das Industrias de Fiação e Tecelagem and reported by USC-SP to SS, July 21, 1927, Box 57, RG 166, USNA.

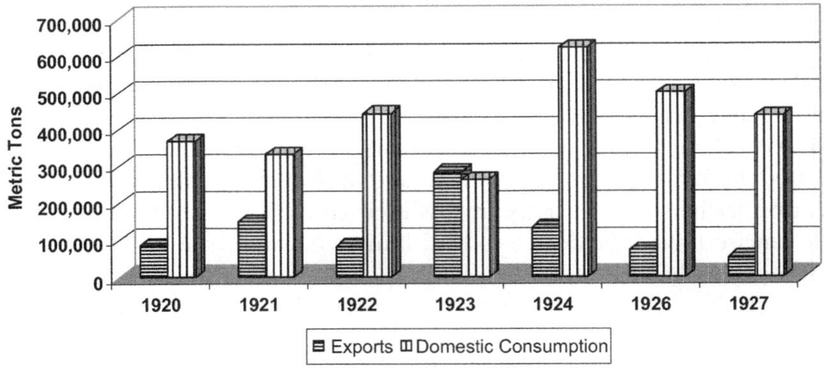

Fig. 9.2 Destinations of Brazilian cotton production, 1920–1926 (*Source* USC-São Paulo to SS, Dec. 26, 1928, RG 166, Box 57, USNA)

to shift production from cotton to coffee.[22] Higher coffee prices and lower cotton prices, coupled with pest infestation in the cotton fields, led to removal of land from cotton production in the state. From 48,407 alqueires (290,442 acres) in cotton cultivation for the 1924–25 crop, total land in cotton shrank 55% to only 21,780 alqueires (140,680 acres) by 1927. The state's cotton production also fell, from over 5.9 million arrobas in 1925 to 3.7 million in 1926 and then 1.9 million arrobas in 1927.[23]

The decreased production of local cotton prompted a response from São Paulo's cotton textile industry, now forced to import large quantities of cotton from northern states. Leading the effort was São Paulo's Bolsa de Mercadorias, a commodities exchange founded in November 1917 to provide an outlet for locally grown cereals, immediately after President Braz's plea for increased production. In 1925, the exchange added a cotton grader in the person of José Garibaldi Dantas (brother of Cristovam Dantas), who had studied cotton growing in Georgia for two years after graduating from Hunnicutt's Lavras school in 1918. From his strategic post, he began to enforce strict commercial standards for São

[22] USC-São Paulo to SS, June 21, 1926, Box 57, RG 166, USNA. On government monetary policy, see Fritsch, *External Constraint*, pp. 110–111.

[23] São Paulostate figures cited in USC-SP to SS, Dec. 28, 1928, pp. 8, 10, Box 57, RG 166, USNA.

Paulo's cotton.[24] The exchange also became heavily involved in cultivation of seeds for future crops by contracting local farmers to create cooperation fields (*campos de cooperação*) that received technical assistance from the exchange. Problems with the cooperation fields' harvest of 1926 highlighted the dilemmas created by low productivity, improper harvesting techniques, and improper baling—lessons useful to the state when it assumed responsibility for the cooperation fields the following year (Fig. 9.3).[25]

São Paulo's merchant community and textile industry then embarked upon a lobbying campaign to elevate the state government's assistance to cotton. The SRB petitioned the state Secretary of Agriculture for relief in early 1926. It argued that the state should create a cotton defense

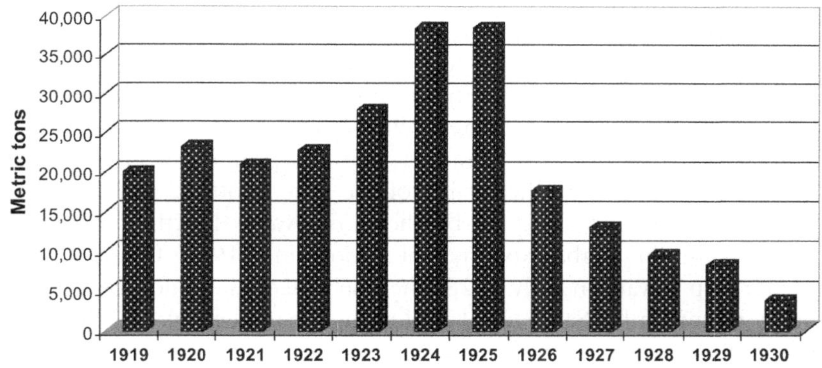

Fig. 9.3 São Paulo cotton production, 1919–1930 (*Source* Rui Henrique Pereira Lima de Albuquerque, *Capital comercial, indústria têxtil e produção agricola: as relações de produção na cotonicultura paulista, 1920–1950* [São Paulo: HUCITEC; Brasilia: Conselho Nacional de Desenvolvimento Científico e Tecnológico, 1983], p. 116)

[24] *O Agricultor*, Vol. 6, No. 1 (1925), 6; Hunnicutt, *Brazil: World Frontier*, p. 120; Bolsa de Mercadorias de São Paulo, *Relatório e contas da Commissão Installadora* (São Paulo: Casa Duprat, 1918), pp. 4–9.

[25] Rui Henrique Pereira Lima de Albuquerque, *Capital comercial, indústria têxtil e produção Agrícola: as relações de produção na cotonicultura paulista, 1920–1950* (São Paulo: HUCITEC; Brasilia: Conselho Nacional de Desenvolvimento Científico e Tecnológico, 1983), pp. 123–127.

institute similar to that functioning for coffee, establish cotton experimental farms statewide, exercise an exclusive right to sell cotton seeds, and be authorized to purchase cotton stocks during periods of lower prices and award prizes for innovations to improve productivity.[26] In July the following year, the state's textile industry urged the legislature to adopt a similar plan. The bulk of its recommendations were incorporated into a decree issued six weeks later that inserted state government directly into the state's cotton growing and processing industry. The decree granted the Secretary of Agriculture control over sales of cotton seeds to ensure cultivation of a uniform variety of cotton. It also required licensing of cotton gins, presses, and storage facilities and that all cotton sold in the state be officially classified. It also created a section within the state's agricultural directorate dedicated to technical support for cotton and other textile-related plants.[27]

Pressure to implement technical standards for São Paulo's cotton crop came from the Bolsa de Mercadorias, where Garibaldi Dantas carried forward his campaign to raise the productivity and marketability of the state's cotton crop as the exchange's chief of classification. Many concepts in September 1927 decree stemmed from his promotion of increasing state support for raising the quality of the state's cotton, aided by technical information provided by brother Cristovam, directing trials with cotton at the Piraçicaba experimental station since 1923. Garibaldi took a major step toward in early 1928 when he issued an opinion on the best variety of cotton for São Paulo based upon experiments at the Piraçicaba station. Responding to many requests for a recommendation on the topic, he stated his conclusion that the Russell "Big Boll" variety imported into São Paulo from the United States by former cotton service director Emilio Castello 20 years earlier best fit local growing conditions. He reported that the "Russell" had been planted "in the most diverse regions of the State" and "shown its true merits and superiority over other varieties introduced during the same period." This variety was especially appropriate for smallholder cultivators in São Paulo, in Garibaldi's opinion,

[26] USC-RJ to SS, Apr. 14, 1926, Box 57, RG 166, USNA.

[27] *O Paiz*, July 27, 1927, p. 4. State of São Paulo decree No. 4.454, Sept. 11, 1928. "Acção dos serviços officaes em prol do algodão nestes últimos tempos," *Annaes da SRB*, Vol. 10, No. 126 (Nov. 1930), 1342–44.

since it could be harvested by farmers "who so far do not use the best mechanical practices."[28]

The São Paulo government responded by stepping up its assistance to cotton cultivation. Continuing breeding experiments at the Instituto Agronômico began to yield high-quality seeds distributed to cooperative fields, now under state authority. By 1927 these fields produced almost 330 tons of seeds, and then an average of over 400 tons per year through 1930. Garibaldi Dantas even suggested in 1928 that cotton could serve as an alternative for coffee planters beset by falling coffee prices. By planting cotton on lands devoted to coffee and on new lands, São Paulo cotton producers could furnish 1.5 million bales for export, equal to one-fourth the U.S. export crop. This would be eminently beneficial, in his opinion, because São Paulo cotton producers enjoyed a 25% advantage over the United States in production costs.[29]

By 1929 the falling price of coffee gave substance to Garibaldi's suggestions. "Low prices for coffee during the past two years have stimulated the planting of cotton," reported the U.S. Consul in 1931.[30] By 1930 São Paulo could claim that it was "a greater [cotton] production center than the Northeast," with cotton that was "easy to export... finding easy placement in any of the most demanding European markets." The state government was "perfectly equipped" to aid those interested in planting cotton by providing seeds for "Texas Big Boll" and "Express" varieties developed through its cooperative fields.[31]

Garibaldi Dantas later summed up the reasons for the phenomenal growth. He cited the fall of coffee as the principal factor convincing Paulista farmers of the need for an alternative. Also important were improvements in seed quality, availability of banking and transportation systems created to serve the coffee sector but available to cotton growers,

[28] "O Algodão," *Correio Paulistano*, Jan, 9, 1928.

[29] USC-SP to SS, Dec. 28, 1928, Box 57, RG 166, USNA. For cooperative fields, the landowners cleared the land and provided animals and some labor necessary for cultivation. The federal and state governments provided seeds, a share of labor costs and machinery for planting and processing the crop. See Brazil, Serviço do Algodão, *Relatório 1920* (Rio de Janeiro: Papaleria Americana, 1920), pp. 51, 57.

[30] USC-SP to SS, July 23, 1931, Box 57, RG 166, USNA.

[31] "A importância da cultura do algodoeiro para São Paulo," *Revista da SRB*, Vol. 10 (1930), 1232; "Acção dos Serviço oficiaes em prol do Algodão nestes últimos tempos," *Revista da SRB*, Vol. 10 (1930), 1343–4.

a lower rate of exchange for the Brazilian currency, technical knowledge, moderate taxation, the availability of new land parcels, and the arrival of new immigrants.[32]

He did not mention the importance of ties between São Paulo's cotton and that of the United States, but these also were obvious. From the initial training of the most prominent cotton experts in the state, including himself and brother Cristovam, to the adoption of U.S. techniques, equipment and most importantly, the same variety of cotton most popular in the United States, the process created an enduring link between the cotton cultivation of both nations.

The Center-South and the Cattle and Meat Packing Sectors

The cattle and beef processing industry of the Center-South underwent a similar transformation toward prosperity during the final eight years of the First Republic. The region enjoyed high local demand, favorable natural conditions, and a renewed external demand for its frozen beef, leading to favorable conditions for those who sold cattle to the São Paulo. Meanwhile, stockmen in Rio Grande do Sul remained dependent upon jerky plants (*charqueadores*) as the principal market outlet for their cattle. Ties with foreign capital remained strong in both regions, but the better results for the cattle and beef processing industry in the Center-South epitomized the benefits attainable from serving Brazil's growing urban population and the dangers of relying on export markets.[33]

The foreign ties of the Center-South's cattle and beef processing industry, like that of efforts to improve the São Paulo's cotton production, were strong. Foreign—predominantly U.S.—capital and U.S.-origin equipment figured prominently in the meat packing industry, dependent upon refrigeration to distribute of its products beyond the reach of traditional slaughterhouse. Two U.S. companies operated plants in suburbs of São Paulo that had arisen from wartime conditions: Continental Products at Presidente Altino (formerly known as Osasco), and Amour at Lapa.

32 *Correio da Manhã*, Mar. 11, 1938, p. 2.

33 See Wilson Cano, *Raizes da concentração industrial em São Paulo*, 4th ed. (Campinas, SP: Unicamp, IE, 1998), pp. 116–132.

The Vestey interests of England operated a plant at Barretos, 435 kilometers northwest of São Paulo, and another at the port of Santos. These foreign-owned packing houses produced over 59% of total packing house products between 1922 and 1930. Two Brazilian entrepreneurs were also engaged in the sector. Antonio Bianco was a wealthy rancher who built a plant at Cruzeiro, 226 kilometers northeast of São Paulo at the junction of railroads serving Minas Gerais and Rio de Janeiro. The plant opened in 1928 with an estimated US$500,000 in U.S.-made machinery and was designed to serve the Rio de Janeiro area. Antonio Simonini erected a plant at his own expense under a concession from the *municipio* of Santo Amaro, near São Paulo, which had a negligible production during this period.[34]

Closely connected to the packing plants were cattle companies—also foreign-owned—possessing often vast tracts of land for preparing animals for delivery to the packing plants. Armour, Continental Products, and the Vestey companies all possessed their own ranches. The Brazilian Land Cattle and Packing Company, formerly owned by Percival Farquhar but in creditors' hands since 1913, maintained extensive tracts of land in Mato Grosso, Minas Gerais, and São Paulo. Two English firms—Waldron and Wood and Tres Barros Syndicate, as well as the U.S.-owned Boston Cattle Company, also raised and pastured cattle within one or more of the three states.[35]

Initially, both stockmen and representatives from the packing sector in the Center-South retained expectations of profiting from foreign markets. Supported by the state's agricultural institutions, they sustained efforts to improve the quality of Brazilian beef by importing both European and Zebu breeds. As a member of the special commission on cattle of the SRB, Continental Products manager Leopoldo Plaut cautioned in 1924 that without improvements "our present type of cattle" Brazilian beef could not compete in the London market. Stockman J. D. Martins, "one of the most energetic and advanced cattle raisers in the state," repeated the need for "developing and perfecting the cattle industry through large-scale importation of breeders of the European races of beef," offering a

[34] USC-SP to SS, Aug. 12, 1930, Box 64, RG 166, USNA.

[35] USC-São Paulo to SS, Feb 18, 1924, Box 64, RG 166, USNA.

promise of higher prices for the resulting better grade of beef.[36] Advocates of the Zebu breed also continued promoting their favored breed. In 1928, the Sociedade Rural do Triangulo Mineiro (the Rural Society of the Minas Triangle) came into being, representing most Zebu breeders in the region. Symbolic of the newly found acceptability of the Zebu was the invitation that the new society extended to Sampiao Vidal, a founding member of the SRB and previous opponent of Zebu imports, as the society's honorary president.[37]

Their efforts and subsidies provided by São Paulo allowed it to boast of improvements in the herd, even though the traditional Caracú breed probably remained dominant. By late 1926, the state Directoria de Industria Pastoril (Bureau of Animal Husbandry) could report to the U.S. Consulate that "during the past ten years our cattle industry has developed greatly." It boasted that "our pastoral industry has attained truly important development" through "zootechnical methods opportunely applied, improvement of pastures by cultivation of new grasses and increased planting of alfalfa, the importation of blooded stock and selection of native stock, [and] the surprising increases in the various branches of the dairy industry," among other measures.[38]

The federal government and other states in the Center-South complemented their support, even though the sector's advocates and observers probably overstated the impact of their efforts. Rio de Janeiro created an animal husbandry section within its Department of Agriculture in July 1924, while private and public efforts in Minas Gerais supported imports of Swiss, Holland, and Holstein cattle, the later for the state's growing dairy industry. The U.S. Consul in Rio de Janeiro reported "great headway" in improving cattle in Minas Gerais, with over 3 million cattle registered in the 1920 census. Breeding in Minas Gerais had been "so beneficial that an added impetus has been given to the industry," he observed. However, the Ministry of Agriculture's actions in support of importing purebreds were decidedly modest. From 1921 through 1926,

[36] *Brazilian-American*, June 10, 1922, quoted in Nash, *The Conquest of Brazil*, p. 271; "Pareceres e consultas," *Revista da SRB*, Vol. 5 (1924), 76.

[37] Joana Medrado, "Do Pastoreio à Pecuária: A invenção da modernização rural nos sertões do Brasil Central" (Diss.: Universidade Federal Fluminense, 2013), pp. 156–157.

[38] USC-São Paulo to SS, Dec. 21, 1926, Box 64, RG 166, USNA.

the Ministry sponsored importation of 1,099 animals, as average of less than 200 per year.[39]

In the end, the superior adaptability of the Zebu breeds led to reliance upon beef of Zebu and Zebu-creole crossbreeds to sustain the packing industry. The excessive costs of improving the herds by importing breeding cattle, erecting fences, silos and cattle dips, and seeding pastures with improved forage crops left Zebu and creole cattle as the dominant breeds. The U.S. Consul in São Paulo reported in 1924 that "Attempts have been made to introduced foreign blood... have met with little success," and "most of the cattle being slaughtered by the large packing houses in São Paulo are the Zebu." He surmised that "although war conditions gave an impetus to cattle raising in Brazil, little has been accomplished in improving the native strain."[40]

Packing houses benefited from a higher demand from both domestic and foreign sources. Metropolitan São Paulo underwent explosive population growth from 604,248 inhabitants in 1920 to 1,119,934 in 1934, becoming a growing market for foodstuffs, including beef.[41] In early 1924, the U.S. Consul in São Paulo estimated that the city consumed 350 to 400 head of cattle per day.[42] The city's proximity to cattle estates in Minas Gerais, Mato Grosso, and parts of Goiás, along with the state's ample grazing lands facilitated supply. As with the state's cotton cultivation, extensive rail networks provided effective transport of animals to market. A federal government decree of December 31, 1924, that limited slaughter of "cows and heifers suitable for breeding," temporarily reduced animals available for consumption, but a growth in production resumed in 1927.[43] Animal sacrifices in São Paulo state packing houses soared between 1922 and 1930, from only 164,775 in 1922 to 523,388 in 1930 (see Fig. 9.4).

[39] Brazil, MAG, *Relatório,* 1929, p. 308; USC-Rio de Janeiro, to SS, Dec. 6, 1926, Box 64, RG 166, USNA.

[40] See Robert W. Wilcox, "Ranching Modernization in Tropical Brazil: Foreign Investment and Environment in Mato Grosso, 1900–1950," *Agricultural History*, Vol. 32, No. 3 (Summer 2008), 366–92.

[41] Flavio Villaça, *Espaço intraurbano no Brasil* (São Paulo: Studio Nobel, 1998), p. 118.

[42] USC-São Paulo to SS, Feb. 18, 1924, in.

[43] Decree 16,740A cited in USC-São Paulo to SS, Feb. 12, 1925, Box 64, RG 166, USNA.

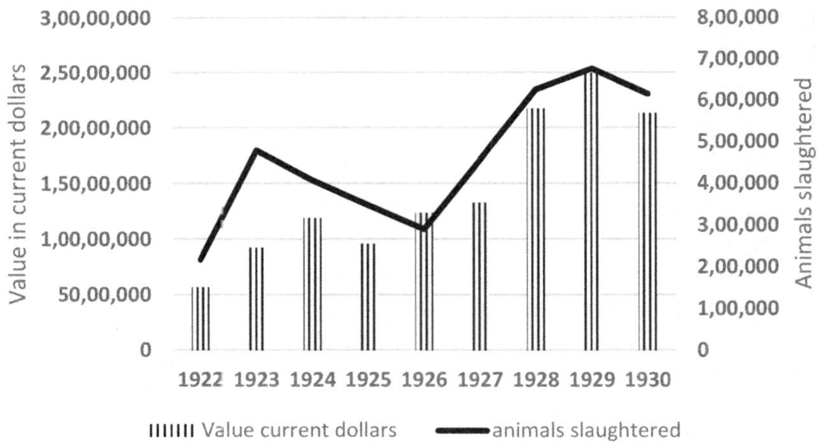

Fig. 9.4 Quantity and value of animals slaughtered in São Paulo Packing Houses, 1922–1930 (*Source* São Paulo [state] Boletim da Directoria de Industria e Commercio, cited in USC-São Paulo to SS, July 14, 1931, Box 65 RG 166, USNA)

Major segments of production were destined for local consumption. From 1928 to 1930, São Paulo packing houses prepared 28% more fresh meat than frozen beef—an annual average of over 55,000 metric tons for the local market. Fresh beef became important to the packing houses' operation. The markets of Santos, Campinas, and São Paulo city consumed an estimated 50,000 head of cattle monthly. The Continental Products plant at Osasco allocated more than one-fourth of its production to fresh meat in 1928, while the Armour plant at Lapa produced 27% more fresh meat than frozen[44] (see Fig. 9.5).

Demand from European markets led to increased imports of Brazilian frozen beef. These climbed consistently from 1927 forward, leading the U.S. Consul in São Paulo to observe that the 1930 production level had been exceeded "only during the years of great activity following the World War, namely 1918 and 1919."[45] Britain was the destination of much of the renewed exports. According to an explanation offered to visitors

[44] Figures cited in USC-SP to SS, Aug. 12, 1930, Box 64, RG 166, USNA.

[45] USC-São Paulo to SS, July 14, 1931, Box 65, RG 166, USNA.

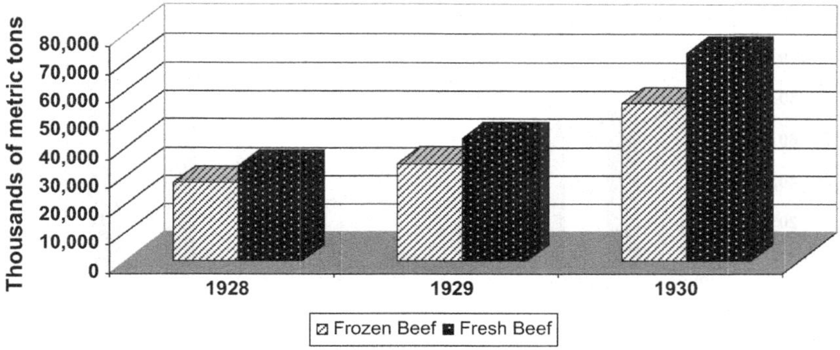

Fig. 9.5 São Paulo Packing House Production of Frozen versus Fresh Beef, 1928–1930 (*Source* São Paulo [state] Boletim da Directoria de Industria e Commercio, cited in USC-São Paulo to SS, July 14, 1931, Box 65 RG 166, USNA)

from the SRB by the staff of the Frigorifico Anglo in Barretos, renewed British imports stemmed from the improved quality of Brazilian beef. They reported that until 1927, Brazilian frozen beef had been "restricted almost exclusively for the consumption of European armies," but scientific breeding methods and the importation of purebred cattle had resulted in a better product.[46] In truth, the renewal of British imports of Brazilian beef was probably due more to improvements in the exchange rate (from the British perspective) and to British concerns in 1927 and 1928 over foot and mouth disease in Argentina, its primary supplier of imported beef. Meat prices in England remained high in 1929 and trade journal references to higher imports of "less expensive frozen beef rather than best chilled beef" almost certainly referred to imports of Brazilian, in lieu of Argentine, beef (Figs. 9.6 and 9.7).[47]

[46] "Sociedade Anonyma Frigorifico Anglo," *Annaes da SRB*, (Dec. 1929), pp. 712–713.

[47] "Producção e consumo mundial de carnes resfriadas e congeladas," Brazil, MAG, *Boletim*, Year 17, Vol. 2, No. 5, 803; *Foreign Crops and Markets*, Vol. 21, No. 8 (1930), 278–279; "High Beef Prices Prevail over World," U.S. Department of Agriculture, *The Official Record*, May 29, 1929, p. 2.

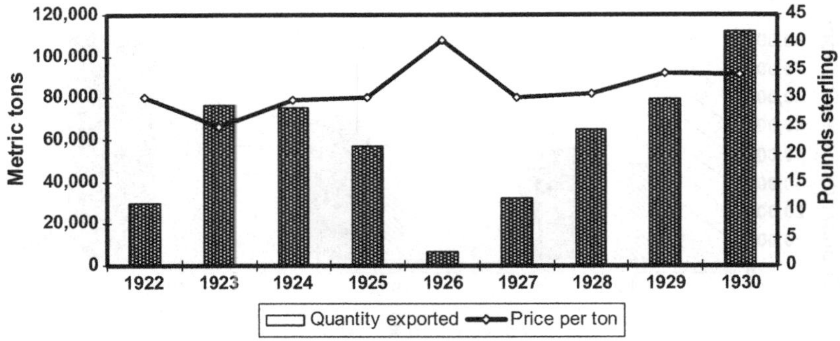

Fig. 9.6 Volume and price per ton of Brazilian Frozen Beef Exports, 1922–1930 (*Source* Brazil, Ministerio da Fazenda, Directoria de Estatística Commercial, *Commercio Exterior do Brasil*, [Rio de Janeiro: Directoria de Estatística Commercial, 1931])

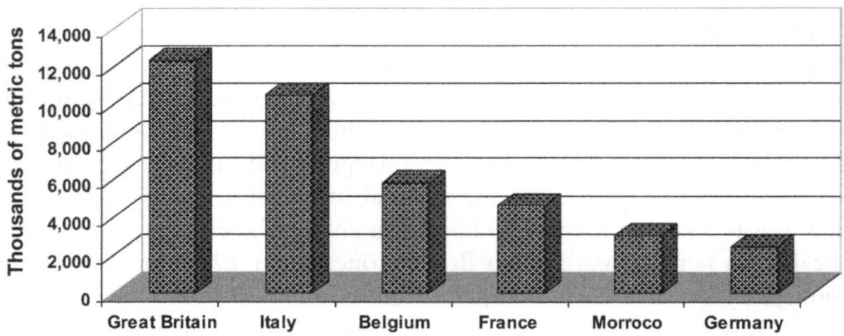

Fig. 9.7 Destination of exports of chilled and frozen beef from São Paulo Packing Houses, 1929 (*Source* São Paulo [state] Boletim da Directoria de Industria e Commercio, cited in USC-São Paulo to SS, July 14, 1931, Box 65 RG 166, USNA)

By 1930 the cattle processing industry of the Center-South, like São Paulo's cotton cultivation, had responded positively to opportunities presented by the region's greater prosperity, access to foreign sources of technology and, in the packing house industry, capital. Ample support from a state infrastructure concerned with creating an agricultural economy marked by "polyculture" in the state was transforming the visions of reformers of earlier years into reality. As with cotton, market realities in the cattle and beef processing industry overtook the notion that Brazil was destined to benefit from its agricultural riches primarily by exporting its products. Domestic demand for cotton drove a focus on the raw material for a burgeoning textile industry. Urbanization in the Center-South, along with extensive transportation networks, allowed mainly foreign capital to utilize new technology to deliver a greater variety of meat products for the domestic markets and profit from changes in foreign market conditions. The argument, put forward at a December 1927 meeting of the SRB, that Brazilian beef had become non-competitive in foreign markets, was proven false.[48] The SRB could correctly state that São Paulo's meat packing industry was enjoying "frank prosperity," with total sales to domestic and foreign markets from 1922 through 1930 of more than US$130 million.[49]

By 1930, the Center-South was achieving higher levels of agriculture-based prosperity than the Northeast and extreme South. Changes facilitated through ties to foreign capital and sources of technology within the cattle, beef, and cotton sectors allowed the Center-South to extract higher value from Brazil's natural endowments. In the First Republic's final years, U.S. capital and educational activities would provide further advantages to the Center-South, thus contributing to the enduring regional imbalance within the nation's agricultural sector.

[48] "Impostos sobre carnes," *Revista da Sociedade Rural Brasileira*, Vol. 8, No. 94 (Mar. 1928), 94.

[49] "Agricultura, Industria e Commercio," *Revista da SRB*, Vol. 10 (1930), 18; Value calculated from São Paulo [state] Boletim da Directoria de Industria e Commercio, cited in USC-São Paulo to SS, July 14, 1931, Box 65 RG 166, USNA.

CHAPTER 10

Education, Extension Services, and Mechanization, 1922–1930

Politicians and bureaucrats during the last eight years of the First Republic also sought to sustain momentum for Brazil's diversified production through substantive changes in services to farmers in the field and adoption of agricultural machinery. Their efforts solidified the role of the Center-South as a national hub of innovation supporting diversified agriculture. In the process, educators from the United States became especially prominent, resulting in higher interaction with U.S. private and public sector entities regarding Brazil's agricultural development needs, especially with respect to technological innovations. U.S. educational methods, extension service practices, and machinery became integral to Brazil's vision as an "essentially agricultural" nation. U.S. educators sought to implant elements of an agricultural extension services with varying degrees of success. Such services would only become viable with intensive federal government support during a forthcoming phase of Brazil's agricultural development.

Rolfs' Extension Services

From his newly inaugurated agricultural school in Minas Gerais, Peter Rolfs took immense pride in outreaching to local farmers and ranchers. The school invited farmers to visit and solicit advice in person and through correspondence. He encouraged them to consider the school

E. R. Downes, *Brazilian Agricultural Development, 1890–1950*,
https://doi.org/10.1007/978-3-031-76992-4_10

"their school," one "destined especially for the instruction of sons of farmers," with students ranging in age from 18 to over 40. In 1930, the "Farmers' Week" (*Semana de Fazendeiros*) hosted 139 farmers and ranchers for several days' instruction in the "most appropriate methods" by the school's professors. The school also processed rice for local farmers lacking appropriate machines. He boasted to the state secretary of agriculture that the Viçosa school was the only school of higher agricultural education in Brazil, "and probably in all of South America," where the farmers and ranchers present themselves for instruction.[1]

Rolf also took a special interest in promoting mechanized agriculture, communicating to his students and the elite of Minas the benefits of mechanization for modern agriculture. He tasked his "Chair of Farm Mechanics" with offering instruction in farm motors of every type, as well as cultivators and harvesting, reaping and milling machinery. As he explained to a gathering at the Viçosa school, "the state of Minas has to adopt mechanical culture or it will always occupy a place of inferiority regarding its agricultural production." He urged every "estate owner [*fazendeiro*], agriculturalist, and farmer to adopt mechanical cultivation."[2]

In Rolfs' opinion, farm owners and foremen [*feitores*] were unaware of the benefits of employing modern implements and machines. Other interests very often "compromise the entire attention" of farm owners who knew "little or nothing about agricultural economics" and cared only about "gross receipts or gross sales." Foremen were "uneducated and frequently illiterate" and jealous of any worker who "manifests an aptitude for becoming a *feitor*," he commented. Furthermore, they regarded with hostility any innovation that threatened their position. "Old time superintendents," wrote Rolfs, when obliged to experiment with farm implements, "consciously or unconsciously ruin the implements or do ruinous work with them." With new methods and improved implements, foremen feared that "their former positions would lose importance." A man who directed two hundred *braços* who used hoes remained more important in the employees' eyes than one directing only ten or fifteen

[1] Escola Superior de Agricultura e Veterinaria do Estado de Minas Gerais, "Annual Report 1928," p. 45; "Annual Report 1930," pp. 8–10, PHRA.

[2] "Conferência realizada 27 de Julho de 1931 a Semana do Fazendeiro...," In Aproveitamento de Braços: Cultura Mecânica de Andrade, Ouividio; Secretario do Agricultura, PHRA.

bracos using modern equipment. Reducing the work gang's size by use of agricultural implements conflicted with the foreman's basis for authority and prestige. The stigma against manual labor, a holdover from slavery, also weighed heavily. "The foreman who directs ten hoe hands," explained Rolfs, "would consider himself forever disgraced to be seen teaching a laborer how to drive a mule and guide a cultivator." This was especially tragic, in Rolfs' opinion, since the foreman alone with a mule and cultivator could have done "even twice as much work and much better, than the ten men with their hoes."[3]

Rolfs illustrated their resistance with an example drawn from his attempt to introduce the plow in cultivation of the school's experimental field. A "young and intelligent Mineiran" charged with preparing the school's experimental field refused to train any of the foreman and nineteen men with hoes assigned for the task. Meanwhile, Rolfs taught a "boy and a native" the use of the disk plow. The illiterate countryman and his son plowed twice the area in a day than the work gang, but the field foreman and the nineteen laborers were "very much displeased by the innovation."[4]

Rolfs also practiced his profession as a citriculturist, focusing on the quality and variety of fruits that could be produced in Brazil as well as their commercialization. Orange cultivation was a topic replete with nationalistic sentiment, as the U.S. success in commercializing oranges shipped from Bahia to the United States by Presbyterian missionary F.J.C. Schneider to California in the 1870 was well known in Brazil. Scholarship student Eugenio Bruck, studying citriculture in Berkeley, California in 1922, had related his encounter with a monument to the first orange tree imported from Bahia into California in Riverside. Bruck regretted that Brazil, despite possessing the "most advantageous conditions of exuberance of natural habitat," was not enriching itself with cultivation of the navel orange. Worse yet, Bruck related, "we regret even more that our golden fruit is not known in world markets as the orange from Bahia,

[3] TS, P. H. Rolfs, "Report to Secretary of Agriculture, Lands, Colonization and Public Works of the State of Minas Gerais," pp. 2–3, May 1930, Box 2, PHRA.

[4] TS, P. H. Rolfs, "Report to Secretary of Agriculture, Lands, Colonization and Public Works of the State of Minas Gerais," pp. 3–4, May 1930, Box 2, PHRA.

or even Bahian Navel, instead of the falsified name of Washington navel orange."[5]

Rolfs engaged in cultivation of Brazilian citrus as an educator, cultivator, and advocate for its commercialization. The Viçosa school presented a complete course on citriculture and offered exhibits of fruits produced on the grounds, including a display of 68 varieties of fruit in June 1927. Rolfs used the school's facilities to produce and sell slips of oranges, limes, and lemons that he had cultivated from plants he imported from the United States. The school sold 1,500 citrus slips in 1927—with a limit of 50 per person, and another 2,500 slips in 1928. Rolfs distributed these to 100 persons and establishments, only partially satisfying total requests for 10,000 shoots.[6] Rolfs also prepared detailed instructions for Brazilian growers on cultivating citrus. He composed a 111-page pamphlet, *A Muda de Citrus* (The Orange Seedling), complete with 37 images, an instruction guide for fruit growers and classroom text.[7]

Rolfs also traveled to the United States as an agent of the Brazilian government to ease restrictions on the importation of Brazilian fruit. Despite the success of a test shipment of Brazilian oranges in 1922, further exports to the United States became impossible because of a U.S. prohibition of imports of oranges from regions that might contain the Mediterranean Fruit Fly. Argentine officials had also embargoed Brazilian fruit based upon recommendations of a USDA consultant.[8] The Ministry of Agriculture commissioned Rolfs to travel to the United States with Felisberto Camargo to argue that the ban be lifted and shipments of Brazilian oranges to Argentine and U.S. ports could resume. The U.S. Federal Horticultural Board listened to the pair's extended

[5] Eugenio Bruck, "A Citricultura na California," *Boletim* (MAG), Vol. XI, No. 3 (Jul.–Sept. 1922), 53.

[6] TS, P. H. Rolfs, "Primeiro Relatório do Director da Escola Superior de Agricultura e Veterinaria de Minas Gerais," 1925, Box 2, PHRA; A. Magarinos Torres, "O estado sanitario das plantas procedentes dos Estados Unidos....," *Boletím* [MAG], 14, No. 6 (1925), 701–707; TS, P. H. Rolfs, "A technical study of Fazenda Retiro of Volta Grande," p. 9, Box 2, PHRA; TS, P. H. Rolfs, "Relatório do Director da Escola Superior de Agricultura e Veterinaria... 1927," PHRA.

[7] TS, P. H. Rolfs, "Relatório do Director da Escola Superior de Agricultura e Veterinaria de Minas Gerais," 1930, PHRA.

[8] R. W. Dunlop [USDA] to SS, Feb. 18, 1926, 811.612/1235, RG 59, USNA; SS to USE-RJ, Mar. 3, 1926, 811.612/1235, USNA; TS, P. H. Rolfs, "Citrus Report" n.d., Box 1, PHRA.

argument and recommended continued study of the matter. Their conclusions apparently agreed with Rolfs' position. Shortly thereafter, Argentina opened its ports to shipments of early oranges, less susceptible to fruit fly infestation.[9]

Brazilian citrus exports climbed steeply after a few years of successful operation of Camargo's São Gonçalo orange packing plant, drawing heavily on U.S.-origin equipment and practices. São Paulo created a citriculture section in 1928, directed by Camargo, and opened experimental sub-stations under direction of the Instituto Agronômico of Campinas at Limeira and Sorocabana. It funded construction of a packing plant in Limeira and turned over its operation to the Citriculture Cooperative of Limeira (Cooperativa dos Citricultores de Limeira), with statutes modeled on those of the California Growers Exchange.[10] In 1929, the Ministry of Agriculture acquired a packing house to be installed in Nova Iguaçu, Rio de Janeiro state, and then obtained three additional packing plants from the United States with support of the USDA to be placed in Rio de Janeiro, Bahia, and Sorocabana, São Paulo. One agronomist-entrepreneur announced plans to plant one million orange trees in 1929. Exports rose sharply. Whereas previous exports of oranges had been to nearby Argentina and Uruguay, exports of Brazilian oranges to Europe rose from 8,000 crates in 1926 to 50,000 by 1928. Total exports shot up from 359,000 crates in 1927 to nearly 900,000 crates in 1930.[11]

[9] TS, Federal Horticultural Board, USDA, "Minutes of May 20, 1926 Meeting," Box 1, PHRA; TS, "Relatório do Director ao Secretário da Agricultura, Industria, Terras, Viação e Obras Públicas," June 10, 1927, Box 1, PHRA; USE-RJ to SS, Apr. 25, 1933, RG 166, USNA. Benjamin Hunnicutt attributed the quarantine on Brazilian oranges to political pressure from Florida and California fruit growers concerned about potential competition from Brazilian oranges. See Benjamin Hunnicutt, *Brazil Looks Forward* (Rio de Janeiro: Serviço Gráfico do Instituto Brasileiro de Geografia e Estatística, 1945), p. 181.

[10] Ramos Filho, Luiz Octávio Ramos Filho, "O papel da pesquisa científica e tecnológica no desenvolvimento da citricultura paulista: análise histórica da atuação do Instituto Agronómico de Campinas (1920–1960)" (Diss: Campinas, SP: 1999), pp. 39–43.

[11] "A laranja brasileira na Europa," *Boletím* [MAG], 18, 1, No. 1 (1929), 120; Eugenio Bruck, "As 'vitaminas' contidas nas laranjas," *Boletím* [MAG], 18, 1, No. 6 (1929), 806; USE-RJ to SS, Apr. 25, 1933, Box 59, RG 166, USNA; *Correio Paulistano*, July 16, 1929, p. 2. São Paulo[state], Departamento de Fomento da Produção Vegetal, *Exposição do Cincoentenario da Immigração de São Paulo: estatística e publicações* (São Paulo: Secretaria da Agricultura, Industria e Commercio do Estado de São Paulo, 1935), p. 21. Brazilian orange production obtained "a stage of relative stability" only with installation of the

Rolfs remained engaged in promoting novel approaches to a broad variety of crops aside from citrus. He served as its director for less than two years and became a technical advisor for the state in 1929, a post he exercised until retiring in 1933 at age 68. During this period, Rolfs converted the school into a resource for the state. In a 96-page set of observations and recommendations for the state secretary of agriculture prepared in early 1930, Rolfs declared that during the previous nine years he had not "spared himself, his time, his money, or his energy" to advance agriculture in the state. He provided recommendations for improving vegetables, coffee, rice, tobacco, beans, sugar, oranges, pineapple, tamarind, tea, silk, and wheat, as well as a variety of animals. He was confident that his recommendations would cheapen production costs and raise the quality of already established products. Combined with increases in worker productivity, they would allow Minas to "open the door of a very rich natural granary." He encouraged the state's leadership to "take advantage of this opportunity, promulgating reforms of fundamental value to the most important industry of the State, Agriculture."[12]

Benjamin Hunnicutt: Extension Services and Mechanization

Rolfs' achievements in establishing an outreach program contrasted sharply with the results of the efforts by Benjamin Hunnicutt, who by 1924 had registered enjoyed considerable progress in establishing the Lavras school. Aided by state, federal, and *municipio* subsidies, Hunnicutt had constructed a small but professional agricultural school that had graduated 53 agronomists, many of whom became resources for the government's diversification efforts, especially with respect to cotton. The school functioned with ten professors, an adequate physics department, an operating farm with a tractor, and a butter factory. Faculty members originated from both Brazil and the United States. John H. Wheelock was an Iowa native who graduated from Texas A&M in 1920 with a

juice industry in the 1960s. See Antonio A. Amaro, *Desenvolvimento da citricultura e localização de novas indústrias para processamento no estado de São Paulo Serie Pesquisa 22* (Piraçicaba, S.P.: Escola Superior de Agricultura "Luiz de Queiroz," 1973), pp. 1–5.

[12] TS, P.H. Rolfs, "A Agricultura Mineira e Seu Melhoramento," pp. ii, v, pp. 95–96, March 1930, PHRA.

degree in agronomy. In 1922 he joined the faculty, along with Oswaldo Emrich, one of the school's first three students in 1911 and the first Lavras graduate to receive a scholarship for study in the United States.[13]

Hunnicutt took his enthusiasm for diversifying Brazil's agriculture beyond the classroom. Improving production of cereals—especially corn—remained a personal objective, as was promoting U.S. equipment for Brazil's farms. Hunnicutt had undertaken the mission of promoting improved cultivation of corn during the wartime era but with lower prices in the early 1920s, enthusiasm for higher corn production corn diminished. Decreasing prices in the cattle market and renewed import of wheat made corn less attractive. The price per ton dropped 30% between 1920 and 1922.[14] Estimated corn production rose slightly and then decreased by over 20% between 1923 and 1926. Difficulties arose in competing with imported Argentina corn because of high freight rates, and corn exports virtually ceased by 1926.[15]

Hunnicutt dedicated himself to an alternative project: establishing an agricultural extension service that would, in his opinion, thoroughly transform Brazilian agriculture. Brazil had 650,000 farms, he wrote, "but only a few hundred students in the agricultural colleges of the country." He envisioned an extension agency "of state, local, and national scope" to educate the "active farmer," supported by donations from interested commercial parties—a type of "Rockefeller Foundation" for agriculture. The extension service would "extend help to an individual requesting it," but to "help him most, who is willing to help himself." Hunnicutt proposed two specific goals for the service: increasing hog production and the use of farm machinery. He then sought a modest US$5,000 per year in financial support.[16]

[13] Michelle Pereira da Silva Rossi, "'Dedicado à Gloria de Deus e ao Progresso Humano': A Gênese Protestante da Universidade Federal de Lavras—UFLA (Lavras, 1892–1938)," (Diss.: Universidade Federal de Uberlândia: 2010), pp. 175–81.

[14] Fundação Instituto Brasileiro de Geografia e Estatística, *Séries estatísticas retrospectivas No. 1* (Rio de Janeiro: IBGE: 1986), p.24.

[15] USC-RJ to SS, May 24, 1927; USC-São Paulo to SS, Apr. 10, 1928, both in Box 60, RG 166, USNA.

[16] TS, "Serviço de Propaganda Agrícola," n.d., attached to minutes, meeting of Mesa dos Curadores, Oct. 8, 1923, GIA; Hunnicutt to Directorate, Aug. 21, 1924, annexed to minutes, Directorate, 1921–1925, GIA. Hunnicutt's concept of a Rockefeller Foundation supported extension service would become reality over 25 years later with the founding of the Associação de Crédito e Assistência Rural in Minas Gerais in 1948.

Promoting U.S. agricultural equipment would be an important function of the service. In 1923 he approached the U.S. trade commissioner with his proposal to institute an agricultural extension service that would distribute information on U.S. farming methods and machinery. The service was to operate with support of local dealers in American farm machinery or American manufacturers. The Agricultural Implements Division of the U.S. Department of Agriculture was naturally enthused about the project, informing the National Association of Farm Equipment Manufacturers in 1923 that Hunnicutt was "in a great position to do work of great value in increasing the use of agricultural implements in that part of Brazil."[17]

A variety of interested parties in Brazil responded to Hunnicutt's pleas for support. Minister of Agriculture Miguel Calmon, the U.S. Chamber of Commerce chapters in Rio de Janeiro and São Paulo, U.S. Ambassador Morgan, Peter Rolfs, and Leo S. Rowe, director of the Pan American Union, all endorsed the idea. In late 1923, six business firms contributed modest amounts to the service: S. L. Allen and Company of Philadelphia (US$100); Continental Products, Armour do Brasil, and Frigorifico Anglo each contributed 15:000$, S.K.F. do Brasil gave 1:800$, and Casa Pratt, a U.S.-owned Rio de Janeiro commercial house, promised a 25% discount on all purchases. By the end of 1924, Hunnicutt had collected a total of 47:988$500, the equivalent of US$4,510. During the first year of the service Hunnicutt was able to register certain accomplishments. He published 40,000 copies of five booklets on corn ("without corn there would be no pigs," he explained), 5,000 copies of a poster on swine raising, and supported establishment of the national swine breeders' association.[18]

By late 1924, though, problems began to arise. The packing houses had agreed to support the service for three years "specifically for the promoting of a campaign to increase hog production." After the first year, though, two companies terminated their support, reducing funds considerably. Undaunted, Hunnicutt planned to tap resources of U.S. farm implement firms that might support the venture as an inroad for future markets. He wrote to G. A. Bell of the Agricultural Implements

[17] Ltr., George F. Kendall, Assistant Chief, Agricultural Implements Division, USDA, to H.S. Sameit, Secretary, National Association of Farm Equipment Manufacturers, Oct. 1, 1923, RG 151, Box 1190, 221.1, USNA.

[18] TS, "Report of the Lavras Agricultural College for the Year 1924," p. 5, OGIA.

Division, USDA, who arranged for publication of news of Hunnicutt's service in a trade journal. Results were meager. Bell reported that "with the exception of the International Harvester Company, there has been but little response." Hunnicutt then proposed to travel to the United States to appeal personally to farm machinery companies with assistance of Bell, who agreed to arrange an itinerary. When Hunnicutt put the suggestion before the school's governing board, however, he encountered a serious limitation. The board judged the trip "not advisable."[19]

Their decision demonstrated the degree of conflict generated within the school by Hunnicutt's frequent absences. Hunnicutt had spent nearly a year in the United States in 1919–1920 with support from the Ministry of Agriculture, and his work with the extension service removed him once again from classroom and administrative responsibilities. Hunnicutt had received permission to operate the service provided he devoted a least a third of his to time the agricultural school and compensate the school financially for his services. The school's financial health was becoming a serious issue, and criticism soon began to mount that the service interfered with his school responsibilities. This caused Hunnicutt to defend his program as "an opportunity to advertise and make known the school all over Brazil" and "the best-known form of agricultural mission work."[20]

During 1925, Hunnicutt came under "considerable criticism... of my work as director of the Escola Agricola, and in connection with my work in the extension department," as he acknowledged in an emotion-packed letter to the Instituto Evangélico's board of directors. He defended his work with the extension service as a "particular line of work that I enjoy and apparently have an aptitude for carrying on." He defended his extensive travel as necessary to meet the program's objectives. He concluded by giving the board "all the freedom in discussing and handling the matter

[19] TS, "Report of the Lavras Agricultural College for the Year 1924," p. 5, OGIA; Hunnicutt to Members of Directorate, Instituto Evangélico, Aug. 21, 1924, GIA; Minutes of the Directorate, Aug. 25, 1924, GIA.

[20] Minutes of the Directorate, Aug. 25, 1924, p. 6, GIA. The Ministry of Agriculture paid 2:000$ for Hunnicutt's 1919–1920 trip for him "to buy animals for this Ministry." See TS, MAG, Directoria Geral da Contabilidade, "Relação das pessoas....," Apr. 8, 1920, 12.00.00 II 15, AISL; "Livro das Actas," May 13, 1920, GIA.

as God may give you," along with his resignation "effective now or as soon as may be desirable."[21]

Hunnicutt withdrew his resignation soon thereafter. While he agreed to give more attention to the school, he continued promoting corn and swine production. The directorate agreed that the extension service could "be continued through 1926 or until funds now on hand can be used up, in the case this can be done without longer demands on Mr. Hunnicutt's time and more and longer absences from Lavras."[22] In August 1925, he organized a Semana de Milho (corn week), an exhibit and contest in São Paulo inaugurated by the state secretary of agriculture and attended by 76 farmers from various parts of Brazil, but especially from cereals-producing states of Rio Grande do Sul, Paraná, and Santa Catarina. In September 1925, he distributed a synopsis of Brazil's agricultural riches, edited by the SNA and published by Rio de Janeiro's *Correio da Manhã*. It highlighted corn as Brazil's second-most important crop and included recommendations on technical issues from various contributors, including the Ministry of Agriculture. Hunnicutt also used the school's journal, *O Agricultor*, to disseminate technical information about corn cultivation and the swine raising, among other topics. Hunnicutt attempted to revive public interest in crop by sponsoring a fifth corn exposition. The Lavras school hosted the event in August 1926, drawing corn samples from 90 entrants from eleven states, including Ceará, Pernambuco, and Rio Grande do Norte, with an estimated attendance of over 2,000. A representative of the Ministry of Agriculture presided and distributed 10 sacks of corn seed "of the best varieties adapted to the climate of Brazil."[23] Indicative of declining interest in the crop was the exhibition's site. Instead of the great halls of capital cities, the setting was the inauspicious grounds of his own agricultural school.[24] In December 1926,

[21] Hunnicutt to Members of the Directorate, Instituto Evangélico, Sept. 8, 1925, in minutes of the Mesa dos Curadores, 1925–1934, GIA.

[22] Minutes of the Directorate, Dec. 7, 1925, GIA.

[23] "A Semana de Milho," *Correio Paulistano*, Aug. 25, 1925; José Normando Gonçalves Meira, "Ciência e Prática: Ensino Agrícola na Educação Presbiteriana em Minas Gerais (1908–1938)," pp. 179–82; "Exposição de Milho," *O Estado de Paraná*, Aug. 22, 1926, p. 2; "Quinta Exposição Nacional de Milho," Brazil, MAG, *Boletim*, Year 17, Vol. 2, No. 2 (Sept. 1926), 378–85.

[24] *O Agricultor*, Vol. 5, No. 1 (1926), p. 28.

Hunnicutt departed for another extended U.S. visit, placing the extension service on hold.

Hunnicutt returned in April 1928 to resume activities of his private agricultural extension service. He carried with him 14 motion picture films acquired from USDA, copies of presentations used by the USDA since 1912 to educate U.S. school children and agricultural societies. Hunnicutt arranged for translation of the films' titles into Portuguese, and they became a centerpiece of his extension service. He held the first exhibit in Rio de Janeiro for the Minister of Agriculture and other dignitaries, followed by showings at the Congresso de Criadores Mineiros (congress of cattle breeders) in Belo Horizonte. In collaboration with the SRB, Hunnicutt then exhibited five films in São Paulo at the SRB's facilities and a local theatre. According to the SRB's weekly bulletin, the films, with topics ranging from treating cattle and swine diseases to the basics of orange cultivation, showed "the many difficulties of the farmer, their solutions, and various ways to take advantage of the productive capacity of a rural establishment."[25] The SRB then requested three additional films on livestock topics.[26] The films were eventually shown in seven cities to a total audience of 4,000.[27]

Hunnicutt also exhibited his films as part of the Lavras School's annual farm exposition, the "Exposição Agro-Pecuaria de Lavras." Held in cooperation with the local agricultural society and reminiscent of a U.S. county fair, in 1928 the five-day event featured extensive displays of domestic goods as well as commercial and industrial products and animals of all variety. Lighting of the display area, provided by the General Electric Company, allowed evening visits to the pavilions with accompaniment of a band of local musicians. Consistent with Hunnicutt's long-term priorities, exhibits displayed varieties of corn and vegetables along with

[25] Sociedade Rural Brasileira, "Informações Semanaes aos Snrs. Associados," No. 24, July 29, 1928; No. 25, Aug. 5, 1928, copies in Volume 94, Records of Foreign Service Posts, Consular Posts, São Paulo, RG, RG 84, USNA.

[26] The USDA loaned the films to the SRB's because it considered the request as a being of a "special nature," but suggested the SRB could purchase additional films from its contracted distributor. Ltr., G. W. Warburton, Director of Extension Work, U.S. Department of Agriculture to SS, Oct. 16, 1928, Volume 94, Records of Foreign Service Posts, Consular Posts, São Paulo, RG, RG 84, USNA.

[27] "Report of the Serviço de Propaganda Agrícola (Extension Department of the Escola Agrícola)," Dec. 7, 1928, in Relatórios Anuais, Annual Reports of the President of the Gammon Institute, GIA.

61 cows, 23 horses, and 57 pigs. Agricultural machinery and electric appliances, including a machine for processing manioc developed by a local farmer, occupied a special section of the exhibit area. Fairgoers could also watch a variety of films, including "Combatting Tics," "The Botfly," "Milk Cows," and "Cooperativism." One observer of the fair credited Hunnicutt with its success, depicting him as "tireless hard worker and propagandist of high merit of the basic principles of agriculture in Brazil."[28]

Hunnicutt also continued his efforts to promote mechanized agriculture through contacts at the U.S. Consulate in São Paulo and the Department of Commerce, but his extension service soon foundered due to lack of support from dealers. According to a long-term Hunnicutt contact at the U.S. Bureau of Foreign and Domestic Commerce, the International Harvester Company had placed several implement engineers in the cotton and coffee regions of Brazil since 1926, as well as a small staff observing Brazilian agriculture. They were approached in late 1928, undoubtedly by Hunnicutt, to ascertain whether they would contribute US$10,000 to form an organization promoting sales of U.S. agricultural equipment in Brazil. They reported that "Brazil was a long way from the point of big business in farm equipment lines." Even though the "country needed a campaign of agricultural education," the company felt that they "could not go into a game of this kind." Neither were the John Deere and J. I. Case companies enthusiastic about the proposal.[29] Hunnicutt discontinued his work with the national swine association but continued to promote mechanization behind the scenes while attending to duties at the Lavras school.

Brazil and Mechanized Agriculture in the 1920s

The notion that Brazil could benefit from mechanized agriculture was not universally accepted. Brazil's 1850 land law had long discouraged adoption of new agricultural technology because large landowners could use their influence to obtain title to new lands. They shifted cultivation to virgin lands once soil exhaustion occurred through rudimentary

[28] *O Paiz,* Aug. 3, 1928, p. 1.

[29] Ltr., George B. Bell, Chief, Agricultural Implements Division, U.S. Bureau of Foreign and Domestic Commerce, to M.A. Cremer, U.S. Trade Commissioner, São Paulo, Jan. 21, 1929, 221.1, RG 151, USNA.

practices, including slash and burn clearing, and the absence of irrigation and fertilizer. An agricultural census of São Paulo state in 1905 revealed that plows and similar implements were present in only 25% of the state's *municipios.*[30] Some owners of large coffee estates in São Paulo saw mechanization as an alternative to maintaining permanent residents or contracting labor from residents of nearly colonias, often more concerned with their own crops. However, the practice of planting cereals between rows of coffee trees restricted use of a weed-killing cultivator, and many considered the tractor an unproven invention. The 1920 national census recorded agricultural machinery in only 15% of the 648,153 "rural establishments" and a nationwide total of only 1,706 tractors.[31] An unsigned article in the SNA's *A Lavoura* argued that a study on tractor use in the United States showed that, for Brazilian farmers, the costs of using tractors far outweighed benefits, since the expensive machines had to be imported, supported by imported fuel, and operated by untrained workers. The author pledged that "we will be, for perhaps long in the future, [supportive of] an anti-tractor policy, which we consider absolutely rational and patriotic."[32]

Countering that argument were observers of U.S. agriculture and pedagogues and practitioners who embraced mechanization, especially tractor technology. They expounded on the benefits of "motocultura." A confidant of Minister Simões Lopes studied U.S. mechanized agriculture during extensive travel as a participant in the ministry's scholarship program. Landulpho Alves de Almeida wrote in a private letter from Chicago to Minister Lopes that visits to farms in the Southwest and California had convinced him of "the very special importance given here to the study of mechanical agriculture." He noted that "the use of the

[30] Leando de Araújo Crestani and Jefferson Andronio Ramundo Staduto, "O Atraso Tecnológico no Setor Agropecuário Brasileiro: Lei de Terras de 1850 em perspectiva," *Revista Eletrônica História em Reflexão,* Vol. 6, No. 12, (Jul.–Dec. 2012); Francisco Vidal Luna, Herbert S. Klein, and William R. Summerhill, "A Agricultura Paulista em 1905," *Estudos Econômicos* (São Paulo), Vol. 44, n. 1 (Jan. Mar. 2014), 157.

[31] See Cláudia Alessandra Tessari, "Trabalhadores temporários para o café: mecanização e núcleos coloniais em São Paulo, 1895–1911," *Estudos Econômicos.* Vol. 44, No. 2 (Apr./ Jun. 2014); Brazil, MAG, *Recenseamento do Brasil Realizado em 1 de Setembro de 1920. Vol. III. Agricultura* (Rio de Janeiro: Typografia da Estatística, 1927), pp. V, 6–7.

[32] "O tractor, na agricultura brasileira, será ainda, por longo tempo, senão para sempre, uma impraticabilidade," *A Lavoura* (May 1926), pp. 205–11.

machine is most common, explaining, as it seems to me, one of the great secrets of its current progress."[33]

Agriculturalists at São Paulo's Luiz de Queiroz school and some large landowners and their allies within the Ministry of Agriculture judged tractors useful for increasing production of cereal and forage crops. The school's 1920 curriculum mandated practical work in utilization of "agricultural machines for soil preparation, sowing, forage cutting, haymaking, [and] harvest of cereals..." as well as using a "tractor with single, double, triple and sub-soil plows." Second year students received grades in "Mechanics and Agricultural Machinery."[34] The chief of the newly created section in the Ministry of Agriculture responsible for seeds for pasture and food assumed an active role in demonstrating the capabilities of tractors. Agronomist Francisco de Assis Iglesias had graduated from Pernambuco's Escola de Agronomia and headed the Superintendência de Sementeiras (seed superintendency), established in 1920. His section sponsored a "tractor contest" to identify tractors most appropriate for Brazil on October 2–3, 1920. The event was repeated the next year with attendance of President Pessoa and the Miguel Calmon, SNA president. The contest supported Assis Iglesias's decision to use tractors in farms he oversaw producing seeds for a variety of grain crops, including corn, rice, beans, and forage crops. Equipment at his seed farms included the "Titan" tractor, an International Harvester machine introduced in the United States in 1915.[35] The ministry also reported effective use of "motorculture" at its seed farm in Lorena, São Paulo, in 1924.[36]

The contest tested five tractors' abilities to plow, till, tow a 2-kiloton truck and traverse a 35-kilometer road trip. Four of the five machines in first event originated in the United States, including Monarch, Allis-Chalmers, Twin-City, and the Titan tractors. A Fiat tractor, first produced

[33] Ltr., Landulpho Alves de Almeida to Simões Lopes, Nov. 5, 1919, ISL 14.12.15, I5, AISL.

[34] F.T. de Souza Reis, *O Ensino na Escola Agrícola Luiz de Queiroz de Piraçicaba* (São Paulo: Typografia da Sociedade da Editora Olegário Ribeiro, 1921), pp. 44, 109.

[35] Assis Iglesias would later exercise prominent roles in Brazil's agricultural support structure. *Rodriguesia, A Revista do Servico Florestal*, Vol. 6, No. 15 (Jun. 1942), 93; Brazil, MAG, *Relatório 1920,* pp. 127–29; "O segundo concurso de tractores Agrícolas," *A Lavoura,* Vol. 25, Nos. 10–11 (Oct.–Nov. 1921), 277–88; Randy Leffingwell, *Classic Farm Tractors: History of the Farm Tractor* (Osceola, WI: MBI Publishing Company, 1996), p. 45.

[36] *Jornal do Brasil*, Aug. 12, 1924, p. 5.

in 1919, was the sole European tractor at the demonstration. Opinions of the five-person jury are not available, but one observer judged the event to have proven the utility of the tractor for Brazilian farmers. It demonstrated the "perfect adaptability to our environment, in detriment to the idea that our natural conditions oppose the utilization of automotors [sic] in our cultivating operations."[37] The next year's event featured five days of competition among four U.S.-built tractors and a German and a French tractor. An observer from the U.S. Embassy judged the U.S.-built tractors to have performed well, even though the event was sparsely attended.[38]

Endorsements for using tractors also came from prominent agriculturalists and bureaucrats. Carlos Botelho had been São Paulo's activist Secretary of Agriculture between 1904 and 1908, supporting reintroduction of cotton cultivation, reform of agricultural education, and improvements to Brazilian cattle. As noted earlier, Botelho was also an admirer of U.S. agriculture. In April 1922 he invited members of local agricultural societies and prominent state official to an exhibition to show the possibility of using cotton seed as a cattle feed after storage in a silo. A central part of the demonstration was use of a Fordson tractor to power a chipper producing the silage.[39] The following year, the serving State Secretary of Agriculture, Heitor Penteado, also promoted mechanization by sponsoring a demonstration of a Citreon tractor acquired by the state's research institute.[40]

Cereal producers in the South and Center-South were also beginning to adopt tractors, especially those from the United States. Nearly half of the tractors counted in the 1920 census were located in Grande do Sul, the nation's largest cereal producer. Its output of corn rice, beans, manioc flour, wheat, the English potato, grapes, tobacco, and onions had earned it a well-deserved reputation as the "granary of the country."[41] German and Italian immigrant farmers, more accustomed to farm implements

[37] "Mechanica Agrícola: Concurso de Tractores Agrícolas," *Brasil Agrícola* (Oct. 1920), pp. 291–94.

[38] U.S. Department of Commerce, *Commerce Reports*, Vol. 1 (Jan. 2, 1922), p. 30.

[39] "Visita ao silo do Jardim de Acclimação," *Correio Paulistano*, Apr. 8, 1922, p. 6.

[40] "Instituto Agronômico de Campinas," *Correio Paulistano*, Nov. 20, 1923, p. 5.

[41] Júlia Elisabete Barden, Darkei Francisco da Silva, Lucildo Ahlert, and Fernanda Cristina Wiebusch, "A Economia do Rio Grande do Sul no Periódo entre 1920 e 1940: Uma Análise da Região do Vale do Taquari," *Estudo e Debate*, Lajeado, RS, Vol. 8, No. 2, (2001), 20–21.

than their countrymen, adopted tractors and other implements mainly to support rice cultivation. The U.S. Consul in Porto Alegre reported in 1921 that tractors, gang and single plows, disk harrows, cultivators, threshers and milling equipment from the United States were becoming "standard for this part of Brazil," especially in the rice industry.[42]

In São Paulo, Henrique P. Ribeiro also adopted tractor technology. Ribeiro was the director of the Companhia Agricola São Martinho, an immense estate in Sertãozinho, 339 kilometers northwest of the city of São Paulo and owned by the Prado-Chavez export house presided over by Antonio Prado. The massive estate boasted the second-largest concentration of coffee plants in Brazil—over 3.4 million bushes in 1908—with a labor force of over 4,000. Damage to the coffee crop from the freeze of 1918 and worries over the continued profitability of coffee led the family to reduce the number of coffee trees to 2.7 million by 1924 and diversify its production.[43] Director-General Ribeiro attested to the utility of tractors when queried in 1920 about his use of a tractor produced by the Wallis Tractor Company of Racine, Wisconsin. Ribeiro was "completely satisfied with the functioning of the two Wallis tractors acquired by me about three months ago." He reported that he had plowed "three hectares of virgin land" in nine hours, resulting in a "perfect" product. The article's author—whose company sold Wallis tractors—concluded that experience showed that tractors could be "most useful, necessary, and indispensable," especially for cultivation of cereals and pastures as well as instruments of transportation.[44]

As the decade progressed, the Ministry of Agriculture became increasingly involved in promoting and implementing "motocultura." In 1924 the ministry's service of development (Serviço de Fomento Agricola) began to transform select cooperation farms (campos de cooperação) into showcases for mechanized agriculture. It provided machines and technical advice for a 35-hectare field operated by Ignacio José de Lemos in

[42] *Brazilian American*, Vol. 3, No3, 70 (Feb. 26, 1921), 15.

[43] Darrell Erville Levi, "The Prados of São Paulo: an elite Brazilian family in a changing society, 1840–1930" (Diss.: Yale University, 1974), pp. 271–271, 278; Rogerio Naques Faleiros, Fronteiras do Café: Fazendeiros e "Colonos" no Interior Paulista (1917–1937) (Diss: Campinas, SP: [s.n.], 2007), pp. 113, 114.

[44] Luiz Silva, "Os tractores Agrícolas enriquicem os seus donos," *Annaes da SRB,* Vol. 1, No. 4 (Aug. 1920), 244, 245; "Demonstrações práticas," *Correio Paulistano*, Apr. 27, 1920, p. 2.

Mesquita, Rio de Janeiro, dedicated to experiments with cotton. The field became a demonstration case for the use of mechanical seeder to prepare a cotton field.[45] Agronomist José Eurico Dias Martins, a 1912 graduate of the Luiz de Queiroz school, who had become chief of the service's directory of machines, proclaimed in mid-1925 that "it can be said that the era of national motorculture has begun."[46] The cooperation fields became the focal point for the next step in promoting mechanized agriculture when the Ministry of Agriculture committed to purchasing major quantities of equipment for its own activities and to be sold at cost to farmers. The ministry decided to "generalize the use of agricultural machinery in the rural centers of the country" by selling the machines and offering instructions at the cooperation fields. Purchases represented commitments of 701:640$900 (US$84,056) in 1928, 112:758$000 (US$13,316) in 1929, and then 1.352:122$680 (US$144,812) in 1930.[47]

The first year's purchase was made in Europe, but some equipment purchased in 1930 originated from the U.S. companies John Deere and Oliver through arrangements of the Brazilian Commercial Attaché in New York, Monteiro Lobato. According to the Assistant U.S. Trade Commissioner in Rio de Janeiro, Benjamin Hunnicutt had been involved in the purchase of "690 cases of agricultural implements" arriving in Rio de Janeiro on October 24, 1930, some of which were destined for the Lavras school.[48]

Importation of U.S. equipment as part of the 1930 purchases was consistent with the prominence of U.S. educators and their endorsement of U.S. agricultural machinery in the implementation of "motorculture." Between 1922 and 1930, some 2,960 tractors were exported from the United States to Brazil, more than double the tractors identified in the 1920 census. U.S. agricultural machinery also figured prominently in the adoption of equipment drawn by horses and mules. The total value of

[45] *O Jornal*, Dec. 10, 1924, p. 3.

[46] *O Jornal*, May 27, 1925, p. 1.

[47] Brazil, MAG, *Relatório 1930–1931*, p. 107.

[48] Ltr., George B. Bell, Chief Implements Division, U.S. Bureau of Foreign and Domestic Commerce, to Dr. Benjamin H. Hunnicutt, July 12, 1930; Ltr., J. Winsor Ives, Assistant Trade Commissioner, Rio de Janeiro, to Director, U.S. Bureau of Foreign and Domestic Commerce, Nov. 4, 1930; Ltr., George B. Bell, Chief Implements Division, U.S. Bureau of Foreign and Domestic Commerce, to Mr. Ives, Nov. 21, 1930, all in 221.1, RG 151, USNA.

U.S. agricultural implement exports to Brazil during this period exceeded US$6.6 million, with a strong concentration on threshers that separate grain from the husks.[49] A U.S. Commerce Department report based on a market surveys in 1924 and 1925 indicated that most tractors sold in Brazil were U.S. made. In addition to their support for cereals cultivation, they were being used for "conventional farm work" and to carry sugar cane to mills in the Campos area of Rio de Janeiro state. São Paulo state offered promise, the report suggested, as "the market [there] has been increasing quite steadily."[50]

The participation of U.S. agricultural educators in promotion and adoption of innovations in Brazilian agriculture between 1922 and 1930, combined with the use of U.S.-origin technical information in São Paulo's cotton cultivation and the presence of U.S. capital in the Center-South's beef processing industry, helped solidify the image of the United States as a reference point for Brazil's agricultural diversification. The process reinforced the notion, nurtured during the wartime, that linkages with U.S. educational and cultivation methods could be adapted to Brazil's environment and yield improvements in Brazil's agriculture. With the inauguration of the Viçosa school in 1926, all three of the First Republic's superior agricultural education institutions used U.S. agricultural education philosophy as the basis for their curricula. The ties that developed in classrooms and fields through the ebb and flow of professors and scholarship students and adoption of U.S. equipment and commercial processes helped sustain the image of the United States as an important source of technical information and practice. This suggested that Brazil would continue to look beyond its shores, and especially to the United States, for ways to sustain "polyculture."

A second important implication of this process was the impetus it gave to the Center-South region as the primary locale for the nation's superior agricultural education and development of agricultural technology. Other regions, notably the Northeast and the South, would lag for reasons of

[49] Calculated from U.S. Department of Commerce, Bureau of Foreign and Domestic Commerce, *Foreign Commerce and Navigation of the United States*, Calendar Years 1919 through 1930.

[50] U.S. Department of Commerce, Bureau of Foreign and Domestic Commerce, *Foreign Markets for Tractors by Charles D. Martin* (N.P: n.p., 1927), pp. 12, 13.

geography and policy. This imbalance in agricultural development would have important political repercussions, contributing to the demise of the First Republic and the end of agricultural development policies created and carried out within a corporatist framework by state elites.

CHAPTER 11

Elite Factionalism and the First Republic's Downfall, 1922–1930

Efforts to support diversified agriculture in the Northeast and extreme South during the final years of the 1920s were less successful than in the Center-South. The Northeast suffered from meager resources and the vagaries of climate affecting its cotton cultivation, while ranchers in the South found competition difficult for sale of their traditional product with the restoration of normal trade conditions. Segments of local elites in both regions became dissatisfied with national policies, attributing their economic problems to favoritism for the Center-South, especially São Paulo. While agricultural diversification efforts continued in all areas, the trials of the cotton sector in the Northeast and the cattle sector in the South contributed to a political backlash and the crumbling of the First Republic. Institutional and technological fragmentation combined with political expediency in the Northeast slowed adoption of innovations beneficial to its cotton. Unfavorable market conditions in the South limited the impact of U.S. capital. Diversification of the First Republic's agriculture through contacts with the United States remained conditioned by political and geographic factors as well as legacy technology.

E. R. Downes, *Brazilian Agricultural Development, 1890–1950*,
https://doi.org/10.1007/978-3-031-76992-4_11

Withdrawing Support for Anti-Drought Works in the Northeast

As the federal president, Artur Bernardes' economic program went beyond supporting coffee cultivation and sponsoring better agricultural education. It also focused on improving Brazil's trade balances by supporting locally favored products and reducing the chronic federal budget deficit. He had long used political office to bolster agriculture in his native Center-South, and, as pointed out in the previous chapter, as president he channeled strong support to agriculture. Such support, however, would take place only within the regionalist parameters guiding the First Republic's politics. His predecessor had attempted to support the Northeast and the South, and Bernardes wasted no time in exercising similar favoritism toward his native Center-South. Moreover, Pessoa's refusal to endorse Bernardes as his successor created a political gulf between the two that would only widen as Bernardes moved toward occupying the presidency. Shortly before entering office, Bernardes expressed frustration with Pessoa's decisions in a private letter to confidant Raul Soares, who had succeeded him as Minas' president. "As far as the financial situation goes... [it was] neither exceeded nor equaled in the Republic!" he penned. "The contracts celebrated in the last days of the past government reach the point of frightening! Of frightening and saddening Brazilians."[1]

Bernardes was most probably referring to contracts implementing Pessoa's massive federal drought relief program for the Northeast, the first casualty of the shift of power back to the Center-South. Even before Pessoa left the presidency, doubts about the program had forced him to adopt a defensive stance. In a speech at the Teatro Municipal in São Paulo in September 1921, he justified his program not only on humanitarian aspects but because "the economic aspect" of the droughts "constitutes a national problem." Those who would resent the effort were either "entirely destitute of public spirit," or never had seen the drought "in its hideous work of destruction and extermination." He later pointed to construction of highways, cart roads, dams, railroads, wells, and port

[1] On the political and economic situation, see Winston Fritsch, *External Constraints on Economic Policy in Brazil, 1889–1930* (Pittsburgh, PA: Univ. of Pittsburgh Press, 1988), pp. 53–76. Ltr, Artur Bernardes to Raul Soares, Oct. 12, 1922, RS22.12.10/1, ARS.

works as evidence that public monies were not "squandered in shady business deals and favors." Pessoa sought validation of the project's worth by appointing an independent commission of three Southerners "to travel throughout the region and to report frankly what they might find there."[2] General Candido M. S. Rondon, head of the Telegraph Commission and a respected pioneer of the Brazilian West, Idlefonso Simões Lopes, who by then had left his post as Minister of Agriculture to return to service as a federal deputy, and engineer Moraes de Barros left Rio de Janeiro on October 25, 1922, for 32 days of travel over nearly 6,000 kilometers in the Northeast.[3]

The commission's mandate implied the need to contest preconceived judgments of waste and mismanagement. The 71 issues to be addressed required compilation of a litany of complex financial and engineering data. It was to report costs of installation relative to the amount of water accumulated, how much material was provided for each work locally and nationally versus imported material, the weight of all imported material, which dams were owned by private individuals versus those owned by the government, all salaries paid to workers at all levels, total surface irrigated by gravity, and the approximate cost of the irrigation systems to be installed, among other a host of other specifics.[4]

To Pessoa's dismay, the commission failed to support his premises about development of the Northeast. Although the commission's work was "expected to be exceptionally impartial," it fell victim to a change in political winds with Bernardes's entry into the presidency. The commission's report, issued on February 2, 1923, nearly three months after Bernardes took office and replete with 36 complex attachments, was highly critical. In its opinion, only one of ten masonry dams should have been undertaken, ports and railroads should have been funded through other means, and simpler and cheaper automobile roads should have been built. The high-quality construction of the roads, with a width of six meters, concrete bridges, and heavy fills to avoid steep grades were criticized as too expensive for "a new country." Cart roads two to four meters wide would have been more applicable, in the commission's opinion. Overall, the commission recommended rapid retrenchment and

[2] Pessoa, *Pela verdade!*, pp. 333–338.

[3] *O Jornal*, Feb. 21, 1923, p. 13.

[4] *O Jornal*, Feb. 21, 1923, p. 13.

that additional expenditures should be incurred only after "careful study and experimentation."[5]

The intent of the Bernardes administration to cease subsidizing Northeastern development through the anti-drought program soon became clear. Even before the commission released its report, the new government began paying Brazilian workers at the dam sites in chits [*vales*] rather than cash. Local merchants discounted these heavily, and soon refused to accept them altogether. By July 1923, a U.S. engineer employed by Dwight P. Robinson on the dam-building contract reported that work on several dams had been interrupted and that "there is a disposition on the part of the Brazilian Federal Government to discontinue work on the northeastern irrigation works entirely." The engineer was appalled that the Brazilian government would abandon several modern power plants already installed but not working, since all would be "a dead loss." He explained that the decision to end work on the project "was due largely to the indisposition of Southern politicians to support heavy expenditures in the North."[6]

The decision was consistent with Bernardes's view of the Pessoa administration, now expressed publicly by his treasury minister. Rafael de Sampaio Vidal was a native of São Carlos in the state of São Paulo, a law school classmate of São Paulo's state President Washington Luiz de Pereira e Souza, and a former São Paulo state Senator. In a statement to Congress in August 1923, Sampaio Vida accused the Pessoa administration of serious malfeasance. He denounced it for creating US$75 million in debts, consumed in a "vortex of the droughts and contracts." Another US$25 million destined for the Central railway was somehow missing, he charged, and "until now, no one knows where they ended up, in which pockets." Contracts had been awarded without public competition, with "onerous" commissions, and public employment had increased by nearly 20,000 "functionaries." In his opinion, it was all a "calamity" [*descalabro*].[7]

Within two years, the Bernardes government phased out most construction, closing dam projects and delaying payments to laborers on

[5] USC-Pernambuco to SS, Mar. 18, 1924, 832.77/126; Apr. 25, 1923, p. 17, 832.6113/4; June 13, 1925, 832.6113/8, RG 59, USNA.

[6] USC-Pernambuco to SS, Aug. 6, 1923, 832.6113/5, RG 59, USNA.

[7] *O Jornal*, Aug. 31, 1923, p. 6.

those few remaining. Federal monies for the drought program's manager, the Inspectoria Federal de Obras Contra as Seccas (IFOCS), fell from 145,947 *contos de reis* in 1922 to 3,827 *contos* in 1925—a reduction of over 97%. The 1925 federal budget authorized sale of equipment for all projects except two dams. Because of the extended inactivity, the remaining equipment was of little value. One interested state government requisitioned construction material acquired for the drought campaign, but when the state engineer arrived to take possession, he found it "mostly useless."[8] Meanwhile, the IFOCS "dove into apathy," and its few remaining employees became "watchmen for great deposits of existing material" in Ceará, Rio Grande do Norte, and Paraíba.[9]

More prominent and enduring in the national political area was the backlash in the Northeastern states created by Bernardes's decision. Northeastern politicians, especially former president Pessoa, raised a "storm of protests." Pessoa criticized the commission for the "dizzy speed" of its inspection trek, leading to neglect of details needed for a complete evaluation of the project's expenditures. Pessoa excoriated the report for failing to mention numerous benefits already rendered to the Northeast by the project, for failing to offer truly accurate statistics on progress and capacity of certain works, and especially for the illogical suggestion that the "construction of highways and ports" be postponed until the Northeast developed its economy further. Other political leaders in the Northeast protested that the commission's findings hampered the industrial and commercial growth of the region.[10]

Observers of the Northeast's economic conditions quickly related the region's problems to suspension of the drought works. The Bank of London and South America reported in 1928 that "some justification for continuing the irrigation works in Ceará, inaugurated during the Presidency of Dr. Epitácio Pessoa, has lately become self-evident." The return of drought had caused "serious loss of cattle and crops," and rice plantations had become "parched," and "in many districts, 50 percent of the beans and 80 percent of the maize crops were lost." With classic British understatement, the bank's observers reported that the "exodus

[8] Bahia, *Mensagem, 1926*, p. 277; USC-Pernambuco to SS, June 13, 1925, 832.6113/8, RG 59, USNA.

[9] Guerra, *A Civilização da seca,* p. 65.

[10] USC-Pernambuco to SS, June 13, 1925, 832.6113/8; Mar. 18, 1924, 832.77/126, both RG 59, USNA; Pessoa, *Pela Verdade!*, pp. 336, 346–61.

of a considerable number of families and individuals from the north" indicated that "conditions in the Northern States are somewhat precarious."[11] In facts, so calamitous was the situation in 1928, according to the U.S. Consul in Rio de Janeiro, that "natives in the interior have banded together and marched on the cities, raiding all possible food supplies to prevent starvation."[12] A Rio de Janeiro journal cited the "suspension of the drought works and irrigation program initiated during the administration of President Dr. Epitácio Pessoa" as having "fatal effects," especially since "nothing that may be done now will alleviate the terrible suffering there."[13]

Further Challenges to the Cotton of the Northeast

Withdrawal of federal support for the anti-drought project was only one of several challenges facing the Northeast's cotton cultivation. Decisions taken by the Bernardes administration and continued through the end of the First Republic further weakened the Northeast's ability to advance its cotton cultivation and compete with cotton from the São Paulo region. As noted earlier, federal and state support for enhancing São Paulo's cotton production was robust. States in the Center-South that enjoyed large resource bases gained an advantage in continuing development of the crop, while smaller and poorer states in the Northeast could muster fewer resources. The cotton service of the state of Alagoas, for example, was established in 1923 with mandates to "increase and perfect the culture of cotton by teaching modern processes of preparing the ground, planting, harvesting, ginning and pressing." However, only five staff members conducted these functions, and four of the five were detailed to oversee the state's cotton seed farms.[14]

Adding to the dysfunction created were its slow implementation of federal reforms to support cotton and the alternative means of association offered to each state. Emissaries from the Ministry of Agriculture

[11] Bank of London and South America Limited, *Monthly Review of Business and Trade Conditions in South America and Portugal,* Vol. 100, No. 118 (Sept. 1928), 359.

[12] USC-RJ to SS, July 28, 1928, Box 57, RG 166, USNA.

[13] *Wileman's Brazilian Review*, July 5, 1928.

[14] USC-Pernambuco, to SS, Apr. 17, 1923, Box 56, RG 166, USNA.

visited each potential cotton-growing state to explain the mechanisms of federal support during 1923 and 1924, reaching agreements with 11 states by the close of 1924. Since states could choose either to operate their own cotton service, with federal subsidy and some federal oversight, or have the federal government operate the service within its borders, two types of state cotton services emerged. Pará, Paraíba, Rio de Janeiro, Minas Gerais, and Bahia accepted federal services, while most Northeastern states—Maranhão, Ceará, Pernambuco, Alagoas, Rio Grande do Norte, and Sergipe—chose to operate their own services.[15]

This mix of bureaucratic arrangements complicated efforts to resolve a central issue detracting from the quality of Northeastern cotton: the great mixture of cotton varieties stemming from localized efforts to breed cotton most acceptable to each state's climactic conditions and satisfy the cotton planters' domestic and international customers. Finding a solution entangled the Northeast in a web of complementary as well as competing research and commercial agendas of both Brazilian and foreign origin. Wild cotton had been present in Brazil when the first Europeans arrived, and Dutch or French colonists commercialized its plantation in the eighteenth century when they imported a variety of cotton from the West Indies known as Sea Island, classified scientifically as *Gossypium barbadense*. This plant, known in Brazil as *Gossypium arboretum* or commonly as arboreo, seridó, or Mocó cotton, became the basis for cotton exports from the Northeast beginning in the eighteenth century, reaching 500 million pounds by 1800. Competing for favor were varieties of short-fibered Upland cotton (termed *algodão herbaceo*), introduced by British agents in the 1860s eager to overcome shortages of U.S.-grown Upland fiber. The Upland variety gained popularity in São Paulo province, and by the 1920s it was being planted in the Northeast to satisfy British demand for short-stapled cotton.[16]

[15] Brazil, MAG, *Relatório 1924*, p. 59.

[16] Sven Beckert, "Emancipation and Empire: Reconstructing the Worldwide Web of Cotton Production in the Age of the American Civil War," *The American Historical Review*, Vol. 109, No. 5 (Dec. 2004), 1410; Cotton Supply Association, *Report of Proceedings at a Conference held on Wednesday, August the 13th, 1862*... (Manchester: John J. Sale, 1862), p. 4. For a scientific discussion of the evolution of cotton varieties in Brazil, see Barbara Pickersgill, Spencer C.H. Barrett, and Dardano de Andrade-Lima, "Wild Cotton in Northeast Brazil," *Biotropica*, Vol. 7, No.1 (Apr. 1975), 42–54. A premier historian of Brazilian agriculture argues that Sea Island was developed initially in Brazil. See Luis

The cotton service's experimental stations and seed farms cultivated a myriad variety of long-, medium-, and short-fiber varieties. The influence of North American agronomists and Brazilians who had studied cotton in the United States led to the widespread planting of short-staple cotton, including "Day's Pedigree," developed by U.S. agronomist Thomas R. Day from seeds of the Russell "Big Boll" species. In 1922, the federal government distributed several thousand copies of Day's 136-page handbook on cotton cultivation, *Manual de Algodão*. Two years later, Day organized the Sergipe's cotton service at an annual salary of 48:000$000 (the equivalent of US$5,251 at 1924 exchange rates).[17] Extensive plantings of "Day's Pedigree" occurred at experimental farms in Sergipe and several other seed farms and experimental stations in the Northeast.

At the same time, the supporters of native long-fiber cotton urged prioritization of research on their favored species. Thomas Pompeu Filho was a member of a family controlling one of the largest textile enterprises in Ceará, Thomaz Pompeu Textil.[18] In 1928, he authored a scathing criticism the director of Ceará's cotton service, English botanist B. C. Gerald Bolland, for his focus on short-stapled varieties. While Bolland was in fact experimenting with multiple species, including the native Mocó variety, Pompeu Filho reasoned that Bolland's experience in Egypt's cotton service had made him enamored of short-staple cotton. According to Pompeu Filho, Bolland disparaged "the fine flower of our product" because of its "disheveled" and wild-like appearance. He criticized the absence of definitive results from Bolland's two years as the service's director, during which Bolland became confronted with "an immensity of varieties that arose in [the cotton service's] plantations, and tired of running after each one, pleaded for the importation of foreign seeds in an effort to provide whatever useful thing while he unraveled the chaos of his cultivations." Moreover, Pompeu wrote, previous experience warned of the danger of trying to compete with North American's short-fibered

Amaral, "Pequena História do Algodão no Brasil (De 1 de Maio de 1500 a 1938)," *Boletim Geográfico*, Vol 7, No. 77 (Aug. 1949), 461–499.

[17] USCG-Rio de Janeiro to SS, Oct.. 4, 1922, 832.6332/10, RG 59, USNA; Brazil, MAG, *Boletim de Ministerio da Agricultura*, Vol. 1, Vol., 15, No. 1, (1926), 332.

[18] Elizabeth Fiúza Aragão, ed., *O Fiar e o Tecer: 120 Anos da Indústria Têxtil no Ceará* (Fortaleza, Ceará: Sinditêxtil—FIEC, 2002), p. 134.

product. The solution lay, in his opinion, in specializing on refining native long-fiber varieties.[19]

The Ministry of Agriculture's experimental and seed farms further complicated the issue by planting and distributing a wide variety of species. The experimental station in Seridó, Rio Grande do Norte was evaluating 12 different species of cotton—six from Egypt, four native, and two from the United States.[20] To provide guidance on the best varieties to plant, it attempted to reach authoritative answers about attributes of 22 short-fiber and three long-fiber species in analyses conducted in its fiber laboratory in 1928 and 1929. Unfortunately, the samples examined yielded "less than satisfactory conclusions." Fiber length fell short of expectations for their categories, and efforts to draw conclusions about the impact of climate and etymological and cryptogrammic (plant breeding) conditions on productivity fell victim to lack of data from some experimental farms. The ministry's analysts were unable to reach definitive conclusions.[21]

As if these limitations were few, state governments in the Northeast also struggled with a limited infrastructure to rationalize cotton production. Paraíba state's president reported in 1929 that the state could classify only a portion of its crop and that the regulation of planting of cotton varieties was a topic that "will not be unperceived by my government." Without a statistical service, the state was unaware of the area under cultivation for cotton or the quantity of cotton produced within its borders. It also struggled with destruction by loose animals wandering into the cotton plots.[22] Pernambuco state also confronted technical issues related to its cotton. "Cotton cultivation has not had, among us, the boom that it needs to animate it, transforming it into one of the most prosperous and most resistant [crops] of our land," reported the state president in 1929. The state had instituted seed and experimental farms, but the persistent

[19] "O algodão no Ceará e os meios empregados para seu desenvolvimento," Brazil, MAG, *Boletim,* Year 16, Vol. 1, No. 1 (Jan. 1927), pp. 39–56; *O Ceará* [Fortaleza], Sept. 2, 1928, pp. 1–9.

[20] Brazil, MAG, *Relatório 1928*, p. 154.

[21] Brazil, MAG, *Relatório 1929,* pp. 137–148.

[22] Parahyba, *Mensagem 1929*, pp. 90–91.

drought had reduced the productivity of the Northeast's traditional Mocó variety.[23]

Other issues challenged production. Interest rates as high as 24% added to problems caused by high state taxes, unreliable rainfall, and the interminable struggle with the *largata rosea* pest, which by early 1923 had infested most of Paraíba's cotton region. Bahia had similar problems in 1925 where the combination of the drought and the *largata rosea* frustrated extensive efforts to improve the state's cotton crop, converting the delivery of ten tons of cotton seeds to the state's farmers into an exercise in futility.[24] Further, discontinuities in appropriations from the federal government restricted efforts to combat the crop's problems. "Important services," complained the chief of the cotton service office in Paraíba, "like the purification of seeds, have to be postponed because the agency does not have the necessary resources to acquire and install the machines."[25]

The volatility of cotton prices during this period caused production to oscillate. When cotton production in the United States returned to normal in 1924, cotton prices fell sharply. From 1921 to 1924 the area planted in cotton in the Northeast had increased steadily, and as late as 1924 one forecast for the future of cotton in Bahia based upon 1923 prices predicted "the laying down of fresh cotton areas on an enormous scale." By 1924 cotton grew on over 600,000 hectares, an increase of 26% of over the 476,360 utilized in 1921. Cotton seed and raw cotton production increased at a similar pace.[26] While the Northeast continued to produce roughly 70% of the nation's crop, the "sudden fall in cotton quotations" created "true anguish" among farmers in Paraíba because these suffered from "quite high production costs," according to a 1925

[23] Pernambuco, *Mensagem 1929*, pp. 50–54.

[24] O.K. Piquet, "Do auxílio financeiro necessário a cultura do Algodão no nordeste," *Annaes da Conferência Internacional*, II, 261; Antidio Guerra, "O Rio Grande do Norte algodoeiro," *Annaes da Conferência Internacional*, II, 435–7; *Diário Oficial* [Sergipe], Jan. 3, 1923, 09.00.07-A3, AISL; Bahia, *Mensagem, 1926*, p. 233.

[25] Paraíba, Serviço do Algodão, *Relatório da delegacia do Serviço Federal do Algodão na Parahyba... 1927* (Paraíba: Imprensa Oficial, 1928), pp. 4, 16, 19, 23.

[26] George M. Chard, "Cotton Development in Brazil," *British Chamber of Commerce Monthly Bulletin*, 6 (1924), 2; Data on cotton production from the Serviço Federal de Algodão and published in "Cotton Growing in Brazil," *British Chamber of Commerce Monthly*, 7 (1925), 459.

federal government report.[27] The combination of unfavorable conditions and lower prices brought especially strong repercussions because export taxes on cotton, as high as 10% ad valorem, provided from fifty to sixty percent of the state's budget. Revenue from cotton export taxes dropped by more than 50% between 1923 and 1925.[28]

Other Northeastern states also suffered severely from drought and cotton prices below their 1924 peak. Drought parched extensive regions of Ceará and Rio Grande do Norte, forcing "a pronounced exodus of the rural population to the cities and for Southern states."[29] The drought was "playing havoc with the crops" and "hundreds of poor people and cattle [are] dying in consequence of drought," the consul reported in 1928, while the cotton crop was "as high as 80 percent destroyed" in some states.[30] Likewise, conditions from 1926 to 1930 proved to be disastrous for Sergipe, where "chronic crisis" meant that "state revenues were not sufficient to cover even expenses of an urgent nature." Even favored concessions suffered, as Trajano S. V. de Medeiros's Companhia Industria de Algodão e Oleos mortgaged its resources in Pernambuco, Paraíba, and Rio Grande do Norte. The company refinanced its original loan, but only by agreeing to surrender 10% of its sales revenues starting six months after refinancing went into effect (Fig. 11.1).[31]

[27] Export prices fell 30% between 1924 and 1925. Brazil, Ministerio de Fazenda, *Relatório 1925*, p. 9; Brazil, Serviço de Inspecção e Fomento Agrícolas, *Relatório 1925* (Rio de Janeiro: Papelaria Americana, 1927), p. 70. For falling commodity prices after 1920, see Walt W. Rostow, *The World Economy: History & Prospect* (Austin: University of Texas, 1978), p. 205.

[28] Paraíba, Serviço do Algodão, *Relatório da delegacia do Serviço Federal do Algodão na Parahyba... 1927* (Paraíba: Imprensa Oficial, 1928), pp. 4, 16, 19, 23.

[29] USC-RJ to SS, July 28, 1928, Box 57, RG 166, USNA.

[30] Article in *Wileman's Brazilian Review*, July 5, 1928, cited in USACG to SS, July 13, 1928, Box 52, RG 166, USNA.

[31] Sergipe, Secretaria de Agricultura, *Apogeu, crise e decadência da cultura algodoeira em Sergipe* (Brasilia: Departamento de Informação e Documentação, 1980), pp. 24–5; *Wileman's Brazilian Review*, July 5, 1928; USC-Pernambuco to SS, Oct. 26, 1929, Box 57, RG 166, USNA; *Boletím* [MAG], 28, 2, (1929), 453. The shift of the Sociedade Algodoeira do Nordeste Brasileiro (SANBRA) from its Northeastern origin to São Pauloin 1933 represented the culmination of the shift toward the South of the nation's cotton production. See "Algodão," *Actualidades SANBRA*, 31, 13.

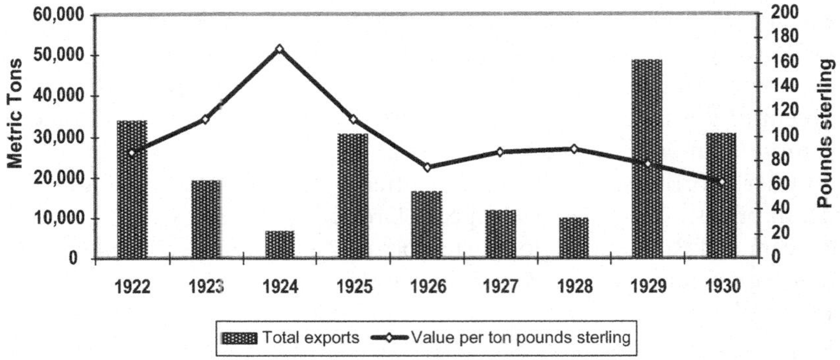

Fig. 11.1 Exports and average price per ton of cotton exported from Brazil, 1922–1930 (*Source* Brazil, Ministerio de Fazenda, *Relatório 1925*, p. 9. *Source* Brazil, Ministerio da Fazenda, Directoria de Estatística Commercial, *Commercio Exterior do Brasil* (Rio de Janeiro: Directoria de Estatística Commercial, 1931))

Compensating Factors

A number of powerful factors overrode the toxic mix of cotton varieties, disease, drought, and funding shortfalls. Although the economic impact of eliminating funding for the Northeast's project remains a much-debated subject, the anti-drought campaigns created tangible benefits by constructing highways into the *sertão*, the arid and semi-arid back country of the Northeast previously dependent upon railroad monopolies to bring products to the coast. Pessoa had justified the project as promoting the region's agricultural development by overcoming its weak transportation infrastructure. Funding road and railroad construction, to support both dam construction and transport of product to market, were critical elements of project. In May 1919, Pessoa had identified the road construction as one of his priorities, since "vast zones of our territory still remain without any means of communication."[32] Prior to the project's suspension, it constructed 2,253 kilometers of roads considered some of the "best existing in the country with respect to technical conditions," according to director Miguel Arrojado Lisboa.[33]

[32] *O Paiz*, May 7, 1919, p. 3.

[33] Presentation to First Pan-American Road Congress by Miguel Arrojado Lisboa, Sept. 23, 1925, in Annex 5, *O Primeiro Congresso Panamericano de Estradas*, (NP: n.p., n. d.).

In Rio Grande do Norte, the IFOCS sponsored highways created two networks for penetration into the *sertão*.[34] In 1923, a journal dedicated to the automobile culture praised the anti-drought works for having created a "grandiose communications network... indispensable for the respective construction and other economic necessities of the region."[35] Paraíba's president expressed satisfaction with roads constructed by IFOCS in a January 30, 1925, telegram to Pessoa. Of the works constructed by the anti-drought campaign, he wrote, "the roads contributed in an obvious way to the extraordinary increase in production of the state naturally because of the ease of transportation." He credited better transportation for allowing sales of cotton sub-products—oil and paste—previously "destined to be consumed in the raw by cattle [or] incinerated to clear out warehouses." The roads also allowed transport of machines for processing those products.[36]

Determining any causal relationship between dam construction, increased irrigation, and cotton production—a central justification for the project—is more problematical. Contemporary observer and cotton industrialist Trajano S. V. de Medeiros argued in 1922 that "completing the irrigation works would add 500,000 hectares of land to cotton cultivation and increased gross revenues by £50,000."[37] Geologist Crandall's survey of previously completed dams in the region attributed the successful cultivation of modest amounts of sugar, corn, potatoes, rice, and cotton to water provided by small, privately owned dams near Pombal, 388 kilometers west of the coast. He observed that any evaluation of the dams' impact should also recognize that they produced "lesser objects, that are truly valuable, like water for cattle and for domestic use" that "should be included that are truly valuable, like water for cattle and for domestic use" that "should be included because with the

[34] Itamara de Souza, *A República Velha no Rio Grande do Norte 1889–1930* (Natal, RGN: Editora da UFRN, 2008), p. 92.

[35] "As grandes estradas do Nordeste," *O Automóvel*, Vol. 8, No. 101 (Jan. 1, 1923), 24.

[36] Tel., João Suassuna to Epitácio Pessoa, Jan. 30, 1925, Pasta 61, AEP.

[37] Trajano S. V. de Medeiros, "O valor econômico dos trabalhos de açudagem e irrigação do nordeste," *Annaes da Conferência Internacional*, II, 355.

Table 11.1 Highways and Carriage Roads constructed by the Inspectoria Federal de Obras Contra as Seccas, 1919–1925

State	*Km of highways constructed*	*Km of carriage roads constructed*
Paraíba	779	1,278
Rio Grande do Norte	517	467
Ceará	479	1,132
Piauí	181	
Pernambuco	152	
Sergipe	103	
Bahia	42	

Source Brazil, Ministerio de Viação e Obras Públicas, Inspectoria Federal de Obras Contra As Seccas, *Estradas de Rodagem e carrocaveis construidas no Nordeste Brasileiro pelo IFOCS aos annos 1919 a 1925* (Rio de Janeiro, 1927)

dam, they would not exist."[38] However, without empirical studies of the cotton production during this period in areas served by completed dams, it is presumptive to attribute production increases to better irrigation (Table 11.1).[39]

Despite the array of complicating factors, cotton production in the three principal cotton-producing states in the region increased significantly between 1922 and 1930. Pernambuco's cotton production

[38] Roderic Crandall, *Geografia, geologia, supprimento d'agua, transportes e açudagem nos estados orientaes do norte do Brasil: Ceará, Rio Grande do Norte, Parahyba* (Rio de Janeiro: Serviço Geológico e Geográfico do Brasil, 1910), pp. 84–87.

[39] The notion that Director Lisboa and other IFOCS engineers "trusted that transferring technological solutions from places like the U.S. West would be sufficient to recreate the Northeast in the image of those societies," expressed by Eve Elizabeth Buckley in "Drought in the sertão as a natural or social phenomenon: establishing the Inspectoria Federal de Obras Contra as Seccas, 1909–1923," *Boletim do Museu Paraense Emílio Goeldi Ciências Humanas,* Vol. 5, No. 2 (May–Aug. 2010), is not supported in remarks in published surveys composed by U.S. geologists. These were replete with recommendations to treat endemic issues associated with poverty and destitution, especially education. For example, Horatio L. Small noted there was "a great need for assistance... to the *sertanejo*, a man of little or no instruction, whose life is tied to a small tract of land that could only poorly be called a *fazenda* and upon whom all our attention should be concentrated." Horatio L. Small, *Geologia e supprimento d'agua subterrânea no Ceará e parte do Piauhy* (Rio de Janeiro, Inspectoria de obras contra as Seccas, 1913), p. 73. There is little doubt that benefits from the anti-drought works accrued disproportionately to the powerful.

doubled between 1922 and 1930. Paraiba's cotton output rose by 138% during the same period, and that of Ceará rose by nearly 27%. Cotton exports to both domestic and foreign destinations from the three principal ports in the region—Recife, Forteleza, and Natal—rose by nearly 70% between 1925 and 1929[40] (see Figs. 11.2 and 11.3).

The agents of increased production were other than major landowners, as Northeast cotton was planted primarily on small plots. Traditionally, sharecroppers (*parceiros*) worked small plots ceded to them by large landowners and surrendered half of their harvest to landlords, selling the remainder to itinerant buyers at the best price possible.[41]

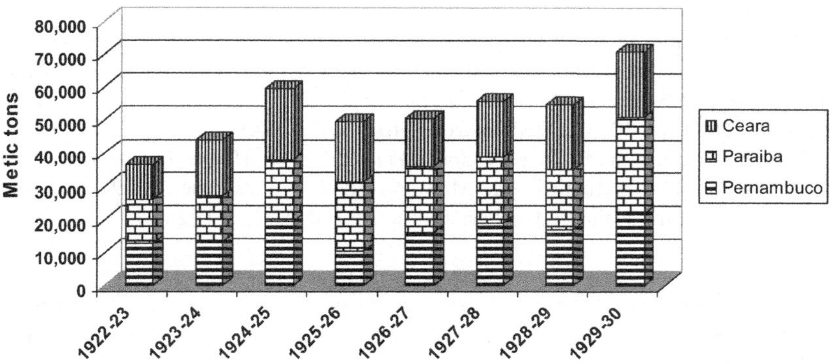

Fig. 11.2 Cotton production in three leading Northwestern Producing States, 1922–23 to 1929–30 (*Source* Rui Henrique Pereira Lima de Albuquerque, *Capital comercial, indústria têxtil e produção agricola: as relações de produção na cotonicultura paulista, 1920–1950* (São Paulo: HUCITEC; Brasilia: Conselho Nacional de Desenvolvimento Científico e Tecnológico, 1983), p. 116)

[40] Recife data from Directoria Geral de Estatística quoted in *A Provincia* [Recife], Jan. 16, 1930, p. 3. Data on Rio Grande do Norte from state presidential messages compiled by Souza, *A República Velha no Rio Grande do Norte,* p. 80. Ceará data from *Annuarios Estatísticos do Ceará* quoted in Memoria do Ceará, *Ceará - A Crise Permanente do Modelo Exportador 1850–1930* (Fortaleza, CE: Instituto da Memória do Povo Cearanese, 1989), pp. 206–7.

[41] Ana Cristina Leite, *O Algodão no Ceará: Estrutura fundiaria e capital comercial (1850/1880)* (Fortaleza, CE: Secretaria da Cultura e Desporto do Estado do Ceará, 1994), p. 65.

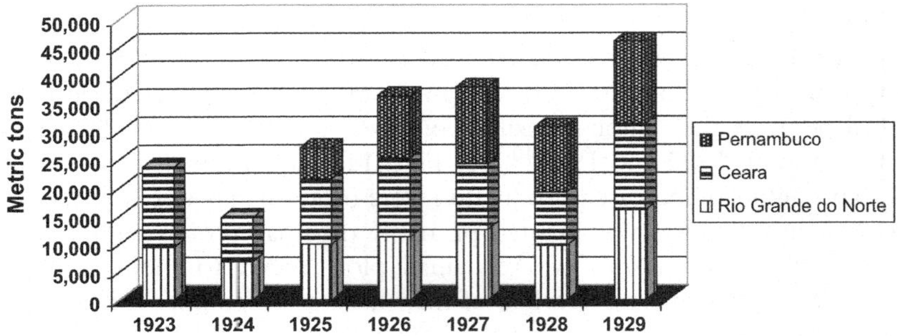

Fig. 11.3 Domestic and foreign cotton exports from Pernambuco, Ceará, and Rio Grande do Norte 1923 to 1929 (*Sources* Recife data from Directoria Geral de Estatística quoted in *A Provincia* [Recife], Jan. 16, 1930, p. 3. Data on Rio Grande do Norte from state presidential messages complied by Itamara de Souza, *A República Velha no Rio Grande do Norte 1889–1930* (Natal, RGN: Editora da UFRN, 2008), p. 80. Ceará data from *Annuarios Estatísticos do Ceará* quoted in Memoria do Ceará, *Ceará—A Crise Permanente do Modelo Exportador 1850–1930* (Fortaleza, CE: Instituto da Memória do Povo Cearense, 1989), pp. 206–207. (No data are available for Pernambuco for 1923 and 1924.))

IFOCS Geologist Horatio Small, traveling in southeast Ceará and Piauí in late 1912, observed substantial amounts of cotton harvested near various towns in Ceará, but that was difficult to appreciate "because the cotton fields do not occupy great areas... but appear in small, isolated fields." An encyclopedic report on Brazil's rural environment by the Ministry of Agriculture in 1922 pointed out that, in Pernambuco, "as a rule," cotton was planted "in small areas, rarely larger than two hectares and in a mixture with other plants (manioc, corn, beans, etc.)." The same ministry, reporting on rural salaries two years later, pointed out that cotton cultivation was "practically in almost its entirety by small farmers '*rendeiros*' (tenants) and sickle carriers [*forceiros*] of small properties."[42]

[42] Horatio L. Small, *Geologia e supprimento d'agua subterranea no Ceará e parte do Piauhy* ([Rio de Janeiro]: Imprensa Ingleza, 1923), p. 66; Brazil. MAG, Serviço de Inspecçao e Fomento Agrícola, *Aspectos da Economia Rural Brasileira* (Rio de Janeiro: Officinas Graphicas Vilas Boas, 1922), p. 322; Brazil. MAG, Serviço de Inspecção e Fomento Agrícola, *Salário de trabalhadores rurais* no *Brasil* (Rio de Janeiro: Imprensa Nacional, 1924), p. 3.

Another factor contributing to increases in Northeast's cotton production was the combined impact of extensive federal and state efforts to improve the Northeast's crop through better regulation and subsidies extended to political favorites. Federal and state technicians of the cotton service successfully created and implemented a classification service in close cooperation with São Paulo's mercantile exchange. The absence of a national classification system for cotton—using uniform standards to describe the physical attributes of raw cotton, especially fiber length and uniformity—complicated its marketing and sale. The harvest and baling of a mixture of varieties dismayed clients expecting uniform fiber length. The issue arose partly from the nature of cotton cultivation in the Northeast, carried out in many cases by poor—itinerant laborers or owners of "minifundos" without access to fertilizer, implements, or sophisticated cultivating techniques. As one observer noted, the "great cotton states of the North" remained "prisoners to a more rudimentary system of planting and harvesting" without a rigorous selection of seeds, comingling planting of short-staple and long-staple varieties of cotton.[43] The Ministry of Agriculture vowed to create a uniform classification system in 1923 in response to presentations at the 1922 cotton conference. Leading the task was José Maria Fernandes, a 1918 graduate of the Luiz de Queiroz school who had completed a six-week course in cotton "classing" at Texas A&M University in 1920. He had urged adoption of a classification system at the 1922 conference. He was assisted by José Garibaldi Dantas, who, as noted earlier, was instrumental in establishing a cotton classification system for São Paulo.[44]

[43] *Jornal do Brasil*, Dec. 14, 1923, copy in RS 23-08-10, ARS; Josué Modesto dos Passos Sobrinho, *História econômica de Sergipe, 1850–1930* (Aracaju, Sergipe: Universidade Federal de Sergipe, 1987), pp. 8–81.

[44] São Paulo (State), Diretoria de Publicidade Agrícola, *Boletim de Agricultura*, Vol. 21 (1920), pp. 524–531; *Jornal do Recife*, Dec. 2, 1924, p. 1. The cotton "classing" course at Texas A&M included study "of the elements which determine the commercial grades of cotton; the influences which affect the price of cotton; the system of financing the crop from field to factory, and the relation of exchanges to the business in general. Each class is furnished with new samples for practice, and the work is patterned after that of a cotton office. The samples used in the summer school are obtained from the cotton states west of the Mississippi river, and an effort is made to familiarize the student with the different characteristics of cotton grown in the southwest." Other Brazilian students in the course—mostly from the Northeast—were Joaquim Mauricio Wanderlay from Pernambuco, João Coimbra from Pernambuco, Floriano A. Freire from Pernambuco, Paulo de Mirando Henriques from Paraíba, Sylvio de Carvalho from Belo Horizonte, and Raphael d'Avila

By June 30, 1925, the ministry had created classification rules and a plan to teach classification. Over 100 students completed the course by 1929, taught by professors who had studied cotton classification in the United States. Ensuring that cotton was indeed classified was another challenge, however, as this required cooperation of both processors and shippers. It took cotton merchants in Campina Grande, Paraíba, nearly three years to resolve to purchase solely classified cotton in response to complaints from merchants in Liverpool about the "lamentable mixture of fibers noted in one lone bale."[45] By 1929, two-thirds of Brazil's overall cotton production was being classified.[46]

Extensive federal and state subsidies improved processing and lowered production costs. In 1922 the federal Serviço de Algodão installed seed disinfecting plants purchased in the United States in Minas Gerais, Paraíba, Pará, and Maranhão.[47] Through a decree of July 1, 1925, dedicated to the "increase of cotton production in the state," Bahia authorized exemption for cotton from all export taxes for ten years, free transportation of agricultural machines, cotton gins, and presses and motors for gins, and free use for five years of state land for agricultural colonies dedicated to cotton cultivation. It also provided agricultural implements and insecticides needed for cotton cultivation at cost.[48] Federal and state governments' experimental stations and seed farms distributed large amounts of seed in the Northeast. In 1925, over 159 tons of seeds were distributed nationwide, of which 73% were distributed in Northeastern states. The next year the governments' cotton service was harvesting cotton on 368 hectares on its farms in Ceará, Pernambuco, Alagoas, and Sergipe and providing 675 kilos of seeds from its experimental station in Seridó, Rio Grande do Norte. In 1928, the governments' seed distributions in the Northeast rose to nearly 183 tons, 78% of the nationwide total.[49]

Oliveira from Rio de Janeiro. See Texas A & M University, *Forty-Fifth Annual Catalogue, Session 1920–21.* Third Series, No. 7 (June 1, 1921), pp. 293–312.

[45] *Diário Nacional* [São Paulo], Jan, 13, 1928, p. 1.

[46] Brazil, MAG, *Relatório 1923*, pp. 57–8; *Relatório 1925*, p. 159; *Relatório 1928*, p. 164; *Relatório 1929*, p. 135.

[47] USC-Pernambuco to SS, Apr. 12, 1922, Box 56, RG 166, USNA.

[48] "Legislação Agrícola e Industrial dos Estados," Brazil, MAG, *Boletim* Vol 2, No. 2 (Aug. 1925), pp. 191–193.

[49] Brazil, MAG, *Relatório 1927*, pp. 131, 133; *1928*, p. 152.

The employment of agronomists trained in cotton practices of the United States also aided production. Hector A. Tavares studied cotton at the University of Georgia and traveled throughout the cotton-producing regions of the U.S. South. In his visit to the Pee Dee experimental station and the Carolina Seed Company, in Florence, South Carolina, he took special note of the use of fertilizers and crop rotation. He spent "the entire day in the fields" of the Pedigree Seed Company in Hartsville, South Carolina, and in Auburn, Alabama, visited Professor E.F. Caruthers, who "opened to me the doors of his laboratory." Tavares wrote a 51-page booklet based on his experiences entitled *Melhoramento do Algodoeiro,* published in 1923. In 1927, he became the director of Sergipe's cotton service, succeeding Day.[50] Octavio Lamartine, a 1924 Lavras graduate who studied cotton at the University of Georgia, directed the Seridó experimental station in Rio Grande do Norte between 1928 and 1930 during the tenure of his father and state governor Juvenal Lamartine.[51]

Finally, the Northeast's cotton production probably rose because of the impact of foreign and domestic investment in its processing. The Wharton Pedrosa company joined forces with Companhia Paraíbana de Beneficiamento e Prensagem de Algodão, of Campina Grande, in 1923. The later firm possessed a "very modern ginning factory," with "three gins of 80 saw blades each," suction pipes and a hydraulic press when visited by British cotton expert Arno S. Pease in 1921.[52] In Paraiba, 580 cotton gins were operating in 1930, and twelve new companies formed in the state between 1922 and 1929 to process cotton. Pernambuco boasted 334 gins and 409 cotton presses in establishments employing

[50] Brazil, MAG, *Boletim,* Vol. 11, No. 4 (Oct.–Nov. 1922), pp. 31–42; Heitor A. Tavares, *Melhoramento do Algodoeiro* (N.P.: n.p., 1923), p. 2: "A cultura do algodão no Estado de Sergipe," Brazil, MAG, *Boletim,* Vol. 1, No. 4 (Apr. 1927), pp. 458–479.

[51] "A classificação do Algodão no Ceará," Brazil, MAG, *Boletim* Vol. 15, No. 4 (Oct. 1926), pp. 419–424; Lauro da Escóssia, *Cronologias mossoroenses* (Mossoró, RGN: Fundação José Augusto, 1981), p. 59.

[52] Paulo Pereira dos Santos, *Um homem admirável: João Severiano da Câmara: o empresário e o político* (N.P.: Departamento Estadual de Imprensa, 1998), pp. 30–35; Arno S. Pearse, *Brazilian Cotton; being the report of the journey of the International cotton mission through the cotton states of São Paulo, Minas Geraes, Bahia, Alagôas, Sergipe, Pernambuco, Parahyba, Rio Grande do Norte by International Federation of Cotton and Allied Textile Industries. International Cotton Mission to Brazil* (Manchester, Eng., Taylor, Garnett, Evans & Co., 1922), p. 157.

around 3,000 workers. As a 1928 account of cotton's status in the Northeast argued, improvements in the quality of the Northeast's cotton had occurred through "a great number of modern cotton mills, belonging to private companies that dedicate themselves to the perfect processing and baling of the product."[53]

Decisions by the federal and state governments between 1922 and 1930 combined with nature's whims created a complex mix of forces. Pressured by the textile industry's lobbying on the Center-South's need for Northeastern cotton, the federal government could not completely withdraw its support. Large landowners and merchants in the Northeast whose fortunes were tied to cotton cultivation, processing, and shipping, pressed successfully for federal and state support. Northeastern-grown cotton benefited from higher levels of support from both state and federal governments, technological expertise and equipment acquired largely through contacts with the United States, and toward the end of the decade, higher levels of global demand for cotton. The Pessoa administration's ambitious public works project provided improvements in transportation infrastructure that may have benefited small holders and large landowners, as well as the owners of cotton processing facilities and exporters. Its abrupt termination reminded those who supported innovation and growth in the Northeast's cotton sector that the nation's political and economic structure favored the Center-South. As the decade's end approached, the Northeast remained Brazil's dominant cotton-producing region, having overcome numerous challenges to emerge as a positive contributor to Brazil's diversified agriculture. When the viability of the *café com leite* political arrangement came into question in 1929 and 1930, members of the Northeast's political elite would remember the depth of its struggle against nature and political favoritism to sustain its version of "white gold."

[53] Irene Rodrigues da Silva Fernandes, *Comércio e Subordinação: A Associação Comercial da Paraíba no Processo Historico Regional -1889/1930* (João Pessoa, PA: Editora Universitaria, 1999), pp. 68, 72; "O algodão em Pernambuco," Brazil, MAG, *Boletim,* Year 18, Vol. 2, No. 2 (Aug. 1929), p. 277; *O Paiz*, Oct. 9, 1929, p. 12.

The Cattle Sector in Rio Grande do Sul

The Northeast's struggles to garner support for its cotton production mirrored the trials of Rio Grande do Sul during the final years of the First Republic. Like the Northeast, the cattle-dependent South suffered from oscillating prices for its principal commodity, exacerbated by a lack of political power. The advantages enjoyed by São Paulo allowed it to side-step the effects of falling cattle prices, but Rio Grande do Sul had no large urban market nearby, endured high transportation costs, and struggled with competition from Uruguay and Argentina. Moreover, sales of its cattle industry's traditional product—charque (beef jerky or salted beef)—were wavering. The domestic market flattened as northeastern states that had imported charque from the Rio Grande do Sul opened their own charque factories, and *gaúcho* charque found difficulty competing in foreign markets with higher quality products from Uruguay and Argentina. Prices for the two principal products of Rio Grande do Sul's cattle sector—refrigerated beef and jerky—continued to slide during this period, extending an atmosphere of crisis developing since mid-decade (see Fig. 11.4).

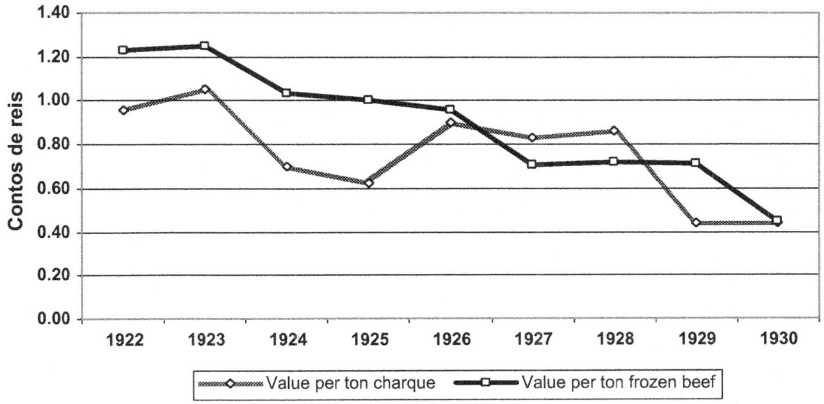

Fig. 11.4 Value per ton Frozen Beef and Charque, Rio Grande do Sul, 1922–1930 (Source: Rio Grande do Sul, Departamento Estadual de Estatística, *Anuario Estatístico do Rio Grande do Sul 1938/39; 1941* (Porto Alegre: DEE, 1939/1940; 1942) cited in Sigfried Emanuel Heiser, *As Relações de Comércio do Rio Grande do Sul – Do Século XIX a 1930* (Porto Alegre: Secretaria de Coordinação e Planejamento, 2004), pp. 109, 122)

The impact of lower prices was especially acute because the cattle industry sold mostly to the charque factories. Low demand for Brazilian beef in foreign markets forced *frigoríficos* in Rio Grande do Sul to purchase a small share total cattle in the market. In 1923, they adsorbed 87,778 cattle, or only 10.3%, of the over 850,000 cattle sacrificed in the state. The 1924 kill included a slightly higher percentage (19.2) dedicated to frozen or even canned beef, but this percentage dropped to 14.8% for 1925.[54] Data on the total production of charque versus chilled and frozen beef (see Fig. 11.5), testify to the overwhelming dependence of the state's cattle sector upon charque production.

Ranchers and owners of beef jerky processing plants in Rio Grande do Sul prioritized political action as a response to the challenges of marketing their beef products. By early 1926, the sector was in a crisis mode. The federal government's decision to allow duty-free imports of Argentine charque left producers with falling prices and stocks of salted beef from

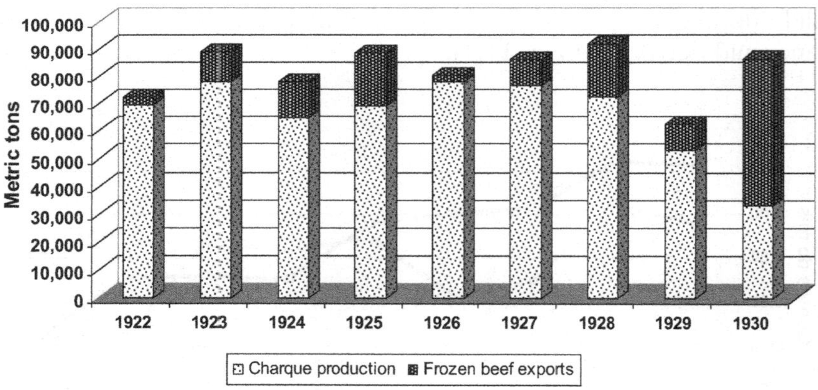

Fig. 11.5 Production of Frozen Beef versus Charque, Rio Grande do Sul, 1922–1930 (Source: Rio Grande do Sul, Departamento Estadual de Estatística, *Anuario Estatístico do Rio Grande do Sul 1938/39; 1941* (Porto Alegre: DEE, 1939/1940; 1942) cited in Sigfried Emanuel Heiser, *As Relações de Comércio do Rio Grande do Sul – Do Século XIX a 1930* (Porto Alegre: Secretaria de Coordinação e Planejamento, 2004), pp. 109, 122)

[54] TS, "Matanzas Totais," Escriptorio Central de Charqueadores do Rio Grande do Sul, Apr. 13, 1926, 12.00.00 VI-5, AISL.

the 1925 slaughter. Meeting in Bagé, Rio Grande do Sul in February 1926, 60 owners and charque plants and ranchers petitioned the federal government to arrange for lower ocean and rail rates and for the state government to reform rules governing the charque industry. Even though President Bernardes arranged for former Minister of Agriculture Ildefonso Simões Lopes, then serving as a federal deputy, to preside over the conference and express the federal government's concern, the ministries of agriculture, treasury, and transport took no actions on the sector's requests.[55]

"The cattle growers are all complaining of unsatisfactory conditions," noted the U.S. Consul in Porto Alegre in early 1927. "The 'Charque' or dried beef plants are not buying as many cattle or paying as much for what they buy as the cattlemen think they should," he reported. He attributed the difficult situation to the lower demand in foreign markets and Brazilian states and smuggling of thousands of cattle from Uruguay into Rio Grande do Sul that were then processed and sold as Brazilian products.[56] Even the Armour plant at Santa Ana do Livramento dedicated about one-sixth of its productive capacity to processing beef for charque in 1928. The Swift plant at Rosario consistently placed third in the ranking of all Rio Grande do Sul jerky producers.[57] In 1928, a prominent Rio Grande do Sul journalist reported that the state's cattle population had risen dramatically—by 32%—since prewar days, while charque exports had fallen. In the meantime, the cold beef export industry had "shattered many hopes" with recent exports of a little more than a thousand tons of beef. To the stockmen's dismay, charque sales represented the overwhelming market for Rio Grande do Sul's cattle industry during this period.[58]

[55] *O Jornal* [Rio de Janeiro], Feb. 16, 1926, p. 1; May 13, 1926, p. 7; May 23, 1926, p. *O Paiz*, Mar. 4, 1926, p. 4.

[56] USC-Porto Alegre to SS, May 1, 1927, Box 64, RG 166, USNA.

[57] TS, Alvara M. Barcellos, "A safra no estado de Rio Grande do Sul," n.d., 12.00.00 VI? 18, AISL; TS, Syndicato dos Xarqueadores do Rio Grande do Sul, "Estatística da exportação do xarque....," 1926, 1927, 1929, 12.00.00 VI 10; VII 9; VII 25, AISL.

[58] Leonardo Truda, "2 Congresso do Criadores do Rio Grande do Sul," *A Lavoura*, Vol. 32 (1928), 230–1.

Political Implications of Regional Inequalities

The problems endured by the cattle industry in Rio Grande do Sul and the cotton-producing states of the Northeast provided the girders for a political bridge for elite politicians of the two regions. In the extreme South, dissatisfaction among ranchers created a political opportunity of national proportions for an astute emerging politician steeped in rural ways. Rio Grande do Sul could count upon the allegiance of Northeastern politicians, clearly resentful of the Northeast's exclusion from economic gains during the Bernardes and Washington Luis administrations.

The contrasts in regional prosperity were readily apparent to an emerging politician with a keen ability to gauge the strength and direction of political currents. Getúlio Vargas viewed Brazil through the perspective of a rancher with acute political insight. While initially not a spokesperson for the cattle sector, he quickly identified with its interests when it became politically expedient to do so. Born in São Borja, in the Rio Grande do Sul cattle-raising district along the Argentine border, Vargas received his political training from his *coronel* father, General Manuel Nascimento Vargas. The elder Vargas was "a perfect product of the land," a tough rancher who not only ruled São Borja in *caudilho* style, but also provided valuable political connections for his son. After an abortive start at a military career, law school in Porto Alegre, and brief apprenticeship in Porto Alegre as a district attorney, Getúlio represented São Borja for two terms in the state legislature. He kept strong local ties by returning to his native town to practice law between terms and throughout his career recalled "fondly the green grass of the region and the days he spent there on horseback."[59]

As a federal officer holder, Vargas remained loyal to his region's interests and traditions. As a federal deputy from 1923 to 1927, and then as Minister of Finance in the Washington Luiz administration, Vargas defended his state's agricultural interests and honed his *caudilho* political skills. When Rio Grande do Sul rice producers found that lower prices and a significant increase in output were threatening their viability in the market, Vargas pushed through a price-support plan that benefited them almost exclusively. As finance minister, Vargas began personally

[59] Jordan M. Young, *The Brazilian Revolution of 1930 and its Aftermath* (New Brunswick, N.J.: Rutgers University Press, 1967), p. 32; John W.F. Dulles, *Vargas: Political Biography* (Austin: University of Texas Press, 1967), p. 17.

receiving individual requests in the best *caudilho* tradition. Political conditions in his home state soon provided the opportunity to employ such skills, and Vargas gained the state governorship unopposed in 1928. Although unspectacular as a federal official, as president of Rio Grande do Sul Vargas quickly strengthened his political base. He astutely cultivated support from associations and cooperatives, including some with urban bases,[60] but paid special attention to the politically powerful cattle sector.

By the time Vargas arrived in office, the state's cattle interests had revitalized their lobbying. A newly heightened sense of crisis stemming from the poor performance of the *frigoríficos* and the falling price of charque in 1926 had reinvigorated the Federação das Associações Ruraes do Estado de Rio Grande do Sul, established in 1921. High on their agenda were the endemic problems of the state's cattle industry, especially the lack of long-term credit at moderate interest rates and competition from charque smuggled from Uruguay. Because of Rio Grande do Sul's poor overland transportation system and high freight costs by sea from Rio Grande to other Brazilian ports, its charque could not compete with Uruguayan imports. Furthermore, false customs receipts allowed much Uruguayan charque to enter without paying customs duties under the guise of being transshipped through Uruguay from Brazilian plants in Mato Grosso. To combat such problems, charque producers organized their own syndicate in 1928, and together with the stockmen asked Vargas for help.[61]

Vargas recognized the plight of stock raisers when he spoke at a Porto Alegre conference of 102 representatives of the cattle sector from 42 municipios on March 28, 1928. He endorsed the "associative spirit" as "one of the most important forces of economic progress" and pledged to "stimulate" and "valorize" the "rise of the associative mentality." He offered multiple solutions to "many problems directly or indirectly related to the cattle industry." He pledged support for improved credit by establishing a state agricultural bank. He also committed to improve the state's

[60] Gunter Axt, "The Origins of an 'Enigma': Getúlio Vargas, Rio Grande do Sul's Decaying *coronelismo*, and the Genesis of the Interventionist State before the 1930 Revolution," in Jens R. Hentschke, ed., *Vargas and Brazil: New Perspectives* (New York: Palgrave Macmillan, 2007), pp. 46–7.

[61] Jahaty Pesavento, *República Velha Gaucha*, pp. 256–7; Love, *Rio Grande do Sul*, pp. 2–3.

transportation system and control smuggling, all with the goals of "facilitating the exploitation of land, the development of agriculture [and] the improvement of the cattle sector." Lest the opportunity be lost, a prominent local journalist reminded Getúlio that the state cattle industry had reached a crossroads, facing either improvement or "annihilation and ruin," with a consequent need for "the remodeling of the whole complex of our pastoral industry."[62]

Vargas soon responded with action at state and federal levels. Assisted by the leader of the state's delegation in Congress, João Neves da Fontoura, Vargas pushed a bill that prohibited transshipment of Brazilian charque through foreign points, making false entry of Uruguayan charque more difficult. Vargas also obtained significant federal assistance for the state's transportation network via three-to-one matching funds for the rail network and acquisition of two port facilities for state use. At the state level, Vargas responded to the call for easier credit by establishing the Banco de Rio Grande do Sul within four months of the close of the Congresso dos Criadores. The bank was to provide pastoral and agricultural interests with low-cost credit. State funds provided for two-thirds of the bank's initial capital. Loans soon began to flow to the cattle sector. The association of charque producers was "much favored by the official actions implemented by the government of Getúlio Vargas."[63] Getúlio's action were entirely consistent with his corporate vision of the relations between capital and state.[64] He soon began to show positive economic and political results, including increased profitability of the charque industry. Vargas also gave moral support to stockmen seeking to establish their own *frigoríficos* and used the state government's apparatus to strengthen the cattle sector across the board.[65]

[62] "2 Congresso de Criadores de Rio Grande do Sul," *A Lavoura*, Vol. 32 (1928), pp. 226, 230–1.

[63] Love, *Rio Grande do Sul*, pp. 220–3; Funds for the bank came from a $42 million loan from White, Weld & Company of New York, see Jahaty Pesavento, *República Velha Gaúcha*, p. 268; Carlos Alberto Di Bernard, *Conseqüências Econômicas e Sociais do Cicle do Charque no Rio Grande do Sul, O Caso da Charqueada de Cruz Alta* (Porto Alegre, RS: Imprensa Livre, 2002), p. 113.

[64] See Joan Lamaysou Bak, "Some Antecedents of Corporatism: State Economic Intervention and rural organization in Brazil: The Case of Rio Grande do Sul, 1890–1937" (Diss.: Yale University, 1977).

[65] Jahaty Pesavento, *República Velha Gaúcha*, p. 289.

Vargas's actions allowed him to approach and eventually make a pact with Assis Brasil that would make Vargas the true representative of the state's rural interests. Assis Brasil had remained prominent in Rio Grande's rural life ever since returning from Washington in 1901. Presiding at rural expositions and striving to improve the state's cattle stock, he breathed deeply from the countryside's political winds. No less than during the 1890s, Assis Brasil championed rural causes and called upon government to meet the rural sector's needs. He presided over founding of the Associação Rural de Bagé in September 1904 and became the group's honorary president. In 1908 he founded the Partido Democrático and unveiled its program at an assembly in Santa Maria, Rio Grande do Sul, in September of that year. Assis Brasil continued his campaign for government attention to education and assistance to agricultural development. He cast his argument in familiar terms, contending that government aid should be directed "principally in terms of agricultural and rural industries" and "peopling of the soil" through a variety of actions, including construction of highways.[66]

Assis Brasil had also remained an impassioned foe of a coffee-based economy and responded vigorously to the crisis in Rio Grande do Sul's cattle sector.[67] In November 1921 he figured prominently in the founding of the Federação das Associações Rurais do Rio Grande do Sul at Bagé. The following year he challenged the government to aid the cattle sector in a speech to stockmen gathered in Porto Alegre. His fellow cattle raisers cheered his call for the government to meet their financial needs by furnishing ample credit on reasonable terms. Assis Brasil then decided to confront the Borges de Medeiros government directly by leading a coalition of liberal democrats, federalists, and disaffected Republicans attempting to unseat the reigning Rio Grande do Sul political clique. He challenged Borges de Medeiros under the banner of the Aliança Libertadora in the 1922 election for state governor. When the forces of Borges de Medeiros manipulated the results, Assis Brasil turned to armed action to end the Borgista grip on the state's political machine. He gathered political support from his status as the state's "most progressive cattle breeder" and as "an authority in political and economic

[66] Fortunato Pimentel, *Joaquim Francisco de Assis Brasil: Emérito Agricultor* (Porto Alegre: Santa Teresinha Ltda., 1950), pp. 114–5; J. F. de Assis Brasil, *Dictadura, parlamentarismo, democracia* (N.P.: Livraria do Globo, n.d.), pp. 8–9.

[67] Assis Brasil, *Attitude do Partido Democrático Nacional*, p. 58.

matters" in the opinion of "many of the larger and wealthier cattle breeders of Rio Grande do Sul." The "leading cattle ranchers" as well as some "professional men" in the state provided him with an estimated US$375,000 to carry out his campaign against Borges de Medeiros.[68]

Agrarian interests beyond Rio Grande do Sul lent important symbolic support. The president of the SRB praised Assis Brasil at a large banquet held in his honor in São Paulo in February 1923. "From the four corners of the country," he asserted, "sympathetic glances converge" upon Assis Brasil, offering "encouragement" and "solidarity" to his cause. The SRB pledged "in chorus with all the strength of the Brazilian nation" that it would continue the support for "Assis Brasil and his courageous companions [that the SRB] spontaneously offered when it saw them armed for combat." The SRB held that "the electoral drama of Rio Grande do Sul" was not a local struggle but "Brazilian," the "first strike for the regeneration of national politics."[69]

Assis Brasil converted such support into an armed movement of such magnitude that the federal government finally intervened to force a truce. The Pact of Piedras Altas of November 1923 ruled out Borges de Medeiros's reelection and provided for stronger representation of the opposition in the state legislature. Although initially a forced truce, the agreement benefited Assis Brasil's supporters because it eventually removed Borges de Medeiros from office. But it also allowed Borges de Medeiros to pick his own successor, and his protégé Getúlio Vargas became governor of the state in January 1928.

Even though Vargas occupied the governor's chair, he soon found that he could not ignore the political power of Assis Brasil. Assis Brasil's status as head of the Aliança Libertadora party had grown significantly when his party united with the Partido Democrático [Democratic Party] of São Paulo in September 1927. The Partido Democático of São Paulo had expressed its support for agriculture in its 1926 founding manifesto. It was agrarian in orientation, although many of its leaders were urban-oriented professionals. Some coffee growers supported the party, but overall, its representation was less export-oriented than that of the

[68] Jahaty Pesavento, *República Velha Gaúcha*, pp. 225–6; Carlos E. Cortes, *Gaucho Politics in Brazil: The Politics of Rio Grande do Sul, 1930–1964* (Albuquerque: University of New Mexico Press, 1974), pp. 14–5; USC-PA to SS, Mar. 19, 1923, 832.00/276, RG 59, USNA.

[69] "Dr. Assis Brasil," *Revista da SRB*, 3 (1923), 85–6.

Partido Republicano Paulista. Significantly, signing the September 21, 1927, alliance with Assis Brasil on behalf of the Partido Democratico was Paulo de Moraes Barros, a prominent advocate of agricultural diversity who, as the Paulista secretary of agriculture between 1913 and 1915, had actively promoted the state's cotton cultivation. The new party called itself the Partido Democrático Nacional [National Democratic Party—hereafter referred to as PDN]—with Assis Brasil as its head. This forced Vargas to lay aside previous disagreements with Assis Brasil and form a strong political alliance that represented the inter-regional pull of Assis Brasil's ideas as well as Vargas's opportunism.[70]

The PDN aimed its political artillery at the national government's highly vulnerable economic policy. It emphasized political reform and pledged attention to the increasing militancy of urban labor, an issue euphemistically termed the "social question." But it also took a strong stand for monetary stability, calling for equilibrium in Brazil's balance of payments and "provisions of economic and financial nature" to stabilize the country's currency. Following conclusion of the alliance with the Paulista element, Assis Brasil incorporated the urban concerns of his São Paulo coalition, a tactic later adopted by Vargas himself. Although the March 1928 platform of Assis Brasil's party retained its emphasis on rural issues, it also promised to "establish in law clear and positive bases for the moral and material progress of workers" through legal protection for unions and provisions for health, training, and disability assistance.[71]

The mechanics of Brazil's national politics soon provided Vargas with reason to draw upon Assis Brasil's coalition of political support. The choice of a successor to National President Washington Luiz had become clouded through squabbling between the Paulistas and Minas Gerais's favorite son, Antonio Carlos Ribeiro de Andrade, of the Partido Mineiro Republicano. According to the informal *café com leite* power-sharing arrangement between Minas and São Paulo, it was time for a Mineiran to occupy the office. Personal and political differences prompted Washington Luiz to break the rules, however, and propose that São Paulo governor Julio Prestes be nominated for the office.

[70] Boris Fausto, *A revolução de 1930: historiografia e história* (São Paulo: Editora Brasiliense, 1970), pp. 32–38; Love, *São Paulo*, p. 165; J.F. Assis Brasil, *Attitude do Partido Democrático Nacional na crise da renovação presidencial para 1930–1934* (Porto Alegre: Livraria do Globo, 1929), p. 109.

[71] Assis Brasil, *Attitude do Partido Democrático Nacional*, pp. 108, 115.

In late 1928 Vargas's lieutenant João Neves probed the possibilities of an alliance with Prestes that would offer Vargas the chance to become a compromise candidate. When Washington Luiz decided to back Prestes, however, Neves allied Vargas with the Partido Republicano Mineiro in June 1929. During the next month and a half, Vargas maneuvered to broaden his base of support still further. He promised to adhere to the platform of Assis Brasil's democrats and gained their endorsement in August. The PDN's directory pledged support for Getúlio because of his "firm promises...... with respect to the essential points of the [PDN's] platform."[72]

To complement the support of Assis Brasil, Vargas also sought an alliance with Paraíban political leaders to broaden his appeal and facilitate his eventual movement into the nation's presidency. Paraíba's political leaders had ample cause of allying with Vargas against the program of the Paulistas. Neglect of the Northeast's needs in the face of oscillating cotton prices and harsh climactic conditions had caused tangible hardships, and, when Getúlio's followers began to sound out Paraíba's President João Pessoa, they found a favorable response. Pessoa was a nephew of former President Epitácio Pessoa and had served since October 1928 as the President of Paraíba. Like his uncle, João Pessoa held great faith in the Northeast's potential for developing cotton and bitterly resented the administration's neglect of the area. "We are sons of the wretched and abandoned Northeast," he explained as he entered the state presidency. He saw the Northeast scourged by banditry, drought, and poverty, but rejected the suggestion that the solution lay in "depopulating the region in favor of the Southern states of the country, more protected by nature and by the public powers." He felt that such an option overlooked the Northeast's assets as "the largest utilizable area of the world for the cultivation of cotton," cotton that "feeds millions of spindles in Brazilian factories." Pessoa had instituted a variety of public works at the state level, including repair of 300 kilometers of roads into the backlands and financing the Banco Hypothecario to support cotton cultivation. Pessoa especially riled at the lack of federal support for his major project,

72 "Resolução do directorio central....," in Assis Brasil, *Attitude do Partido Democrático Nacional*, p. 122.

the construction of the port of Cabedello, one that would allow direct shipment by sea of Paraíba's cotton.[73]

Vargas's supporters sought to take leverage Pessoa's disillusionment with the current government to broaden their candidate's national appeal. After telegraphic consultations, the Vargas group offered the vice-presidential candidacy to João Pessoa, who accepting after duly consulting his uncle, then a world court judge at The Hague.[74] The Paraíbanos entered the Vargas coalition largely at the urging of Epitácio, who, in the opinion of Boris Fausto, "was a figure with the national prestige to enter into an alliance of opposition."[75] The move added a strong ally from a second region equally neglected by the Minas Gerais-São Paulo axis. Vargas's party's platform, adopted at its September 1929 national convention, displayed its debt to its allies, particularly Assis Brasil and Pessoa. In addition to political reforms, the Aliança Liberal stood for "aid to agriculture, not only coffee," renewal of irrigation projects in the Northeast, improving transportation, ending balance of payments deficits, freedom to unionize, protection for child and women workers, and autonomy for the Federal District.[76]

Vargas himself identified the regional pillars of his support to a throng gathered in Rio de Janeiro on January 2, 1930. He expressed his concern that Brazilian agriculture suffered from "a lack of organization and method" while "little, which is almost nothing" had been done for the cattle industry. He renewed his support for "the ideas of eminent Senator Pessoa" and berated the federal government for not extending aid to the Northeast to overcome the "periodic punishment of the droughts." While coffee should be supported, he added, it was nevertheless unwise "to overlook market conditions and to ignore completely the economic laws that regulate production and distribution." While in Rio de Janeiro,

[73] Adhemar Vidal, *1930: História da revolução na Parahyba* (São Paulo: Editora Nacional, 1933), pp. 22, 29–31.

[74] Vidal, *1930: História da revolução na Parahyba,* pp. 40–43.

[75] Boris Fausto, "Tranformações Econômico-sociais e Revolução de 30 no Brasil," In Abguar Bastos, et al., *João Pessoa, A Paraíba e a Revolução de 30.* Intro. Tarcísio de Miranda Burity (Paraíba: Secretaria da Educação e Cultura, 1979), p. 144.

[76] Agnes I. Waddell, "The Revolution in Brazil," *Foreign Policy Association Information Service,* Vol. 6 (1931), 493; Michael L. Coniff, *Urban Politics in Brazil: The Rise of Populism* (Pittsburgh: University of Pittsburg Press, 1981), p. 79.

Vargas attended a lunch for all liberal candidates hosted by former President Pessoa, now back in Brazil, and then undertook triumphal visits to São Paulo and Santos in company of his vice presidential candidate.[77]

The pivotal roles of Assis Brasil and João and Epitácio Pessoa in Vargas's coalition testify to the importance of regional issues in the 1930 revolt. Not only did regional elites who supported agricultural diversification sustain Vargas's political program, their actions were crucial to placing Vargas in the presidential palace by November 3, 1930. Vargas lost the March 1, 1930, election to the officially backed candidate from São Paulo, Julio Prestes, but his supporters refused to accept defeat. At the invitation of Vargas's confidants, army Lieutenant Colonel and Northeast native Pedro Aurelio Goes Monteiro agreed to support an armed overthrow of the government. He gathered other military reformers, known as *tenentes* [lieutenants] to the cause. Plotting for a revolt that would overturn the election results remained confined to subtle maneuvering, however, until a Paraíban politician who enjoyed Washington Luiz's support assassinated Vargas's running mate, João Pessoa, in late July. Plans for an armed revolution gathered momentum during several months of tension. Finally, military action on October 3 and then a statement by Vargas himself, proclaimed the onset of revolution. After a month of intense struggle, Vargas occupied the presidential palace.[78]

The revolution Vargas headed signified the triumph of those elites from regions who struggled throughout the First Republic for more power and influence against the Center-South. While at the turn of the century they were satisfied with additional federal and private resources dedicated to building wealth in their regions, at the end of a decade of favoritism for coffee and limited attention to their own interests, they clearly wanted more. The rush of events and the presence of allies in urban areas gave the movement additional strength, and Vargas's co-optation of the desire of the *tenentes* for thorough reform gave him the military sinews to implement his political designs. Vargas also probably benefited from a general disillusionment within the coffee sector itself, especially after Washington Luiz failed to come to its aid in the accelerating coffee crisis of 1929 and

[77] Getúlio Vargas, *A nova política do Brasil I: da Aliança Liberal as realizações do 1 ano do governo 1930–31* (Rio de Janeiro: José Olympio Editora, 1938), pp. 35–6, 38, 41, 46, 51.

[78] Jordan, *The Revolution of 1930*, pp. 47–63.

1930.[79] Failure of the *café com leite* alliance to overcome the impact of weak prices for the primary products of the Northeast and Rio Grande do Sul provided a common basis for political action by disaffected rural-based regional elites. As Oswaldo Aranha, one of Vargas's closest supporters, explained during the turmoil of October 1930, the previous government had "centered its support on the production of coffee.... to the detriment of other products of the country" and "favored only the state of São Paulo."[80]

As the final days of 1930 approached, it was clear that policies of the previous decade had reshaped Brazil's economic and political reality. Disillusionment and political turmoil supplanted the exuberance of the immediate postwar period, especially in the Northeast and Rio Grande do Sul. Weak prices for non-coffee commodities caused marginal producers to suffer and recoil against the threat of further destitution. Dissatisfied ranchers and beef processors in Rio Grande do Sul joined with Northeastern politicians to build an agrarian-based coalition to challenge the direction of the national political economy. Meanwhile, the nation's richest state—São Paulo—improved its economic standing still further through access to political power, the higher coffee prices, continued research into new products, and a newly found interest in the internal market aided by U.S. capital and technical information. The First Republic withered on the vine and died, choked, in many ways by elites dissatisfied with agricultural policies that ignored their regionally defined preferences. Brazil's agriculture then began a transformation, driven by a state corporatism that rejected policies that ignored regional economic inequities and intent upon co-opting the state elites' approach to producing wealth from the Brazilian countryside.

[79] See Mauricio A. Font, Coffee, *Contention, and Change: The Making of Modern Brazil* (Cambridge, MA: Basil Blackwell, 1990), pp. 248–252.

[80] *NYT*, Oct. 12, 1930, p. 24, col. 1.

CHAPTER 12

Vargas: Institutional Restructuring, 1930–1937

The collapse of the First Republic initially did little to alter the structure of Brazilian agriculture despite the political posturing of Getúlio Vargas and his allies. The champion of the *putsch* to appropriate the presidency was yet another member of the land-owing elite that had manipulated the resources of the state to further its agricultural pursuits. However, rural issues no longer dominated the political agenda. New economic and demographic realities, especially the ongoing international commodities crisis, were beginning to force changes in the nation's political economy. Accelerating urbanization generated pressure on food supplies. Domestically trained agronomists became available to harness the increasingly technical sophistication of food and fiber production. Foreign investors—especially from the United States—began seeking new sources of profits from Brazil's natural endowments.

Vargas responded with the agility of a talented tactician, attending to new political forces as well as to a sector responsible for his entry into national politics. During the first seven years of his presidency, he set aside the *laissez-faire* approach of the First Republic and increased and centralized the federal government's role in the economy, including its relations to agriculture. From 1930 forward, relations between the state and agriculture enter the second stage of corporatist development marked by "differentiated demands from regional oligarchies." The unitary model of traditional corporatism represented by the SNA and SRB fragments

E. R. Downes, *Brazilian Agricultural Development, 1890–1950*,
https://doi.org/10.1007/978-3-031-76992-4_12

became less relevant before the increasing specialization and diversity of the agricultural sector itself.[1]

Formulating Brazil's reaction to the global commodities crisis became a prime task for Vargas's agrarian-based provisional government. His pre-revolution pronouncements and the arrival on horseback in Rio de Janeiro of a contingent of his supporters, clad in wide-brimmed hats, ponchos, and red bandanas following the overthrow of the previous government, implied primacy for rural prerogatives. After all, the platform of Vargas' Liberal Alliance had proclaimed that "the economic problem can be summarized in one word: produce, produce much and produce cheaply, the largest number of recommendable articles, to supply the internal markets and export that which is excess to our necessities."[2] Moreover, the revolutionaries' manifesto of the October 3, 1930, embraced agrarian causes, including "promoting the polyculture of the soil, orienting the activity of the agriculturalist toward the management of the most productive activities, [having] abandoned as much as possible the mirage of monoculture of exotic products, artificially valorized by government support."[3]

The rhetoric and initial actions of the revolution's victors also implied central government activism in fostering changes on multiple issues, including Brazil's agriculture. The priorities Vargas outlined in his first speech included "intensifying production through polyculture" and promoting the "progressive extinction of the latifundia."[4] He named Assis Brasil Minister of Agriculture and charged him with "complete reorganization" of the ministry's services. He instituted the Ministerio de Trabalho, Commercio e Industria [Ministry of Labor, Commerce, and Industry] and the Ministerio da Educação e Saúde Pública [Ministry of Education and Public Health] to satisfy his urban supporters. To placate

[1] Antonio Cesar Ortega, "Corporatism and New Forms of Representing Agricultural interests: A Theoretical Approach," *Revista de Economia e Sociologia Rural*, Vol. 36, No. 4 (1996), 152–53.

[2] See James P. Woodard, "'All for São Paulo: All for Brazil': Vargas, the Paulistas, and the Historiography of Twentieth Century Brazil," in Jens R. Hentschke, ed., *Vargas and Brazil: New Perspectives* (New York: Palgrave Macmillan, 2006), p. 88; Edgard Luiz de Barros, *Getúlio!* (São Paulo: Nankin Editorial, 2004), p. 32.

[3] Maria Cecilia Spina Forjaz, *Tenentismo e as Forças Armadas na Revolução de 1930* (Rio de Janeiro: Forense Universitária, 1988), p. 91.

[4] Brazil, Biblioteca da Presidência da República. *Discurso Pronunciado pelo Dr. Getúlio Vargas... 3 de Novembro de 1930.* (NP: n.d.), p. 19.

the Northeast, he installed Pessoa confidant José America de Almeida as Minister of Public Works and Transportation and commissioned *tenente* Juarez Távora to bring about extensive reform and economic change throughout the Northeast.[5]

Combating the Commodities Crises

The ramifications of the global commodities crisis forced Vargas to prioritize retaining political power and set aside support promised for polyculture. The crisis had a strong impact on "essentially agricultural" Brazil, dependent upon coffee exports for over 60% of its foreign exchange and heavily invested in exports of cacao, tobacco, and other commodities to garner foreign exchange to pay foreign creditors. The foreign debt burden was high—£259 million—and debt service equaled 25% of export earnings. Foreign exchange reserves fell precipitously after September 1929 and reached zero in the month following the revolution's triumph. The sharp decline in prices for coffee, sugar, and cacao from 1928 forward created a fiscal and political crisis for the new government.[6]

Vargas approached these crises with an activist philosophy that would eventually transform the relationship between the state and the nation's economy. He had long questioned *laissez-faire* liberalism, and his experience during the final years of the First Republic as President of Rio Grande do Sul demonstrated benefits of a more interventionist role for the State in the economy. He declared in 1927 that "the government cannot lack the necessary mental agility [for] a continuous capacity of adaption to the irrepressible demands of progress." In his opinion, the "State could no longer limit itself to the concept of Spencer of maintaining order and distributing justice." His creation of the state-run Banco do Estado de Rio Grande do Sul in 1928 allowed him to provide long-term credit at reasonable interest rates to the state's producers. His support for the establishment of producer cooperatives under the tutelage of the state promoted price stability while at the same time

[5] Dulles, *Vargas: A Political Biography*, p. 79; Vargas, *A nova política*, pp. 219–27.

[6] Marcelo de Paiva Abreu, "The Brazilian Economy, 1930–1945," University of Oxford Centre for Brazilian Studies Working Paper Series, Paper CBS-03-99(E), pp. 1–5.

allowing state oversight. Such innovation allowed him to meld the interests of competing political factions through institutional structures that supported a developmental agenda (Fig. 12.1).[7]

He adopted this approach while sustaining a fragile coalition of civilian liberal democrats and junior socialist-minded military revolutionaries known as *tenentes*, who had rebelled against precepts of the First Republic for nearly a decade. Their military leadership had been critical to success of the 1930 revolution, and Vargas sought to retain their support by placing

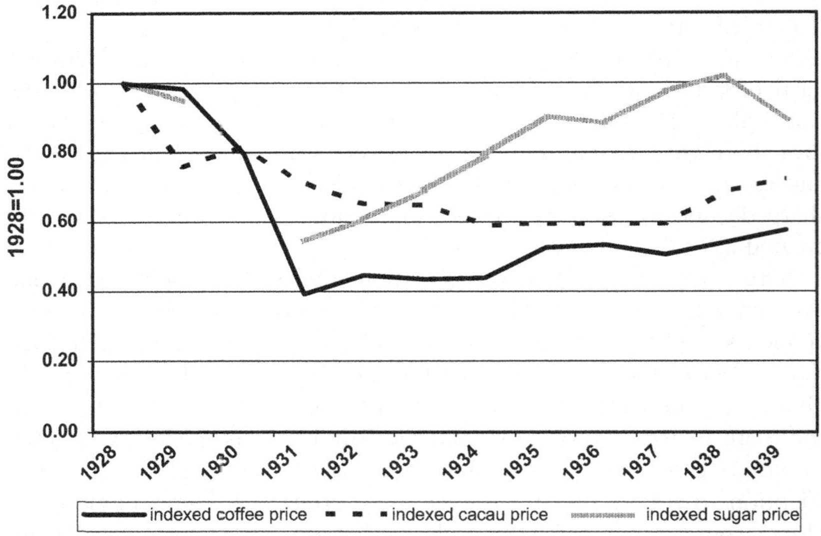

Fig. 12.1 Indexed prices for coffee, sugar, and cocoa, 1928–1939 (*Sources* Coffee and Cocoa prices from Instituto Brasileiro de Geografia e Estatística, Reportório Estatístico do Brasil, Quadros Respectivos, No. 1 (Separata do Anuário Estatístico do Brasil, Ano V, 1939/40 (Rio de Janeiro: Serviço Gráfico do Instituto Brasiliero de Geografia e Estatística, 1941), p. 23. Sugar prices from Brazil. Instituto do Açúcar e do Álcool, *Anuário Açucareiro 1939* (Rio de Janeiro, Brasil Açucareiro, n.d.), p. 95)

[7] Pedro Paulo Zahluth Bastos, "Ortodoxia e Heterodoxia antes e durante a Era Vargas," in Pedro Paulo Zahluth Bastos and Pedro Cezar Dutra Fonseca, eds., *A Era Vargas: Desenvolvimento, Economia e Sociedade* (São Paulo: Editora Unesp, 2011), pp. 199, 200, 217.

them in governing positions, especially as military governors (*interventor*) in almost all Brazilian states. He also called on trusted civilian supporters from his native Rio Grande do Sul both before and during the revolution, as well as members of his political alliance from Minas Gerais and the Northeastern states. Throughout this period, he struggled against intrigues spun by fascist-minded Integralists, Communists supported by the Soviet Union, regional elites disillusioned with their fall in political status and influence, and a military ever cognizant of its role as Vargas' principal power base.[8]

Within this political cauldron, responses to the global commodities crisis by both Vargas and U.S. government restructured Brazil's agricultural priorities. Countering the impact of collapsing prices of export commodities became a prime concern for Vargas as he attempted to consolidate his rule while promoting foreign markets for traditional and non-traditional exports. The political power of regional elites engaged in producing and marketing coffee, sugar, and cacao forced Vargas to assume an unprecedented preeminent role for the central government in agricultural matters, even at the local level. Meanwhile, rising international tensions regarding Germany gave him increased leverage on international agricultural trade, as did U.S. measures to overcome the "crisis of cotton," a commodity with strong domestic political support within the United States.

The most immediate pleas for action came from Northeastern plantation and sugar mill owners in São Paulo, Minas Gerais, and Rio de Janeiro. Improvements in sugar cane disease control and a better processing had generated massive production increases throughout the 1920s. The harvest reached a record of 19 million sacks in 1930, followed by 17 million sacks the following year. With the global collapse of commodity prices, prices for Brazilian sugar fell by 40% between 1930 and 1931 and nearly all sugar-producing states, except Alagoas, appealed to Vargas for a solution.[9]

[8] See Lira Neto, *Getúlio 1930–1945: Do Governo Provisório à ditadura do Estado Novo* (São Paulo: Companhia de Letras, 2013).

[9] Brazil. Instituto do Açucar e do Álcool, *Anuário Açucareiro 1939* (Rio de Janeiro, Brasil Açucareiro, n.d.), pp. 95, 239. Agronomist Jose Vizioli, who had studied phitopathology in the United States, introduced numerous foreign varieties of sugar cane into the São Paulo sugar cane experimental station in the 1920s that led to a major increase in production. See "A introdução de novas variedades de cana de açucar e seu

Vargas responded by instituting control over sugar production through a commission and then an institute under central government direction but with participation of sugar refiners and growers. His December 1931 decree created the Comissão de Defesa da Produçâo Açucareira (Commission for the Defense of Sugar Production) and placed a tax on each bag of sugar refined. The commission also set quotas for sugar processing at each refinery and purchased 742,520 sacks of Northeastern sugar that was sold off to export markets in small lots stocks to quell the "superabundance" of sugar. Nearly simultaneously, the Ministry of Agriculture purchased land for an experimental farm focusing on sugar cultivation in Pernambuco and a seed production field for sugar cane in Ceará.[10]

Vargas provided further support for the sugar sector by aggressively promoting alcohol as an additive to gasoline. In January 1931 he showed his enthusiasm for using alcohol in autos with a highly publicized auto excursion to Mangarabita, 65 miles west of Rio de Janeiro, accompanied by ministers of agriculture, labor, and transportation. The following month Vargas decreed that gasoline for public sales should contain 5% of alcohol and that fuel for public vehicles should contain at least 10% alcohol, lessening the need for gasoline imports and consuming a portion of excess sugar stocks. Further support for alcohol production came the following year when his government exempted equipment necessary for producing anhydrous alcohol from import duties and taxes. The Vargas government then formalized its support for managing sugar and alcohol production in a single entity by replacing the commission with the Instituto do Açúcar e do Álcool (Sugar and Alcohol Institute) to "guide, promote, and control" the production of sugar and alcohol nationwide in June 1933.

The institutions created by Vargas to manage the sugar sector patronized the Northeastern sugar elites through support for cultivation fields and by incorporating them as subordinate members of oversight institutions. Vargas loyalist and gaúcho journalist Leonardo Truda presided over the commission's delegates from the ministries of treasury, industry, labor,

comportamento no estado de São Paulo," *Revista de Agricultura,* XI (Apr. 1936), pp. 79–88, and São Paulo, Secretaria da Agricultura, Industria e Commercio do Estado de São Paulo, Departamento de Produção Vegetal, *Estatísticas e Publicações, Secções Technicas* (c. 1936), pp. 1–3.

[10] *Anuário Açucareiro 1939*, p. 241. Brazil. Ministerio da Agricultura. *Relatório 24 Oct. 1930 to 31 Dec. 1931* (Rio de Janerio: Imprensa Nacional, 1932), p. 21.

and commerce, the banking sector, Pernambuco, Alagoas, and the states of Rio de Janeiro and São Paulo. Truda went on the head the Institute as well, whose members included a Bahian nominated by the military governor because of family ties despite having no connections with the sugar or alcohol sectors. Through 1939, seven Northeastern states (Paraíba, Pernambuco, Ceará, Maranhão, Rio Grande do Norte, and Bahia) received over 70% of the Institute's funds allocated for cooperation fields[11] (see Fig. 12.2).

Vargas's intervention into the sugar crisis generated success on several fronts. The price of sugar began to recover with sales of the harvests of 1932/1933, surpassing the 1929/1930 figure by the harvest of 1938/1939. It also stimulated production of alcohol for automotive use, and output reached over 92 million liters by 1938/1939. Vargas's action also generated political support of sugar mill owners of the Northeast who had

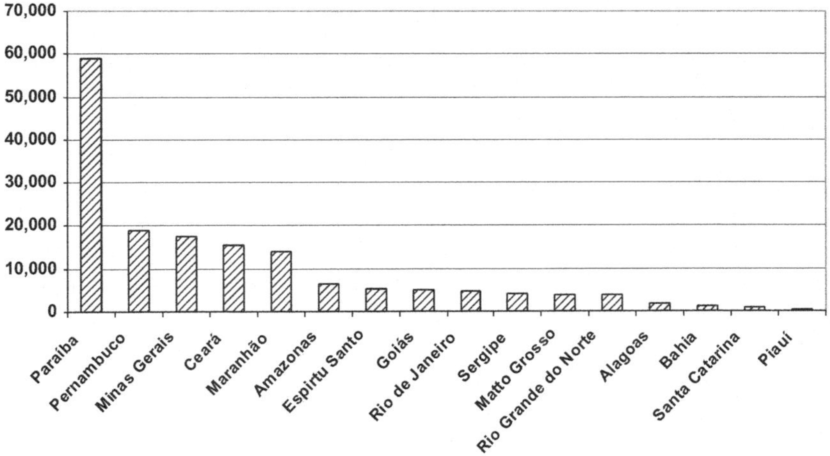

Fig. 12.2 Allocations of central government expenditures for sugar cane cooperation fields, c. 1933–1939 (*Source Anuário Açucareiro 1939*, p. 57)

[11] *Anuário Açucareiro 1939*, p. 239; TS, Oscar Vianna to Juarez Távora, Aug. 30, 1933, in Juarez Távora Archive, JT 1932.12.09, de História Contemporânea do Brasil.

argued that Institute would benefit the Northeast as a whole, a region whose support was critical to the success of the Vargas government.[12]

Far more consequential than the sugar crisis was addressing the dilemma created by the massive overproduction of coffee, the foremost economic challenge confronting victors of the 1930 revolution. Federal and state defense of coffee prices through "valorization" during the First Republic had incentivized strong production increases. With respectable prices guaranteed, planters invested in improved fertilizing and harvesting techniques and replaced exhausted coffee plants with new bushes. At the planters' behest, the states continued to buffer market forces by using foreign loans to purchase excess stocks that were then sold off during years of lean production.[13] Coffee production soared, increasing by 33% between 1922/23 and 1925/26, when it reached over 21 million bags.[14]

The support system soon proved unsustainable. Valorization functioned satisfactorily through 1926, but the 1927/28 harvest of over 34 million sacks far surpassed market demand, requiring financing of storage of over 10 million of sacks of coffee. The crisis accelerated when the Wall Street crash of October 1929 reduced credit to finance purchases of excess stock. The search for solutions led to raucous debates among planters clamoring for reduced taxes, increased financing, limited export of low-grade coffees, abandonment of older plantings, and even an easily transportable coffee extract using lower grade coffees. A far-fetched proposal was offered in September 1930 by Brazilian banker Decio de Paula Machado at an international conference. He argued that coffee-producing countries should boost international demand by opening new

[12] Maria de Nazareth Baudel, *Capital e propriedade fundiária: suas articulações na economia açucareira de Pernambuco* (Rio de Janeiro: Paz e Terra, 1978), pp. 56–57, cited in Forjaz, *Tenentismo e as Forças Armadas*, p. 20.

[13] A robust literature exists on the coffee crisis of the 1920s and early 1930s. This discussion is drawn from Marcello Martins and E. Johnston, *150 anos de café* 2nd rev. ed. (N.P: Salamandra Consultoria Editorial S.A., 1990), pp. 240, 241; Antonio Delfim Netto, *O Problema do Cafe no Brasil* (São Paulo: Instituto de Pesquisas Econômicas, 1981), pp. 115–45; Mauricio A. Font, *Coffee, Contention, and Change in the Making of Modern Brazil* (Cambridge, MA: Blackwell, 1990), pp. 192–268; João de Scantimburgo, *O café e o desenvolvimento do Brasil* (São Paulo: Melhoramentos: Secretaria de Estado da Cultura, 1980), pp. 137–70. Export earnings are from Affonso de E. Taunay, *Pequena História do Café no* Brasil (Rio de Janeiro: Departamento Nacional de Cafe, 1945) p. 549.

[14] Scantimburgo, *O café e o desenvolvimento do Brasil, p. 134.*

markets. "How about China with all its millions?" he queried. "Who has tried to show them how to drink coffee?".[15]

The outlook for coffee continued to deteriorate on the eve of the Vargas revolution. Overlooking the inelasticity of demand for coffee, politicians and the leadership of the São Paulo coffee institute mistakenly argued that lower prices would lead to higher consumption. While export quantities for 1930 rose slightly, prices and revenue continued to plunge. Santos coffee fell from 22.4 cents per pound in September 1929 to 12 cents per pound for the second half of 1930 and revenue from coffee exports fell by nearly 40% from 1929 to 1930. São Paulo contracted for a 20 million pounds sterling loan in July 1930, but the massive stock of stored coffee—21 million bags—coupled with falling prices and low confidence in the Brazilian currency reduced foreign exchange earnings. The consequent inability to import industrial goods and meet foreign debt obligations transformed the resolution of the coffee crisis from a regional to national imperative.[16]

Vargas entertained a variety of potential solutions before moving to consolidate federal control over coffee production and ending the valorization program. Months prior to the revolution, he had criticized the price-support scheme for creating the "illusion of profit" and benefiting other countries far more than Brazil. He called for lowering taxes, decreasing production and transportation costs, and limiting intermediaries.[17] Less than two months after assuming office, he received a proposal from Treasury Minister José María Whitaker and the São Paulo treasury secretary recommending purchase of excess stocks through credits issued by the Bank of Brazil. Vargas initially opposed the maneuver, observing in his diary that "I made various objections to the request for the emission [of credits], arguing that we should not repeat the errors of past

[15] Font, *Coffee, Contention, and Change*, pp. 240–50. "Exposição de Paulo de Morais Barros sobre a situação da produção cafeeira, incluindo: posição estatística do café; política da retenção; trabalho e custeio atrícola; financiamento; o Instituto do Café, crise e providências," GVA, GVc1930.12.00, de História Contemporânea do Brasil; *Final Report of the Delegates of the United States Of America To The Inter-American Conference On Agriculture Held at Washington, D. C., September 8–20, 1930* (Washington: GPO, 1930), p. 37.

[16] Netto, *O Problema do Café no Brasi*, pp. 129–42; Martins and E. Johnston, *150 anos de café*, p. 148.

[17] Edgard Luiz de Barros, *Getúlio!* (São Paulo: Nankin Editorial, 2004), p. 35.

governments wanting to force the valorization and retention of coffee."[18] After raising various other objections, Vargas relented and approved the request. Two other maneuvers soon removed additional coffee from government accounts. In February 1931 Hard and Rand coffee exporters contracted to receive 1,350,000 sacks of coffee, followed seven months later by a barter agreement for another 1,275,000 sacks of coffee in return for 25,000,000 bushels of wheat furnished by the Grain Stabilization Corporation and the Bush Terminal Company of New York.[19]

Vargas then established federal control over the coffee sector. In February 1931 he announced the demise of the previous system by declaring that the government would purchase excess coffee stocks from São Paulo, tax on future exports and new coffee trees planted in the next five years, and encourage importing countries to reduce duties on coffee.[20] Shortly thereafter, Vargas instituted the Conselho Nacional de Café, renamed the Departamento Nacional de Café in February 1933. These entities gradually assumed responsibilities for managing the nation's coffee crop previously exercised by the states, a change not welcomed by coffee planters in São Paulo and Minas Gerais. Getúlio resisted their demands for a higher price, telling São Paulo's secretary of treasury Sousa Dantas in a May 1, 1931, meeting that the federal government would maintain the price of coffee at 8 cents [per pound], to which it had fallen, instead of the 12 cents as pleaded by the Paulista government.[21] By far the most revolutionary step was the decision that the federal government purchase and burn excess coffee, an idea proposed by several planters who traveled to Rio de Janeiro in early November 1931. Vargas adopted the tactic as a necessity, as he explained in a speech on the first year anniversary of his revolt, because the retention of coffee threatened the nation with "economic collapse," causing suffering among coffee planters, tenant farmers, rural businesses, and wholesalers alike.[22] Privately, Vargas explained that he acted in the face of "constant appeals"

[18] Entry for Dec. 22, 1930. *Getúlio Vargas, Diário*, Vol. 1, 1930–1939 (Rio de Janeiro: Fundação Getúlio Vargas, 1995), p. 34.

[19] Netto, *O Problema do Cafe no Brasil*, p. 143; *Wileman's Brazilian Review*, Aug. 17, 1932, pp. 770–71.

[20] Decree 19.688 of February 11, 1931.

[21] Entry for Mar. 1, 1931. *Getúlio Vargas, Diário*, Vol. 1, 1930–1936, p. 51.

[22] Scantimburgo, *O café e o desenvolvimento do Brasil*, pp. 148, 149. See also "Coffee Problem," U.S. Consul General, São Paulo, to Secretary of State, Nov. 20, 1931, RG

to assume direction of coffee policy ["*a política do café*"] from national and foreign commerce.[23]

Vargas's coffee policy held multiple ramifications for the coffee sector and the entire nation. Destruction of 78.2 million sacks of coffee between June 1931 and July 1944 allowed the international price of coffee to move slightly upward. However, the price fell again between 1938 and 1940, recovering only marginally with the advent of the Second World War. The volume of exports remained stable at around 15 million sacks, similar to pre-1930 totals. The total area planted in coffee decreased by 38% between 1931 and 1945[24] (see Figs. 12.3 and 12.4).

Vargas's coffee policy generated a political backlash among coffee planters that contributed to unrest and then open revolt in São Paulo in 1932. Planters were unable to reach a unified political front during the 1930 electoral campaign despite intense activism by various factions of planters.[25] However, the provisional government's treatment of the state as an occupied territory directed by a military governor [*interventor*], along with the coffee elite's dissatisfaction with Vargas's coffee policy unified the Paulista upper class against Vargas. The failure of the Constitutionalist revolt, waged from July through October 1932, allowed Vargas to reassert control over the state, but the Paulista upper class retained a "deep sense of resentment and betrayal" toward Vargas.[26]

229, Office of Inter-American Affairs, Records of the Division of Agriculture, Box 1479, USNA.

[23] Ltr., Getúlio Vargas to Olegario Maciel, Feb. 13, 1933, GVA, CPDOC, GV33.02.12 X40.

[24] Brazil, Instituto Brasileiro de Geografia e Estatística. Estatísticas Históricas Do Brasil, Séries Econômicas, Demográficas e Sociais de 1550 a 1985 (Rio de Janeiro: IBGE, 1987), p. 291.

[25] Font, *Coffee, Contention, and Change*, pp. 218–68; Maria Ligia Coelho Prado, *A democracia ilustrada (O Partido Democrático de São Paulo, 1928–1934)* (São Paulo: Editora Ática, 1986), pp. 141–49.

[26] Woodard, "All for São Paulo: All for Brazil", p. 94. See also Boris Fausto, *Getúlio Vargas: O poder e o sorriso* (São Paulo: Companhia das Letras, 2006), p. 63; Scmrecsányi, *Pequena história da agricultura*, p. 43. The impact of Vargas's coffee policy on Brazil's economic development has generated a robust literature. Celso Furtado and Werner Baer conclude the funds transferred to the coffee growers by the federal government stimulated income growth and industrial production, while Carlos M. Pelaez argues that payments to growers originated from the tax on coffee exports and was prejudicial to industrial growth. See Werner Baer, *The Brazilian Economy*, 5th ed. (Westport, CN: Praeger, 2001),

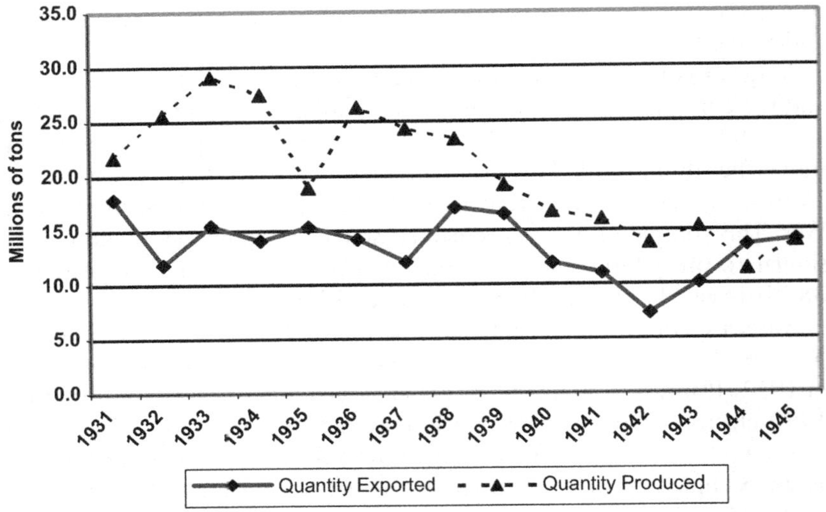

Fig. 12.3 Brazilian coffee production and export, 1931–1945 (*Source* Charles C. Mueller, *Das Oligarquias Agrárias ao Predomínio Urbano-Industrial: Um estudo do Processo da Formação de Políticas Agrícolas no Brasil* (Rio de Janeiro: IPEA/IPES, 1983), pp. 225, 227)

Vargas faced a similar call to action from the planters of cocoa, a crop cultivated in Bahia since the eighteenth century. Bahia's fertile soil and warm, wet climate allowed production in the same land for as long as 80 years, allowing Bahia to become by the 1930s one of the "foremost producing cocoa regions of the world."[27] During the late nineteenth century thousands of peasants from the drought-stricken Northeast had migrated to Bahia and planted cocoa as a subsistence crop. They contributed to an explosive rise in cocoa exports during the 1920s, which reached over 75,000 tons in 1927, a five-fold increase over the 1901 total. Prices underwent an "unexpected and dizzying" fall in 1928

pp. 36–38, and Wilson Cano, "Crise de 1929, Soberania na Política Econômica e Industrialização," in Pedro Paulo Zahluth Bastos and Pedro Cezar Dutra Fonseca, eds., *A Era Vargas: Desenvolvimento, Economia e Sociedade* (São Paulo: Editora Unesp, 2011), pp. 144–54.

27 "Bahia Cocoa Industry," U.S. Consul General Bahia to Secretary of State, Dec. 28, 1944, RG 166, FAS, Narrative Reports (1950–1954), USNA, pp. 14–15.

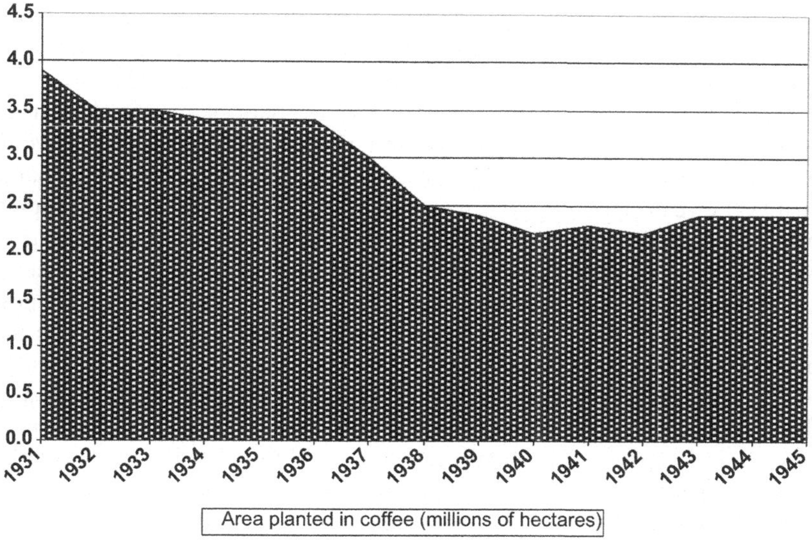

Fig. 12.4 Total Area Planted in Coffee (millions of hectares) 1931–1945 (*Source* Brazil Instituto Brasileiro de Geografia e Estatística. *Estatísticas Históricas Do Brasil, Séries Econômicas, Demográficas e Sociais de 1550 a 1985* (Rio de Janeiro: IBGE, 1987), p. 291)

and further declines by 1930. Export revenue measured in pounds sterling fell 55% from 1927 to 1930. The drop in prices, combined with a perennial lack of agricultural credit, hit growers in Bahia, source of nearly 60% of cocoa exports in 1930, especially hard.[28]

Representatives of the Bahia growers, with support of the Associação Commercial of Bahia, appealed to Vargas on February 5, 1931, for 10,000 *contos* of agricultural credit to counter the effect of lower prices. The provisional government initially failed to accept the proposal

[28] Victor V. Valla, "Factores relacionados com a distribuição fundiária na região cacaueira da Bahia," *A Propriedade Rural, Anais do VIII Simpósio Nacional dos Professores Universitários de História*, Vol. II, pp. 465–73; Bahia, Secretaria da Agricultura, Instituto de Cacau da Bahia. *Instituto de Cacau da Bahia: Meio Século de História*. Anglina Nobre Rolim Garcez (Salvador, Bahia: 1981), p. 42; Brazil, Ministerio de Relações Exteriores, *Brasil: Estatísticas Recursos,* Posibilidades (Rio de Janeiro: NP, 1936), p. 137; Brazil, Ministerio da Fazenda, Directoria de Estatística Commercial, *Commercio Exterior do Brasil* 1930–1934 (Rio de Janeiro: 1935), p. 130.

but responded favorably after Bahia's secretary of agriculture proposed creation of the Instituto da Defesa do Cacau e Fomento Agricola [Institute for the Defense of Cocoa and Agricultural Development] financed by taxing each bag of exported cocoa. Support for Bahia's request came from military governor of the Northeast and Vargas confidant Juarez Távora. Távora appealed to Vargas to have the Banco do Brasil "provide Bahia [with] the reasonable support it is requesting of us."[29] Távora's support proved important, as Arthur Neiva, *interventor* for Bahia, noted in a May telegram thanking Távora for his "patriotic intervention in the cacao case." In the opinion of *interventor*, the solution "foreshadowed a new era of reconstruction [for] this state, assuring peace and tranquility in the most productive zone of the state."[30]

The interest-free loan allowed the Institute to begin functioning as a financial backer for growers, a broker for their products, and a source of technical support. The Institute gained additional federal support the following year with a new loan of 25,000 *contos* that allowed retirement of the original loan. By 1936 the Institute controlled 30% of production, had established itself throughout the cocoa-growing zone and constructed a four-story, 4,000 square meter "monumental warehouse and office building" capable of storing and processing up to 250,000 bags of cocoa. Though the Institute proved unable to shield the cocoa industry from fluctuations in the world cocoa market during the 1930s, in supporters' eyes it became "the only visible instrument of action, capable of minimizing the effects of the crisis and of rescuing the crop."[31]

Sustaining Political Support from the Cattle Sector

Though the cattle sector was not in crisis, Vargas offered similarly favored treatment to the beef cattle industry, reflecting his origins as the son of a *fazendeiro* and a native of Brazil's largest cattle state with an estimated 8

[29] Ltr., Juarez Távora to Getúlio Vargas, May 20, 1931, GV 31.05.30, GVA, CPDOC.

[30] Bahia, *Instituto de Cacau da Bahia,* pp. 40, 41, 52; *Diário de Pernambuco,* Nov. 9, 1935, pp. 8, 9; Arthur Neves to Jaurez Távora, May 4, 1931, JTdpf 1930.12.08, Juarez Távora Archive, CPDOC.

[31] Bahia, *Instituto de Cacau da Bahia,* p. 53; "Bahia Cocoa Industry," U.S. Consul General Bahia, pp. 15–26.

million head of cattle in 1930.[32] Shortly after the revolution's victory, he ordered 200 tons of beef previously designated for export to European markets to be distributed to the poor in Rio de Janeiro.[33] His federal government moved to subsidize grassland development, silo construction, genealogical registries of various cattle breeds, and imports of purebred cattle. The number of government-registered breeding stations rose from 137 in 1930 to over 1,100 in 1938. The ministry nearly doubled the number of experimental farms devoted to cattle development created since the founding of the Serviço de Industria Pastoril [The Pastoral Industry Service] in 1921. In 1936 Vargas and his minister of agriculture appeared at the second congress of cattle raising in July and helped inaugurate the national exposition of animals, an event re-instituted after a 14-year hiatus. At the animal exposition Vargas attended the parade of prized animals and inspected cattle in company of the agriculture minister and director of the pastoral service. On another occasion, he joined the agriculture minister in a Sunday afternoon jaunt to inspect cattle imported from Argentina and Uruguay.[34]

The combination of official support and rising demand from a growing urban population supported a strong increase in beef production for local consumption by 1938. Over 600,000 immigrants entered Brazil between 1926 and 1935, and the population of Brazil's six largest cities grew by an estimated 33% between 1931 and 1935, an absolute increase of over one half million inhabitants.[35] Between 1933 and 1938 production of fresh beef and pork for local consumption in establishments registered with the ministry of agriculture rose an estimated 150 and 140%, respectively.[36] Beef consumption in the city of Rio de Janeiro increased 36%

[32] Brazil. Ministério da Agricultura, Industria e Commercio. Instituto de Expansão Commercial. *O Brasil Atual. Brazil of Today.* (Rio de Janeiro: 1930), p. 96.

[33] Brazil. Ministério da Agricultura, *Relatório na Vigência do Governo Provisório (1930–1933)* (Rio de Janeiro: Oficinas Gráficas da Directoria de Estatística e Publicidade, 1933), pp. 65, 66.

[34] Brazil. Ministério da Agricultura. *O Ministério da Agricultura no Governo Getúlio* Vargas (Rio de Janeiro: Ministério da Agricultura, 1945), pp. 89–105; *Relatório 1938*, p. 392; Entries for Dec. 15, 1935 and July 18, 1936. *Getúlio Vargas, Diário*, Vol. 1, 1930–1936, pp. 455, 524.

[35] Brazil. Ministério de Relações Exteriores. *Brasil Estatísticas Recursos Posibilidades* (Rio de Janeiro: Ministério de Relações Exteriores, c 1937), pp. 33, 38.

[36] Brazil. Ministério da Agricultura, *Relatório 1938*, p. 410.

between 1930 and 1938.[37] The former minister of agriculture recognized the newly discovered power of the internal market for Brazilian beef. Speaking at the second national cattle conference in July 1936, Ildefonso Simões Lopes declared that the increase in beef consumption by the domestic market "evidences the relevance of our interior market…."[38]

Restructuring Agricultural Research and Education

Vargas's personal support to products linked to regional elites stands in stark contrast with his penurious treatment of two activities essential to fulfilling his promise of promoting polyculture: agricultural research and agricultural education. Throughout the seven years of the first Vargas era, the agriculture ministry served principally as another tool for consolidating political power, mainly through symbolic visits to ministry activities, and sponsorship of institutions of regional importance but under central government control. Though entries in Vargas' diary attest that he met frequently with his ministers of agriculture, Vargas' choices for agriculture minister and the budgets allocated for the ministry precluded an aggressive developmental role. The ministry declared its dedication to improving non-traditional crops and products, but shortcomings in leadership and budgets limited its ability to advance essential research and higher agricultural education.

Vargas's selection of 73-year-old Joaquim Francisco de Assis Brasil as his first agriculture minister demonstrated his penchant for placing political allies in the position in lieu of qualified agriculturalists. Assis Brasil had long championed agrarian reform, but notations in Vargas's diary made during his first year as provisional president indicate that Assis Brasil functioned primarily as a political adviser. Meanwhile, the ministry suffered turbulence, as Vargas removed labor, commerce, and industry matters from its portfolio with the creation of the Ministerio de Trabalho, Commercio e Industria [Ministry of Labor, Commerce, and Industry] to satisfy urban supporters. Assis Brasil's assignment as Ambassador to Argentina in December 1931 left leadership of the newly reformed

[37] Brazil. Instituto Brasileiro de Geografia e Estatística, *Repertório Estatístico do Brasil, Quadros Retrospectivos No. 1* (Rio de Janeiro: IGBE, 1941), p. 95.

[38] TS, ISL 00.00, IX 14a, Ildefonso Simões Lopes Archive, CPDOC.

ministry vacant. Three months later, Assis Brasil resigned after unsuccessfully attempting to mediate a dispute between Vargas and disillusioned power brokers in Rio Grande do Sul. His resignation letter contained no references to agriculture programs, explaining only that "circumstances have overcome my good wishes and sincere personal affection."[39]

Vargas's selection of *tenente* Juarez do Nascimento Fernandes Távora (1898–1975) as Assis Brasil's successor primarily gave Vargas an effective tool for retaining political loyalty in the Northeast who, nevertheless, lacked training as an agriculturalist. Távora was a native of Ceará and a *tenente* who had commanded support for Vargas in the Northeast during the 1930 revolution. Vargas named him chief of military governors in the Northeast on December 12, 1930, and Távora became known as the "Viceroy of the North." The 34-year-old responded positively to the invitation to serve as agriculture minister because of his "love of the North" and his desire to facilitate coordination among the military governors of the Northeast and the Ministry of Transport to address the region's problems. He also requested assurances of "weighty budgetary resources" and rationalization of the ministry's complicated bureaucratic workings.[40] In accepting the position, Távora admitted that he did not possess "specialized knowledge about the material" but that he would "surround himself with the best technicians that could be at hand inside or outside of the rosters of the Ministry."[41]

The most visible aspect of Távora's tenure was completion of the ministerial reorganization originally tasked to Assis Brasil. Less than one year into his tenure, Távora unveiled his reorganization plan at Rio de Janeiro's Escola Polytechnica. After endorsing the Vargas's approach to governance by instituting a complex of *conselhos* (councils) to guide government policy, Távora explained that he had used the latest scientific principles to reconfigure the reporting relationships within the ministry to improve internal communication and coordination. He closed the presentation by citing previous statements by Vargas appealing to the nation's

[39] Lira Neto, *Getúlio 1930–1945*, pp. 48, 49. Ltr., Assis Brasil to Getúlio Vargas, GVA, GV 32.03.19/5, CPDOC.

[40] Ltr., Juarez Távora to Getúlio Vargas, Dec. 11, 1932, GV c32.12.11. IX-52, GVA, CPDOC.

[41] Juarez Távora, *Uma Vida e Muitas Lutas*, Vol. II (Rio de Janeiro: Coleção Documentos Brasileiros, 1974), p. 92.

university students to collaborate with "men of good faith in the organization of the country...." Távora apparently made no reference to the degree of increased efficiency expected through the reforms. For 1933, the ministry's budget to support animal development had already registered a 39% reduction from that of 1930. Funds for vegetal development and production had fallen by 29%, and funds for agricultural education had suffered a whopping 64% reduction since 1930. To stress material over personnel expenditures, the reform eliminated 135 positions, leaving the ministry with 2,129 staffers.[42]

During his two-year tenure, Távora found that his budgetary resources were far from weighty. He struggled to respond to requests for assistance, many from his beloved Northeast. In a memo to the treasury minister complaining about the 1934 budget proposed for the ministry, Távora railed against the lack of funding. He noted that his predecessor had classified the ministry's budget as "miserable" in his only official report on the ministry's activities. The proposed budget precluded the ministry's "adequate equipping [*aparalhamento*] for fulfillment of its role as the most eminent driver and coordinator of the national economy in its three sources of production—mineral, vegetable and animal...." So meager was the budget that the ministry was in danger of becoming an "object of national shame." He noted that even though Brazil was "recognizedly an agricultural country," the largest budget allocation for the ministry of agriculture—that of 1930—represented only 2.3% of the central government's budgetary expenditures.[43] The approved budget for 1934 fell 40.000:000$ short of what he had requested.[44]

Despite meager resources at his disposal, Távora proved his usefulness to Vargas by making a special effort to satisfy requests originating in the Northeast, as already noted in the case of the crisis in the cocoa sector. In response to a plea from the military governor of Amazonas,

[42] Brazil. Ministerio da Agricultura. *A Reforma do Ministerio da Agricultura (1933)* (Rio de Janeiro: Directoria de Estatística e Publicidade, 1933), pp. 8, 17–27. The Ministry of Agriculture underwent 90 structural reforms from its founding in 1860 through 1978. See Mario Olinto Campos De Araújo "Evolução administrativa da pesquisa agropecuária no âmbito do Ministério da Agricultura no período 1938/1978: Um estudo de caso," (NP: Fundação Getúlio Vargas, 1979), p. 14.

[43] "Exposição ao Ministro da Fazenda com proposta orçamentaria para 1934," Dec. 2, 1933, Juarez Távora Archive, JT dpf 1931.12.02, Vargas Archive, CPDOC.

[44] TS, Távora to Dr. Mario Camara, Mar. 31, 1934, Juarez Távora Archive, JT dpf 1932.12.09, CPDOC.

Távora arranged for a credit of 200:000$ for purchase of cotton gin and promised to send several of his principal directors to study the region's agricultural needs.[45] He also assured the military governor of Paraíba that federal funding supporting cotton cultivation in his state in 1934 had been respected. He intervened with Vargas to gain central government support for destitute residents of the Northeast fleeing the drought-stricken interior. Vargas approved a broad program of relief that included creation of "artificial" public works jobs and sweeping measures to control the supply and prices of food. He charged Távora's ministry with implementing a two million *conto* grant for credit cooperatives to support local agriculture.[46]

When Távora exited the post after two years in office, the position was then offered to another Vargas political ally, Odilon Braga (1894–1954), of Minas Gerais with equally weak professional credentials. Lawyer Braga had supported Vargas' Aliança Liberal during the 1930 campaign and played a pivotal role in the victory of Vargas's forces in Minas Gerais as the state's secretary of the interior. Vargas invited Braga to become minister of agriculture in August 1934, noting in his diary that the agriculture ministry (as well as the education ministry) had been reserved for Minas Gerais, undoubtedly as a reward for support from Braga and his native state during the 1932 São Paulo uprising.[47]

Other than political activism in support of Vargas, Braga held no obvious qualifications for the position. He is remembered for a 1936 study on the possibility of petroleum deposits, *Bases para o inquérito sobre petroleo,* a product of his ministry's portfolio as keeper of nation's mineral deposits. He extended federal intervention in the coffee sector in 1935 by inaugurating construction of the federal center for coffee research. The Estação Experimental de Café [Experimental Station for Coffee] in Botucatu, São Paulo state, had been authorized during Távora's ministry. Research activities began only after Bragas left the ministry in 1937 after Vargas's assumption of dictatorial powers under the *Estado Novo.* Vargas interacted with Braga often, but on one occasion complained that Braga

[45] TS, Távora to "Presado Barata," Aug. 8, 1933, Juarez Távora Archive, JT dpf 1932.12.09, CPDOC.

[46] Frederico de Castro Neves, "Getúlio e a seca: políticas emergenciais na era Vargas," *Revista Brasileira de História,* Vol. 21, No. 40 (2001); Entry for Jan. 20, 1933. *Getúlio Vargas, Diário.* Vol. I, p. 180.

[47] Entry for July 22, 1934. *Getúlio Vargas, Diário.* Vol. I, p. 309.

"likes to talk, has no notion of time, and stays to deal with things that are not the concern of his ministry, principally political affairs."[48]

The federal government acknowledged the deficiencies of the agriculture ministry in general and especially its lack of technical expertise. Juarez Távora's first annual report highlighted a "complexity of factors" contributing to the "lack of practical productivity of the Ministry." These included bureaucracy, technical disorganization, a lack of technical elements, and an impropriety in installation of establishments of a technical nature." Third-party interests had guided the location of experimental farms and cooperation fields, the biology and chemistry sections lacked laboratories, and administrators without technical backgrounds directed important research installations. He argued that most divisions of the ministry had been created "to serve interests and accommodations of a political nature."[49]

Vargas openly embraced the reforms presented by Távora to remedy the situation, as he explained to the November 1933 constitutional assembly. In a review of the performance of the provisional government, he detailed the rational for reform of the agriculture ministry and identified primary tasks for the future. These included support for "improving our agricultural conditions by selecting the species and choice of the most favorable habitat for their development," as well as "studying the adaption of exotic plants and animals to our environment" and "modifying the mentality of our agricultural and pastoral environment by technical-professional instruction."[50]

Providing resources to fulfilling those promises, as well his initial commitment to polyculture, proved difficult. Only a trickle of trained agronomists was graduating from the federally funded Escola Nacional de Agronomia. Twelve graduated in 1934; 17 the following year. In 1935, only 53 students were enrolled in all four years of the agricultural engineer program. Those who did graduate possessed limited training, as the school's urban location at the foot of Sugar Loaf in Praia Vermelha, Rio

[48] Jefferson de Lara Sanches Junior, "As Estações Experimentais No Início Do Processo De Modernização Agrícola Brasileiro: Diversificação, Racionalização e Qualidade"; Entry for Oct. 22, 1935. *Getúlio Vargas, Diário*. Vol. I, p. 431.

[49] Brazil. Ministério da Agricultura, *Relatório 1930–1933*, p. 146.

[50] Getúlio Vargas, *A Nova Política Do Brasil, III. A Realidade Nacional em 1933: Retrospecto das realizações do Governo, em 1934* (Rio de Janeiro: Livraria José Olympio Editora, n.d.), p. 108.

de Janeiro, lacked fields for experimentation and facilities for research.[51] Moreover, as one journalist observed, finding agronomists accustomed to city life as students who would then be willing to serve in rural environments proved difficult.[52]

Federally sponsored research that could have supported additional diversification instead remained dedicated to supporting crops and products with important political backing: sugar, textiles, and coffee, and cattle raising, although the ministry devoted some resources to fruit, wine, and silk experimental stations. Personnel expenditures consumed almost 80% of the budgets of the ministry's research institutes for 1935, and the ministry admitted that results for most experimental stations "left much desired" because of bureaucratic requirements of the ministry itself. The federal research effort also fell victim to at least one case of poaching of personnel. German researcher Paul Vegeler left his federal position to accept a position with São Paulo Instituto Agronômico.[53]

Prosperous states, meanwhile, were conducting far more robust research, education, and extension programs. Graduates from state-sponsored superior agricultural schools in Minas Gerais and São Paulo totaled 52 in 1935 and boasted more than 400 total students enrolled in courses.[54] São Paulo's state agricultural secretariat had implemented reforms since 1927 that transformed the quality and quality of its research and educational programs. State agricultural secretary and 1907 Piraçicaba graduate Fernando Costa charged a reorganized Instituto Agronômico with overseeing all agricultural research and development throughout the state, providing results of its research to the state's agriculturalists, and distributing seeds and seedlings to the state's seed fields. He endowed the Institute with laboratories appropriate for technical analyses and oversaw programs of studies related to fertilizers, diverse fruits including citrus, as well as cotton. He instituted a council to supervise agricultural education in the state, transformed the veterinary institute into a school of veterinary medicine, and instituted a campaign to protect

[51] Brazil. Ministério da Agricultura, *Relatório 1938*, pp. 143, 145.

[52] Luís Amaral, *Aspectos fundamentaes da vida rural brasileira* (São Paulo: Revista dos Tribunaes, 1936), pp. 286, 287.

[53] Brazil. Ministério da Agricultura, *Relatório 1934–1935*, pp. 13–35.

[54] George W. Ware and Lincoln Monteiro Rodrigues, *Relatório Sôbre as Escolas de Agricultura e Veterinária do Brasil (Report on the Agricultural and Veterinary Colleges of Brazil)* (Rio de Janeiro: Escritório Técnico de Agricultura (ETA), 1954), Table No. 5.

the state's forests through a reformed state forest service. He created the *Instituto Biológico de Defesa Agricola e Animal* [The Biological Institute for Agricultural and Animal Defense] with various sections to assure the health and scientific soundness of the state's agriculture. He also established a directorate for agricultural inspection and development to collect information about the state's agriculture, promote adoption of new techniques, and organize expositions and contests to promote quality within the sector.[55] His activities as São Paulo's state secretary of agriculture were a prelude to his activism as Getúlio Vargas's minister of agriculture during early years of the Estado Novo.

Dissemination of the results of agriculture research conducted in São Paulo and elsewhere occurred through the *Revista da Agricultura*, founded in 1926 and published in São Paulo by Nicolas Athanassof, a former professor at the Luiz de Queiroz school in Piraçicaba. The journal disseminated technical data with practical applications for a wide variety of agricultural pursuits. One typical 150-page issue carried reports on the coffee borer, silk cultivation, goat milk, cotton and ticks, and a "simple method for the theoretical calculations of sugar production."[56] Journal articles attested to the diversity and quality of research underway under state auspices. One article on experiments underway at the genetics section of the Instituto since 1932 cited methods for improving Brazilian corn through application of internationally proven techniques. This was the product of the decision of the Instituto in 1932 to send São Paulo native Carlos Arnaldo Krug to Cornell where he completed a Master of Science degree specializing in plant genetics. Another article probed the economics of mechanization by documenting the cost of one day of farming using animal traction. Other articles advocated additional support for agricultural research and education. The journal published an article by Arthur Torres, SNA president, who argued that "without scientific investigation, we will not bring to the economic domain the solution for the innumerable technical problems of agriculture. Or, even better,

[55] Carlos Borges Schmidt and José Reis, *Rasgando Horizontes: A Secretaria da Agricultura no Seu Cinquentenário* (São Paulo: Secretaria da Agricultura, Industria e Comércio, 1942), pp. 38–55.

[56] *Revista da Agricultura*, XIII (Oct. Nov. Dec. 1931).

without experimental science applied to agriculture, we cannot have agricultural instruction."[57] In another article, a professor at the Luiz de Queiroz school urged commitment to genetics research by creation of a dedicated chair at the Piraçicaba school.[58]

Similar state-level activism supporting agricultural development was underway within Minas Gerais, centered on the Escola Superior de Agricultura at Viçosa and sponsored by the state's directorate of agriculture. In 1931, 1932, and 1933 the state organized tours for farmers that included instruction in the classrooms of the Viçosa school during the "Semana de Fazendeiro," supplemented by visits to coffee and beef processing plans in São Paulo state and a tour of the Instituto Agronômico at Campinas. The state also invited farmers to extension meetings led by technicians who offered instructions to farmers "on a variety of issues of practical interest." High attendance at sessions—1,218 in 1931, 2,687 in 1932, and 888 in 1933—reflected their popularity.[59]

By 1935 the robust programs of São Paulo and Minas Gerais states, along with others conducted in Pernambuco, Bahia, and Rio Grande do Sul, convinced the Ministry of Agriculture of the need to integrate state-supported activities into federal efforts to fulfill the sector's research and educational needs. The states were allocating more funds than the federal government on superior education, scientific research, and experimentation. As pointed out in Fig. 12.5, the states' spending on experimentation was more than doubled that of the federal government. In its 1935 report, the ministry admitted that the reform plan outlined by Távora may have been "theoretically magnificent," but it could only be implemented by adding technicians or tripling or quadrupling the ministry's budget. At the same time, states undergoing economic expansion were carrying out programs equivalent to those of the federal government. It was necessary, in the ministry's opinion, to forge a compact with the states based upon a division of labors. The federal government would retain responsibility for instruction, especially at the superior level, as well as research and experimentation, classification and standardization of products, and organization and defense of production, but such services would be conducted

57 "O ensino de agricultura e a profissão agronômica," *Revista da Agricultura*, VIII (Jan. Feb. 1933), p. 70.

58 S.T. Piza Junior, "A Genética e a Evolução da Agricultura em São Paulo," *Revista de Agricultura*, VI (April 1932), pp. 129–34.

59 *Jornal do Commercio*, April 29, 1934, p. 10.

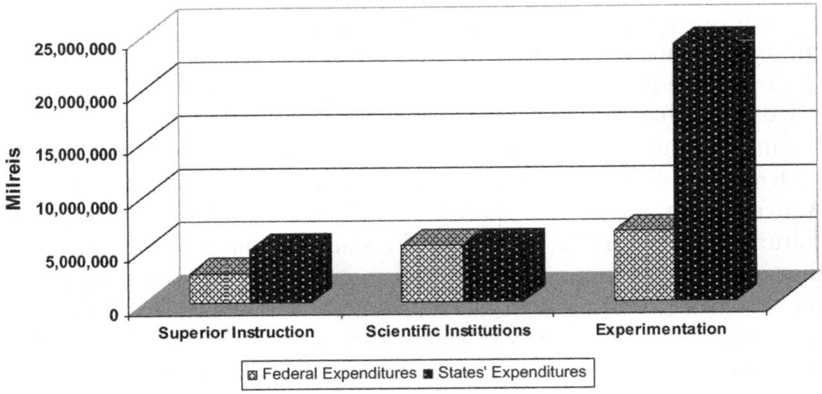

Fig. 12.5 Federal versus States' Allocations on Superior Education, Scientific Institutes and Experimentation in Agriculture, 1935 (*Source* Brazil. Ministério da Agricultura, *Relatório 1934–1935*, p. 169)

by the states. Other functions, such as practical instruction, and demonstration, seed, and cooperation fields would become the responsibility of the states under federal guidance.[60]

Conclusion

The Vargas government shifted control of Brazil's corporatist economic politics from the private sector to the federal government. Always the astute negotiator and devoid of ideological binders, Vargas superimposed state agencies onto the governing mechanisms of commodities previously controlled by private producers. He astutely increased the central government's power while eroding the power of the previously dominant agrarian elites—even while currying their political support by creating institutions and processes that aided coffee, sugar, Northeastern cotton, cacao, beef cattle, and other products. Vargas's successful introduction of central government-controlled institutions dedicated to moderating market forces initiated a new development model for the nation's industry and agriculture.

[60] Brazil. Ministério da Agricultura, *Relatório 1934–1935*, pp. 172–174.

Vargas' support for elite-centered traditional products did not include funding for more broad-based agricultural development. He remained committed to balancing the budget and limiting federal expenditures. His proclaimed commitments to diversifying agriculture and supporting broad-based agrarian interests proved largely rhetorical. Absent strong central government support, state agricultural secretaries, and schools of higher agricultural education elevated commitments to diversified agriculture and began path-breaking research programs. Declining federal and state government revenue in an era of falling prices for most agricultural products—especially coffee—severely restricted funds for agricultural research, education, extension, and the importation of agricultural machinery. The Ministry of Agriculture suffered continual resource shortages and endless bureaucratic reshuffling. Lobbying groups founded during the First Republic, including the SNA and SRB, remained vocal advocates for large land-owning farmers and ranchers but crop-specific institutes founded by Vargas to gain the political support of specific elites rose to importance. Vargas' failure to implement a comprehensive agricultural credit system—despite elaborate preparations during the ministry of Juarez Távora—deprived "agrarian activities" of the support enjoyed by commercial and industrial interests, in Távora's opinion.[61]

Despite such challenges, efforts initiated during the First Republic to improve agricultural education and technical expertise sustained modest production increases for crops raised primarily for domestic consumption. Compared with production averages for 1925–1929, by 1937 Brazil registered major gains in the production of basic food crops and oranges. Rice production rose 42%. The production of potatoes increased by 27%; corn output rose by 21%; bean production was up 24%; and the production of oranges rose an astounding 469% during the period.[62]

Brazil's agriculture made little progress between 1930 and 1937 toward embracing the mechanical, biological, and chemical revolutions underway in global agriculture. The initiation of genetic research at São Paulo's Instituto Agronômico and trials with various fertilizers at experimental farms only hinted of future progress. Despite imports of agricultural implements and machinery, mainly from the United States, mechanization remained a distant goal. The lack of resources dedicated

[61] Távora, *Uma Vida e Muitas Lutas*, Vol. II, p. 96.

[62] Brazil, Ministério da Agricultura, *Relatório 1938*, p. 17.

to agricultural research and education deprived the "essentially agricultural" nation of the technical bases to transform its primary source of wealth. Such a transformation would only occur if the political leadership supported a more aggressive and better resourced effort to diversify agriculture. Vargas increased the federal government's control of the Brazilian corporate state by becoming the interface between producer and market for select crops with high political visibility. The result was a bifurcated organizational arrangement that removed power from the state elites without committing to a nationally directed and funded program for improving agriculture.

Vargas did lend attention to one crop, however, that offered intriguing possibilities for increasing wealth derived from agriculture. The federal government would once again turn its attention to "white gold," but with more robust participation from U.S. capital.

CHAPTER 13

Vargas: The Cotton Alternative and the United States, 1930–1937

The increasing profitability of cotton as an alternative to the traditional dependence upon coffee engendered modifications to Vargas's politically weighted approach toward agriculture. Vargas strengthened federal support for the much-troubled cotton industry in the Northeast, demonstrating a personal interest in its fate to sustain the government's legitimacy and political control in the politically volatile region that had formed part of his pre-1930 coalition. Despite his strong support for cotton in the Northeast, South-Central Brazil—especially São Paulo—soon became the dominant producer for both domestic and external markets.

Northeastern cotton in the early 1930s continued to struggle with unique environmental and institutional challenges. Transportation remained a major impediment, as highways were unimproved and many farmers still resorted to oxcarts or pack trains to deliver product to market. Efforts to adhere to uniform classification standards instituted during the previous decade were only partially successful. Processors often mixed fibers from Upland cotton cultivated along the coast and those of the traditional tree-based cotton grown in the region's interior. As a visiting

E. R. Downes, *Brazilian Agricultural Development, 1890–1950*,
https://doi.org/10.1007/978-3-031-76992-4_13

USDA analyst noted, such mixing resulted in a "staple that is noticeably lacking in uniformity."[1] Carelessness by classifiers led to complaints from customers forced to downgrade major portions of purchased lots. In October 1932, the president of the Centro de Fiação e Teclagem of Uberlandia, Minas Gerais, requested assurances that the Ministry of Agriculture would act "in defense of the good name of a service of undeniable utility." Several of the center's affiliated companies had received cotton processed in Campina Grande, Paraíba, with undeservedly high grades, forcing downgrading of various lots.[2] Improving Northeastern cotton was a long-term challenge, as cotton expert William Coelho de Souza explained in 1936. Coelho de Souza had demonstrated the utility of proper classification to local businesses as the technical director of agriculture for the state of Maranhão in 1931. Much to his dismay, five years later he reported that "no progress had been attempted, neither in the increase in production nor improvement in the type and length of its fibers."[3]

The return of severe drought in 1932 further complicated efforts to produce a marketable product. In April 1932 the Cotton Service's delegate in Paraíba reported the results of his visits to cooperation fields maintained by the service. "The situation is really desolate in that zone," he reported. Farmers, including small landowners and *fazendeiros,* were "suffering major destitution, abandoning their homes and belongings to search for resources that would guarantee subsistence and thereby avoid starving to death."[4]

Vargas's provisional government demonstrated a keen interest in Northeastern cotton at every opportunity. Shortly after assuming power, it mandated the classification of all cotton intended for export, a measure that benefited Northeastern cotton given that São Paulo's classification system was already functioning. The federal government opened new classification stations in Pará and Piauí, adding to the 19 federal installations already functioning throughout the Northeast and the Federal District. The ministry assumed an active role in the distribution of seeds

[1] Percy K. Norris, *Cotton Production in Northeastern Brazil* (Washington, DC: U.S. Department of Agriculture, 1939), pp. 10, 14.

[2] *Jornal do Commercio*[Rio de Janeiro], Oct. 6, 1932, p. 4.

[3] William Coelho de Souza, "O algodão na economia brasileira," *O Observador Econômico e Financeiro,* Vol. XXI (1936), 88–97.

[4] *Jornal do Commercio* [Rio de Janeiro], Apr. 23, 1932, p. 4.

throughout the Northeast and Minas Gerais. For the 1933–1934 harvest, cotton growers in the northeastern states received over 55% of the 2,112 tons of cotton seed provided by the federal government. Federally sponsored research on cotton took place almost exclusively at experimental stations in Ceará, Rio Grande do Norte, Paraíba, Pernambuco, Alagoas, Sergipe, and Bahia.[5]

Vargas also lent his personal prestige to the cotton effort in the Northeast during travel to the region in September 1933, a trip designed to reward his supporters in the North and Northeast who had stood by him during the 1930 revolution and the 1932 São Paulo revolt. It was also designed to build support for Vargas in the upcoming constitutional assembly. In addition to participating in tumultuous receptions, banquets, and festivities, he visited the cotton experimental station in Alagoas, textile plants in Pernambuco and Paraíba, and a cotton press in Rio Grande do Norte, as well as various water reservoirs reconstructed to attenuate the impact of the 1932 drought.[6]

Vargas's support for Northeastern cotton helped increase the region's output during his government's early years. The region's cotton production rose an average of 50% between 1930 and 1939, largely because of increased planting. Consumption in textile mills also increased, rising from nearly 120,000 bales in 1933 to over 167,000 bales in 1937. As USDA analyst Percy Norris noted, "the decrees regulating the distribution of seed, the treatment of seed for the eradication of the pink boll worm, the inspection and licensing of cotton gins, and the classification of cotton exported have had an influence on increasing the quantity and improving the quality of Northeastern Brazilian cotton."[7]

Vargas's support, however, could not overcome the substantial advantages of cotton in São Paulo. As noted earlier, São Paulo devoted important resources to cotton research based largely upon the U.S. experience with upland cotton. This research created a slightly longer variety of Upland cotton more suitable to demands of both the national textile

[5] Brazil. Ministério da Agricultura. *Relatório,* 1930–1933, pp. 173, 198; 1933–1934, p. 173; 1934–1935, p. 88.

[6] Lira Neto, *Getúlio 1930–1945,* p. 147; Entries for Aug. 29 to Sept. 20, 1933. *Getúlio Vargas, Diário*. Vol. 1, pp. 239–44.

[7] Norris, *Cotton Production in Northeastern Brazil,* pp. 3, 10, 12.

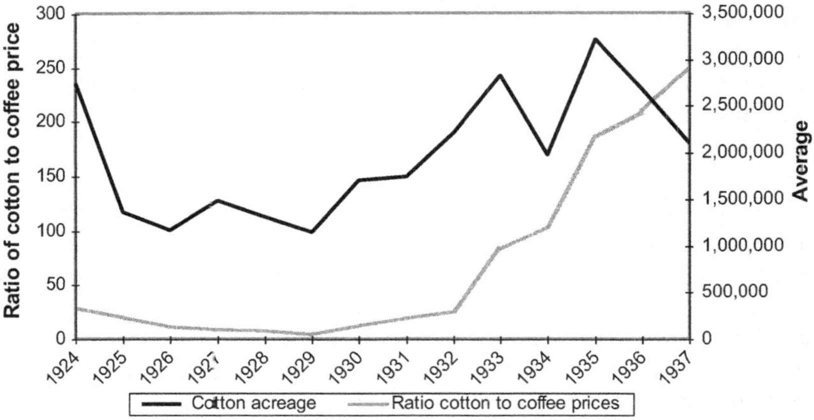

Fig. 13.1 Ratio of cotton to coffee prices and cotton acreage in São Paulo state, 1924–1937 (*Source* Compiled from reports of the São Paulo Merchandise Exchange and the Ministry of Agriculture. Cited in Percy K. Norris, *Cotton Production in Southern Brazil.* U.S. Department of Agriculture Office of Foreign Agricultural Relations (Washington DC, Sept 1939), p. 16)

industry and export.[8] Moreover, measures taken to remedy the coffee crisis, especially restriction of coffee plantings, contributed to a shift of resources from coffee to cotton cultivation. USDA observer Norris reported that cotton cultivation had expanded during the 1920s when coffee prices fell largely through planting of cotton between rows of coffee trees. However, the expansion of cotton planting that occurred in São Paulo state from 1933 until 1937 was influenced strongly by restrictions on planting coffee on land previously cleared for coffee. Figure 13.1 depicts Norris's calculations on the relationship.

Research on cotton genetics at the Instituto Agronômico expanded in 1935 with the hiring of a specialist in cotton genetics with a lengthy list of publications and extensive experimentation. The state offered an attractive US$9,000 per year salary to Sidney Cross Harland, an Englishman serving as a cotton researcher for Britain's Imperial Department of Agriculture for the West Indies, and an expert on long-staple cotton. Harland's

[8] Annibal Villanova Villela and Wilson Suzigan, *Política do governo e crescimento da economia brasileira 1889–1945*, 2nd ed. (Rio de Janeiro: IPEA/INPES, 1975), p. 185.

work on cotton breeding generated immediate and long-term results, despite conflicts with another section of the institute with a similar charter directed by Raimundo Cruz Martins, whom Harland described as "a malevolent individual."[9]

William Clayton and Brazilian Cotton

The opportunities for cotton cultivation in Brazil were obvious to powerful Houston cotton broker William L. Clayton. Clayton was exuberant about the cotton that he observed while traveling by automobile in the central São Paulo on February 10, 1937. "The cotton looked very good to me," he confided to the Houston headquarters of his Anderson Clayton Company. "Practically very field was well fruited—the cotton grows right up to the road so you can see it easily—and blooming like a flower garden."[10] The 57-year-old Clayton was optimistic about his company's prospects in Brazil. Three years earlier, the company had established Anderson, Clayton & Companhia Limitada in partnership with Brazilian businessman Ruy Campista to engage in the cotton trade. The company's experience was to mirror its other foreign and domestic ventures designed to take advantage of new realities regarding cotton prices in the world market and land use in São Paulo. Brazilian and U.S. reaction to the vicissitudes of the depression-era commodities crisis had created an opportunity that Clayton felt he could not overlook.

Brazilian cotton cultivation reacted favorably to U.S. government measures to mitigate a commodities crisis threatening the livelihood of millions in the U.S. South. The U.S. federal government attempted to restrict supply and thereby raise the price of cotton, experiencing strong increases in production and dramatically falling prices. The price of cotton fell from 29 cents a pound in 1923 to 6.5 cents in 1932, casting economic uncertainty over the future of 1.6 million U.S. farmers raising cotton. Federal and state governments struggled for a solution. On June 30, 1930, the federal government's newly formed Cotton Stabilization Corporation took 1.3 million bales off the market. Production continued unabated. The 1931 crop registered a near record 16 million bales.

[9] Sydney Cross Harland, *Nine Lives: the Autobiography of a Yorkshire Scientist*. Max Millard, ed. (Raleigh, NC: Boson Books, 2001), pp. 101–103.

[10] Emphasis in original. Ltr., William L. Clayton to AC&Co, Houston, Feb. 10, 1937, in William Clayton Papers, Rice University Manuscript Collection, Box 99.

Southern politicians, led by firebrand Louisiana governor Huey P. Long, attempted to organize a "cotton holiday," a commitment by cotton-growing states to forego planting cotton in 1932 in hopes that reduced supplies would raise prices to a suitable level. When Texas refused to adhere to the proposal, cotton farmers were once again left to vicissitudes of the market.[11]

The incoming Roosevelt administration took action that dramatically lowered the U.S. production of cotton by the 1933–1934 crop season. The Agricultural Adjustment Act of 1933 allowed the Secretary of Agriculture to reach agreements with cotton growers to plow under 10,000,000 acres of cotton and reduce plantings by 40% for 1934 in return for cash payments. As a result, U.S. cotton production plummeted from over 18 million bales in 1932–1933 to 9.6 million bales from the 1933–1934 harvest, a drop of over 46%. Cotton prices recovered from 6 to 11 cents by 1933–1934, but the push to restrict cotton planting, coupled with high tariffs that made it difficult for foreign buyers to obtain foreign exchange to purchase U.S. cotton, led to a marked decrease in U.S. cotton exports. Passage of the Cotton Control Act of 1934 removed additional lands from cotton cultivation. By 1936, U.S. cotton exports declined by over 31% of the 1926 and 1930 average. Meanwhile, cotton production outside the United States by the 1933–1934 harvest increased by nearly 2.5 million bales over the previous year's harvest.[12]

William Lockhart Clayton (1880–1966), chairman of Anderson Clayton & Company, was well prepared to take advantage of the consequences of Congress' action. Clayton had grown up in cotton. His father had been a cotton farmer in Tupelo, Mississippi, and Clayton's first job as a manager with the American Cotton Company in New York had immersed him in the international cotton market. Together with two

[11] See Robert E. Snyder, *The Cotton Crisis* (Chapel Hill, NC: Univ. of North Carolina Press, 1984).

[12] Supply and price figures from U.S. Department of Agriculture, Bureau of Agricultural Economics. *The World Cotton Situation: Foreign Cotton Production* (Washington, DC: 1935), pp. 13, Table 1; Export Figures from U.S. Department of Commerce, Bureau of Foreign and Domestic Commerce, *Foreign Trade of the United States Calendar Year 1936* (Washington, DC: GPO, 1936), p. 36.

brothers in law who also contributed $3,000 each, at age 24 he founded Anderson, Clayton, and Company in Oklahoma City in 1904.[13]

The company's business model focused on ginning cotton and crushing cotton seeds to produce multiple byproducts, a formula later applied in Brazil. It invested in ginning and oil seed milling equipment, including an advanced press that compacted the cotton more thoroughly and reduced shipping costs. In its first year the company recorded a US$10,000 profit and within three years the company's value soared to over US$178,000. The company's financial strength and Clayton's global perspective enabled it to buy and store large quantities of processed cotton for sale to worldwide customers. The firm's horizons broadened when World War I brought financial difficulties for European firms that had traditionally dominated the trade. The company moved its office to Houston in 1916 and established agencies in Canada, France, Japan, and China, offering stocks that met spinners' immediate needs as well as financing where risks warranted. By 1933, the company and its subsidiaries controlled 3.5 million bales of cotton.[14]

The Agricultural Adjustment Act forced the company to expand its scope. Instead of focusing on selling U.S.-produced cotton to foreign markets, the company began purchasing and processing foreign cotton for global sale. Clayton cited his understanding of the reasons for "the rapid loss of our foreign markets for cotton" in a letter to a confidant in Washington D.C. in November 1934. "I respectfully submit," he wrote, "that the only tenable explanation is that we have priced our cotton out of the world market."[15] The new realities of reduced supply and increased price of U.S. cotton not only made foreign cotton more competitive, but they also mandated a choice by Anderson Clayton: either expand to new locations or seriously reduce its staff. After successful trial sales of Brazilian cotton in England and the European continent, in 1934 the company

[13] TS, J.A. Stillwell, "Story of the Anderson Clayton Company, The Founders," Anderson, Clayton and Company Collection, HMRC, Box 6; Ellen Clayton Garwood, *Will Clayton: A Short Biography* (Freeport, NY: Books for Libraries Press, 1958), p. 78.

[14] TS, Lamar Fleming, "Growth of the Business of Anderson Clayton and Company," pp. 18–19, Anderson, Clayton and Company Collection, HMRC, Box 7; Stillwell, "The Founders."

[15] Ltr., William L. Clayton to Chester Davis, Nov. 21, 1934, Anderson, Clayton and Company Collection, HMRC, Box 7.

decided to open operations in Brazil and market Brazilian cotton to global customers.[16]

São Paulo research helped create plentiful cotton harvests and provided the quality raw material for the Anderson Clayton's investments in the state. Also critical to the company's rapid rise in status was its competitive advantages over local processors. The limited financial resources of Brazilian cotton growers and processors made them vulnerable to poor harvests caused by pests or adverse weather. In an era when Brazilian federal government agricultural financing was unavailable, Anderson Clayton purchased gins from struggling small processors and extended financing to planters, charging them eight percent interest on plantings plus a 15% commission on delivered product. In its first year of Brazil operations, Anderson Clayton obtained a banking charter, allowing it to charge interest rates lower than those of private lenders. Its financing of cotton growers drew praise from the local press, citing Anderson Clayton's decision to "finance freely and frankly the cost of cotton production" even while the federal government had refused to do the same.[17]

The firm also enjoyed a technological advantage important to achieving prominence in Brazil's economy, not only as a cotton processor but also as a supplier of food and cattle nutrients. Unlike many local processors, the company had extensive experience in utilizing every element of the cotton boll. Once the company separated the seed from the lint in its gins, it produced multiple byproducts at cotton seed mills. The residual lint extracted from the seed was sold for upholstery, bedding, or felt. The hull of the seed was marketed as fuel or roughage feed. Oil removed from the seed by crushing was combined with other ingredients to prepare margarine, soap, salad oil, or shortening. Finally, seed residue became cake or meal for high-protein foods. Despite the rapid spread of cotton cultivation in the São Paulo countryside, the number of gins and cotton seed mills remained limited. While Brazil's cotton processors had long extracted and marketed cotton seed oil, Anderson Clayton's superior financial resources allowed it to install modern gins and cotton seed mills, providing an edge over buyers without the capital to process the

[16] Fleming, "Growth of the Business of Anderson Clayton and Company," p. 36.

[17] TS, Sebastião Gonçalves da Silva, "History of Anderson, Clayton & Cia Ltda.," Anderson, Clayton and Company Collection, HMRC, Box 39; *Correio Paulistano*, Dec. 15, 1935, p. 5.

cotton into similar byproducts. The oil mills contributed substantially to the company's profitability.[18]

The company moved quickly from creation in November 1934 to operations by the next harvest. In 1935, it installed five gins in the São Paulo cities of Jaboticabal, Piratininga, Avaré, Cerqueira César, and Curinhos and acquired plants in Duartina and Cândido Rodrigues. It established two oil extraction mills in the state's interior at Bauru and Avaré, reducing transportation costs to urban markets by separating lint from seed closer to harvest sites. The company also invested in 15 gins in the Northeast after opening an office in Recife. It installed new gins in Ceará, Pernambuco, Alagoas, Rio Grande do Norte, and a gin and warehouse in Campina Grande, Paraíba. In 1935, the company purchased over 60,000 bales of 500 pounds of cotton, and over 212,000 bales the following year. By February 1937, the company's investment in Brazil totaled approximately $10 million.[19]

Clayton's preference for the São Paulo area became apparent in an evaluation he conducted after visiting his company's facilities in Brazil in 1937. Less than two years after entering Brazil, it was clear to Clayton that southern Brazil held a brighter future than the company's ventures in the Brazilian Northeast. Clayton confided to key staff at his Houston headquarters that "despite many disappointments, I am optimistic about our future in Brazil." He was confident that the firm's activities in Southern Brazil "will show a profit this season," but he cautioned that "it is going to be sometime before any of us will be proud of North Brazil" where conditions were "so different and the risks much greater."[20] His outline showed the seed mills were generating substantial profits: US$769,766 by January 1937. Each bale of cotton was creating a profit of US$3.33. Meanwhile, operations in Northern Brazil were losing money: US$196,234. Costs for infrastructure, interest expenses on the

[18] TS, "Notes on the Activities of Anderson Clayton & Co.," p. 2, c. 1944–1945, Anderson, Clayton and Company Collection, HMRC, Box 8.

[19] TS, "Notes on the Activities of Anderson Clayton & Co.," p. 2; TS, Sebastião Gonçalves da Silva, "History of Anderson, Clayton & Cia. Ltda.," p. 2, Anderson, Clayton and Company Collection, HMRC, Box 39; Investment figure from Ltr., William L. Clayton to ACCO Houston, Feb. 11, 1937, Anderson, Clayton and Company Collection, HMRC, Box 99.

[20] Ltr., William L. Clayton to AC&Co, Houston, Feb. 10, 1937, in William Clayton Papers, Rice University Manuscript Collection, Box 99.

company's investments, and reserves for bad loans led to a net loss for the company's operations in Brazil through February 1937 of US$431,234. Clayton was especially disappointed with Northeastern Brazil, surmising that "we would have been wise not to invest any money there at present, confining our activities to cotton merchandising, with low overhead." He complained that political conditions there were unfavorable, as it was "too easy for local competitors, in these little states in the North, to stir up political action against us."[21] (Fig. 13.2).

Clayton's partiality for investing in the São Paulo area reflected a similar preference among other cotton cultivators and processors. The number of gins for processing cotton in the state rose from 240 in 1934 to more than 400 several years later. São Paulo's production reached nearly one million bales by 1937, seven times the amount produced

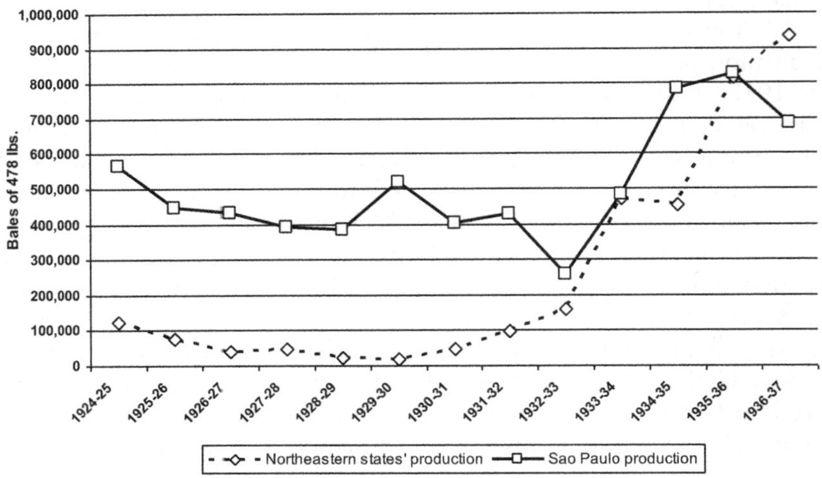

Fig. 13.2 Cotton production in São Paulo versus Northeastern States, 1924–1925 to 1936–1937 (*Source* Percy K. Norris, *Cotton Production in Southern Brazil.* U.S. Department of Agriculture Office of Foreign Agricultural Relations (Washington DC, Sept. 1939), p. 7)

[21] TS, William L. Clayton, "Memo on South America Trip," Mar. 10, 1937, in William Clayton Papers, Rice University Manuscript Collection, Box 99.

in 1925, the most productive year of the 1920s, and surpassing the Northeast's production by 1937 by nearly 250,000 bales.[22]

The Implications of the Cotton Boom

The expansion of cotton cultivation in both southern and northeastern Brazil altered the structure of Brazilian exports and presented an early example of the power of the agribusiness model. Through the activities of Anderson Clayton and other foreign and domestic cotton merchandisers, especially the Sociedade Algodoeira do Nordeste Brasileiro, operating in Brazil since 1923, and Wharton Pedrosa, Brazilian cotton exports rose precipitously from 1933 forward. Exports increased from a mere 11,693 metric tons in 1933 to 236,181 metric tons in 1937. The share of cotton in Brazil's exports rose from 2.1% of the value of total exports during 1925–1929 to 18.8% in 1937. Coffee's share of Brazil's exports, meanwhile, shrank to 42%.[23]

The explosion in cotton production also furnished the raw material for expansion of the domestic textile industry. The industry grew at a rate of 11.5% during the 1930s, producing 914.5 million meters of cotton in 1936, an increase of about 54% over 1927.[24] Domestic consumption of cotton rose from approximately 200,000 bales in the early 1930s to 828,000 bales in 1937.[25] Anderson Clayton exported most of its cotton purchased in Brazil, but it also sold to the domestic market. Chairman Clayton reported in 1937 that the company had sold "possibly" 20,000 bales to textiles mills in Northeastern Brazil, where mills consumed 167,540 bales of cotton in 1937. The domestic market also consumed cotton byproducts. The company's most profitable venture was

[22] Source: Percy K. Norris, *Cotton Production in Southern Brazil*. U.S. Department of Agriculture, Office of Foreign Agricultural Relations (Washington DC, Sept 1939), pp. 5, 7.

[23] Export figures from Brazil, Ministerio da Fazenda, Serviço de Estatística Econômica e Financeira do Tesouro Nacional, *Comércio Exterior do Brasil 1933–1937* (Rio de Janeiro: Tipografia do Serviço de Estatística Econômica e Financeira, 1940), pp. 766, 767; Villela and Suzigan, *Política do governo*, p. 187; Brazilian government data cited in *Brazilian Business*, Vol. 18, No. 1 (Mar. 1938), 46.

[24] Villela and Suzigan, *Política do governo e crescimento*, p. 195.

[25] Royall Brandis, "Cotton Competition: U.S. and Brazil: 1929–1948," *Journal of Farm Economics*, Vol. 34, No. 1 (Feb. 1952), p. 80; Norris, *Cotton Production in Northeastern Brazil*, p. 10.

its cotton seed oil mills, allowing it to market cooking oil sold under the brand "Saude' [health]. Ads promised that the oil "would not alter the natural flavor of food" and that it was "refined through an exclusive system of de-odorizing" leaving it "absolutely without a smell."[26]

Finally, Brazil's embrace of cotton cultivation with a heavy emphasis on the Upland cotton produced in the United States tied the fate of cotton developed by the two countries even more closely. As show in Fig. 13.3, prices for Brazilian cotton at the Liverpool market generally reflected the price of U.S. cotton. Prices for both rose nearly 6 cents per pound following the U.S. decision to reduce its cotton crop in 1933. A high percentage of Brazil's new cotton exports were destined for three markets where U.S. cotton had traditionally dominated: Britain, Japan, and especially Germany. U.S officials in Japan reported in 1936 that "Cotton from Brazil is available in greater volume" and that "the smaller takings of American cotton during the year, were chiefly due to a price relationship unfavorable to the American."[27] Brazil sold nearly 36% of its cotton exports between 1933 and 1937 to Germany while U.S. cotton exports to Germany fell by 1.1 million pounds. While partly attributable to U.S. trade restrictions imposed upon Germany, the similarity of U.S. and Brazilian cotton as well as Brazilian willingness to barter created a market for Brazilian cotton in what had been a prominent U.S. market.[28] According to USDA calculations, Brazil's share of the world cotton production rose from one percent from the 1920s through 1932 to eight percent by 1937.[29] So positive was the outlook for cotton during this period that a Brazilian Foreign Ministry publication proclaimed that "national cotton constitutes, currently, the exploration of greatest interest in the complex of Brazilian agriculture."[30] At least as far as exports were concerned, Brazil was no longer just the land of coffee.

[26] TS, William L. Clayton, "Memo on South America Trip," Mar. 10, 1937, in William Clayton Papers, Rice University Manuscript Collection, Box 99; See ad in *Correio Paulistano,* Aug. 12, 1938, p. 4.

[27] U.S.Department of Agriculture, *Foreign Crops and Markets* (Nov. 2, 1936), p. 511.

[28] Brandis, "Cotton Competition: U.S. and Brazil: 1929–1948," p. 75.

[29] U.S.Department of Agriculture, *Foreign Crops and Markets*, Vol. 35, No. 12, p. 182.

[30] Brazil, Ministério da Fazenda, *Comércio Exterior do Brazil 1933–1937*, pp. 766, 767; Brazil, Ministério de Relações Exteriores, *Brasil: Estatísticas Recursos Possibilidades* (Rio de Janeiro: NP, 1936), p. 108.

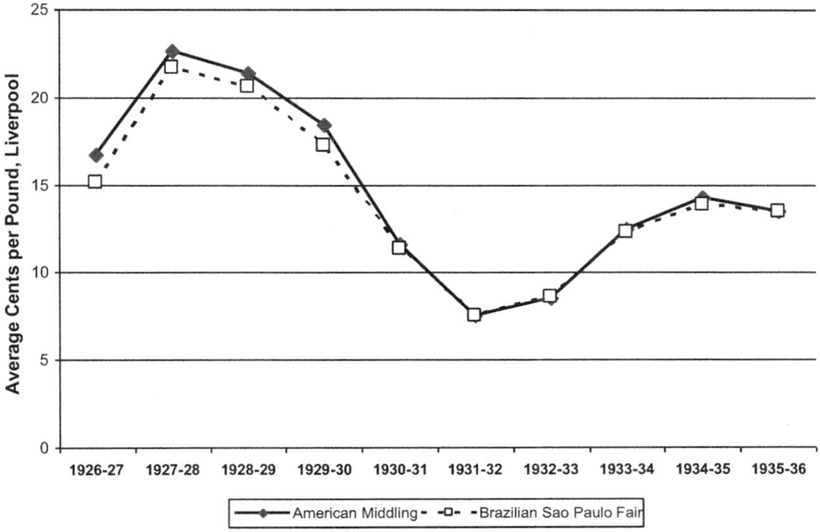

Fig. 13.3 Price per pound for U.S. and Brazilian Cotton, Liverpool, 1926–1927 to 1935–1936 (*Source* U.S. Department of Agriculture. *Agriculture Statistics 1937* (Washington, DC: GPO, 1937), p. 100)

CHAPTER 14

The *Estado Novo*, Agriculture and the United States, 1937–1942

At 2:25 pm on Saturday, November 13, 1937, the first cabinet meeting of Brazil's newly self-proclaimed dictator Getúlio Vargas convened at the Catete presidential palace. Three days earlier Vargas had closed congress, installed a new constitution and proclaimed a drastically reconfigured Brazilian nation state: the *Estado Novo* [New State]. Saturday's weather forecast for the Rio de Janeiro area called for storms with rain, an outlook consistent with disturbances brewing in Europe and Asia foreshadowing even darker days ahead. The first cabinet officer to arrive was the new minister of agriculture, Fernando de Souza Costa. Paulista Sousa Costa had been sworn in three hours earlier, after departing his previous post as head of the Conselho Nacional de Café [The National Coffee Council]. He joined Francisco Campos, minister of justice, and other ministers to discuss national coffee policy and another high-interest topic involving agriculture: how to suppress the communist threat, including using agricultural colonies as internment camps.[1]

Two days later, Vargas and Souza Costa met again. This time they discussed technical and policy issues related to agriculture: wheat, fish, fertilizers, a study of phosphates, and organization of agricultural cooperatives, among other topics. Gone were the days when Vargas' previous

[1] *Correio da Manhã*, Nov. 14, 1937, p. 1.

E. R. Downes, *Brazilian Agricultural Development, 1890–1950*,
https://doi.org/10.1007/978-3-031-76992-4_14

minister of agriculture tested the president's patience by raising political issues beyond his portfolio. Also gone were the days when Vargas' ministers of agriculture had no formal education to prepare for the position. Vargas's new agricultural minister was an agronomist, respected former secretary of agriculture of São Paulo and owner of a textile mill in an inland town in São Paulo. The choice symbolized renewed seriousness about agriculture's role in the new political order. Vargas was even willing to overlook Souza Costa's support for the 1932 São Paulo uprising when he attempted to rally neighboring Minas Gerais against the Vargas government. As the first agronomist to serve as the nation's minister of agriculture, Souza Costa was a valuable political asset, essential to fulfilling Vargas' newly defined vision of the Brazilian state.[2] Agriculture would be the primary tool to fulfill a new institutional mandate: extending the federal government's reach into the nation's vast and largely uninhabited interior.

The Estado Novo and Agriculture

The *Estado Novo* arose primarily from Vargas' frustrations with the endless political maneuvering that had characterized his governments since the 1930 revolution. He had long wished for a more authoritarian mandate, and the communist uprising of November 1935 presented further justification for centralizing power, a process underway since the 1930 revolution. Squabbling among candidates to succeed Vargas in the presidential election set for January 3, 1938—encouraged by Vargas' own political machinations—threw more fuel on the national political bonfire. The following month he added to the political turmoil by denouncing a falsified plan outlining communist plans to install an extreme leftist government. Public revelation of the "Plano Cohen," concocted by a member of the right-wing Integralist party and promoted as valid by senior military commanders, prompted congress to vote for a return to a state of war. Six weeks later, Vargas took to the national radio airways to announce a new political reality. Under a new constitution scripted at his

[2] Jornal do Commercio, Nov., 13, 1937, p. 5; Entry for Nov. 16, 1937. *Getúlio Vargas, Diário. Vol. II, 1937–1942* (Rio de Janeiro: Fundação Getúlio Vargas, 1995), p. 84; Verbete,"Fernando de Souza Costa," CPDOC, Fundação Getúlio Vargas. http://www.fgv.br/cpdoc/acervo/dicionarios/verbete-biografico/fernando-de-sousa-costa.

direction, the *Estado Novo* abolished political parties, prohibited formation of civilian militias, closed congress, and placed governors and mayors under central government control. The 1938 elections were canceled. President-dictator Getúlio Vargas began to exercise his expanded political and economic powers.[3]

During the next three years, the new national political structure combined with the international pressures of an increasingly global conflict endowed agriculture with even more importance. Agriculture benefited from Vargas' new authority as the sole arbiter of the Brazilian nation and his push for enhanced national unity, symbolized by burning state flags in a ceremony on November 27, 1937, an event overshadowed by a national emblem 20 meters in height. Less there be any doubt, featured speaker minister of justice and author of the 1937 constitution, Francisco Campos, explained the event's significance. The nation's flag stood for "the new unity of Brazil... the order of a single way of thinking of a single authority, the thinking and authority of Brazil."[4] The power of state elites to shape agricultural policy, like ashen remnants of their state flags, became reminders of a bygone era.

Agriculture and Brazil's natural resources played a central role in the indigenous ideology Vargas embraced, one constructed upon a glorious image of Brazil's past when expeditionary parties—*bandeirantes*—had penetrated the nation's immense interior in search of fortune. This vision had been brewing during the 1920s as intellectuals countered the emphasis on regional identities dominant in literature to offer a vision of a greater Brazil. The *Verde-Amarelo* [Green-Yellow] group during the 1920s embraced a nationalist vision of the Brazilian state under São Paulo's hegemony. After the failed 1932 revolt, they transferred their vision of mystical nationalism to the central government. Cassiano Ricardo, Cândido do Motta Filho, and Menotti del Picchia provided Vargas' *Estado Novo* with an ideological basis for an authoritarian, nationalist, corporatist state dedicated to recovering Brazil's greatness.[5] The ideology drew from a perennial notion that endowed the nation's geographic expanse "with novelty, recognition and the future, as if the

[3] See Lira Neto, *Getúlio 1930–1945: Do Governo Provisório à ditadura do Estado Novo* (São Paulo: Companhia de Letras, 2013), pp. 304–319.

[4] *A Noite*, Nov. 27, 1937, p. 3.

[5] Mônica Pimenta Velloso, *A Brasilidade Verde-Amarela: nacionalismo e regionalismo paulista*, 2nd ed. (Rio de Janeiro: Fundação Getúlio Vargas, CPDOC, 1990).

vastness of the territory implied the discovery of new identities and forms of life."[6] The movement reinforced this concept by attempting to create an identification between Brazil's open spaces and the promise of a more powerful and wealthy state. It was the country's vast geographic expanse that held the secret to achieving the nation-state's true potential. Only a modern-day *bandeirante*—none other than Getúlio Vargas—could lead the nation to its predestined greatness.[7]

Vargas moved quickly to gain acceptance for utilizing Brazil's natural resources to create a more powerful state. In his January 1, 1938, national address, he proclaimed the need to transform Brazil's "potential riches into effective resources." He explained that the country's riches and activity had too long remained concentrated along its vast shoreline. Now there was an "urgent reality" to "cross the mountains, transform the plains, and expand ourselves in terms of latitudes." He urged "retaking the paths of the pioneers who, in an epic and vigorous accomplishment, planted the markers of our frontier territories in the heart the continent." It was necessary, he argued, to "once again overcome obstacles, shorten distances, open roads, and extend the economic frontiers, definitely consolidating the foundations of the Nation."[8] Central to this process, as he later stressed, was a harmonious relationship between the state and the individual, a relationship severed, according to his supporters, by the tenets of liberalism.[9]

Vargas projected a grand vision for Brazil's natural resources. With help of his publicists, Vargas began popularizing his image of a nation-state expanding into the nation's interior as essential to restoring Brazil's greatness. His declaration that the true sense of Brazilianness was a March to the West [*Marcha para o Oeste*] became a clarion call for colonizing the nation's vast interior. Essential to success of the march were roads of penetration, continuing the struggle against the drought in the Northeast, incorporating the Amazon more securely under central government

[6] João Marcelo Ehlert Maia, *A terra como invenção: O espaço no pensamento brasileiro* (Rio de Janeiro: Jorge Zahar Editora, 2008), P. 43.

[7] Pimenta Velloso, *A Brasilidade Verde-Amarela,* p. 16.

[8] *Correio da Manhã*, Jan. 1, 1938, p. 1.

[9] Ângela Maria de Castro Gomes, "O Redescrimento do Brasil," in Lúcia Lippi Oliveira, Mônica Pimenta Velloso, and Ângela Maria Castro Gomes, *Estado Novo: Ideologia e Poder* (Rio de Janeiro: Zahar Editores, 1982), p. 116.

control, and not incidentally, protecting sub-soil resources essential to reequipping the nation's military.[10]

The March to the West also countered fears of insecurity created by Brazil's largely vacant borderlands and that the nation's seaside capital was far more vulnerable than a land-bound city within Brazil's vast inland spaces.[11] Through speeches and a torrent of published and broadcast material created by his Department of Press and Propaganda [Departamento de Imprensa e Propaganda], founded in December 1939, Vargas generated a vision of an energized Brazil moving to occupy virgin lands and stimulating new production to satisfy its growing population. Aside from pamphlets, posters, newspapers, magazines, films, and technical journals, radio became a new tool for reaching the masses, including illiterate rural workers. A series of "cultural conferences" broadcast by radio linked the March to the West to a brighter national future and lionized Vargas as the movement's inspiration. On April 19, 1941, poet Harold Daltro exclaimed that the "Chief of the Nation" had set the example by "opening roads to true patriots." The March to the West "was not just a sentence," but instead "the expansion of Brazil within its own borders." It meant "cultivation of the soil" and "civilization penetrating the backlands." Brazil was "producing throughout its territory" and "raising itself up with all its strength."[12] Accompanying the rhetoric was practical advice on agriculture. Radio Inconfidência in Minas Gerais began daily transmissions on rural topics in 1940 and Radio Mayrink Veiga of Rio de Janeiro provided weekly broadcasts on agricultural notes and commentaries with support of the Ministry of Agriculture.[13]

Appeals to agricultural development embodied in the March to the West campaign were not just political imagery. While Vargas's attention to agriculture prior to 1937 had been a largely tool to control regional elites,

[10] Paulo de Figueiredo, *Aspectos Ideológicos do Estado Novo* (Brasilia: Centro Gráfico—Senado Federal, 1984), p. 67; Lourdes Sola, "O Golpe de 37 e o Estado Novo," in Carlos Guilherme Mota, ed., *Brasil em Perspectiva*, 19th ed. (Rio de Janeiro: Editora Bertrand, 1990), p. 265.

[11] Liliane da Costa Freitag, *Fronteiras Perigosas: Migração e brasilidade no extremo-oeste paranaense* (Cascavel, PR: EDUNIOESTE, 2001), p. 35.

[12] Brazil. Ministério da Agricultura. Serviço de Documentação. *Marcha para o Oeste (Conferências Culturais) Vol. I, 1939–1943* (Rio de Janeiro: Ministério da Agricultura, 1946), p. 161.

[13] Brazil. Ministério da Agricultura. *Atividades do Ministerio da Agricultura em 1942*, Vol. II (Rio de Janeiro: Ministério da Agricultura, 1943), p. 262.

under the *Estado Novo*, he began serious efforts to stimulate production. His government responded to the needs of an increasingly urbanized population as well as to create substitutes for food imports under the pressure of a continuing foreign exchange crisis.

Critical to the effort was appropriation of an organization concept that had tied immigrants to the land during the Empire and First Republic: settlement colonies [*nucleos colonias*]. In some settlements, immigrant settlers exchanged labor for the small plots of land owned by the state or large landowners. In others, they purchased plots outright with the expectation they would contribute to the local agricultural production. In the 1860s various provincial governments established agricultural settlements for drought victims or Paraguayan war veterans to populate Brazil's vast interior. The First Republic's governments had established agricultural settlements for various purposes, including housing inmates and populating border areas. Japanese immigrants flowed into central and southern Brazil in the first three decades of the twentieth century and became agriculturalists. In 1923, São Paulo counted 4,828 Japanese colonist families planting or harvesting coffee, cotton, rice, and potatoes.[14]

Vargas advocated creation of agricultural settlements even before his victory in the 1930 revolution, based upon his knowledge of settlements in his native Rio Grande do Sul. On January 2, 1930, Vargas evoked an image of a suffering rural populace before a large crowd in Rio de Janeiro during a speech on the platform of the Liberal Alliance. He drew attention to the needs of "thousands of Brazilians who live in the backlands, without instruction, without hygiene, poorly fed, [and] poorly dressed," whose only contact with public powers was through the payment of "extortive taxes." He proclaimed that it was "necessary to group them

[14] Antônio Gavião Gonzaga, "Contribuição para o estudo das imigrações no Brasil, *Revista de Imigração e Colonização,* Vol. III, No. 1 (April 1942), p. 90; Marinês Zandavalli Grando, "Narração Do Processo De Formação De Uma Colônia Agrícola No Rio Grande Do Sul, No Século XIX—A Colônia São Feliciano (1861–1880)," *Ensaios FEE*, Vol. 76, No, 2 (1986), 101–132, 1986; Johny Santana de Araújo, "O Estabelecimento De Colônias Agrícolas Civis e Militares Na Província Do Piauí No Pós-Guerra Do Paraguai (1865–1888)," *EDIPUCRS*, Porto Alegre, Vol. 6, No. 2 (July–Dec. 2013), 57–77; Vinicius Rajão da Fonseca, "Discussões acerca da necessidade de instalação de colônias agrícolas no sul de Mato Grosso (1889–1920)," *Revista Catarinense de História* [online], Florianópolis, No. 23 (2014), pp. 145–63, 2014; Myrian Sepúlveda dos Santos, "Os Porões da República: A colônia Correcional de Dois Rios entre 1908 e 1930," *TOPOI*, Vol. 7, No. 13 (Jul–Dec. 2006), 445–76.

together by instituting agricultural settlements, invest them in the ownership of land, providing them with the instruments of work, easy transport, for the sale of production excess to their needs...."[15] Two years later, his provision government took the first steps toward providing settlers with land ownership in the backlands via a decree proposed by minister of labor Lindolfo Collor that allowed settlers to lease lands in Piauí for a modest sum.[16]

While those who populated the agricultural settlements were to engage in farming, a more subtle motivation was the state's concerns for public security. The provisional government supported agricultural settlements in the Baixada Fluminense, a region bordering the Federal District, not only for producing fruits and vegetables for the internal market, but also to resettle unemployed urban workers and prisoners condemned as revolutionaries.[17] The correction colony on Ilha Grande, a 75 square-mile island off Rio de Janeiro state, became an agricultural settlement where prisoners assembled at four am to begin work in the fields and elsewhere. In 1938 the central government took control of an agricultural settlement on the island of Fernando de Noronha established by the state government eight years earlier. Now under central government control, the colony housed political prisoners condemned by the national security tribunal [*Tribunal de Segurança Nacional*] for participation, imagined or otherwise, in the 1935 communist uprising. Two hundred eight political prisoners were dispatched to the island on October 26, 1938, to cultivate manioc, corn, beans, coconuts, and various fruits.[18] In Osasco, outside of the city of São Paulo, an agricultural settlement dedicated to "re-education," housed 300 persons rounded up by local police for begging in the city's streets.[19]

[15] Brazil. Câmara de Deputados. *Getúlio Vargas* (Brasilia: Biblioteca Digital da Câmara de Deputados, 2011), p. 286.

[16] Maria Yedda Linhares and Francisco Carlos Teixeira de Silva, *Terra Prometida: Uma História da Questão Agraria no Brasil* (Rio de Janeiro: Editora Campus, 1999), p. 113.

[17] P.S. Rose, *One of the Forgotten Things: Getúlio Vargas and Brazilian Social Control, 1930–1954* (Westport, CN: Greenwood Press, 2000), p. 17; Henrique Dias Sobral Silva, "Uma semente no campo do Vargas: A questão agrária e social da colônia agrícola de Santa Cruz (1930–1945)," *Anais do XV Encontro da História Regional da ANPUH-Rio* (c.2012), pp. 9–10.

[18] *Correio Paulistano*, Apr. 3, 1938, p. 24; Aug. 25, 1938, p. 4; Oct. 27, 1938, p. 2.

[19] *Correio Paulistano*, May 26, 1938, p. 15; Mar. 23, 1939, p. 15.

Vargas aggressively expanded support for agricultural settlements under the March to the West banner. On February 9, 1940, the government decreed its support for "colonial nuclei" [*núcleos coloniais*] settlements consisting of plots of land in rural areas located near cities and transportation links. Plots ranging from 10 to 50 hectares could be purchased by Brazilians and foreign agriculturalists willing to dedicate themselves to agriculture. The settlements were to consist of demonstration fields, rural schools, wood and metal shops, an infirmary, and cooperatives for credit and sale and purchase of goods. Agricultural machinery, implements and tools, as well as seeds, fertilizers, insecticides, and fungicides would be made available at cost. Payments for land could occur over ten years, with the first payment not due until the last day of the settler's third year of occupying the land.[20]

Vargas expanded the program with a new decree in February 1940, several months after a dramatic seven-day foray into the hinterland of Goiás. He charged the minister of agriculture with installing large national agricultural colonies [*colonias agricolas nacionais*] for Brazilians who were "recognizably poor" and displayed aptitude for agricultural work as well as, exceptionally, foreign agriculturalists. The size of lots available for purchase expanded to between 20 and 50 hectares, and settlements were also to maintain shops where settlers and their children could learn skills necessary for rural life. During their first year, settlers were to receive salaries for employment and the loan of agricultural machinery and implements and working animals. The agricultural focus of the settlement was made clear by the requirement that each be administered by an agronomist "of recognized professional capacity and unblemished reputation."[21] Reaction was highly favorable, in Vargas' opinion. He confided to his diary about the "excellent impression" generated by the measure, a product of the "orientation that I brought back after my trip to the backland of Goiás."[22]

[20] Decree-Law No. 2.009, FeBRUA, ry 9, 1940. Brasil. Ministry of Agriculture. National Department for Vegetable Production, Land and Colonization Division. *Questions and Other Information Concerning the Admittance of Foreigners into Brazilin the Capacity of Farmers* (Rio de Janeiro, 1940), p. 4.

[21] Decree-Law 3,059. FeBRUA, ry 14, 1941.

[22] *Vargas, Diário. Vol. II, 1937–1942*, p. 378.

Public endorsement of the program became a high priority for Vargas and his confidants. Press accounts highlighted Vargas' personal engagement selection of lands for future "great agricultural settlements." Newspaper reports highlighted how the Director of Land and Colonization, José de Oliveira Marques, personally briefed Vargas on surveys for settlements in Northern states. Vargas responded with decisions based on the "perfect documentation of the motives that should prevail for the definite location of the referenced colonies."[23] Land dedicated to production there doubled between 1937 and 1939, where one hectare planted in English potato by a farmer working his plot with his wife and three sons yielded 140 sacks of potatoes and a handsome profit. Getúlio's brother Viriato expressed surprise following a visit in early 1941 to the settlement when shown the large amounts of rice, tomatoes, hay, oranges, and vegetables produced by the settlers.[24] In the opinion of the Director of Lands and Colonization, Brazil was well on its way to establishing "a vast network of agricultural centers" that would become "advanced outposts of the March to the West."[25]

Expanding Federal Support for Agriculture

If opening new lands to agriculture under the banner of the March to the West contributed to regime legitimacy, it was also necessary to raise agricultural productivity for economic reasons. The first two topics of the November 16, 1937, meeting between Vargas and Minister Fernando de Souza Costa highlighted the dilemmas facing the new government. The first was the coffee situation. Increased production of higher-grade coffees in Africa and other parts of Latin America in the 1930s had pressured Brazilian coffee revenues, and between 1936 and 1937 coffee exports fell by over 7% in quantity and over 12% in value.[26] Failure to sustain a 1936 agreement on differentiating prices between competing Brazilian

[23] *Correio Paulistano,* Oct. 31, 1941, p. 4.

[24] Fernando Costa, *A Ministério da Agricultura no Primeiro Decênio Governamental de Presidente Vargas. Conferência Pronunciada no DIP em 20-12-940*, p. 26; *Correio Paulistano,* Mar. 2, 1941, p. 7; Apr. 10, 1941, p. 7.

[25] *A Manhã*, Dec. 15, 1942, p. 3.

[26] Instituto Brasileiro de Geografia e Estatística, *Reportório Estatístico do Brasil, Quadros Respectivos, No. 1 (Separata do Anuário Estatístico do Brasil, Ano V, 1939/40* (Rio de Janeiro: Serviço Gráfico do Instituto Brasiliero de Geografia e Estatística, 1941), p. 23.

and Colombian coffee grades prompted Vargas to shift course. Along with proclaiming the *Estado Novo,* Vargas declared an end to limiting production by burning excess coffee stocks. Simultaneously, he declared a moratorium on paying the foreign debt, further limiting access to foreign exchange. The consequent burden to limit imports probably led to the second topic discussed by Vargas and Souza Costa: the need to stimulate domestic wheat production. In 1937, Brazil had imported nearly one million tons of wheat and wheat flour at a cost of nearly £5.5 million.[27]

Fernando de Souza Costa was aware of such challenges. Soon after assuming office he had outlined the tasks facing Brazilian agriculture. Brazil was a powerful agricultural nation, he boasted, endowed with the "vastness of its land" as well as a "variety of climates" and "diverse geological formations" that was "perfectly capable of producing almost all the categories of crops of the world." It was necessary, though, to embark upon a "program of action that stimulates in each promising land, crops adapted and intensified according to today's techniques." He called for greater understanding of the soil and sub-soil and more trained agronomists and geologists. He highlighted the need for improvements in cattle raising and production of honey, sugar cane, coffee, tobacco, and cotton. Recalling his role as São Paulo's secretary of agriculture, he reminded his audience of the value of seed selection and experiments with fertilizers as well as the benefits of research in animal and plant science. Consistent with his earlier discussions, he summarized his previous successes in advancing cultivation of cereals, especially wheat.[28]

Souza Costa wasted no time in advancing an aggressive agenda supporting the cultivation of wheat, foreshadowing tactics applied to other products of domestic consumption. Ten days after Souza Costa's meeting with Vargas, the government ordered bakers to mix imported wheat flour with up to 30% of nationally produced starch or wheat.[29] The ministry increased the number of wheat experimental stations from one, established in Rio Grande do Sul in 1934, to four, with additional stations created in São Paulo, Paraná, and Minas Gerais. Before leaving for the 1938 Easter holidays on his farm in Pirassununga, São Paulo, Costa

[27] *Brazilian Business*, Vol. 19 (April 1939), p. p. 226.

[28] *Jornal do Commercio*, Nov. 14, 1937, p. 9.

[29] Decree Law No. 26, Nov. 30, 1937.

informed Vargas that "wheat campaign is progressing with great optimism" in Rio Grande do Sul and that he was attempting to recruit noted Italian agronomist Girolani Azzi to assist in creating experimental fields on wheat. He was also conducting a "rigorous inquiry" into activities of various departments of the ministry to identify accomplishments as well as deficiencies. His ministry was also assisting farmers in the perennial struggle against ants, advancing plans for a national agricultural school, investigating the feasibility of cultivating dates, and constructing housing for workers at the Santa Cruz agricultural settlement.[30]

The wheat program soon benefited from the ministry's contracting foreign experts in wheat cultivation and dilution of the wheat content for bread. With Professor Azzi unavailable, the ministry contracted a noted expert in wheat cultivation from neighboring Uruguay to direct "better oriented research with respect to the competition among varieties" and studies on the impact of fertilizers. The following year it engaged Professor Evin Charles Stakman of the University of Minnesota, a noted plant pathologist and specialist in combating wheat stem rust. The government began furnishing machinery to improve wheat planting and harvesting. A December 1938 decree established a minimum price for native wheat, and a nationwide campaign called for mixing manioc flour with wheat to produce "mixed bread" [*pão mixto*]. The percentage of manioc flour mixed with wheat flour rose from 2% in 1938 to 15% by 1941. Beginning in 1939, corn and rice flour were also mixed with wheat in varying percentages.[31]

The combination of more intensive experimentation, fixed prices, widespread distribution of seeds, and the mixing of other grains into bread production led to a major increase in wheat production in Santa Catarina and Rio Grande do Sul as well as decreased imports of wheat flour. The ministry distributed nearly 800,000 metric tons of seeds to farmers in 1939. As shown in Fig. 14.1, by 1943 wheat production rose by a factor of four in Santa Catarina and by over 100% in Rio Grande do Sul. Overall, Brazil's wheat production increased by 120,000 metric tons between 1939 and 1943. The use of manioc, corn, and rice flours

[30] Attachment to Ltr, Fernando Costa to Getúlio Vargas, Apr. 8, 1938, in AGV, CPDOC, Lv 38.04.08.

[31] Ministerio da Agricultura Brazil. Ministério da Agricultura. *O Ministério da Agricultura no Governo de Getúlio Vargas (1930–1944)* (Rio de Janeiro: Ministério da Agricultura, 1945), pp. 83–85, 262.

lessened wheat imports between 1939 and 1943 by an estimated 467,000 metric tons.[32]

Meanwhile, the ministry continued efforts to improve cultivation of manioc, oats, corn, beans, rye, barley, various fruits, sugar, coffee, cotton, jute, and flax, as well as conducting trials with various fertilizers and silkworm development. To raise the productivity of these and other crops, Souza Costa embarked upon a campaign to place the nation's agricultural research and educational facilities under centralized control. In December 1938, the government instituted the Centro Nacional de Ensino e Pesquisas Agronômicas (CNEPA) [National Center of Agronomic Teaching and Research], to supervise all agricultural research and agricultural and veterinary teaching at the superior level. The institute assumed direction of research at experimental stations previously controlled by the ministry's various services. Further coordination of

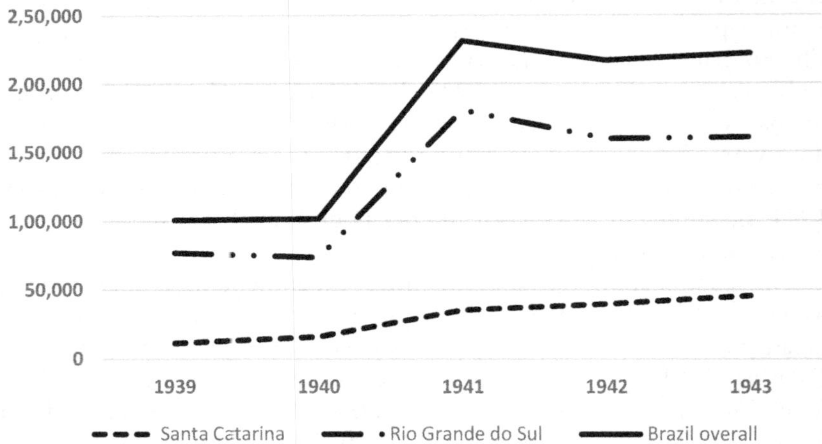

Fig. 14.1 Wheat Production in Santa Catarina, Rio Grande do Sul and Brazil Overall, 1939–1943 (metric tons) (*Source* Brazil. Instituto Brasileiro de Geografia e Estatística. *Anuário Estatístico do Brasil Ano VI—1941–1945* (Rio de Janeiro: Instituto Brasileiro de Geografia e Estatística, 1946), p. 96)

[32] Brazil. Ministério da Agricultura. *As Atividades Agrícolas do Brasil em 1939, Vol. I* (Rio de Janeiro: Ministério da Agricultura, 1940), p. 18; Brazil. Ministerio da Agricultura. *O Ministério da Agricultura no Governo de Getúlio Vargas (1930–1944)*, pp. 83–85, 262.

research on a regional basis became the responsibility of regional agronomic institutes under central government control, marking the realization, for the first time in the nation's history, that Brazil's wide diversity of climates required a more regionalized approach to agricultural research. The ministry envisioned five regional institutes, the first being the Instituto Agronômico do Norte in Belem, Pará.

Souza Costa also followed through on his observations about the need for more agronomists and veterinarians. The Ministry of Agriculture gained authority over the higher schools of agriculture and veterinary studies via Decree-Law 933 of December 7, 1938. The decree empowered the ministry to approve the curriculum and functioning of the schools, limiting professional certification of agronomists and veterinarians to graduates of approved institutions. In November 1938, the ministry also committed to construct the national agricultural school, following approval of the plans for the school by Vargas himself, to be located at kilometer 47 on the Rio de Janeiro-São Paulo highway. The complex was to house the national agricultural and veterinary schools, major research facilities, experimental farms, a cattle breeding station, and housing for students and staff. During his tenure as minister, Souza Costa frequently visited the construction site, located in Santa Cruz on grounds of the former Imperial farm. Costa aggressively supported the site's development, which required draining of swamps and removal of residences of the former agricultural settlement.[33]

Souza Costa's program to expand production of a broad variety of crops soon benefited from measures taken by the Banco do Brasil to broaden its financial support of national production of both agricultural and industrial products. While the coffee, cacao, and sugar sectors benefited from credit during the first seven years of the Vargas government, commercial lenders, and the banks remained reluctant to finance other crops because of their susceptibility to market fluctuations and bankruptcy. In the face of expanding production of other crops, in 1936 the Banco do Brasil recognized the need to provide credit for agricultural

[33] *A Noite,* July 20, 1938, p. 5; *O Observador Econômico e Financeiro,* LXXXV (February 1943), pp. 31–32. Legal battles slowed construction of the school and accompanying institutes. Only during the last three wartime years did construction at the site move toward completion. Transfer of the schools to the new site occurred in February 1948. *Jornal do Commercio,* Feb. 28, 1948, p. 2. The U.S. Embassy estimated the cost of the complex at US$20 million. See U.S. Embassy, Rio de Janeiro, to Secretary of State, Mar. 28, 1947. USDA, FAS Narrative Reports, 1946–1949, USNA, RG 166, Box 518.

activities. The following year legislation created instruments of guarantees for the lender: a rural mortgage (*penhor rural*) and a land title (*cédula pignatorícia*). The law authorized financial assistance for acquiring seeds and fertilizers, cattle, and payment of crop costs. With the *Estado Novo* less than two months old, another decree law gave additional legal status to the rural mortgage. The way was now clear for the *Carteira de Credito Agricola e Industrial* [Department of Agricultural and Industrial Credit]: "to develop an increase in the national wealth and provide direct financial assistance to agriculture, ranching and industry."[34]

Most of the CR$724,500 in loans extended through 1940 served traditional sectors: the beef cattle sector received 30.31%; coffee 24.43%; and sugar 18.3%—a combined total of over 73% of the value of loans. But loans also supported cultivation of a wide variety of crops and products, many for domestic consumption, including manioc (as a substitute for wheat), cotton, fruits, corn, tomatoes, black acacia (a gum producing tree), agave, alfalfa, garlic, peanuts, oats, peat, onions, barley, tea, coconut, mate, peas, anis, sesame, tobacco, Ceasar weed (for rope), jute, fire wood, flaxseed, flax, hops, mint, rami (a fiber), hops, castor, cabbage, wheat, silk, and grapes.[35] Federal government support for financing polyculture was beginning to become a reality.

Changes in the International Environment and Agriculture (1937–1939)

Increasing support for agricultural diversification occurred within a dynamic international environment. Minister Souza Costa correctly noted in his report to President Vargas on his ministry's activities in 1939, that "It is quite true that the current European conflict has opened wide horizons for our exports, but that alone would not suffice to justify the surge

[34] Paulo Roberto Beskow, "O Crédito Rural Público Numa Economia Em Transformação: Estudo Histórico e Avaliação Econômica das Atividades de Financiamento Agropecuário da CREAI/BB, de 1937 a 1965" (Diss: Univ. de Campinas, 1994), pp. 189, 201.

[35] Banco do Brasil figures cited in Centrais Elétricas Brasileiras, S.A., "O papel do Banco do Brasil via CREAI no financiamento do desenvolvimento econômico brasileiro (1937–1952)" https://www.arpec.org.br/.../000-7c3dae1a4bd4b31eaa7e2bfb4abf.., Table III; Beskow, "O Crédito Rural Público," p. 22, Table III.1.

of progress we are experiencing."[36] Souza Costa was well aware that international conflict would generate higher demand for raw materials, as had occurred during the "Great War," and create additional benefits for Brazilian producers. Critical to improving the productivity of Brazil's agriculture was the acquisition of additional technical information, especially from a nation that would gradually become Brazil's strategic partner: the United States.

Brazilian agriculture's ties with the United States had remained strong during the first seven years of the Vargas government. The role of the United States as the primary purchaser of Brazil's agricultural exports strongly conditioned trade relationships between the two countries. Brazil entered into a commercial trade agreement that lowered import duties on U.S. goods in 1935 under the threat of imposition of a duty on Brazilian coffee entering the United States. The United States continued as the prime customer for two of the nation's primary exports, importing over 55% of Brazil's coffee exports and more than 85% of its cocoa bean exports in 1937.[37] In 1936 and 1937, the United States remained the main source for Brazil's agricultural implement and machinery imports. Brazil purchased 21,486 horse and power plows from the United States in 1936 and 1937, as well as 681 tractors. U.S. suppliers garnered an average of 87.5% of all tractors and tractor parts imported into Brazil during those years. U.S. machinery was also prominent in processing the nation's burgeoning cotton cultivation. Few cotton farmers had mechanized the actual cultivation of the crop, but the market for cotton gins, cotton presses, and cotton seed oil presses was thriving. In 1936 Brazil imported 1,496 gins and other U.S. cotton processing machines, followed by 1,145 similar machines the following year. The U.S. exporters captured 92 and 88%, respectively, of the Brazilian market in those two years for such machines, far ahead of leading competitor Germany.[38]

[36] Brazil. Ministério da Agricultura. *As Atividades Agrícolas do Brasil em 1939, Vol. I*, p. 3.

[37] William H. Ukers, *Ten Years of Coffee Progress: the Highlights of Coffee Developments During the Decade, 1935–1944* (New York: Pan-American Coffee Bureau, 1945), p. 30; Brazil, Ministerio da Fazenda, *Comércio Exterior do Brasil 1933–1937*, pp. 781, 782.

[38] U.S. Commercial Attaché, Rio de Janeiro to Department of State, "The Brazilian Market for Farm Equipment," Sept. 19, 1940, USNA, Department of Agriculture, Records of the FAS, RG 166, "Narrative Reports," Box 16; USBFDC, *Trade of the United States with Brazil in 1938* (Washington: 1939), p. 4.

Moreover, the U.S. experience in agriculture remained a prominent reference point for policy decisions related to agriculture. The provisions of Vargas' program to aid coffee farmers through an "economic readjustment" law [Reajustamento Econômico] drew heavily from the example of the U.S. Agricultural Adjustment Act of 1933. The 1933 decision of the Ministry of Agriculture to create an agricultural statistics unit (*Diretoria da Estatística da Produção*) cited the U.S. intervention in agricultural affairs via the Agricultural Adjustment Act. In the ministry's opinion, the U.S. act exemplified the need for a more powerful state that should "control more and more the means of production and the distribution of riches."[39] Former minister of agriculture Ildefonso Simões Lopes argued that Brazil should shift its focus from export agriculture and attend to the internal market just as done in the "United States of North America...."[40]

Such ties came under pressure between 1937 and September 1939 when Brazil hedged its international political and economic bets, seeking to benefit from trade with both Germany and the United States. One year after signing a commercial treaty with the United States, Vargas agreed to trade with Germany on a barter basis and began to export large amounts of cotton, leather, and other agricultural products. Brazil's trade with Germany rose by 170% between 1933 and 1937 and its value reached nearly 70% of the value of U.S. trade by 1937.[41] Meanwhile, Brazil's pro-Axis military leaders, Vargas's primary supporters within the *Estado Novo*, clamored for German war materiel for the nation's woefully inadequate military. By early 1939, this policy of "pragmatic equilibrium" was reaching a decision point driven by twin uncertainties: Axis intentions regarding Brazil's large German minority in Southern Brazil, and whether the United States was willing to support one of Vargas's major goals, establishment of a domestic steel industry.[42]

[39] Villela and Suzigan, *Política do governo*, pp. 182, 183; Brazil. Ministerio da Agricultura. *Relatório 1933–1934*, p. 76.

[40] TS, ISL 00.00, IX 14a, Ildefonso Simões Lopes Archive, CPDOC.

[41] Brazil. Ministério da Fazenda. *Comércio Exterior do Brasil. Foreign Trade of Brazil. Commerce Exterieur du Brasil 1933–1937* (Rio de Janeiro: Typografia do Serviço de Estatística Econômica e Financeira, 1940), pp. 31–35.

[42] Gerson Moura. *Brazilian foreign relations:1939–1950: the changing nature of Brazil-United States relations during and after the Second World War* (Brasília: FUNAG, 2013.), p. 71; Stanley Hilton, *Oswaldo Aranha: Uma Biografia* (Rio de Janeiro: Objetiva, 1994),

Vargas confidant Oswaldo Aranha was instrumental in tipping the scale toward the United States and inserting higher levels of U.S. technical expertise into Brazil's development plans, starting with support for the ongoing transformation of Brazil's agriculture. A native of a small rural municipio in Rio Grande do Sul, lawyer Aranha played vital roles in the October 1930 revolution and the 1934 constitutional convention. As Vargas' finance minister from November of 1931 to July of 1934, he had suggested creation of the *Conselho Federal de Comércio Exterior* [Federal Council of Foreign Trade] to promote exports and diversify the nation's economy.[43]

Aranha became Vargas' ambassador to Washington in September 1934 and immersed himself in the economic and political realities of Brazil's major trading partner, realities he grew to admire. War clouds on the horizon in Europe and Asia and Brazil's uncertain relationship with neighboring Argentina convinced him that Brazil's would benefit from a strong partnership with the United States. After Vargas invited him to become the *Estado Novo's* foreign minister in March 1938, Aranha leveraged contacts with senior U.S. officials by reminding them of the "tradition" of "U.S. assistance to Brazil in the politics of South America and of the cooperation of Brazil with the United States on international issues."[44] U.S. officials, meanwhile, were highly concerned about possible Nazi penetration of the South Atlantic and even civil war within Brazil or, in the worst case, an overthrow of the Vargas government provoked by Nazi agents.[45]

The environment was right for Brazil to seek U.S. economic support consistent with goals of the *Estado Novo*. When President Roosevelt invited Aranha to Washington for consultations in early 1939, Aranha came prepared to raise the possibilities of closer relations with the Axis powers if Washington proved insensitive to Brazil's development needs. He was carrying a portfolio of recommendations from various ministers—including agriculture minister Souza Costa—about possible support

pp. 282–304; Neto, *Getúlio 1930–1945,* pp. 345–49; Frank D. McCann, Jr. *The Brazilian-American Alliance, 1937–1945* (Princeton, NJ: Princeton Univ. Press, 1973), pp. 114–116.

[43] Hilton, *Oswaldo Aranha*, p. 187.

[44] Aranha to Sumner Wells, Sept. 9, 1938, Oswaldo Aranha Archive, cited by Hilton, *Oswaldo Aranha*, p. 298.

[45] Hilton, *Oswaldo Aranha*, p. 305.

from Washington.[46] Souza Costa had provided Aranha with a plethora of proposals designed to remedy the "most sensible need of the Ministry: the lack of technicians." He advocated having the United States agree to send Brazilian technicians to the United States for specialization, who would then work with U.S. technicians in Brazil. He also recommended seeking a 15 thousand conto credit [approximately US$900,000] for purchase of agricultural machinery and a similar credit to purchase breeding cattle. The United States could also assist Brazil by identifying which Brazilian products held the most promise for the U.S. market. Finally, he argued that Aranha should arrange for "white, American agriculturalists" specialized in products of most interest in Brazil—especially wheat and fruit—to emigrate to Brazil. To implement the idea, Costa's ministry resolved to admit up to 3,000 U.S. immigrants annually, 80% of whom would be dedicated to farming or providing technical information to other farmers.[47]

Aranha followed through on at least one of the proposals and discussed possible U.S. assistance for Brazil's agricultural development with the officials of the departments of state and agriculture. He informed his U.S. counterparts that Brazil was "especially desirous of stimulating the systematic large-scale production of agricultural products native to Brazil or capable of successful introduction to Brazil." Negotiations resulted in commitments by Brazil to establish a central bank and finance purchases in the United States. The United States pledged to loan Brazil over US$19 million to pay off debts and open credits to capitalize the central bank and support imports of Brazilian products. The United States also agreed to detail technicians to conduct surveys of "agricultural possibilities, including the development of tropical hardwoods, rubber, and other products" as well as "the coincidental study of many additional native products of Brazil."[48]

[46] Hilton, *Oswaldo Aranha*, p. 303.

[47] Fernando de Sousa Costa to Oswaldo Aranha, Jan. 28, 1939, in AGV, CPDOC, Gv c.1939.01.09; Memo, José de Oliveira Marques, Diretor, Serviço de Irrigação, Reflorestamento, e Colonização, Jan. 27, 1939, AGV, CPDOC, Gv c.1939.01.0.

[48] Aranha to Vargas, Mar. 27, 1939, GVA, CPDOC, GV 39.01.09c; Aranha to the Secretary of State [Translation], Mar. 8, 1939, U.S. Department of State, *Foreign Relations of the United States Diplomatic Papers, 1939, The American Republics, Volume V*, 832.51/1406.

The first fruits of Aranha's agreement for official U.S. support to Brazil's agriculture was an extended visit by a renowned U.S. plant geneticist and world authority on citrus and plant hybridization. Walter Tennyson Swingle (1871–1952) was an advocate of closer U.S.-Brazil relations related to agriculture who, in July 1936, had provided Aranha with information on his accomplishments and seven bundles of publications related to agriculture. Two months after Aranha concluded his negotiations and departed Washington for Brazil, Swingle accepted an invitation from Aranha and embarked for Brazil. His stated mission was to advise the Ministry of Agriculture on the commercial potential of plants that could be grown in Brazilian soil. On board ship enroute to Brazil, Swingle explained that he intended to focus on two crops: quinine and rubber. Quinine was native to South America, but the British had become the main cultivators of the crop after spiriting seeds away to India from its native habitat in Peru. Swingle had acquired quinine seeds from the East Indies, cultivated them in Puerto Rico, and arranged for shipment of 1000 seedlings to Brazil in September 1938. The plants offered Brazil an opportunity to produce commercial quantities of a quinine-based drug known as "totaquina," effective in treating malaria. As he explained to a Washington newspaper reporter, "I am sure fine quinine can be grown in Brazil for distribution at a low price."[49]

Swingle was also embarking on a more strategic mission, supported by both Brazil and the United States: promoting production of natural rubber. Japanese occupation of China had raised the specter of threats to the Southeast Asia rubber trade, and the U.S. Rubber Manufacturers Association began seeking emergency supplies of rubber. In April 1939, the United States reached a barter agreement with the United Kingdom to exchange 500,000 bales of cotton for 90,000 tons of rubber for use in event of a wartime emergency.[50] Swingle raised the same concern the following month, reasoning that a general war might cut off the United States from its Asian rubber supply. True to Brazil's understanding of his mission, Swingle also expressed hope that, in addition to growing quinine and rubber in commercial quantities, Brazil could soon be producing

[49] WarrenDean, *Brazil and the Struggle for Rubber: A Study in Environmental History* (New York: Cambridge University Press, 1987), p. 12; *Washington Evening Star*, May 4, 1939.

[50] Paul Wendt, "The Control of Rubber in World War II," *Southern Economic Journal*, Vol. 13, No. 3 (Jan. 1947), 203.

other tropical products for the U.S. market. The U.S. market, he pointed out, could become a viable substitute for Brazil's European markets disrupted by war.[51]

Swingle opened his visit with a call on Minister Souza Costa in company of the director of the National Agricultural School, followed by a seven-week tour of various facilities in São Paulo including a tung oil (a dryer for paints) plantation in Limeira. Prior to departing, he urged Souza Costa consider an Asian crop producing good results, especially as substitute for cow's milk: soy.[52] Upon returning to the United States, Swingle issued a glowing report on Brazil's agricultural possibilities. He surmised that Brazil could increase exports of tropical products by more than ten-fold by adopting "intelligent and progressive agricultural methods." Brazil's exports of rubber, vegetable oils, and medicinal plants, could reach as high as US$300 million per year.[53] He was also confident that Brazil's rubber industry, aided by U.S. technical experts, could develop large-scale production of rubber and supply most U.S. rubber needs within ten years, as he wrote in a report published by the Ministry of Foreign Relations. Brazil could also benefit from producing

[51] *Washington Evening Star*, May 4, 1939.

[52] *Diário de Pernambuco*, June 29, 1939, p. 6. The first Brazilian experiments with soy took place at the Instituto Agronômico of Campinas in the 1890s. Early linkages with U.S. soy resources were strong. F.G. Craig, a U.S. instructor at Escola Superior de Agronomia e Veterinaria of the Universidade Técnica in Porto Alegre, experimented with soy at the school in 1914. Henrique Lóbbe, director of an experimental seed farm in São Simão, São Paulo state, conducted trials with 48 varieties of seeds imported from the United States starting in 1926, publishing comprehensive results in 1935. See Empresa Brasileira de Pesquisa Agropecuária, *A Soja no Brasil: História e Estatística* (Londrina, PR: Centro Nacional de Pesquisa de Soja, 1987), pp. 8, 9; J.R. Jardim Freire, J.A. Costa, and J.G. Stammel. "Principais fatores que propiciaram a expansão da soja no Brasil." http://www.plantiodireto.com.br/?body=cont_int&id=713;

João Rui Jardim Freire, Francisco De Jesus Vernetti, "A Pesquisa Com Soja, A Seleção De Rizóbio e a Produção De Inoculantes No Brasil," www.fepagro.rs.gov.br/upload/1398909703_art_14.pdf. Benjamin Hunnicutt advocated cultivating soy in a state sponsored publication in Minas Gerais in 1930. He correctly predicted that "in view of its value as a forage crop, as an oil, and for human consumption, its cultivation [of soybeans] is destined to become very generalized in Brazil." Benjamin H. Hunnicutt, "Feijão Soja," *Boletim de Agricultura, Zootécnica e Veterinaria*, Ano III, Nos. 9–12 (Sept.–Dec. 1930), 41.

[53] *O Jornal*, Aug. 18, 1939, p. 3; Aug. 26, 1939, p. 4.

large quantities of quinine and oiticia oil, an ingredient in industrial oil paints.[54]

Swingle was convinced that Brazil and the United States shared compatible interests in Brazil's agricultural development that could serve as the basis for a de facto agricultural alliance. Like other U.S. agronomists who became engaged in Brazilian agricultural development, he reasoned that Brazil and the United States had compatible interests. In his view, the two nations competed only in cotton and that "the United States and Brazil can supplement each other if they only would."[55] He reasoned that Brazil could become a vast storehouse of tropical plant products, allowing the United States to free itself from dependence upon Asian supplies of tropical goods. Brazil possessed the "largest area of easily farmed tropical and subtropical land of any New World country," he wrote after returning to the United States. Further, "no other country with a large population of capable agriculturalists situated in the tropical zone has such advantages." He proposed that Brazil create a tung oil industry, cultivate more Manila hemp and quinine, and create a plant introduction service modeled on the U.S. example. He pledged that "all that has been learned is freely at the disposal of Brazilian experts."[56]

Agriculture's Role in Rise of a De Facto Alliance (1939–1940)

Wartime events soon intensified Brazilian interest in raising agricultural production with or without U.S. cooperation. The German invasion of Poland on September 1, 1939, stirred Vargas and his cabinet to enumerate Brazil's actions in the face of a European war that was "threatening to involve in the conflict nations of other Continents."

[54] *A Noite*, June 28, 1939, p. 2; *Diário de Notícias*, Nov. 11, 1939, p. 4. U.S. imports of Oiticia oil surged to an estimated 900 million tons in 1941 after losing access to Asian supplies. See Seth Garfield, "The Environment of Wartime Migration: Labor Transfers from The Brazilian Northeast to The Amazon During World War II," *Journal of Social History*, Vol. 43, No. 4 (Summer 2010), 997.

[55] *Washington Evening Star*, May 4, 1939.

[56] TS, "Complementary Crops for Brazil," Sept. 10, 1940, Walter Tennyson Swingle Collection, University of Miami, Folder 11, p 1, and TS, "Need for a Brazilian Plant Introduction Service," Aug. 22, 1940, Walter Tennyson Swingle Collection, University of Miami, Folder 13, p. 1.

In a confidential memorandum prepared after cabinet meetings in early September, the government specified how it would deal with the international and domestic consequences of the spreading conflict. Its terms mirrored Brazil's response to international market distortions created by World War I. While pledging to be "strictly neutral," Brazil reserved the right to conduct business with countries in either belligerent camp involving the "excess of its production and primary materials." Brazil would develop its economic potential "through all means" and determine the nation's capacity for exporting agricultural products without prejudicing domestic market needs. The Ministry of Agriculture became responsible for "promoting and stimulating the intensification, on a large scale, the agricultural, pastoral, and mineral production" to meet domestic needs but also to supply "countries menaced by war." These would be required, in the cabinet's judgment, "to make large orders to Brazilian markets."[57] To carry out the directive, Vargas met separately with Minister Souza Costa on September 12 to consider "the development of certain products" as well as ways to "avoid increases in the cost of living."[58]

Brazil mobilized to meet the opportunities and challenges related to agriculture created by the new international environment. Throughout 1940, the Ministry of Agriculture was "active in promoting and developing any crop showing real economic potential," in the opinion of the U.S. assistant commercial attaché in Rio de Janeiro. "Much work" took place in support of "wheat, oil seeds, and other crops, fisheries, [and] textiles," while "various model food distribution stations were built for handling, by improved methods, perishable commodities such as fish, vegetables and meat," he reported. The ministry was also "encouraging farmers to perfect plans which might prove to be of individual or collective interest, including ideas relating to diversification and standardization." In 1940 disruption of Brazil's European trade led to a 26% drop in coffee exports, a 30% reduction in exports of cotton, a 15% fall in cocoa exports, and a 50% drop in tobacco exports.[59] The drop in exports was

[57] TS, "Diretrizes Gerais No. 1 Aos Ministérios," Sept. 12, 1939, Gustavo Capanema Archive, CPDOC, GCi 1939.07.06.

[58] Entry for Sept. 12, 1939, in *Getúlio Vargas, Diário. Vol. II*,p. 255.

[59] TS, "Annual Economic Review, 1940," U.S. Assistant Commercial Attaché, Rio de Janeiro, Feb 8, 1941, RG 166, USDA, FAS, Narrative Reports (1920–1941), Box 16, USNA, pp. 38–44.

accompanied by changes in the destination of Brazil's trade. The value of exports to European countries fell by 74% between 1938 and 1941, while exports to the Americas more than doubled during the same period.[60] The U.S. market gained new prominence as the government explored the opportunities for increasing U.S. imports of Brazilian products, including guaraná, a tropical fruit drink.

Building Brazilian production through U.S. Ties. The increased prominence of the United States as a trading partner was accompanied by Brazilians' conviction that close collaboration with the United States was essential to boosting the output of agricultural and extractive products. With economic ties between Brazil and Germany hindered by Germany's interference in internal Brazilian politics, securing technical expertise and equipment from the United States became the primary option for Brazilian economic planners. From the U.S. viewpoint, the fear of a German beachhead in the Americas via an invasion of Northeastern Brazil, and the U.S. perception that Brazil's decisions would influence events in the Americas in any forthcoming conflict made securing the support of Brazil a political priority for the Roosevelt administration. Within this charged political and economic environment, the mutual search for ways to increase the output of agricultural and extractive products created an important incentive for wartime cooperation perceived by many of its proponents as merely a prelude to a broader economic alliance. Both Brazilian and U.S. advocates of more intense economic ties took advantage of their respective governments' interests in meeting the short-term demands of the war consistent with their long-term interests. Fundamental to a more intense relationship was Vargas's commitment to increasing the federal government's presence in developing the Amazon and the nearly simultaneous realization by the U.S. government that the Amazon could meet its need for a secure supply of critical strategic resource: natural rubber.

First Rubber, then Beans and Rice. Cooperation toward mutually defined strategic goals began with the pursuit of increased production of rubber. With full-scale U.S. production of the synthetic rubber still several years away and the May 1940 German invasion of the Netherlands

[60] Instituto Brasileiro de Geografia e Estatística, *Annuário Estatístico do Brasil Ano VI 1941/1945* (Rio de Janeiro: Serviço Gráfico do Instituto Brasileiro de Geografia e Estatística, 1946), p. 278.

threatening the supply from the Dutch East Indies, the U.S. government began a frantic search for new sources for natural rubber. On the surface, at least, Brazil seemed to be logical choice. Henry Ford had been attempting to establish a high-yield, disease-resistant variety of a natural rubber since acquiring rights in 1927 to over one million acres of land on the Tapajós River upstream from Belém. Experimental plantings of 5,000,000 seedlings had yielded disappointing results, as the plantation style format of the gardens facilitated propagation of a destructive fungus—South American Leaf Blight—while allowing hordes of insects to devour easily obtained food sources. By 1940, results of experiments combining the attributes of various species of rubber at Ford's plantation at Belterra through labor-intensive grafting offered little hope for producing significant quantities of rubber. Labor unrest spurred by Ford's insensitivity to local cultural norms and the persistent decimation of leaf blight were converting Ford's venture into a business nightmare. Nevertheless, the manager of the Belterra plantation remained publicly optimistic. Harry Braunstein suggested to Getúlio Vargas during his visit to the plantation in October 1940 that, despite setbacks, revival of the latex economy "may possibly mean the re-birth of the Amazon Valley."[61]

It was clear to Vargas that expanding the economy of the Amazon region could extend his *Estado Novo* into a region historically neglected by Brazil's rulers. He was reluctant, however, to commit the region's future solely to rubber. The mandate of his government's newly founded Amazon research station—the Instituto Agronômico do Norte—included experimenting not only with rubber, but with other tropical crops. This would preclude other tropical regions, including India, Africa, and even other South American countries from displacing Brazil as a primary producer. On its 3,000 plus hectare estate, the institute was also to focus on technical issues related to the profitable cultivation for export of Brazil nuts and plants producing fiber, oils, legumes, and natural pesticides.[62]

Consistent with his March to the West campaign, Vargas touted the potential contributions to the region of agricultural colonization. The challenge of the government, in his view, was to transform all that had

[61] Quoted in Gregg Grandin, *Fordlandia: The Rise and Fall of Henry Ford's Forgotten Jungle City* (New York: Metropolitan Books, 2009), p. 338.

[62] Brazil. Ministério da Agricultura. As *Atividades Agrícolas do Brasil em 1939 Vol. I* (Rio de Janeiro: Ministério da Agricultura, 1940), pp. 121–23; Costa, *A Ministério da Agricultura no Primeiro Decênio Governamental de Presidente Vargas*, p. 32.

been done in the region—whether related to extractive products or agriculture—into a rational process. His visit to Belterra may have convinced him that such a vision was feasible. His diary record of his day and a half visit noted the "medical services, plantations, workers' festivities, speeches, [and] creation of a children's nursery" as well as the "banquet, speeches, workers' dance, burnings, the shelter for the retirees."[63] As Vargas explained in Manaus two days after visiting Belterra, the task before his government consisted of converting the "nomadism" of rubber gatherers and the economic instability of the residents of river banks via "settlements of agricultural cultivation." It was there, he argued, that the agricultural colonist, having received his land freely, could "establish a family with health and comfort."[64]

The first director of the Instituto Agronômico do Norte (IAN) shared Vargas' hopes for linking agricultural development with colonization throughout the valley. Felisberto Camargo (1896–1977) was a Brazilian agronomist whose U.S. training had molded his vision of agriculture's potential social impact. As pointed out earlier, Camargo had studied citrus culture for two years at University of Florida and worked with Peter Rolfs in the 1920s to develop citrus exports. Camargo remained in contact with Rolfs in the early 1930s while directing the fruit research institute at Deodoro on the outskirts of Rio de Janeiro. He promoted fruit culture and research for São Paulo from 1936 to 1938. In February 1939, minister Souza Costa promoted him to director of the Instituto de Experimentação Agricola [Institute of Agricultural Experimentation], supervising the newly created Instituto Agrônomico do Norte [IAN]. Two years later Camargo became the IAN's director.[65]

In correspondence with a USDA researcher, Camargo explained that establishing a "Rubber Institute" had been debated and set aside in favor of a broader agenda. This "new cycle in the technical evolution of the Ministry of Agriculture" meant conducting research on a geographic instead of a product basis. The institute's mandate included nearly fifty percent of the nation's land mass and "the largest equatorial region in the entire world, all suitable for agricultural and pastoral development." The institute was to study plants, but also collaborate with and coordinate

[63] Entry for Oct. 8, 1940, in *Vargas, Diário. Vol. II, 1937–1942*, p. 343.

[64] *Correio Paulistano*, Oct. 12, 1940, p. 1.

[65] *O Jornal*, Feb. 16, 1939, p. 4.

"Agricultural Economics, Meteorology, Immigration and Colonization, Fish and Game, Agricultural Development, Ecology, Agricultural Education, etc." To fulfill its mission, Camargo offered a bold vision of an institute of five divisions, including a technology division charged with investigating not only natural rubber but also starch and cacao, "matters of great importance in the Amazon."[66]

The Search for a Viable Rubber Species. The exigencies of war soon created opportunities for testing the Amazon region's potential for both extractive products and agricultural development as well as the IAN's capabilities. The U.S. quest for natural rubber became a vehicle for establishing a presence of U.S. researchers within Brazil's agricultural institutions as well as a motive for creating a joint commission promoting agricultural development in the Amazon region, the Brazilian Northeast, and even in portions of South-Central Brazil. In May 1940, the United States appropriated US$500,000 to explore the possibilities of increasing natural rubber production in the Americas. Thirteen nations eventually cooperated in the venture, which adopted a research model practiced in U.S. agriculture: a regional focus with cooperation of interested governments and private firms. The USDA established an extensive research network anchored by centers in Costa Rica, Guatemala, and Haiti and incorporated into the survey already established activities at the Ford plantations in Brazil and the planned resources of the IAN. Encouragement for Brazilian participation had already been forthcoming from Walter Swingle, who informed Oswaldo Aranha in 1939 that "rubber can undoubtedly be grown now at a profit in two regions of Brazil, (1) the lower Amazon valley, and (2) the rain-forests of the coastal Eastern States from Pernambuco to Espirito Santo."[67]

On the same day Getúlio Vargas returned to Rio de Janeiro from travels in the Amazon valley, his Ministry of Agriculture agreed in principle to allow USDA's Bureau of Plant Industry to conduct surveys of "lacticiferous plants" and establish an experimental nursery at the IAN. Leading the negotiations was Dr. Barcelos Fagundes, the ministry's director of agricultural research, who had studied at Cornell prior to

[66] TS, Felisberto Camargo, "The Northern Institute of Agriculture," [translation], Sept 9, 1941, U.S. Department of State, Office of Interamerican Affairs, RG 229, General Records, Country Files Brazil, USNA, Box 82, pp. 1–5.

[67] Emphasis in original. Ltr., Walter T. Swingle to Oswaldo Aranha, Dec. 26, 1939, Walter Tennyson Swingle Collection, University of Miami, Box 27, Folder 2.

earning a doctorate at Rutgers. Also participating was the institute's future director, Felisberto Camargo, who was destined to become the primary interface with U.S. technicians at his institute. By the end of the month, the parties signed a formal agreement to cooperate on rubber research.[68]

The agreement between the agricultural ministries reflected conviction that a relationship based upon mutual research interests was a long-term commitment, especially since rubber plants reached full-scale production only after nine years of growth. Plant scientists from the USDA and the State Department planners accepted a long-term vision of their presence, apparently convinced that higher production of natural products by other counties in the Americas would raise living standards, greatly increase inter-American trade and strengthen U.S. national security. As Walter Swingle commented to the head of a New York philanthropic institute, sponsoring the study of Brazilian agriculturalists in the United States would "train men able to supervise the very necessary shift in Agriculture to export crops that can be marketed in the United States and thereby secure capital to purchase all kinds of machinery: automobiles, tractors, etc. from us."[69] In the view of a State Department economist, establishing the United States as the primary market for the region's products would also "remove, or greatly reduce, the economic dependence of Canada and Latin America on Europe."[70]

Such views gained support from Vice President Henry A. Wallace, a University of Iowa graduate and an accomplished agricultural economist who had served as secretary of agriculture between 1933 and 1940. In July 1941, Wallace became chair of the Economic Defense Board, a position that assumed broader responsibilities for coordinating wartime supplies of strategic materials when transformed, ten days after Japan's attack on Pearl Harbor, into the Bureau of Economic Warfare (BEW). Wallace used his influence as board president to advance his conviction

[68] TS, "Proposed Agreement between the United States Department of Agriculture and the Brazilian Ministry of Agriculture....," Dec. 15, 1947, USDA, FAS, RG 166, Narrative Reports 1946–1949, Box 518, p. 5; Dean, *Brazil and the Struggle for Rubber*, p. 88.

[69] Ltr., Walter T. Swingle to H. A. Moe, Nov. 9, 1939, Walter Tennyson Swingle Collection, Univ. of Miami, Box 27, Folder 2.

[70] Francis A. Linville, "An Agricultural Policy for Hemisphere Defense," *Journal of Farm Economics,* Vol. 23, No. 4 (Nov. 1941), 726. See Also Dean, *Brazil and the Struggle for Rubber*, p. 88.

that superior U.S. agricultural technology could be applied to the needs of a postwar world. He personally supported creation of a hemispheric-wide "American Institute of Tropical Agriculture," convinced, as he later reflected, that "food and our technology skills properly used can help the crowded hungry lands into a position to help themselves."[71]

Also endorsing a longer-term vision of closer relationships between the United States and Latin America were members of the U.S. agricultural education community, eager to encourage a broader adoption of scientific principles of agriculture and, incidentally, increase enrollment in their agricultural education programs. E. J. Kyle, Dean of the College of Agriculture at Texas A&M University, traveled to nine Latin American countries in mid-1941 on a 14-week trip sponsored by the State Department's Office of Inter-American Affairs, Anderson Clayton, and Standard Oil. Intent on "helping them improve their agricultural schools," Kyle visited agricultural colleges and research stations in Manaus, Belém, Recife, Bahia, Rio de Janeiro, Campinas, Piraçicaba, and Porto Alegre.[72] Kyle returned to report that "when we win the war, as we most assuredly will do, we must be prepared to use the full extent of our wealth and influence in aiding them [people of "temperate" and "tropical" America] in the further development of their natural resources and in so placing their surplus products on the markets of the world that there will be no disastrous competition between us."[73]

[71] Ltr., Walter T. Swingle to Arthur F. Fischer, Aug. 7, 1940, Walter Tennyson Swingle Collection, University of Miami, Box 27, Folder 5; Henry A. Wallace, "The Department as I have Known it," Address at the U.S. Department of Agriculture, Oct. 18, 1961, cited Harold Carl Knoblauch, E. M. Law, Werner P. Meyer, *State Agricultural Experiment Stations: A History of Research Policy and Procedure* (Washington, DC: U.S. Department of Agriculture, 1962), p. 211. See also Donald G. Stevens, "Organizing For Economic Defense: Henry Wallace and the Board of Economic Warfare's Foreign Policy Initiatives, 1942," *Presidential Studies Quarterly*, Vol. 26, No. 4, (Fall, 1996), 1126–139; Mordecai Ezekiel, "Henry A. Wallace, Agricultural Economist," *Journal of Farm Economics*, Vol. 48, No. 4, Part 1 (Nov. 1966), 789–802; Seth Garfield, *In Search of the Amazon: Brazil, the United States, and the Nature of a Region* (Durham, NC: Duke University Press, 2013), p. 66.

[72] Ltr., E. J. Kyle to W. L. Clayton, Mar. 5, 1941; TS, E.J. Kyle, "A Tour of Central and South America, July 28 –Nov. 6, 1941," USNA, RG 229, U.S. Department of State, Office of Inter-American Affairs, General Records, Box 76.

[73] TS, Kyle, "A Tour of Central and South America."

Among those meeting with Kyle was Felisberto Camargo, who also promoted an enduring vision of ties between the U.S. and Brazilian agricultural communities through his position at the IAN. In communications with U.S. counterparts, Camargo borrowed from concepts elaborated nearly a century earlier by Matthew Maury in promoting U.S. commitment to developing the Amazon as the "natural economic element of the Mississippi." While acknowledging the immediate need to raise rubber production, he considered long-term interaction as most important. In a November 29, 1941, letter to a senior U.S. official, he stressed economic opportunities offered to U.S. interests by the Amazon, including "fibers for coarse textiles... meat of every sort to be obtained from the transformation of the forests of the low Amazon into ever green pastures... aluminum in the form of an island... vegetable oils, fish, [and] entomologic plants.... everything that can represent the wealth of an immense Empire... which today clamors disparately for American action." He argued that "It is urgent to open up Amazonia and to prepare ourselves to receive the groups of men, who, when the war is over, will not meet a better region than the Amazon to flee from the hunger and misery which will pervade Europe." American collaboration, he wrote, could consist of an "Economics Division" encompassing a "broader field of study and practice." He suggested that the United States agree to stationing a geneticist, two ichthyologists [fish scientists], two economists, a sanitation specialist, a zootechnical geneticist, and a nutrition expert.[74]

As amply established by Warren Dean and others,[75] Camargo's institute initially received robust cooperation from both the USDA and commercial companies searching for a reliable source of natural rubber. Cooperation benefited from the June 1940 appropriation of US$500,000 that bankrolled a robust trans-national network of trials and experimentation. Researchers exchanged seeds and seedlings to evaluate the productivity and disease resistance of *Hevea brasiliensis* and other natural rubber species in varied climates and environments. U.S. and Brazilian

[74] Ltr., Felisberto Camargo to Berente Friele [translation], Nov. 29, 1941, RG 229, U.S. Department of State, Office of Inter-American Affairs, General Records, Box 76, USNA.

[75] Harry J. Fuller, "War-Time Rubber Exploitation in Tropical America," *Economic Botany*, Vol. 5, No. 4 (Oct.–Dec. 1951), pp. 311–37; Dean, *Brazil and the Struggle for Rubber*; USDA, *Progress Report on the Cooperative Hevea Rubber Development Program in Latin America. Circular No. 976* (Washington, D.C.: GPO, 1955).

researchers embarked upon a comprehensive survey of rubber varieties in the Amazon valley.

The U.S. government's decision to finance the search for additional supplies of rubber in the Amazon valley breathed new life into Vargas's push to increase the federal government's presence in the region, an initiative that had yielded few results since the president's speeches of October 1940. The U.S. interest in the Amazon rose further with the Japanese invasion of rubber producing regions of Southeast Asia, the source of 97% of U.S. rubber imports in 1941, causing a "rubber famine" in the United States.[76] The United States focused its search for rubber on existing stands of rubber trees in the Americas, but especially in Brazil, with an estimated 200 million wild rubber trees sprinkled throughout the Amazon basin. The U.S. Rubber Development Commission estimated in 1941 that 100,000 tons of rubber might be harvested by inserting thousands of new laborers into the vast Amazon basin.[77] However, harvesting an additional 100,000 tons of natural rubber would require another 100,000 *seringueiro* rubber tappers, imposing a crushing burden on the already fragile Amazon social infrastructure.[78]

The agreements to support research on rubber at Brazil's Instituto Agronômico do Norte foreshadowed a far more substantial mutual commitment regarding agricultural cooperation to arise from the flow of wartime events. With the rise of Nazi aggression in Europe, the notion that the United States should contribute to Latin America's economic growth through financial assistance and economic programs gathered strength. On June 15, 1940, President Roosevelt asked for guidance from his secretaries of State, Commerce, and Treasury as to the "action this government should take" regarding the economic relations with Latin America. The result was a memorandum on "Hemispheric Economic Policy" urging emergency measures to absorb surplus agricultural and mineral outputs, promote free trade, and increase investments. The memorandum argued that protection of U.S. international interests

[76] Paul Wendt, "The Control of Rubber in World War II," *The Southern Economic Journal*, Vol. XIII, No. 3l (Jan. 1947), 203.

[77] Dean, *Brazil and the Battle for Rubber*, p. 93.

[78] Dean, *Brazil and the Battle for Rubber*, p. 93.

required a system of economic cooperation and interdependence among the nations of the Americas.[79]

The memorandum's author was the politically connected 32-year-old son of petroleum mogul John D. Rockefeller. Nelson A. Rockefeller had become a vocal advocate of closer ties with Latin America after visits to a Venezuelan subsidiary of the family's Standard Oil Company and travels in Brazil, Argentina, Chile, and Peru in 1937. For his Brazil travels, Rockefeller benefited from advice of William Clayton, who opened Anderson Clayton's cotton plantations and processing plants in São Paulo to his well-healed visitor. Rockefeller also visited coffee plantations and left impressed with the potential of Brazil's agriculture. The experience left him enthralled with Latin America and Latin Americans but dismayed by his own firm's treatment of its Venezuelan workers and concerned about its potential nationalization. Over the next two years, he implemented improvements in the workers' social conditions and required its executives to learn Spanish. Simultaneously, he gained a better appreciation of U.S.-Latin American relations, especially of the threat posed to U.S. interests by Nazi influence in the region.[80]

Rockefeller soon gained the political power necessary to push for a closer economic relationship between the United States and Latin America. A consensus among Roosevelt's advisors to implement the recommendations contained in Rockefeller's memo led to creation of the office of the Coordinator of Inter-American Affairs (CIAA) and appointment of Nelson as the Coordinator on July 3, 1941. Reporting directly to the President, Rockefeller's office wielded broad authority to conduct an aggressive program of pro-Allied propaganda. It also was to support public health and food development in the Americas through 18 corporations that Rockefeller established with support of U.S. and local governments. Rockefeller recruited a plethora of business executives

[79] Charles A. Gauld, *History of the Coordinator of Inter-American affairs: Historical Reports on War Administration* (Washington, GPO, 1947), pp. 4, 5.

[80] Antonio Pedro Tota, *O Amigo Americano: Nelson Rockefeller e o Brasil* (São Paulo: Companhia de Letras, 2014), pp. 77–78; Cary Reich, *The Life of Nelson A. Rockefeller: Worlds to Conquer 1908–1958* (New York: Doubleday, 1996), pp. 167–73; Elizabeth Ann Cobbs, *The Rich Neighbor Policy: Rockefeller and Kaiser in Brazil* (New Haven, CN: Yale Univ. Press, 1992), p. 33; Joseph E. Persico, *The Imperial Rockefeller: A Biography of Nelson A. Rockefeller* (New York: Simon and Schuster, 1982), p. 32.

to direct its various divisions in his drive to implement a "long range, continuing program of economic development and cooperation."[81]

As head of the CIAA, Rockefeller initially focused on purchasing strategic materials and commodities—"hides, wool, nitrates, manganese, tin, and numerous other commodities"[82]—previously adsorbed by European markets. He also promoted U.S. business investment and increased U.S. tourism. He told the Economic Club of Chicago on May 7, 1941, that the United States should "direct our efforts toward finding means to strengthen our neighbors in their resistance against forces that thrive on economic weakness."[83] Formation of the CIAA's Agricultural and Mineral Technical Advisory Service in October 1941 created a mechanism for increasing cooperation in agriculture, supported by 30 agricultural and technical assistants hired immediately after U.S. entry into the war.[84]

Simultaneously, Rockefeller gained insight into the Vargas government's interest in broad-based development of the Amazon valley through detailed reporting by the U.S. Embassy in Rio de Janeiro. Embassy memos recounted Vargas's mention of possible U.S. participation in the basin's development in speeches during his Amazon tour of October 1940 and of deliberations in June 1941 within Conselho Federal do Comercio on advancing the federal government's presence in the Amazon.[85] In August 1941 staffers within the CIAA revived a 1926 U.S. Department of Agriculture study on possibilities of agricultural development in the basin, and in September Rockefeller obtained support of Vice President Wallace to explore cooperation with the Brazilian government in the "opening up and development of the Amazon Basin."[86]

[81] Gauld, *History of the Coordinator of Inter-American Affairs*, p. 282; Cobbs, *The Rich Neighbor Policy*, p. 41.

[82] Gauld, *History of the Coordinator of Inter-American Affairs*, p. 12.

[83] TS, "Address of Nelson A. Rockefeller before the Economic Club of Chicago," May 7, 1941, USNA, RG 229, Office of Inter-American Affairs, Coordination Committee for Brazil, Box 1259.

[84] Gauld, *History of the Coordinator of Inter-American affairs*, p. 18.

[85] See attachments to TS, "Proposed Amazon Basin Survey," RG 229, Office of Inter-American Affairs, Basic Economy, Box 76.

[86] TS, Miss Harmon to Mr. Emerson, Aug. 14, 1941, USNA, RG 229, Office of Inter-American Affairs, Basic Economy, Box 76.

TS, Nelson Rockefeller to Berent Friele, Sept. 24, 1941, USNA, RG 229, Office of Inter-American Affairs, Basic Economy, Box 76.

In late 1941 the CIAA began drafting a proposal for a joint survey of the economic potential of the Amazon valley to serve as a precursor to a joint development project with the endorsement of U.S. Ambassador to Brazil Jefferson Caffrey, The CIAA's director in Brazil, Berent Friele, president of a Brazilian coffee brokerage firm, reported on October 29, 1941, that "officials of the Ministry of Agriculture are extremely well disposed toward the possibilities of the cooperation of the United States in the development of the Amazon Valley...."[87] The project envisioned participation of U.S. technicians with experience in agriculture, tropical diseases, agricultural settlements, transportation, nutrition, agricultural economics, and labor with a proposed initial annual budget of US$200,000. Undersecretary of State Sumner Welles presented the proposal to President Vargas on January 28, 1942, affirming that he had been "deeply impressed by the tremendous possibilities which the development of your great Amazon Basin appears to offer...." The project would supplement, according to Welles, the just concluded agreement on "a plan of assistance for rubber development...."[88] Reaching an agreement on that issue and a host of other economic measures, including cooperation related to agriculture, would hinge upon reaction by the United States and Brazil to the confluence of events in early 1942.

[87] TS, Berent Friele and Frank Nattier, "Amazon Development Project," Oct. 29, 1941, in USNA, RG 229, Office of Inter-American Affairs, Central Files, Box 76.

[88] TS, Creswell F. Micou, "Project Authorization," Feb 12, 1942, USNA, RG 229, Office of Inter-American Affairs, Basic Economy, Box 76; TS, Sumner Welles, "My dear Mr. President," Jan. 28, 1942, USNA, RG 229, Office of Inter-American Affairs, Basic Economy, Box 76.

CHAPTER 15

Wartime Agricultural Cooperation, 1942–1945

The October 1940 agreement between the United States and Brazil supporting rubber research at Brazil's Instituto Agronômico do Norte foreshadowed a far more substantial mutual commitment driven by wartime events. Of overwhelming consequence for Brazilian agriculture was the implementation of a joint agricultural development program, stemming from the U.S. political leadership's conviction that closer economic ties with Latin America, and especially with Brazil, were essential to preventing an Axis beachhead in the Americas. Increased agricultural cooperation was but one of the economic incentives offered to Brazil to abandon its calculated stance of neutrality and side with Washington against Germany and its allies.

The pace of cooperation between U.S. and Brazilian governments accelerated during the first three months of 1942 in step with events in Europe and Asia. Most consequential was a U.S. commitment to aid Brazil's economic development. Along with interaction in the military and economic spheres, agricultural cooperation increased incrementally,

An earlier version of this chapter was published in Diálogos Latinoamericanos, Vol. 30 (2021): "The Great Agro-Acceleration in the making: transnational and global histories of agricultural modernization in Brazil (since 1940)." Reprinted with permission.

E. R. Downes, *Brazilian Agricultural Development, 1890–1950*,
https://doi.org/10.1007/978-3-031-76992-4_15

driven by complementary objectives. The United States needed vital raw materials and political support from the hemisphere's most influential nation. Brazil, meanwhile, welcomed additional resources supporting extension of central government's power into the hinterland, overcoming the impact of rising prices for foodstuffs and offsetting devastation wrought by the return of the drought to the Northeast, the very region most imperiled, in the minds of U.S defense planners, by the conquests of Axis powers.

The Joint Food Commission

The U.S. entry in the war presented Nelson Rockefeller with a new scenario for implementing his vision for broad U.S.-Brazil economic cooperation. In the days following Pearl Harbor, he pressed his vision of solidifying Brazil's support for U.S. wartime goals by complementing Vargas's development plans for the Amazon despite temporary setbacks. The first occurred in January 1942 at the Rio de Janeiro foreign ministers meeting, followed in March by the results of discussions between Vargas's finance minister, Artur de Souza Costa, and Undersecretary Welles in Washington. At the January meeting, Welles agreed to a "cooperative program for the development of strategic and basic materials" financed by a US$100 million credit from Washington.[1] Six weeks later, Welles acceded to Brazilian concerns that Rockefeller's proposed development commission would intrude upon Brazilian sovereignty in the Amazon. Instead, as part of a comprehensive set of agreements that became known as the "Washington Accords," the United States committed to providing US$100 million to support increased production of "strategic materials and other basic materials." A subsequent agreement allocated US$ five million to stimulate increased rubber production.[2]

[1] TS, "Memorandum by Mr. Emilio G. Collado to the Under Secretary of State (Welles)," *Foreign Relations of the United States: Diplomatic Papers, 1942, The American Republics*, Vol. V, p. 45

[2] The Washingtonaccords consummated years of negotiations between Braziland Washingtonstrongly influenced by U.S.fears of Nazi penetration of the South Atlantic and Brazil's difficulties in sustaining ties with Germany. From mid-1940 onward Brazilagreed to allow the United Statesto construct airfields in Brazilian northeast to support ferry, supply and patrol missions, and utilize Brazilian ports to support anti-submarine patrols. In return, the United Statesresponded positively to the Brazilian military's request for armaments and furnished economic support designed to reinforce Brazil's status as

Despite promises of higher funding levels to support increased production of rubber from already standing trees, this prospect faced challenges as formidable as those confronting researchers at the Instituto Agronômico do Norte (IAN). This entity had been created in 1939 to promote production of rubber as well as other tropical crops to preclude other tropical regions, including India, Africa, and even other South American countries from displacing Brazil as a primary producer. New rubber tappers were essential for an increase in production, but these could hardly be expected to arrive via the Vargas government's promotion of migration into the valley. Between October 1940 and July 1942 only 435 migrants reached the Amazon.[3] Moreover, providing incentives for migrants to leave other parts of Brazil—primarily the drought-parched Northeast—and become productive laborers in the Amazon—required subsidies, transportation, and major improvements in health, sanitation, and the supply of food.

The needs of additional workers engaged in higher rubber production gave Rockefeller an inroad for implementing aspects of his original development proposal. As part of the Washington Accords, the CIAA received US$ five million to improve health and sanitary conditions in the valley and train Brazilian health and sanitation experts.[4] Seizing the initiative, Rockefeller ordered a comprehensive survey of the valley in April and May 1942 by confidant Caldwell King. The study revealed the supply

an ally. See Frank McCann, *The Brazilian-American Alliance 1937–1945* (Princeton, NJ: Princeton University Press, 1973); Gerson Moura, *Relações Exteriores Do Brasil 1939–1950: Mudanças na natureza das relações Brasil-Estados Unidos durante e após a Segunda Guerra Mundial* (Brasilia: Fundação Alexandre de Gusmão, 2012); Stanley E. Hilton, "Brazilian Diplomacy and the Washington-Rio de Janeiro 'Axis' during the World War II Era," *The Hispanic American Historical Review*, Vol. 59, No. 2 (May 1979); Dennison de Oliveira, *Aliança Brasil-EUA: Nova História do Brasil na Segunda Guerra Mundial* (Curitiba, PA: Juruá Editora, 2015); and Stetson Conn and Byron Fairchild, *The United States Army in World War II; The Western Hemisphere; The Framework of Hemispheric Defense* (Washington, DC: Center of Military History United States Army, 1989), pp. 265–330. For a nuanced view of the impact of the de facto alliance on Brazil's national character, see Antonio Pedro Tota, *The Seduction of Brazil: The Americanization of Brazilduring World War II*. Trans. Lorena B. Ellis (Austin, TX: Teresa Lozano Long Institute of Latin American Studies, 2009).

[3] Seth Garfield, "The Environment of Wartime Migration: Labor Transfers from The Brazilian Northeast To The Amazon During World War II," *Journal of Social History*, Vol. 43, No. 4 (Summer 2010), 1003.

[4] Wilkinson, "Tapping the Amazon for Victory, pp. 112–114.

of labor to be the most pressing issue, accompanied by logistical issues created by necessary increases in the labor supply and gathering and transporting higher amounts of latex. King reported that "if we are to get all the rubber that can be gotten with sufficient manpower, a half million people must be moved into the valley in the next 12 months, fed, clothed, sheltered, supplied with materials for work." He concluded that "a public health program alone is not the full answer as these people must have food as well."[5]

Supplying food for an expanded work force faced formidable obstacles. King reported that there was "a growing shortage, caused by less planting, increased production and high prices."[6] Steps to accelerate the arrival of new rubber workers threatened to exacerbate the situation. Almost immediately after the signing of the agreement to support rubber production, the Vargas government began encouraging migrants into the Amazon from drought-stricken Ceará. Per a December 1942 agreement with the Rubber Development Corporation (RDC), the Brazilian government promised to support the transfer of 50,000 laborers into the Amazon by May 1943. The RDC was to provide a US$100 per man subsidy for the transfer of laborers and provide foodstuffs at discounted prices.[7] On April 9, 1942, Vargas announced that rural workers migrating to the Amazon would "be able to count on technical, economic and financial assistance."[8]

Supporting new workers in the region, however, also depended heavily upon the viability of Brazil's coastal shipping trade, a doubtful proposition. A member of Vargas's inner circle reasoned that any interruption in transport would reduce food supplies from southern Brazil and raise the cost of living in major cities in the Center-South and North.[9] Such was the situation by early 1942, when shortages of fuel for shipping and

[5] TS, John C. McClintock to Mr. Nelson A. Rockefeller, May 21, 1942, USNA, RG 229, Office of Inter-American Affairs, Basic Economy, Box 76.

[6] TS, I. CaldwellKing to Mr. Nelson Rockefeller, June 17, 1942, in USNA, RG 229, Office of Inter-American Affairs, Basic Economy, Box 76, p. 2.

[7] Garfield, *In Search of the Amazon*, p. 74.

[8] TS, "Memorandum Co. No. 865," Apr. 13, 1942, in USNA, RG 229, Office of Inter-American Affairs, Basic Economy, Box 76.

[9] TS, "Relatório sobre atos e resoluções governmentais que visaram garantir a estabilidade socio-econômica do Brasil durante o período de Guerra," GV Confid 1942.00.00/3, p. 23. GVA, CPDOC.

rail transport reduced the transport of food to the Northeast, which, according to the U.S. Embassy, depended upon coastal shipping for at least 50% of its staples. Drought conditions depleted supplies in Natal, and purchases by U.S. Navy ships created shortages of vegetables in Pernambuco.[10]

The increasing presence of Brazilian and U.S. military personnel in Northeast also raised pressure for a coordinated food production effort beyond the Amazon valley. The War Department judged that protecting air bases in Northeastern Brazil, constructed surreptitiously in the prewar era, to rank in priority just below protecting the continental United States, Hawaii, and the Panama Canal Zone. In its view, the "occupation of Natal by American forces in considerable strength" was essential to maintaining communication in the South Atlantic and providing a launch point for airplanes enroute to Africa, the Middle East and the Far East.[11]

In March 1942, Vargas approved the stationing of an additional 800 U.S. military forces in the region, and by July over 18,000 Brazilian military personnel were dispersed throughout the Northeast. The sinking of five Brazilian merchant ships by German submarines between August 14 and 17, 1942, followed by Brazil's declaration of war on Germany and Italy on August 22, intensified apprehensions about the ability of coastal shipping to supply the Northeast's food needs.[12] Unrestricted submarine warfare against Brazil's shipping, in the CIAA's opinion, could lead to "drastic food supply shortages in areas of strategic importance to this government."[13] By June 1942, food shortages in the rubber-gathering

[10] Telegram, Ambassador Caffery to the Secretary of State, May 13, 1942, USNA, RG 229, Office of Inter-American Affairs, Basic Economy, Box 82.

[11] Diary of Henry Stimson, entry for Dec. 17, 1941, cited in Stetson Conn and Bryon Fairchild. *The United States Army in World War II. Western Hemisphere. The Framework of Hemispheric Defense* (Washington D.C.: Center of Military History, United States Army, 1989), p. 307.

[12] Conn and Fairchild, *The United States Army in World War II; The Western Hemisphere; The Framework of Hemispheric Defense,* pp. 317, 321. By 1943, the total contingent of U.S. military forces in Manaus, Belem, and various cities in the Northeast, Brazil reached 15,000. Frank D. McCann, "Brazil and World War II: The Forgotten Ally. What did you do in the war, Zé Carioca?" *Estudios Interdisciplinarios de América Latina y el Caribe*, [Tel Aviv], Vol. 6, No. 2; http://eial.tau.ac.il/index.php/eial/issue/view/82.

[13] TS, George Doherty to Alfred E. Hurt, Sept. 4, 1942, USNA, RG 229, Office of Inter-American Affairs, Basic Economy, Box 82.

region prompted the governor of Amazonas to encourage rubber gatherers to plant subsistence crops. The average price of key food goods (sugar, rice, beans, manioc flour, and fresh beef) in Brazil's 22 capital cities rose by 50% between 1941 and 1942, a trend that would continue to war's end.[14] (See Fig. 15.1).

The CIAA's evaluation of the situation led it to propose an activist role for the agency with a solution drawing from the U.S. agricultural experience. Despite the State Department's argument that "food production in the rubber producing areas be increased but feels that this is a

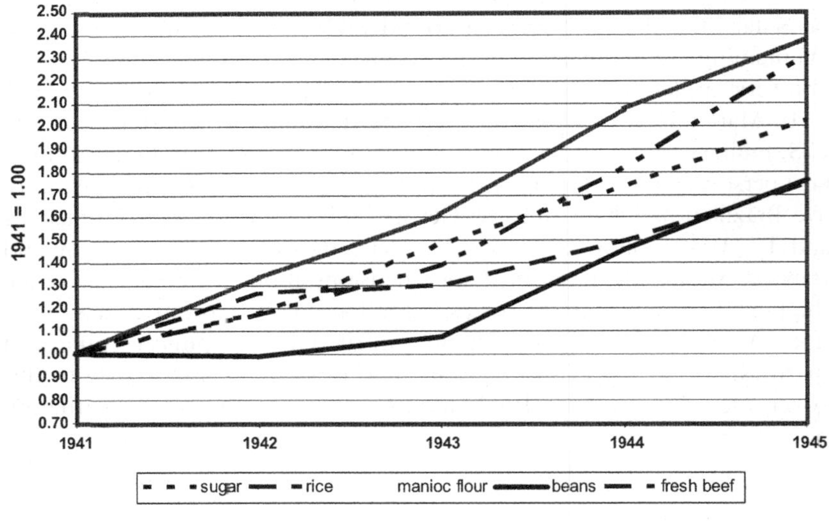

Fig. 15.1 Indexed prices for key food goods in Brazil's 22 capital cities (1941–1945) (*Source* Calculated from Instituto Brasileiro de Geografia e Estatística. Conselho Nacional de Estatística. *Anuário Estatístico do Brasil Ano VII 1946* (Rio de Janeiro: Serviço Gráfico do IBGE, 1947), pp. 357–60)

[14] TS, Memo, Caldwell King to Mr. Nelson Rockefeller, June 17, 1942, USNA, RG 229, Office of Inter-American Affairs, Coordination Committee for Brazil, Box 1272; Fiona Gordon-Ashworth, "Agricultural Commodity Control under Vargas in Brazil, 1930–1945, *Journal of Latin American Studies*, Vol. 12, No. 1 (May 1980), 96–97; Instituto Brasileiro de Geografia e Estatística. Conselho Nacional de Estatística. *Anuário Estatístico do Brasil Ano VII 1946* (Rio de Janeiro: Serviço Gráfico do IBGE, 1947), pp. 357–60.

Brazilian responsibility and should be affected primarily by Brazilian initiative through Brazilian agencies...," Rockefeller's CIAA advocated a more aggressive U.S. role. It gained support when the Board of Economic Warfare charged the CIAA with responsibility for food supply issues in the Americas and recognized that "the production of subsistence food crops in the Amazon Basin was of extreme importance."[15] In July 1942 the CIAA urged setting up "field centers for the production and distribution of supplies... for the purpose of encouraging the growth of subsistence foods in the Amazon valley."[16] The CIAA then dispatched executive director John McClintock and James D. LeCron, director of its food supply division, to Brazil to consult with Ambassador Caffery and Brazilian government officials about "the means whereby we may assist in overcoming some of their more critical and immediate food supply problems."[17]

Planners predictably considered U.S. practices applicable to Brazilian agricultural development needs. The Brazil Division recognized in May 1942 that "Agriculture in Brazil offers an equally important field for cooperation between the two countries and for extending a knowledge and appreciation of United States methods." Director LeCron reasoned that "In some ways our own experience may provide us with a background for attacking the problems of food production and distribution along the Amazon." In his view, the combination of local and federal support, especially in the U.S. South, could serve as a model for Brazil. This arrangement had shown the utility of "promoting home production and preservation of highly nutritive foods and the supplementation of local production with foods shipped in by the Surplus Commodities Corporation."[18]

[15] TS, Alfred M. Hurt to George Doherty, "Food Production, Supply, Storage and Distribution Problems in Brazil," Sept. 4, 1942, USNA, RG 229, Office of Inter-American Affairs, Basic Economy, Box 82.

[16] Attachment to TS, J.C. McClintock to Board of Directors, Institute for Inter-American Affairs, July 22, 1942, in USNA, RG 229, Office of Inter-American Affairs, Basic Economy, Box 82; TS, Secretary Hull to Nelson Rockefeller, July 27, 1942, USNA, RG 229, Office of Inter-American Affairs, Basic Economy, Box 82.

[17] TS, Alfred M. Hurt to George Doherty, "Food Production, Supply, Storage and Distribution Problems in Brazil," Sept. 4, 1942, USNA, RG 229, Office of Inter-American Affairs, Basic Economy, Box 82.

[18] Memorandum, J.D. LeCron to John G. McClintock, Aug. 11, 1942, USNA, RG 229, Office of Inter-American Affairs, Basic Economy, Box 82.

After preliminary discussions, on September 3, 1942, President Vargas approved creation of the Comissão Brasileiro-Americana de Produção de Géneros Alimentícios, the Brazilian-American Food Production Commission.[19] The agreement called for "stimulation of production of foodstuffs in Brazil, especially in the Amazon area, and north and northeastern Brazil, including Bahia, where war and transport difficulties have created deficiencies in foodstuffs." It called for technical assistance for producing foodstuffs, the provisioning of equipment, insecticides, support for establishing an effective extension service, assistance in developing plans for irrigation, technical and financial assistance for agricultural colonization, and assistance in bettering the nutrition of populations covered by the agreement.[20] It committed Brazil to expend the equivalent of US$1.4 million during the program's first two years and for the United States to provide food production specialists and contribute US$2 million through September 1943.[21] The agreement also required payment by the United States of US$500,000 to an account at the Bank of Brazil under control of the Ministry of Agriculture.[22]

Implementation of the Agreement

Rockefeller's staffers quickly used the agreement's mandate to adopt parameters like those proposed for the defunct Amazon development corporation. For the CIAA, there was no question that the "food problem" in the Amazon as "enormous," given that production of food for the estimated million and a half residents of the valley was limited by allocation of only 100,000 acres of valley's land for food production. Staffers

[19] United States Department of State, *United States Statues at Large, Containing the Laws and Concurrent Resolutions Enacted during the Second Session of the Seventy-Six Congress of the United States of America, 1942, Vol. 56, Part II* (Washington, D.C.: GPO, 1943), pp. 1876–882.

[20] Mr. Nelson Rockefeller's Visit to Brazil," *Brazilian Business*, Vol. XXII, No. 9 (Sept. 1942), 22–25; "Foodstuffs Production," 56 Stat. 1875. Charles L. Bevans, ed., *Treaties and Other International Agreements of the United States of America 1776–1949*, Vol. V (Washington, DC: U.S. Department of State, 1970), pp. 932–35.

[21] 832.5018/7: Telegram, Ambassador Caffery to the Secretary of State, Aug 31, 1942, *Foreign Relations of The United States: Diplomatic Papers, 1942, The American Republics, Volume V*, pp. 688, 689.

[22] Ltr., John C. McClintock to John E. Lockwood, Sept 4, 1942, USNA, RG 229, U.S. Department of State, Office of Inter-American Affairs, General Records, Box 76.

estimated the need to overcome a deficient of 350,000 tons of food per year for the Amazon region alone.[23] Nevertheless, the office immediately sought to widen the project's scope through discussions on "an over-all project for collaboration with the Brazilian Government to meet food shortages and develop subsistence agriculture in other parts of Brazil."[24]

Rockefeller's concern for raising food production for the rubber-gathering effort coincided with the Vargas government's efforts to improve the standard of living, not only in Amazonia but also the Northeast. Since the 1930s Vargas had directing relief efforts to demonstrate his responsiveness to the Northeast's needs. The approach typified Vargas's crisis-driven support for the Northeast that focused on infrastructure projects (dams, roads, and railroads) without addressing historic inequities in land holding.[25] His new agricultural minister, appointed in February 1942, was a native Northeasterner with strong regional ties. Professional agronomist Apolônio Sales (1904–1982) had graduated from Bahia's Escola Superior de Agricultura de São Bento in 1924 and served as secretary of agriculture of Pernambuco from 1937 to 1942. He was acutely aware of the challenges created for the Northeast by wartime conditions and familiar as well with U.S. agricultural practices. An expert in sugar cane and irrigation, Sales had traveled several times to the continental United States and Hawaii. The U.S. Embassy considered him "pro-American" with status in Brazilian circles as "a competent scientist and able executive." He proved eager to cooperate, departing shortly after the agreement's signing with key members of the CIAA staff for an extended survey of the Northeast's food needs.[26]

[23] TS, Alfred M. Hurt to George Doherty, "Food Production, Supply, Storage and Distribution Problems in Brazil," Sept. 4, 1942, USNA, RG 229, Office of Inter-American Affairs, Basic Economy, Box 82.

[24] TS, Alfred M. Hurt to George Doherty, "Food Production, Supply, Storage and Distribution Problems in Brazil," Sept. 4, 1942, USNA, RG 229, Office of Inter-American Affairs, Basic Economy, Box 82.

[25] Eve E. Buckley, *Technocrats and the Politics of Drought and Development in Twentieth Century Brazil* (Chapel Hill, NC: University of North Carolina Press, 2017), pp. 125–77. Buckley points out that the engineers overseeing the various entities established to counter the impact of the drought attempted to encourage support for small holders, but such efforts foundered because they ran counter to the interests of politically influential large land holders.

[26] *Jornal do Brasil*, Feb. 20, 1942, p. 6; TS, John F. Simmons to Secretary of State, "Appointment of Dr. Antonio Sales as Minister of Agriculture," Feb. 20, 1942, USNA,

Sales adroitly leveraged the resources of the food commission to provide an important subsidy to Vargas's ongoing *plano de emergência*, implemented in early 1942 to combat the scourges of the Northeast's latest devastating droughts. The 1941–1942 drought in Ceará wreaked havoc on thousands of sharecroppers and small holders who lost their crops and animals. With little hope for a harvest, small cotton producers were unable to acquire advances for food, forcing them to abandon their houses, lands, and plantings. Destitute farmers migrated to cities and small towns, often resorting to begging to survive.[27] Tenant farmers who remained on irrigated lands surrendered half their harvest to the lands' owners and worked three days per week for starvation wages, all the while residing in wattle and daub houses with gasoline cans as typically their only furniture.[28]

Minister Sales placed special emphasis on aiding the Northeast. Soon after assuming office, Sales named a trusted aid from the Northeast to serve as head of the Division of Development of Vegetal Production [Divisão de Fomento da Produção Vegetal]. Agronomist and Paraíba native Oscar Espinola Guedes had been integral to efforts to increase food

RG 166, Foreign Agricultural Service Narrative Reports, Brazil (1942–1945), Box 50; TS, "Travel of Agricultural Attaché Erwin P. Keeler, in Northern Brazil," July 9, 1941. USNA, RG 166, Foreign Agricultural Service, Narrative Reports, (1920–1941), Box 16; Ltr., John C. McClintock to John E. Lockwood, Sept 4, 1942, USNA, RG 229, U.S. Department of State, Office of Inter-American Affairs, General Records, Box 76; Coordinator of Inter-American Affairs, *Weekly Report on Activities,* Oct. 10, 1942. p. 1. Sales communicated freely with CIAA's officers. In December 1942, he forwarded a copy of a poem he had written while flying up the Amazon to the director of the CIAA food program. See Ltr., John D. LeCron to Apolônio Sales, Dec. 9, 1942, USNA, RG 229, Office of Inter-American Affairs, Basic Economy, Box 82. Sales remained in contact with the U.S.agriculture after leaving the ministry in 1945. While serving as a senator for his native Pernambuco state in 1949, Sales requested State Department assistance in acquiring copious data on sugar cane experiments in Hawaii. See Telegram, U.S. Embassy, Rio de Janeiro, "Request for Sugar Cane Information," July 6, 1949, USNA, RG 166, Foreign Agricultural Service, Narrative Reports 1946–1949, Box 536; "Apolonio Sales," https://cpdoc.fgv.br/producao/dossies/AEraVargas2/biografias/Apolonio_Sales. Sales would become an important link between the United States and Brazil in 1955, briefly serving as the Brazilian coordinator for technical cooperation between the two countries.

[27] Garfield, *In Search of the Amazon*, p. 132; T. Lynn Smith, *Brazil, People and Institutions*, Rev. ed (Baton Rouge, LA: Louisiana State University Press, 1952, pp. 130–32.

[28] Buckley, *Technocrats and the Politics of Drought*, p. 159.

production as Sales's assistant in Pernambuco. Sales soon arranged for Vargas to approve a RS$2.5 million subsidy for "productive forces," principally in the Northeast, to stimulate increased production of vegetable and animal sources of food. The funds, destined for five Northeastern states, supported purchase of small tools (hoes, root pullers, and scythes), insecticides, small irrigation pumps, and machines for processing rice, corn and beans, and construction of grain storage facilities. Leading the effort to coordinate the federal government's response with the state directors of development [*fomento*] and serving as primary interface with U.S. members of the commission was Oscar Guedes.[29]

Working relations between Brazilian and the U.S. members of the commission—termed within U.S. correspondence as the "CBA"—ranged from friction to admiration. In the commission's early days, U.S. members complained that commission President Guedes was "away from Rio a great deal of time and when he leaves, all authority to buy or make decisions goes with him."[30] A prominent U.S. member of the CBA, probably John B. Griffing, observed that "instead of the easy going, suave, polite individual we have come to expect," Guedes was "more blunt, brusque, and aggressive than North Americans." Guedes fired or transferred or fined subordinates did not get results "with ruthless vigor." He was "loyal to Brazilian ways with an intense nationalism, and somewhat reluctant to endorse innovations from the U.S. until they can be proven." Nevertheless, Guedes's division was "remarkably active and efficient as compared with other departments."[31]

At the regional level, U.S. members of the CBA encountered cooperative approaches from agriculturalists previously exposed to U.S. practices. Antônio Secundino São José de Araujo, an early graduate of the Viçosa agricultural school, had studied corn hybridization while obtaining a

[29] *Jornal do Brasil*, Feb. 20, 1942, p. 6; *A Manhã*, Mar. 14, 1942, p. 3; *Jornal do Brasil*, Apr. 5, 1942, p. 11; *A Manhã*, Apr. 22, 1942, p. 5.

[30] TS, Coordinator of Inter-American Affairs, Food and Nutrition, Brazilian Division, Monthly Report for March 1943," in USNA, RG 286, Records of the Agency for International Development and Predecessor Agencies, IIA Periodic Reports, 1942–1953, Box 2.

[31] TS, "Dr. Oscar Espinola Guedes," n.d., in USNA, RG 286, Records of the Agency for International Development and Predecessor Agencies, IIA Periodic Reports, 1942–1950, Box 4.

master's degree from the University of Iowa. Secundino served as a technical advisor to the commission. Otavio Gomes de Moraes Vasconcelos, educated in Georgia and California, directed the Federal Fruit Experimental Station in Itapirema, Pernambuco. A U.S. commission member reported that Otavio was "one of the best authorities on the climate, soils, and crop plants, particularly horticulture, of Northeast Brazil." He "enjoys contacts with North Americans and spares no pains in rendering such assistance as they may request." Equally helpful was Julio Silvério Gonçalves, Director of the Estação Experimental de Frio in Recife. A former student at the Colorado and New Mexico schools of mines, Gonçalves was "cordial to North Americans" with "a great admiration for ways of doing things in the United States." He noted that "there is no Brazilian more desirous of introducing new ideas from the United States."[32]

Beyond aggressive planning, little was achieved during the first few months of the commission's existence. By December, though, implementation of the agreement slowly gained momentum. The commission prioritized production of beans, rice, corn, tuberous plants, vegetables fruits, and peanuts while committing to free distribution of seeds, trees, tools, insecticides, and technical assistance to small farmers. CBA planners overlooked the possibility that the region's fish reserves could provide additional nutrition, since it considered the typical resident's diet to consist of "manioc flour, black beans and rice, with small quantities of jerked beef, dried fish, lard, sugar and coffee."[33]

Technicians from the United States experienced in livestock and poultry development began arriving in December 1942, followed by mid-1943 by engineers, and specialists in irrigation, general farming, nutrition, grass and forage crops, and training and extension as well as an entomologist. Especially valuable for the commission's work was John B. Griffing, a Kansan with extensive experience in Brazilian agriculture. Griffing had graduated from Kansas State College with a degree in agronomy in 1904

[32] http://www.personagens.ufv.br/?area=antonioSecundino; TS, "Dr. Otavio Gomes de Moraes Vasconcelos," "Dr. Julio Silvério Goncalves," "José Guimarães Duque," and "Dr. Heitor Tavares," all in USNA, RG 286, Records of the Agency for International Development and Predecessor Agencies, IIA Periodic Reports, 1942–1950, Box 4.

[33] TS, "Brazilian-American Food Production Committee Report No. 1," Jan. 1942, USNA, RG 286, Records of the Agency for International Development and Predecessor Agencies, IIA Periodic Reports, 1942–1953, Box 2.

and became an agricultural missionary, serving in Nanking, China, from 1919 to 1927. He succeeded Peter Rolfs as director of the Escola Superior da Agricultura e Veterinária in Viçosa, Minas Gerais from 1936 to 1939 when Rolfs' collaborator João Carlos Belo Lisboa fell out of favor with the state government.[34] Praised in the Vargas-friendly *A Manhã* newspaper as "a renowned technician to whom Brazilian agriculture owes much," Griffing became the CIAA's representative for its Division V, encompassing four key northeastern states. He also served as a personal link to Oscar Guedes. Griffing interacted with several of his former agricultural school's graduates who, by 1943, had attained important positions in various agricultural entities in the Northeast.[35]

Moving from planning to creating increased food supplies required overcoming a myriad of technical and market-based obstacles, beginning with the minister himself. Sales preferred supporting his native Northeast and initially was "not outstandingly sympathetic to the production of foodstuffs in the Amazon." In an April 14, 1943, meeting with U.S. administrators of the commission, Sales outlined steps his ministry had taken to support food production in the Amazon but noted that he would "leave the handling of the food production program in the Amazon largely in the hands of Mr. Kadow," the U.S. representative.[36]

The commission faced other challenges. The lack of U.S. personnel and their limited familiarity with Brazilian agriculture hindered program development.[37] The U.S. livestock specialist seeking to increase production and distribution of meat in the Amazon region found it a "very, very

[34] *Kansas Industrialist*, Sept 23, 1926, p. 2; Lucas Paulo de Freitas, "Entre o Evangelho e o Ensino: O Colégio Presbiteriano Buriti (1923–1965), (Diss.: Univ. Federal de Mato Grosso, 2013), p. 58; TS, Erwin F. Keeler, "Order of the Coordinator of Economic Mobilization...," Mar. 19, 1943, USNA, RG 166, Foreign Agricultural Service Narrative Reports, Brazil(1942–1945), Box. 90.

[35] *A Manhã*, Feb. 6, 1942, p. 7; Brazilian Ministry of Agriculture and Office of the Coordinator of Inter-American Affairs, "A Summary Report of the Activities of the Comissão Brasileiro-Americano de Produção de Gêneros Alimenticios," Sept. 3, 1942, to Dec. 21, 1944. "John Benjamin Griffing," http://www.personagens.ufv.br/?area=john.

[36] TS, U.S. Embassy Rio de Janeiro to Secretary of State, "Brazilian American Foodstuffs Production Agreement," Apr. 17, 1943, USNA, RG 166, Reports from Agricultural Attaches Relating to International Conferences and Congress, 1931–1958, Box 15.

[37] TS, K.J.Kadow, "C.B.A. Activities in the Amazon: Special Report," Aug. 18, 1943, in USNA, RG 286, Records of the Agency for International Development and Predecessor Agencies, IIA Periodic Reports, 1942–1953, Box 2.

difficult task." Perhaps unaware that all of Brazil's eleven *xarque* [dried beef] plants were located in distant southern states, he reported that preparation of *xarque* in the humid atmosphere of the Amazon was unfeasible and that no refrigeration was available.[38] The lack of transportation and widespread flooding in late 1942 and 1943 hindered delivery of supplies.[39] Hopes that the Instituto Agronômico do Norte in Belém would aid production of vegetables faltered when its workers abandoned the Institute for higher wages in the local municipality, thus ending "a wonderful opportunity to produce corn and rice for the Belém area."[40]

Commission members also encountered resistance from established interests. Increasing production at Santarem incurred opposition of local merchants "who control 80% of the commerce within a closely guarded ring, which drives out of the district by threats, slander, and taxes all growers who refuse to sell to them." As the merchants never paid cash, "crop values must be taken out in merchandise from their stores."[41] In Recife, efforts to increase production of vegetables conflicted with the local farmers' cooperative, "a first-rate monopoly." The cooperative limited production quotas to "keep prices where they want them," allowing no one to "produce or sell farm products in the state of Pernambuco unless it clears through the cooperative." As the monopoly buyer and seller of produce, the cooperative sold the farmers' goods for as much as a 1,200% markup. The issue was infused with political tensions, as Minister Sales had championed cooperatives as the state's secretary of agriculture. U.S. members of the commission stayed clear, reporting that the situation was "so full of dynamite that our boys are keeping their hands out of it 100%." Resolution came through creation of a committee

[38] Brazil. Ministério da Agricultura, *Boletim* Ano 30, No. 6 (June 1941), p. 69; TS, Kenneth J. Kadow to James D. LeCron, "Monthly Report," Mar. 16, 1943, USNA, RG 286, Records of the Agency for International Development and Predecessor Agencies, IIA Periodic Reports, 1942–1953, Box 2.

[39] TS, K. J. Kadow, "CBA Activities in the Amazon Special Report," Aug. 18, 1943, USNA, RG 286, Records of the Agency for International Development and Predecessor Agencies, IIA Periodic Reports, 1942–1953, Box 2.

[40] TS, Kenneth J. Kadow to James D. LeCron, "Weekly Report," Mar. 1, 1943, USNA, RG 286, Records of the Agency for International Development and Predecessor Agencies, IIA Periodic Reports, 1942–1953, Box 2.

[41] TS, Kenneth J. Kadow to James D. LeCron, "Monthly Report," Mar. 16, 1943, USNA, RG 286, Records of the Agency for International Development and Predecessor Agencies, IIA Periodic Reports, 1942–1953, Box 2.

of representatives of the state government, the local military region, the Ministry of Agriculture and the food commission, under guidance of the local military commander. This led to "perfect cooperation and the maximum increase in production."[42]

The commission did, however, advance its mandate by working through its primary contacts at the Ministry of Agriculture, the Divisão de Fomento Agricola [Agricultural Development Division] and by reaching out to educational and religious groups. In October 1942, the commission's ministry contacts purchased a large amount of hand tools in the São Paulo area for shipment to the Amazon region, and several thousand pounds of seeds and ten tons of dry milk were enroute from the United States. The ministry contracted with cooperatives to grow rice, beans, corn, and manioc in the North and Northeast, establish a farm for milk and vegetable production near Natal, and install several chicken farms.[43]

By May 1943, the commission reported that over 200,000 hectares of new land placed into cultivation through commission financing by farmers on small plots in Ceará and Pernambuco and in the Amazon region.[44] The commission also launched a Victory Garden program, mirroring a similar U.S. program, through the Legião Brasileria de Assistência, chaired by Vargas's wife Darci. Portions of the 1,300 pounds of seeds shipped to the commission in Belém were forwarded to the bishop of Guajara Mirim, Mato Grosso, for distribution to rubber workers. Other seed packets went to residents of Manaus, a school master on the Rio Negro, and a bishop on the upper Solimões tributary of the Amazon near the Bolivian border.[45] Ironically, the commission's efforts to promote

[42] *A Manhã*, Mar. 16, 1943, p. 4; TS, Kenneth J. Kadow to James D. LeCron, "Weekly Report," Mar. 1, 1943, USNA, RG 286, Records of the Agency for International Development and Predecessor Agencies, IIA Periodic Reports, 1942–1953, Box 2; TS, Kenneth J. Kadow to James D. LeCron, "Monthly Report," Mar. 16, 1943, USNA, RG 286, Records of the Agency for International Development and Predecessor Agencies, IIA Periodic Reports, 1942–1953, Box 2.

[43] Coordinator of Inter-American Affairs, *Weekly Report on Activities*, Jan. 2, 1943, pp.1, 2.

[44] Coordinator of Inter-American Affairs, *Weekly Report on Activities*, May 8, 1943, p.1.

[45] TS, Memo, Berent Friele to the Ambassador, "Annual Report of the Activities of the Office of the Coordinator of Inter-American Affairs..., Mar. 2, 1944, in USNA, RG 229, Office of Inter-American Affairs, Records of the Department of Information, Coordination Committee for Brazil, TS, Box 1259; Kenneth J. Kadow to James D.

agriculture may have adversely affected rubber production. Migrant workers arriving in Manaus insisted on engaging in farm work rather than tapping rubber. More than half the migrant workers imported into the Amazon region by March 1943 settled in the Bragança agricultural region near Belém.[46]

Despite its slow start, by the first-year anniversary of the program administrators claimed a variety of results. For the 1942–1943 growing season, 345,077 farmers received seeds of corn, beans, rice, and potatoes or cuttings of manioc, resulting in a total of over 450,000 acres of new plantings. Over 400 landowners received seeds, tools, insecticides, transportation, and technical advice through the ministry's cooperative farming program, planting 6,416 acres of vegetables and over 550,000 fruit trees and plants. Clearing of land in Pará, commenced in December 1942, allowed for planting of nearly 600 acres for seeds of corn, rice, manioc, and sweet potatoes. By mid-1943, distribution of the seeds to local farmers yielded nearly 7,000 tons of corn, beans, and rice. The commission began development of a hog farm near the air base at Belém with between 300 and 600 hogs and sponsored construction of 20 grain silos in Pará, along with a 25-acre vegetable farm to supply rubber workers at Tapanã, on the outskirts of Belém.[47] To overcome the lack of loans for farmers, the commission extended US$265,000 in small loans. It also furnished over 100,000 hoes, 1,212 axes, 733 pieces of animal drawn equipment and over 80 tons of arsenic, an insecticide. By the end of its first year, the commission's roles had expanded to 800 employees of the Division of Vegetable Development, over 1,000 farm laborers, and 23 U.S. employees, including clerical help.[48]

LeCron, "Weekly Report," Mar. 1, 1943, USNA, RG 286, Records of the Agency for International Development and Predecessor Agencies, IIA Periodic Reports, 1942–1953, Box 2.

[46] Garfield, *In Search of the Amazon*, p. 195.

[47] Brazilian Ministry of Agriculture and Office of the Coordinator of Inter-American Affairs, "A Summary Report of the Activities of the Comissão Brasileiro-Americano de Produção de Gêneros Alimenticios," Sept. 3, 1942 to Dec. 21, 1944; TS, K. J. Kadow, "CBA Activities in the Amazon Special Report," Aug. 18, 1943, USNA, RG 286, Records of the Agency for International Development and Predecessor Agencies, IIA Periodic Reports, 1942–1953, Box 2.

[48] Memorandum, Berent Friele to the Ambassador, "Annual Report of the Activities of the Office of the Coordinator of Inter-American Affairs...," Mar. 2, 1944, in USNA,

Results of the first year of the commission's efforts gained praise from Sales but registered few results for the rubber workers for whom the project was nominally intended. The minister expressed appreciation privately to U.S. administrators for the "work which is being done" and credited the Brazilian farmer for the commission's accomplishments. In a joint press conference, he heralded the commission's work as "not just a typical effort of war," but instead signifying the "launching of the bases of a ruralist movement of great importance for the renovation of agriculture in the vast area from Bahia to the Acre territory."[49]

Results varied regionally. Pará benefited from nearby agricultural lands and a good distribution network, but rubber tappers in the western Amazon suffered from food shortages and abuses of a distribution system manipulated by intermediaries. Recent migrants from the Northeast were unfamiliar with their new habitats and knew little of the hunting lifestyle that sustained local residents. Malaria, tuberculosis, and parasitic infections led to high mortality rates.[50] Sales gave priority to the Northeastern states for subsidies provided by the commission. This decision reflected not only Sales preference for developing the Northeast, but also the difficulty of clearing land and planting on inhospitable soil within the Amazon's tropical rainforest. According to an observer, in 1942 Amazonian agriculturists limited their planting to soil left along the banks of receding rivers that shifted from year to year.[51] Three decades later, impediments to large-scale agriculture in the Amazon would also hamper the Médici government's efforts to open the Amazon to agriculture. Sixty percent of subsidies distributed in 1944 flowed to Northeastern states (See Fig. 15.2).

Poultry production received special emphasis as a rapid solution to protein deficiency resulting from shortages in the beef supply. The CBA

RG 229, Office of Inter-American Affairs, Records of the Department of Information, Coordination Committee for Brazil, TS, Box 1259, p. 41.

49 *A Noite*, Sept 3, 1943, pp. 1, 8; TS, Memo to the Coordinator from the Brazilian Division, Dec. 24, 1943, in USNA, RG 229, Office of Inter-American Affairs, General Records, Basic Economy, Box 76.

50 Seth Garfield, *In Search of the Amazon: Brazil, the United States, and the Nature of a Region* (Durham, NC: Duke University Press, 2013), pp. 188.

51 T. Lynn Smith, *Brazil: People and Institutions* (Baton Rouge, LA: Louisiana State University Press, 1946). p. 108.

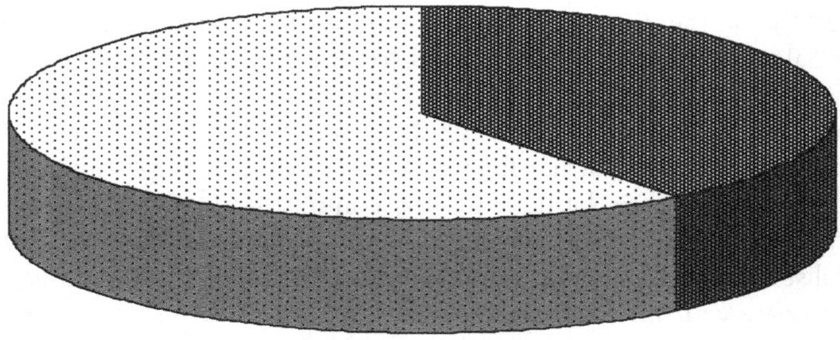

Fig. 15.2 Destination by region of subsidies distributed by the Brazilian-American Food Production Commission, 1944 (Source: TS, "Ministerio da Agricultura, Trabalhos em Execução nos Estados e Respectivas Dotações Orçamentarias," Getúlio Vargas Archive, Centro de Pesquisa e Documentação de História Contemporânea do Brasil (CPDOC), Fundação Getúlio Vargas, GV MinA,44.06.00)

reconditioned existing aviaries and ordered construction of new installations, resulting in 19 new poultry production units with a capacity of 34,000 birds. The CBA imported new breeds of chickens from the United States along with two large flocks of turkeys and small flocks of Peking ducks. The Ministry of Agriculture and the CBA organized a three-month course on practical poultry farming attended by 62 individuals. The CBA also sought inexpensive ways of maintaining high production while researching more nutritious bird feed. After two years and the dedication of over US$100,000 to its poultry program, the CBA concluded that "the success of the CBA poultry efforts, along with the high interest in this field by farmers, bids well for the future of this industry in Brazil."[52]

By the end of its second year, the CBA could boast of successful projects in the Northeast and Amazonia. In Pará, the commission was

[52] TS, Memo to Mr. Kinports from W.G. Casseres, May 21, 1944, in USNA, RG 229, Office or Inter-American Affairs, General Records, Basic Economy, Brazil, Box. 82; TS, John B. Griffing, "Two-year Comprehensive Report," Dec. 1, 1944, in USNA, RG 286, Records of the Agency for International Development and Predecessor Agencies, IIA, Periodic Reports, 1942–1950, Brazil, Box 3; Brazilian Ministry of Agriculture and Office of the Coordinator of Inter-American Affairs, "A Summary Report of the Activities, p. 46.

operating two poultry farms, a large vegetable garden and a pork project with the capacity for 1,000 hogs. In São Luis de Maranhão, the CBA was maintaining a large farm producing fruits, vegetables and eggs, while in Fortaleza it operated two farms producing vegetables, fruits, and fresh eggs for the U.S. military mission. In Rio Grande do Norte, the CBA operated two farms that produced a variety of vegetables and over 82,000 pounds of pork. In Paraíba, the CBA's farms were meeting the food demands of the Brazilian military forces as well as much of the population of João Pessoa. In Pernambuco, the CBA maintained large pork and poultry projects, organized a large vegetable garden, and planted thousands of fruit trees. In Alagoas, the commission operated three farms producing fruits and vegetables, as well as turkeys and ducks, for Brazilian and U.S. armed forces. The commission's reach extended even to the island of Fernando Noronha, where CBA members provided technical assistance, seeds, tools, and fertilizers.[53]

True to Rockefeller's vision, the CBA extended its activities to other regions of Brazil. In the Rio Doce river valley of Minas Gerais, the boom in mining strategically important high-grade iron ore, mica, and quartz crystals and related railroad and road construction had diverted workers from agricultural pursuits, leading to food shortages exacerbated by the lack of transportation. Moreover, as one CBA staff member commented, "not only is there a shortage of food, but the increased earning power of the workers induces them to eat a great deal more than before, which adds to the demand."[54] With the support of CBA technicians, schools and railroad construction camps in the region created vegetable gardens. The CBA distributed seeds for cereals, beans, and vegetables as well as small tools, insecticides, and agricultural machinery. Its agronomists worked with county governments to increase food production.[55]

53 Brazilian Ministry of Agriculture and Office of the Coordinator of Inter-American Affairs, "A Summary Report of the Activities of the Comissão..., pp. 81–87.

54 TS, "Meetings of the Weekly Policy Meeting," Mar. 22, 1944, in USNA, RG 229, Office of Inter-American Affairs, Coordination Committee for Brazil, Box 1272.

55 Brazilian Ministry of Agriculture and Office of the Coordinator of Inter-American Affairs, "A Summary Report of the Activities of the Comissão..., pp. 81–87; Office of the Coordinator of Inter-American Affairs, *Weekly Report of Activities*, July 11, 1944, p. 5.

Gaining Support for U.S. Agricultural Practices

A far more enduring impact resulted from the commission's special emphasis on the education and training of Brazilians in U.S. agricultural techniques, in both Brazil and the United States, a program that evolved from long-established ties related to agricultural education in São Paulo and Minas Gerais. The training program was crucial to supporting U.S. long-term regional objectives. As explained by an anonymous document prepared by Rockefeller's staff, increasing the food production in Latin America would lead to higher "levels of living," and the resulting increase in purchasing power "will thus create new and expanded markets for the United States." One staffer reasoned that while the commission's efforts to introduce the benefits of North American techniques" were important, the program also sought to "further the spirit of good will existing between Brazil and the United States through the means of an operating agricultural program."[56]

Training agriculturalists and nutritionists would create the capability to "carry on the program of food production after the Institute's assistance has ended." Even prior to establishment of the agreement, Rockefeller and the Ambassador Caffery used the CIAA to expose Brazilian agricultural students to U.S. agricultural education. In 1941, the office provided US$15,000 to support a tour of U.S. agricultural facilities by 48 students of the Piraçicaba agricultural school, resulting in ringing endorsements of U.S. agricultural practices. School director and escort Jose de Mello Moraes was impressed a luncheon meeting with Nelson Rockefeller and a chance encounter in the capitol with Vice President (and agronomist) Henry Wallace, who discussed corn hybridization with Mello Moraes prior to joining the students in a chorus of the Piraçicaba's school song on the capitol steps. Upon return, Mello Moraes, commented positively on U.S. agricultural practices in his weekly column in São Paulo's *Folha da Manhã,* focusing on "agriculture in general, stock and poultry raising, and forestation... as practiced in the United States."[57]

[56] Memo, Berent Friele to the Ambassador, "Annual Report of the Activities of the Office of the Coordinator of Inter-American Affairs..., Mar. 2, 1944, in USNA, RG 229, Office of Inter-American Affairs, Records of the Department of Information, Coordination Committee for Brazil, TS, Box 1259.

[57] TS, "Project Authorization," Oct. 9, 1941; TS, "Memo to the Coordinator from the Brazilian Division," June 5, 1942; Ltr., Arnold Taschudy to the Coordinator, Mar. 20, 1943; Ltr., Miguel Bechara to Nelson Rockefeller, Feb. 19, 1942, all in USNA, RG

The food commission's program reached multiple Brazilians by offering training in both Brazil and the United States under the motto of "learning by doing." The in-Brazil training program utilized the commission's seed production and demonstration farms producing hogs, poultry, cattle, fruits, vegetables, and cereals, as training sites for future farm managers. Nine units located in the Northeast and Amazonia hosted between 16 and 24 trainees each. Because none of the trainees could read or write, the commission instituted a night course in reading and writing. The commission also established a specialized unit in Maranhão with a one-year course for 16 students focused on poultry development in all aspects: incubation, egg production, and broiler production.[58]

Trainees selected to travel to the United States received a far more comprehensive introduction to U.S. farming. The training, funded solely by the U.S. government, was designed to "provide a means of practical agriculture and home economics training for worthy boys and girls and boys" through six to nine months with "a county agriculture or home demonstration agent." After rudimentary English classes, trainees received a monthly stipend (US$135 if single, US$195 with dependents) and engaged in a "wide range of practical farm enterprises." By mid-1944, 49 Brazilians were participating in program. Thirty-three focused on livestock, poultry, fruits, vegetables, dairy products, farm machinery, and processing byproducts, while another 10 concentrated on public services, including extension services, organization of 4H clubs, and research. Six were studying home economics and nutrition.[59]

Participants experienced U.S. farm life through contacts with farm families and local agricultural organizations. Ceará native Francisco Diogenes Nogueira lived at the 60,000-acre Painter Hereford Company Ranch, home to 1,000 cattle, near Greeley, Colorado, and spent a month at a dairy farm in Weld County. He visited the local county agent in

229, Office of Inter-American Affairs, General Records, Basic Economy, Brazil, Box. 82; *A Noite* [Rio de Janeiro], Dec. 4, 1941, p. 1; *A Manhã*, Feb. 5, 1942, pp. 3, 8. For an example see "A Agricultura na América do Norte," *Folha da Manhã*, Apr. 30, 1942, p. 8.

[58] Brazilian Ministry of Agriculture and Office of the Coordinator of Inter-American Affairs, "Summary Report," p. 61.

[59] Ltr., W.C. Brister to Kenneth J. Kadow, Dec. 17, 1943, in USNA, RG 229, Office of Inter-American Affairs, Basic Economy, Country Files Brazil, Box 82; Brazilian Ministry of Agriculture and Office of the Coordinator of Inter-American Affairs, "Summary Report," p. 69.

Greeley who was president of the National Association of County Agents, an association of agricultural extension specialists. Hugo Frota lived with the family of the president of the local farm bureau active in 4H work near Fort Collins and assisted his host family prepare for the annual Western Livestock Show in Denver in January 1944. At least one trainee promoted a better understanding of Brazil to local communities. Pará native and medical doctor Eduard Cattete Pinheiro, training in Mariana, Arkansas, made presentations to multiple local business, church, and civic groups.[60]

The long-term impact of the new perspectives obtained by these and the other 39 agriculturalists and nutritionists who participated in the program through 1944 cannot be precisely measured. In the very least, their experiences in the United States oriented their thinking about agricultural practices and reinforced the notion that the U.S. model of agriculture held relevance for Brazil. Ozaman Frederico Marra, upon returning from a year's exposure to U.S. agricultural practices, especially poultry raising, in Delaware, Ohio, New Jersey, and New Hampshire, remarked that "for me, no activity could have been more beneficial; I acquired, then, a stock of experiences that, I am certain, will be most useful in Brazil in view of the problems of our still depressed poultry industry."[61] Other participants returned to Brazil to become leaders in agricultural education, home economics education, and the burgeoning poultry industry.[62]

The endorsement of U.S. agricultural practices also occurred at the policy level through the visit of minister Sales to the United States in mid-1944. Accompanied by Oscar Guedes and a personal secretary, Sales embarked upon a 45-day tour of agricultural facilities at the invitation of Nelson Rockefeller and Secretary of Agriculture Claude R. Wickard. He marveled at experiments underway at the Beltsville, Maryland, agriculture research station, especially "the most interesting" machines being

[60] *The Tribune* [Greely, CO], April 5, 2012; Ltr., W.C. Brister to Kenneth J. Kadow, Dec. 17, 1943, in USNA, RG 229, Office of Inter-American Affairs, Basic Economy, Box 82.

[61] *Diário de Pernambuco,* Oct. 20, 1944, p. 3.

[62] Ltr., W.C. Brister to Kenneth J. Kadow, Dec. 17, 1943, in USNA, RG 229, Office of Inter-American Affairs, Basic Economy, Box 82; Brazilian Ministry of Agriculture and Office of the Coordinator of Inter-American Affairs, "Summary Report," pp. 69–70.

tested for future application on various crops.[63] He visited a poultry farm in Newark, Delaware, and observed hydroelectric plants in Schenectady, New York, and those of the Tennessee Valley Authority in Knoxville, Tennessee. In Ames, Sales was honored at a University of Iowa forum attended by 200 Iowa farmers, gathering information on corn hybridization in the process. He also visited the King Ranch in Texas and large-scale vegetable projects in Illinois, met with Chicago manufacturers of farm equipment, and toured vegetable and soup canning installations in Pittsburg.[64]

Sales's visit added to his conviction that Brazil needed to increase the technical knowledge and mechanization of its agriculture. At a press conference upon his return, he proclaimed that "It is not an exaggeration to say that the technician, upon standing on North American soil, feels enveloped in an aura of confidence in technique and work." In his own words, Sales had seen the "most prosperous agricultural nation of the world." He returned to advocate a stronger federal government role in both the mechanization of agriculture and electrification of the São Francisco river valley, a topic of vital interest to his Pernambucan base. He met with Vargas soon after returning to recommend an agricultural development plan to assure "the rapid penetration of the technical, principally mechanization, in farming and agricultural resources from "north to south."[65]

[63] Apolônio Sales, *Viagem aos Estados Unidos (Aspectos da produção agropecuário e do electrifição rural)* Rio de Janeiro: Serviço de Informação Agricola, Ministerio da Agricultura, 1944), pp. 3–7; *Correio da Manhã*, July 28, 1944, p. 1; *Diario de Pernambuco*, July 30, 1944, pp. 2, 3.

[64] "Brazilian Minister of Agriculture Tours the United States," *Weekly Report of Activities* [Coordinator of Inter-American Affairs], July 4, 1944, p. 1.

[65] Sales, *Viagem aos Estados Unidos*, p. 3; *Correio da Manhã*, July 28, 1944, pp. 1, 3. Oscar Guedes returned also convinced of the applicability of the U.S. experience to the needs of Brazilian agricultural needs after visits to the King Ranch in Texas and observing machinery at work in the fields of Iowa. He reported that he carefully observed "the agricultural organization in the states that I visited with the view of transplanting—adapting, of course to our conditions—everything that I found interesting in the visited zones." He also visited with several Brazilian trainees sponsored by the CBA who reported that they were satisfied with the program and looking forward to taking advantage of their new knowledge. *Diário de Pernambuco*, July 30, 1944, p. 2. The CBA also gave substantial support to development of a large "agro-industrial colony" at Itaparica in the São Francisco Valley. By December 1944, the colony housed several hundred colonists and boasted a slaughterhouse and *xarque* plant capable of processing 200 cattle per day. From 1943 forward, Sales campaigned for the development of the hydroelectric resources

Sales's embrace of mechanization complemented measures proposed six months earlier by the *Conselho Federal de Comercio Exterior* [Federal Council of Foreign Trade] to subsidize the national manufacture of farm equipment. After studying national agricultural machinery production, the council judged that "the precarious situation of the industry of agricultural machines" and the "scarcity of agricultural implements," required urgent measures. Production of agricultural machines was to be standardized, with profits controlled at both the manufacturer and retail levels. For 1944, the government was to purchase a modest five million *cruzeiros* worth of equipment (about US$250,000). Specifications for each equipment item to be developed cited exact models of imported equipment, although the council affirmed that "we do not wish to intimate that the national industry is going to copy the type indicted."[66] However, the decree's impact was limited. A serious effort to develop an agricultural machinery industry, focusing on the manufacture of tractors, was still decades away.[67]

The Demise of the Commission

The flurry of activity of the two years of the food commission soon faded as events in Europe and Asia lowered the perceived threat to Northeastern Brazil and increases in food production stabilized prices, albeit at levels higher than during prewar years. In October 1943, Berent Friele informed the U.S. staff of the commission that "the feeling in Washington was that the food shortage emergency in the Northeast was now over." The remainder of funds allocated for the program, he recommended, "should be used more to cover Brazil's need for nutritional and agricultural education."[68]

of the river's Paulo Affonso waterfalls. Brazilian Ministry of Agriculture and Office of the Coordinator of Inter-American Affairs, "Summary Report," p. 87. "Apolônio Sales," https://cpdoc.fgv.br/producao/dossies/AEraVargas2/biografias/Apolonio_Sales.

66 TS, Jack B. Neathery, "Brazilian Government Provides a Subsidy for the Agricultural Machinery Industry," Jan. 18, 1943, in RG 229, Office of Inter-American Affairs, Basic Economy, Box 82.

67 See Secretaria da Agricultura do Estado de São Paulo, *Anais do I Simpósio sobre Fabricação do Trator e Implemento Agricola no Brasil, 16 20 de Novembro de 1959* (N.P: n.p., c1960).

68 TS, "Meeting of Staff of Brazilian Division," Oct. 20, 1943, USNA, RG 229, Office of Inter-American Affairs, Coordination Committee for Brazil, Box 1272.

Moreover, the commission was quickly losing relevance. One of its principal mandates—providing food for migrant rubber workers—was becoming less urgent as the flow of workers into the rubber-gathering effort fell far short of Caldwell King's estimate that a half million new residents would relocate to the Amazon to gather rubber. Between late 1942 and December 1945, less than 35,000 "rubber soldiers" and their dependents migrated to the Amazon area under government sponsorship.[69] By April 1944, consideration was clearly being given to terminating the program, but staff members argued that "the job cannot be stopped at this point until the eight training schools and the thirty-one other stations are running smoothly." The agreement was extended for an addition year through June 30, 1945, allowing for continuation of "various projects in operation which will not be concluded at the expiration of the present agreement."[70]

Undeterred, Brazilian agriculturalists and Rockefeller himself continued to envision a further extension of the agreement. Despite a February 1945 request from Fernando Costa, former agriculture minister and since 1942 appointed governor (*interventor*) of São Paulo, for U.S. participation in a large-scale agricultural development plan, both governments agreed to end the program by June 30, 1945. The commission closed the books on pending expenditures and transferred funds from the sale of CBA facilities to the Ministry of Agriculture to maintain works in progress.[71] The joint food production commission closed its doors, but Rockefeller would continue to be a factor in Brazilian agriculture for decades to come.[72]

[69] Wilkinson, "Tapping the Amazon For Victory," p. 158.

[70] TS, "CIAA-Brazilian Division Meeting of the Policy Committee," Nov. 19, 1943; TS, Minutes of Weekly Policy Meeting," Apr. 3, 1944, all in USNA, RG 229, Office of Inter-American Affairs, Coordination Committee for Brazil, Box 1272; Ltr., G. C. Dunham to Apolônio Sales, July 24, 1944, USNA, RG 286, Records of the Agency for International Development and Predecessor Agencies, IIA Periodic Reports, 1942–1953, Box 2.

[71] Memo, William B Gotaas to the Board of Directors, CIAA, June 23, 1945, USNA, RG 229, Office of Inter-American Affairs, Country Files, Brazil, Box 82.

[72] See Claiton Marcio da Silva, *De Agricultor a Farmer: Nelson Rockefeller e a Modernização da Agricultura no Brasil* (Curitiba, PR: Editora UFPR, 2015).

Brazilian Agriculture at War's End

As the commission's work was winding down, friends and colleagues of Apolônio Sales gathered on February 28, 1945, to celebrate his third anniversary as agriculture minister. Aside from praising his plans for mechanizing agriculture and constructing grain silos, they highlighted his work with the food commission as having brought "great benefits" to Brazil "from Bahia to Acre."[73] In a broader perspective, the activities of the joint food production commission were part and parcel of the unprecedented intervention of the federal government into the agriculture sector.

This process had begun in September 1939, when the federal government established the Commission of National Economic Defense [Comissão da Defesa da Economia Nacional] to control the economic impact of the war on the nation's population. It was charged with tracking food stocks, promoting exports, and controlling shipping and transport fees. Far from achieving "a complete unity of the productive forces and the effective collaboration of public powers for a framework of immediate action that would possibly normalize our social life without great clashes and without many surprises,"[74] the program opened a wide fissure between producers and policy planners. No longer would government intervention focus only on remedying the ills of specific crops, now it would attempt to control the destiny of the entire agricultural sector.

The level of intervention sparked concern among business sectors and generated unintended consequences. The *Coordinação*'s setting of prices for bread, sugar, and beef in May 1943 generated protests from producers and provoked the formation of a black market. Business groups allied under the umbrella the Commercial Association of Rio de Janeiro organized the First Brazilian Economic Conference in late November and early December 1943, ostensibly to examine the relations between government and the economy. According to a confidential report prepared by a U.S. Embassy observer, the meeting stemmed in part from businesses' wish to register a "rebuke to Government controls,

[73] *A Manhã*, Mar. 1, 1945, p. 6.

[74] Brazil. Coordinação da Mobilização Econômica, *Economia de Guerra No Brasil: O Que Fêz A Coordenação da Mobilização Econômica, Vol. II, Setor Abstecimento*, (N.P.: n.p., c. 1946), p. 42.

taxation, and mismanagement,"[75] forecasting a political reaction that would eventually result in the Vargas government's downfall. In one analyst's opinion, the federal government's efforts to promote alternatives to the scarcity and high prices of goods had resulted in an unsatisfactory situation marked by long lines, high prices, and rationing.[76]

Despite such turbulence, the *Coordinação* did offset some of the negative impact of the war on Brazil's agriculture by agreements with the United States to buy commodities deprived of usual markets. In October 1942, the U.S Commodity Credit Corporation agreed to buy US$100 million worth of Brazilian coffee and smaller amounts of Brazil nuts, cacao, and cotton oil. In May 1944, in cooperation with the United Kingdom, the United States also agreed to supply a US$2.5 million loan to support increased cultivation of rice in Rio Grande do Sul.[77]

The status of Brazilian plantings for 1945 reflected a dynamic agricultural sector beginning to diversify away from a dependence upon coffee while trying to meet the demands of domestic and global markets within an uncertain political environment. Spurred by a five-fold increase in agricultural credit by the Bank of Brazil's Portfolio of Agricultural and Industrial Credit [Carteira de Crédito Agricola e Industrial],[78] and the continuing availability of virgin lands, farmers brought nearly one million hectares of new land into cultivation between 1939 and 1945.[79] With the assistance of the CBA, the output of several major crops—manioc roots, tomatoes, sugar cane wheat, barley, cotton, and beans—expanded despite

[75] TS, Reginald S. Kazanjian, "The First Brazilian Economic Conference," Dec. 10, 1943, USNA, RG 166, Foreign Agricultural Service, Narrative Reports 1942–1945, Brazil, Box. 50.

[76] Alzira Alves de Abreu, Dicionário histórico-biográfico da Primeira República (1889–1930); Luciano B. Meron, "Racionamentos e Carestia de Alimentos na Bahia durante a II Guerra Mundial," p. 18. http://www.uel.br/cch/his/ISNHM/AnaisPDF/luizbmeron.pdf.

[77] USDA, *Foreign Crops and Markets*, Vol. 45, No. 16 (Oct. 19, 1942); Vol. 46, No. 13 (Mar. 29, 1943); Vol. 50, No. 9 (Feb. 26, 1945); Vol. 48, No. 20 (May 27, 1944), p. 267; TS, "Relação dos produtos cujos projetos de acordo já forma encaminhados ao governo dos estados unidos pela comissão de control," GVA, CPDOC, Fundação Getúlio Vargas, GV Confid 1943.00.00, Relação da Commissão de Controle.

[78] Salamão L. Quadros da Silva, " A Era Vargas e a Economia," in Maria Celina D'Araujo, eds., *As Instituições Brasileira da Era Vargas* (Rio de Janeiro: Editora FGV, 1999), p. 149.

[79] Brazil: *Agricultural Production and Trade Statistics* (Washington, D.C.: USDA, 1951), p. 4, 7.

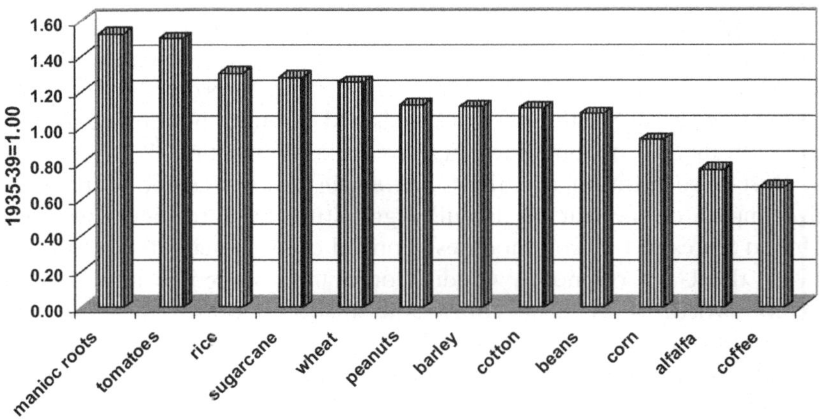

Fig. 15.3 Indexed change in production major crops, average production 1940–1944 versus 1935–1939 (*Source Brazil*: Agricultural Production and Trade Statistics (Washington, DC: USDA, 1951), p. 7)

the vicissitudes of war. Meanwhile, coffee production fell by 34%. Cotton and food crops provided more attractive returns. (See Fig. 15.3).

Conclusion

Reponses by the Brazilian and U.S. governments to wartime conditions fundamentally altered the course of Brazil's agricultural development. Aside from the leading to expansion of foodstuffs and greater intervention of the government into agricultural decision making, actions of the Ministry of Agriculture, and the joint food production commission exposed multitudes of farmers to the benefits of increased federal governmental support. Efforts by the ministry and the CBA to introduce even rudimentary agricultural implements accelerated the replacement of the digging stick with the hoe and marked the beginnings of a shift toward favoring capital-intensive cultivation. The Brazilian government leveraged U.S. strategic concerns not only to obtain important subsidies for research on rubber development, but also to receive major subsidies for a relief program for the politically volatile and drought-stricken Northeast. Thus, the joint food production program stands as a clear example of Gerson

Moura's observation that Brazil was able to manipulate its relationship with the United States to obtain political and economic success.[80]

It also supported U.S. geopolitical goals. The United States gained not only access to a dependable source of raw materials—especially rubber—but also a supportive political and economic partner within an American system under U.S. leadership. Closer ties with the Vargas government reduced chances of a German beachhead in the Americas and laid the basis for a broader vision of Pan-Americanism in the immediate postwar period.[81] Within this charged political and economic environment, the search for ways to increase the output of Brazil's agricultural and extractive products, especially those related to the Amazon, created an important incentive for wartime cooperation. Many of its proponents considered the effort merely a prelude to a broader economic alliance.

[80] Moura, *Relações Exteriores Do Brasil 1939–1950*, p. 206.

[81] W. Michael Weis, "Pan American Shift: Oswaldo Aranha and the Demise of the Brazilian-American Alliance," in David Shenin, ed., *Beyond the Ideal: Pan Americanism in Inter-American Affairs* (Westport CN: Greenwood Press, 2000), pp. 133, 134.

CHAPTER 16

Industrialization and the Agricultural Revolution, 1945–1950

Brazilian agriculture emerged from the disruptions of a wartime economy confronting competing pressures. Political tensions arose from urban classes suffering from rising food prices, a trend that continued despite war's end. Meanwhile, producers chafed against the ineffectiveness of Brazil's agricultural bureaucracy. The nation's business leaders promoted a liberal definition of the path forward at a May 1945 conference of over 900 delegates from 680 industrial, commercial and agricultural entities of the self-denominated "productive classes." They called for joint action by private initiative and the state to raise Brazil's income and "to realize through safe and adequate measures the industrialization of the country." Government's role was to be limited to circumstances beyond the "power, capacity, or convenience of private initiative." Brazil's agricultural policy should be defined by the "rural classes" but still provide better transportation, lower taxes, and access to land, credit, technical assistance, and equipment for mechanization.[1]

Private sector pressure to prioritize industrialization coincided with a severe reduction in official U.S. support for Brazilian agricultural development, no longer a U.S. strategic priority. Nevertheless, U.S. private actors—especially Nelson Rockefeller—remained engaged in the sector's

[1] *Carta Econômica de Teresópolis: Conferência das Classes Produtoras do Brasil. Teresópolis, E. do Rio de Janeiro, 1–6 de Maio de 1945*, pp. 2–4.

E. R. Downes, *Brazilian Agricultural Development, 1890–1950*,
https://doi.org/10.1007/978-3-031-76992-4_16

institutional development to further U.S. geopolitical interests. U.S. private capital also adapted to new market conditions and regulatory demands to expand their presence in the domestic market for beef cattle and cotton products. Renewed official U.S. interest in Brazil's agriculture would only come with the intensification of global political competition.

Agriculture and the New Reality

In forging a path forward for agriculture, Brazil's political leaders and agriculturalists faced a new reality. The continuing pressures of rural to urban migration and lessons of the war reminded Brazilian political leaders and agriculturalists that the country needed to produce more foodstuffs. Food prices in São Paulo exchanges rose precipitously following the war. Between years end 1945 and 1947, corn rose by 46 percent, cooking oil by 27 percent, sugar by 25 percent, manioc flour by 41 percent, and wheat by a whopping 121 percent.[2] Food prices in São Paulo nearly doubled between 1945 and 1950[3] and average prices for principal crops between 1946 and 1950 rose by between 50 percent (for rice) and nearly 200 percent (for cotton).[4] (See Fig. 16.1).

Defining and implementing an agricultural policy to deal with these pressures suffered from political uncertainty following ouster of Vargas from the presidency on October 29, 1945. Elaboration of a new national constitution following the election of General Eurico Gaspar Dutra to the presidency in January 1946 delayed broad initiatives related to agriculture. Candidate Dutra had declared that Brazil's era as an "essentially agricultural nation" had passed, as "essential agricultural countries are countries of pauperism." Even though Brazil needed to develop "mass production of vital raw materials, seeking a great expansion of internal consumers and exports to nearby countries," it should emphasize

[2] *Conjuntura Econômica*, Vol. 2, No. 5 (1948), 6.

[3] Fundação Instituto Brasileiro de Geografia e Estatística, *Estatísticas históricas do Brasil: séries econômicas, demográficas e sociais de 1550 a 1988 2nd ed. Rev. of Vol. 3 de Séries Estatísticas Retrospectivas* (Rio de Janeiro: IBGE, 1990), p. 286.

[4] Calculated from Fundação Instituto Brasileiro de Geografia e Estatística, *Estatísticas históricas do Brasil: séries econômicas, demográficas e sociais de 1550 a 1988 2nd ed. Rev. of Vol. 3 de Séries Estatísticas Retrospectivas* (Rio de Janeiro: IBGE, 1990), pp. 322–24, 326, 327, 329–30, 332, 335.

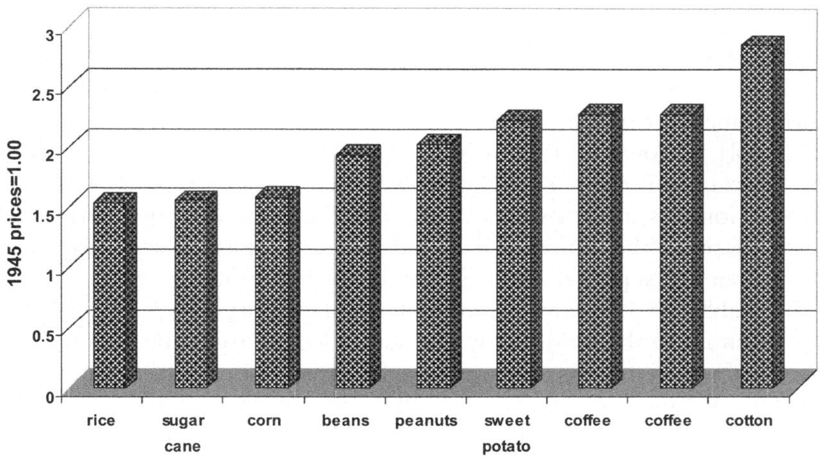

Fig. 16.1 Indexed average price increases for various crops, 1946–1950 (1945 = 1.00) (*Source* Calculated from Fundação IBGE, Estatísticas históricas do Brasil: séries econômicas, demográficas e sociais de 1550 a 1988 2nd ed. Rev. of Vol. 3 de Séries Estatísticas Retrospectivas (Rio de Janeiro: IBGE, 1990), pp. 322–24, 326, 327, 329, 330, 332, 335)

importing manufactured goods for the nation's industrial park.[5] But any program to support expansion of raw materials production suffered from turbulence in key ministerial posts, including finance, transportation, and agriculture. A U.S. embassy observer noted "little continuity or consistency in the conversion and rehabilitation program of the Government and progress was retarded by these changes."[6] After months of deliberation, in September 1946 a new constitution returned some political power back toward the states, but to a lesser degree than enjoyed under the First Republic.[7]

[5] Mauro Renault Leite and Novelli Júnior, eds. *Marechal Eurico Gaspar Dutra: O Dever da Verdade* (Rio de Janeiro: Editora Nova Fronteira, 1983), pp. 698, 699.

[6] TS, DuWayne G. Clark, "Annual Economic Review for the Year 1946," Feb. 21, 1947, USNA, RG 166, FAS Narrative Reports, 1946–1949, Box. 518.

[7] Thomas E. Skidmore, *Brazil: Five Centuries of Change* (New York: Oxford Univ. Press, 1999), p. 129.

The primary agricultural issue facing the post-Vargas governments was the issue of higher food prices. The first minister of agriculture in the Dutra government, Manoel Neto Campelo Junior, a Recife native and former member of the Alcohol and Sugar Institute [Instituto de Açúcar e Álcool], announced a drive to increase food production and improve transportation in March 1946. He expressed commitment to increasing production "as a means of overcoming the high cost of living" and asserted that "the Ministry had undertaken all justifiable measures in order that the supply of meat is carried out in accordance with the new plan established."[8] Campelo Junior blamed transportation bottlenecks for contributing to the food supply problem. Like its Argentine counterpart, the Dutra government soon spent substantial amounts of accumulated foreign exchange to purchase the Ilheus-Conquista, Leopoldina, Great Western, and São Paulo railways from their British owners.

Equally compelling was the need to increase production by encouraging greater mechanization of Brazil's farms, and Campelo Junior began implementing the plan for mechanizing agriculture outlined by Sales in 1944. He was facing a daunting task: a 1946 survey indicated Brazil's nearly two million agricultural establishments possessed a mere 3,380 tractors. Moreover, 74 percent lacked even plows. Harrowers—machines to pulverize and smooth the soil—were present on less than seven percent of the properties. Aside from their scarcity, the nation's tractors were unevenly distributed. A full 78 percent were in São Paulo, Paraná, Santa Catarina, and Rio Grande do Sul, with only 177 tractors situated in all seven northeastern states.[9] In June the ministry arranged purchase of "agricultural machinery, such as tractors, harvesters, graders, etc." in the United States and sought U.S. Embassy assistance to accelerate delivery to make the equipment available for the next planting season. The ministry assumed control of the sale of CR$40 million worth of agricultural machinery imported by the Bank of Brazil, pledging to use proceeds from sales to create a revolving fund to promote further mechanization,

[8] TS, U.S. Embassy, Rio de Janeiro, "Minister of Agriculture Press Conference," Mar. 15, in 1946, USNA, RG 166, FAS, Narrative Reports 1946–1949, Box 518.

[9] Encl. 1 to Report 194, May 16, 1947, "Census of Rural Establishments in Brazil, Showing Number and Type of Agricultural Implements Employed," USNA, RG 166, FAS, Narrative Reports 1946–1949, Box 535.

a necessary step "since there is a lack of manpower due to the exodus of the rural population."[10]

The appointment of Daniel de Carvalho as agriculture minister in October 1946 promised a dramatic departure from piecemeal approaches to agricultural development. Carvalho was a Minas Gerais native with broad experience in agriculture, government, and commerce, having served as state secretary of agriculture for Minas Gerais from 1922 to 1926 and overseen construction of the Viçosa agricultural school. In addition to stints as a federal deputy from Minas Gerais, he had served as director-secretary of the fledgling national steel mill project at Volta Redonda from 1943 to 1943 and vice president of the Commercial Association of Rio de Janeiro from 1945 to 1946.[11]

Carvalho faced multiple challenges as agriculture minister. Despite lofty rhetoric about agriculture's importance, the federal government allocated it only meager financial support—less than five percent of the federal government's budget outlay went for agriculture since 1940. More than half the ministry's budget for 1947 was consumed by personnel expenses.[12] Fiscal policies discriminated against some crops in favor of others. The combination of price controls on cotton sales and a 30 cents per kilo "special quota" tax on raw cotton, established in 1943, forced cotton producers to absorb cost of the tax. Since similar price controls were not levied on peanuts and peanut oil, cotton planting declined in favor of peanuts. Peanut production increased four-fold between 1944 and 1948 while cotton production fell by 47 percent.[13] A publicist for cotton processor Anderson Clayton judged the policies as endangering not only production of cooking oil produced from cotton "but also cotton planting itself" as well as the textile industry.[14]

[10] *Diário Official*, June 26, 1946, translated and cited in TS, M.A. Wilson, "Ministry of Agriculture to Import American Farm Machinery Instead of Bank of Brazil," July 9, 1946, USNA, RG 166, FAS Narrative Reports 1946–1949, Box 535.

[11] Carvalho, Daniel De, cpdoc.fgv.br.

[12] Brazil. Ministério da Agricultura, *Atividades do Ministerio da Agricultura, 1946–1950*. (Rio de Janeiro: Serviço de Informação Agrícola, 1951,) pp. 176–78.

[13] Fundação Instituto Brasileiro de Geografia e Estatística, *Estatísticas históricas do Brasil*, pp. 284-5.

[14] TS, RLPS, "Details for the History of ACCO Limitada," p. 11, n.d., Anderson Clayton & Co. Collection, HMRC, Box 39.

The Federation of Rural Societies of São Paulo [*Federação de Associações Rurais do Estado de São Paulo*] specified weaknesses of the state's agriculture in response to a questionnaire from a joint congressional commission investigating the agricultural market. The association cited lack of credit, deficiencies in transportation, absence of price guarantees, lack of machines and tools, reductions in soil fertility, deficiencies in the supply of fertilizer, lack of conservation practices, and the resurgence of insect plagues. Poor compensation caused by low output per unit planted, in the opinion of the federation, created "discouragement with respect to the advantages of rural activities."[15]

Agriculture also suffered financially from the lack of investment and distortions generated by the Bank of Brazil's allocation of crop financing. In 1947, the Bank dedicated 77 percent of support provided to farming by its Carteira Agricola e Industrial to four crops, three of which were tied to export markets: cotton, rice, coffee, and sugar.[16] Support was also heavily skewed in favor of large producers. Between 1940 and 1947, creditors receiving small loans (less than 30,000 *cruzeiros*), received an average of less than 10 percent of the bank's rural credit, while those borrowing 100,000 *cruzeiros* or more benefited from over 73 percent of the bank's rural financing.[17] Moreover, a lack of capital investment precluded major changes. A U.S. government report prepared in 1946 cited an immediate need for "more adequate transportation facilities, agricultural machinery and technicians." As the report noted, "the natural resources of the country can be adequately developed only by the employment of large sums of capital."[18]

Carvalho also confronted structural challenges related to deficiencies in rural education, extension, research and the ministry's bureaucracy. Responses to a survey conducted in 1948 as part of a joint U.S.-Brazil study of the nation's economy (The Abbink Commission) reflected broad

[15] Ltr, Iris Meinberg, President of the Federação de Associações Rurais do Estado de São Paulo, to Ernâni Amaral Peixoto, Chair of the Comissão Mixta de Investigação da Produção Agrícola e Respectivo Financiamento, Câmara de Deputados. May 10, 1948, EAP dfl 1948.01.11, Ernâni Amaral Peixoto Archive, CPDOC, Fundação Getúlio Vargas.

[16] *Conjuntura Econômica*, Vol. 3, No. 10 (1949), p. 6.

[17] *Conjuntura Econômica*, Vol. 5, No. 11 (1951), pp. 7, 8.

[18] U.S. Tariff Commission, *Agricultural, Pastoral and Forest Productions in Brazil* (Washington, DC: U.S. Tariff Commission, 1946), p. 77.

dissatisfaction with the ministry. Respondents complained that "the ever-increasing and overwhelming Brazilian bureaucracy causes more damage than erosion itself." They cited difficulties created by complex records, the lack of freedom of action, eccentric procedures, poor hiring practices, shortages of technicians, agronomists and veterinarians, and delays in approvals for purchase of necessary equipment.[19]

Carvalho sought to break the mold of previous practices and strengthen the state's role, going beyond the call of the "productive classes" for joint action by state and private initiative. He acknowledged that Brazilian agriculture was undergoing "a real crisis" marked by the fall of average output per unit of land. He reasoned Brazil was facing "the imposition of special circumstances in the postwar, when the supply crisis demonstrated the urgent necessity of changing the traditional course of our agricultural, oriented toward export products." He called for reorienting agriculture away from exporting "determined raw materials" toward "internal supply," giving preference to "assuring the full supply of food goods." Key to intensifying and improving the production of Brazil's agriculture was application of science and know-how [*técnica*] and direct assistance to farmers and ranchers through cooperation with the states and municipalities.[20]

To carry out this vision, Carvalho gathered directors of his ministry's services together in the final days of 1946 to develop a three-year plan of agricultural development. The plan placed the government squarely in the forefront of the struggle to overcome the sector's deficiencies and specified preferred allocations by project. Mechanization stood at the top of the list, with provisions calling for purchase and reselling of appropriate machines, training for operators and formation of roving "mechanization patrols." These were to prepare the soil, assist with irrigation projects and plant and even harvest crops, with farmers reimbursing costs incurred.[21]

[19] U.S. Department of State, *Report of the Joint Brazil-United States Technical Commission Rio de Janeiro, Brazil, February 7, 1949* (Washington, DC: U.S. Department of State, 1949), pp. 213–15.

[20] Brazil. Ministério da Agricultura, *Atividades do Ministerio da Agricultura, 1946–1950*. pp. 166–67.

[21] José Teixeira de Oliveira, *O Governo Dutra: Algumas realizações Diretrizes doutrinárias Um período de paz* (Rio de Janeiro: Editora Civilização Brasileira, 1956), p. 91.

The patrols also were to demonstrate the benefits of mechanization, a concept not fully embraced in the field.

The Dutra government supported mechanization by importing another 1,684 tractors by 1949 and creating 34 training centers to teach tractor operation, partially funded by the joint commission on rural education. In 1947 the government instituted courses in rural engineering and tractor operation at the Ipanema Fazenda in São Paulo state.[22] During an installation visit in October 1947, Minister Carvalho praised the teaching of soil conversation, drainage, irrigation and mechanized agriculture that would mark the beginning of "a great campaign of reform of agricultural practices."[23]

The emphasis on mechanization was integral to Carvalho's campaign to increase wheat production. Over 300 of the imported tractors, along with 683 mechanized seed machines, 305 reapers and 549 threshers were to support wheat cultivation. Intensive federal government support, including construction of storage silos and provisioning of specialized financing, led to a wheat harvest of over 500,000 tons in 1949, a nearly three-fold increase over the 1944 total. Carvalho's ministry also combated coffee rust, a grasshopper plague in Santa Catarina and Rio Grande do Sul, diseases of sugar cane and cacao plants, and various pork and cattle infirmities, including hoof and mouth disease.[24]

Carvalho attempted to project an optimistic image of the results of his actions in a July 1, 1949, speech at the Army's General Staff school. He pointed out that previous statistical summaries had imparted a far too pessimistic vision of Brazil's agriculture by ignoring production outside the formal economy. Government tables overlooked production of meat, fish, milk, cheese, eggs, and honey for local consumption, obscuring the reality that agricultural output was becoming increasingly diversified and bountiful. Carvalho touted progress in agricultural research and training and production of wine, cereals, and fruits. His ministry was aggressively working to reverse the "primitive and empirical methods of cultivation," shortages of tractors and accessories, the lack of fertilizer, and absence of credit facilities in many regions. Moving forward required greater government commitment to overcome the "anarchical nature of

[22] Teixeira de Oliveira, *O Governo Dutra,* p. 92.

[23] *A Manhã*, Oct. 23, 1947, pp. 1, 2.

[24] Teixeira de Oliveira, *O Governo Dutra,* pp. 95–97.

our individualism," promote measures to guide farmers, and increase sophistication of research. Increased production would occur through cooperation among all levels of the government and by making the "benefits of techniques and science directly accessible to the farmer."[25]

Postwar Official Ties Regarding Agriculture

One potential source of new techniques and science was a remnant of the cooperative relationship between the USDA and Brazil's Ministry of Agriculture. Vestiges of bilateral cooperation that had flourished during the war remained, albeit greatly reduced in intensity. Among the few cooperative ventures was the assignment of U.S. agrostologist Jason R. Swallen to study native pasture grasses in Rio Grande do Sul, Santa Catarina, and Paraná. He supported the newly established Instituto Agronômico do Sul from September 1945 to September 1946. Swallen gathered 2,400 samples of grasses to form the basis for possible improvements in the region's pastures, while also collecting 40 packets of grass seeds for possible planting in U.S. southern states.[26] The two nations agreed to extend cooperative research in natural rubber at the Instituto Agronômico do Norte for an additional ten years in 1947, despite a decidedly negative evaluation of the IAN's management by a departing U.S. botanist.[27] In 1948 the Department also provided a supervisor for the rural engineering courses at the newly instituted Fazenda Ipanema. William C. Tucker served as director of the center, supporting training in the operation, repair, and maintenance of farm machinery.[28]

[25] Daniel de Carvalho, *Brazilian Agriculture: Lecture given before the School of the General Staff of the Army* (Montreal: Brazilian Government Trade Bureau, c.1950), pp. 7–14.

[26] TS, US Embassy Rio de Janeiro, "Jason R. Swallen Concludes Assignment to Instituto Agronômico do Sul," Sept. 19, 1946, USNA, RG 166, FAS, Narrative Reports 1946–1949, Box 525.

[27] Enclosure to Ltr. 50, U.S. Consulate Belem do Pará, Feb. 25, 1946, USNA, RG 166, FAS, Narrative Reports 1950–1954, Brazil, Crop Estimates, Box 53; TS, "Proposed Agreement Between the United States Department of Agriculture and the Brazilian Ministry of Agriculture...," Dec. 15, 1947, USNA, RG 166, FAS, Narrative Reports 1946–1949, Brazil, Box 518.

[28] *Diário de Noticias*, May 24, 1949; Telex, U.S.Embassy Rio de Janeiro, "Assignment of Agricultural Specialists in Brazil," Apr. 6, 1950, USNA, RG 166, FAS, Reports from Agricultural Attaches Relating to International Agricultural Conferences and Congresses,

Additional official U.S. support for Brazil's agricultural development fell victim to a reordering of U.S. priorities following war's end. Fragments of mechanisms established by Rockefeller's Office of the Coordinator of Inter-American Affairs sustained, albeit temporarily, cooperation in the agriculture through the Institute for Inter-American Affairs, integrated into the State Department on August 31, 1945. On October 20, 1945, the Institute signed a three-year agreement with minister Sales designed to develop "closer relations between teachers of vocational agriculture" and engage in other rural education projects. The United States promised US$250,000 in funding while Brazil pledged an additional US$750,000 to support the program. Minister Sales cited success of the bilateral food commission and expressed a conviction that the new agreement would produce similar results. Even though the Institute overseeing the project had the support of U.S. Ambassador and staunch anti-Communist William Pawley, who described the IIAA's program as "one of the greatest undertakings the United States has made,"[29] the IIAA's funding was soon severely reduced. The rural education program proved short-lived. The Truman administration's push to reduce government spending resulted in termination of the program when the U.S. entity supporting it, the Inter-American Education Foundation, was abolished as a cost savings measure in June 1948.[30]

1931–1958, Box 13; U.S. Congress, 89th Congress, 1st session, *Special Missionto Brazilto Attend the Inauguration of His Excellency President Getúlio Dornellas Vargas, Jan. 31, 1951* (Washington, DC: GPO, 1951), pp. 12.

[29] Ltr., William D. Pawley to the Secretary of State, Dec. 20, 1946, in USNA, RG 263, Records of the Central Intelligence Agency, The Murphy Collection on International Communism, Brazil, Box 203.

[30] Harry S. Truman, *Public Papers of the President of the United States, Harry S. Truman*, Vol. 3 (1947), p. 95; Elizabeth A. Cobbs, *The Rich Neighbor Policy: Rockefeller and Kaiser in Brazil* (New Haven, CN: Yale University Press, 1992), p. 103. The Inter-American Education Foundation was one of five government corporations set up by Rockefeller as Coordinator of Inter-American Affairs. See *History of the Office of the Coordinator of Inter-American Affairs*. (Washington, DC: U.S.GPO, 1947.), p. 100. The appropriation for the Coordinator's Office during its last year of existence (1946) was $13 million. For fiscal year 1947, total funding for the IIAA's health and sanitation, education, and agricultural programs amounted to a little over $6 million—a million dollars less than contributions expected from collaborating countries. *History of the Office of the Coordinator of Inter-American Affairs*. (Washington, DC.: GPO, 1947), p. 266; *The program of the IIA*. (Washington, DC: IIA, 1949), Appendix 2.

Rockefeller Renews His Engagement

The languishing of official U.S. support for Brazil agricultural development clashed with Nelson Rockefeller's vision for future of Brazil and U.S.-Brazilian relations. Though Rockefeller had been summarily dismissed from his U.S. government position in August 1945 in disputes over the future of inter-American relations, he continued advocating U.S. involvement in South America in general and in Brazil in particular. Convinced that the U.S. government's priorities would be long focused on Europe against the rising power of communism, Rockefeller embarked upon a private assistance program building upon contacts established during the war and his reputation as a friend of Brazil.

Rockefeller envisioned creating private corporations that would become vital weapons in the evolving struggle between capitalism and communism. Even before war's end, Rockefeller's CIAA had considered ways to sustain the U.S. presence in Brazil. A study prepared by the coordinator's office in 1944 cited potential U.S. contributions in a variety of fields, including "provide technical assistance in the study of crop diversification and improvement of agricultural techniques."[31] Correctly foreseeing a retrenchment of official U.S. government support, the office raised the possibility of private funding for assistance programs, suggesting that "wherever practical, such programs should be carried out by other than government financing."[32]

Dismissed from government, Rockefeller and cohorts from his former office set about creating an organization to "see if wartime unity and cooperation with the United States could be translated into peacetime cooperation for economic development and a rising standard of living."[33] Its fostering of Latin American business ventures would combat ignorance, poverty, and illness, and convince Latin Americans that "their best interests and opportunity for the future are identified with our country and our way of life." This view was consistent with that of Truman's Assistant Secretary of State, Spruille Braden, who testified in June 1947

[31] TS, Office of the Coordinator of Inter-American Affairs, "Brazil: United States Activities and Future Possibilities July 1944." RAC, Nelson A. Rockefeller Personal Papers, Washington, DC, RG III 40, Series 0, FAR 350, Box 4, Folder 30.

[32] *History of the Office of the Coordinator of Inter-American Affairs*, p. 273.

[33] Martha Dalrymple, *The AIA Story: Two Decades of International Cooperation* (New York: American Association for Economic and Social Development, 1968), p. 8.

that abandoning wartime cooperative programs would substantiate Latin American criticism that these programs were merely wartime expedients. Cooperative programs with Latin American nations, in his opinion, represented "one of our most effective methods to counteract the spread of communism among the masses, with the growth of anti-American feeling."[34]

Rockefeller's Programs for Brazilian Agriculture

Rockefeller created two organizations to sustain promotion of democratic capitalism and long-term U.S. interests in the hemisphere—the American International Association for Economic and Social Development (AIA) and the International Basic Economy Corporation (IBEC). The AIA's charter, approved on July 1, 1946, described its philosophy as being "based upon a faith in the inherent dignity and worth of the individual and in the capacity and desire for self-improvement of human beings…." The corporation intended to "enter into such fields as agriculture, land use and conservation, public health, sanitation, literacy, industry, trade and other fields as it may determine."[35] Six months later, as recommended by lawyer John Lockwood, Rockefeller agreed to create a separate for-profit corporation—the IBEC—dedicated to business activities, leaving the AIA to focus on charitable ventures. Nevertheless, the IBEC retained a social mandate to "promote the economic development of various parts of the world" and better living standards of those touched

[34] Cary Reich, *The life of Nelson A. Rockefeller: worlds to conquer, 1908-1958.* Vol. 1 (New York: Doubleday, 1996–1997), p. 407; United States House of Representatives, *Hearings of Subcommittee No. 4—State Department Organization and Personnel, Committee on Foreign Affairs, House of Representatives, Eightieth Congress, First Session, On H. R. 4168, A Bill To Provide For The Reincorporation Of The IIA, And For Other Purposes June 20 and 27, 1947* (Washington, DC: GPO, 1947), pp. 29, 30. For a detailed discussion of the contemporaneous theory of development, see Claiton Marcio da Silva, "Agricultura e Cooperação Internacional: a Atuação da American International Cooperation for Economic and Social Development (AIA) e os Programas de Modernização no Brasil (1946-1961) (Diss.: Casa de Oswaldo Cruz-Fiocruz, 2009), pp. 23–40.

[35] "Certification of Incorporation of American International Association for Economic and Social Development," Encl. 1 to TS, Gary L. Bush, US Embassy, Rio de Janeiro, "New Association Exploring Possibilities of Developing Enterprises in Brazil," Sept. 5, 1946, in USNA, RG 166, FAS, Narrative Reports, 1946–1949, Box 524.

by the corporation's projects.[36] Both companies supported Brazilian agriculture, especially enhancing food production for local consumption. The AIA focused on the rural family, while the IBEC prioritized overall agricultural productivity.[37]

Rockefeller focused his corporations' activities on two countries: Venezuela, because of his ties with Creole Petroleum, and Brazil, which he considered a vital strategic partner of the United States and where he had experience and contacts. Rockefeller's extensive web of high-level contacts in Brazil and availability of colleagues from the wartime food commission facilitated a commitment to action. After Rockefeller's resignation from the State Department, his wartime friend, and now president, Eurico Gaspar Dutra, told Beret Friele that "We have to get Nelson to visit Brazil." Dutra extended a personal invitation for him to do so.[38] Rockefeller associate Kenneth Kadow, a plant pathologist who had support the food commission's program in Brazil and who was prominent in planning the two corporations, in May 1946 wrote that "I have the necessary facts and information to allow an immediate start there."[39]

Rockefeller searched for ways to reverse the flow of rural migrants to Brazil's cities and their notorious shanty towns as he contemplated a program for Brazil. "What can we do to get the people more dedicated to the area in which they were born?" he asked confidant Berent Friele.[40] He sought advice from Simon Hanson, a Washington consultant who had supported the CIAA's wartime program. Hanson offered an alarming panorama of Brazil in November 1946. The increased cost of

[36] Reich, *The life of Nelson A. Rockefeller*, p. 408. There are multiple comprehensive accounts of AIA's and IBEC's formation and development that need not be repeated here. This account focuses principally on actions directly affecting agricultural production. See Dalrymple, *The AIA Story*; Cobbs, *The Rich Neighbor Policy*; Antonio Pedra Tota, *O amigo Americano: Nelson Rockefeller e o Brasil* (São Paulo: Companhia das Letras, 2014); Claiton Marcio Da Silva, "Agricultura e Cooperação Internacional"; Margaret C. Boardman, "The Man, The Girl and the Jeep AIA: Nelson Rockefeller's Precursor Non-Profit Model for Private U.S. Foreign Aid," http://www.profmex.org/mexicoandtheworld/volume6/1winter01/01boardman1.html.

[37] Cobbs, *The Rich Neighbor Policy*, p. 146.

[38] Berent Friele Oral History Interview, Nov. 28, 1979, p. 59.

[39] Kenneth Kadow to John R. Camp, May 10, 1946, RAC, John R. Camp Papers, Box 1, Folder 2, cited in Cobbs, *The Rich Neighbor Policy*, p. 103, n. 8.

[40] Berent Friele Oral History Interview, Nov. 28, 1979, p. 51, RAC, Nelson A. Rockefeller Personal Papers, RG III 4, Series Q, FA 352, Box 1, Folder 8.

living in Brazilian cities was a possible time bomb that could be exploited by communist propaganda, he informed Rockefeller. "Genuine shortages of foodstuffs are developing," while "crop forecasts indicate that the food situation may deteriorate further in 1947." Meanwhile, rural workers leagues were forming, part of "the communist program to organize the large part of Brazilian labor that was practically ignored by others."[41]

The projected support for Brazilian agriculture centered on transferring elements of the agricultural revolution to Brazil and creating a cooperative program of credit and extension facilities to support small farmers. The non-profit AIA would serve as a catalyst in promoting mechanisms to assist farmers and rural works in all aspects of rural life through partnerships with local governments. Funding from local governments was to increase gradually, allowing the AIA to withdraw and shift its resources to other projects. The IBEC, on the other hand, would depend upon capital from U.S. and Brazilian investors to "set a pattern" for raising living standards in Brazil and other countries. The IBEC's six subsidiaries would be engaged in producing high-grade seeds and phosphates for fertilizer, facilitating transport for agricultural goods, creating vegetable gardens near large cities, hog raising, and producing condensed milk.[42]

"Financial support for the Brazil program would be provided by IBEC and whenever possible, in collaboration with Brazilian capital and such American private enterprise or individual capital as may be available."[43] During a November 1946 visit to Brazil that included a call of President Dutra, Rockefeller explained that "it is my hope to bring here the technical knowledge and managerial experience, together with capital, to cooperate with people here in undertaking projects in fields which are essential to the economic and social security of the country."[44] He assured state secretaries of agriculture that his purpose was to "found carefully worked out Brazilian companies, serving the public through increased

[41] Memo, "The Brazilian Situation," Simon G. Hanson to Nelson A. Rockefeller, Nov, 4, 1947, RAC, Nelson A. Rockefeller Personal Papers, RG 4, Series E, FA 341, Box 10, Folder 69.

[42] Joe Alex Morris, *Nelson Rockefeller: A Biography* (New York: Harper and Brothers, 1960), pp. 242, 243; *New York Times*, Jan. 10, 1947.

[43] "Memorandum on International Basic Economy Corporation," July 22, 1948, RCA, Office of Messrs. Rockefeller, RG 2F, FA 315, Box 1, Folder 8A.

[44] *New York Times*, Nov. 19, 1946, p. 27.

production at reasonable prices and contributing to rising standards of living."[45]

The AIA and the IBEC undertook several projects to establish credibility during their first three years of activities. The AIA responded vigorously to an outbreak of hog cholera in Brazil's southern states a month after its incorporation. With the nation's hog industry threatened with extinction by dwindling vaccine supplies and a shortage of foreign exchange to purchase new vaccine, the AIA conducted an emergency campaign to contain the disease. The association flew in a specialist on the disease who worked with Brazilian experts to devise rules and procedures for producing vaccine and other control measures.[46] The AIA also began experiments with fertilizer in Paraná, São Paulo, and Rio de Janeiro states on corn, soybeans, wheat, and alfalfa crops. Neighboring farmers (*fazendeiros*), extension workers and "agricultural leaders" observed the results, allowing the AIA to judge the experiments to have been "an important educational device." When trials expanded, the association engaged the cooperation of federal and state experimental stations. In 1948, the AIA contacted the USDA to experiment with various insecticides for controlling livestock parasites, a project fully discussed with Minister Carvalho. By the end of 1948, 35 herds were being sprayed. Project results appeared in *A Fazenda* magazine and a U.S. professional journal. The association also opened extension services in Santa Rita do Passo Quarto, São Paulo, and Belo Horizonte, Minas Gerais.[47]

A cooperative venture with Brazilian geneticists soon provided another opportunity to test Rockefeller's model. The IBEC began collaboration with Brazilian geneticists Antonio Secundino São José de Araujo and Gladstone Drummond. As noted earlier, Secundino was an early graduate of the Viçosa agricultural school and had advised the joint food commission during the war. Like Secundino, Drummond had earned an advanced

[45] "Speech by Nelson A. Rockefeller at a meeting of State Secretaries of Agriculture, Rio de Janeiro, Brazil, Nov. 20, 1946," RCA, RG 4, Series E, FAR 338, Box 145, Folder 1578.

[46] Dalrymple, *The AIA Story*, p. 17.

[47] TS, The American International Association for Economic and Social Development, "Annual Report 1948," Rockefeller archive, American Association for Economic and Social Development, RG IV3B2.11, Series 1, FA 079, Box 1, Folder 2; TS, John B. Griffing, Air View of the Forest," n.d, Rockefeller Archive, The American International Association for Economic and Social Development, RG IV3B2.11, Series 1, FA079, Box 2, Folder 12, p. 2.

degree in corn hybridization from Iowa State College. On September 19, 1945, Secundino and Drummond joined with Dr. Dee William Jackson, an economist supporting Rockefeller's Brazilian activities, John Ware, a chemist employed by General Mills, and Adylio Vitarelli, an agricultural technician, to create Agroceres Limitada, a company dedicated to advance experiments with hybrid corn. Soon thereafter, the IBEC invested the equivalent of US$108,000 to create a joint venture known as Sementes Agroceres, S.A., with the provision that Agroceres shareholders could eventually secure a majority holding in the firm. The IBEC would benefit from the company's sales in return for providing management services.[48]

Positive results came quickly. By 1949, the hybrid corn had proven its superiority over traditional varieties by withstanding a prolonged hot dry spell. Company director and Rockefeller confidant John B. Griffing explained that "the past dry season which has brought disaster to so many farmers has been a means of impressing everyone with the superior qualities of the hybrid." Responding to strong demand, the company planned to market 1,500 tons of seed for 1950, 50 times the amount harvested in 1948.[49]

The IBEC quickly ventured into other areas. Increasing hog production was the objective of a US$326,000 investment in another company founded by IBEC, S.A. Fomento Agro-Pecuário. Like Agroceres, this company's leadership benefited from experience obtained by the joint food commission and education imparted by the Viçosa agricultural school in the person of Ozaman Federico Marra. During the war, the CIAA had sponsored Viçosa graduate Marra for a year's study of U.S. agricultural practices in Delaware, Ohio, New Jersey, and New Hampshire. As supervisor of the company's Fazenda São Carlos, he explained that the company's purpose was "to show farmers that it is possible to

[48] Dalrymple, *The AIA Story*, p. 17; "Memorandum on International Basic Economy Corporation," July 22, 1948, RCA, Office of Messrs. Rockefeller, RG 2F, FA 315, Box 1, Folder 8A; "Roberto Andrade discursa em homenagem aos 70 anos da Agroceres," Dec. 15, 2015, http://www.robertoandrade.net.br/discurso-de-roberto-andrade-em-homenagem-a-agroceres/; Cobbs, *The Rich Neighbor Policy*, pp. 151–52; Jaine Menoncin, "O Caso Das Sementes Agroceres (1945–1960): Uma Abordagem Da História Ambiental," XVI Encontro Estadual de História da ANPUH-SC: História e Movimentos Sociais, June 7–10, 2016.

[49] "Nature's Frowns Give Hybrid Chance to Prove its Quality," Encl. to TS, John F. Root, U.S. Consulate São Paulo "The International Basic Economy Corporation," May 9, 1949, USNA, RG 166, FAS, Narrative Reports, Brazil, Box 536.

have modern hog raising without tremendous capital." The farm set out to demonstrate how electrified fences, drinking troughs, and automatic feeders could improve efficiency. It introduced Sudan grass grown from seeds imported from the United States as a nutrient, along with soy, mucuna beans (*Mucuna pruriens*), and hybrid corn.[50] Six of the major meatpacking companies in Brazil found the prospect of better hog raising attractive, subscribing to 86 and 2/3 percent of the preferred stock and 33 and 1/3 percent of the common stock.[51] At a 1947 meeting with stockholders, Director Quartim Barbosa explained that the company's main objective was "to transfer scientific technique into routine: thus it can and will be copied because the farmer can see results."[52]

The IBEC also began to implement Rockefeller's vision of capitalist agriculture by promoting improved storage facilities and mechanization through contacts with U.S. businesses. In an agreement with Cargill Incorporated of Minneapolis, Minnesota, the IBEC arranged for establishment of Cargill Agricola e Comercial, dedicated to the purchase, storage, and sale of grain. Cargill and the IBEC each provided 33 and 1/3 percent of the company's capital of US$979,000, with the remaining one-third of stock offered to Brazilian investors. The company's president was a professional agronomist with access to financial resources. By July 1949, the company had constructed two grain storage elevators with a capacity of 150,000 bushels of corn to serve farmers in northwestern Paraná and an adjacent section of São Paulo. Cargill's storage facilities utilized elevators and tubes that raised the grain forty meters high, allowing gravity to support outflow. The elevators also contained drying and shelling elements for accelerated processing and sale of corn as well as fumigation equipment to reduce weevil damage. The Cargill elevators competed with established grain dealers who processed stocks

[50] From *Diário de São Paulo,* Feb 17, 1949, translated and enclosed to TS, John F. Root, U.S. Consulate São Paulo "The International Basic Economy Corporation," May 9, 1949, USNA, RG 166, FAS, Narrative Reports, Brazil, Box 536.

[51] "Memorandum on International Basic Economy Corporation," July 22, 1948, RCA, Office of Messrs. Rockefeller, RG 2F, FA 315, Box 1, Folder 8A.

[52] Memo, Dee W. Jackson, "Semi-Monthly Progress Report," Nov. 21, 1947, RCA, RG III 4, Series B, FA 339, Box 12, Folder 124. Emphasis in original.

manually. They protested the Cargill installations as American "intervention." Communists, meanwhile, denounced the elevators as "Rockefeller Capitalist Infiltration."[53]

The IBEC also worked closely with major U.S. agricultural implement manufacturer to establish a company dedicated to employing agricultural machinery in virtually all functions of agriculture. The Empresa Mecanização Agricola (EMA) was designed to provide equipment for clearing, destumping, plowing, terracing, cultivation, and harvesting. Capital for the company was equally allocated between the IBEC, which provided 50 percent of funds, and private Brazilian and U.S. subscribers. Extensive consultations with International Harvester resulted in contracting a technician experienced in land clearing to prepare an operations plan. By mid-1949, the company had imported tractors, seeding and harvesting machines, and disk cultivators, and set up headquarters in Jacarezinho, Paraná, through agreement with the Paraná government. Over 500 *alqueires* (approximately 1,210 hectares) of land were cleared for planting, and farmers in the region were buying tractors to work the cleared land.[54]

The company's initial impact on the region was small, but the changes it introduced hinted that mechanization could bring about major social and economic changes. A local coffee grower contracted the company to care for 200,000 coffee trees, using a tractor to plow between rows of 3,000 trees per day. The tractor did the work of 15 laborers, reducing labor costs but also raising the question of the livelihood of the displaced workers. The company employed ten graduates of local agricultural schools as tractor operators, maintenance workers, and mechanics.[55]

[53] TS, John F. Root, U.S. Consulate São Paulo "The International Basic Economy Corporation," May 9, 1949, Enclosure 3, Enclosure 3, USNA, RG 166, FAS, Narrative Reports, Brazil, Box 536; TS, Oscar C. Moore, U.S. Consulate São Paulo, "Recent Agricultural Trends in Northwestern Parana," July 8, 1949, USNA, RG 166, FAS, Narrative Reports, Brazil, 1946–1949, Box 518.

[54] TS, John F. Root, U.S. Consulate São Paulo "The International Basic Economy Corporation," May 9, 1949, Enclosure 2, USNA, RG 166, FAS, Narrative Reports, Brazil, Box 536.

[55] TS, John F. Root, U.S. Consulate São Paulo "The International Basic Economy Corporation," May 9, 1949, Enclosure 2, USNA, RG 166, FAS, Narrative Reports, Brazil, Box 536. IBEC also explored the possibility of funding a packing plant, erecting a manioc starch mill, and improving wheat production. It also invested US$342,000 in a one-year cattle fattening program in cooperation with Frigorifico Cruzeiro, a company

Rockefeller was not content with the activities of the AIA and IBEC dedicated to increasing the productivity of Brazilian agriculture. With cooperation of the governor of Minas Gerais, Rockefeller instituted an extension service under AIA auspices to assist small farmers with the intricacies of modern agriculture. The Associação de Crédito e Assistência Rural (ACAR) stemmed from an agreement between Rockefeller and Milton Campos, governor of Minas Gerais, and took effect on January 1, 1949. Modeled loosely after the New Deal's Farm Security Administration and jointly financed by equal contributions of the AIA and the state government, the association was an autonomous organization that worked closely local organizations and state governments and cooperated with state health and sanitation programs. ACAR provided low-interest credit accompanied by technical assistance that guided the farmers' use of the loans, unlike existing state agricultural services that responded to requests for technical assistance from farmers and ranchers. As in other activities of the AIA and IBEC, ACAR benefited from resources of the Viçosa agricultural school (renamed the Universidade Rural do Estado de Minas Gerais in 1948) which taught a "theoretical-practical" course in late 1948 to train agronomists and technicians to support ACAR's mission. Many technicians at nearby research facilities had also studied at Viçosa, some of whom had "very good training at some of our Middle Western agricultural colleges" in the opinion of a visitor. The Minas Gerais government contributed to the program's success when its Caixa Econômica agreed to provide mortgage loans at six percent interest and non-mortgage loans at eight percent.[56]

During its first year, ACAR opened offices in four *municipios* from where an ACAR supervisor and a home economics specialist reached out

directed by Teodoro Quartim Barbosa, a consultant to IBEC. Ltr. From Joe Jenne, Dec. 2, 1947, RCA, Office of Mssrs. Rockefeller, RG 2, Series F, FA 315, Box 1, Folder 8; "Memorandum on International Basic Economy Corporation," July 22, 1948, RCA, Office of Messrs. Rockefeller, RG 2F, FA 315, Box 1, Folder 8A.

[56] José Paulo Ribeiro, *A saga da extensão rural em Minas Gerais* (São Paulo: Annablume, 2000), p. 23; Associação de Crédito e Asistência Rural, *Resenha Estatística, Periodo 1949–1957* (NP: n.d.p, n.d.), Quadro II; TS, "Memorando para o Doutor Ary Torres," n.d., USNA, RG 286, USAID Mission to Brazil Executive Office, Entry #P221, Central Subject Files, Container 5; Memo, James G. Maddox to Mr. Robert Hudgens, Apr. 18, 1949, RCA, Office of Mssrs. Rockefeller, RG 2, Series F, FAR 315, Box 1; TS, The American International Association for Economic and Social Development, "Annual Report 1948," p. 24.

to farmers and their families, traveling by jeep throughout the countryside. In that year, ACAR provided technical services to 40 families, held 242 meetings, assisted in the medical treatment of another 1,768, and even oversaw the installation of seven privies. By the end of 1949, ACAR had arranged for 67 loan approvals and made home visits to 125 borrowers and non-borrowers. The success of the association's two years in operation led to its expansion into an additional four *municipios* in 1950.[57]

The arrangement demonstrated how small farmers could enter capitalist agriculture. In a typical case outlined in the association's second annual report, a small farmer used a loan from ACAR to replace his oxen for newer animals, clear his pasture more extensively, plant hybrid corn, and improve his potable water supply. The ACAR supervisor and the home economics specialist visited his farm regularly, and after one year the farmer paid back the loan in full as well as a previous debt. The results convinced the farmer that he could continue to maintain his family on the plot he was working.[58]

[57] Associação de Crédito e Asistência Rural, *Segundo Relatório Anual da ACAR* 1950 (Belo Horizonte, MG: ACAR, n.d.), p. 9.

[58] ACAR, *Segundo Relatório Anual,* p. 9.

CHAPTER 17

The New Model: Capital and Technical Assistance

The presence of private U.S. investment and the technical assistance provided by Rockefeller's programs marked the beginning of a new U.S. model to support Brazilian agricultural development. Brazil's economic development prior to the onset of the Cold War. Programs sponsored by Nelson Rockefeller and various U.S. government agencies were supplemented by the strong presence of private U.S. capital. Three already established private U.S. firms—Anderson Clayton, Swift, and Armour—maintained a strong presence in their respective sectors. Cotton processor Anderson Clayton sustained its position as one of the leading processors and exporters of Brazilian cotton with benefits of favorable financing from the government. The company's exports accounted for 33% of cotton exports from the port of Santos in 1946 and 31% of a reduced crop in 1947. It also broadened its presence in the commodities market by creating a coffee brokerage in 1949. For the domestic market, the company complemented its already established offerings of cooking oil and margarine with "the most delicious peanut butter you've ever tasted," Pasta de Amendoim Saude.[1] Its efforts were apparently successful, despite

[1] *Jornal de Notícias*, June 16, 1946, p. 7; *Fundamentos: Revista de Cultura Moderna*, Vol. 3, No. 2 (Aug. 1948), p. 185; *Correio da Manhã*, Aug. 3, 1949, p. 6; *Brazilian Business*, Vol. 30, No. 11 (Nov. 1950), p. 45.

E. R. Downes, *Brazilian Agricultural Development, 1890–1950*,
https://doi.org/10.1007/978-3-031-76992-4_17

the travails of the postwar cotton crop. The value of Anderson Clayton's investment in Brazil rose markedly–from US$27 million in 1946 to US$35 million by mid-1949.[2] By mid-1949 the company was exploring purchasing land in Mato Grosso to introduce mechanized cotton cultivation.[3]

U.S. investment in Brazil's beef cattle industry benefited from greater availability of cattle—up from an estimated 46. 3 million in 1945 to 53.7 million in 1950,[4] reflecting the end of wartime restrictions on slaughtering. Ranchers pressured the Ministry of Agriculture to allow increased distribution of beef and consumption of beef returned to prewar levels.[5] The industry remained saddled, though, by price controls, taxes to finance operation of the Fresh Meat Department [Departamento de Carne Verde] of Rio Grande do Sul, and the need for export licenses.[6] In addition to exporting frozen beef, Armour and Swift offered canned meat for local markets, including deviled and canned ham, beef with chili, cattle tongue, liver pate, and Vienna sausage. Profits for Armour's plant in 1948 stood at US$2.2 million for 1947 and slightly less than US$ two million for 1948.[7]

U.S. capital also began its venture into mechanization of Brazilian agriculture with construction of an International Harvester tractor factory in Santo André, outside São Paulo. The plant was dedicated to assembling tractors, trucks, and farm and road building equipment. International Harvester had a long sold imported equipment in Brazil, but the plant marked the company's first venture in assembling products within Brazil. Its presence marked the initiation of a domestic tractor industry, a venture that had gotten off to an uncertain start when the National Motors

[2] Anderson Clayton & Company, "Report to the President and Stockholders and Financial Statements, Year Ending July 31, 1945," p. 12; "Year Ending July 31, 1949," p. 20, Anderson Clayton Special Collection, M.D. Anderson Library, Univ. of Houston.

[3] *A Manhã*, Aug. 16, 1949, p. 9.

[4] *Conjunta Econômica*, Vol. 5, No. 7 (1951), p. 8.

[5] *Conjunta Econômica*, Vol. 5, No. 7 (1951), p. 6.

[6] TS, U.S. Consul Porto Alegre, "1949 Slaughter Season in Rio Grande do Sul....") Oct. 4, 1949, USNA RG 166, FAS, Narrative Reports, 1946–49, Box 524.

[7] "1949 Slaughter Season in Rio Grande do Sul"; *Brazilian Business*, Vol. 31, No. 7 (1949).

Factory [Fábrica Nacional de Motores] began producing trucks instead of farm tractors as envisioned by a January 1946 Decree-Law.[8]

Fully engaged with the reconstruction of Europe, the Truman administration prioritized the role of private capital in Latin American development, much to the disappointment of Brazilians who felt their wartime cooperation merited substantial financial support. Within this limitation, the United States advanced the notion that technical assistance could serve as a means of reshaping Brazil's development programs, including agriculture. The 1949 report of the Joint Brazilian-United States Technical Commission (the "Abbink Commission") identified the "improvement of agricultural production and of the transportation and commercial distribution of foodstuffs" as "one of Brazil's greatest problems." Initial meetings of the agricultural subcommittee recognized the need for "expansion of research and educational activities, particularly to attract and train competent technicians in agriculture."[9] The commission's final report cited the need for improving agricultural education in Brazil and for providing technical assistance for mechanization, soil and water conservation, fertilizer use, irrigation, plant and animal improvement, insect and disease control, forestry, rural property organization, rural industrialization, and commercial development of economically important products.[10]

Going beyond exhortations required a high-level commitment to action supported by allocation of official U.S. resources, a controversial proposition given the stridency of U.S. insistence on promoting private capital to meet Brazil's development needs. The possibility of greater U.S. assistance did arise, however, with the President Truman's 1949 inaugural address, prepared amidst growing fears of Soviet expansionism and potential East–West conflict. On the eve of the speech, a former staff member of Rockefeller's CIAA Brazil team convinced Truman to include a commitment to "making the benefits of our scientific advances and industrial

[8] *Brazilian Business*, Vol. 26, No 3 (1946), pp. 22–24.

[9] TS, John C. Cady, U.S. Embassy Rio de Janeiro, "Summary of the Work of the United States Delegation for Period Ending September 30, 1948," Oct. 14, 1948, USNA, RG 166, FAS, Narrative Reports, 1946–49, Box 518.

[10] Joint Brazil-United States Technical Commission, *Report of the Joint Brazil-United States Technical Commission with appendixes approved by the Central Cammission [sic] at Rio de Janeiro, Brazil, February 7, 1949* (Washington, D.C.: Dept. of State, Division of Publications, Office of Public Affairs: 1949), pp. 201–2.

progress available for the improvement and growth of underdeveloped areas." Ben Hardy urged Truman to utilize a "powerful weapon in the present struggle.... the employment of America's immense technological resources through the medium of Technical Cooperation."[11] Truman accepted the idea and pledged that the United States would combat the "false philosophy" of communism and "undertake new projects to strengthen a free world." He announced that U.S. "business, private capital, agriculture, and labor" stood ready to "help the free peoples of the world, through their own efforts, to produce more food, more clothing, more materials for housing, and more mechanical power to lighten their burdens."[12] Implementing the declaration, which became known as "Point Four"—the fourth course of action spelled out in Truman's speech—languished for 18 months by Congressional and State Department opposition. The program became law on June 5, 1950, but with a miniscule $35 million budget.

The new U.S. framework for international cooperation offered Brazilian and U.S. advocates of Brazilian development the opportunity to explore closer ties. In mid-April 1950, the former U.S. head of the Abbink Commission suggested to Assistant Secretary of State for Inter-American Affairs, Edward G. Miller, that joint technical talks on Brazilian development "if possible, be reconstituted in some form because the Brazilians badly need help."[13] Following passage into law of the Point Four program, the U.S. delegation met on August 31, 1950, with their Brazilian counterparts, including prominent Brazilian economists Eugenio Gudin and Otávio Gouveia de Bulhões, former chief of the Brazilian delegation to the joint technical commission. The proposal presented to the Brazilian delegation cited language of the Point Four law allowing for establishment of a joint commission for economic development at the request of a foreign government. Technical skills to be

[11] Ben Hardy, "Use of U.S. Technological Resources as a Weapon in the Struggle with International Communism," RCA, Nelson A. Rockefeller Personal Papers, RG III 4, Series O, FA 350, Box 39, Folder 357.

[12] Truman's Inaugural Address, January 20, 1949, https://www.trumanlibrary.org/whistlestop/50yr_archive/inagural20jan1949.htm

[13] "Memorandum by Mr. John U. Abbink of the Interim Office for Technical Cooperation and Development to the Assistant Secretary of State for Inter-American Affairs (Miller)," *FRUS, The United Nations; The Western Hemisphere, Volume II*. Document 399.

represented by U.S. members on such a commission would include an economist skilled in finance who would serve as the U.S. delegation chief, as well as experts in transportation, agriculture and engineering. The unsigned U.S. note further suggested that the United States would respond favorably to a note the "Brazilian Government might wish to send the government of the United States requesting the establishment of a Joint United-States-Brazilian Economic Development Commission."[14]

Aside from the seeking to sustain Brazil's political support for an ever-challenging global political environment, retain access to strategic materials, and respond to continual diplomatic pressure from Dutra's ministers, the embassy's submission of this proposal may have influenced by lobbying by Nelson Rockefeller. Rockefeller passed through Brazil in early July on a mission to review the progress of his AIA and IBEC ventures. Only a few weeks before, he had endorsed Point Four during congressional hearings considering its passage.[15] Once in Brazil, he interacted with the "upper bourgeois of carioca and Paulista society," including President Dutra and U.S. Ambassador Herschel Vespasian Johnson, as a guest speaker at the inauguration of the Museu da Arte [Art Museum] of São Paulo on July 5, 1950. The following week Rockefeller was honored at a "magnificent dinner" in Rio de Janeiro attended by President Dutra, Foreign Minister Fernandes, Ambassador Johnson, and other influential Brazilians. Prior to departing, Rockefeller publicly declared that the United States "had a proposal" that would allow for the "continuation of the collaboration that proved advantageous in the war" consisting of "a plan of cooperation that would profoundly interest Brazilians and Americans." Rockefeller personally briefed President Truman on July 24 on impressions gained from the trip and conversed about the future of Point Four.[16] Deliberations between U.S. and Brazilian delegations eventually led to a request for formation of a joint development commission through an exchange of notes on December 19, 1950.

[14] Enclosure 1 to TS, Sheldon T. Mills, "Second Meeting of the Brazilian Government-Embassy Informal Group," Sept. 6, 1950, USNA, RG 16, Records of the FAS, Narrative Reports, 1940–1954, Box 4.

[15] Robert Carlyle Beyer, "Point Four and Latin America, " *University of Miami Law Review*, June 1, 1950.

[16] *Jornal de Noticias,* July 7, 1950, p. 7; *Diário Carioca*, July 6, 1950, p. 2; July 11, 1950, p. 6; *Diário de Noticias,* July 8, 1850, p. 1; Reich, *The life of Nelson A. Rockefeller*, p. 448.

The push to improve the production and productivity of Brazil's agriculture during the Dutra administration registered limited successes, including advances stemming from the promotion of non-traditional food crops. Peanut production increased markedly as the government encouraged farmers to shift from planting cotton to peanuts following three consecutive years of below average cotton yields.[17] Soybean production received federal support in April 1947 through a plan announced by Minister Carvalho.[18] A soybean processing plant opened that year in São Paulo, and the 1948 soybean crop totaled an estimated 690,000 bushels, a nearly five-fold increase over the amount harvested in 1946.[19] The average production of 13 major crops (excluding coffee) between 1945 and 1949 increased an average of over 33% above the average produced during 1940–44. Of these, peanuts registered the greatest increase (180%), followed by wheat (55%), sweet potatoes (51%), manioc, (44%), English potatoes (32%), sugar cane (28%), rice (26%), and tobacco (21%). Only the average production of cotton, beset by heavy rain, additional taxes, insect attacks and the migration of farm workers to urban areas, fell (-37%) when compared with that of the previous period[20] (See Fig. 17.1).

Increases in production were achieved largely by using ever greater areas of land to cultivate crops. The average land area for growing 13 major crops between 1945 and 1949 expanded by more than 38% over the average area planted in the same crops during the wartime years[21] (See Fig. 17.2). All crops listed here, except corn, coffee, and cotton, registered major increases in cultivated area. Only one—cotton—registered a decrease in area cultivated. Correlating the two indices—averaged increased production versus average increased planting area—suggests that most increases were positively related to increases in planting area. (See Fig. 17.2). Only peanuts, wheat, sweet potatoes, and sugar cane registered average production levels higher than the average increases in

[17] *Foreign Crops and Markets*, Vol. 57 (1948), p. 286.

[18] *O Jornal*, May 4, 1947, p. 6.

[19] *Foreign Crops and Markets*, Vol. 57 (1948), p. 463.

[20] *Foreign Crops and Markets*, Vol. 55 (1947), p. 110; Vol. 58, p. 473.

[21] Calculated from Table 4, in Dwight R. Bishop, *Brazil: Agricultural Production and Trade Statistics* (Washington, DC: U.S. Dept. of Agriculture, Office of Foreign Agricultural Relations, 1951), p. 4.

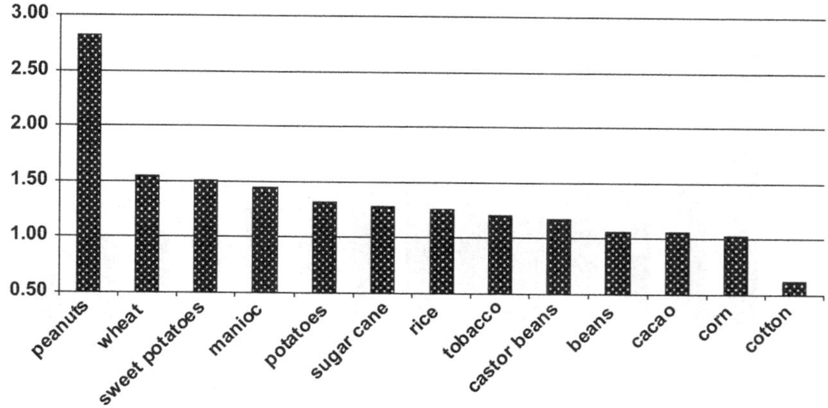

Fig. 17.1 Average increases in production for various crops, 1945–49 versus 1940–44 (Average production 1940–44 = 1.00) (*Source* Calculated from Tables 6, in Dwight R. Bishop, *Brazil: Agricultural Production and Trade Statistics* (Washington, DC: U.S. Dept. of Agriculture, Office of Foreign Agricultural Relations, 1951), p. 6)

planting area. For the remainder of the crops listed here (potatoes, rice tobacco, castor beans, cacao, and corn), planting crops in greater areas yielded less (or nearly equal, in the case of corn) product per hectare. These declines in productivity for major crops suggest that few improvements in techniques accompanied the opening of new lands, as noted in a 1950 analysis: "We planted a larger area and we had a bigger production, [but with] a small decline in yield per hectare."[22]

These data suggest that progress in integrating key elements of the agricultural revolution into Brazil's agriculture from 1945 to 1950 made little headway. Implementation of plans for mechanizing agriculture developed during the war moved forward slowly. Reaching higher levels of mechanization remained stymied by the lack of a domestic tractor manufacturing capability, subjecting the supply of tractors and spare parts to the volatility of Brazil's trade balances. By 1950, imports raised the number of tractors to 8,372, a substantial increase over the 3,380 reported in the 1946 survey, but mechanization reached only a small

[22] *Conjuntura Econômica*, Vol. 5, No. 1 (1951), p. 6.

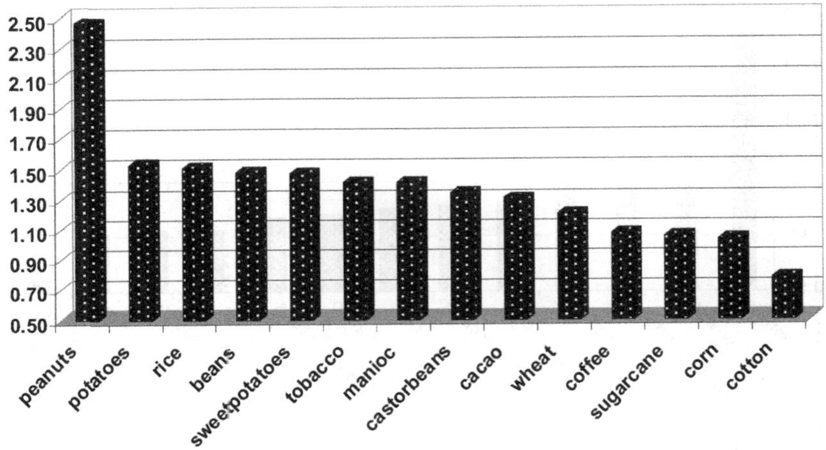

Fig. 17.2 Average increases in area cultivated for specific crops, 1945–49 Compared to average 1940–44 plantings (1940–44 average—1.00) (*Source* Calculated from Table 4, in Dwight R. Bishop, *Brazil: Agricultural Production and Trade Statistics* (Washington, DC: U.S. Dept. of Agriculture, Office of Foreign Agricultural Relations, 1951), p. 4)

percentage of farms. Seventy-three percent of all farms operated with only humans employing hand-operated tools. Steel plows and even wood plows were absent from three-fourths of the farms (Fig. 17.3).[23]

The push for mechanization had to overcome both resource and social barriers. Government efforts to encourage mechanization through the rural engineering course at Fazenda Ipenema yielded only a trickle of graduates—80 students completed the course by the end of 1950, including some from neighboring countries.[24] Moreover, many large landowners refused to make the capital investment required to mechanize their establishments, content to have sharecroppers and day laborers perform farm tasks via primitive methods. A large plantation owner in

[23] Fundação Instituto Brasileiro De Geografia e Estatística, *Estatísticas Históricas do Brasil Séries Econômicas, Demográficas e Sociais: Séries Estatísticas Retrospectivas,* Vol. 3 (Rio de Janeiro: IBGE.

1987), p. 282; G. Edward Schuh, *The Agricultural Development of Brazil* (New York: Praeger, 1970), pp. 282–283.

[24] *Correio da Manhã*, Mar. 2, 1951, p. 11.

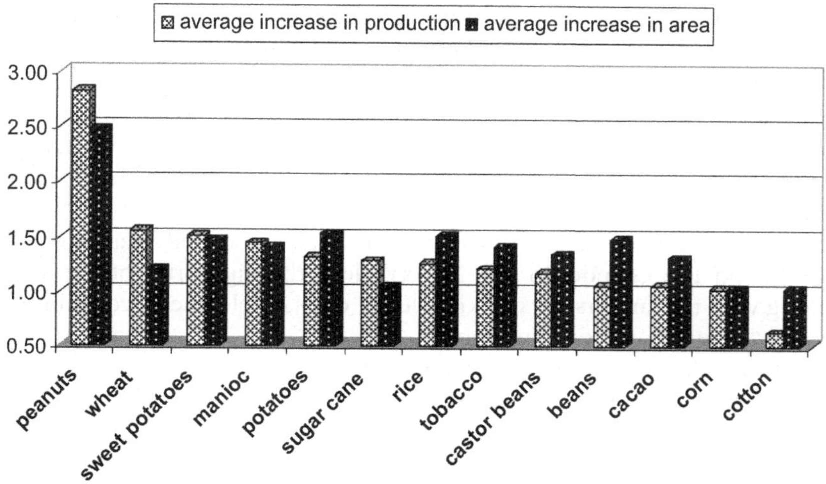

Fig. 17.3 Average increases in production versus average increases in cultivated area for specific crops, 1945–49 (1940–44 averages compared to 1945–49 averages) (*Source* Calculated from Tables 4 and 6, in Dwight R. Bishop, *Brazil: Agricultural Production and Trade Statistics* (Washington, DC: U.S. Dept. of Agriculture, Office of Foreign Agricultural Relations, 1951), pp. 4, 6)

São Paulo, Paraná, and Goiás expressed such sentiments when interviewed by a São Paulo newspaper in 1949. Jeremia Lunardelli, owner of over one million coffee trees and known as the "king of coffee," explained that most of his coffee crop was cultivated by tenant farmers working "exclusively with hoes and rakes drawn by animals, oxen, or even human power." Without understanding that mechanization could generate greater productivity, Lunardelli reasoned that "mechanization must be subordinated to economic necessities."[25]

Further complicating efforts to raise productivity was the scarcity and high cost of fertilizer. Brazil depending heavily upon imports of all three varieties of fertilizer (nitrate, phosphate, and potassium), and imports

[25] Harold M. Clements, *The Mechanization of Agriculture in Brazil: A Sociological Study of Minas Gerais* (Gainesville, FL: Univ. of Florida Press, 1969), p. 55; TS, U.S. Consul General, São Paulo, "Views of Leading Brazilian 'Fazendeiro' on Agriculture in Brazil and a Description of His Fazendas," Apr. 25, 1949, USNA, RG 166, FAS, Narrative Reports, Box 535.

made up 94% of nitrogen and 88% of phosphate fertilizers employed in Brazil in 1950. Along with 23,000 tons of imported potassium fertilizer, Brazil imported a total of 81,796 tons of fertilizer that year. The high costs of the imported fertilizer prohibited its use by most Brazilian farmers, prompting the Abbink commission to identify "the lack of adequate supplies of commercial fertilizers at costs farmers can afford to pay" as a major deficiency. A domestic fertilizer industry, small "when compared with the necessities of the country," operated plants in São Paulo and Rio Grande do Sul. Nevertheless, the high price of fertilizer, along with the farmers' lack of knowledge of its employment, contributed to its "insignificant consumption."[26]

Finally, the continuing lack of adequate transportation facilities diminished benefits from increasing area devoted to crops. The U.S. Embassy in Rio de Janeiro reported in December 1945 that the planned expansion of planting areas for corn and other would not necessarily result in greater supply. Much of the increase in areas planted in corn "has been at points too far in the interior to move to markets with normal transportation facilities," while surpluses of rice were "likely to develop again this year at points in Central Brazil too far from ports…."[27]

By contrast, intensification of the biological component of the agricultural revolution began to make headway, especially, as noted, with development of hybrid corn. Research on "biological" topics received almost half the resources dedicated to research between 1940 and 1949. Research increased on potatoes and vegetables, while coffee, citrus, sugar cane, and cotton garnered the highest commitments among crops.[28] Research initiated in 1942 to develop an improved cotton derived from two U.S.-grown varieties proceeded at the Instituto Agronômico de Campinas.[29] Research begun at the turn of the century on improving

[26] Fundação Instituto Brasileiro de Geografia e Estatística, *Estatísticas históricas,* Vol. 3, p. 305; U.S. Department of State, *Report of the Joint Brazil-United States Technical Commission,* p. 71; *Conjuntura Econômica,* Vol. 4, No. 8 (1950), pp. 11–13.

[27] Memo A-1589, Secretary of State, Dec. 27, 1945, in USNA, RG 166, FAS Narrative Reports 1946–49 Brazil, Box 518.

[28] R.E. Evenson, "Observations on Brazilian agricultural research and productivity," in Levon Yeganiantz, ed., *Brazilian Agriculture and Agricultural Research* (Brasilia: EMBRAPA, 1984), pp. 250–251.

[29] Results—that eventually proved unsatisfactory– would not be determined until 1956. See O. S. Neves, P. A. Cavaleri, I. L. Gridi-Papp, C. A. M. Ferraz, "Melhoramento Das Variedades Paulistas De Algodão.

soybeans garnered federal sponsorship at the Instituto Agrônomico do Sul in 1948, and trials began at the experimental station in Pelotas, Rio Grande do Sul.[30]

Conclusion

In the five years after World War II, Brazil reordered its economic priorities. Government support for Brazilian agriculture took second place to industrialism as developmentalist strategies gradually replaced the classic liberal approach adopted immediately after the war.[31] This strategy sought to transform Brazil from an "essentially agricultural" to predominantly industrial. Consequently, agriculture received little more than token attention from a federal government. Agricultural production grew far more slowly than industrial output, and even fell nearly one percent on a per capita basis between 1940–42 and 1950–52.[32]

Brazilian officials sought U.S. assistance for its development plans based upon the belief—ultimately proved mistaken—that the United States was willing to finance Brazilian growth in gratitude for Brazil's wartime support. The Dutra administration obtained only US$136 million in U.S. financial support in two loans in 1946 and 1947, despite the Itamaraty's 1946 request for a five-year, US$ one billion loan. A 1949

Criação Da Iac-12," *Bragantia-Boletim Científico do Instituto Agronômico de Estado de S. Paulo*, Vol. 28, No. 24 (Aug. 1969).

[30] João Rui Jardim Freire, Francisco De Jesus Vernetti, "A Pesquisa Com Soja, A Seleção De Rizóbio E A Produção De Inoculantes No Brasil." http://www.fepagro.rs.gov.br/upload/1398909703_art_14.pdf.

[31] On the transition from a liberal to a developmentalist approach by the Dutra government, see Luhan Martins Reigoto, "Governo Dutra: cenário externo, debate interno e política econômica (1946–1951)," XII Congresso Brasileiro de História Econômica & 13ª Conferência Internacional de História de Empresas.

Governo Dutra: cenário externo, debate interno e política econômica (1946–1951)," www.abphe.org.br/congresso/xii-congresso-niteroi/resultados. See also Ricardo Bielschowsky, "Brazilian Economic Thought (1945–1964) -The Ideological Cycle Of Developmentalism," (Diss., Univ. of Leicester (1985); and Fausto Saretta, "A Política Econômica Brasileira 1946/1950," *Revista de Sociologia e Política*, No. 4/5 (1995) and Paulo R. Beskow, "Agricultura e política agrícola no contexto brasileiro da industrialização do pós-guerra (1946–1964)," *Estudos Sociedade e Agricultura*, 12, April 1999: pp. 56–79.

[32] Data from *A Industria de Alimentação no Brasil* (Rio de Janeiro, CCN IBTR, FGV, 1966), cited in Schuh, *The Agricultural Development of Brazil*, p. 75.

U.S. visit by President Dutra resulted in a mere US$14.5 million credit at the Export–Import bank.[33]

Private U.S. actors attempted to compensate for diminished official U.S. government support and transfer elements of the agricultural revolution to Brazil in support of U.S. global political objectives, but resources were limited and results, by 1950, were uncertain. U.S. private investors sustained positions in production and processing of beef cattle and cotton while expanding a presence in the Brazilian marketplace. The construction of a tractor assembly plant and grain storage silos funded by U.S. private capital suggested a more prominent role for private U.S. investment in Brazil's future agricultural development. However, neither Brazilian nor U.S. advocates of Brazil's agricultural development could harness the resources necessary to effect fundamental changes. By 1950, it was clear that official US. and Brazilian efforts were more rhetorical than substantive even as production grew from the stimulus of increased internal demand.

[33] See Stanley E. Hilton, "Brazil's International Economic Strategy, 1945–1960: Revival of the German Option," *The Hispanic American Historical Review*, Vol. 66, No. 2 (May 1986), pp. 287–318.

Bibliography

Archives and Collections of Private Papers

Anderson, Clayton and Company Collection, Houston Metropolitan Research Center, Houston, Texas.

Merwin L Bohan papers, Harry S. Truman Presidential Library, Independence, Missouri.

John Casper Branner Papers, Stanford University Archives, Palo Alto, California.

Brown University Opening the Archives: Documenting U.S.-Brazil Relations, 1960s–80s [online].

William Clayton Papers, Rice University Manuscript Collection, Houston, Texas.

Domício da Gama Papers, Instituto Histórico e Geográfico Brasileiro, Rio de Janeiro.

Itamaratí Historical Archive, Rio de Janeiro, Brazil.

Ildefonso Simões Lopes Archive, Centro de Pesquisa e Documentação de História Contemporânea do Brasil (CPDOC), Fundação Getúlio Vargas, Rio de Janeiro.

Minutes of the Mesa de Curadores, Instituto Evangélico, Lavras, Minas Gerais.

Nilo Peçanha Archive, Museu da República, Rio de Janeiro.

Epitácio Pessoa Archive, Instituto Geográfico e Histórico Brasileiro, Rio de Janeiro.

Rockefeller Archive Center, Sleepy Hollow, New York.

Peter Henry Rolfs Archive, University of Florida Archives, Gainesville, Florida.

G. Edward Schuh Papers, University of Minnesota Libraries, St. Paul, Minnesota.

E. R. Downes, *Brazilian Agricultural Development, 1890–1950*, https://doi.org/10.1007/978-3-031-76992-4

Secretaria da Agricultura, Industria, Terras, Viacão e Obras Públicas, Minas Gerais, paper and account books, Public Archive, State of Minas Gerais, Belo Horizonte, MG.
Raul Soares Archive, Centro de Pesquisa e Documentação de História Contemporânea do Brasil Social, Fundação Getúlio Vargas, Rio de Janeiro.
Walter Tennyson Swingle Collection, University of Miami.
Juarez Távora Archive. Centro de Pesquisa e Documentação de História Contemporânea do Brasil (CPDOC), Fundação Getúlio Vargas, Rio de Janeiro.
U.S. Central Intelligence Agency, various reports [online].
U.S. Department of Agriculture, Record Group 166, Foreign Agricultural Service, U.S. National Archives.
U.S. Department of State, Record Group 59, Diplomatic Correspondence, Brazil, U.S. National Archives.
U.S. Department of State, Record Group 229, Office of Inter-American Affairs, US. National Archives.
U.S. National Archives, Record Group 286, U.S. Agency for International Development.
U.S. National Archives, Record Group 469, U.S. Foreign Assistance Agencies.
U.S. Navy, Office of Naval Intelligence, Record Group 45, Subject Group 1911–1927, U.S. National Archives.
Getúlio Vargas Archive, Centro de Pesquisa e Documentação de História Contemporânea, Fundação Getúlio Vargas, Rio de Janeiro.
Jerry Voorhis Papers, Claremont University, Claremont, California.

Official Government Publications

Amazonas. President do Estado. Mensagem Lida perante a assembleia legislativa ... 1914–1915. Manaus. Obras da Imprensa Pública.
Bahia. Governador do Estado. Mensagem apresentado ... Assembleia Geral Legislativa ... 1926. Bahia: Imprensa Official, 1926.
———. Secretaria de Agricultura, Industria, Commercio, Viação e Obras Públicas. Boletim Agricultura, Commercio e Industria.1917–1920.
Brazil. Câmara dos Deputados. Deputados Brasileiros 1826–1976. Brasilia: Senado Federal, Centro Grafica, 1976.
———. Câmara dos Deputados. Questões econômico-financeiras: Trabalhos do Deputado Paulista Dr. Cincinato Braga. São Paulo: Dupret & Co., 1915.
———. Conselho Nacional de Protecção aos Indios. Relatório dos trabalhos realizados de 1900–1906 pela Commissão de Linhas Telegraphicas do Estado de Matto Grosso. Rio de Janeiro: Imprensa Nacional, 1949.
———. Directoria de Estatística Commercial. Commercio Exterior do Brasil. 1913–1923, 1926–1930. Rio de Janeiro: Estatística Commercial.

———. Directoria Geral de Estatística. Estimativa da produccão do milho no Brazil (Safra de 1916–17). Rio de Janeiro: Typographia da Estatística, 1918.
———. Directoria Geral de Estatística. Recenseamento do Brazil 1920. Rio de Janeiro: Typographia da Estatística, 1922.
———. Directoria Geral de Estatística. Relatório, 1916–1917. Rio de Janeiro: Typographia da Estatística, 1920.
———. Directoria Geral de Estatística. Resumo de várias estatísticas econômo-financeiras. Rio de Janeiro: Typographia da Estatística, 1924.
———. Directoria Geral de Estatística. Valor das terras no Brazil segundo o censo agricola realizada em 1 de Setembro de 1920. Rio de Janeiro: Typografia de Estatística, 1924.
———. Escriptorio de Informações do Brazil em Pariz. Relatório dos Trabalhos, 1914. N.P.: n.p., nd.
———. Estrada de Ferro Central do Brasil. Relatório referente ao anno de 1915. Rio de Janeiro: E.F. Central do Brasil, 1917.
———. Instituto Brasileiro do Café. Bibliografia do Café. Brasilia: EMBRATER, 1977.
———. Instituto Brasileiro de Geografia e Estatística. Anuário Estatístico do Brasil. Various Years. Rio de Janeiro: Serviço Grafico, IBGE, n.d.
———. Inspectoria de Obras Contra as Seccas. Perfurações de Poços. Rio de Janeiro: Inspectoria de Obras Contra as Seccas, 1912.
———. Inspectoria Federal das Estradas. Estatística das Estradas de Ferro do Brasil Relativo ao anno de 1934. Araguary, MG: Ministerio de Viação e Obras Públicas, 1936.
———. Inspectoria Federal de Obras Contra as Seccas. Estradas de Rodagem e Carrocaveis construídas no Nordeste Brasileiro pela Inspectoria Federal do Obras Contra as Seccas nos annos 1919 a 1925. Rio de Janeiro: n.p., 1927.
———. Lloyd Brasileiro. Relatório … 1916. Rio de Janeiro: Jornal do Commercio, 1916.
———. Ministério da Agricultura, Industria e Commercio. Boletim.
———. Ministério da Agricultura. O Ministério da Agricultura no Governo de Getúlio Vargas (1930–1944). Rio de Janeiro: Ministério da Agricultura, 1945.
———. Ministerio da Agricultura, Industria e Commercio. Escola de Agricola annexa ao Posto Zootechnico Federal de "Pinheiro." São Paulo: Vanordem, 1912.
———. Ministerio da Agricultura, Industria e Commercio. Relatório. Various years.
———. Ministerio da Fazenda. Economical Data about Brazil, 1910–1928. Rio de Janeiro: Impr. Nac., 1929.
———. Ministerio das Relações Exteriores. Relatório. 1914–1930.

———. Ministerio do Trabalho, Industria e Commercio. Sociedades Mercantis autorizadas a funcionar no Brasil (1808–1946). Rio de Janeiro: Departamento Nacional de Industria e Commercio, 1947.

———. Serviço de Informações Agricola. 1 centenario do Ministerio da Agricultura, 1860–1960. Rio de Janeiro: Ministerio da Agricultura, 1960.

———. Serviço de Informações. Salários Ruraes: Inquérito organizado pelo Serviço de Inspeccão e Fomento Agricolas.... Rio de Janeiro: Ministerio da Agricultura, 1927.

———. Serviço de Inspeccão e Defesa Agricola. Questionarios sobre as condições da agricultura dos municipios do Estado de Goyaz. Rio de Janeiro: Serviço de Estatística, 1913.

———. Serviço de Inspeccão e Fomento Agricolas. Circulação dos produtos agricolas e custa da vida em relação aos artigos de alimentação, no Brasil, 1921–1923. Rio de Janeiro: Imprensa Nacional, 1925.

———. Serviço de Inspeccão e Fomento Agricolas. Estudo dos fatores da produccão nos municipios brasileiros e condições econômicas em relação aos artigos de alimentação, no Brasil, 1921–1923. Rio de Janeiro: Imprensa Nacional, 1922.

———. Serviço de Inspeccão e Fomento Agricolas. Estudo dos fatores da produccão nos municipios brasileiros e condições econômicas em cada um ... Municipio de Santa Luzia do Rio das Velhas, Minas Gerais. Rio de Janeiro: Imprensa Nacional, 1921.

———. Serviço de Inspeccão e Fomento Agricolas. Relatório. 1921–1930.

———. Serviço do Algodão. Relatório. 1920. Rio de Janeiro: Papelaria Americana, 1920.

———. Secretaria de Planejamento, Secretaria de Controle das Empresas Estatais (SEST), Relatório das Atividades de SEST 1981. N.P.: n.p.,n.d.

Ceará. Presidente do Estado. Mensagem apresentada a assembleia legislativo do Ceará ... 1917. N.P.: n.p., n.d.

Maranhão. Presidente do Estado. Mensagem apresentado ao congresso legislativo de Maranhão ... 1916. Maranhão: Imprensa Oficial, 1916.

Minas Gerais. A assistência a infância desvalida em Minas Gerais. Belo Horizonte: Imprensa Oficial, 1930.

———. Presidente do Estado. Mensagem dirigida pelo presidente do Estado ... 1915–1917. Belo Horizonte: Imprensa Oficial.

———. Secretaria da Agricultura do Estado de Minas Gerais. A agropecuária mineira: sua história, sua evolução. N.P.: Secretaria de Estado de Agricultura, 1979.

Organization of American States. Comitê Interamericano de desenvolvimento Agricola. Posse e uso da terra e desenvolvimento socio-economico do sector agricola, Brasil. Washington: Pan American Union, 1966.

Paraíba. Serviço do Algodão. Relatório da Delegacia do Serviço Federal do Algodão na Parhyba, apresentado ao Superintendente F. L. Alves Costa. Anno 1927. Paraíba: Imprensa Oficial, 1928.

Paraná. Presidente do Estado. Mensagem dirigida ao Congresso Legislativo do Estado ... 1916–1917. Curitiba: Typografia da A República.

———. Secretaria d'Estado dos Negócios, Fazenda, Agricultura e Obras Públicas. Relatório. 1916–1917. Curitiba: Typografia da A República.

Rio de Janeiro. Presidente do Estado. Mensagem apresentada a assembleia legislativa do estado do Rio de Janeiro.... 1917. Rio de Janeiro: N.P., n.d.

Rio Grande do Sul. Presidente do Estado. Mensagem a Assembleia de representantes do Estado de Rio Grande do Sul.... 1912–1930. Porto Alegre: A Federação, 1922–1930.

São Paulo. Departamento Estadual do Trabalho. Localizacão dos trabalhadores nacionaes. São Paulo: Typographia Brasil, 1917.

———. Instituto Agronômico do Estado de São Paulo em Campinas. Boletim. São Paulo: Diário Oficial, 1898.

———. Presidente do Estado. Presidente Altino Arantes. Mensagens 1916–1919. N. P.: N.p., n.d.

———. Secretaria da Agricultura. Desenvolvimento da agricultura paulista. São Paulo: Instituto de economia agricola, 1972.

Sergipe. Secretaria de Agricultura. Apogeu, crise e decadência da cultura algodoeira em Sergipe. Brasilia: Departamento de Informacão e Documentação, 1980.

United States. Bureau of Foreign and Domestic Commerce. Foreign Commerce and Navigation of the United States. 1914–1930. Washington: GPO.

———. Congress. House of Representatives. Report of the Federal Trade Commission on the Meat Packing Industry. Part II. Evidence of Combination Among Packers. H. Doc. 1297. 65th Cong. 2nd Sess. Washington: GPO, 1918.

———. Department of Agriculture. Yearbook. Various years. Washington: GPO.

———. Department of Agriculture, Bureau of Agricultural Economics. The World Cotton Situation: Foreign Cotton Production. Washington, DC: 1935.

———. Department of State. Foreign Relations of the United States.

———. Report of the Joint Brazil-United States Technical Commission Rio de Janeiro, Brazil, February 7, 1949 (Washington, DC: U.S. Department of State, 1949.

———. National Academy of Sciences, Science and Brazilian Development: Report of the Third Workshop on Contribution of Science and Technology to Development. Washington: National Academy of Sciences, 1969.

———. Senate, Committee on Foreign Relations, Subcommittee on the American Republics. Survey of the Alliance for Progress, The Problems of Agriculture. Washington, D.C: GPO, 1967.

Government Publications Cited by Author

Andrade Alves, Eliseu Roberto de and others. Pesquisa Agropecuária: Novos Rumos. Brasilia, DF: EMBRAPA, 1985.

———. Prosa com Eliseu: Entrevista a Jorge Duarte. Brasilia: EMPRAPA, 2018.

Baruch, Bernard M. U.S. War Industries Board. American Industry in the War: A Report of the War Industries Board. Richard H. Hipplehauser, ed. New York: Prentice-Hall, 1941.

Belleza, Newton. Evolução do Ministerio da Agricultura. Rio de Janeiro: Serviço de Informacão Agraria, 1955.

Branner, John C. Cotton in the Empire of Brazil: The Antiquity, Methods and Extent of its Cultivation; Together with Statistics of Exportation and Home Consumption. Washington: GPO, 1886.

Carmo, A. Gomes. Considerações históricas sobre a agricultura no Brasil. Rio de Janeiro: Serviço de Publicidade Agricola, 1939.

———. O estado moderno e a agricultura. Rio de Janeiro: Imprensa Nacional, 1908.

Coelho de Souza, William W. Brazil. Serviço do Algodão. Possibilidades da cultura algodoeira no Brasil. Rio de Janeiro: Imprensa Nacional, 1922.

Crandall, Roderic. Brazil. Inspectoria de Obras Contra as Seccas. Geografia, geologia, supprimento d'agua, transportes e açudagem nos estados orientaes do norte do Brasil: Ceará, Rio Grande do Norte, Parahyba. Rio de Janeiro: 1923: rpt: N.P.: Departamento Nacional de Obras Contra as Seccas, 1977.

Dantas, Garibaldi. Brazil. Ministerio da Agricultura. O algodão en São Paulo. São Paulo: Irmãos Spina, 1935.

Fernandes, Jose Maria. São Paulo. Secretaria da Agricultura, Commercio e Obras Públicas. Classificação commercial do algodão. São Paulo: Secretaria da Agricultura, 1923.

Gross, David R. "Agricultural Higher Education in Brazil, AID Working Paper No. 127." N.P.: U.S. Agency for International Development, 1989.

Hunnicutt, Benjamin H. Brazil Looks Forward. Rio de Janeiro: Instituto Brasileiro de Geografia e Estatística, 1945.

Martins, Dias. A producção das nossas terras. Rio de Janeiro: Directoria de Estatistica, 1915.

Redfield, Arthur. United States. Bureau of Foreign and Domestic Commerce. Economic Studies of Countries during the War: Brazil, A Study of Economic Conditions Since 1913. Washington: GPO, 1920.

Sales, Apolônio. Viagem aos Estados Unidos (Aspectos da produção agropecuário e da eletrificação rural). Rio de Janeiro: Serviço de Informação Agricola, Ministerio da Agricultura, 1944.

Schmidt, Carlos Borges and Jose Reis. Rasgando horizontes: A Secretaria da Agricultura no seu cinquentenario. São Paulo: Directoria de Publicidade Agricola, 1942.

Tavares, Heitor A. São Paulo. Secretaria da Agricultura, Commercio e Obras Públicas. Melhoramento do algodoeiro. São Paulo: Secretaria da Agricultura, 1923.

Torres Filho, Arthur. Brazil. Ministerio da Agricultura, Industria e Commercio. O ensino agricola no Brasil (Seu estado atual e a necessidade de sua reforma). Rio de Janeiro: Imprensa Nacional, 1926.

Tosta, Ignacio. Brazil. Câmara de Deputados. Organização agronômica: Parecer da Commissão de Finanças sobre o orçamento do Ministerio da Industria, Viação e Obras Públicas.... Rio de Janeiro: Cia. Litho-Typographia, 1905.

Von Motz, F. H. United States. Bureau of Foreign and Domestic Commerce. Markets for Agricultural Implements and Machinery in Brazil. Special Agents Series 140. Washington: GPO, 1917.

Waring, Geraldo A. Brazil. Inspectoria de Obras Contra as Seccas. Supprimento d'Agua no Nordeste do Brasil. Publication No. 23. Rio de Janeiro: Inspectoria de Obras Contra as Seccas, 1912.

Williams, Horace E. Brazil. Serviço Geológico e Mineralógico. Notas sobre a geologia e os recursos minerais do norte do Ceará. Bulletin 16. Rio de Janeiro: Imprensa Nacional, 1926.

Newspapers and Journals

O Agricultor. Lavras, Minas Gerais, 1922–1930.

Annaes da Sociedade Rural Brasileira.

Boletim [Ministerio de Agricultura, Industria e Commercio].

Boletim Mensal da Sociedade Mineira de Agricultura. Belo Horizonte, 1917.

Boletim da Sociedade de Agricultura do Paraná. Curitiba, 1918.

Brasil Agricola.

Brasil Industrial.

Brazil. New York, 1927–1930.

Brazil News. Liverpool, 1919–1928.

Brazilian - American.

Brazilian Business.

Bulletin of the Pan-American Union. Washington, 1910–1930.

Bulletin of the U. S. Chamber of Commerce, S. Paulo. São Paulo, 1921–1922.

Correio Brasiliense.

Correio Paulistano

O Criador Paulista.

O Estado de São Paulo.

A evolução agricola. São Paulo, 1906–1916.

Foreign Crops and Markets [U.S. Department of Agriculture]

A Industria e Commercio.

Jornal do Commercio.

A Lavoura.
A Manhã.
O Milho.
Monthly Bulletin of the British Chamber of Commerce in Brazil. Rio de Janeiro, 1919–1927.
New York Times.
O Observador Econômico e Financeiro.
O Progresso.
The Quarterly [American Chamber of Commerce for Brazil]. Rio de Janeiro, 1916–1917.
Revista de Comercio e Industria.
O Sul Rural.
The Times.

Dissertations and Other Sources

Abranches, Dunshee de. Brazil and the Munroe Doctrine. Rio de Janeiro: Imprensa Nacional. 1915.

———. A cultura do arroz e o proteccionismo agricola.... São Paulo: Topografia Brazil de Rothschild & Cia., 1916.

———. Expansão econômica e o commercio exterior do Brazil. Rio de Janeiro: Imprensa Nacional, 1915.

———. Governos e Congressos dos Estados Unidos do Brasil. São Paulo: n.p., 1918.

Albuquerque, Jose Medeiros E. O perigo americano: Conferência realizada no Teatro Phenix.... Rio de Janeiro: Leite, Ribeiro & Maurillo, 1919.

Alexander, Robert J. "Brazilian 'Tenentismo,'" Hispanic American Historical Review, 34 (1956), 229–42.

Amato Neto, João. "A indústria de máquinas agrícolas no Brasil- origem e evolução" Revista de Administração de Empresas, Vol. 25, No. 3 (July–Sept. 1985).

Almeida, Jose. A implantação da indústria automobilística no Brasil. Rio de Janeiro: Fundação Getúlio Vargas, 1972.

Almeida, Miguel Calmon du Pin e. Ideias econômicas de Miguel Calmon. Intro. Francisco de Assis Barbosa. Brasilia: Senado Federal, 1980.

Amaral, Luis. História geral da agricultura brasileira no tríplice aspecto político-social-economico. São Paulo: Editora Nacional, 1939.

Andrade, Darcy Bessone de Oliveira. Wenceslau: Um pescador na presidência. N.P.: Sociedade de Estudos Históricos Pedro II, 1968.

Andrade, Valente de. A aliança necessaria entre o Brasil e a América do Norte: O Brasil e o Pan-Americanismo. São Paulo: n.p., 1917.

Assis Brasil, J. F. de. Attitude do Partido Democratico Nacional na crise da renovação presidencial para 1930–1934. Porto Alegre: Livraria do Globo, 1929.

———. Cultura dos campos. 3rd ed. Paris: Mounier, Jeanbin & Co., 1910.

———. Ditadura, parlamentarismo, democracia. N.P.: Livraria do Globo, n.d.

———. Do governo presidencial na república brasileira. Rio de Janeiro: Calvino Filho, 1934.

———. Idea da Pátria. São Paulo: Typographia Piratininga, 1918.

———. A vida do campo e a reforma rural. Belo Horizonte: Imprensa Oficial, 1916.

Associação Commercial de Rio de Janeiro. O momento econômico e financeiro (Representações das classes produtores ao exco. Sr. Dr. Wenceslau Braz. Rio de Janeiro: Typographia do Jornal do Commercio, 1917.

Azevedo, Fernando de. Brazilian Culture: An Introduction to the Study of Culture in Brazil. Trans. William Rex Crawford. New York: MacMillan, 1950.

Baer, Werner and Annibal V. Villela. "Industrial Growth and Industrialization: Revisions in the Stages of Brazil's Economic Development." Journal of Developing Areas, 7 (1973), 217–34.

Baer, Werner. The Brazilian Economy: Growth and Development 7th ed. Boulder, CO: Lynne Rienner Publishers, 2014.

Barreto, Luiz Pereira. O século XX sob o ponto de vista brasileiro. São Paulo: O Estado de São Paulo, 1901.

Barros, Roque Spencer Maciel de. A evolucão do pensamento de Pereira Barreto. São Paulo: Editorial Grijalba Ltda., 1967.

Bartels, Alberto Xavier and Jose Reginaldo Figueiredo Reis. Livro da turma dos engenheiros agronômicos 1966, Escola Superior de Agricultura. Viçosa, MG: Universidade Rural do Estado de Minas Gerais, 1966.

Beskow, Paulo Roberto. "O Crédito Rural Público Numa Economia Em Transformação: Estudo Histórico e Avaliação Econômica das Atividades de Financiamento Agropecuário da CREAI/BB, de 1937 a 1965." Diss.: University de Campinas, 1994.

———. "Agricultura e política agrícola no contexto brasileiro da industrialização do pós-guerra (1946–1964)." Estudos Sociedade e Agricultura, Vol. 12, April 1999.

Bielschowsky, Richard. "Brazilian Economic Thought (1945–1964)—The Ideological Cycle Of Developmentalism." Diss.: University of Leicester 1985.

Bourne, Richard. Getúlio Vargas of Brazil, 1983-1954: Sphinx of the Pampas. London: Charles Knight & Co. Ltd, 1974.

Branner, John C. Geologia elementar preparada com referência especial aos estudantes brasileiros e a geologia do Brasil. 2nd ed. Rio de Janeiro: Francisco Alves, 1915.

———. "Memorial of Orville A. Derby." Bulletin of the Geological Society of America, 27 (1916), 15–21.

Brooke, G. Nigel and Mary Witoshynsky, eds. Os 40 Anos da Fundação Ford no Brasil: uma parceria para a mudança social. São Paulo: Editora da Universidade de São Paulo, 2002.

Buckley, Eve E. Technocrats and the Politics of Drought and Development in Twentieth Century Brazil. Chapel Hill, NC: University of North Carolina Press, 2017.

Burns, E. Bradford. "As relações internacionaes do Brasil durante a Primeira República," in Boris Fausto, ed., Sociedade e Instituições. Vol. 2 of O Brasil Republicano. Tome 3 of História Geral da Civilização Brasileira. Rio de Janeiro: DIFEL, 1978. pp. 375–400.

———. The Unwritten Alliance: Rio Branco and Brazilian-American Relations. New York: Columbia University Press, 1966.

Cabral, J. Irineu. Sol de Manhã: Memoria da Embrapa. Brasilia: UNESCO, 2005.

Calogeras, João Pandia. Problemas de administração: Relatório confidencial apresentado em 1918 .... São Paulo: Editora Nacional, 1933.

———. Problemas do governo. São Paulo: Rossetti Lta., 1928.

Câmara do Commercio Internacional do Brasil. O problema econômico do Brazil. Rio de Janeiro: Jornal do Commercio, 1914.

———. O problema econômico e financeiro do Brasil (Impressões de uma Palestra com o Sr. Dr . Wenceslau Braz). Rio de Janeiro: Edifício da Bolsa, 1915.

Cano, Wilson. "Da Década de 1920 à de 1930: Transição Rumo à Crise e a Industrialização no Brasil," Revista EconomiA, Brasilia, DF, Vol. 13, No. 3b (Sept.–Dec. 2012).

Caputo, Ana Cláudia and Hildete Pereira de Melo, "A Industrialização Brasileira nos Anos de 1950: Uma Análise da Instrução 113 da SUMOC" Estudos econômicos, Vol. 39, No. 3 (Jul.–Sept. 2009).

Cardim, Fernão. Tratados da terra e gente do Brasil. Intr. Batista Caetano, Capistrano de Abreu and Rodolfo Garcia 3rd ed. São Paulo: Editora Nacional/ MEC, 1978.

Carone, Edgard, ed. Pensamento industrial no Brasil (1880–1945). Rio de Janeiro: DIFEL, 1977.

———. A República Velha. II. Evolução política (1889–1930). 3rd ed. Rio de Janeiro: DIFEL/Difusão Editorial, S.A., 1977.

———. A República Velha. (Instituições e classes sociaes). São Paulo: DIFEL, 1970.

Carvalho, Ronald de. Pequena história da literatura brasileira. Pref. Medeiros e Albuquerque. 3rd. ed. Rio de Janeiro: Briguiet, 1925.

Castro, Ana Celia. As empresas estrangeiras no Brasil, 1860–1913. Rio de Janeiro: Zahar Editores, 1979.

Centro Commerical de Cereaes [Rio de Janeiro]. Relatório. 1908, 1910, 1914–1916.
Cobbs, Elizabeth Ann. The Rich Neighbor Policy: Rockefeller and Kaiser in Brazil. New Haven, CN: Yale University Press, 1992.
Cortes, Carlos E. Gaucho Politics in Brazil: The Politics of Rio Grande do Sul, 1930–1964. Albuquerque: University of New Mexico Press, 1974.
Costa, Cruz, Joao. Contribuição a história das ideias no Brasil. 2nd ed. Rio de Janeiro: Editora Civilização Brasileira, 1967.
Davis, Shelton H. Victims of the Miracle: Development and the Indians of Brazil. Cambridge, UK: Cambridge Univ. Press, 1977.
Day, Thomas R. Manual do algodão: Meio século de experiencia em Texas e no Brasil. 3rd.ed. N.p.: n.p., 1926.
———. Plantas forrageiras. N.P.: Repartição Industrial da Leopoldina Railway, 1915.
D'Araujo, Selena de and Celso Corrêia Pinto de Castro, eds., *Ernesto Geisel,* 3rd ed. Rio de Janeiro: Editora Fundação Getúlio Vargas, 1997.
Dean, Warren. The Industrialization of São Paulo, 1880–1945. Austin: University of Texas Press, 1969.
———. "Latifundia and Land Policy in Nineteenth-Century Brazil," Hispanic American Historical Review, 51 (1971), 606–25.
———. Brazil and the Struggle for Rubber: A Study in Environmental History. New York: Cambridge University Press, 1987.
Denis, Pierre. Brazil. Trans. Bernard Miall. London: T. Fisher Unwin, 1914.
Dias, Manuel Nunes et al. Brasil em perspectiva. São Paulo: DIFEL, 1968.
Dulles, John W. F. Vargas of Brazil: A Political Biography. Austin: University of Texas Press, 1967.
Duncan, Julian S. Public and Private Operation of Railways in Brazil. New York: Columbia Univ, Press, 1932.
Elliott [Joyce], Lillian Elwyn. Brazil Today and Tomorrow. New York: MacMillan, 1917.
Fausto, Boris. A revolução de 1930: Historiografia e história. São Paulo: Editora Brasiliense, 1970.
———. Trabalho urbano e conflito social (1890–1920). São Paulo: DIFE, 1976.
Federacão das Associaçoes Commerciaes do Brasil. Relatório 1916. Rio de Janeiro: Jornal do Commercio, 1916.
Fernandes dos Anjos, Antônio. "Sociedade, o Estado e a Ciência na Apropriação e na Diferenciação socioespacial do Cerrado." Thesis: Universidade Federal de Goiás, 2016.
Ferraz, Mario de Sampaio. Piracicaba e sua Escola Agricola. 2nd ed. São Paulo: Typographia Brazil de Rothschild, 1916.
Fite, Gilbert C. and Jim E. Reese. An Economic History of the United States. 3rd ed. Boston: Houghton Mifflin, 1973.

Fleuiss, Max. História administrativa do Brasil. 2nd ed. São Paulo: Melhoramentos de S. Paulo, 1922.

Font, Mauricio A. Coffee, Contention, and Change in the Making of Modern Brazil Cambridge, MA: Blackwell, 1990.

Foweraker, Joe. The Struggle for Land: A Political Economy of the Pioneer Frontier in Brazil from 1930 to the Present Day. Cambridge, UK: Cambridge Univsity Press, 1981.

Freire de Souza, Iván Sergio. Organismos de investigação agropecuária nos países do Cone Sul: O caso de EMBRAPA. Montevideo, UR: IICA-Procesir, 1991.

Fundação Instituto Brasileiro de Geografia e Estatística, Anuário Estatístico do Brasil. Various years.

———. Estatísticas Históricas do Brasil, Séries Econômicas, Demográficas e Sociais de 1550 a 1985, Vol. 3. Rio de Janeiro: IBGE, 1997.

Furtado, Celso. Manual of Programming and Economic Development Promotion. Rio de Janeiro: Economic Commission of Latin American, 1956.

Gallo, Ezequiel. "Agrarian Expansion and Industrial Development in Argentina, 1880–1930." in Raymond Carr, ed. Latin American Affairs. Oxford: Oxford Univsity Press, 1970.

Garfield, Seth. In Search of the Amazon: Brazil, the United States, and the Nature of a Region. Durham, NC: Duke University Press, 2013.

Gaspari, Elio. A Ditadura Envergonhada. São Paulo: Companhia das Letras, 2002.

Gauld, Charles A. History of the Coordinator of Inter-American Affairs: Historical Reports on War Administration. Washington, GPO, 1947.

———. The Last Titan: Percival Farquhar, American Entrepreneur in Latin America. Stanford: Stanford University Institute of Hispanic American and Luso Brazilian Studies, 1964.

Girão, Raimundo. História econômica do Ceará. N.P.: Editora "Instituto do Ceará," 1947.

Gomes, Raul and L. Rocha Junior. O milho no Paraná. Curitiba: Papelaria Globo, 1918.

Graham, Richard. "Brazil: The National Period." in Roberto Ezquenazi-Mayo and Michael C. Meyer. Latin American Scholarship since World War II: Trends in History, Political Science. Lincoln, N.E.: University of Nebraska Press, 1971.

———. Britain and the Onset of Modernization in Brazil, 1850–1914. Cambridge: Cambridge Univsity Press, 1968.

Grandin, Gregg. Fordlandia: The Rise and Fall of Henry Ford's Forgotten Jungle City. New York: Metropolitan Books, 2009.

Guimarães da Silva, Felipe Maia. "Questão agraria e modernização do Brasil." Diss.: Universidade do Estado do Rio de Janeiro, 2014.

Haas, Werner. Os investimentos estrangeiros no Brasil. Trans. ed. Jearn Bernet and Roland A. Bossart. Rio de Janeiro: n.p., 1958.
Haddad, Claudio L. S. "Growth of the Brazilian Real Product, 1900–1947." Diss.: Univsity of Chicago, 1974.
Hanson, Simon G. "The Farquhar Syndicate in South America." Hispanic American Historic Review, 17 (1937), 314–26.
Harris, Marvin. Town and Country in Brazil. New York: Columbia Univsity Press, 1956.
Hasse. G. and F. Bueno: O Brasil da Soja: Opening Frontiers, Sowing Cities. Porto Alegre, RGS: L&PM Editors, S.A., 1996.
Helfand, Steven M. "The Distribution of Subsidized Credit in Brazil: Do Interest Groups Really Matter?" Development and Change, Vol. 32 (2001)
Hentschke, Jens R. ed., Vargas and Brazil: New Perspectives. New York: Palgrave MacMillan, 2007.
Hilton, Stanley E. "Brazil and the Post-Versailles World: Elite Images and Foreign Policy Strategy, 1919–1929." Journal of Latin American Studies, 12 (1980), 341–64.
———. Oswaldo Aranha: Uma Biografia. Rio de Janeiro: Objetiva, 1994.
Holloway, Thomas H. The Brazilian Coffee Valorization of 1906: Regional Politics and Economic Dependence. Madison: The State Historical Society of Wisconsin, 1975.
———. Immigrants on the Land: Coffee and Society in São Paulo, 1886–1934. Chapel Hill: Univ. of North Carolina Press, 1980.
Hosono, Akio and Carlos Magno Campos da Rocha, and Yutaka Hongo, eds., Development for Sustainable Agriculture: The Brazilian Cerrado. New York: Palgrave MacMillan, 2016.
House, Lewis. "Edwin V. Morgan and Brazilian-American Diplomatic Relations, 1912–1933." Diss.: New York Univsity, 1969.
Hunnicutt, Benjamin H. Algodão: cultivo e commercio. São Paulo: Editora Ltda., 1936.
———. Brazil, World Frontier. New York: D. Van Nostrand, 1949.
———. O livro do milho. N.P.: n.p., 1916.
———. As machinas agricolas essenciaes para uma lavoura racional. Rio de Janeiro: Jornal do Commercio, 1918.
———. O milho: Sua cultura e aproveitamento. Lavras, M.G.: Imprensa Gammon, 1933.
——— and William Watkins Reid. The Story of Agricultural Missions. New York: Missionary Education Movement of the United States and Canada, 1931.
Hymowitz, Theodore and Francisco de Jesus Vernetti, and Henry L. Shands, "The Brazilian national soybean program," Soybean Digest (May 1968).
Instituto Agricola Brasileiro. Annuario Commercial Industria e Agricola. Rio de Janeiro: Instituto Agricola Brasileira, 1923.

Jackle, Frank Robert. "John Casper Branner and Brazil." Diss.: Stanford University, 1967.
James, Herman G. Brazil after a Century of Independence. New York: MacMillan, 1925.
Jornal do Commercio. 1 Centenário do Jornal do Commercio, 1827-Octubro-1927. Rio de Janeiro: 1928.
———. Retrospecto Commercial do "Jornal do Commercio." 1914–1930.
Ladeira, J. R. Pela grandeza econômica do Brasil. Vol. I. 1918–1930. Rio de Janeiro: Ferreira, Ladeira & Cia., 1930.
The Leopoldina Railway Company Limited. Relatório da diretoria relativo ao anno de 1911.... Rio de Janeiro: Jornal do Commercio, c. 1912.
Levine, Robert M. Historical Dictionary of Brazil. Metuchen, N.J.: The Scarecrow Press, 1979.
———. Pernambuco in the Brazilian Federation, 1889–1937. Stanford, CA: Stanford University Press, 1978.
———. The Vargas Regime: The Critical Years, 1934–1938. New York: Columbia University Press, 1970.
Lima, A. Saboia. Alberto Torres e a sua obra. Rio de Janeiro: Labor, 1918.
Lima, José Custodio Alves de. Aproximação racional entre o Brasil e os Estados Unidos da América. São Paulo: n.p., 1918.
———. Cartas Americanas. Rio de Janeiro: Imprensa Nacional, 1914.
———. Problemas sociaes e econômicas. Buenos Aires: Ricardo Radaelli, 1915.
Lima, Manoel de Oliveira. Relations of Brazil with the United States. New York: American Association for International Conciliation, 1913.
Lima, Heitor Ferreira. História política-econômica e industrial do Brasil. São Paulo: Editora Nacional, 1970.
Linhares, Maria Yedda Leite. História do abastecimento: uma problemática em questão (1918–1974). Brasilia: BINAGRI, 1979.
——— and Francisco Carlos Teixeira da Silva. História política do abastecimento (1918–1974). Brasilia: BINAGRI, 1979.
Lloyd, Reginald, ed. Twentieth Century Impressions of Brazil: Its History, People, Commerce, Industry and Resources. London: Lloyd's Greater Britain Publishing Co., 1913.
Lobo, Euallia Maria Lahmeyer. História político-administrativa da agricultura brasileira. Brasilia: Ministerio da Agricultura, n.d.
Lobo [Leite Pereira], Hélio. Brasilianos & Yankees. Rio de Janeiro: Pimenta & Cia., 1926.
———. Cousas americanas e brasileiras. Rio de Janeiro: Imprensa Nacional, 1923.
———. A passo do gigante. Rio de Janeiro: Imprensa Nacional, 1925.
———. "As relações entre os Estados - Unidos e o Brasil," Revista Americana 7, No. 2 (1917), 79–102.

Lombardi, Mary. "The Frontier in Brazilian History: An Historiographical Essay." Pacific Historic Review, 44 (1975), 437–57.

Love, Joseph L. Rio Grande do Sul and Brazilian Regionalism, 1882–1930. Stanford, CA: Stanford, University Press, 1971.

———. São Paulo in the Brazilian Federation, 1889–1937. Stanford: Stanford University Press, 1980.

Macauley, Neill. The Prestes Column: Revolution in Brazil. New York: New Viewpoints, 1974.

Machado, Barry F. "Farquhar and Ford in Brazil: Studies in Business Expansion and Foreign Policy." Diss.: Northwestern Univsity, 1975.

Magalhaes, Amilcar A. Botelho. Impressões da Commissão Rondon. 4th. ed. Porto Alegre: Livraria do Globo, 1929.

Mandall, Paul I. The Rise of the Modern Brazilian Rice Industry. Stanford: Food Research Institute, Stanford University, 1971.

Maram, Sheldon. "Juscelino Kubitschek and the Politics of Exuberance, 1956–1961" Luso-Brazilian Review, Vol. 27, No. 1 (Summer, 1990).

Macarini, José Pedro. "Crise e política econômica: o Governo Figueiredo (1979–1984)." Campinas, SP: IE/UNICAMP, June 2008.

Marcio da Silva, Claiton. "Agricultura e Cooperação Internacional: a Atuação da American International Cooperation for Economic and Social Development (AIA) e os Programas de Modernização no Brasil (1946–1961). Diss.: Casa de Oswaldo Cruz-Fiocruz, 2009.

———. De Agricultor a Farmer: Nelson Rockefeller e a Modernização da Agricultura no Brasil. Curitiba, PR: Editora UFPR, 2015.

———. "The Barren Side of Brazil: Science, Water Resources, and the Debate on the (In)Fertile Soils of the Brazilian Cerrado, 1892–1942," História, Ciências, Saúde—Manguinhos, Vol. 26, No. 2 (Apr.–Jun. 2019).

Marineli, Felipe. " O pensamento de Antônio Delfim Netto e o milagre econômico brasileiro (1968–1973)." Diss.: Universidade de São Paul, 2017.

Margolis, Maxine L. Moving Frontier: Social and Economic Change in a Southern Brazil Community. Gainesville: University of Florida Press, 1973.

Mascarenhas, Hipólito Assunção Antônio. "Contribuição de três pesquisadores dos Estados Unidos na produção de soja no Brasil," O Agronômico, Vol. 56, No. 1 (2004).

Massuqueti, Angélica. "A mudança no padrão de financiamento da agricultura brasileira no período 1965–97." Diss.: Universidade Federal do Rio Grande do Sul, 1998.

McCann, Jr., Frank D. The Brazilian-American Alliance, 1937–1945. Princeton, NJ: Princeton University Press, 1973.

———. "Brazil and World War II: The Forgotten Ally. What did you do in the war, Zé Carioca?" Estudios Interdisciplinarios de América Latina y el Caribe, [Tel Aviv], Vol. 6, No. 2.

Mendonca, Salvador de. A situação internacional do Brasil. Rio de Janeiro: Livraria Garner, 1913.

Mengel, Alex Alexandre. "A Modernização da Agricultura e Pesquisa no Brasil: A Empresa Brasileira de Pesquisa Agropecuária EMBRAPA." Diss.: Universidade Federal de Rio de Janeiro, 2015.

Moacir, Manoel. "The Processo of Agricultural Technology Generation in Brazil: A Social Audit." Diss.: University of Sussex, 1997.

Moniz Bandeira, Luiz Alberto. Presença dos Estados Unidos no Brasil. (Dois séculos de história.) Rio de Janeiro: Civilização Brasileira, 1973.

Moog, Vianna. Bandeirantes e pioneiros: paralelo entre duas culturas. Rio de Janeiro: Editora Globo, 1954.

Morse, Richard M. From Community to Metropolis: A Biography of São Paulo, Brazil. Rev. ed. New York: Octagon Books, 1974.

Moura, Gerson. Brazilian Foreign Relations:1939–1950: The Changing Nature of Brazil-United States Relations during and after the Second World War. Brasília: FUNAG, 2013.

Nash, Roy. The Conquest of Brazil. New York: Biblo and Tannen, 1968.

Neto, Lira. Getúlio 1930–1945: Do Governo Provisório à ditadura do Estado Novo. São Paulo: Companhia de Letras, 2013.

Nicholls, William H. "The Agricultural Frontier in Modern Brazilian History: The State of Paraná, 1920–65." in Merrill Rippy, ed. Cultural Change in Brazil: Papers from the Midwest Association for Latin American Studies. Muncie, In.: Ball State University, 1969.

Nogueira, Jose A. Sonho do gigante. São Paulo: Monteiro Lobato & Cia., 1922.

Normano, João F. Brazil: A Study of Economic Types. Chapel Hill, NC: University of North Carolina Press, 1935.

———. The Struggle for South America: Economy and Ideology. London: George Allen & Unwin Ltd., 1931.

Oakenfull, J. C. Brazil: A Century of Independence, 1822–1922. Freiburg, Ger.: Wagner, 1922.

Paiva Abreu, Marcel de. "The Brazilian Economy, 1930–1945," University of Oxford Centre for Brazilian Studies Working Paper Series, Paper CBS-03-99(E).

——— ed. Ordem do progresso Cem Anos de Política Econômica Republicana: 1889–1989. Rio de Janeiro: Editora Campus, 1990.

Pang, Eul-Soo. Bahia in the First Brazilian Republic: Coronelismo and Oligarchies, 1889–1934. Gainesville, FL: University of Florida Press, 1979.

Pearce, W. M. The Matador Land and Cattle Company. Norman, OK: University of Oklahoma Press, 1964.

Pearse, Arno S. Brazilian Cotton. Manchester, Eng.: International Federation of Master Cotton Spinners and Manufacturers Associations, 1923.

———. Cotton in North Brazil, Being the Report of the Journey through the States of Ceará, Maranhão and Pará, Together with a Synopsis of the Whole of Brazil's Cotton Potentialities. Pref. Miguel Calmon. Manchester, Eng.: Taylor Garnett Evans & Co., n.d.

Pelaez, Carlos Manuel. "The State, the Great Depression, and the Industrialization of Brazil." Diss.: Columbia University, 1968.

Pereira, Baptista. Brasil e Estados Unidos: Affinidades históricas entre os dois paizes. Rio de Janeiro: Jornal do Brasil, 1930.

Pereira, Waldick. Cana, café & laranja: História econômica de Nova Iguaçu. Rio de Janeiro: Fundação Getúlio Vargas, 1977.

Persico, Joseph E. The Imperial Rockefeller: A Biography of Nelson A. Rockefeller New York: Simon and Schuster, 1982.

Pesavento, Sandra Jatahy. República Velha Gaúcha: Charquiadas, frigoríficos, criadores. Porto Alegre: Movimento, 1980.

Pessoa, Epitácio. Pela Verdade. Rio de Janeiro: Livraria Francisco Alves, 1925.

Pimenta Velloso, Mônica. A Brasilidade Verde-Amarela: nacionalismo e regionalismo paulista, 2nd ed. Rio de Janeiro: Fundação Getúlio Vargas, CPDOC, 1990.

Pimentel, Fortunato. Joaquim Francisco de Assis Brasil: Emérito agricultor. Porto Alegre: Santa Teresinha Ltda., 1950.

Poliano, L. Marques. A Sociedade Nacional de Agricultura: Resumo histórico. Rio de Janeiro: Sociedade Nacional de Agricultura, 1942.

Porto, Hannibal. Aspectos econômicos do Brasil: Retrospecto de 1921 a 1923, considerações sobre as nossas possibilidades mercantis. Rio de Janeiro: Annuario do Brasil, 1924.

Prado, Eduardo. A ilusão americana. 3rd. ed. São Paulo: Typographia Salesiana, 1902.

Prado Junior, Caio. História econômica do Brasil. 11th ed. Rio de Janeiro: Editora Brasiliense, 1967.

Putnam, Samuel. Marvelous Journey: A Survey of Four Centuries of Brazilian Writing. New York: Alfred A. Knopf, 1948.

Quirós, Eca de. A cidade e as serras. Rio de Janeiro: Biblioteca Manancial, 1971.

Ramos, Augusto. O café no Brasil e no estrangeiro. Rio de Janeiro: Santa Helena, 1923.

Reich, Cary. The Life of Nelson A. Rockefeller: Worlds to Conquer 1908–1958. New York: Doubleday, 1996.

Reis, F. T. de Souza. O ensino na Escola Agricola "Luiz de Queiroz" de Piracicaba. São Paulo: Sociedade Editora Olegário Ribeiro, 1920.

Reis Velloso, João Paulo. "A Estratégia de Desenvolvimento e o Programa de Integração Nacional." Revista Do Serviço Público, Vol. 105, No. 2 (1970).

Rodrigues, José Honório. "Brazilian Historiography: Present Trends and Research Requirements." in Diegues Junior, Manuel and Bryce Wood, eds.

Social Science Research in Latin America: Papers Presented at the Conference on Latin American Studies. New York: Columbia University Press, 1966. pp. 217–39.

Rodrigues, Roberto. ed. Ney Bittencourt: o dínamo do agribusiness. N.P.: n.p., 1996.

Rosenberg, Emily S. "Anglo-American Economic Rivalry in Brazil during World War I," Diplomatic History, 2, No. 2 (1978), 131–52.

———. "World War I and 'Continental Solidarity'" Americas , 31 (1975), 313–34.

Rostow, Walt W. The World Economy: History and Prospect. Austin: University of Texas Press, 1978.

Santos, Jose Maria dos. A política geral do Brasil. São Paulo: J. Magalhaes, 1930.

Schuh, G. Edward and Eliseu Alves. The Agricultural Development of Brazil. New York: Praeger, 1970.

Schwartzman, Simon. A Space for Science—The Development of the Scientific Community in Brazil. University Park, PA: The Pennsylvania State Univeristy Press, 1991.

Simonsen, Roberto C. Brazil's Industrial Evolution. São Paulo: Escola Livre de Sociologia e Política, 1939.

———. História econômica do Brasil (1500/1825). São Paulo: Editora Nacional, 1967.

Singer, Paulo. Desenvolvimento econômico e evolução urbana: análise da evolução econômica de São Paulo, Blumenau, Porto Alegre, Belo Horizonte e Recife. São Paulo: Editora Nacional, 1968.

Skidmore, Thomas E. Black into White: Race and Nationality in Brazilian Thought. New York: Oxford University Press, 1974.

———. Brazil: Five Centuries of Change. New York: Oxford University Press, 1999.

Smith, T. Lynn. Brazil: People and Institutions. 4th ed. Baton Rouge: Louisiana State University Press, 1972.

Sociedade Nacional de Agricultura. Annaes do Congresso Nacional de Agricultura installado a 20 de Setembro de 1901 no Rio de Janeiro. Rio de Janeiro: Imprensa Nacional, 1907.

———. Annaes da Primeira Conferência Algodoeira. São Paulo: O Estado de São Paulo, n.d.

———. Immigracão. Inquérito promovido pela Sociedade Nacional Agricultura. Rio de Janeiro: Villam & Barbero, 1926.

Sociedade Rural Brasileira. Estatutos 1930. São Paulo: Irmãos Ferraz, 1930.

Souza Pires Munoz, Viviane Carla de. "A Educação Superior em Agricultura no Brasil como Terreno Fértil para os Estados Unidos: A Fundação Ford na UREMG/UFV (1964–1976)." Diss.: Universidade Federal de Viçosa, 2017.

Stauffer, David H. "The Origin and Establishment of Brazil's Indian Service, 1889–1910." Diss.: University of Texas at Austin, 1955.
Stein, Stanley J. The Brazilian Cotton Manufacture: Textile Enterprise in an Underdeveloped Area, 1850–1950. Cambridge: Harvard University Press, 1957.
———. Vassouras: A Brazilian Coffee County, 1850–1900. Cambridge: Harvard University Press, 1957.
Strauss, Norman. "Rise of American Growth in Brazil: Decade of the 1870s." Americas, 32 (1976), 437–44.
Suzigan, Wilson. "Industrialization and Economic Policy in Historical Perspective," Brazilian Economic Studies, 2 (1976), 5–34.
Sweigert, Joseph E. Rev. of Warren Dean, The Industrialization of São Paulo, 188–1945. TS, Austin, Texas, 1974.
Taunay, Affonso de E. Pequena história do café no Brasil (1727–1937). Rio de Janeiro: Departamento Nacional do Café, 1945.
Teixeira de Oliveira, José. O Governo Dutra: Algumas realizações Diretrizes doutrinárias Um período de paz. Rio de Janeiro: Editora Civilização Brasileira, 1956.
Topik, Steven C. "Economic Nationalism and the State in an Underdeveloped Country: Brazil, 1889–1930." Diss.: University of Texas at Austin, 1978.
———. "The Evolution of the Economic Role of the Brazilian State." Journal of Latin American Studies, 2 (1979), 325–42.
Torres, Alberto. As fontes de vida no Brazil. Rio de Janeiro: Papelaria Brazil, 1915.
———. A organização nacional: Primeira parte, a constituição. Rio de Janeiro: Imprensa Nacional, 1914.
———. O problema nacional brasileiro: Introduccão a um programa de organização nacional. 3rd. ed. São Paulo: Editora Nacional, 1978.
Torres Filho, Arthur E. M. Expansão econômica do Brasil: Organização interna-situação internacional. Rio de Janeiro: Calvino Filho, 1935.
Tota, Antonio Pedro. The Seduction of Brazil: The Americanization of Brazil during World War II. Trans. Lorena B. Ellis. Austin, TX: Teresa Lozano Long Institute of Latin American Studies, 2009.
———.. O Amigo Americano: Nelson Rockefeller e o Brasil. São Paulo: Companhia de Letras, 2014.
Truda, R. de Leonardo. O Brasil e a doutrina de Monroe. São Paulo: Editora Monteiro Lobato, 1924.
Tulchin, Joseph S. World War I and U. S. Policy Toward Latin America. New York: New York University Press, 1971.
Universidade Rural do Estado de Minas Gerais. Escola Superior de Agricultura: Origem, desenvolvimento, atualidade. Viçosa, M.G.: Universidade Rural do Estado de Minas Gerais, c. 1968.

D'Utra, Gustavo R. P. Cultura do algodoeira. São Paulo: Redaccão da Revista Agricola, 1904.

Vargas, Getúlio. Diário. Vol. II, 1937–1942. Rio de Janeiro: Fundação Getúlio Vargas, 1995.

———. A nova política do Brasil: I da Aliança Liberal as realizações do 1° ano do governo. Rio de Janeiro: Jose Olympio Editora, 1938.

Vargas do Amaral Peixoto, Alzira. Getúlio Vargas, meu pai. Porto Alegre: Livraria do Globo, 1960.

Vidal, Adhemar. História da revolução na Parahyba. São Paulo: Editora Nacional, 1933.

Villela, Annibal Villanova. "Surto industrial durante a guerra de 1914–1918." in Ensaios econômicos: Homenagem a Octavio Gouvêa de Bulhões . Rio de Janeiro: APEC Editora, 1972, pp. 535–49.

——— and Wilson Suzigan. Government Policy and Economic Growth of Brazil, 1889–1945. Rio de Janeiro: IPEA/IPES, 1977.

Valla, Victor. A penetração norte-americana na economia brasileira, 1898–1928: Sempre de acordo ou nobre emulação? Rio de Janeiro: Ao Livro Técnico, 1978.

———. "Subsídios para uma melhor compreensão da entrada do Brasil na Primeira Guerra Mundial," Estudos Históricos, 15 (1976), 29–46.

Vieira Lima, Ricardo and Luciana Quillett Heymann, Da monocultura a o agribusiness: a história da Sociedade Nacional de Agricultura (SNA). Brasilia: Embrapa Informação Tecnológica, 2005.

Waddell, Agnes S. "The Revolution in Brazil," Foreign Policy Association Information Service, 6 (1931), 489–506.

Wagley, Charles. An Introduction to Brazil. New York: Columbia University Press, 1963.

Weis, W. Michael. Cold Warriors and coups d'etat: Brazilian-American Relations 1945–1964. Albuquerque, NM: University of New Mexico Press, 1993.

Werneck Sodré, Nelson. História da literatura brasileira: seus fundamentos econômicos. 2nd ed. Rio de Janeiro: Jose Olympio Editora, 1940.

Wickizer, V. D. The World Coffee Economy, with Special Reference to Control Schemes. Stanford: Food Research Institute, Stanford University, 1943.

Wileman, J. P. The Brazilian Yearbook, 1909. London: McCorquodale & Co., n.d.

Wirth, John D. Minas Gerais in the Brazilian Federation: 1889–1937. Stanford: Stanford University Press, 1977.

———. "Tenentismo in the Brazilian Revolution of 1930." Hispanic American Historical Review, 44 (1964), 161–79.

Wood, Charles H. and Marianne Schmink, "The Military and the Environment in the Brazilian Amazon," Journal of Political and Military Sociology, Vol. 21, No. 1 (Summer 1993).

Yedda Linhares, Maria and Francisco Carlos Teixeira de Silva, Terra Prometida: Uma História da Questão Agraria no Brasil. Rio de Janeiro: Editora Campus, 1999.

Yeganiantz, Levon ed. Brazilian Agriculture and Agricultural Research. Brasilia: EMBRAPA, 1984.

——— ed. Pesquisa agropecuária: questionamentos, consolidação e perspectivas. Brasilia, D.F.: EMBRAPA, 1988.

Young, Jordan M. The Brazilian Revolution of 1930 and the Aftermath. New Brunswick, N.J.: Rutgers University Press, 1967.

Zahluth Bastos, Pedro Paulo and Pedro Cezar Dutra Fonseca, eds. A Era Vargas: Desenvolvimento, Economia e Sociedade. São Paulo: Editora Unesp, 2011.

Zweig, Stefan. Brasil: Pais do futuro. Trans. Odilon Galloti. Rio de Janeiro: Editora Guanabara, 1941.

The manufacturer's authorised representat ve in the EU is Springer
Nature Customer Service Centre GmbH, E ıropaplatz 3, 69115 Heidelberg,
Germany. If you have any concerns regard ng our products, please
contact ProductSafety@springernature.com

Printed and bound by CPI Group (UK) Ltd, Croydon, CR0 4YY
30/09/2026
02225502-0015